ton.

The Final Schedule Revealed

In the Fall Feasts and Festivals

By

Maureen G. Metcalf

authorHOUSE

1663 LIBERTY DRIVE, SUITE 200
BLOOMINGTON, INDIANA 47403
(800) 839-8640
www.authorhouse.com

© 2004 Maureen G. Metcalf.
All Rights Reserved.

No part of this book may be reproduced, stored in a retrieval system, or transmitted by any means without the written permission of the author.

First published by AuthorHouse 08/05/04

ISBN: 1-4184-5134-7 (sc)

Printed in the United States of America
Bloomington, Indiana

This book is printed on acid-free paper.

All Scriptures used in this document are quoted from the King James Version of the Bible. Underlining and/or bold emphases are mine throughout.

Dedicated to:

My loving and supportive husband, Alistair, and to Marilynn, Brian, and Cheryl for your encouragement, prayers, and input. Together, you have made writing this book a joy.

May God indeed bless you for your great patience and assistance with this project.

Love you all!

Mom

TABLE OF CONTENTS

PART 1 1
   INTRODUCTION 3
   CHAPTER 1 A PROPHETIC MID-SENTENCE PAUSE.........................7
   CHAPTER 2 HEBREW VERSUS WESTERN PERCEPTION 11
   CHAPTER 3 HOLY CONVOCATIONS; DIVINE APPOINTMENTS...15
   CHAPTER 4 THE FALL FEASTS AND FESTIVALS 21
   CHAPTER 5 THE WEDDING CONNECTION 59
   CHAPTER 6 SIGNS...69
   CHAPTER 7 THE OLIVET DISCOURSE 95
   CHAPTER 8 THE KEYS (CLUES)...109
   CHAPTER 9 SEVENTY WEEKS DETERMINED................................115
   CHAPTER 10 THE CONTROVERSY REGARDING THE ABRAHAMIC COVENANT...137
   CHAPTER 11 TENTS OF JUDAH, and GOG AND MAGOG 149
   CHAPTER 12 CONFIRMATION OF THE COVENANT 183

PART 2: THE REVELATION EXPLANATION 195
   THE PURPOSE OF THE BOOK OF REVELATION............................197
   CHAPTER 13 THE SEVEN CHURCHES..199
   CHAPTER 14 THE THRONE ROOM, and THE SEALED BOOK 225
   CHAPTER 15 THE SEALS..235
   CHAPTER 16: THE SEVENTH SEAL...281
   CHAPTER 17 MEASUREMENTS, WITNESSES, and AN EARTHQUAKE...303
   CHAPTER 18 TEKIAH HA GADOL, THE SEVENTH TRUMPET, THIRD WOE..313
   CHAPTER 19 THE TWO BEASTS OF REVELATION 13...................329
   CHAPTER 20 THE OFFICIAL WELCOMING DIGNITARIES 351
   CHAPTER 21 THE SICKLE HARVESTS, and THE JUDGMENT OF THE NATIONS 371
   CHAPTER 22 THE VIALS OF WRATH..377
   CHAPTER 23 THE FALL OF THE WHORE, BABYLON 387
   CHAPTER 24 THE BRIDE, ISRAEL, AND THE TIMES AND SEASONS 407
   CHAPTER 25 THE TIMES AND SEASONS EXPLAINED IN THE PSALMS..413
   CHAPTER 26 JESUS CHRIST, VICTORIOUS KING 441
   CHAPTER 27 IRAQ, SYRIA, and ISRAEL'S SHORTCOMINGS 457
   CHAPTER 28 'PALESTINA'..489
   CHAPTER 29 TREACHERY 509
   CHAPTER 30 PERSONAL TESHUVAH..521

"WATCHMAN, WHAT OF THE NIGHT?"

What enemies are abroad?
Errors are a numerous horde, and new ones appear every hour:
Against what heresy am I to be on my guard?
Sins creep from their lurking places when the darkness reigns;
I must myself mount the watch-tower, and watch unto prayer.
Our heavenly Protector foresees all the attacks which are to be made upon us,
And when as yet the evil designed us is but in the desire of Satan,
He prays for us that our faith fail not, when we are sifted as wheat.
Continue, O gracious Watchman, to forwarn us of our foes,
And for Zion's sake hold not thy peace.

"Watchman, what of the night?"
What weather is coming for the Church?
Are the clouds lowering, or is it all clear and fair overhead?
We must care for the Church of God with anxious love;
And now that the Popery and infidelity are both threatening,
Let us observe the signs of the times and prepare for conflict.

"Watchman, what of the night?"
What stars are visible?
What precious promises suit our present case?
You sound the alarm, give us the consolation also.
Christ, the Polestar, is ever fixed in His place,
And all the stars are secure in the right hand of their Lord.

But, Watchman, when comes the morning?
The Bridegroom tarries.
Are there no signs of His coming forth as the Sun of Righteousness?
Has not the Morning Star arisen as the pledge of day?
When will the day dawn, and the shadows flee away?
O Jesus, if Thou come not in person to Thy waiting Church this day,
Yet come in Spirit to my sighing heart, and make it sing for joy.

"Now all the earth is bright and glad with fresh morn;
But all my heart is cold, and dark, and sad:

Sun of the soul, let me behold Thy dawn!
Come, Jesus, Lord,
O quickly come, according to Thy word."

By Charles Spurgeon

PART 1

INTRODUCTION

For the majority of folk, the rapid changes unfolding in our world appear to be the logical course of events resulting from the evolution of a global society. Increasingly we are made aware that no person, government, or country; no political ideology or religious philosophy, and certainly no monetary system, can now endure without interacting with all others on the planet. But such interaction is obviously a breeding ground for disharmony, mistrust, and animosities, rather than peaceful synchronism. Taken solely from man's perspective, there really does not appear to be any absolute foundations of society left. This realization leaves all of us with the uneasy sense that no one has the ability to take things decisively in hand, and create a truly just global society. In fact, in our search for this illusive utopia, we have magnified, and birthed, the exact opposite.

There can never be common ground without repentance before God, and a turning wholeheartedly to the principles of the Scriptures. Very few world leaders want to acknowledge God or His Word, or even entertain the concept that He may have an opinion, or that He will ultimately, and shortly, insert Himself directly into the affairs of mankind.

Meanwhile, the battle is not only being waged on the level of saber-rattling military/political posturing and international terrorism, but in the religious arena as well. East against West, Muslim against Christian and Jew. This latter arena has definite opposing sides emerging, not just ideologically, but also geographically, with the line of demarcation drawn between whole groups of nations. Is man's existence headed somewhere? And what does this journey mean for the individual, the Church, the Jews, and for the entire family of nations?

Much has been, and is being discussed and written about these troubling issues. The Bible-believing Christian must play a major role, by providing the world with the prophetic interpretation of the scene according to Scripture. Although that interpretive role is very much a part of our mandate in taking the Gospel to the whole world, we have perhaps been guilty of delivering our message with only a partial emphasis. We have capitalized on the eternal destiny of man, without also delivering the warnings, as John the Baptist queried the religious leaders, asking them, *"...who hath warned you to flee from the wrath to come?"* Luke 3: 7b. This is not just a warning to flee from eternal damnation, which is the ultimate judgment, but to also flee from the wrath of God that is to be shortly poured out upon the nations of the whole earth before Christ's Second

Coming. This aspect of our mandated message must be restored, because it is the generation who is alive just prior to the Second Coming of Christ that especially needs to hear it. This generation needs to know there is definite hope, and a route to deliverance. *"That you may be accounted worthy to escape all these things that shall come to pass, and to stand before the Son of man."* Luke 23:36.

However, within the ranks of Christendom there is a groundswell of chosen apathy that is even more disturbing than the issues we all face. Because much of our discussion has not necessarily been with love, or even with a desire to understand, many within the Church have given up on Bible prophecy altogether, feeling that all will ultimately be fulfilled anyway, so it really does not much matter what we, or the world around us, believes or understands. How tragic! We stand on the threshold of the most dramatic fulfillment of Bible prophecy, and suddenly a vast number of Christians tune-out! Not only is this stance not scriptural, it is dangerous!

We have been exhorted by Jesus and Paul to be awake and aware; to *"look up"* when the world scene gets to the stage where there appears to be no definitive answers on the horizon, because our *"redemption draweth nigh."* We truly live in an era when we are able to observe God's hand at work! Since 9/11, the pace of prophetic fulfillment has indeed sped up. Are we paying attention? Are we ready to meet The LORD? Are our friends and neighbors ready? Are we motivated to take the Gospel with increased fervor?

The purpose of the following pages is to take another look at the prophetic Scriptures, and interpret them in the light of current world events as related to the time-table set out by God Himself. In examining the books of Daniel and Revelation, along with the other prophets, and by placing ourselves in a position to 'hear' the words of Jesus Christ as revealed in the light of the Feasts and Festivals, we are able to revisit some of the obscure or controversial passages, and attempt to see where they fit.

Without a doubt, there will certainly be some who will challenge and disagree with the position I take on some issues regarding the days in which we now live. But my purpose is not so much to make everyone agree with my views, as to stir the waters sufficiently to create a fresh hunger to open the Word of God, and re-examine our doctrines regarding end-times. If you find yourself with opposing or alternate views, fine; but lets not take sides merely to have an argument. Enough of that already! Rather, we need to enter into fair and honest examination of doctrinal positions, in order to bring ourselves to clarification. Not simply to entrench traditional exegesis, but to have a heart to really arrive at the truth of what Scripture is saying, and to encourage one another. My challenge is that those who do not necessarily agree with my interpretation, will at least enjoy the debate. If nothing else, lets relish the pursuit as we look into Scripture.

In researching for this book, I have found myself arriving at some startling conclusions that certainly were not what I thought I believed. I have verified some views, changed my interpretation in others, and left some questions open to debate . I trust you will find similar challenges in what is presented in the following pages.

CHAPTER 1
A PROPHETIC MID-SENTENCE PAUSE

Jesus' Ascension had taken place ten days earlier. One hundred and twenty of His devout followers, in obedience to His directive, were gathered together in an Upper Room in Jerusalem, to await the empowerment of the Holy Spirit. Suddenly, the sound of rushing wind filled the room, and each was anointed with a burning flame. At the same time, their tongues were loosed, and they began glorifying and praising God in languages they had never learned.

Many Jewish pilgrims from surrounding nations were also present at the Temple to keep the Feast of Shavuot (Pentecost.) They were amazed to hear the praises of God in their own languages! How could this be? In Acts chapter 2, verses 16 to 21, we read a passage Peter quoted from Joel as part of his explanation. Peter was quick to point out that those assembled in the Upper Room that morning were not drunk! Then he went on to explain to the gathered crowd, that what they were hearing and witnessing was the inaugural outpouring fulfillment of prophecies regarding the Holy Spirit in what is known as 'the last days.'

Peter's explanation highlighted a prophetic significance that I had never really noticed before in regard to The Church Age. So I turned to the book of Joel to examine the prophecy within its original context.

I. The Comparison:

A. Acts 2:16 to 21. *"But this is that which was spoken by the prophet Joel;* Verse 17. *And it shall come to pass in the last days, saith God, I will pour out of my spirit upon all flesh: and your sons and your daughters shall prophesy, and your young men shall see visions, and your old men shall dream dreams:* Verse 18. *and on my servants and on my handmaidens I will pour out in those days of my spirit; and they shall prophesy:* Verse 19. *and I will show wonders in heaven above, and signs in the earth beneath: blood, and fire, and vapor of smoke:* Verse 20. *the sun shall be turned into darkness, and the moon into blood, before that great and notable day of the Lord come:* Verse 21. *and it shall come to pass, that whosoever shall call on the name of the Lord shall be saved."* KJV.

B. Joel 2: 28 to 32. *"And it shall come to pass afterward, that I will pour out my spirit upon all flesh; and your sons and your daughters shall prophesy, your old men shall dream dreams, your young men shall see visions:* Verse 29. *And* *also upon the servants and upon the handmaids in those days will I pour out my spirit. Verse 30. And I will show wonders in the heavens and in the earth, <u>blood, and fire, and pillars of smoke</u>. Verse 31. <u>The sun shall be turned into darkness and the moon into blood, before the great and terrible day of the LORD come</u>. Verse 32a. And it shall come to pass, that whosoever shall call on the name of the LORD shall be delivered:..."* KJV. Underlining mine.

But Joel continues his prophecy. Verse 32b. " *<u>for in mount Zion and in Jerusalem shall be deliverance</u>, as the LORD hath said, and in <u>the remnant whom the LORD shall call</u>.*" Let's continue reading to verse 2 of Joel chapter 3, " *For behold, in those days, and in that time, <u>when I shall bring again the captivity of</u>* **Judah and Jerusalem,** *Verse 2. I will also gather all nations, and will bring them down into the valley of Jehosephat, and I will plead with them there* **for my people and for my heritage Israel,** *whom they have scattered among the nations, and* **parted my land."** KJV. Emphases mine.

Peter, in his Pentecost sermon, quoted Joel verbatim. However notice Peter stopped quoting part-way through Joel 2:32, <u>right in the middle of a sentence</u>! Now I do not believe that Peter figured he had quoted far enough, so arbitrarily quit. <u>Where he ended his quote is just as significant as where he began quoting Joel's prophecy</u>. In other words, Peter, under the anointing of the Spirit, was giving more than simply an explanation for the manifestations of the Holy Spirit as relevant only to that particular Day of Pentecost.

The revealed presence of the Holy Spirit was the fulfillment of Jesus' promise that His followers would receive power after the Spirit would be poured out on them, to witness the Gospel to the world -- beginning at Jerusalem, then extending to Judea, to Samaria, and to the far reaches of the earth, according to Acts 1:8. " *But ye shall receive power after that the Holy Ghost is come upon you, and ye shall be witnesses unto me both in Jerusalem, and in all Judea, and in Samaria, and unto the uttermost part of the earth."*

This outpouring was in fulfillment of Jesus' promise to send The Comforter as indicated in John 15: 26-27. *"But when the Comforter is come whom I will send unto you from the Father, even the Spirit of truth, which proceedeth from the Father, he shall testify of me; and ye also shall bear witness, because ye have been with me from the beginning."* Thus was inaugurated the anointing enablement and empowerment for the Church that has lasted throughout The Age of Grace. The Holy Spirit is the abiding Comforter and Helper for the Church until the Rapture.

Of course we know that when the restraining influence of the Holy Spirit will be removed from the world, The Church-Bride of necessity will be removed also, because Jesus said He would not leave us comfortless. In fact, the Holy Spirit has the role of one of Two Friends of The Bridegroom.

A PROPHETIC MID-SENTENCE PAUSE

This one Friend is assigned with the mandate to assist The Bride in her preparations for the upcoming Wedding in compliance with The Bridegroom's and The Father's wishes. He speaks and acts on behalf of both The Son and The Father, specifically giving glory and honor to The Son, Jesus Christ. He is the 'Eleazar' who will present The Bride to The Son in the Clouds of Glory at the Rapture. The mandate of taking the Gospel message to the entire earth is part of the preparations of The Bride, and the empowerment of the Holy Spirit is vital to carrying out this command.

What struck me is the realization that Peter's quote indicates <u>the duration</u> of the dispensation of the empowerment of the Holy Spirit, and therefore <u>the duration of The Church Age</u>. Peter, by quoting Joel, tells us when The Church Age began, and also provides us with specific signs as to when it will end. So what is the time-frame of The Church Age?

The Church Age extends from the outpouring of the Holy Spirit on The Day of Pentecost in Jerusalem in the Upper Room, <u>until the sun is darkened and the moon is turned to the color of blood</u>. After that particular sign, Peter quotes, *"and whosoever shall call upon the name of the Lord shall be delivered,...."* End of quote. Those who call upon the Name of the LORD are delivered from what? Answer: the coming wrath of God that will be poured out on the ungodly.

The question is, since we generally consider a sentence to be a complete thought, why didn't Peter continue quoting at least to the end of the sentence?

Joel continues the sentence, but his prophecy shifts completely to <u>focus upon Mount Zion and Jerusalem</u>, and speaks of the deliverance *"of the remnant whom the LORD shall call."* Joel 2:32b. Joel then continues his prophecy into chapter 3, revealing that the LORD will bring again the captivity of <u>Judah and Jerusalem</u>, then He will gather all nations together into The Valley of Jehosephat to plead with them for <u>His heritage Israel</u>, referring specifically to <u>His Covenant of The Land with the descendants of Abraham</u>, <u>Isaac, and Jacob</u>. This God-given Covenant addresses the inheritance, both for the Israelis as a people and nation, and of the geographical Land of Promise. The specific cause for this gathering and pleading with the nations of the world, will be regarding the parting of His Land, and the scattering of His people into all nations, both in reference to past dispersions, as well as in <u>the desire of Israel's enemies</u> <u>to do so again</u>. All nations will have input into this dispute, and God will entice all of them into The Middle East to plead with them over these specific issues.

However, where does the Holy Spirit and the Church fit into this scenario? The Bride is not participant beyond Joel chapter 2:32a. Obviously, since Peter quit quoting <u>exactly</u> where he did, something occurs between the first half of the sentence of Joel chapter 2 verse 32, and the last half. The full anointing of the Holy Spirit upon the Church that began on The Day of Pentecost in The Upper Room, ends. The mandate of the Holy Spirit's anointing and empowerment upon the Church to preach the Gospel of Grace and deliverance from sin, beginning in Jerusalem, then extending to Judea, then to Samaria, and ultimately to the ends of the earth, <u>comes to an abrupt halt</u>. God changes His emphasis to focus upon **deliverance for Jerusalem and Mount Zion**. So the full anointing and empowerment of the Holy Spirit <u>began</u> in Jerusalem in the Upper Room, and <u>will end</u> at a time when God's prophetic calendar regarding Israel will pick up again, focusing particularly on Jerusalem and Mount Zion. Interesting!

So what becomes of the Church in the middle of Joel's sentence where Peter quits quoting? Notice the King James translators used the word *"delivered"* in Joel, and *"saved"* in Peter's quote. Obviously, since Peter is quoting Joel, these two words mean the same thing. Peter is not simply referring to salvation from sin as in the receiving of Christ as Savior, although that is primarily significant for all those who call upon the Name of the LORD in repentance, and therefore is definitely the major factor in qualifying for deliverance. Rather, <u>the context in Joel indicates there is a very real earthly scenario that those who call upon the Name of the LORD are delivered (saved) from</u>. This scenario of world events occurs following The Church Age, during a prophetic period known as Yamim Nora'Im, The Days of Awe. All those who call upon the Name of the LORD are delivered, then, from what? From the coming wrath of God that will be poured out upon the unrepentant people and nations of the earth. This deliverance that takes place for all those who call upon the Name of the LORD during the Age of the fullness of the Holy Spirit's anointing, is the Rapture of the Church, and God's Prophetic Appointment Schedule explains the details.

CHAPTER 2
HEBREW VERSUS WESTERN PERCEPTION

I. The Prophetic Spiral:

Before proceeding further with this discussion, it would help if we briefly examine the difference between philosophical Hebrew thinking regarding prophetic presentation, verses Western reasoning. We must remember that God gave His Word to the entire world primarily through the Jews, so to think in Hebrew philosophic methodology helps in interpreting prophecy.

Our Western mind-set in examining almost anything, whether historic or prophetic, is to consider the details in terms of a straight time-line, where sequence is always progressively chronological. Although this approach has validity, it does tend to limit us when we begin to read the prophetic Scriptures. The Hebrew approach is more like looking at a multi-layered spiral. This spiral allows one to traverse much of the same territory more than once, while also progressing forward. Each time one passes around the spiral, new information, and/or more complex and more complete fulfillment is able to occur, while building upon similar, or even the same elements.

This allows for an interpretive approach we have come to recognize as The Law of Multiple Fulfillment. In other words, <u>God is able to have history repeat itself</u>, <u>with progressive results</u>. We must look at all the Prophets in this manner. When we do, we realize for example, that Daniel and Revelation, as well as all the prophetic Scriptures, are not necessarily consecutive narratives with one written prophetic incident always following in chronological sequence upon another, but are progressive layers of data incorporating chronological sequential events, building upon, and sometimes repeating, but also spanning the course of God's intervening Hand in the affairs of mankind throughout the Ages, until fulfillment of the prophecies are complete.

Jesus illustrated this particular type of interpretive thinking for us when he pointed out in His Olivet Discourse on the end times, *"When ye therefore shall see the abomination of desolation, spoken of by Daniel the prophet, stand in the holy place, (whoso readeth, let him understand:)..."* Matthew 24:15. Obviously, Jesus was referring to Daniel 9:27, *"...and in the midst of the week he shall cause the sacrifice and the oblation to cease, and for the overspreading of abominations he shall make it desolate, even until the consummation, and that determined shall be poured upon the desolate."* And Daniel 11:31, *"...and they shall pollute the sanctuary of strength, and shall take away the daily sacrifice, and they shall place the abomination that maketh desolate."*

When most Jews and Christians consider this incident, we understand that it already has been fulfilled by Antiochus Epiphanes in 167 to 165 B.C.E., when he entered and desecrated the Temple in Jerusalem, and sacrificed female swine (sacrificially unclean animals according to The Mosaic Law) on the altar, rendering the Temple and the altar ceremonially unclean for the Jews to carry out their worship, thus causing the daily sacrifices to abruptly halt.

However, Jesus was not speaking historically, but prophetically. He obviously was referring to <u>a future event</u> where a similar desecration scenario will occur. Jesus could not interpret Daniel futuristically if the 167 to 165 B.C.E. incident was the only possible fulfillment. Antiochus' desecration of The Temple was 167 years <u>B</u>efore <u>C</u>hrist was born, so how could he refer to this incident in future terms if it was already totally fulfilled? In fact, the 167 B.C.E. incident was only an incomplete shadow of what will yet be fulfilled, because when we read Daniel, we realize all the pieces were not completely in place in 167 B.C.E. However, we certainly are able to observe that in fulfillment of this particular prophecy, the Temple and the Jews, have 'gone around the mountain' at least once already.

The truth is, God knows the human race never does seem to 'get it the first time.' We must have certain things repeated with increasing detail for us to finally understand. By using the example from Daniel, Jesus illustrates this spiral principle, and tells us (actually, more specifically the disciples, who were themselves Jews, and through them the rest of the world) to pay attention!

So when we read Daniel, Ezekiel, or Revelation, or any of the Prophets, we must keep this spiral in mind. We are not looking at a sequence of prophecies that always follow chronologically in a straight line, but at a progressive spiral helix that contains strands and layers of sequential chronological events. Then these prophetic Scriptures begin to make more sense.

The helix spiral illustration is not at all unlike looking at a DNA molecule! The DNA double helix forms a spiral ladder of genetic information necessary for all life. God's double helix DNA molecule is His finger-print on all living things. However, His spiral finger-print is not limited to the genetic level, but it is also very evident within the inanimate heavens, because we are able to observe the helixical spirals of far off galaxies. In other words, God is the Author of all Creation, and He has orchestrated how all will ultimately unfold within the entire Universe. He is The Creator of Heaven and Earth! It is no wonder that all Scripture is also marked with His fingerprint, revealing His Plan for the Ages.

II. Flash-back / Layer / Overlap Techniques:

The writers if the Scriptures often used flash-back / layer/ overlap techniques. These literary tools are particularly useful when explaining a myriad of interconnected complex details, and/or situations, which occur within a particular time-frame or sequence, or overlap connectively -- weaving into one another. The Prophets, and The Book of Revelation particularly, show evidence of making proclamations, then going back, sometimes several times, revealing additional information of what will occur during a particular time-period, or overlap connectively from one time-period to the next. If we read these Scriptures thinking all that is mentioned is sequential only, we quickly become confused, because we realize the sequences do not make sense. But if we look for literary and prophetic clues and details, we are able to see where the writers, under the inspiration of the Holy Spirit, have 'flash backed,' 'layered,' and /or 'overlapped' information, giving added detail and/or clarification of concurrent, but progressive fulfillment. So in traveling around and along the prophetic spiral, we also must realize each cycle of the progressive helix has multiple layers, and inter-woven overlaps as well.

Often the details of each layer are explained by using a different metaphor or identifiable feature(s). For example, in reading The Book of Revelation we realize the Seals give an overview, while the Trumpets, Woes, Vials, and Sickles explain more detail regarding much the same time-period covered. Some is exact layer, while some is progressive overlap. When we 'layer' and 'overlap' them, a clear, detailed picture emerges. The obvious reason these techniques are used in prophetic Scripture, is that in order to explain the many prophecies that are significant for a particular portion of the spiral sequence, there has to be a way to separate the details out from one another. Prophecy explains God's Plan for the Ages, only much of it indicates complicated interactive elements and events. Life is multifaceted and complex. So too are the prophecies.

CHAPTER 3
HOLY CONVOCATIONS; DIVINE APPOINTMENTS

Inherent within the prophetic spiral is definite progress and chronology. The Feasts and Festivals are <u>a schedule revealing the order in which all prophecy regarding Messiah will ultimately be fulfilled</u>. Actually, the Feasts are referred to by God as His <u>Holy Convocations</u> regarding <u>His Divinely set Appointments</u> with mankind, which were, and are, to be celebrated accordingly.

What is a Holy Convocation? The word 'convocation,' according to [1]Webster's New Complete Dictionary, literally means "a ceremonial assembly (as of the clergy.)" [2]Therefore, a convocation is a religious ceremonial assembly. Now, a sacred ceremony means there is a specific, practiced agenda, that is presented in a ritualistic, pre-ordained manner, and it carries an air of great import and/or purpose. Such ceremony is rooted in set tradition, and has been practiced (rehearsed) over many previous assemblies, so that the importance becomes liturgically based.

Whenever a convocation is presented, all who attend and participate know something of serious importance is taking place, and that this ceremony has life-changing, life-long ramifications. A convocation, then, not only draws from history or religious tradition, but sets the stage for the future. A convocation is therefore not the absolute reality of ramification in and of itself, but the venue whereby preparation for future fulfilled reality takes place.

The Holy Convocations refer to the Old Testament Feasts and Festivals that were ordained by God. Therefore, a Holy Convocation ordained by God Himself, is not simply a rehearsal as in the 'rehearsing' of information, although that is part of the meaning, but is a <u>rehearsal of preparation</u> for a pre-scheduled God-ordained Appointment of prophetic consequence. [3]The word, 'Feast' is translated from the Hebrew "mo-'ed," literally meaning "an appointed time," and "a festival gathering." The Holy Convocations

---

[1] Webster's New Complete Dictionary, Ed, Merriam-Webster, SMITHMARK Publishers, 1995, New york, NY.
[2] Evangelical Dictionary of Theology, Walter A. Elwell, Editor, Baker Book House, 1987, Grand Rapids, Michigan. . p 273.
[3] The Zondervan Pictorial Encyclopedia of the Bible, Volume 2, 1976, Regency Reference Library, Grand Rapids, Michigan. p. 521.

of the Feasts and Festivals are therefore 'Holy Rehearsals' for God's 'Divine Appointments,' and God Himself is The Director. The Holy Convocations as given by God to Israel, then, are Holy Rehearsals which will culminate in actual prophetic appointed presentation.

We know from involvement in drama or special music, that rehearsals are very necessary if we wish for a presentation to be polished, enjoyable, and affective in delivering a message, and for everyone involved to be prepared and ready to do their part. But just the rehearsals themselves would not be sufficient, because <u>rehearsing is not an end in itself</u>. We must eventually have <u>the real production</u>, or all the ceremonial rehearsing in the world is in vain. The diligent rehearsals of the Feasts as given by God were, and are, to provide <u>a detailed schedule</u> of the prophetic sequence to Israel, and through them, to all nations. The main actors were, and are primarily, the people of Israel. But not just Israel. There are other invited guest participants as well -- the Gentile Nations, and the Church. At every Feast and Festival as given by God, there was always a place for the 'stranger' or non-Israeli to take part. Deuteronomy 16:14 states, *"And thou shalt rejoice in thy feast, thou, and thy son, and thy daughter, and thy manservant, and thy maidservant, and the Levite, <u>the stranger</u>, and the fatherless, and the widow, that are within thy gates."* KJV. Underlining mine. The Feasts were given as rehearsals of prophetic truth for all, both Israeli, and *"the stranger,"* and they are to be rehearsed in a specific sequence, because each is for a <u>Time Appointed</u>.

These Holy Convocations also contain an artists ability to look back at previous Divine Appointments (mo'ed) with mankind, particularly with the nation of Israel, and draw parallels, types, and messages forward to portray events to come. The final artistically orchestrated presentations will take place at Appointed Times determined by God Himself. The Feasts then, indicate God has a specific set of Divine Appointments with mankind that <u>will come to pass</u>. We cannot change, either by time, or by content, these Divine Appointments. The program is entirely His. <u>Mankind will have to face these Appointments</u>. It would be greatly advantageous then, for all who must participate, to gain an understanding of <u>The Holy Rehearsals</u> in preparation for <u>the Scheduled Appointments</u>!

The problem we encounter is that three errors have taken place regarding The Holy Convocations. First of all, the Church has thrown out the Feasts and Festivals as Old Testament Jewish Cultural Law and tradition, and therefore irrelevant for the Christian. As far as the necessity for the Church to rehearse these Feasts and Festivals in a legalistic manner is concerned, <u>we are definitely not to be caught up in legalism.</u> <u>Rather, our rehearsal is to recognize the work of Jesus Christ prophetically in these</u>

HOLY CONVOCATIONS; DIVINE APPOINTMENTS

<u>Feasts and Festivals</u>. But it has become a closed topic for anyone in the Church to make reference to the Feasts, other than in a fleeting manner, or be accused of Judaizing. This is unfortunate, because we have ignored a most detailed explanation and sequence for the actual presentation of fulfillment of the Divine Appointments in and through Jesus Christ.

These Feasts were not dreamed-up by the Israelis themselves. They were dictated, appointed, and directed by God. Leviticus 23: 1-2. *"And the LORD spake unto Moses, saying, Speak unto the children of Israel, and say unto them, Concerning the feasts of the LORD, which ye shall proclaim to be holy convocations, even these are my feasts."* And verse 4. *"These are the feasts of the LORD, even holy convocations, which ye shall proclaim in their <u>seasons</u>."* How can we close The Bible and ignore them as we have done over the course of most of The Church Age? It is time to take out Scripture and examine these Convocations again, <u>because the actual performance and fulfillment of The Fall Feasts and Festivals is about to unfold,</u> and we need to be prepared.

As believers in the fact that Jesus Christ is the true incarnate Word of God, we have been given the Holy Spirit who *"will guide you into all truth."* John 16:13. We must allow the Holy Spirit to illuminate the Feasts and Festivals to us, so we can spread the truth about them to those who need to hear.

Assigning these Convocations solely to the Jews, who generally up to this point in time do not accept Jesus as Messiah, is the first mistake. The rehearsals have been called, and we have ignored them. It is pretty difficult for those who do show up for rehearsal (the Jews) to understand, when part of the cast (the Church) never attends. So we cannot put the entire blame for lack of perception on the Jews alone! Now is the time for the Church to again become informed, because it is time for the partial blindness to begin to be lifted for the Jews.

The second mistake is that the Jews have claimed the Feasts and Festivals solely for themselves, and consider anyone other than themselves studying, or trying to understand them, or especially participating in any way, as being out of line. In the Jewish religious mind-set, the rehearsals are only for them to attend! <u>They also fail to realize the Feasts and Festivals culminate in Divine Appointments</u>, <u>not only for themselves</u>, <u>but for all nations of the world</u>. They have lost sight of the reason God gave these Holy Convocations in the first place! It would appear the Jews want to be the only ones to be both the actors and audience, and no one else is allowed in. Strange! Every great production needs both players and audience, and <u>both must be participant</u> for the real message to be presented and received. These Convocations are specifically meant for all people and nations to participate in, because they rehearse the prophetic sequence and details as <u>fulfilled in Christ</u> for all mankind. Jews are Jews. But they also must come to recognize the fact that they have been chosen by God to be an object lesson to the nations, to proclaim righteousness, and to be the nation through whom Messiah, The Redeemer, has, and will come. They hold on to their Feasts with such an iron fist, that they actually miss the importance of their own rehearsals! They forget these Holy Convocations will eventually culminate in actual appointed production; not merely serve as historical remembrance.

Another mistake is that both the Church and the Jews have totally missed the ramifications of the rehearsals. The Church misses, because we have ignored the rehearsals entirely, so don't even know what is being rehearsed! In fact most Christians do not know the rehearsals have been called! So we have adopted our own times of celebration throughout the year as Christian holidays, that also are used to spread the Gospel. That in itself is not necessarily out of line; but we should not totally ignore what God gave as His own Feasts and Festivals! He has not called us to mere celebration, but to rehearse for a very important program ahead. His purpose is rehearsal for events He has prepared in advance, and placed on His Appointment Calendar of The Ages.

The Jews miss the point because they are so busy rehearsing, and adding in their own lines, the message has become lost. Nothing like 'not being able to see the forest for the trees!' If the Jews actually recognized the message they are supposed to be portraying, they would have long ago accepted Jesus as Messiah, because He has fulfilled all the Spring Feasts to the letter already! Then they would be looking forward to the fulfillment of The Fall Feasts and Festivals with great anticipation, and with some dread, because the Fall Feasts rehearse the ingathering and resurrection of The Wholly Righteous, the Wedding and Coronation of the KING, the set-up of The Millennial Reign of Christ, and the sobering fact that Messiah is The Righteous Judge.

They would realize The Spring Feasts have already had their appointed presentation, so The Fall Feasts should now take precedence in rehearsal, because they are now going to soon be brought to their full presentation fulfillment. But the Jews still place a great deal of emphasis on rehearsing for what already has taken place regarding their own history, and missing the fulfillment of what has already been fulfilled in and through Jesus Christ, and what is shortly to come to pass in the Revelation of Messiah, and the Restoration of The Kingdom to Israel!

Many of us also miss why they have been chosen to be the people-group through which much of the unfolding of the Schedule will take place. They are no better, and definitely no worse, than any other ethnic group. They are simply chosen by the LORD to be the focal-point through which He reveals Himself to the entire world; much like a teacher will choose a student or group of students from among classmates to be the vehicle to distribute and illustrate necessary information to all the students, themselves included. They are not 'teacher's pets,' but are chosen from among equals to do a specific job, for a specific purpose. If they weren't chosen, someone else would have been. Therefore, there is no room for animosity or jealousy on anyone's part! Also, we cannot ignore the intended illustration simply because a specific people-group was chosen to reveal God's redemptive plan of salvation, and the unfolding of the prophetic time-table. Let's get our attention on the intention, not just on the conscripts!

Meanwhile, the Church debates and argues over sequences and time-lines of prophecy, while the order of the actual Appointed Schedule has already been printed and distributed. All we need do is read the Program! When we recognize this, the apparent discrepancies between the accounts of Matthew, Mark, and Luke actually make sense, and prophecy from both Old and New Testaments becomes more understandable. In other words, the program not only gives the schedule of actual events being rehearsed, but also explains the fact that these presentations have specified Divinely Appointed Times when they will be accomplished. *"At the time appointed," "For the appointed time," "in that day," "the day," "at that time," "the appointed day of ,"* etc. When we see this type of wording, some aspect of the fulfillment of one of the Feasts and Festivals has, is, will be, or will again be, taking place. Jesus came in the *"fullness of time."* Look for these clues!

The rehearsals do lead to actual appointed final presentation. Each Feast and Festival, and even the days that lie between them, is God's appointed rehearsal, because He has a REAL appointment that will FULFILL each Feast and Festival. Christ fulfilled The Spring Feasts when He came the first time as Prophet and Redeemer, and as the prophetically fulfilled Passover Lamb of God. He has yet to completely fulfill The Fall Feasts and Festivals when He reveals Himself as: The Risen Lamb, The Lion of The Tribe of Judah, The Righteous Judge, The Eternal High Priest, The KING, LORD, and Bridegroom. We are to rehearse carefully, and thoroughly, so we are ready for the appointed fulfillments. This goes for the Christian as well as for the Jew! And both have an ultimate obligation to reveal the truth to all nations and peoples, because we are the ones who have direct access to the Scriptures!

CHAPTER 4
THE FALL FEASTS AND FESTIVALS

Jesus Christ fulfilled all The Spring Feasts exactly as specified in Scripture, right down to the intricate details of each. That being the case, there is no reason to believe He will change His approach concerning fulfillment of The Fall Feasts. In light of this fact, it is interesting to note some important prophetic characteristics regarding The Fall Feasts. This is not an exhaustive study, but hopefully the aspects discussed here will help in understanding the prophetic sequence as revealed by these God-ordained Convocations.

I. The Agricultural Significance of The Feasts:

The Feasts are agricultural in orientation, having to do with the harvests in particular. Jesus often spoke prophetically, using grain and fruit as metaphors, because these symbols are rooted within the agricultural base of Israeli society. Barley is a Spring crop referring specifically to Israel, so is a regionally localized, relatively small crop. The Fall harvests are broader in meaning. The wheat crop produces a large harvest, so represents all people of the earth. Corn speaks of the vastness of humanity made up of identifiable individuals. Fruit is generally in reference to the harvests gathered from vines and trees, so represents the nations and their leaders.

A. The Seasonal Rains:

There are two seasons of planting and harvest in Israel. The Spring, and the Fall. The bounty of these two seasons depends solely upon the seasonal rains sent by God, since the Land of Israel has no readily available water supply, other than what comes from rain. Even the Kinneret, which is Israel's main domestic and industrial water source, depends to a large extent on rainfall. 'Thus, Israel must depend upon God for sustenance. The greatest threat to the Israeli economy is either lack of precipitation, or unseasonal rain. That is why God often used either drought or flooding to chastise Israel and Judah.

---

[4] Jewish Heritage Online Magazine, Jeffrey H. Tigay, *How Israelite Rain is different From All Other Rain*, www.jhom.com/topics/rain/different.html

The Final Schedule Revealed

1. The "Early" and "Latter" Rains:

[5]There are two seasons of rain in Israel. The "early" or "former rain," and the "latter rains."

The "early" or" former" rains, "are called [6] "yoreh" or "moreh" in Hebrew, and are further broken down into two sub-seasons, the Fall rains, and the "Geshem" Winter rains. The "early rains" range in intensity and volume from relatively moderate in late Fall, to very heavy in Winter. The first sub-season for "the"early rains" is <u>from late October through November</u>. The second sub-season for "the early rains" lasts throughout the Winter from <u>December to early March</u>. The seeds planted in the Fall <u>produce the Spring Harvests</u> (the Spring Feasts.) The seeds for the Spring crops, then, must be germinated and stabilized by the Fall early rains before the heavier Winter rains arrive.

[7]The Fall Feasts (Fall Harvests) result from an early Spring planting, germinated by the "Malqosh" "latter rains" which fall in the <u>early Spring from March approximately through to the end of April</u>. The "latter rains" serve to germinate the seeds of the Fall crops that are planted in the early Spring, and at the same time continue to water the Spring crops, maturing them until they are ready for Spring harvest.

Therefore, the amount of water deposited in the soil and aquifers by the "early or former rains" falling from late Fall through the Winter, provides the bulk of the nation's annual water supply. Whereas the Spring "latter rains" prevent the soil from becoming parched, providing just enough irrigation to last throughout the drier late Spring and Summer months until the Fall Harvests. The timing of the ingathering for the Fall crops, must take place within a very short time-period before the "early rains" begin again in late Fall. So, the Fall crops especially, must be harvested quickly, <u>at the appointed times</u>, or they could be ruined. The Fall always has some risk of stormy weather and squalls, indicating the prophetic fulfillment of The Fall Feasts and Festivals will occur during a short, but specific time of duress.

The prophetic significance of these rains relates directly to how God will deal with Israel, and all nations. When the seasons of rain are upset in their timing, and/or in their volume, God's judgment is in play. Either the withholding of rain, or the orchestration of unseasonable deluge, can cause famine and great hardship. When the people forgot God's blessings

---

[5]   Sacred Text Bible Index, www.sacred-texts.com/bib/ebd/305.htm.
[6]   Sacred Texts Bible Index, *Rain*, www.sacred-texts.com/bib/ebd/ebd305.htm
[7]   The Latter Rain Page, http:/latter- ain/eschae/latter.htm.

and became complacent or disobedient, God changed the pattern of precipitation. Jeremiah 5:24 *"Neither say they in their heart, Let us now fear the LORD our God, that giveth rain, both the former and the latter, in his season: he reserveth unto us the appointed weeks of the harvest."* God sends the rains. He also <u>appoints</u> the times of harvest. Therefore, both His discipline as well as His blessings are prophetically exhibited through these seasons of rain and appointed harvests.

Joel makes an interesting prophetic proclamation in chapter 2, verses 23 to 27. *"Be glad then, ye children of Zion, and rejoice in the LORD your God: for he hath given you the former rain moderately, and he will cause to come down for you the rain, the former rain, <u>and</u> the latter rain <u>in the first month</u>. Verse 24. And the floors shall be full of wheat, and the vats shall overflow with wine and oil. Verse 25. And I will restore to you the years that the locust hath eaten, and the cankerworm, and the caterpillar, and the palmerworm, my great army which I sent among you. Verse 26. And ye shall eat plenty, and be satisfied, and praise the name of the LORD your God, that hath dealt wondrously with you: and my people shall never be ashamed. Verse 27. And ye shall know that I am in the midst of Israel, and that I am the LORD your God, and none else: and my people shall never be ashamed."* KJV. Underlining mine.

Since the "former rain" comes in the late Fall and Winter, and the "latter rain" comes in the Spring, how is it that <u>both will fall in the first month, and will usher in a time of renewal</u>? This passage in Joel, in context, just precedes the passage Peter quoted on the Day of Pentecost, from which Joel continues beyond Peter's quote through to the restoration of Israel under Christ. In other words, this <u>appointed time of combined "former" and "latter" rains</u> will be an alteration of the usual seasons of precipitation, meaning, <u>God's discipline is in play</u>. The fact that this discipline will take place in the first month (Tishrei), means these former and latter rains together will accompany the Fall Harvests (Feasts), and will ultimately usher in the blessing and restoration of The Kingdom of Israel under the rule and reign of Messiah. This time-period is the prophetic fulfillment of the Tishrei High Holy Days, the Yamim Nora'Im from Rosh HaShanah to Yom Kippur, which will be followed by Sukkot and Shemini Atzeret - Simchat Torah. There will be a Fall Season of harvests, coupled with God's wrath, <u>followed by great everlasting blessing</u>.

Some may argue that rain represents the work and presence of the Holy Spirit. Yes, it does. But we must also remember the fact that the Holy Spirit anointed the prophets, and will expedite all that the prophets have spoken and written, to bring all to fulfillment through Jesus Christ. In order to understand, we must not only look at how the Holy Spirit has been poured out upon the Church, but at the prophetic context of how all will be brought to completion for the Church, for Israel, and for all nations. In other words, the work of the Holy Spirit does not begin and end with the Church!

Although the Church has a specific Holy Spirit anointing to take the Gospel to the entire world, there is a much broader picture of the ministry of the Holy Spirit than just during the Church Age. The Church does not have an exclusive corner on the work and ministry of the Holy Spirit! He deals with all people of all Ages. Therefore, "The Latter Rain" movements touted by many groups are often slightly erroneous, because they have wrested the concept of the "former" and "latter" rains out of their prophetic context, which is rooted within the agricultural year and annual harvests of Israel. The cycles of the Times and Seasons of the rains, winds, and the harvests, are to portray God's prophetic Plan of the Ages, revealed through Israel as the object lesson to all nations. The Holy Spirit expedites the entire program!

II. "Mo'ed:"

The Spring Feasts (Harvests, Convocations) are now historical, because Messiah has already fulfilled them at His First Coming. The Fall Feasts (Harvests) are yet to come, and Messiah is yet to complete their appointed fulfillment.

All the Feasts occur on specified dates throughout the Jewish Calendar year, and the dates on which they fall are called "mo'ed," which means "appointed time," or "set time," so each is an "appointment of the LORD," or " a day of fulfillment," or similar wording. In fact, The Fall Feasts especially are relatively easy to spot, because their fulfillment accompanies the "Day of Judgment," the "Day of Trouble and Distress," the "Great and Notable Day of the LORD," the "Day of Christ," etc., referring to a coming time of unprecedented difficulty when God will pour out His wrath upon the earth. So The Fall Feasts come with warnings of impending judgment on the unrepentant, but at the same time, promise tremendous blessing for the righteous.

The Fall Feasts take place during the month of Tishrei. In fact, they do not take up the entire month. The High Holy Days are from Rosh HaShanah to Yom Kippur, Tishrei 1-10. Sukkot, The Feast of Tabernacles, is celebrated five days later; followed immediately by Shemini Atzeret, The Eighth Day, and Simchat Torah, the honoring of the written Word of God as revealed to Moses on Mount Sinai.

III. Teshuvah:

The Jewish religious calendar has a particular season called Teshuvah, which is 40 days of repentance and reconciliation between God and man, between man and his family members, between friends and neighbors, and even reaches out toward enemies in desire for peace. [8]"The word "teshuvah" literally means "to return." This period begins on Elul 1, and ends on Tishrei 10. That's approximately August to September. The Ten Days of Awe from Rosh HaShanah to Yom Kippur are the most sobering and awesome of these 40 days of repentance. These final ten days of Teshuvah, known as the "High Holy Days," or Yamim Nora'Im, "The Days of Awe," also referred to as "Jacob's Trouble," are the days we are addressing specifically in this book.

A. Calendar Differences:

Let me insert an interesting observation revealing why prophecy, at this juncture, cannot necessarily be pin-pointed exactly to the day or hour. However, when The Fall Feasts literally begin to be fulfilled, the calculation of events to follow will then become easy to peg on a calendar. The Jewish calendar does not line up exactly with our Gregorian calendar, so the dates compared to our calendar slide each year, until an added thirteenth month is inserted to correct for the seasons. A prophetic year is 360 days, based on the 24 hour seven days of Creation and original perfection within the universe. The Jewish calendar year is 354 days, based on the lunar cycle. Our Gregorian calendar is calibrated according to a solar year of 365.25 days. [10]"To accommodate seasonal adjustment, the correction month, Ve Adar, is inserted seven times every nineteen years. Prophetic calculation becomes somewhat of a challenge because of these calendar differences. According to Jesus and Paul, we ought to be able to discern the Times and the Seasons, even though we cannot know the exact day or hour of Christ's return for His Bride at the Rapture. These calendar discrepancies are allowed by God to make sure we are kept on our toes.

---

[8] .www.aish.com/hhgrowth/hhgrowthDefault/Teshuvah_Dry_Clea... Rabbi Shraga Simmons. *Growth and Renewal, Teshuvah, Dry cleaning for the Soul*,#1 of 16 in the Aish.com High Holidays Growth Series .

[9] RoshHaShanah and the Messianic Kingcdom to Come, Joseph Good, 1989, HaTikva Ministries, Port Arthur, TX. P.87,197.

[10] .The New Encyclopedic Reference Edition of The Holy Bible, Zodervan Publishing House, Grand Rapids, Michigan, Royal Publishers, Inc. 1966. The Jewish Calendar, p, 813.

The Final Schedule Revealed

To further complicate things, the Jews have four ways of interpreting their own calendar. Most of the time they use two of the four, the Sacred Calendar, and the Civil Calendar. Therefore, Elul is the middle month of the Sacred Calendar, and also is the final month of the Civil Calendar. The following month, Tishrei, is the seventh month of the Sacred Calendar, and the first month of a new Civil year. So Teshuvah (a forty day time of repentance)falls in the lead-up to, and during the first ten days of the Civil year, and in the middle of a Sacred year. Repentance is necessary in the middle of our busy daily lives, but ultimately will be the foundation for the inauguration of a new era of relationship with Christ, the LORD.

When the Fall Feasts and Festivals are referred to as taking place during the first month, we know Tishrei is being considered from the perspective of the Civil year. When they are referred to as taking place in the seventh month, the Sacred year is the frame of reverence. Therefore, Rosh HaShanah can be referred to as a celebration of the beginning of a new Civil year (like a New Years), or as the inauguration of a time-out for repentance mid-way through the Sacred year.

B. Teshuvah Greetings:

The Forty Days of Teshuvah are divided into two distinct periods: The Thirty Days of the month Elul, followed by Yamim Nora'Im, The Ten Days of Awe, The High Holy Days of Tishrei 1-10. "To highlight the significance of these two distinct periods of Teshuvah, there are two greetings used. During the Thirty Days of Elul, the greeting is,[12] "May you're name be inscribed in The Book of The Wholly Righteous." The significance of this greeting is that it is imperative to repent of all sin to be assured of inscription in The Book of Life before Rosh HaShanah, also known as Yom HaDin, The Day of Judgment, so that when Ha Teruah Shofar (The Last Trump) sounds, one will be qualified to be Tzadika (wholly righteous), and therefore considered worthy to participate in the benefits of the <u>first</u> Fall Harvest (resurrection and ingathering) unto the LORD. Those who are the living righteous receive incorruptible bodies, and are gathered unto the LORD along with the resurrected righteous. All of those gathered unto the LORD at Rosh HaShanah, are hidden from the wrath of God that is to be poured out during The Ten Days of Awe, Jacob's Trouble.

---

[11] , Rosh HaShanah and the Messianic Kingdom to Come, Joseph Good, 1989, HaTikva ministries, Port Arthur, TX. P.51.

[12] A Quick Overview of the High Holidays, Rabbi Shraga Simmons, www.aosh.com/hhElulDefault/a_quick_overview_of_the...

THE FALL FEASTS AND FESTIVALS

If one has not repented, so must remain to go through The Days of Awe, the second greeting used during the Tishrei Ten Days of Teshuvah applies. [13] "May you be sealed unto the Day of Redemption." This greeting highlights the fact that there are only ten more 'Days' remaining, and it is absolutely imperative to now repent, or face eternal punishment, because at Yom Kippur, The Day of Atonement, (also known as The Day of Redemption) the eternal destiny of each person who remained to go through The Days of Awe is sealed.

If one repents during The Days of Awe, their name will be entered into, or not be blotted-out of, The Book of The Wholly Righteous (The Book of Life.) And if the repentant die during these Ten Days, they will be resurrected at the sounding of Tekiah HaGadol, The Great Shofar, and will enter into the Kingdom along with the changed living righteous. If one does not repent, their name is not entered into The Book of Life. Or, if in the past one had repented, but fell into unrepentant sin, their name will be blotted out, and they will be accounted as Rashim (Wicked) and sealed unto eternal damnation. So this greeting covers the aspect of being sealed regardless of whether one repents, or does not repent, so one's eternal destiny will be permanently sealed on Yom Kippur, The Day of Redemption. The crop is either in-gathered or destroyed. One's sealed destiny depends entirely on the decision of repentance, or lack of repentance, on the part of the individual before God. This greeting is both an urgent invitation to repent, and a warning, because all who go through The Ten Days (years) of Awe will be sealed one way or the other on Yom Kippur.

So we see the entire Season of Teshuvah carries a strong message of the necessity for repentance before God, and the invitation to reconciliation, both with God and with man. This reconciliation can only be expedited by repentance of all sin, and by faith receiving The Atonement of the blood of Christ. The Church Age is the patient grace and mercy of God calling all unto repentance and salvation before the resurrection and ingathering of Rosh HaShanah, when The Last Trump of the Feast will sound. (Some Jewish Rabbis place The Last Trump at Yom Kippur. However, the weight of Scripture appears to be in agreement that The Last Trump is blown at Rosh HaShanah, and most Jews adhere to this interpretation. The conclusion is, The Last Trump of Rosh Hashanah, and The Great Shofar of Yom Kippur are actually the same instrument, but it is blown more

---

[13] Rosh HaShanah and the Messianic Kingdom to Come, Joseph Good, 1990, Teshuvah. P.87-98.

than once with significance. I will explain this later.) The Age of Grace is pictured by the Days of Elul.

Psalm 103:8-9 states: *"The LORD is merciful and gracious, slow to anger, and plenteous in mercy. He will not always chide: neither will he keep his anger for ever."* The LORD's longsuffering and patience is certainly great during these Elul Days of Grace, but He will not withhold His anger forever. The Ten Tishrei Days of Awe are coming soon upon all who are not repentant. Following Rosh HaShanah, prophetically, there will only be ten more years remaining for mankind to turn to God in repentance unto salvation before all are finally sealed on Yom Kippur. This is a clear and strong message, and no one will be able to plead lack of understanding, or of opportunity, so long as the message is preached. It is the mission of the Church to take this message to all nations until the LORD comes for the ingathering harvest of Rosh HaShanah. Then it will be the mandate of the 144,000 to take this message of repentance to the entire world once more during the final Ten Days (years) of Teshuvah, The Ten Days of Awe, before The Second Coming of Christ, The Redeemer and Righteous Judge, at Yom Kippur.

Are you ready? Those who repent during The Elul Days of Teshuvah (the current Church Age) will be most blessed. Those who repent during The Ten Tishrei Teshuvah Days of Awe will suffer greatly, and will be martyred for their faith in Jesus Christ. It is best to repent NOW! *"Behold now is the accepted time; behold now is the day of salvation."* 2 Corinthians 6: 2b.

[14]The Elul period of Teshuvah has another notable significance for those who repent before Rosh Hashanah. Elul is the month of the Bridegroom and the Bride, which is significant since Elul Teshuvah pictures the Age of Grace, which is the Age of the Church, the period of prophetic time when the Bridegroom chooses and courts His Bride. The Hebrew letters for Elul, Alef-Lamed-Vav-Lamed, are an acronym. "Ani l'dodi v'dodi li." Translated into English, this means, "I am my Beloved's, and my Beloved is mine." The word "Elul" itself means "search," carrying the message that those who search their hearts earnestly, in repentance, will find forgiveness, and will enter into a relationship of love with the LORD Jesus Christ, the Beloved Bridegroom. Those who repent during this Age of Grace will be the Bride of Christ!

Toward the wrap-up of the thirty days of Elul Teshuvah, there is a crescendo of urgency felt, and Selichot prayers are offered. The urgency

---

[14] Judaism 101, The Month of Elul and Selichot,Level: Basic. www.jewfaq.org/elul.htm.

for repentance builds, because the Elul Days are drawing to a close, and Rosh Hashanah is rapidly approaching. The Selichot prayers recite the "Thirteen Attributes of Mercy," revealing God's character traits of mercy and forgiveness. These Selichot prayers are offered daily throughout the Days of Awe until Yom Kippur, the Day of Atonement.

What are the Thirteen Attributes of Mercy that were revealed to Moses? After the tablets of stone were complete on Mount Sinai, then smashed by Moses because of sin in the camp, Moses was again taken back up the Mount, and given the commandments again. *"The Lord descended in the cloud, and stood with him there, and <u>proclaimed the name of the LORD</u>. Verse 6. And the LORD passed by before him, and proclaimed, <u>The LORD, The LORD God</u>, merciful and gracious, long-suffering, and abundant in goodness and truth, Verse 7. Keeping mercy for thousands, forgiving iniquity, and transgression, and sin, and that will by no means clear the guilty;"* Exodus 34:5-7. Underlining mine. *"The LORD"* here is translated from the Hebrew 'Ha Shem" which literally means "The Name," and in this passage is used to denote the LORD's attributes of grace and mercy. [15] "Ha Shem is doubled in verse 6, and placed in conjunction with the Hebrew "El" meaning "The Almighty God." "Ha Shem, Ha Shem El." "The LORD, The LORD God Almighty." He is The Almighty God, the strong all powerful Ruler of the universe, yet He is full of grace and mercy.

[16] The Thirteen Attributes of Mercy are the attributes that God revealed to Moses as the LORD descended on Mount Sinai and communed with him. But the urgency of cashing-in on these attributes of the mercy and grace of the LORD, the Almighty, is also portrayed in the double repetition, revealing the fact that there is a sense of timing involved. [17] The mercy of the LORD, although intrinsic to His nature, reveals His justice. The LORD is not a mamby-pamby sugar-daddy, turning a blind eye to

---

[15] Judaism 101, The Month of Elul and Selichot, Level: Basic. Www.jewfaq.org/elul.htm.
[16] Yeshivat Har Etzion, www.vbm-torah.org/roshandyk/13-eb.htm., Rav Ezra Bick, The Israel Koschitky Virtual Beit Midrash, *The Secret of Selichot: The Thirteen Attributes of Mercy.*
[17] Hadrash Ve-Haiyun - The Torah Page, http://members.aol.com/eylevine/5763pinchas.htm., The Reisha rav HaGoan R' Aaron Levine zt"1, Torah Insights on the Weekly Parsha, Pinchas 5763, In our prayers we sometimes address Hashem as "our Father." At other times we address Him as "our King." Throughout the Torah we find that Hashem is addressed with many different titles. Indeed, the Thirteen Attributes of Mercy are nothing other than thirteen different titles of Hashem..." "This conveys our awareness that Hashem is the True Judge."

iniquity. Mercy, in a court of law, is extended toward one that has been proven guilty. In other words, the LORD is the Righteous Judge! The Almighty cannot forgive those who do not repent, but choose to remain in their guilt. Therefore, the message of mercy and grace also carries the sobering underlying warning of impending judgment on those who do not repent. The Rosh HaShanah "Day of Judgment" is imminent, then the Yom Kippur judgment will soon follow. Hence, the double emphasis. The Books will be opened at both these judgments.

II. Rosh HaShanah:

[18] Rosh HaShanah, 'Rosh' meaning 'Head,' 'Shana' meaning 'year,' is The 'New Years' of the Jewish Civil Calendar, and takes place on the first day of the Fall month of Tishrei. Depending on which branch of Judaism is adhered to, Rosh HaShanah may be celebrated variously from one to four days, indicating a degree of flexibility for the time of the ingathering Rapture. Such an ingathering of a harvest (Natzal) is built into Judaic practices. Tishrei, being the seventh month of the Jewish Sacred Calendar, is significant in that seven is the number of completion. Therefore Rosh HaShanah is both the first day of a new Civil year, and the completion of all things pertaining to the spiritual affairs of mankind over the past Season. The significance for us is that The Church Age (the prophetic Season we are currently in) is about to be wrapped up, and the ushering in of a new Dispensation is soon to take place. This God-Appointed Convocation calls everyone to examine themselves, to repent of sin, return to God, and to reach out to others in love, blessing, and forgiveness. Rosh HaShanah is the beginning of the final Ten Days of The Season of Teshuvah, the last chance for mankind to repent and turn to Christ.

Rosh HaShanah also is called Yom HaDin, The Day of Judgment, and is accompanied by trumpets calling all to repentance, the significant trumpet of the Feast being Ha Teruah Shofar, also known as "The Last Trump." So this Feast is known as "Yom Teruah," meaning The Day of the Trumpet, so is called "The Feast of Trumpets." Rosh HaShanah is a judgment Feast when the hearts of all mankind are examined before God, and at the sounding of The Last Trump, all are judged according to what is written in The Books.

---

[18] Rosh Hashanah and the Messianic Kingdom to Come, Joseph Good, 1990, HaTikvah Ministries, Port Arthur Tx. P. 81-86.

A. The Books are Opened:

[19]Several Books are opened at this time. One Book for the Tzadikim (Wholly Righteous), one Book for the intermediates, and one Book for the Rashim (Wicked) according to Judaic belief. Whether there is a real designation of a specific 'Book' for the intermediate group is debatable, but it is obvious there are many such folk in this world, and the fact that they will not be raptured (Natzal, meaning ingathered) at Rosh HaShanah along with the Tzadikim (Wholly Righteous), shows this group does receive judgment at this juncture.

[20]One other significant Book is opened during Rosh HaShanah. Another name for Rosh HaShanah is "Yom HaZikkaron," meaning "The Day of Remembrance." There is a ceremony during Rosh HaShanah called "Zikhronot," "Divine Remembrance," where everyone is reminded that God keeps the Books. The Book of Remembrance is one of these written records. *"Then they that feared the LORD spake often one to another: and the LORD hearkened, and heard it, and a <u>book of remembrance was written before him for them that feared the LORD</u>, and that thought upon his name."* Malachi 3:16. This tells us that God keeps a detailed record of our conversations and lifestyle regarding Himself and His Word, and He will reward us accordingly.

How do we know this Book of Remembrance is opened at Rosh HaShanah? Let's continue in Malachi chapter 3, reading verses 17-18. *"And they shall be mine, saith the LORD of hosts, <u>in the day</u> when I make up my jewels; <u>and I will spare them, as a man spareth his own son that serveth him</u>. Verse 18. <u>Then shall ye return</u>, and <u>discern between the righteous and the wicked, between him that serveth God, and him that serveth him not</u>."* KJV. Underlining mine.

---

[19] Growth and Renewal, Rabbi Ari Khan, *Power of Tzesakah*, www.aish.com/hhGrowth/hhGrowthDefault/Power_of_Tzedaka. The Talmud: "Rabbi Kruspedai said in the name of Rabbi Yochanan: "Three books are opened (in heaven) on Rosh HaShanah – one for the thoroughly wicked, one for the thoroughly righteous, and one for the intermediate. The thoroughly righteous are immediately inscribed definitively in the Book of Life. The thoroughly wicked are immediately inscribed definitively in the Book of Death. The doom of the intermediate is suspended from Rosh HaShana until Yom Kippur, the Day of Atonement. If they deserve well, they are inscribed on the Book of Life. If they do not deserve well, they are inscribed in the book of Death." Rosh Hashana 16.b.)

[20] Rosh HaShanah and the Messianic Kingdom to Come, Joseph Good, 1990, HaTikvah Ministries, Port Arthur Tx. P.84-85.

Notice, the *"Jewels"* are those who have spoken to one another remembering the LORD. It is these that He has been keeping written record regarding, and He is going to assemble them <u>on a specific day</u> (Appointed Day). Why? <u>Because He is going to spare them as a man spares his son</u>. Spare them from what? The Wrath of God. <u>This is the Rosh HaShanah judgment</u>.

But the next verse goes on to state *"Then shall ye return..."* Who returns? The LORD and His righteous Jewels. In order to return, they first must have gone somewhere. Where have they been? They all have been in Heaven. Then they come back, and <u>a subsequent judgment hearing</u> takes place at Yom Kippur when the LORD will bring final judgment upon those who were remaining on the earth. He, along with those who return with Him, will <u>discern between the Righteous and the Wicked</u>; between those who serve God, and those who don't.

So the sequence of the two separate judgments of The Fall Feasts of Rosh HaShanah and Yom Kippur is being described here, with the emphasis in this passage being on the blessings of the first judgment when The Book of Remembrance is opened, and the Righteous are judged according to their works of righteousness and remembrance of the LORD.

One of the first activities the Righteous will participate in upon entering the halls of Heaven following the Rapture, will be the Judgment Seat of Christ, known as the Beama Seat Judgment. This is not a judgment regarding sin, but of reward for righteousness according to our deeds. Romans 14:10. *"But why dost thou judge thy brother? or why dost thou set at nought thy brother? "* <u>*For we shall all appear before the judgment seat of Christ*</u>, *that every one may receive the things done in his body, according to that he hath done, whether it be good or bad."* 2 Corinthians 5:10. *"Every man's works shall be made manifest: <u>for the day</u>* (a specific appointed day) *shall declare it, because it shall be revealed by fire; and the fire shall try every man's work of what sort it is. If any man's work abide which he hath built thereupon, he shall receive a reward. If any man's work shall be burned, he shall suffer loss: but he himself shall be saved; yet so as by fire."* 1 Corinthians 3: 13-15. Emphasis mine. This opening of <u>The Book of Remembrance</u> for the Tzadikim (Righteous) is at once sobering, and joyful, and our works will be tried by fire to see what they are made of, and whether they will remain.

B. Trumpet Blasts:

There are several trumpet blasts sounded, beginning during the thirty day Elul Teshuvah lead-up to The Days of Awe, and sounding also from Rosh HaShanah to Yom Kippur. These blasts are specific <u>sequences of notes within a score of music for a trumpet orchestra</u>, or ensemble, <u>to play</u>.

THE FALL FEASTS AND FESTIVALS

The Last Trump, HaTeurah Shofar, is the lead voice blast in the orchestra at Rosh HaShanah, The Feast of Trumpets, calling the Wholly Righteous together unto the LORD. Tekiah HaGadol is the lead voice trumpet blast at Yom Kippur, announcing The Second Coming of Messiah to the earth.

In this trumpet orchestra, there are several patterns of notes sounded, and <u>the lead trumpet</u>, along with other trumpets, plays all these notes at specified times within the music score, and the total number of trumpet blasts adds up to one hundred.

1. Tekiah Notes:

[21]A 'Tekiah' blast is a long sound <u>heralding the Royal Coronation and Crowning of the LORD as the KING</u>. This Coronation-Wedding Ceremony takes place in Heaven. A Tekiah blast will also take place at Yom Kippur when Christ returns to earth as KING of Kings and LORD of Lords, and the nations will have to recognize Him as the rightful, Royal Anointed One. HaTekiah was sounded at Creation, so reveals God as Creator.

2. Shevarim Notes:

Then there is the sounding of the 'shevarim' notes. These are three short blasts indicating sobbing, and they represent remorse for sin, and are thus a call to final repentance, because all, both righteous and unrighteous, eventually will stand before God. These shevarim blasts sound throughout the entire Forty Days of Teshuvah, but are most piercing at Rosh HaShanah, when these shevarim notes are the announcement that the last Ten Days of Teshuvah have now arrived, and the time for repentance is now urgent. These blasts speak of impending trials, and ultimate judgment. The shevarim blasts also sound the call for Assembly to Battle. Sounding at Rosh HaShanah, these shevarim clarion notes will begin the process of assembling the nations into The Middle East, where God will deal with them regarding His Covenant with Israel. Shevarim blasts announce the End of Battle also, so these notes will be played again at the accounting of Yom Kippur.

---

[21] The Jerusalem Post Internet Edition, Sep.9,2002, Jonathan Rosenbleum, *THINK AGAIN, Conservatism's incredible shrinking God.* "Our primary task on Rosh HaShana is to crown God as King over us. The cantor begins his prayers by calling out dramatically, "O King," and throughout the prayers we implore God to reveal Himself in His full glory as King over all that He has created." "The King who we are addressing holds the power of life and death, as we acknowledge repeatedly in our prayers."

3. Teruah Notes:

The third type of trumpet blast is 'teruah,' which is "a wake-up call arousing from slumber." These nine quick blasts, [22]"like an alarm clock going off, call the Righteous dead to resurrection. 'HaTeruah' is the name specifically given to the lead voice trumpet of Rosh HaShanah, The Last Trump, because it is the ingathering harvest-call for the Wholly Righteous. The awakening blast, Ha Teruah, signals several things. First of all, it separates the righteous from the unrighteous at Rosh HaShanah, so it announces a great awakening of the righteous dead, a resurrection and ingathering harvest unto the LORD. It also announces the fact that the appointed time of the Wrath of God upon the unrepentant is come, and the Ten Days of Awe are now to begin. The 'teruah' notes will again be played at Yom Kippur, awakening the martyred Tribulation Saints when Christ returns to the earth.

What we have then, is <u>a music score</u> being played during the entire Season of Teshuvah, rising in crescendo at Rosh Hashanah, The Feast of Trumpets, then sounding at pre-ordained times during The Days of Awe, culminating in profound orchestration at Yom Kippur. In essence, these blasts are a series of notes having significant meaning, and have the ability to be played by several trumpets, <u>along with One Specific Lead Trumpet Voice known as The Seventh Trumpet</u>. I will explain this more when we look into the Seven Trumpets of Revelation.

C. The Three Groups of Mankind:

Rosh HaShanah, also called Yom HaDin, The Day of Judgment, is the Feast that separates out the [23]three levels of mankind: the Rashim (Wicked), the Intermediates (secular nominal average persons), and the Tzadikim (the Wholly Righteous). The Tzadikim from the Age of Grace already have their names entered into The Book of Life <u>before</u> Rosh HaShanah. However, most folk fit into the nominal, intermediate category. And some are Rashim, so they will be judged accordingly.

1. The Rashim:

The Rashim, the Totally Wicked, are sealed to their fate when The Books are opened at Rosh Hashanah, and their names are <u>not found</u> entered into

---

[22] . A quick Overview of the High Holidays, Rabbi Shraga Simmons, www.aish.com/hhElul/hhElulDefault's_quick_overview_of_the_...

[23] Rosh HaShanah and the Messianic Kingdom to Come, Joseph Good, 1990, HaTikvah Ministries, Port Arthur, TX. P. 115-119.

The Book of Life. The dead Rashim are left in their graves until The Great White Throne Judgment, and the living Rashim are allowed to continue to live through The Days of Awe until Yom Kippur, but their fate is sealed at Rosh HaShanah unless they wake up to the truth of their fateful eternal damnation, and honestly repent by Yom Kippur. This is a wonderful picture of the grace and long-suffering of Christ, Who is not willing that any perish, but that all come to repentance.

2. The Intermediates, the Nominal Persons:

Then there is a large group of people who are not righteous, but are not total unbelievers either. They are average law-abiding citizens who believe God exists, but do not put too much emphasis on their spiritual condition most of the time. They may simply be going through life not really giving much thought to anything godly. These are given a final chance to examine their hearts during Yamim Nora'Im, the final ten days of Teshuvah, The Days of Awe, also referred to as Jacob's Trouble, The High Holy Days, from Rosh HaShanah to Yom Kippur. If they repent, and appropriate the atonement that was offered for their sin through Christ's redemptive shed blood, which fulfilled the required sin offering of The Day of Atonement (Yom Kippur), they will be appointed their portion with the Righteous in the Kingdom of God on Yom Kippur, and their names will be inscribed in The Book of Life. Meanwhile, they must endure The Days of Awe along with the Rashim. It is from this Intermediate group that most of the Tribulation Saints will come when they finally realize the seriousness of their spiritual condition, but most will pay for their faith through martyrdom during The Days of Awe. When the intermediates wake up to the fact that they have missed the Rapture, they will be very sorrowful. But some will be angry.

Could this be what Jesus was referring to when He stated in Matthew 8:11&12, *"...many shall come from the east and west, and shall sit down with Abraham, and Isaac, and Jacob, in the kingdom of heaven. But the children of the kingdom shall be cast out into outer darkness: there shall be weeping and gnashing of teeth."* Luke 13:28-30, *"There shall be weeping and gnashing of teeth, when ye shall see Abraham, and Isaac, and Jacob, and all the prophets, in the kingdom of God, and you yourselves thrust out. And they shall come from the east, and from the west, and from the north, and from the south, and shall sit down in the kingdom of God. And, behold, there are last which shall be first, and there are first which shall be last."* KJV.

When the wholly righteous Tzadikim are invited from all over the earth to sit down with the Patriarchs in The Kingdom of Heaven at the time of the Rapture, to participate in the Coronation and Wedding of the KING, there will be some on earth who actually recognize what has occurred, and will realize they have been rejected, and left behind to go through The Days of Awe along with the Wicked. They will weep and gnash their teeth because of their ambivalence and unbelief, and will be assigned to partake in the darkness of Jacob's Trouble. These people will be cognizant of the ramifications. Some will be cold, unrepentant individuals who thought they were OK simply because they lived relatively good lives, and they will be angry at God, because after all, they were not so terribly bad.

Many of those who understand will be Jews who have had access to the truth of the Gospel, but did not give heed to it, or believe in Jesus Christ as their true Messiah and Bridegroom. The *"last who are first"* are the predominantly Gentile Church. They will go into The Kingdom ahead of the *"first which are last,"* meaning Israel. Thus the *"blindness in part,"* which Paul mentions in Romans 11:25, begins to be removed from Israel when the Rapture occurs, and when Israel again controls Jerusalem and Mount Zion. This blindness is lifted gradually until *"...all Israel shall be saved: as it is written, There shall come out of Zion, the Deliverer, and shall turn away ungodliness from Jacob: For this is my covenant unto them, when I shall take away their sins."* Romans 11:26-27. KJV. Unfortunately, most Jews will need to go through The Days of Awe to recognize Messiah, and come to complete repentance.

Also notice Luke 12:46, *"The lord of that servant shall come in a day when he looks not for him, and at an hour when he is not aware, and will cut him in sunder, and will appoint him his portion with the unbelievers."* Jesus says of the man who did not have on a wedding garment, indicating the stance of the unrepentant, Matthew 22: 12&13, *" Friend, how camest thou in not having a wedding garment? And he was speechless. Then said the king to the servants, Bind him hand and foot, and take him away, and cast him into outer darkness: there shall be weeping and gnashing of teeth."* Also, Matthew 24:50-51, *"The lord of that servant shall come in a day when he looketh not for him, and in a hour that he is not aware of, And shall cut him asunder, and appoint him his portion with the hypocrites: there shall be weeping and gnashing of teeth."*

And finally, during the Tribulation, Revelation 16: 9-11, *"And men were scorched with great heat, and blasphemed the name of God, which has power over these plagues: and they repented not to give him glory. And the fifth angel poured out his vial upon the seat of the beast; and <u>his kingdom was full of darkness</u>; <u>and they gnawed their tongues for pain</u>, and blasphemed the God of heaven because of their pains and their sores, and repented not of their deeds."*

This darkness occurs during the outpouring of God's wrath on the disobedient. A great many of those left behind after the Rapture of the Church, do not turn to God, so are sealed with the Wicked when Christ

THE FALL FEASTS AND FESTIVALS

returns at Yom Kippur. But those who do repent and accept the message of Christ, become Tribulation Saints. It appears pretty much all of the Tribulation Saints are martyred by AntiChrist's regime. However, there are those of the tribes of Israel who actually make it to enter The Kingdom of Messiah on earth. These include the 144,000, along with a great many other Jews who suddenly, and finally, wake up to the fact that Jesus is Messiah, and start to call out to Him for deliverance. There will also be some who repent from other nations as well. All the nations do exist when Christ returns, some "sheep," and some "goats."

Most Jews do expect Messiah, the Anointed One, to come, but they believe He will be a man, not God in the flesh. This misidentification is partially why they will be easily deceived by the AntiChrist, who at first they will receive as a type of Messiah, because he will broker peace, and allow them to worship in The Temple in Jerusalem. (So there will be a Temple in place before the seven year Tribulation segment of The Ten Days (years) of Awe Dispensation. I will explain later approximately when this construction of The Temple will likely take place. It's a wonder we have not picked up on the timing of this necessary fulfillment long ago, but perhaps it was not to be recognized until just prior to when it is to be accomplished, being one of the prophecies recorded in Daniel that are to become clear at the time of the end, according to Gabriel's explanation to Daniel.) But when AntiChrist and his cohorts desecrate The Temple, the Israelis will then realize they have been duped. Many will begin to listen to The Two Witnesses, and to the 144,000 sealed Evangelists, and by the time Armageddon occurs, they will know Messiah is the only One Who can help them, and they will cry out to Him for deliverance.

So all told, The Days of Awe from Rosh HaShanah to Yom Kippur, prophetically, will be a total time of soul-searching, both for the Jews, as well as for the remaining people of all nations. Some will repent, and some will rebel. Whichever they do, their fates will ultimately be sealed on Yom Kippur at The Second Coming of Messiah.

3. The Tzadikim:

Then there are the wholly Righteous. These have repented, and have kept themselves pure from The Day of Atonement (Yom Kippur) of the <u>previous</u> year (the previous year prophetically representing the former Dispensation of The Church Age, the Dispensation of Grace) until Rosh HaShanah, so <u>they already are entered into The Book of Life</u>. The Tzadikim who have died throughout The Church Age are resurrected at the Last Trump, Ha Teruah Shofar of Rosh HaShanah, to join with the living righteous. The living righteous are changed to have incorruptible bodies. Together, they will be caught up to meet Christ in the air.

It is interesting to note that it is the previous year's Day of Atonement that is significant. The Day of Atonement, Yom Kippur, <u>is the one Fall Feast that Jesus has already partially</u> fulfilled by being <u>The Perfect Lamb of God</u>, and by His position as The Righteous High Priest. He fulfilled atonement once and for all by becoming the perfect sacrifice for all sin. <u>He accomplished this perfect atonement at Passover</u>, fulfilling the Spring Feast, because He was The Perfect Sacrificial Lamb for all sin forever. <u>He no longer must sacrifice for atonement on Yom Kippur</u>, the Fall Feast Day of Atonement. <u>A further Yom Kippur sacrifice would be redundant</u>, so He was able, as The Perfect Pascal Lamb, to be resurrected as The Firstfruits of the coming harvests. As The Eternal High Priest, He entered at that time into The Holy of Holies in the Heavenlies, sprinkling His own blood on the Heavenly Mercy Seat once and for all. <u>So the atonement of Yom Kippur was accomplished once and for all at Passover</u>. Jesus Christ, <u>The Lamb of God</u>, did not have to **twice** give His life and blood as atonement for our sin.

But there is more to Yom Kippur to be fulfilled when Christ returns -- not in sacrificial Atonement, but in demonstration of the complete victory and authority of The Risen Lamb, The Lion of The Tribe of Judah, The KING of Kings, and The Righteous Judge. Of course the Jews do not yet believe Jesus is The Lamb of God Who shed His blood as the perfect atonement for all sin, fulfilling the promise to Isaac by Abraham that *"God will provide <u>himself a lamb</u> for a burnt offering."* Genesis 22:8. They still have The Day of Atonement sprinkling of the blood on The Mercy Seat once a year at Yom Kippur in mind when they keep these Feasts. They therefore do not accept Christians as Tzadikim. When they finally accept Jesus as Messiah, they will also recognize His atonement as The True Lamb of God Who takes away the sin of the world, as John the Baptist preached. He pointed to Jesus and stated, *"Behold the Lamb of God which taketh away the sin of the world."* John 1:29. The Akeida Lamb became the substitute sacrifice in place of Isaac, the son of promise for many nations. The Jews, to this day, do not yet accept John's proclamation of Who The Lamb of God is. But they will! The Days of Awe from Rosh HaShanah to Yom Kippur will ultimately, and unquestionably, reveal His identity for all to behold.

<u>The Book of The Wholly Righteous</u>, also referred to as <u>The Book of Life</u>, is opened on Rosh HaShanah. The Wholly Righteous whose names are found written there, are given special privileges. At the Last Trump (HaTeruah Shofar) of the Feast, they are gathered to the Wedding and Coronation of The KING. This celebration takes place in Heaven. Paul

refers to HaTeurah Shofar in 1 Corinthians 15:51,52. *"Behold I show you a mystery, we shall not all sleep, but we shall be changed, in a moment, in the twinkling of an eye, at **the last trump**: for **the trumpet** shall sound, and the dead shall be raised incorruptible, and we shall be changed."* The Last Trump of Rosh HaShanah summons all the righteous dead back to life, and changes the righteous living from corruptible to incorruptible. Then together they are snatched away to meet The Bridegroom in clouds of Glory, and taken into the Father's House in Heaven for the Wedding-Coronation of Jesus Christ, The KING of Kings, and LORD of Lords. What an event to look forward to, and it will take place very soon! So there are Jews who do believe in a Rapture (Natzal, ingathering harvest) of the Righteous, and this event takes place at the blowing of HaTeruah, The Last Trump of Rosh HaShanah.

There is only one group who obviously qualifies for this event, and that is the Bride-Church who is deemed completely righteous because of faith in the finished work of Christ on the Cross, when He fulfilled the sacrificial requirements of The Day of Atonement once and for all. It's unfortunate, but no Jews, unless they have come to Christ before the Rapture, will have this privilege, but will have to go through The Ten Days of Awe.

The important question is, are you Tzadika? Because of the LORD's great love and mercy You can be. All you must do is recognize you are totally unworthy and sinful. Then repent of your sin. That means you must turn away from sin, and turn to Christ. By faith pray, and admit your sinful condition. Pray, and accept Jesus Christ as your Savior and Lord; asking Him to cleanse you from your sin and make you a new, righteous person through the atonement of Christ's blood which He shed for you on the cross. If you really mean it, He will wash away your sin, and you will be born a new person into the family of God. You will become Tzadika, a Wholly Righteous One.

III. Yom HaKeseh, a Special Rosh HaChodesh:

There is a Festival that accompanies Rosh HaShanah that few Christians give much thought to, because few have even heard of it, let alone understand its significance. This Festival is [24]Yom HaKeseh, <u>The Day of Concealment</u>.

Throughout the Jewish year, there are monthly Festivals referred to as New Moon Feasts. [25]These are called Rosh HaChodesh, Head of the Month

---

[24] Jewish Heritage Online, *The day of the Concealed Moon*. www.jhom.com/calendar/tishrei/concealment.htm.
[25] Judaism 101, *Rosh Chodesh, Level Basic*, www.jewfaq.org/chodesh.htm

('Rosh' meaning head, and 'Chodesh' meaning month.) Each New Moon ushers-in the next complete monthly cycle of the moon. Each New Moon also is a picture of the wedding of a bridegroom (sun) and bride (moon), and many traditional Jewish weddings were purposely scheduled to take place on a Rosh HaChodesh.

As we all know, when there is a New Moon, the light of the moon actually is eclipsed by the shadow of the earth, so the moon is hidden from the view of those on the earth. [26]Yom HaKeseh, The Day of Concealment, ("Yom" meaning "Day," "Keseh" meaning hidden or concealed") is a special Rosh HaChodesh shadowing of the moon that falls either on, or close to Rosh HaShanah, the Civil Calendar New Years. The reason Yom HaKeseh may fall close to, but not necessarily always on Tishrei 1, the first day of Rosh HaShanah, is because the Jewish months are generally 29 or 30 days, and the cycle of the moon is approximately 28 days. So this Festival slides slightly in the present Jewish Calendar, according to the cycles of the moon. Prophetically, this fits with the timing of the Rosh HaShanah harvest ingathering Natzal, Rapture.

There are four quarters to the phases of the moon. Two quarters phase-in until we have a full moon revealed, then two quarters phase-out to the complete shadow, referred to as the New Moon. We know from Joel and Peter that just prior to the Rapture the moon will appear blood-red. Whether this phenomenon will take place only during the last quarter leading up to the New Moon, or will last for an entire 28 day cycle, or take place from the Full-Moon until the New-Moon, is somewhat debatable, but it will appear for a time-frame that is long enough to be recognized. I tend to feel the red-moon will be visible from the time of the Full Moon, because there will come a time in God's prophetic time-table when the Church (Wholly Righteous) will be complete (full). Our mandate will then be finished, so the Church will be revealed in fullness (Full Moon), indicating the end of The Age of Grace. The Holy Spirit, the Friend of the Bridegroom Who assists the Bride by His role as the Paraclete, will then be ready to present the Bride to the Bridegroom. The cry will then go out, *"Behold the Bridegroom Cometh! Go ye out to meet Him!"* Matthew 25: 6. This cry will go out during the time period when the moon appears red, because this Sign will indicate the end of The Church Age has arrived, and deliverance from the coming wrath is now the next item on the agenda. This deliverance is for those who have called upon The Name of the LORD during The Age

---

[26] Prophetech, Digital Missions, *The Rapture of the Church. The Rapture of the Bride of Christ: A Digital Missions Fact Sheet.* www.prophetech.com/institute/rapture.htm.

THE FALL FEASTS AND FESTIVALS

of the Holy Spirit, according to Joel and Peter. So following, and possibly including the Full Moon, the moon will appear red during the third and fourth phases leading to Rosh HaChodesh (the New Moon). Yom HaKeseh (The Day of Concealment) of Rosh HaShanah, is the Yom HaChodesh (New Moon) close to which the Rapture will very possibly occur.

This cosmic sign for the Church is not unlike the fact that there was a significant star in the heavens heralding Christ's First Coming at His birth, and the Magi recognized it as indicative of The Coming of Messiah, The Newborn KING. The blood-red moon will herald the imminent coming of Messiah, The Bridegroom, to receive His Bride! Although we cannot be dogmatic regarding the exact day or hour of the Rapture, we are able, because of this Sign in the moon, <u>to be aware of the Appointed Times we are living in,</u> and The Fall Season fulfilling the onset of The Fall Feasts. Therefore, we have a very observable sign, not just a spiritual reason, to *"look-up for your redemption draweth nigh."*

The calendar discrepancies make the exact timing of this Rosh HaShanah event somewhat hazy. Our calendars may be close, but not exact, so even the Hebrew calendar date of Tishrei 1 may be out slightly. But the catching away of the Righteous will clarify the prophetic countdown for Israel, and for the nations. So the specific Sign for the Church to watch for is the blood-red moon which will phase toward the New Moon Yom HaKeseh, The Day of Concealment. The Sign for Israel will be the Rapture of the Righteous, indicated by the sounding of Ha Teurah Shofar, The Last Trump of Rosh HaShanah. Rosh HaChodesh -Yom HaKeseh, will indicate the arrival of The Ten Days of Awe.

So, Yom HaKeseh is the pre-eminent New Moon of a Sacred Year. This is exciting because it speaks about the Concealment of the Wholly Righteous as one would refer to a Bride ushered to her Wedding with her Bridegroom, to be followed by a new life together. The Church, The Bride of Christ, is hidden from the earth as she is wedded to her Bridegroom in Heaven. The moon typifies the Righteous, therefore the moon is a type of the Church reflecting the Light of the Son of God on the earth. The fact that the moon is hidden at the time of the call of The Last Trump of Rosh HaShanah, coinciding with The Day of Concealment, is a complete picture of The Bride and Bridegroom, who are referred to as King and Queen during their wedding festivities, and are hidden away from the rest of the world in the Chupah (Wedding Chambers) prepared by the groom in his Father's estate. The Kedushin (wedding ceremony) is referred to as a Wedding-Coronation. What a picture of Christ and the Church!

There is more than one prophetic sequence of the prophetic spiral taking place here. The Church will be raptured, according to the prophetic fulfillment of Rosh HaShanah, at The Last Trump, when the trumpet is blown at the New Moon. But remember, <u>each year</u> has a Rosh HaShanah with a <u>closely accompanying</u> Rosh HaChodesh (new moon) - Yom HaKeseh (Day of Concealment.) From Rosh HaShanah to Yom Kippur prophetically, there are ten years, and three of these years <u>precede</u> The Tribulation week, which is the final seven years of that ten year Dispensation. So further Rosh HaShanah - Rosh HaChodesh - Yom HaKeseh's continue to occur annually during this ten year period. I am not being totally dogmatic here, but I am suggesting that the actual Wedding in Heaven will take place when the moon is <u>in absolute Concealment exactly on</u>, <u>not just close to</u>, <u>Rosh HaShanah</u>, because there is a specific Day of Concealment which is part of The Wedding Ceremonial proceedings. The third year following the Rapture of Rosh HaShanah may be the year when the insertion of the additional month, a practice which already takes place for seasonal adjustment, places <u>Rosh Ha Chodesh -Yom HaKeseh in absolute conjunction with Rosh HaShanah</u>. This conjunction will <u>be exact</u> at that time, because the Israeli calendar, at the recognition of Rosh HaShanah fulfilled at the Rapture, will be able to be correctly pegged according to The Fall Feast sequence.

    The initial Rosh HaChodesh -Yom HaKeseh (New Moon Day of Concealment) will be important for the Bride, because it will <u>coincide closely</u> with Rosh HaShanah at the time of the Rapture. But notice Psalm 81:3. *"Blow up the trumpet in the new moon, in <u>the time appointed</u>, <u>on our solemn feast day</u>."* This verse indicates there is coming an Appointed Time (mo'ed) when the trumpet will be blown in Rosh HaChodesh (the New Moon) at the Appointed Time <u>exactly on</u> The Feast of Rosh HaShanah. The Wedding in Heaven will therefore take place <u>on an exact Rosh HaShanah-Rosh HaChodesh -Yom HaKeseh</u>, indicated by the trumpet blown directly at the new moon, <u>*"in the time appointed* **on the solemn feast day**</u>*."* This time, <u>the Concealment of the moon (Yom HaKeseh) will coincide **exactly** with The Feast Day</u>. This verse is a prophecy, so has the ability to be fulfilled in more than one Convocational Appointment sequence involving the same players.

    This is revealing, since <u>Psalm 81 appears to be a Wedding Psalm</u>, indicated by the singing, and the music of the harp and timbrel used specifically at wedding celebrations. The LORD will come suddenly for His Bride in typical procession, complete with trumpets, shouts, and music, and usher her into Heaven for the Wedding. But He comes at the Rosh HaShanah that ushers in The Days of Awe on the earth -- meaning, He comes for His Betrothed to also protect Her from the Appointed Days of Wrath to be poured out on the ungodly.

THE FALL FEASTS AND FESTIVALS

But the Days of Awe are ten years prophetically. In a Jewish wedding, the Bride is ceremonially taken to the Father's House, and of course she must be totally prepared to leave at a moments notice for this significant event. Then the final joint preparations are made, settling the Bride into her surroundings in the Father's house, following which the actual wedding takes place. The joint preparations do take time. Therefore, the final preparations plus the Wedding and Concealment Week may easily add up to ten days total for the entire proceedings and celebrations. It is very possible this sequence will take place for Christ and His Bride.

This means then, in Heaven the Bride may have a short period (three years) of orientation, adjustment, and finishing preparations just prior to the actual Wedding, coinciding with the first three years of The Ten Days of Awe on earth. So there is time allotted for The Judgment Seat of Christ to take place in Heaven before the actual Wedding Week. The Wedding Week of seven years will then coincide exactly with the Seven Year Tribulation period on earth. Thus the Wedding in Heaven would have the ability to take place at the literal conjunction of Rosh HaShanah - Rosh HaChodesh -Yom HaKeseh. The Bride and Bridegroom will indeed be hidden for a full Wedding Week in the Wedding Chambers the Bridegroom has prepared for His Bride in His Father's House. Following the Concealed Wedding Week, the now Married Royal Couple will emerge from the Wedding Chambers exactly at Yom Kippur, and return to the earth to take up their rule and reign from The Throne of David in Jerusalem. It's amazing how the Convocations of the Feasts and Festivals given by the LORD have the ability to be so accurate, right down to the number of days (years)!

Notice the sequence in Isaiah 26:19-21. *"Thy dead men shall live, together with my dead body shall they arise. Awake and sing, ye that dwell in dust: for thy dew is as the dew of herbs, and the earth shall cast out the dead.* Verse 20. *Come, my people, enter thou into thy chambers, and shut thy doors about thee: hide thyself as it were for a little moment, until the indignation be overpast.* Verse 21. *For, behold, the LORD cometh out of his place to punish the inhabitants of the earth for their iniquity: the earth also shall disclose her blood, and shall no more cover her slain."* These verses describe the resurrection of the righteous which takes place at the sounding of HaTeruah (an awakening blast) at Rosh HaShanah, of which Jesus was the firstfruits. This is subsequently followed by the righteous entering into The Wedding Chambers at the invitation (formal Wedding) of the LORD, to be hidden for a little season. He shuts the doors until the indignation (Tribulation) is over. Verse 21 takes us next to Yom Kippur. The LORD comes *"out of his place to punish the inhabitants of the earth for their iniquity."* Then another resurrection takes place indicated by, *"the earth also shall disclose her blood, and shall no more cover her slain."* This is the Yom Kippur resurrection, because up until when He returns, Christ is also hidden in the Wedding Chambers with His Bride. So there is definite sequence portrayed here.

But notice verse 4 of Psalm 81, which is prophetically significant in how Christ will ultimately relate to Israel. *"For this was a statute for Israel, and a law of the God of Jacob."* Originally, this Wedding was scheduled to take place between God and Israel, but they rejected their Bridegroom. Psalm 81:11, *"But my people would not hearken to my voice; and Israel would have none of me. So I gave them up unto their own counsels. Verse 12. Oh that my people had hearkened unto me, and Israel had walked in my ways!"*

Israel was betrothed, but broke the sanctification of the betrothal through the sin of rejecting the LORD and His statutes, by following after (committing spiritual fornication with) false gods. So He divorced Israel, which means He officially broke off the binding engagement with a written Divorce Document. Jeremiah 3:8-9 *"And I saw, when for all the causes whereby backsliding Israel committed adultery I had put her away, and given her a bill of divorce: yet her treacherous sister Judah feared not, but went and played the harlot also."* This situation is not allowance for divorce and re-marriage by the way, because this divorcement is rooted in Torah Law regarding what we term engagement, which requires a betrothal be ended with a written document called a Bill of Divorcement. This document issued at the LORD's betrothal break-up is therefore not a divorcement from a consummated marriage Covenant. The LORD has not yet entered into Covenant consummated marriage, because His formal Wedding has not yet taken place. It will take place in Heaven at His Coronation. He therefore was able to issue this Bill of Divorcement from betrothal, and subsequently enter into another betrothal leading to His Wedding. This He has done, and has taken to Himself a new Betrothed Bride, the Church. His marriage proposal to the Church took place at The Last Supper. Does this mean He has totally rejected Israel? No. He does choose Israel again! They will be saved, and God will complete His Covenant of the Land, and of His Kingship with them, but they will not be His Wedded Bride.

So Yom HaKeseh, The Day of Concealment of Rosh HaShanah, speaks both of the Bridegroom coming to claim His Bride, concealing her from the coming wrath to be poured out, and of the Wedding of Christ and the Church, complete with the concealment of the Bride and Bridegroom in the Chupah (Wedding Chambers) in the Father's House in Heaven while the wrath of God is being poured out on the ungodly on the earth.

IV. Yamim Nora'im: The Days of Awe:

These are The Ten Days of Awe, also referred to as Jacob's Trouble, The High Holy Days, or The Days of Judgment, The Day of the Wrath of God. These are days when those who were not found worthy on Rosh HaShanah realize they have ten days until Yom Kippur to examine their hearts before God, and to repent, and accept the atonement for their sins before the coming Day of Atonement of Yom Kippur. This then, is a conscious decision deliberately made by the one who is repenting. Meanwhile, these are difficult days of testing and trials, full of many temptations. One must focus on the Scriptures and on prayer, avoiding the distractions of worldly pleasures, seeking God's truth. They must develop a heart that is toward God, and a real desire for forgiveness, both from God, and of others. They must also seek to offer forgiveness to those who have wronged them.

Yamim Nora'Im are the difficult days those left behind will have to face and endure in this world after the wholly righteous are taken. In carefully examining what Christ says in His messages to the Seven Churches of Revelation, it would appear there may be some who were entered into The Book of Life who will be left behind, if they are not prepared as the Bride, ready for Rosh HaShanah. These will have to go through The Ten Days of Awe along with the wicked. (Please do not shoot me yet! I will explain this more when we look at the Seven Churches of Revelation.)

Those left behind must turn their hearts back to God, and to His Word, while facing severe trials and tribulation; and prepare to receive their Redeemer and KING, the Messiah. These Ten Days (years) of Awe also are prophetic of the period of discipline that Israel as a nation will face, thus these days are referred to as Jacob's Trouble. Much of Daniel and Revelation, along with the other prophets, speak to this time period for Israel and for the entire world. For Israel, and for the nations left behind after the Rapture, HaTeruah, The Last Trump, accompanied closely by four other trumpets mentioned in The Book of Revelation, will be the announcement of having to face The Ten Days of Awe, the call to battle the forces of evil during Daniel's Tribulation Seventieth Week, and the call to assembly before God, and of the need to repent, and of the coming judgment of Yom Kippur.

The Final Schedule Revealed

V. Yom Kippur:

[27]Ten Days after Rosh HaShanah is Yom Kippur, The Day of Atonement, The Day of Redemption,[28] also known as "That Day," and "The Great Fast." This is the most solemn Convocation of the year. It is a Day of fasting and repentance, and of seeking God for forgiveness, and of making sacrifice for sin. Christ, The Perfect Lamb of God, already has fulfilled the need for sacrificial Atonement for sin. All we need do is accept His provision with a truly repentant heart. Israel still must come to acceptance of Jesus Christ's shed blood on the cross as the perfect Atonement, so the fulfillment of Yom Kippur will be of particular significance to them.

This Convocation also is announced with the blowing of a significant trumpet voice, Tekiah HaGadol, The Great Shophar, which announces the final call of judgment separating the righteous from the unrighteous of The Days of Awe Dispensation. The Book of Life is again opened, and all who are now entered there are welcomed into The Kingdom of God, and those who truly repented, but have suffered death during The Days of Awe, are resurrected. This is the resurrection of the Tribulation Saints. Those not found written in The Book of Life, the wicked (Rashim) are sealed for eternal judgment. There even are some whose names are <u>blotted out</u> of The Book of Life, indicating their names were written there at one time, but they were not prepared to be part of the Bride, and have subsequently chosen to remain in an unrepentant condition during The Days of Awe, so their names are removed. Notice, there is no 'intermediate' nominal designation for the judgment of Yom Kippur.

Tekiah HaGadol also announces the Coming of Messiah, The KING, to take up His earthly Throne, inaugurating His rule and reign from The Throne of David. It also is a blast announcing the wrap-up of The Battle of Armageddon, when all the nations will be defeated, and brought under the rule of Christ. The AntiChrist and False Prophet will be cast alive into The Lake of Fire, and Satan will be bound, and cast into The Bottomless Pit. Yom Kippur then, is the final drama of the fulfillment of The Mystery of Righteousness, placing the kingdoms of this world into the hands of the LORD forever.

---

[27] Jewish Heritage Online Magazine, *Yom Kippur Basics*, <u>www.jhom.com/ calendar/tishrei/yk/basics.html.</u>

[28] Workable Calendar And Fact Sheet On the Feasts of Judaism. Www.velocity.net/edju/PForum/Calendar.htm.

VI. Sukkot: The Feast of Tabernacles:

[29]Five days following Yom Kippur is Sukkot, The Feast of Tabernacles, also called The Feast of Booths, The Feast of Dedication, and The Feast of Lights. This amazing Convocation is a tremendous celebration entered into by everyone who has been welcomed into The Kingdom. The booths commemorate the protection and sustenance of God while the Children of Israel wandered in the wilderness, living in tents.

In keeping this rehearsal, each family builds a temporary shelter, usually in their backyard, and spends the week-long Feast outside enjoying God's provision and creation. Family activities are planned to take place in the booth. The daily meals are eaten there. Sometimes family members may sleep overnight in the booth. Basically, the whole community takes a break from old routines and pressures, and takes an at-home holiday. But this is not a complete holiday. Those who have jobs still attend to their duties. In other words, what is pictured is a new era, a new beginning, a restored Kingdom of Righteousness, remembering and honoring God, The Creator of Heaven and Earth, and The Provider of all that is good, Who ultimately is in control.

The roof of the booth is constructed in such a way as to give protection, but is flimsy enough so one is able to lie or sit back, and view the night sky and the stars. Generally the roof is constructed from branches which shed water easily, but which can be seen through at the same time. The walls are constructed of willow branches, or whatever materials are handy. So the booth gives protection, but it also allows one to reflect on the vastness and awesomeness of Creation and The Creator, in a relaxed atmosphere.

This Fall Feast is the final celebration of the Fall harvests of grain and fruit, and the meals reflect the goodness and abundance. Friends and neighbors, and even strangers, are invited to take part in Sukkot, and everyone has a lot of good, clean fun. This is the happiest of the Feasts. After the solemn Days of Awe, and all that will be taking place surrounding the previous two Fall Feasts, the world will be in need of some shared happiness, and a renewed vision of a changed world under Christ. Encouragement will definitely be in order!

A. Beit HaShoevah:

In ancient Israel, a special ceremony took place at The Temple during Sukkot. Every day during the Feast, Beit HaShoevah, The House of the Waterpouring, was conducted. Priests were sent out to The Valley

---

[29] Rosh HaShanah and the Messianic Kingdom to Come, Joseph Good, 1990, Hatikvah Ministries, Port Arthur, TX, p 44-49.

of Motza to cut very long willow branches. Then they would align themselves in several rows about thirty feet apart, and ascend up to the City gate toward The Temple, waving the willow branches in unison. This waving of the willow branches produced a loud sound of rushing wind as they approached The Temple.

At the same time, the High Priest and his Assistant would go through The Water Gate to The Pool of Siloam to draw water. They would pour this water into a golden vessel. (It is interesting to note that The Gihon Spring feeds the pool from which the water is drawn, and carries the same name as one of the four rivers that surrounded The Garden of Eden, so ties in with the fact that God is The Creator of Heaven and Earth. Is The Gihon Spring a vestige of The Gihon River? Perhaps, but we cannot be certain.) The water that was drawn from the pool was termed 'Mayim HaYim,' meaning 'Living Water.' The Assistant to The High Priest present at the water-drawing ceremony, also held a silver vessel filled with wine. Together, they would then proceed toward The Temple.

Each party, those waving the willow branches, and those carrying the water and the wine, would enter into The Temple Compound via their respective separate gates, and the shofar was blown, and a flute would begin to play. The priests who performed the animal sacrifices would ascend the altar to place their offerings on the fire. Those with the willow branches circled the altar seven times, then placed their branches against the altar in the form of a Sukkah (booth) to cover the altar, and The High Priest ascended the altar to pour out the water and the wine.

The water represents Jesus, The Living Water. The golden vessel represents His Deity. The High Priest represents Christ's High Priestly position. The wine in the silver vessel represents the blood of Christ and the presence of the Holy Spirit. The silver vessel represents Jesus' purity and perfect humanity. The Priest Assistant represents the servanthood of Christ. The pouring out of both the water and the wine onto the altar represents Jesus, our High Priest, pouring out His life and shedding His blood as the perfect sacrifice for sin for all mankind. Matthew 19:34. *"But one of the soldiers with a spear pierced his side, and forthwith came there out blood and water."*

The people sang Isaiah 12:3. *"Therefore with joy shall you draw water out of the wells of salvation."* Jesus referred to this ceremony and its significance when He stood in The Temple on The Great Day of the Feast and shouted, *"If any man thirst, let him come unto me, and drink. He that believeth on me, out of his belly shall flow rivers of living water."* John 7:37-39. He also gave this same message to the Samaritan woman at the well. What is being portrayed here is the fact that Jesus is The Living Water, the perfect Sacrifice, the

Robert Ludlum

IF YOU LIKE
ROBERT LUDLUM
TRY THESE AUTHORS

Desmond Bagley
Vance Bourjaily
James Carroll
Tom Clancy
Richard Condon
Clive Cussler
Len Deighton
Peter Driscoll
Clive Egleton
Peter Evans
Ken Follett
Colin Forbes
Frederick Forsyth
Bill Granger
Nicolas Guild

William Heffernan
Reginald Hill
Tony Hillerman
Thomas Keneally
Fletcher Knebel
John Le Carre
Elmore Leonard
Alistair MacLean
Charles McCarry
David Morrell
Martin Cruz Smith
Robert Stone
Ross Thomas
Trevanian
Morris West

 FRASER VALLEY REGIONAL LIBRARY

THE FALL FEASTS AND FESTIVALS

Giver of the wine of the Holy Spirit, and the Sender of the rushing wind which is the anointing and power of the Holy Spirit. Jesus is The Eternal High Priest who ascended into the Heavenly Temple sprinkling His blood as the perfect atonement for sin. The sacrifice on the altar shows Christ as the perfect sinless Lamb of God, slain and offered as the sin offering for all mankind, so man does not have to face eternal judgment in The Lake of Fire. The symbolism of Sukkot centers completely on Christ and on what He has done, and what He will do when He reigns. In other words, <u>Sukkot represents Salvation -- complete redemption and reconciliation between God and man</u>.

Sukkot is also known as The Feast of Dedication, because it commemorates the dedication of the First and Second Temples. It is very likely The Third Temple, which will be The Tribulation Temple, will be dedicated on Sukkot. Will Messiah dedicate His Temple, which will be The Fourth and final Temple on Mount Zion, as His earthly Palace on Sukkot when He sets up His reign? I believe He will. He has fulfilled all up to this juncture. There is no reason to believe He will not fulfill this also.

The altar represents a place of sacrifice, but it will become a place of beauty and rest, illustrated by the placing of the willow branches around it in the form of a Sukka (booth.) When Christ fulfills Sukkot, also called The Feast of Tabernacles (Booths), He Who is The Creator of Heaven and Earth will Himself be present and rest in His Temple, and He will be approachable. Mankind will be able to sit and commune directly with Him, and partake of His abundance. The fact that the priests waving the willow branches circle the altar seven times shows completion of redemption for all ages, the seven Dispensations of God's Spirit dealing with mankind, carefully formed and brought to fruition at the sacrificial altar of Salvation through Christ's atonement. Man will rest from his labors of sin, and lay down his willow branches (his own flimsy attempts to build a good and righteous life) facilitated by reconciliation through the work and wind of the Holy Spirit drawing man to Christ. This laying down will not be arbitrary or scattered, but will carefully form the place of rest, sustenance, and communion with Christ Himself around the altar of completed sacrifice.

Another custom was to place four great lights in the Temple during Sukkot, thus it is referred to as The Feast of Lights. It was during Sukkot that Jesus declared Himself to be The Light of the World. Jesus did not just bring the light into the world, but <u>He is The Light of the World</u>. Anyone dwelling in His presence walks in The Light, and darkness has no place where He is. He will physically fulfill this aspect also as He dwells in the Temple during Sukkot, making His home and Palace here on the earth.

The fact that there are four great lights present shows He is The Sun of Righteousness, fulfilling the cosmic sign of the light of the sun that was created on Day Four along with the other heavenly lights, to light the way for mankind, and write His message in the universe for all to be amazed at, and sense the greatness of His Creation and power. Jesus, The Sun of Righteousness, The Light of the World, The Creator, The Word, The One Who spread out the universe for all to see, will make His abode among men. <u>Thus the full revelation of The Creator and God Almighty</u>, <u>reconciled with His crowning creation</u>, <u>man</u>, <u>is portrayed at Sukkot</u>.

The Jews will come to realize the true significance of this prophetic depiction they have celebrated annually. Of course the practices of Sukkot involving The Temple have been omitted by the Jews, because there has been no Temple in Jerusalem for approximately two thousand years. But the truths of what took place are remembered. When The Temple is rebuilt, Sukkot will be re-instated completely, and the Jews will then be prepared for understanding the fulfillment when Christ returns to set up His rule and reign. At that time, The Feast of Tabernacles will not be simply a celebration of remembrance, but will be the Inauguration Ceremonies when Messiah ascends His Throne. Six times, and six Dispensations have come with mankind having to circle the altar for forgiveness. The seventh encirclement will see this altar transformed as we lay down our willow branches at the altar, and see them built into a Sukka of blessing. Christ's perfect provision for man will be physically, not just spiritually, viewed in approachable glory.

So Sukkot shows overtones of the fulfillment of Messiah's earthly inauguration as KING of Kings. His Feast of Tabernacles will be a time of great rejoicing, merriment, feasting, and fun; accompanied by much music and dancing. Sukkot is reminiscent of a Wedding-Coronation Feast, so will be the great Inaugural Feast of celebrating His Ascension to The Throne of David in Jerusalem with His Bride, The Church, at His side. This is not the Wedding-Coronation Ceremony and celebration itself (which takes place in Heaven), but a subsequent earthly celebration of His Marriage and Ascension to The Throne, revealing and declaring what has already taken place in the Heavenlies.

Others will be invited to join in. In fact, The Feast of Tabernacles is the one Feast that will be required attendance of all nations every year. The LORD has decreed that all nations must send representatives to Jerusalem to give honor to The KING, or suffer the consequences of drought and plague for the following year as discipline! Zechariah 14:16-19. *"And it shall come to pass, that every one that is left for all the nations which came against Jerusalem shall even go up from year to year to worship the King, the LORD of*

THE FALL FEASTS AND FESTIVALS

hosts, and to keep the feast of tabernacles. Verse 17. And it shall be that whoso will not come up of all the families of the earth unto Jerusalem to worship the King, the LORD of hosts, even upon them shall be no rain. Verse 18. And if the family of Egypt go not up, and come not, that have no rain; there shall be the plague, wherewith the LORD will smite the heathen that come not up to keep the feast of tabernacles. Verse 19. This shall be the punishment of Egypt, and the punishment of all nations that come not up to keep the feast of tabernacles." Messiah will require honor and respect, but will also require all nations take part in the celebration of freedom, and the bounty of the harvest of righteousness. They will come to participate in all His blessings, and honor Messiah, The KING. They will sit back and gaze upon the beauty of Creation in the presence of the Creator, Jesus Christ, God Incarnate. Israel will obviously benefit first and foremost, and all nations will be made to recognize Israel as the nation chosen and blessed of God.

VII. Shemini Atzeret - Simchat Torah:

The Day following Sukkot Week is known as Shemini Atzeret, The Eighth Day. On this day the King would physically, and purposefully ascend to his Throne, to pick up his responsibilities, and <u>begin the serious business of daily administrative government</u>. Shemini Atzeret will be significant when Christ rules and reigns. All nations will be required to celebrate Sukkot, following which He will get on with the job of ruling and reigning along with His Bride, the Church, in a new era, The Millennium. Also, The Eighth Day celebration will come to its complete fulfillment in The New Heaven and The New Earth, when the LORD will reign from The New Jerusalem for eternity during the Eighth Dispensation, so again we observe a Spiral of fulfillment.

A. Heeding God's Word:

[30] Shemini Atzeret (The Eighth Day) and Simchat Torah (the celebrations honoring Torah) are two celebrations referred to as Yom Tov. In Israel, Yom Tov Shemini Atzaret is celebrated along with Yom Tov Simchat Torah, <u>on the same day</u>, whereas, in most Jewish Diaspora congregations there are two days of Yom Tov, so Simchat Torah is celebrated the day following Shemini Atzeret. But the real <u>appointed time for both these celebrations is on The Eighth Day</u>.

---

[30]   Judaism 101, Shemini Atzeret and SimkhatTorah, Level Basic, www.jewfaq.org/holiday6.htm.

[31]The significance of Simchat Torah is that this is the end of the daily Torah readings for the year, and a new year of Torah reading is begun. A new focus of reading and heeding the Word of God is set in place. Because Shemini Atzeret - Simchat Torah has not been fully celebrated since The Second Temple was destroyed, this aspect of heeding and reading Torah has sometimes been celebrated among Diaspora Jews on Rosh HaShanah. They do still keep some of the ritualistic water ceremonies, praying on Shemini Atzeret for the rains of the coming year to fall in due season. New Torah Scrolls, and/or parade ceremonies honoring the Torah, take place on Simchat Torah.

When Christ returns and celebrates Shemini Atzeret - Simchat Torah, He will be recognized as both The Living Water and The Living Word of God given to a new era of righteousness, and all men will hear His Word, and give Him heed. God, who gave The Torah to Moses, will then dwell Himself among men, and will Himself be the recognized Giver of The Law of His own administration. The Living Word Himself indeed will dwell among us on Mount Zion, and His Word will proceed from Jerusalem into all the earth! Micah 4:1-2. *"But in the last days it shall come to pass, that the mountain of the house of the LORD shall be established in the top of the mountains, and it shall be exalted above the hills: and people shall flow unto it. Verse 2. And many nations shall come, and say, Come, and let us go up to the mountain of the LORD, and to the house of the God of Jacob; and he will teach us of his ways, and we will walk in his paths: for the law shall go forth of Zion, and the word of the LORD from Jerusalem."*

B. Forgiveness Extended:

According to John 8:1-11, on the day following Sukkot, on Shemini Atzeret - Simchat Torah, Jesus was teaching in The Temple, and He was presented with a situation that required His evaluation and judgment. On this Eighth Day when The Torah is honored, a mob of Scribes and Pharisees came to Jesus, dragging a woman caught in adultery. This group of pious, self-righteous men purposely assembled before Him, bent on bringing judgment against this woman who obviously was in breach of Torah Law. She deserved to be stoned!

Throughout the previous week, they had celebrated the Sukkot ceremonies regarding The Living Water, picturing cleansing and forgiveness. But they were not willing to forgive. What they refused to accept, and believe, was the claim Jesus had made that He is The Living

---

[31] Workable Calendar and Fact Sheet On The Feasts Of Judaism, www.velocity.net/_edju/PForum/Calender.htm.

THE FALL FEASTS AND FESTIVALS

Water. On the last day of Sukkot, just the day before, John records, *"In the last day, that great day of the feast, Jesus stood, and cried, saying, If any man thirst, let him come unto me and drink. He that believeth on me, as the scripture hath said, out of his belly shall flow rivers of living water."* John 7: 37-38. They had chosen to reject this message, and the implied identification of The Messenger, because they obviously were not displaying anything akin to allowing the Living Water of forgiveness to flow out of their own lives toward this woman. Jesus rebuked them stating, *"He that is without sin among you, let him first cast a stone at her."* John 8:7b. Of all those standing there, who was without sin according to Torah, which they now should be honoring according to Simchat Torah on this Shemini Atzeret? Only Jesus. In fulfillment of the requirement of absolute righteousness, giving legal license for the accuser to take up stones against someone caught in adultery, He certainly would have qualified. But Jesus was not about to cast the first stone! Instead, He bent down and began writing in the dust of the ground.

What was He doing? He was fulfilling Jeremiah 17:12-13. *"A glorious high throne from the beginning is the place of our sanctuary. O LORD, the hope of Israel, all that forsake thee shall be ashamed, and <u>they that depart from me shall be written in the earth</u>, because they have forsaken the LORD, the fountain of living water."* The LORD, Who Himself is The Living Water fulfilling Sukkot, and The Living Word fulfilling Shemini Atzeret -Simchat Torah, had just revealed Himself to them, and they had rejected His claims. Jesus was letting these accusers know they were being hypocritical in sentencing another, while they themselves were caught in the throes of sin by rejecting The Revealed Living Water, and not honoring The Revealed Word of God. Jesus fulfilled Jeremiah's prophecy by writing the names of these proud religious leaders who had rejected Him, in the dust of the ground. They reluctantly put down their stones and left, beginning with the eldest (revered elder) unto the youngest, because, according to John, they were *"convicted by their own conscience."* John 8:9a.

But notice, they did not repent, but witnessed Jesus forgive the sin of the woman. He did not discount her sin, but acknowledged her sinfulness, while at the same time extending forgiveness by telling her *"neither do I condemn thee, go and sin no more."* John 8:11b. Jesus, in fulfilling Jeremiah's prophecy on Simchat Torah - Shemini Atzeret, condemned the religious leaders who thought they had it all figured out, but who did not receive or acknowledge <u>The Redeemer and KING Who will ascend The Throne in The Sanctuary</u>. Many Jews to this day still take the stance of these religious leaders. But one day they will have to acknowledge the fact that Jesus is indeed The Fountain of Living Water and The True Living Word. Thus they will have to fully, and willingly, recognize His claims of Deity and Identity on Shemini Atzeret - Simchat Torah, when Christ ascends to His Throne, and takes up the reigns of government in His Sanctuary, fulfilling the Prophets and Torah Law completely.

I would like to point out one other ramification of the above incident. The religious leaders had taken up stones to stone the woman. But Jesus bent down to write their names in the dust, thus condemning them. He was leaving Himself wide open here. <u>No one but God Himself has the ultimate right to exercise this power of condemnation by writing the names of those who forsake the LORD in the dust of the earth</u>. The self-righteous religious leaders knew this. Now what were they going to do? Would they further refuse to recognize His authority and Deity by turning on Him? According to Torah, they would have the right to stone anyone falsely claiming to be God, because such a claim would be considered blasphemy. Jesus' forgiveness of the woman, stating, *"Neither do I condemn thee, go and sin no more,"* was itself a provocation, because no one can forgive sin but God Himself. <u>Jesus was proclaiming Himself to be God</u>, <u>both by writing their names in the dust, and by forgiving the woman</u>. He shifted self-righteous condemnation away from the woman, causing her accusers to focus on Himself, and <u>on Who He really is</u>, thus incurring the possibility of being stoned Himself. But His time was not yet. He came with a specific mission -- to go to the Cross as the ultimate atonement sacrifice for all sin. He did not come to be stoned by religious bigots! This incident at the Temple was an important revelation of Who Jesus is. He is The Living Water. He is The Living incarnate Word of God. He is HaShem El, the LORD, God Almighty, full of mercy. He is Messiah. He is The Righteous Judge.

Just because these religious leaders turned and walked away does not mean they were not angry and full of self-righteousness. This incident just cemented in their minds what they wanted to accomplish in getting rid of Jesus. What was their ultimate accusation at Jesus' trial? Blasphemy! Making Himself out to be God! So what Jesus did, and said, was not lost on them! They ultimately did turn Jesus' claims against Him, even though He had every right, as God in the flesh, to make these claims.

Will the religious leaders of the Jews still have to answer for this rejection and lack of recognition? Yes. Jesus will pose this ultimate question as to His identity when He returns. Every knee will bow, and every tongue will confess that Jesus Christ is LORD! Will this take place at the Temple? The Court Rooms for Justice were situated in The Temple Complex on Mount Zion. He will preside as The Righteous Judge from His Judicial Seat of Judgment located in The Temple Courts. Indeed He will inaugurate a new judicial era of absolute righteousness, and a rightful celebration of

The Word of God Himself, uttered in their hearing, and totally revealed in their midst. He again will say to a 'woman' taken in adultery, *"neither do I condemn thee, go and sin no more."* Who is this woman He will confront and forgive? Israel, who committed fornication against the LORD Himself! At that time, all stones of accusation will be thrown down, from the eldest (those most steeped in their ways, traditions, and interpretations) unto the youngest (those most desirous to follow what is true and right, and to follow righteous example.) At that time, no one will dare cry blasphemy! This will be absolute fulfillment of Simchat Torah - Shemini Atzeret, when The Righteous Judge, the LORD Himself, is revealed and forgives Israel.

VIII. The Root of Christianity:

Allow me to reiterate what I have already mentioned. The removal of the Church from our Jewish Scriptural roots certainly has done us a disfavor! We would understand so much more of doctrine and prophecy if we understood these Feasts and Festivals! The Feasts were given by God with a specific purpose. They were not just Jewish traditions, but were to be rehearsed as object lessons to the entire world, to reveal God's plan of redemption, and to reveal Christ. There was always to be a place in each Feast for the 'stranger' (Gentile) to participate. But we have relegated these celebrations to Judaic religiosity and tradition, not to be examined by Christians for fear of 'Judaising' the Church.

Certainly we are not to embrace Judaic tradition just for the sake of religious ritual. Merely ceremonially keeping these Feasts is not enough, and in fact the Church is <u>not</u> <u>required</u> to do so in order to obtain any favor with God. But not keeping the Feasts does not automatically mean we shouldn't seek to <u>understand their significance</u>! Obviously, even the Jews who do carefully celebrate these Convocations, still tend to miss the implications of their prophetic fulfillment as well. But the Church has completely thrown them out! We need to remember the Feasts were given by God Himself, and are part of the Scriptures.

Since, according to 2 Timothy 3, verses 16 to 17, <u>all</u> Scripture is profitable for doctrine, correction, and the revealing of truth, to equip us for living effective lives of godliness, we really should examine the Feasts in light of their <u>prophetic fulfillment in Christ</u>, and we will uncover eschatological doctrinal truths that for centuries have been misunderstood, and even fought over in our Churches! Actually, the Church has been guilty of not preaching all that the Scriptures have said. The results have often been devastating doctrinally, and our interpretations divisive.

IX. The Prophetic Significance of Yom Kippur and Sukkot:

At the end of The Ten Days of Awe, Yom Kippur occurs. Christ comes back to Earth. On this Day of Atonement, everyone's eternal destiny up to that juncture in human existence is finitely sealed at the sounding of The Great Shofar. Tekiah HaGadol will announce the Second Coming of Messiah with His Bride, and will signal the involvement of Christ and His forces in The Battle of Armageddon which occurs toward the end of the Tribulation. Jesus Christ will stop this terrible war before all mankind obliterates himself from the planet.

Tekiah HaGadol, The Great Shofar, is also the trumpet of the ingathering of the Sons of Jacob to their inheritance. The ingathering that is taking place now is only a gathering of the remnant of Israelis to The Days of Awe, and specifically to the final 70th Week of discipline for Israel, and the Wrath of God upon the nations. Tekiah HaGadol sounding at the inauguration of Christ's return when He fulfills Yom Kippur, will call all Jews out of all nations. Then they will turn their hearts completely to the LORD, and finally recognize Him as Messiah, Redeemer, Righteous Judge, LORD and KING. This initially will not be a joyful experience for them, because Scripture indicates they will weep and mourn. They repent of their refusal to receive The Suffering Messiah and His redemptive work when He came the first time, and their rejection of Him down through the centuries since. This will be a time of shameful recognition of their own inadequacies and unbelief. But their repentance will be complete, thus also fulfilling Tishrei Teshuvah, which ends on Yom Kippur.

Also, the sounding of Tekiah HaGadol will 'awake' the martyred Tribulation Saints.

The inauguration of the prophesied Reign of Messiah will be celebrated during Sukkot, which begins five days after Yom Kippur. There are two ways to interpret this sequence, and <u>both are correct in their spiral order</u>. First of all it is likely Sukkot, in a limited but significantly decisive fashion, will be fulfilled <u>literally</u> five days after Yom Kippur when Christ returns. He will indeed enter in victory through The Golden Gate, and walk again on Mount Zion as The rightful Victorious Ruler.

However this initial, immediate Sukkot will not be a universally festive celebration fitting for Messiah's Royal Inauguration and Ascent to The Throne of David. From purely a practical point of view, taking into account the obvious devastation the whole world will have suffered during The Days of Awe, and the need for replacing the desecrated Tribulation Temple, and the result of the earthquake that will split The Mount of Olives and The Temple grounds of Mount Zion -- all but destroying Old Jerusalem, a more official Sukkot celebration will take place later.

THE FALL FEASTS AND FESTIVALS

Since The Days of Awe have been prophetically interpreted to be one day for one year, we may in fact state the same prophetic principle for the five days from Yom Kippur to Sukkot. It is possible <u>the official international celebration of the inauguration of Christ's Millennial Reign and Ascension to The Throne of David,</u> <u>will take place five earthly years after His Yom Kippur Second Coming</u>. Although Christ returns at Yom Kippur, and takes up His rightful position as KING of Kings literally five days later at Sukkot, it may <u>actually take another five years for all the nations of the world to come to total recognition of His sovereignty</u>, and for the devastation of The Days of Awe judgments to be repaired completely, and for the earth to be placed back into a state of cosmic stability. Messiah does not wave any magic wands. He could simply speak everything back into stability and order. But He allows His own built-in repair program of working along with His ordained scientific laws of natural replenishment, coupled with the co-operation of mankind, both among themselves and with His leadership, to bring order out of chaos. The resulting World Order will actually be much more stable and equitable for all of Creation, including: mankind, the earth itself, plants, animals, and even the Solar System, than it has been for many centuries. In essence, Creation will be brought into a similar equilibrium as was evident pre-Noahic Flood. But it will not happen overnight.

Also, Messiah will want every Jew from all the nations of the entire world to be ingathered, and living comfortably in Israel in their allotted inheritance according to Tribe. There will be much to organize. The Nation of Israel will encompass the entire Land of Covenant given to Abraham, Isaac, and Jacob, and will be fruitful. The whole world will be at peace. Once this equilibrium is reached, and mankind has settled down, and recognizes Jesus as truly Messiah, Judge, Priest, Redeemer, KING of Kings, and LORD of Lords, then the whole earth can, and will, celebrate His rule and reign. The entire family of nations will be invited to the biggest, most lavish Sukkot to ever take place in Israel. Jesus Christ Himself, The Light of the World, The Living Water, The Righteous Judge, and The KING of Kings, will preside from His Palace on Mount Zion -- the amazing Millennial Temple Ezekiel describes. So Jesus, the Victorious Messiah, will immediately take the reigns of government for Israel, fulfilling Sukkot five literal days after His return. But the official international Sukkot ceremonies of His Ascension to The Throne of David may well be celebrated five years later.

CHAPTER 5
THE WEDDING CONNECTION

The [32]traditional Jewish Proposal and Wedding shed much light on the sequence of end-time prophecy, so in order to gain a better understanding of the role and position of the Church-Bride, it is helpful for us to have some idea of what takes place during these celebrations.

The prospective groom must approach the family of his chosen bride with several things: a bride-price, a legal document explaining his intentions, a proposal speech, a wine-skin of wine, and adornment gifts for his bride. Jesus came with all of these. He came all the way from His Father's House in Heaven to the human earthly family to call out a Bride for Himself.

I. The Proposal Package:

The young man comes to the Proposal Meeting armed with several necessary items which he must provide for, and present to his intended betrothed. These bountiful gifts are indicative of his honor, love, and absolute devotion, showing he is intentionally, sacrificially, and willingly offering himself, and sanctifying himself exclusively unto his chosen beloved. He provides all that is necessary for The Betrothal. The young lady needs only to accept his love, and receive the gifts. She has nothing to bring but herself

A. The Bride-Price.

Jesus came with the intent to pay the Bride-Price (Mohar) for His Bride. He paid the ultimate price for our sin by dying on the cross, thus purchasing our redemption, and consecrating to Himself a pure, sinless Bride. Since Christ has bought His Bride with the Bride-Price, we are now separated, sanctified, set-apart unto Him. Consequently, the Bride, preparing for her Wedding, sets aside counter-productive and distracting activities, and focuses on her objective. She therefore becomes an example of righteousness to others. We are a purchased Bride! Jesus Christ has purchased and cleansed us. He has sanctified us to Himself, a beautiful, pure, sinless Bride. We belong to Him, and are willingly subject to Him! We now come under His Headship, because He is our Redeemer. Jude

---

[32] Rosh Hashanah and the Messianic Kingdom toCcome, Joseph Good,1990, Hatikvah Ministries, Port arthur, TX, The Wedding of the Messiah, p, 147156.

says in verse 24, "*...to present you faultless before the presence of his glory with exceeding joy,...*" He is excited about His faultless Bride, and has gone to prepare for His Glorious Church to be presented to Himself at The Wedding in Heaven! Yes, He certainly did pay the Bride-Price, and because He did, we are not our own, but His in Sealed Betrothal!

B. The Shitre Erusin:

The Shitre Erusin legal document of His Betrothal and subsequent intentions is obvious. He has in His Hand all The Law and The Prophets that explain Who He is, and what He has come for. It is His promised Covenant with us who are The Bride. His purpose is to redeem mankind and bring us back into full relationship with God. Jesus Christ came to fulfill this mission by giving Himself as the ultimate sacrifice for our sin, paying in full, thus providing a way for us to come to The Father. His intention is that He call out a spotless, sinless Bride, and present Her in the heavenlies to His Father. He intends, after the Wedding, to spend the rest of eternity with His Bride. Wherever He is, She will always be. He is The KING of Kings, and LORD of Lords, and He intends to have Her rule and reign with Him over the nations. All is to be carried out exactly as written. All Scripture is to be exactly, and completely fulfilled through Him. His Bride will be clothed in a robe of exceedingly white righteousness, because He and His Father have provided the Wedding Garments. She will be showered with all His promises of blessing and honor. She will experience no more death, pain or suffering, or sinfulness, and will receive crowns that she will humbly, and with all love, honor and respect, lay at His feet. We could go on and on, but I think we all get the picture. He has come and ratified the Shitre Erusin of Betrothal.

C. The Proposal Speech.

Jesus, at The Last Supper, states that His desire is not just that the Church understand that He must suffer, but because of His suffering there is hope, and now the fulfillment of all things is about to unfold. So He proposes to the Church. Now that is strange! But, not only did the disciples fail to totally understand the import of what He said at The Last Supper (being Jews, they surely would have recognized the proposal routine,) but we miss it as well because we do not recognize and understand Jewish betrothal. In keeping with His own 'Exception Clause,' He was not in sin to choose a new Bride, because His marriage to Israel was not complete, since He divorced her during betrothal. But where in Scripture do we actually see this new betrothal take place?

THE WEDDING CONNECTION

In The New Testament, we see Jesus, who is God incarnate, the LORD in human flesh, giving His Betrothal Speech to His Chosen -- represented by His disciples, the founders of the Church. This speech begins in John chapter 14 and ends with Jesus' High Priestly Prayer in John chapter 17. We usually view this dissertation and series of events as Jesus presiding over The Passover Last Supper with His disciples, and so it is. But because we have become separated from Jewish custom, we have lost some of the significance of The Last Supper, and the implications of what He did and said during this *particular* Passover Seder. He stated *"With desire have I desired to eat this Passover with you before I suffer."* Luke 22:15. We focus on only one aspect of this statement -- the suffer part, and miss the full implication of <u>his desire</u>. Jesus surely is about to go through the most difficult experience anyone ever has, or ever will have to face. He is about to carry out the very mission He came for. He is celebrating this Passover Feast with His disciples, who ultimately become the core from which the Church arises. They represent His Chosen Bride.

This is very much like a young man escorting his beloved to a celebration feast or dinner, but of course this Feast is much more significant and meaningful. This is the Passover of all Passovers. It is the ultimate celebration, because this Passover is fulfillment, not just reflection! All previous Passovers have pointed in type to this particular celebration. This indeed is extra special! He capitalizes on this occasion to explain to His Chosen that everything she has ever celebrated about Passover, He is now going to fulfill in reality! And its all for her! But that is not all he desires to tell her. He has promises and plans for her as well, because what He is about to go through is not the end, but the beginning of the fulfillment of all that has ever been celebrated in the Passover, and all the other Laws and other Feasts as well! He is going to fulfill them literally!

Let's look a little more closely at a key aspects of His betrothal speech, starting particularly in John 14:1-3 where Jesus says: *"Let not your heart be troubled; you believe in God, believe in me also. In my Father's house are many mansions; if it were not so, I would have told you. I go to prepare a place for you. And if I go and prepare a place for you, I will come again, and receive you unto myself; that where I am, there you may be also."* He is the Bridegroom explaining that He is going to His Father's house to prepare a 'chupah' a wedding suite, 'a place,' in His Father's house, and He will return for her when all is finished and ready so that where He is she will have the privilege of being as well. Isn't that the desire of any bride and groom, to eternally be with each other?

D. The Wine-Skin and Wine.

Then there is the wine-skin of wine. As with all the Jewish Feasts, wine was very significant, and usually there were four cups of wine at every Passover celebration, or, one cup filled and re-filled enough times to last through the significance of the entire festive meal. Each aspect had tremendous meaning, and wine was supped to emphasize the significance of each progressive step. This was much like a toast, but carried much greater meaning.

The first cup of wine for Passover was the cup of sanctification, and signified remembering God's deliverance and separation of the Children of Israel from the slavery and oppression of the Egyptians, and God choosing them out as a special people for Himself. In essence, this was God's proposal for Israel, which betrothal Israel broke through fornication with pagan gods and practices. But, we, the betrothed Church, see this cup as the deliverance from sin (Egypt) by the blood of Christ, which has purchased us by His atoning blood.

The second cup of wine, the cup of instruction, focused on the directives given regarding the sacrificial death of the Paschal Lamb. Its blood became the covering that protected them from the judgment of God when He sent the Death Angel throughout Egypt. So this cup of wine speaks both of deliverance and judgment. The <u>unleavened bread</u> served with this cup signified the Paschal Lamb which became their meat to eat to strengthen them for the journey ahead. Matzot has some physical features that are significant. If one holds it up to the light, one sees pricks of light shining through. This is because the bread has been pierced so that the steam will escape and it will bake evenly because it is unleavened. Jesus, who was Himself sinless but bore the sins of the whole world, was pierced by the shards of glass and sharp metal woven into the scourging whip, and by the nails, and by the Roman sword, and from His body flowed blood and water. The cross became sprinkled with His blood, and from His body flowed a cleansing redemptive stream that washes our sins away forever.

Also, the Matzot appears to be stripe after it is baked, and is porous because of the pin-pricks purposely inflicted on the dough before it is baked. When held up to the light, these pricks can be seen. Jesus bore in His body the stripes of the Roman lashings. His body was bruised and torn for our healing. Through all of this, the light of redemption shines through, especially when Jesus is lifted up. The significance of this cup and the bread we are fully aware of. The bread symbolizes Christ's broken body, His burial, and His resurrection. There are three chunks or large crackers of Matzot. The middle cracker (called the Afikoman) is removed from between the other two, broken, then wrapped in a napkin and hidden.

Jesus, the Second Person of the Trinity, in physical body as The Bread of Life, was broken for us, and His body was wrapped in linen grave-clothes and hidden in a grave.

Then there was the cup of redemption (salvation). It was savored so its flavor would linger, reminding them that they were delivered, clean before God, and a new life in the blessings of the Promised Land awaited them. Along with this cup of wine, the wrapped broken bread (Afikoman) was taken from its hiding place (its tomb), unwrapped (the grave and grave-clothes have no hold on Him), and eaten with gladness. This speaks of the resurrection, and new life! It also speaks of <u>the promise</u> of Christ's return for His Bride, because those who will be gathered in righteousness at Rosh HaShanah are His Bride!

The final cup of wine is the cup of blessing and thanksgiving, also called the cup of hope and rejoicing, and points to hope of a life of peace and joy, and promised blessings to look forward to in the Promised Land. This speaks of our eternal position as the Bride of Christ, and blessings forevermore that we will constantly be thankful for.

We could enumerate much more on each of these cups, and how Christ has, and will, fulfill each of them. What is important for us, His Bride, is that the wine of Passover was brought by Jesus, and poured out for us to partake of. The wine-skin was His body. The wine was His blood shed for us. The significance of the wine as the blood of Christ has remained right throughout this Church Age. What seems to have almost been lost, and certainly it shouldn't be, is the Bridegroom connection.

The fact that the wine that He offers to His disciples is a betrothal seal to be partaken of by the Bride, is indicated by Jesus words in Matthew 26: 29,"*But I say unto you, I will not drink henceforth of this fruit of the vine, until that day when I drink it new with you in my Father's kingdom.*" Mark 14:25, "*Verily I say unto you, I will drink no more of the fruit of the vine, until I drink it new in the kingdom of God.* Luke 22:18 states the same thing. These all are Gospel accounts of the same event, as Jesus sat with His disciples celebrating the Passover before His death. The cup of wine offered by Christ revealed the cup of sanctification, instruction, redemption, blessing and thanksgiving all rolled into one great proposal and loving promise to His Bride! The wine is the cup of the Passover which He says is now The New Testament (Covenant) of His blood shed for the remission of sins.

But also, it is the cup of the hope of His return, and He indicates He will not drink of it again until He will share it later in His Father's kingdom. This is the promise of a Bridegroom. He went to the cross and shed His blood, fulfilling Passover and all the sacrificial requirements of the Law, so He could redeem those who would become His Bride. We partake of this wine spiritually when we accept Christ's shed blood for the remission of our sin. We partake symbolically of this wine every time we participate in a Communion Service. One day, we will partake with our Bridegroom at The Wedding Feast of The Lamb in His Father's House in Heaven!

Remember, Israel had been chosen out of sin and slavery to become a holy nation, separated, betrothed unto the LORD. But when the LORD came to His own people, they rejected Him! John 1:11 says, *"He came unto his own, and his own received him not."* Isaiah 53:3 *"He is despised and rejected of men; a man of sorrows, and acquainted with grief; and we hid as it were our faces from him; he was despised, and we esteemed him not."* The Bridegroom was present with them, but Israel did not recognize nor receive Him, and they still do not to this very day. So, Jesus took the opportunity of the Passover Last Supper to betroth to Himself a new Bride, one that He has chosen and freed from sin and death with His own blood, and strengthened and healed by His own body. This Bride is not the Israeli Nation, but all those who are called out of all nations, The Church. He partakes of the wine because He Is the Lamb of God that takes away the sin of the world. 1Corinthians 11:25 shows He drank of this cup. *"After the same manner also he took the cup, when he had supped, saying, This is the New Testament in my blood: this do ye as oft as ye drink of it, in remembrance of me."* So the Bridegroom has provided the wine, and the Bride has sealed this betrothal by partaking of the cup with Him.

The early Church called the Communion Service an Agape Feast. Every time we partake of Communion, we are reminded of the betrothal, and all it means to us, as well as all Christ has already done for us by His death and resurrection. The Last Supper was the Passover before The Lamb of God shed His blood and gave His life for us. It is the Seder where He told His disciples to drink of the wine, and promised He would not drink again of it Himself until He drinks it new in His Father's house with them. The Marriage Supper of the Lamb is where He will celebrate His victory, and perform His marriage vows to His redeemed Bride, The Church. Meanwhile, the Bride savors this cup and all it signifies, remembering her Bridegroom, Jesus Christ, until He returns. We are to do this whenever we have a chance to take Communion. Somehow, this particular significance is often overlooked when we take Communion. We treat the cup of Communion with its due respect as representing the blood of Christ and our redemption, but we miss the joy we look forward to in celebrating Christ's return to claim His Bride.

He will come in true Jewish fashion: with a shout, and with the sound of the trumpet, and it will be a slight surprise because we are not sure of the exact day or hour! If we remembered this significance, we would focus more on <u>our own preparations</u> to be a Bride of holiness, worthy of Him! A Bride that is without spot and without wrinkle. <u>A Bride that has made herself ready</u>! We would look forward to His return with great anticipation. After all, He gave us the cup of Communion to seal our betrothal, and He even told us we could partake of it as often as we want! The Church really should look forward to Communion, because it keeps us in touch with our absentee Bridegroom, (absent in body, but in touch with us through His Spirit.) He certainly doesn't want us to forget about Him, or grow cold toward Him.

He really is coming back, in person, in His resurrected body, for us! We really will see Him face to face soon, and then we will be with Him forever! What more could a Bride ask for? Why have I taken the time to explain this? Because we, the Church, must understand who we are in Christ! We are His Beloved, His Betrothed!

E. Gifts of adornment.

And what about gifts of adornment? Yes, Jesus has provided these as well. He has given us the garment of Salvation. He has given us robes of righteousness, pure and white. He has even taken away our old filthy tattered clothes and provided us with a new, clean wardrobe. Now, that is a complete make-over for the One who is to be His wife!

II. Friends of The Bridegroom:

The Groom has two "Best Men' assigned to assist him with his wedding preparations, making sure the wedding itself goes as planned. One Friend he assigns to the Bride, and both Friends officiate during the wedding ceremony itself. Before Jesus ascended, He promised to send another Comforter to assist the Church. This Comforter is the Holy Spirit who guides and helps us daily; <u>to prepare us as the righteous Bride for when our Bridegroom comes to receive us unto Himself</u>. When this Friend is called to complete His ceremonial duties, the Bride will obviously be taken with Him, to be presented to the Bridegroom. This is not mere interpretive speculation. That is His role -- to prepare the Bride, and then to present her to the Bridegroom without spot or wrinkle.

The Second Friend has the important position of standing at the door of the Chupah (Wedding Chamber) to hear the voice of the Groom, thus telling all that the marriage is consummated. According to Joseph Good, John The Baptist appears to be the one who has this privilege. John 3:27-29. *" John answered and said, A man can receive nothing, except it be given him from Heaven. Ye yourselves bear me witness, that I said, I am not the Christ, but that I* have been sent before him. He that hath the bride is the bridegroom; <u>but the friend of the bridegroom which standeth and heareth him, rejoiceth greatly because of the bridegroom's voice: this my joy therefore is fulfilled</u>." John is obviously excited to have this role, and says so. The resurrection and rapture are coming, so John will be the Friend to have this privilege in Heaven.

III. The Wedding Proceedings Contain an Element of Surprise:

What is really significant for us, is the fact that Jesus Christ is going to come back for His Church, and take us to Heaven where we will be married to Him, and He will become not only our eternal Husband, but will also be our Sovereign KING, and we will ultimately return with Him to rule and reign at His side.

But, the Bride does not know for certain when her Bridegroom is going to come for her. He has gone away to prepare a place (Chupah) in His Father's House, so He is making His own appropriate Wedding preparations according to His Father's, and His own wishes. It is <u>up to the Father to pronounce when all is ready</u>, <u>and when the Groom may return to</u> <u>receive His Bride</u>. This was what Jesus was referring to when He stated, "*But of that day and hour knoweth no man, no, not the angels of heaven, but my Father only.*" Matthew 24:36. True to the Jewish ancient traditional wedding, Jesus, as The Son of Man, does not know the exact day or hour when He is going to return for His Bride, the Church. He has a pretty good idea when the approximate time will be though, because He is in the Father's House, and knows pretty much when all the preparations are complete. <u>He just must wait until the Father gives the signal</u>. Notice, Jesus does not say He does not know the month or the year, just the day or the hour. This is also traitionally typical.

There is an interesting tradition in this sequence that is note-worthy. The Bride understands, traditionally, that the Groom and His entourage generally will return for her whenever the Father of the Groom indicates. However, the Bride must prepare for his return at any time. This has been the stance of the Church since Christ ascended. The general traditional waiting period for a Bride is usually from one to two years, but seldom longer, or the Bride becomes understandably anxious as to whether the wedding really is going to take place. We have been expecting Christ's return for approximately 2,000 years! If we use a prophetic time-metaphor of one year equals one thousand years, the Church has been waiting for approximately two metaphorical prophetic years. We then must conclude we are really close to the return of Jesus Christ, our Bridegroom, for us!

As the Bride waits however, she is not idle, nor is she alone. She has the help of the appointed Friend of the Bridegroom, who assists her in

THE WEDDING CONNECTION

her preparations according to the Groom's and Father's wishes. <u>This Friend also has somewhat of an inside track that the Bride can use to her advantage</u>. He has access to pertinent information regarding the preparations which are being made in the Father's House. In other words, the Friend is acting as a liaison to co-ordinate the preparations of the Bride in concert with the preparations of the Groom. The Bride then, **takes comfort** in the fact that if she **listens carefully to the Friend**, she will have a pretty reliable set of clues available to her indicating how close she is to the Groom's return for her. The Holy Spirit fulfills this role for the Church, and He has given us some clues. (But, as a true Friend, He will not take the fun out of the Father's and Groom's plans by telling the Bride when the actual time is. He certainly is party to the secret, but He is not going to 'snitch!') This is a pretty good reason to listen to the Voice of the Spirit speaking to us through the inspired Scriptures, as well as in our hearts! If we observe and listen, we will have a fairly accurate indication of when Christ is going to return for us. We just are not given an exact day or hour of the return of the Bridegroom. That much is kept as a special surprise! Until all the preparations are complete, the Groom does not know for sure either, because that department of the Wedding is the prerogative of The Father. But we at least are able to know <u>almost</u> as much as The Groom does, because we have the Friend to tell us what He knows from His end! The Holy Spirit is the communication pipe-line available between us, and He truly is a Friend, not just to the Groom, but to us as well!

Also, Paul shares an interesting observation in 2 Thessalonians 2:1-4 that echos Daniel 9:26 & 27. He says, *"Now we beseech you, brethren, by the coming of our Lord Jesus Christ, and <u>by our gathering together unto him</u>, that you be not soon shaken in mind, or be troubled, neither by spirit, nor by word, nor by letter from us, as that the day of Christ is at hand. Let no man deceive you by any means: for that day shall not come, <u>except there come a falling away first</u>, and that man of sin be revealed, the son of perdition: Who opposes and exalts himself above all that is called God, or that is worshiped; so that he as God sitteth in the temple of God, showing himself that he is God."* KJV. Underlining mine.

When we examine these verses, we are made aware of several things at once. Even though we do not know the day or the hour of Christ's coming at the Rapture, <u>we do have the ability to know the Times and the Seasons</u>, so that Day will not come as a complete surprise to the Bride who is watching and ready. In other words, we should have an extremely good idea when the Rapture will take place by reading the signs in the world around us.

The Final Schedule Revealed

[33]Using the analogy indicated by both Jesus and Paul, <u>the Thief is not to the Church, but to the worldly unbelievers who will not be expecting the departure of the Bride</u>. The Father is the only One Who knows for sure when Christ will snatch His Bride from the Earth. Even Jesus indicates neither He nor His angels know the day or the hour, but only His Father. Therefore, we are able to look at what the Holy Spirit is saying in regard to the signs that will qualify the approximate time of the Rapture from the perspective of the Christian Church, and know when our, 'Beloved Bridegroom-Thief' will come to 'steal us away' in thoroughly Judaic fashion!

Now that we have taken a look at some of the characteristics of The Fall Feasts and Festivals, and the Betrothal and Wedding of the Bride and Bridegroom, the sequence of prophetic events to be shortly unfolded should become clearer.

---

[33] I Thessalonians 5: 1-11. Luke 12:39-40.

CHAPTER 6
SIGNS

I. The Church is Given Signs for the End of the Age:

A. The Whole World will hear the Message of the Gospel

The first sign given by Jesus Christ for us to watch for indicating the end of the Church period, is that the Gospel must be preached throughout the entire world, and then the end of the Age will come. The main purpose of the empowerment of the Holy Spirit is to prepare a people called out and set apart in righteousness unto the LORD from among all nations, tongues, and peoples. The whole world must have access to the message of salvation before Christ will return for His Bride at the Rapture, and therefore this specific accomplishment brought to fruition will herald the soon departure of the Church, because her mandate is then complete. In Matthew 24: 14, Jesus states, *"And this gospel of the kingdom shall be preached in all the world for a witness unto all nations; and then shall the end come."*

B. Other Signs:

[34]Jesus gives many other signs as well. Wars, rumors of war, signs in the heavens, pestilence, famines, earthquakes, distress of nations, perplexity, etc. As we near the end of the Church Age, these signs will become more intense and closer together. But we must pay attention to <u>all</u> the signs revealed in Scripture. Some of these signs the Church will live through, and some the Church will only observe the lead-up to. Joel and Peter, under the inspiration of the Holy Spirit, shed light on a couple of signs specifically for the Church Age that have direct relevance to the work and presence of the Holy Spirit, The first Friend of the Bridegroom, in fullness. It is imperative that the Church in particular pays attention to these signs, because they indicate the approximate duration of The Age of Grace.

[35]1. Joel's and Peter's Two Signs for the Church:

There are two specific signs for the end of The Church Age of the Holy Spirit's full empowerment quoted by Peter from Joel. They both are physically observable.

    a. Blood, fire, and pillars of smoke.

---

[34] Matthew 24:4-7.
[35] Joel 2:31, Acts 2:20.

b. The sun darkened, and the moon appearing the color of blood.

I believe that both these signs are pre-Trib, and the Rapture of the Church is pre-Trib. Actually, to use the term 'Tribulation' as in 'pre-Trib, mid-Trib, post-Trib' etc., does not describe accurately the Dispensation of Wrath decreed for Israel and the nations following the Rapture of the Church. The terminology is somewhat misleading, but we often use these terms anyway. The entire period from the Rapture of the Church to the Second Coming of Christ is more accurately identified in Scripture as 'Jacob's Trouble,' or as the Jews describe it, 'The Days of Awe,' also referred to as the 'High Holy Days.' <u>The Tribulation is Daniel's 70th Week which is the final seven years of the Dispensation of The Ten Days (years) of Awe</u>. So the Rapture takes place pre-Days of Awe, making these particular signs regarding the dispensation of the Holy Spirit's empowerment of the Church imminently pre-Rapture.

Notice, because there are 10 days from Rosh HaShanah to Yom Kippur, and these days are referred to as Yamim Nora'Im, The Days of Awe, The Holy High Days, or Jacob's Trouble, what we actually have is 10 years (one prophetic day for one year) from the Rapture of the Church to The Second Coming of Christ. This means the Church will be absent from the earth for at least 10 years, not just the 7 years of Daniel's 70th Week of Tribulation.

The three years following the Rapture are a transition period from The Church Age to The Tribulation. That gives time for the leader known as the Raiser of Taxes (Daniel 11:20) to have tenure, and allows time for The Third Temple to be built on Mount Zion in Jerusalem, with Temple Worship reinstated. Following these three years, AntiChrist will rise to power as the Tribulation 70th Week actually begins. The three years account for the Period of Calm during The Sixth Seal of Revelation chapter 6, when the 144,000 Evangelists of the Tribes of Israel are sealed following The Battle of Gog and Magog.

Also, these three years would allow for the ceremonies surrounding The Judgment Seat of Christ to take place in Heaven, when the Righteous will be given their rewards and crowns to lay at the feet of The Lamb. Then the Wedding Ceremony will follow according to Jewish tradition, and the Bride and Bridegroom will enter the Chupah, where they will be hidden for the full seven years of Wedding Celebration. All of these prophetic events take place during The Ten Days (years) of Jacob's Trouble. So it appears the Church very well could be raptured approximately mid-69th Week, not at the beginning of the 70th Week as we have generally thought.

a. Blood. Fire, and Pillars of Smoke:

In keeping with the spiral of fulfillment, we have seen this scenario at least a couple of times already. The detonation of the atomic bombs that destroyed Hiroshima and Nagasaki during World War II produced pillars of billowing mushroom-shaped clouds, and many people lost their lives through fire and radiation sickness. But Hiroshima and Nagasaki were not the only time these warheads were detonated. These deadly mushroom clouds were released a number of times during atomic warhead testings, and the world has subsequently been living with resultant massive radiation pollution in areas near where these tests were done, or from the fall-out from contaminated air-streams which have been tracked virtually around the world. So in a measure, this prophecy began to be fulfilled during World War II, interestingly around the same time-period that Israel was re-born as a Nation.

We have just lived through another prophetic warning fulfillment of this prophecy, accomplished, not by atomic bombs, but through the use of aircraft as the weapons. There may be further manifestations of this sign the closer we come to the end of The Church Age, and the ushering-in of the time of Jacob's Trouble. The sign of *"blood, and fire, and pillars of smoke"* Acts 2:20, that just precedes the reference to the sun and moon lends some significance to the timing and order of the prophetic signs within the framework of the dispensation itself, and therefore must be examined. There is nothing arbitrary in Scripture.

Many students and teachers of Bible prophecy believe the terrorist attack on the World Trade Center in New York was a direct fulfillment of this prophecy. No one can deny the fact that the attack on the World Trade Center combined all three elements of devastation that Joel mentions. There was definitely **blood**. Many lives were lost, as well as a vast number were injured, both of folk who were in the Trade Center complex, as well as of rescue, fire, and police personnel. There was **fire** and **smoke**. And, most startling, these appeared as actual **pillars of smoke** and noxious vapors billowing in the distinct shape of the Twin Towers during their collapse. These images are etched indelibly into the minds of everyone world-wide. Something incredible has occurred here, because of the effect this single event has had on all mankind. We seem to know instinctively that this one particular event has ushered in a changed world on every level of human endeavor. **This was a history-changing circumstance, and the world, as a result, will never return to its former innocence and complacency.**

We have had many horrible disasters and wars in our world, and multitudes of situations that have actually taken far more lives. But somehow, the terrorist attack on The World Trade Center eclipses them all **because of its impact upon the entire world.** If this event had happened to the Eiffel Tower, or the CN Tower, or the Seattle Space Needle, the effect would not have been the same. I believe this event is a fulfillment of [36]Joel's prophecy. The Trade Towers became **literal pillars of blood, fire, and smoke!** There may still be more similar incidents to come, and we certainly hope not, but now that this event has taken place in Manhattan, anything similar following will somehow seem subsequent (but no less important) in significance.

This terrorist attack was carried out using **aircraft**. The Trade Towers were only one target. The Pentagon also was severely damaged, and a fourth aircraft appeared to be heading toward either the White House, Camp David, or just as scary, a nearby communications installation. Wherever it was really headed, we probably will never know for sure, but even if it had reached any one of these destinations, there would have been severe and lasting repercussions both for the USA as well as for the entire world. As it is, there are enough world problems as a result of what was on target. [37]Peter and Joel state there will be *"wonders in the heavens."* coupled with blood, fire, and pillars of smoke. Aircraft fly in the heavens!

The aircraft used by the terrorists were not the only ones to be affected. Almost all commercial and international flights were grounded immediately. World-wide there were no aircraft, except for military surveillance, allowed to fly! This also has never occurred before. What effect did this have on our world?

People's travel plans were delayed, re-routed on the ground, or just plain halted. This was devastating for those already en-route, as well as for people trying to do business, or going to or from jobs or homes. What about the ruined vacations and other important plans both private and public? And what about the movement of goods and services, mail, and anything else that is generally transported by air? All this was interrupted!

Many airlines have subsequently suffered monetary loss. United Airlines, the North American largest domestic air carrier, was affected to the point they filed for bankruptcy. Some airlines no longer exist!

The tourism industry on all levels has suffered a major blow. People have lost jobs, and companies have lost billions of dollars.

The world economy in general has taken a nose-dive. It really wasn't doing overly well before September 11, 2001, but it has slid into a further recession since the attacks. The stock markets and international economic

---

[36] Joel 2:30.
[37] Joel 3:20, Acts 2: 19.

trading stopped within one hour of the attacks. Observe the parallels of this event with Revelation 18: 15-19: *"The merchants of these things, which were made rich by her, shall stand afar off for the fear of her torment, weeping and wailing, Verse 16. And saying, Alas, alas, that great city, that was clothed in fine linen, and purple, and scarlet, and decked with gold and precious stones, and pearls! Verse 17. <u>For in one hour is so great riches come to nought</u>. And every shipmaster and all the company in ships, and sailors, and as many as trade by sea, stood afar off, Verse 18. And cried when they saw the smoke of her burning, saying, What city is like unto this great city! Verse 19. And they cast dust on their heads, and cried, weeping and wailing, saying, Alas, Alas, that great city, wherein were made rich all that had ships in the sea by reason of her costliness! For in one hour is she made desolate."* KJV. Underlining mine.

Many would argue that these verses refer to a city called Babylon, and well they may in future, but we must keep in mind that prophecies have the ability to have more than one fulfillment. Some Bible scholars indeed have referred to New York as the modern day Babylon because of her being the center of world-trade and commerce, and because she harbors much that reflects her wealth, and even debauchery. It is for sure, the markets of the entire world were affected, and world trade came to an abrupt and decisive halt within the hour that the Twin Towers were hit. There was not one major stock-exchange world-wide that remained efficiently operating, and the effect of this event on the markets has been lasting! Even now, more than two and one-half years later, the stock markets continue to fluctuate beyond normal. Certainly there are other factors now effecting the world economies, but the real pendulum swings began pretty much with the events of September 11, 2001.

Also, many of the world's seaports were sealed and searched, and surveillance set up. This happened extremely fast in New York, Halifax, Vancouver, and other North American ports. Many ports of other nations that ship and receive goods by water also closed, or were put under heightened security.

The nations mourned! This world-wide response <u>has never</u> transpired before <u>over a single incident</u>. But the impact of the event was not isolated just to the USA. After all, the World Trade Center was exactly that. It was the nerve-center for almost all world trade! Almost every country and most major corporations had offices in the Twin Towers Complex. Official services of mourning and remembrance were held internationally. [38]Nations were

---

[38] Hineni, A Wake-Up Call – Choose Life. Rebbetzin Esther Jungreis, www.hineni.org/rcolumn_view.asp?id+54&category=1. "On 9/11, the President called upon the nations to pray, and quoted Psalm 23."

73

called to prayer. Christians, Jews, and Muslims, and those of other religions, found themselves seated together in memorial services of mourning, particularly in Washington, London, and even in Ottawa. Many other cities around the world held ceremonies and somber services of mourning and remembrance as well. <u>This international response was absolutely unprecedented</u>! Condolences were voiced by leaders from nations around the entire globe. Heads of state from many nations made pilgrimage to the site of the World Trade Center to pay their respects to the dead, to view 'ground zero,' and to offer support to those who lost loved ones.

Out of this incident has arisen a kindred spirit between many nations of the world as all have been trying to make some sense out of the awfulness, and are trying to strengthen their resolve to never let it happen again, and to bring terrorists to justice. New alliances have been forged between nations. There have also been new animosities and old grievances dusted off. Along with the increase in resultant terrorism and terrorist threats, nations have been forced to choose sides either with or against one another.

People world-wide have come to the realization that we live in a dangerous world. Security has taken precedence over freedom and rights. Folk around the world find themselves willing to accept, and even request, methods of surveillance they previously would have considered encroachment on their personal privacy and national sovereignty. Somehow we all know the world has changed, and will never be the same again. Even on the second anniversary of the attack on the World Trade Center, world leaders were still adamantly voicing this sentiment, and vowing to take up their respective support for the war on terrorism.

Many more effects could be cited, but these are enough to realize September 11, 2001 was indeed a prophetic fulfillment indicating that the LORD is coming very soon to rapture His Church, and very soon The Days of Awe will begin.

[39]Notice the numerical implication of September 11. That is the **11**th day of the **9**th month. In month/day sequence it is **9/11**. What important

---

[39]   Hineni, Rebbetzin Esther Jungreis, Dec.9,2002, *A Wake-Up Call.* " ... But there is one line which seemed to slip by most people, and that was a quote from the Torah: "I have set before you life and death – therefore, choose life." Deuteronomy 39:19, the very protion that was read on 0/11/01. It is most significant that it was with these words that the President concluded his address."
"We have a cabalistic teaching that propounds that G_d often sends His messages through the most unexpected sources. The normal channels for such wake-up calls should, of course, be the clergy, but alas, they no longer command

number in society world-wide is **911**? It is <u>the number to call if there is an emergency or crisis</u>! The terrorists may have chosen this particular day to carry out their attacks for whatever their own reasons, but God knew this crises would happen. It occurred on 9/11. **Was God calling 911 because there is an emergency to be reported, and for people to do something about it?** Something like, **"Repent, or face the wrath of the coming Day of the LORD?"** Also, I wonder if God was trying to remind us <u>He is there on the other end of the crises line</u>! All we need to do is call on Him, and He will deliver. Joel, and subsequently Peter when he quotes Joel, states: ***"Whosoever shall call on the name of the*** LORD ***shall be delivered."*** It's

---

attention. And so, the wake-up call must come from a source that everyone heeds. When the President of the United States speaks, the world listens. From that horrific day of 9/11 to 6/25, sprinkled in his addresses have been messages, that are totally unrelated to politics or foreign policy, messages to which we have yet to attune our spiritual antennae. "

"On 9/11, the President called upon the nation to pray, and quoted Psalem 23. What is the meaning behind this call to prayer?"

"...Prayer is not just "give me, "do for me," or even" forgive me." In the Hebrew language, prayer means to stand before G_d, to be judged, to give an accounting of our lives."

"The very same week, Friday, September 14, the President convened a prayer service at the Washington Cathedral, and the invocation delivered was a passage from the prophet Jeremiah – the very words that, just a few days later, Jews the world-over would chant during the High Holy Day, Rosh HaShanah services. The quote depicts the matriarch Rachel weeping on high, waiting for her childrn to come home to their borders, and G_d promising that they would."

"That Divine promise lends a metaphysical dimension to the Jewish people's return to their ancient land. It defies logic. It transcends all political negotiations and mocks all the rules of warfare. There is no parallel for it in the annals of mankind. Millions have come to understand this. It is the basis for the total support of the Christian Right, and the reason why Evangelicals have made Israel their priority."

"The messages continued. That very same week, there was a call to all Americans to light candles at 7:00pm on Friday nicht, when Jews traditionally kindle the Sabbath lights – a clear reminder of the fourth commandment to our people to re-institute the Sabbath in their lives."

"But above and beyond that, there was a message to all of us, "I have set before you life and death – therefore, choose life." Deuteronomy 30:19. And when the Torah says, "choose life," it is not referring to mere existence, but rather, the Covenant sealed at Sinai."

"We are living in the most momentous time in history. G_d is sending us His wake-up call...."

time for the world to be reminded that there is Someone they can call on for eternal deliverance. **There is a Heavenly 911 !**

b. The Sun Darkened, and the Moon Turned to Blood:

The very next sign the Church is to look for following the *"blood, fire, and pillars of smoke,"* is *"the sun shall be turned into darkness, and the moon into blood, before the great and notable day of the Lord come:"* Acts 2:20. This is the next major cosmic indicator to watch for following 9/11 in the sequence of Joel's prophecy as quoted by Peter. I am aware that there are those who may use this particular sign in the heavens to suggest a post-Trib Rapture position, or at the least, mid-Trib. However, I am of the persuasion that the Rapture of the Church is pre-Ten Days of Awe. Notice this prophecy states, "*before* the Day of the Lord come." In fact, the Rapture may occur several (at least three) years pre-Daniel's 70th Week. The explanation for this position will become clear as we proceed.

So let's look at some Scriptures regarding the prophesied changes which are to take place in the sun and moon.

1. Two Scenarios Involving the Sun and Moon:

Most teachings on end-time prophecy present the darkening of the sun, and the moon appearing as the color of blood, as an event that takes place during the Tribulation. Actually, there appears to be at least <u>two separate cosmic events</u> that involve the sun, the moon, the stars, and the earth shaking. Most folk put these cosmic prophecies regarding the sun and the moon all together as one and the same event, because they both appear to be mentioned in relation to war and/or judgment. Joel, and subsequently Peter, clarify to us that there are two separate events involving signs in the heavens. And yes, both accompany war and judgment.

The first set of changes to the sun, moon, and stars, are signs to the Church, indicating when the Age of the fullness of the Holy Spirit is over, and the deliverance of the Church from coming wrath is about to take place. *"the sun shall be turned into darkness, and the moon into blood before that great and notable day of the Lord come: and it shall come to pass , that <u>whosoever shall call on the name of the Lord shall be delivered</u>."* Acts 2:20-21. The Day of the Lord is The Day of God's Wrath. Paul states in regard to the born-again believers in Christ, *"For God has not appointed us to wrath, but to obtain salvation by our Lord Jesus Christ."* 1 Thessalonians 5:9. Underlining mine. These first cosmic changes also are <u>a warning</u> to Israel and the Nations that the wrath of God <u>is about to be poured out</u>. Let's take a look at some of these prophecies.

This is not an exhaustive list for each of the following categories, but rather examples of what to look for in interpreting when the cosmic changes take place. Once we become aware of the surrounding circumstances of each, we are able to interpret many other passages where the sun, moon and stars are used as signs.

a. The Pre-Days of Awe Sun/Moon Prophecies:

Joel 2:31-32a, *"The sun shall be turned into darkness, <u>and the moon into blood, before <i>the great and terrible day of the LORD come</i></u>. And it shall come to pass that whosoever shall call on the name of the LORD shall be delivered:"* KJV. Emphasis mine. These verses are pre-Days of Awe! Then Joel continues, *"for in mount Zion and in Jerusalem shall be deliverance, as the LORD hath said, and in the remnant whom the LORD shall call."* Joel 2:32b. Underlining mine. The deliverance for Mount Zion and Jerusalem comes as the result of battle. The battle delivers Mount Zion and Jerusalem into the hands of the Israelis, the *"remnant whom the LORD shall call."* [40] It is of great significance to note there are those in Israel today who recognize themselves as the 'remnant.' Here, the sun is darkened and the moon turned to blood, just as Peter quotes is a sign to the Church that the wrap-up of the Age of the Fullness of the Holy Spirit's earthly ministry to and through the Church is imminent.

Two circumstances will occur along with this Sign. The Rapture, and The Battle of Gog and Magog, resulting in the temporary deliverance of Mount Zion and Jerusalem. I will explain more about this deliverance for Israel later, and why it is temporary at the time of the sun being darkened and the moon blood-colored. Although Mount Zion and Jerusalem are delivered, there is no mention that the LORD Himself is physically present to reign from Mount Zion at this juncture. So these cosmic Signs occur during The Battle of Gog and Magog, near the time of the Rapture, during the time when the Remnant of Israel have been ingathered; as opposed to

---

[40] Hineni, Rebbetzin Esther Jungreis. Not Just Tilim – Missiles, But Tehillim – Psalms. "We are a generation that has witnessed civilization at its lowest ebb, but we are also a generation that has been provleged to behold the fulfillment of prophecy – from Auschwitz to Jerusalem in one breath. It's dizzying.. It's mind boggling. After two thousand years of persecution and oppression, G_d has gathered our remnant, returned us to our ancient land, and redeemed our holy soil. But somehow, we have failed to grasp the miracle of it all, and we live our lives as though there is nothing unusual about our history or that which we have seen unfold before our very eyes."

the ingathering of the Elect at the end of The Days of Awe when the sun is darkened and the moon does not shine at all.

Revelation 8:12. *"And the fourth angel sounded, and the **third part of the sun was smitten, and the third part of the moon**, and the **third part of the stars; so as the third part of them was darkened**, and the **day shone not for a third part of it, and the night likewise."* KJV. Emphases mine. Notice that light is still visible from the sun, moon, and stars, but it is dimmed by one-third. The moon does give off some light here, as it is still effectively giving off about one-third of its glow.

Zephaniah 1:14-15: *"The great day of the LORD **is near, it is near, and hasteth greatly**, even the voice of the day of the LORD: the mighty man shall cry there bitterly. That **day** is a day of wrath, a day of trouble and distress, a day of darkness and gloominess, a day of clouds and thick darkness, **A day of the trumpet and alarm against the fenced cities**, and against the high towers."* KJV. Emphases mine. Zephaniah appears to speak of an imminent coming of The Day of The LORD, because he states, *"the day of the LORD is near, it is near, and hasteth greatly."* He indicates that day will be accompanied by trouble and distress, thick clouds and thick darkness. He also mentions *"the voice of the Day of the LORD"* and *"a day of the trumpet, and alarm against the fenced cities."* (I will explain later the significance of these fenced cities under attack at the time of the rapture of Rosh HaShanah.) The Shout of the Lord and the Voice of the Archangel, coupled with Ha Teruah (The Last Trump) blast of Rosh HaShanah, are referred to by Paul the Apostle. *"Behold, I show you a mystery, We shall not all sleep, but we shall all be changed, in a moment, in the twinkling of an eye, at the last trump, for the trumpet shall sound, and the dead shall be raised incorruptible,...."* 1 Corinthians 15:51-52.

Notice the Voice and the Trumpet Paul mentions in regard to the resurrection and rapture of the Saints in I Thessalonians 4:16-17. *"For the Lord himself shall descend from heaven with a shout, with the voice of the archangel, and with the trump of God, and the dead in Christ shall rise first: Then we which are alive and remain shall be caught up together with them in the clouds, to meet the Lord in the air: and so shall we ever be with the Lord."* So, it would appear that about the time of the Rapture, there is a reduction in the light given off by the sun, moon, and stars; along with a Shout, a Voice, a Trumpet, and a massive resurrection and departure of Saints from the earth. These all usher in The Day of the LORD, The Day of Wrath, trouble, and distress. This day of The Last Trump is also called Yom HaDin, The Day of Judgment -- another name for Rosh HaShanah.

Also notice Zephaniah 2:3. *"Seek ye the LORD, all ye meek of the earth, which have wrought his judgment; seek righteousness, seek meekness: **it may be ye shall be hid in the day of the LORD's anger**."* KJV. The departure that takes place at this time would appear to be <u>necessary to hide the righteous from coming judgment</u>. There is a prepared place where the Righteous are to be taken, so that they do not have to endure The Day of the LORD's Anger. They must be taken to this place of safety <u>before</u> the Days of Awe begin.

Revelation 6:12-17, *"And I beheld when he had opened the sixth seal, and, lo, there was a great earthquake; <u>and the sun became black as sackcloth of hair, and the moon became as blood</u>; Verse 13. And the stars of heaven fell unto the earth, even as a fig tree casts her untimely figs, when she is shaken of a mighty wind. Verse 14. And the heaven departed as a scroll when it is rolled together; and every mountain and island were moved out of their places. Verse 15. And the kings of the earth, and the mighty men, and every bondman, and every free man, hid themselves in the dens and in the ricks of the mountains; Verse 16. And said to the mountains and rocks, Fall on us, and hide us from the face of him that sitteth on the throne, and from the wrath of the Lamb: Verse 17. For the great day of his wrath is come; and who shall be able to stand?"* KJV. Underlining mine.

The changes in the sun and moon make them appear to be veiled as with sackcloth. Accompanying these cosmic phenomena are a series of disasters on the earth, very likely the result of whatever has caused the sun and moon to appear as described. Perhaps this is the result of a nuclear exchange such as seems to be indicated in Ezekiel chapter 38 during The Battle of Gog and Magog, <u>coupled with</u> the devastations caused by a huge earthquake, <u>in conjunction with</u> a massive meteorite shower. The people remaining on the earth interpret all these phenomena as 'acts of God,' so desire to hide.

b. Examples of End of Days of Awe Sun/Moon Changes:

Isaiah 5:26-30 speaks of the coming assembling to battle, and verse 30 states, *"And in that day they shall roar against them* (Israel) *like the roaring of the sea; and if one look unto the land, behold darkness and sorrow, and the light is darkened in the heavens thereof."* Isaiah is referring to the land of Israel being darkened due to a battle that has such a prolific use of weaponry, both cosmic and man-made, that the lights (sun, moon and stars) are as if someone turned them out. Now, this passage, according to the prophetic spiral, could be referring to both the beginning and the end of The Days of Awe, because the sun and moon are darkened at both. But ultimately this is referring to The Battle of Armageddon, because verse 25 of the same chapter indicates Isaiah is speaking about the *"... anger of the LORD kindled against his people, and he hath stretched out his hand against them, and hath smitten them; and the hills did tremble, and their carcasses were torn in the midst of the streets.*" What streets? The streets of a city. The streets of Jerusalem. Gog and Magog does not result in the streets of Jerusalem so completely devastated, because at that time the armies are stopped on the mountains of The West Bank. But during The Battle of Armageddon, even Jerusalem appears to be lost, and would be completely destroyed, except that Messiah returns to end this battle. <u>So we would interpret this darkening of the heavens as taking place at the end of The Tribulation Week.</u>

Isaiah 13:9-13. *"Behold, <u>the day of the Lord cometh</u>, <u>cruel both with wrath and fierce anger</u>, to lay the land desolate: and he shall destroy the sinners thereof out of it. Verse 10.* **For the stars of heaven and the constellations thereof shall not give their light: the sun shall be darkened in his going forth, and the moon shall not cause her light to shine.** *Verse 11. And I will punish the world for their evil, and the wicked for their iniquity; and I will cause the arrogancy of the proud to cease, and will lay low the haughtiness of the terrible. Verse 12. I will make a man more precious than fine gold; even a man than the golden wedge of Ophir. Verse 13. Therefore* **I will shake the heavens, and the earth shall remove out of her place,** <u>in the wrath of the LORD of hosts, and in the day of his fierce anger.</u>" KJV. Emphases mine.

These verses speak of the wrath of the LORD, so refer to the period of The Days of Awe. But notice, the sun is darkened, and the moon does not *"cause her light to shine."* This is not the same as the sun darkened, and the moon appearing blood-red. To further illustrate the end of the period, the haughtiness of the terrible and the arrogancy of the proud, evil and iniquity are ceased. This would refer to the arrogancy and haughtiness of AntiChrist and his henchmen, and the evil and iniquity of his corrupt system. These are abruptly caused to cease. Christ Himself ends the careers of AntiChrist and his crew, and brings their evils to an absolute end at Armageddon.

Isaiah 24: 19-23. *"The earth is utterly broken down, the earth is clean dissolved, the earth is moved exceedingly. Verse 20. The earth shall reel to and fro like a drunkard, and shall be removed like a cottage; and the transgression thereof shall be heavy upon it; and it shall fall, and not rise again. Verse 21. And it shall come to pass in that day, that the LORD shall punish the host of the high ones that are on high,* (Satan and his fallen angels) *and the kings of the earth upon the earth.* (The Leaders of all nations.) *Verse 22. And they shall be gathered together, as prisoners are gathered in the pit, and shall be shut up in the prison, and after many days shall they be visited. Verse 23.* **Then the moon shall be confounded, and the sun ashamed,** <u>when the LORD of hosts shall reign in mount Zion, and in Jerusalem, and before his ancients gloriously.</u>" KJV. Emphases mine.

This sequence is the same as is described in The Book of Revelation when Christ returns, ends The Battle of Armageddon, and defeats the forces of Satan and the nations. Then He has Satan bound and thrown into The Bottomless Pit, to be released a thousand years later to again try the nations. Notice these verses refer to the moon being confounded, and the sun ashamed at the time the LORD sets up His reign in Zion and Jerusalem, and He reigns gloriously in the presence of the Angels and twenty-four elders, *"ancients."* This occurs at Yom Kippur. So these cosmic changes in the sun and moon occur at the end of the Tribulation period of The Days of Awe.

Ezekiel 32: 7-8. *"And when I shall put thee out, I will cover the heaven, and make the stars thereof dark;* **I will cover the sun with a cloud, and <u>the moon shall not give her light</u>. <u>All the bright lights of heaven will I make dark over thee, and set darkness upon thy land,</u>** *saith the Lord God."* KJV. The moon does not give off any light, so this situation occurs at the end of the Tribulation. All these end-of Tribulation cosmic references describe the plaque of darkness of the Fifth Vial of Revelation 16:10.

Matthew 24:29-31. *"Immediately <u>after the tribulation of those days shall the sun be darkened, and the moon shall not give her light, and the stars shall fall from heaven, and the powers of the heavens shall be shaken:</u> And then shall appear the sign of the Son of man in heaven: and then shall all the tribes of the earth mourn, and they shall see the Son of man coming in the clouds of heaven with power and great glory. And he shall send his angels with a great sound of a trumpet, and they shall gather together his elect from the four winds, from one end of heaven to the other."* KJV. Emphasis mine. This ingathering will not be just a remnant as it was previously, but all Israelis, and takes place at the wrap-up of the Tribulation, because verse 29 states specifically, *"<u>after</u> the tribulation of those days."* Then all Israel will be gathered from the four corners of the earth. Notice again the difference here in the moon especially. The sun is darkened, and the moon does not give off any light.

Mark 13:24-27. *"But in those days, <u>after that tribulation</u>, the sun shall be darkened, and the <u>moon shall not give her light</u>, And the stars of heaven shall fall, and the powers that are in heaven shall be shaken. And then shall they see the Son of man coming in the clouds with great power and glory. And then shall he send his angels, and shall gather together his elect from the four winds, from the uttermost part of the earth to the uttermost part of heaven."* This is similar to the explanation in Matthew 24 which obviously refers to *"<u>after the tribulation</u> of those days."*

Joel 3:12-17. *"Let the heathen be wakened, and come up to the valley of Jehosephat: for there will I sit to judge all the heathen round about. Verse 13. Put ye in the sickle, for the harvest is ripe: come, get you down; for the press is full, the vats overflow; for their wickedness is great.* Verse 14. *Multitudes, multitudes in the valley of decision: for the day of the LORD is near in the valley of decision.* Verse 15. **The sun and the moon shall be darkened, and the stars shall withdraw their shining.** Verse 16. *The LORD also shall roar out of Zion, and utter his voice from Jerusalem; and the heavens and the earth shall shake: but the LORD will be the hope of his people, and the strength of the children of Israel.* Verse 17. *So shall ye know that I am the LORD your God dwelling in Zion, my holy mountain: then shall Jerusalem be holy, and there shall no strangers pass through her any more."*

Joel refers to a second round of changes to the sun, moon, and stars. This is not a repeat of what he mentions in verse 31 of Joel chapter 2, but a subsequent series of events with a further battle regarding pretty much the same issues, and taking place centered eventually in The Valley of Jehosephat. It will take the LORD roaring <u>from Zion</u>, and uttering his voice <u>from Jerusalem</u> to end this conflict. He comes, actually setting His feet upon the earth and ascending Mount Zion in Jerusalem, to end The Battle of Armageddon at the end of the Tribulation. So in Joel chapters 2 & 3 we see <u>both</u> sets of circumstances where the sun and moon are involved. One is mentioned in chapter 2, and the other in the latter half of chapter 3. The second set indicates that God's wrath is overwhelmingly thorough and complete, and Christ Himself returns to put an end to the chaos of the nations, and to set up His rule and reign in Jerusalem from Mount Zion. This also is referred to as a Sickle judgment of the nations being gathered. This Sickle judgment of the nations (multitudes in The Valley of Decision) is the Second Sickle of Revelation 14:18-20, where the clusters of grapes (nations) are thrown into the winepress of the wrath of God.

c. A Prophecy that Appears to Apply to both Before and at the End of the Days of Awe : The Prophetic Spiral in Play.

Jeremiah 4: 27-28, *"For thus hath the LORD said, The whole land shall be desolate; yet will I not make a full end. For this shall the earth mourn, and* **the heavens be black***: because I have spoken it, I have purposed it, and will not repent, neither will I turn back from it."* KJV. Bold emphasis mine. The context of these verses appears to be during a time when the very existence of Jerusalem is at stake. This is one prophecy that very well <u>may have more than one fulfillment</u>, but it does have a couple of clues that indicate it could actually be fulfilled at the time of Gog and Magog. *Verses 30 - 31 of this chapter states, "... thy lovers will despise thee,* <u>they will seek thy life</u>. *For I have heard the voice as of a woman in travail, and the anguish as of her that bringeth forth her first child, the voice of the daughter of Zion, that bewaileth* *herself, that spreads her hands, saying, Woe is me now! for my soul is wearied because of murderers."* KJV. Underlining mine.

First of all, who seeks the life of Israel? [41]"The Islamic Arabs who feel they have a right to The Land by decree of Allah. Who is the woman in travail? Israel. [42]The travail is as one who brings forth her first child. Who is the child? Messiah, Jesus Christ. It will take travail for Israel to accept the fact that Jesus is truly Messiah. But notice, it is the <u>Daughter of Zion, present-day Israel</u>, that is wailing. There are those that seek her life. They wish to annihilate her. And she is weary of soul because of murderers. Who are the murderers? They are the terrorists and suicide bombers who are carrying out Jihad against Israel because they do not want Israel to exist. The reason this prophecy could have further fulfillment is because this situation will continue until Messiah returns.

The context speaking of the Daughter of Zion would indicate this prophecy refers to a sovereign nation status of a revived Israel. The original nation was the "mother" but the offspring is the "Daughter." This reference then, would indicate the Nation of Israel since 1948. What I am emphasizing is the fact that the *"heavens shall be black"* indicating the prophetic fulfillment will work itself out in war, accompanied by God-ordained cosmic disasters that darken the skies over Israel, but visibly observable world-wide. The double fulfillment is that this scenario may take place at both The Battle of Gog and Magog pre Days of Awe, and again at Armageddon which is waged during the final days of the Tribulation. The skies are darkened at both. The issues are pretty much the same for both, being the sovereignty of Israel's borders, and the involvement of the nations of the world in the deliberations and exercise of this sovereignty.

2. The Olivet Discourse Regarding the Sun/Moon Events:

When we read the accounts of The Olivet Discourse, we tend to lump together all of the information Jesus gave as describing only one series of events. But we must remember that although Matthew, Mark, and Luke all give basically similar accounts of what Jesus explained, the <u>particulars are not completely identical</u> in each Gospel, especially in regard to the when of the changes in the sun and moon, and in explaining the appearance of The

---

[41] The Jerusalem Post, Sept.11, 2003, Regional Media, Translated by Shira Guttgold, Editorials From The Arab Press: *To Annihilate the Infidels is a divine decree.* "...Allah will torture them Himself or at our hands. (Koran 9:52.)" "...The belief in "annihilating the country of heresy" therefore opens up for us a window of hope by setting a goal that is in the realm of the possible."

[42] Jeremiah 4:30-31, Jeremiah 6:24. Micah 4:9-10, Revelation 12, 1-2.

Son of Man in the clouds. Is this a discrepancy? No. It just means Matthew and Mark recorded information emphasizing The Second Coming, and Luke recorded the sequence leading up to the Rapture, and described also some of the details regarding the Tribulation period and The Second Coming. The fact is, Jesus actually addressed both scenarios.

The reason we tend to amalgamate these events into one and the same time-frame is because the surrounding circumstances are so similar in both scenarios. The pre-Days of Awe events are only a warning, and an indication of the severe judgments about to come on the earth during The Days of Awe. But the particulars are magnified and full-blown during The Days of Awe, especially during the seven year Tribulation Week segment. Luke clarifies the pre-account of what Jesus said. Matthew and Mark specifically state *"after the tribulation..."* Luke is not out on a limb by himself, because the Prophets also indicate there is a difference between the two cosmic events, one introducing Yamim Nora'Im, The Days of Awe, one wrapping them up.

Also notice the admonitional warning given by Jesus in his end times Discourse in Luke 21:36, *"Watch ye therefore, and pray always, that ye may be accounted worthy to escape all these things that shall come to pass, and to stand before the Son of man."* Underline mine. Zephaniah 2:3 states basically the same thing regarding those who are righteous and meek. *"Seek ye the LORD, all ye meek of the earth, which have wrought his judgment; seek righteousness, seek meekness: it may be ye shall be hid in the day of the LORD's anger."* Underlining mine.

What are the righteous hidden from? The Day of the LORD's Anger; Jacob's Trouble, Yamim Nora'Im, The Days of Awe, and all they entail. So, it would appear that the Church does have a cosmic sign in the sun and moon, and this sign will take place just prior to The Ten Days of Awe.

For comparison of both scenarios involving the sun and moon notice what Jesus says in **Matthew 24:2.**, *"Immediately after the tribulation of those days shall the sun be darkened, and the moon shall not give her light, and the stars shall fall from heaven, and the powers of the heavens shall be shaken."* Notice something about this verse. First of all, Jesus is referring to a cosmic event that takes place immediately *"after the tribulation of those days!"* The time-frame is immediately after the Tribulation segment of the Days of Awe. Also note that this event has the sun darkened and the moon **refusing** to give her light, and the stars falling from the heavens. **This is different than the cosmic sun and moon sign of Joel chapter 2 that Peter quotes in Acts chapter 2!** They indicate that the sun is darkened and the moon is **blood-colored BEFORE** the Day of the LORD comes.

Therefore, there appears to be <u>two end-time prophetic scenarios that involve the sun and the moon, and these are at different times, and under similar, but different circumstances</u>. Peter's message for the Church was that The Church Age, under the leading and empowerment of the Holy Spirit, was now born and would continue until the sun was darkened and the moon turned to blood *" before the great and terrible Day of the LORD comes, and whosoever shall call upon the name of the Lord <u>shall be delivered</u>."* So the sun is darkened, and the moon is turned to the color of blood **before** the Days of Awe begin. And the sun is darkened and <u>the moon does not give off any light</u> at **the end** of the Days of Awe. Therefore, the Church does have a physical cosmic sign in the heavens to indicate the end of the Church Age!

In order for the moon to give off any light at all, it must reflect the light from the sun. In Joel's description in chapter 2, the moon does give off light, albeit with a red color, suggesting that there is some light to reflect, but it has been severely reduced in intensity and appears red, indicating there is much air pollution of dust and debris particles. This is not the same as the moon not giving any light at all which Jesus speaks about in Matthew and Mark's accounts. But if we continue to read beyond Joel chapter 3:15, we see a reference to the sun and moon that is similar to Jesus' Matthew description . *"The sun and the moon shall be darkened, and the stars shall withdraw their shining."* In this latter instance the sun and moon are darkened, suggesting one will not see much light from either one, and the stars will not even be observable.

Actually the red moon of Joel chapter 2 and Acts chapter 2 is not at all out of character with the possible air-pollution which may take place during The Battle of Gog and Magog if there is a concentrated use of missiles and/or nuclear weapons. (Some refer to this war as The Russian Invasion of Israel.) The inference, then, in both Joel chapter 2 and Acts chapter 2 is that the Church may very well be around while this battle takes place, or at least for its beginning. The reasons for this battle are described in Joel chapter 3: 1-8, and Ezekiel 38 and 39 calls it The Battle of Gog and Magog. But during The Battle of Armageddon, described in Joel 3: 9-17, the sun and moon are darkened and the stars refuse to shine, suggesting unprecedented air pollution <u>worse</u> than during The Battle of Gog and Magog. The saints come back with Christ to end this battle at the end of the Tribulation. (The saints cannot come back unless they have first gone somewhere!) The Rapture takes place shortly after the first changes appearing in the sun and moon at Gog and Magog, and then the Church returns with Christ at The Second Coming, which appears to be at the same time as the second set of cosmic changes. So in essence, the Church will observe both, but at opposite ends of The Ten Days of Awe.

Also, <u>the first</u> darkening of the sun, and the moon's red color, is **a sign to the Jews that God's final discipline upon Israel, and His wrath against the nations of the whole world, is soon to begin,** because <u>Joel's prophetic focus then shifts to dwell on Mount Zion and Jerusalem for deliverance</u>. Both deliverances (first of the Church, and of Zion and Jerusalem) are different from each other, but occur pretty much simultaneously. The Church is delivered <u>from</u> the coming wrath of God, while Israel is <u>delivered</u> to <u>the coming period of discipline</u>, and <u>Jerusalem and Judah</u> are delivered into her jurisdiction for Israel's preparations to take place. There is a deliverance for Zion and Jerusalem that occurs at the time that the sun is darkened and the moon is turned blood-red according to Joel 2:32 to 3: 1-8, <u>but it is only a temporary deliverance</u> in bringing some relief to The Middle East situation. Zion and Jerusalem, and ultimately all Covenant Lands, will finally and totally be delivered following the return of Messiah at The Battle of Armageddon, and at that time again there will be changes in the sun, moon, and stars.

So what we appear to observe are two situations regarding Israel and the whole earth that involve the sun, moon, and stars. I would propose that the signs in the sun and moon at the end of The Church Age are a wake-up call to Israel, because the Rapture of the Church immediately following will trigger <u>some</u> of the Jews to realize it is only born-again Christians who have disappeared, so they will scurry to the Scriptures to re-examine their beliefs regarding the significance of their own eschatology.

We must remember, Joel's message primarily was directed toward the Jews, while Peter's explanation was directed to the Jews who were in Jerusalem celebrating Shavuot, but his remarks and quote were regarding the pouring out of the Spirit on those who accept Jesus as Messiah. The fact that the explanation by Peter was a dissertation to the believers in Jesus Christ as to what was being fulfilled, and what will prophetically follow, was a double-edged message. To the Jews it was a sign of fulfillment of the prophetic message given by Joel, as well as the truth of Jesus Christ's words proving His Messianic role, which the Jews were in danger of misinterpreting and ultimately rejecting. Somehow when the Jews finally recognize Jesus as their true Messiah, this Shavuot event, (and indeed the entire life and ministry of Christ) will surely come back to mind, and they will finally realize what they have missed out on, and what the Church has been blessed with -- namely the outpouring of the Holy Spirit in His full power and presence, and His role as the One who prepares and takes The Bride to The <u>Bridegroom</u>.

Certainly many Jews who were in the audience accepted Peter's words, and became followers of Jesus, The Messiah. [43]The first converts were all Jews, and three thousand of them believed that Shavuot day! Great numbers accepted Christ in the days following as well. [44]After the healing of the lame man at The Temple gate, Peter again preached a sermon, and five thousand more believed. However, this initial trend among the Jews did not last long.

As a result, the Church now is predominantly Gentile, and most Jews do not accept Jesus as Messiah. **But the Jews do have access, through The Law and Prophets, to the meaning of the events that will occur when the Rapture takes place**. When these events unfold, those who are familiar with The Law and Prophets will recognize that something of apocalyptic significance has occurred, and many will begin to search the Scriptures to explain these events. <u>The Rapture of the Church will begin this awakening for Israel</u>. The Abomination of Desolation will wake-up many more, and The Battle of Armageddon will cause the majority of the Jews to finally cry out for deliverance, and for Messiah to come. Then they will finally, officially, recognize Jesus as LORD, Messiah, Redeemer, Bridegroom, and KING.

God has always spoken to mankind through His Creation to show His complete and unquestionable power and sovereignty. The changes in the sun, moon, and stars are in keeping with Genesis 1:14 of day four's Creation Week explanation that the lights in the sky were to be *"for signs, and for seasons, and for days, and for years."* When we think about it, every Dispensation has had accompanying *"signs"* in the heavens to indicate a change from one Dispensation to another, and to herald God's hand at work in the affairs of mankind. Some involved the sun or moon. Some involved the stars as well. The transition from the Church Age to The Ten Days of Awe will then be no different! Also, the transition from The Days of Awe to The Millennium will be with cosmic signs in the heavens. Otherwise, Genesis 1:14 would be incorrect and totally irrelevant!

The sun, moon, and stars are not only to be for lights, but they are for the counting of days and years, and for signs. The signs aspect is pretty much ignored by most Jews and Christians, because the occult has used the cosmos for astrology and erroneous interpretations, ascribing intrinsically to things created, powers that are not there. The universe is not in place for fortune-telling, but to indicate God is at work in all His Creation, <u>revealing a time-table for this universe</u>, the judgment of God

---

[43] Acts 2:41.
[44] Acts 4:4.

upon the unrighteous, and <u>the ultimate reconciliation of man to God</u>. We are to read the signs according to God's revealed Word so we know where we fit into the scheme of things, and also to recognize His awesome power and sovereignty!

So to summarize, there are changes in the sun and moon both **before** The Ten Days of Awe, **as well as at the end** of The Days of Awe. Both of these cosmic events appear to be accompanied by war. The pre-Jacob's Trouble war which accompanies cosmic signs, and signals the end of The Church Age and imminent Rapture, and the inevitable soon pouring out of the Wrath of God, is The Battle of Gog and Magog, which ushers in The Days of Awe Period, sets the stage for the rebuilding of The Temple, and the subsequent rise of AntiChrist to power. The war that ends The Days of Awe is The Battle of Armageddon accompanied by signs in the sun and moon, and these signal The Second Coming of Christ, and the complete restoration of Israel in fulfillment of The Covenant.

3. Cosmic Symbolism in the Sun, Moon, and Stars:

The symbolism attributed to these heavenly bodies is important, and assists us in understanding the prophetic significance of specific times and seasons as revealed in Scripture.

The sun symbolizes <u>Christ</u> who is The Light of the World. He is the Sun of Righteousness. *"For the LORD God is a sun and shield"* Psalm 84:11a. *"But unto you that fear my name shall the Sun of Righteousness arise with healing in his wings:"* Malachi 4:2a.

The moon symbolizes <u>the wholly righteous</u>, and the stars symbolize the celestial beings of God's Creation that influence this world, namely <u>the angelic dimension</u>, both good and evil.

The moon symbol is interesting, because in observing the changes that occur to the moon, we are able to arrive at an understanding of <u>what unfolds for the wholly righteous</u>. Generally we say that the moon is symbolic for The Church, <u>but the symbol is more broad-based</u>. It is obvious when we read Scripture, that indeed there were those who were considered righteous before The Church Age. The cross of Christ is central to God's redemptive plan. The Lamb of God offered on this cross, and shedding His own blood, is the perfect atonement for all sin for all time, both before and after the cross. Those before the cross are redeemed by the shed blood of Christ if they indeed repented, and accepted by faith the covering of the blood of the sacrificial atonement which ultimately was fulfilled in Christ's death and resurrection. They are deemed righteous, but they are not part of The Church-Bride who are of the redeemed of

The Church Age. We realize many more will be washed in the blood of The Lamb during The Days of Awe, but they also will not be part of the Bride. Thus, the moon represents the Righteous of all ages. Therefore, the signs regarding the moon indicate coming prophetic seasonal fulfillments regarding all who are Righteous, whether part of the Church or not.

Certainly the Church is wholly righteous through the blood of Christ, but the Church is removed prior to The Days of Awe. So the brightness of the testimony of the righteous is first dimmed at the time of the Rapture. The Full Moon indicates the mandate of the Church is complete.

The dimming of the moon (righteous) at this juncture in the prophetic time-table, will actually be a strong testimony to the truth of Jesus Christ, and the atonement He procured for all who will accept His redemptive work. Hence <u>the blood-red color</u> of the moon which will be visible <u>during the phase-out of the moon</u> to Rosh HaChodesh - Yom HaKeseh (The New Moon Day of Concealment.) However this is <u>only a dimming</u>, because the Gospel message will still be preached throughout the world by the 144,000 sealed Jewish Evangelists after the Rapture, and many more will come to true repentance world-wide.

The majority of converts who become righteous through the blood of The Lamb during The Ten Days of Awe will be martyred. Their martyrdom will be pretty much complete, especially during the final three and one-half years of the seven year Tribulation. Therefore, at the end of the Tribulation period the moon (righteous) will be rendered not visible (darkened) from the perspective of those on the earth. So we are able to observe the significance for the righteous, indicated by the two separate cosmic signs of the moon, and in the same sequence as the actual literal changes to the moon that will be observable in the sky.

The sun as used in Scripture metaphorically, refers to The Light of The Redeemer. Even the light from the sun will <u>first be dimmed</u> after the Rapture, <u>then</u> ultimately will almost be obliterated (darkness) during the final days of the Tribulation. So the <u>two physical signs regarding the sun (Jesus Christ) also will be prophetically significant, and physically observable</u>. Just prior to Christ's Second Coming, the message of salvation through Jesus Christ <u>will almost not be visible</u> on the earth. *"...Nevertheless, when the Son of Man cometh, shall he find faith on the earth?"* Luke 18:8.

This question is posed along with the parable of the Unrighteous Judge. In explanation Jesus says, *"And shall not God avenge his own elect, which cry day and night unto him, though he bear long with them? I tell you he will avenge them speedily."* Luke 18:7-8. Who are *"his own elect who cry day and night?"*

There are three groups of 'elect.' First, there are those who have been martyred for their faith during The Church Age. They stand under the altar in Heaven, and cry out for avengement of their blood. Revelation 6: 10. *"How long, O Lord, holy and true, dost thou not judge and avenge our blood on them that dwell on the earth?"* The second and third groups of 'elect' are of Israel, and of the righteous out of all nations from The Days of Awe period, so represent the cry of Israel, as well as the martyred Tribulation Saints. Revelation 16: 5-6 *"And I heard the angel of the waters say, Thou art righteous, O Lord, which art, and wast, and shalt be, because thou hast judged thus. For they have shed the blood of saints and prophets, and thou hast given them blood to drink; for they are worthy."* These also cry for blood-avengement.

Although metaphorically the 'light' of the righteous and of The Son of God, portrayed by the moon and the sun, are almost obliterated, Christ Himself will break through in Clouds of Glory, and every eye shall see Him. He will avenge all His Elect at His Second Coming at the end of The Days of Awe!

But in order for Israel to have a glimmer of faith, their eyes of understanding must begin to be opened. This illumination for Israel begins before the wrath of God is poured out, but comes to completion at the end of The Days of Awe when Jerusalem appears to have been brought under Gentile domination again, so must be delivered. Notice what Jesus says in **Luke 21:24-36.** *"And they shall fall by the edge of the sword, and shall be led away captive into all nations; and Jerusalem shall be trodden down of the Gentiles, until the times of the Gentiles be fulfilled. Verse 25. And there shall be <u>signs in the sun, and in the moon, and in the stars</u>; and upon the earth distress of nations, with perplexity; the sea and the waves roaring; Verse 26. Men's hearts failing them for fear, and for looking after those things <u>which are coming on the earth</u>: <u>for the powers of heaven shall be shaken</u>. Verse 27.* ***And then shall they see the Son of man coming in a cloud with power and great glory.*** *Verse 28.* <u>*And when these things begin to come to pass, then look up, and lift up your heads; for your redemption draweth nigh*</u>*. Verse 29. And he spake to them a parable; Behold the fig tree, and all the trees; Verse 30. When they now shoot forth, ye see and know of your own selves that summer is now nigh at hand. Verse 31. So likewise ye, when ye see these things come to pass, know ye that the kingdom of God is nigh at hand. Verse 32. Verily I say unto you,* <u>*This generation shall not pass away, till all be fulfilled*</u>*. Verse 33. Heaven and earth shall pass away: but my words shall not pass away. Verse 34. Take heed to yourselves, lest at any time your hearts be overcharged with surfeiting and drunkenness, and cares of this life, and so that day come upon you unawares. Verse 35. For as a snare shall it come on all them that dwell on the face of the whole earth. Verse 36. Watch ye therefore, and pray always, that ye may be accounted worthy to escape all these things that shall come to pass, and to stand before the Son of man."* KJV. All emphases mine.

The changes to the sun and moon indicated by this passage, are <u>warnings of judgments to follow</u>. In other words, men's hearts will fail them for fear, because they will be scared silly by what is transpiring, and <u>afraid of what more will follow</u>. When the Church sees these things beginning to take place, we are to *"<u>look up, for your redemption draweth nigh</u>."*

The specific prophetic sign indicating fulfillment <u>is about to take place</u>, is the sign of the Fig Tree shooting forth new leaves. This is the rebirth of Israel, heralding the imminent end of The Age of Grace, and the approach of The Days of Awe.

In His Olivet Discourse, Jesus explained the destruction of The Second Temple, and of Jerusalem, resulting in further dispersion of Jews into all nations. However, the resultant dispersion was not a destruction of Israel as a sovereign Nation, because Israel was only a puppet to Rome already. Rather, Jesus was referring specifically to what was imminently about to transpire in regard to The Second Temple Complex, and the devastation that would result for many centuries afterward for the Jews. [45]This prophecy was fulfilled in 68-70 C.E. under Titus, during the Roman destruction of Jerusalem and The Temple.

Subsequently, The Temple Mount and Jerusalem have been downtrodden of the Gentiles for many centuries. This situation will continue until The Times of The Gentiles ends, at which time Jerusalem and The Temple Mount will be restored to the jurisdiction of the Jews. Therefore, Israel must exist as a recognized sovereign Nation for this prophecy to be ultimately fulfilled, and Israel must eventually <u>control</u> The Temple Mount! We have seen part of this scenario come to pass already. Israel again is a sovereign Nation, and at this juncture, Jerusalem is in Israel's hands, but The Temple Mount is questionable as long a Muslim presence remains there, and the Palestinian Authority maintains control on The Mount.

But throughout the intervening Church Age, [46]Jesus indicated there would be distress of nations, perplexity, wars and rumors of wars, becoming more and more intense as the end of the Age approached. [47] At the end of this Age, men's hearts would fail them for fear because of the awful things that are <u>about to transpire</u>.

[45] The Zondervan Pictoral Encyclopedia of The Bible, 1976, Vol. 5, Tenney, Merrill C. Gen. Ed. The Zondervan corporation, Regency Reference Library, Grand Rapids, Michigan. P. 653, 654.
[46] Matthew 24:6-8, Mark 13:7-8, Luke 21:10.
[47] Luke 21:26.

This fear will accompany war and cosmic changes according to Revelation 6:12 to 17. I will explain this passage more later. [48]Joel and Peter indicate the sun will be darkened, and the moon will be turned blood-red at the end of The Age of The Holy Spirit, the Church Age of Grace, because the focus of world tensions will begin to center around the sovereign Israeli Nation. This will result in a conflict, Gog and Magog, which will involve many nations, and will bring about deliverance to Mount Zion, Jerusalem, and Judea.

The Rapture will occur around this same time. The account in Luke is especially significant for the Church, because he records Jesus' statements regarding these prophetic signs with a somewhat different emphasis than Matthew and Mark. In other words, Luke reveals a nuance of Jesus' Discourse that Matthew and Mark do not emphasize, namely, that the Coming of the Son of Man in Clouds of Glory <u>will follow</u> the heavens being shaken, and <u>this shaking is what men are dreading</u>. One can only dread what appears <u>to be coming</u>, <u>but has not yet taken place</u>. One does not dread the things of the past, except only in memory. *"...Men's hearts failing them for fear, and for looking after those things <u>which are coming on the earth</u>: for the powers of heaven shall be shaken. Verse 27. And then shall they see the Son of man coming in a cloud with power and great glory."* Luke 21:26-27. However, the very next verse places a qualification on what is stated, revealing the Spiral of Prophecy is definitely in play. Verse 28, *"And when these things <u>begin</u> to come to pass, then look up, and lift up your heads; for you redemption draweth nigh."* Underlining mine.

In other words, these events have a Season when they <u>begin</u>. The Days of Awe begin with the sun and the moon darkened, distress of nations, perplexity, and unusual weather patterns where the sea and waves roar. The beginning of these devastations is one-third of normal, compared to the total devastation which will strike the earth during the Tribulation period. So, it is when these warning judgments <u>begin</u> that we are to look up, because our redemption is nearing. Notice, <u>Luke's emphasis is the Rosh HaShanah sequence</u>. *"And take heed to yourselves, lest at any time your hearts be overwhelmed with surfeiting, and drunkenness, and cares of this life, and so that day come upon you unawares. Verse 36. For as a snare shall it come on all them that dwell on the face of the whole earth. Verse 36. Watch ye therefore, and pray always, <u>that ye may be accounted worthy to escape</u> all these things that shall come to pass, and to stand before the Son of man."* Underline mine. The 'escape' is the Yom HaKeseh Concealment which fulfills the ingathering of Rosh HaShanah. When do the escaped righteous stand before the Son

---

[48] Joel 2:28-32, Acts 2:17-21.

of Man? At Rosh HaShanah, and they assemble around The Throne in Heaven! Following the Rapture, those who know Scripture will realize this harvest escape has taken place, because many born-again Christians will have disappeared.

Then will follow The Ten Days of Awe (one year for each prophetic day), the last seven years of which are Daniel's 70 Week, the seven years of Tribulation, ending with The Battle of Armageddon, and with the sun and moon almost obliterated from view, and Jerusalem appearing to be lost to Gentile forces. <u>The same list of devastations will apply</u>, only this time they will be full-blown, fulfilling <u>what was dreaded</u>! At the end of The Ten Days of Awe, The Second Coming of Christ will take place. He will come with His Church-Bride accompanying Him, to set up His rule and reign on the earth, and Jerusalem will be permanently delivered. At that time <u>every eye shall see The Son of Man</u> as He descends in Clouds of Glory. Yom Kippur. Matthew and Mark emphasize the Yom Kippur sequence.

Notice, the Church is to take note of when these things *"<u>begin to come to pass</u>."* Very important! The Church-Bride does not remain on the earth through all of this, but only sees from earthly perspective, the beginnings of the sequence.

CHAPTER 7
THE OLIVET DISCOURSE

In His Olivet Discourse, Jesus answered the disciples questions regarding when certain fulfillments will occur. It is helpful to place His explanation in its original setting to understand what Jesus was saying. We travel with Jesus and His disciples from The Temple to The Mount of Olives as He explains what is to come to pass.

I. The Temple:

Jesus and His disciples were in Jerusalem for Passover. This was not just any Passover as usual, but was The Passover that Jesus fulfilled through His death as The Lamb of God. This was a <u>'mo'ed'</u> Passover Feast, meaning it was <u>a Divine Appointment</u> of complete fulfillment. Jesus knew what was about to transpire during this particular Passover, even though the disciples did not know that in just a few days, before the week would end, Jesus, the One who they were now convinced was indeed Messiah, would go to the cross.

Jesus' Triumphal Entry into Jerusalem had just taken place, and He and His disciples had gone to The Temple. The Temple Complex was undergoing major renovation and expansion. This restoration and renovation project had been ongoing for many years, but was not yet complete, even though Herod the Great, who commissioned the project, had been dead many years. Herod, the great King of the Jews, died the year Christ was born, in 4 B.C.E. Now, Jesus, the true KING of the Jews, visited the very Temple that [49]Herod had commissioned to become a lasting reminder and memorial of his own inflated personal greatness. But Herod's Temple complex was destroyed. The true KING of Kings, Jesus, Messiah, will be the One to receive all the glory forever, and will dwell in His Temple, and His Name will be forever magnified!

Following this Temple visit, we find Jesus had left the Temple Mount area, but the disciples brought Him back to the Complex, because they had arranged a tour to show Him the progress of the renovations on the buildings and grounds. *"And Jesus went out, and departed from the temple: and his disciples came to him for to show him the buildings of the temple."* Matthew 24:1. In the course of this tour Jesus observed, *"See ye not all these things?"*

---

[49]   The Zondervan Pictorial Encyclopedia, Volume 5, 1976, Tenney, Merrill C., Gen. Ed. The Zondervan Corporation, Regency Reference Library, Grand Rapids, Michigan. Herod's Temple, p. 645-646, 653.

The Final Schedule Revealed

Verily I say unto you, There shall not be here one stone left upon another, that shall not be thrown down." Matthew 24:2.

II. The Disciples Questions:

This comment by Jesus, referring to what was obviously a future destruction of the entire Temple Complex, tweaked the disciples curiosity. Although the fate of The Temple was certainly part of their questions, they had broader concerns as well. They waited until they were assembled privately on The Mount of Olives overlooking The Temple grounds, and then their questions were voiced. These questions were given in a specific sequence, and Jesus answered them in the order they were asked. What were the questions? *"Tell us, when shall these things be? and what shall be the sign of thy coming,? and of the end of the world?"* Matthew 24: 3.

These three questions were not arbitrary, but obviously were directed by the Holy Spirit. The queries also were both for personal information to satisfy the disciples own fears and curiosity, as well as were based in two distinct affiliations. First of all, the disciples were asking as Jews, concerned for the deliverance of their people from the oppression of their enemies, and wonderment about the prophesied Messianic Kingdom. Had the time now arrived? And, would Jesus now ascend to The Throne of David, now that He had been hailed King by the people? Secondly, they were asking on behalf of the fact that they were disciples of Jesus, so were concerned how prophecy would unfold for the followers of Christ. When we keep these affiliations in mind, we are able to see where the Jews, and the nations of the world, as well as the Church, all fit into the answers Jesus gives.

Primarily, His answers are given in reference to the Jews, because the Jews are the people who God <u>has chosen to be the international object lesson and vehicle through which the Redeemer came</u>, <u>and will ultimately again come</u>. Therefore, we must keep in mind the fact that Jesus was Himself a Jew, and indeed is The Messiah who will rule and reign from Mount Zion in Jerusalem, from The Throne of David. So of course He would understand the Jewish concerns here. As prophecy unfolds for the Jews (Israelis) we are able to understand where the Church, as well as all nations, fit into the spiral of prophetic fulfillment.

Jesus' answers center around Jerusalem and The Temple Complex, and he later makes a key reference to The Abomination of Desolation recorded in The Book of Daniel, indicating the obvious need for a Temple in the future. It is as if what was to happen regarding the prophesied

⁵⁰destruction of The Second Temple Complex, which destruction took place when Titus lay siege to Jerusalem in 68-70 C.E., was answered by His previous statement while they were on their inspection tour.

But His Olivet response to their questions was more far-reaching, both for the Church as well as for the Jews. Jesus' answers were probably overwhelming to the disciples, because He launched into a very detailed explanation of situations and events, and reasons for these events. He explained first of all what will unfold for those who have faith, and who take the Gospel message to the world; and the political / religious/ spiritual climate that will transpire throughout The Church Age. This was to encourage, as well as to warn His disciples.

Remember, there are three questions. Jesus answers these questions by making overall statements, then He goes back and adds more detail. The Spiral of Prophecy is in play, so <u>a portion</u> of His answer to each question is for the Church to pay attention to. However, <u>all is for the Jews to discern</u>. So, we must keep the unfolding of these prophecies for the Jews in mind. <u>They also have undergone persecutions, and endured much over the past 2000 years to fulfill these prophecies. However, the majority of them have not named The Name of Christ</u>. So any reference to the Gospel, and what will transpire regarding those who have The Testimony of the Name of Christ, obviously refers to Christians, both of the Bride, and 'after' for the Tribulation Saints. Actually, what Jesus was saying is that both Jews and Christians will be persecuted throughout what we refer to as The Church Age, and subsequently during The Days of Awe. It is ironic that much of the difficulties endured by both Christians and Jews have arisen, and very well may continue to arise, from intrinsic animosities generated against each other, just as much as from outside forces!

So in understanding Jesus' Discourse, we are able to observe world events, and interpret them in the light of the prophecies contained in God's Word. Some folk feel that we cannot accurately point to the succinct fulfillment of any end-time prophecy, because we may come at our conclusion from a pre-conceived standpoint, and therefore ought to avoid any dogmatic conclusions just in case we may be wrong. Although that approach appears to have some logical caution and validity, it puts blinders on our eyes, and from what we observe Jesus saying to His disciples, <u>we are not to have blinders on, rather are to be awake, aware, and watching</u>. That means then, we must be able to peg-down the fulfillment of a good portion

---

⁵⁰   The Zondervan Pictorial Encyclopedia, Volume 5, 1976, Tenney, Merrill C., Gen. Ed. The Zondervan Corporation, Regency Reference Library, Grand Rapids, Michigan. P. The History from A.D. 30 to A.D. 70. P. 653.

of these prophecies, or we will not have a clue where we are on God's time-table. If we cannot exercise any discernment, it also would mean that Jesus' admonition to understand, and His warnings given right down to the details, would be invalid. So Jesus would have wasted His breath even talking about what would transpire. We do not have an option of putting our intellectual and interpretive heads in the sand, saying, "Whatever transpires will transpire whether I understand it or not, so I won't bother myself and others with trying to interpret Bible prophecy."

Unfortunately, there are a great number of Christians who adhere to this passive approach. Probably it is because there have been excesses and wrong date-setting by many, and they do not wish to ever make any interpretive mistake, so choose to ignore the whole matter. Its not that they do not believe Bible prophecy is true, but just that they do not think we have any business trying to figure it out. That is a travesty, because these folk actually miss out on the blessings and purifying effects that come with looking into God's Word with a heart to try to understand. The fact is, there are events and situations happening all around us that point to the imminent Rapture of the Church, and we ought to be aware of these events and their prophetic significance. Sometimes we may peg them erroneously, or place them into a wrong context, but the closer we come to the end of this Age, I feel we will become more adept at calling the appropriateness of the matter, because [51] according to Gabriel's explanation to Daniel, it will all become clear at the time of the end of The Age. There comes a time for every prophecy when it really is finally and totally fulfilled. We must learn to recognize when this actually happens, and be willing to say so. Otherwise, even the Church will be caught sleeping!

Therefore, when we read Jesus' response to the disciples' questions, we must interpret His answers in the light of all end-time prophecy from all prophetic Scripture. This is a challenge, because much of Scripture is prophetic in metaphorical type, or in direct statement, and sometimes in both of these at once; and often as we have already observed, in more than one fulfillment cycle of the prophetic spiral. From our perspective, we are able to look back on a great deal of prophecy and see its fulfillment already, such as the re-formation of the nation of Israel in 1948, with the resulting ingathering of the remnant taking place before our eyes. Current fulfillment is more difficult to recognize until we are able to gain some degree of perspective. Future fulfillment is much more illusive, but we are able to follow signs that are indicating the lead-up to fulfillment. The unrest and controversy in The Middle East between Israel and her Arab

---

[51] Daniel 12:8-10.

Muslim neighbors, and the Palestinians in particular, are signs that we know are leading up to the fulfillment of prophecy, and the end of The Church Age. We may sometimes put varying degrees of interpretation and significance on these signs, but the truth that none can deny is that the signs are there nonetheless. So interpretation aside, we are nearing the end of The Age!

The Church will both observe, and participate in, the signs up to and including the sun being darkened and the moon appearing as blood. Then the Church will <u>experience</u> the initial Sign of The Son of Man coming in a Cloud of Glory. Jesus appears to indicate there are two scenarios involving His coming in Clouds of Glory. Luke 21: 27 does not say specifically that every eye observes the first event, but those who live to see the signs He has just mentioned in Luke 21:25-26, namely the signs in the sun, moon, and stars, distress of nations, perplexity, the sea and waves roaring, men's hearts failing them for fear of what is obviously <u>going to come to pass</u> on the earth; these are the ones who *"...shall see the Son of man coming in a cloud with power and great glory."* It is the Church here that sees Him, and rises to meet Him in The Cloud of Glory! It does not say in Luke's passage anything about Jesus setting foot on earth at this time, or even that everyone on earth will physically observe this Sign. Luke only writes the fact that this powerful Sign of the LORD coming in a Cloud with power and great glory does occur. The context in Luke is regarding the events <u>leading up to this Rosh HaShanah appearing</u>.

The second time Christ appears in Clouds of Glory will be at His Second Coming, and then **every eye shall see Him** according to Matthew and Mark, who both mention The Son of Man coming in Clouds of Glory and power AFTER the Tribulation. Matthew 24:29-31, "*<u>Immediately after the tribulation of those days shall <u>the sun be darkened</u>, and the moon shall not give her light</u>, and the stars shall fall from heaven, and the powers of the heavens shall be shaken: <u>And then shall appear the sign of the Son of Man in heaven</u>: and then shall all the tribes of the earth mourne, and they shall see the Son of Man coming in the clouds of heaven with power and great glory.*" Underlining mine. Mark 13:24-26 states the same sequence. This is the Yom Kippur sequence.

The ethnic identity of the writer of each of the Gospels, along with the identification of who each was addressing, also plays a role in understanding and interpreting Jesus' Olivet Discourse. Matthew and Mark were Jewish followers of Christ, and under the leading of the Holy Spirit wrote their Gospel accounts primarily to Jewish readers, with the Jewish mind-set and understanding. Matthew, and probably Mark, would have been among those present during The Temple tour, and immediately following on The Mount of Olives when Jesus gave His Discourse on the end times.

The Jewish mind-set is that The Day of Atonement, Yom Kippur, which is the culmination of The High Holy Days, is of great significance, being the final day of The Forty Days of Teshuvah. So <u>Rosh HaShanah</u>, that takes place <u>ten days before</u> Yom Kippur, <u>is the final wake-up call</u>. According to the Jews, beginning with Rosh HaShanah, there are ten days (The High Holy Days) of Teshuvah (repentance) left. <u>This is most significant, because in actual fact prophetically, this is how it will ultimately play out for Israel</u>! Therefore, Matthew and Mark capitalize on the prophetic sequence emphasizing the fulfillment of Yom Kippur. Their emphasis is on The Atonement, and the promise of The Messianic Kingdom which will be set up at the coming of Messiah. Because they were Jews themselves, they would automatically have had this orientation in their minds, so would logically write their accounts accordingly.

It is not that Matthew and Mark totally ignore any reference to Rosh HaShanah, because they record the fact that Jesus obviously explained it in terms of the Thief coming to break up the house of the one not watching. Matthew mentions the Thief, and both Matthew and Mark mention the importance of watching and not sleeping, so as not to be caught unawares. They both also record Jesus' warnings regarding the coming wrath of God on the nations, and on the ungodly. But their emphasis on Yom Kippur explains why they hinge their accounts on the Coming of the Lord in The Clouds of Glory and power <u>after</u> the Tribulation. That event will ultimately be of great importance to Israel.

But Luke was a Greek physician. He addresses his account from a different perspective. Luke's Gospel was written to convey the truth of the life and ministry of Christ to Theophilus, who also was a Greek. He is therefore writing primarily to the believer in Christ who is Gentile. The focus of importance for the Church is therefore Rosh HaShanah, the catching away ingathering of the Tzadikim (wholly righteous) at the sounding of Ha Teurah Shofar (The Last Trump), when the Saints are to be hidden from the Wrath of God that is to be poured out during Jacob's Trouble. The Church will be participant in The Wedding-Coronation of The KING in The Father's House in Heaven, so <u>is hidden from</u> the coming Wrath of God. So his account is written accordingly. He also does not ignore Jesus' warnings regarding the Wrath of God, or The Second Coming. Actually, Luke's account illustrates the Spiral of fulfillment. Devastations occur both in the lead-up to Rosh HaShanah when the LORD will be revealed in Clouds of Glory to the totally righteous saints, as well as precede Yom Kippur when the LORD will be revealed to the whole world.

The Tzadikim were considered wholly righteous if they had no sin ascribed to them throughout the year since the previous Day of Atonement of Yom Kippur. It becomes obvious, no one of himself can maintain such an absolutely righteous position through personal works. Righteousness must be attained by accepting the atoning finished work of Christ unto salvation by grace through faith. The significance of The Day of Atonement of Yom Kippur for the Christian is that he has already availed himself of what Christ fulfilled in obtaining redemption through His death and His resurrection. The believer has already repented, so therefore already has his name entered into The Book of Life. He no longer must focus on Yom Kippur to come, because Jesus Christ has fulfilled the required atonement of Yom Kippur already at Passover, which for the Church is the betrothal, so the Christian has a more immediate celebration awaiting. When The Books are opened on Rosh HaShanah, he already is inscribed in The Book of The Wholly Righteous, so qualifies as Tzadika - a wholly righteous one through the complete atonement of the Blood of The Lamb unto salvation. So he looks forward to The Last Trump of Rosh HaShanah, to be taken into the Father's House in Heaven to participate in the Coronation and Wedding of the Bridegroom. In fact, the Church is also referred to as the Bride of Christ, presented in purity and holiness to the Bridegroom. She is promised she does not have to live through The Days of Awe judgment on earth, but is hidden from it. Yom HaKeseh. The Day of Concealment. Now that's the love of a Bridegroom!

Therefore it is logical that Luke, a Gentile, would record Jesus' account from the perspective of the coming of The Son of Man for His Church, so he explains The Clouds of the Glory and power of the coming of The Son of Man before the Tribulation, indicating the Rapture, ingathering, of Rosh HaShanah. The believer is encouraged to watch the signs, so as not to be caught unawares. But the watching of the believer is like the watching and waiting of a Bride for her Bridegroom, so she must always be prepared, wearing her robes of righteousness that Her Betrothed Bridegroom has provided.

III. Jesus Gave the Entire Perspective:

Jesus, in His Olivet Discourse, gave the entire perspective, because all the points are necessary for the fulfillment of The Fall Feasts. For us to understand the entire magnitude of His Discourse, we must read all the Gospel accounts of it. There is no discrepancy, just different emphasis in each account. In not understanding the Jewish root connection, we tend to argue pre, mid, and post trib, millennial, a-millennial etc. positions, because we have lost the understanding of the common basis which in fact brings all the sequences in the accounts together into a logical prophetic drama. This is not an accusation against the Church for not physically keeping these Feasts, but rather in not at least understanding the truths portrayed by the Feasts, and rehearsing these truths frequently, so as to be prepared in understanding for the events themselves when they are fulfilled. The ongoing dispute is not necessary when we take the whole Discourse into consideration, placing Jesus' words into their original Judaic Scriptural and ethnic setting. The Church is not to become 'Jewish,' but must understand, because we are participants in the actual appointed fulfillment sequence.

Both Jesus and Paul liken the Rapture to that of a Thief coming to break up the house. In Matthew 24:43 Jesus states: *"But know this, that if the goodman of the house had known in what watch the thief would come, he would not have suffered his house to be broken up. Therefore be ye ready; for in such an hour as ye think not the Son of man cometh."* This Discourse to the disciples regarding the end times, <u>was primarily given in relation to the Jews</u>. <u>They</u> will not be expecting the LORD to catch away the righteous (Tzadikim) at this time, so *"in such an hour as ye think not, the Son of man Cometh."* This indictment is against the Jews and unbelievers in particular, not the born-again Christians who are righteous in Christ, and thus will be taken. The Christian will be watching, the Jew won't. In fact, Paul states in I Thessalonians 5:1-4 in regard to the Christian, *"But of the times and seasons, brethren, I have no need that I write unto you. For yourselves know perfectly that the day of the Lord so cometh as a thief in the night. For when they shall say <u>peace and safety</u>; then sudden destruction <u>cometh upon them</u>, as travail upon a woman with child; and <u>they</u> shall not escape.* **But ye brethren are not in darkness, that that day should overtake you as a thief."** And in verse 9, *"For God hath not <u>appointed</u> us to wrath, but to obtain salvation (deliverance) by our Lord Jesus Christ."* Emphases mine. Who are *"they"* who won't escape? The Jews and the unbelievers, and those who are not in love with Christ. The Jews though, have little excuse, because they do have access to the truth if they will just honestly look at it.

Also notice the mo'ed (appointment) mentioned by Paul. He tells us what we are not appointed to! The Appointment of Wrath, because the darkness that is to fall upon the whole world is for those who remain and find the Lord came as a Thief, taking His Bride when they were not watching. Sudden destruction ensues upon those left behind. Rather, our appointment is deliverance! Rosh HaShanah!

Who does the destruction come upon? Those who are busy attempting to bring about, and perhaps in a measure achieve, *"peace and safety."* Now isn't that the whole reason why everyone, including Israel, is working on implementing a peace plan that includes the formation of a Palestinian State? Somehow everyone is under the false impression that peace in The Middle East will be achieved if the Palestinians have their own state with internationally recognized borders. However, this will be peace under false pretenses, because in actual fact the Palestinians, along with most of the Arab World, do not even want Israel to exist. This *"peace and safety"* will only be used by them to re-group to bring about their real objective, which is to 'push Israel into the sea.' This *"peace and safety"* is the cornerstone of 'The Road Map' now under negotiation by 'The Quartet,' which includes the USA, Russia, the EU, and the United Nations. When the world finally heaves a sigh of relief that 'peace and safety' has been achieved in The Middle East, then sudden destruction will ensue. Therefore the cries we are now hearing regarding Peace in The Middle East through 'The Road Map' plan, may indeed be a sign to the Church that the Rapture is shortly to take place!

A. Which Trumpet Blast?

However, when we read the accounts of The Olivet Discourse, we must be careful to discern which trumpet blast is being sounded in order to understand what part of the Divine Appointment sequence is being explained. We must keep the trumpets and their significance in mind. Rosh HaShanah, which takes place <u>at the beginning of</u> The Ten Days of Awe, is a depiction of the Rapture, and sounds Ha Teruah Shofar, The Last Trump, as an awakening blast calling the righteous to The Coronation -Wedding ceremonies of the KING in Heaven. Yom Kippur sounds Tekiah HaGadol, The Great Shofar, the announcement of the final tally of the Righteous called to their eternal destiny, and the inauguration of the rule and reign of The KING of Kings on earth. <u>The Ten Days of Awe lie between these two distinct trumpet blasts of judgment and in-gathering of Rosh HaShanah and Yom Kippur</u>.

Both Matthew and Mark, who capitalize on Yom Kippur, give further clues to the timing of the second appearance of The Son of Man in The Clouds of Glory, because the sound of a trumpet accompanies this incident, and an ingathering of The Elect from the four corners of the earth, and from the far-reaches of the heavens takes place. See Matthew 24:31, *"And he shall send his angels with a **great** sound of a **trumpet**, and they shall gather together his elect from the four winds, from one end of heaven to the other."* and Mark 13: 27. *"And then shall he send his angels, and <u>shall gather together his elect from the four winds, from the uttermost part of the earth to the uttermost part of heaven</u>."* Emphases mine. This makes logical sense when we remember that Yom

Kippur, at the end of The Days of Awe, sounds a significant trumpet of the final sealing of the righteous, called Tekiah HaGadol, The Great Shofar.

But the admonition given in Luke's account of Jesus' Discourse is clarified in verse 36 of chapter 21, so is directed to those who have the possibility *"to escape those things that are about to come on the earth."* In other words, to escape having to live through the Yamim Nora'Im during which time the Wrath of God is to be poured out on the nations of the earth, particularly during the final seven years. Many people will be preoccupied with daily personal issues, suggesting that life generally up to the Rapture carries on with some semblance of uneasy normalcy as far as human endeavors and day to day activities, and even war and distress of nations is concerned. A great many will miss the signs because they are caught up with *"surfeiting, drunkeness, and cares of this life,"* so that the day when Christ appears at the Rapture will occur when they are not aware. Thus we have Jesus coming as a Thief in the night. The Thief is not to those who know He is coming for them, but to those left behind. But everyone will be totally aware of The Second Coming of Christ!

B. The End of The Times of The Gentiles:

Jesus mentions the [52]culmination of The Times of The Gentiles. There is a great deal of debate about when The Times of The Gentiles will be fulfilled, which some place in 1948, some in 1967, and many place at the time of the Rapture, and some at the end of the Tribulation. Actually, there is evidence to indicate that the <u>wrap up of The Times of The Gentiles is more of a process involving a series of events</u>, <u>rather than one single event</u>. Of course, when the focus of prophetic attention shifts entirely onto Israel following the Rapture of the Church, we <u>could</u> say The Times of The Gentile will be ceased at that juncture.

However, this prophecy is not specifically contingent upon the departure of the Church, but rather on <u>who controls Jerusalem</u>. *"Jerusalem shall be trodden down of the Gentiles, until the times of the Gentiles be fulfilled."* Luke 21:24. This criteria partially was fulfilled as a result of The Six Day War of 1967, and it will partially be fulfilled as a result of The Battle of Gog and Magog, and will completely be fulfilled at The Second Coming of Christ. <u>In order for The Times of The Gentiles to cease</u>, <u>Jerusalem must be totally in the hands of the Israelis</u>. So the sign to watch for is **who controls**

---

[52] Luke 21:24. "And they shall fall by the edge of the sword, and shall be led away captive into all nations: and Jerusalem shall be trodden down of the Gentiles, until the times of the Gentiles be fulfilled."

THE OLIVET DISCOURSE

Jerusalem, not just most of the city, but ALL of Jerusalem; including the modern city, The Old City, and The Temple Mount. This jurisdiction of the Jews over all of Jerusalem has already taken place once in 1967. Briefly. Did this end The Times of The Gentiles? Well, for about 12 hours. Then Israel gave up her absolute sovereign right to The Temple Mount. However the prophetic spiral continues, so who controls Jerusalem in total will come around again -- not just once, but twice.

In Romans 11:25-27 Paul states in regard to Israel, *"For I would not, brethren, that ye should be ignorant of this mystery, lest ye should be wise in your own conceits; that blindness in part is happened to Israel, until the fulness of the Gentiles be come in.* Verse 26. *And so all Israel shall be saved: as it is written, There shall come out of Zion the Deliverer, and shall turn away ungodliness from Jacob:* Verse 27. *for this is my covenant unto them, when I shall take away their sins."* Underlining Mine. Where and when is this complete deliverance to take place? When The Age of Gentile domination over Jerusalem is complete. And when will that be? When the blindness is removed from Israel's understanding, and ungodliness is removed from Jacob. This will occur when the Deliverer, The Messiah, comes out of Zion. When does He come out of Zion? At His Second Coming when He returns to end The Battle of Armageddon, and to take up His rule and reign from Mount Zion. Notice Paul does not say that the presence of The Temple is specifically necessary, only that Mount Zion is the place from which the Deliverer comes, and that requires one necessary development. His Second Coming will return Mount Zion and Jerusalem to full Israeli possession!

Israel's possession of Mount Zion is indeed a process. The Israeli's had the entire Mount in their hands in June of 1967, but gave up total jurisdictional control. They will regain this control, and will be able to build a Temple on Mount Zion following The Battle of Gog and Magog. Then they will again lose jurisdiction of Jerusalem, The Temple, and The Temple Mount, to the AntiChrist and his regime mid-70th Week, when AntiChrist desecrates that facility. Ultimately, Mount Zion will permanently be restored to Israel when Messiah comes. Then all blindness will be removed, because the Deliverer *"shall turn away ungodliness from Jacob."* At that time The Covenant will be complete when He takes away their sins. But how will all this come about?

Before we are able to answer this question, we must remind ourselves of a couple of exegetical details which allow us to grasp the ramifications of what Jesus was teaching.

C. Scripture Cannot be Altered, Added to, or Replaced.

Christianity did not exist as a separate religious entity from Biblical Judaism during the life and ministry of Jesus Christ. Now don't be too startled, but I would like to point out an amazing fact. Jesus Christ was not a 'Christian!' Jesus was a Jew <u>by Divine Appointment</u> at His birth. He was born, ministered, died, and arose as a Jew, fulfilling The Spring Feasts and Festivals. He still must fulfill The Fall Feasts and Festivals. He practiced Judaism, but threw out the traditions of men, setting Himself apart from all the Scribes, Pharisees, Sadducees and other Rabbis. He was considered a great Rabbi. His Judaism was pure because it was based on His Own Word, The Scriptures. He came as The Emanuel, God in the flesh, to absolutely fulfill The Law and The Prophets, not to eradicate them. He stated in Matthew 5:17-20, "*Think not that I am come to destroy the law, or the prophets. <u>I am not come to destroy, but to fulfill</u>. For verily I say unto you, till heaven and earth pass, one jot or one tittle shall in no wise pass from the law, till all be fulfilled.*" Have heaven and earth passed away? No! Has all been fulfilled? Not yet. So The Law and Prophets still stand, **but only as fulfilled, and to be fulfilled, in and through Christ**! We often lose sight of these facts.

Christianity is not a separate religion per se' from Judaism, <u>but a seamless continuuium of the fulfillment of The Law and Prophets,</u> <u>the root being true Scriptural Judaism</u> brought to completion <u>in and through Jesus Christ</u>. The first Christians were predominantly Jews, and continued to practice almost all aspects of Judaism, including keeping the Feasts and Festivals. When one honestly thinks about it, there was no other orientation upon which to build, and no other Scriptural foundation would have sufficed. The Early Church obviously did not continue with the sacrificial system, because they rightly realized Christ fulfilled all the sacrificial requirements regarding sin and iniquity. But they did keep the Celebrations. This basis and orientation was originally introduced to Gentile believers who were brought out of paganism.

Massive persecution of <u>both</u> the believers in Christ <u>and</u> traditional Jews began under Titus with Jerusalem being sacked, and The Temple destroyed in 68 to 70 C.E. This persecution continued unabated until Constantine, and beyond under successive repressive regimes. However, these persecutions became a great tool in spreading the Gospel, <u>because they forced first Jewish believers,</u> <u>then Gentile believers to disperse</u>, and they took the Gospel with them. Now the Gospel has reached around the world.

Certainly the traditional religious Jews developed animosities quickly toward 'Christian' Jews, but as far as the world around them was concerned, these 'Christians' were simply a renegade sect of Judaism. Some of the animosities were in fact due to misinterpreted inclusion of Gentile believers in Early Church Judaic practices. The connection was not entirely severed until the time of Constantine when the Church was basically segregated, and paganized with Gentile orientation; and <u>Judaic practices, both for Christians as well as for traditional Judaic Jews, were banned</u> throughout the entire Roman Empire.

[53]However, long before Constantine, Paul and subsequently Peter, James, and The Council in Jerusalem, recognized the difficulty regarding what Gentile believers were to adhere to in relation to traditional Judaic religious practices as related to The Law. They realized the belief structure in regard to the doctrines of The Scriptures must remain intact for Gentile believers. They concluded that Gentile believers did not have to keep <u>the letter of The Law</u>, but the <u>Spirit of The Law</u> as fulfilled in and through Christ. <u>Actually, they came to the conclusion that this stance was the necessity even for Jewish believers.</u> <u>The works of The Law do not save, but justification is by faith in Jesus Christ and His finished work of sacrificial atonement</u>. The Early Church understood this, and we understand this.

The difficulty is that the Church generally has set aside <u>our understanding of the doctrinal and prophetic interpretations</u> of certain Scriptures, both Old and New. Christians have shunned much of what we consider to be <u>cultural Judaic Law,</u> thus divorcing ourselves from much that sheds light on prophecy and doctrine. The greatest example is our general lack of understanding in regard to The Feasts and Festivals which were given by God to reveal Himself to all nations through Israel. Our stance is indeed unfortunate. We must remember these celebrations were given by God, to be Holy Convocations. Leviticus 23:2 *"Speak unto the children of Israel, and say unto them, Concerning the feasts of the LORD, which ye shall proclaim to be holy convocations, even these are my feasts."* <u>They were not simply Judaic cultural traditions.</u> <u>They have particular prophetic doctrinal meaning for us as Christians</u>, and even for the nations in general.

---

[53] Evangelical Dictionary of Theology, Walter A. Elwell, Editor, Baker Book House, Grand Rapids, Michigan, 1987. P. 590. "Paul opposed Peter at Antioch because Peter refused to eat with Gentile Christians. Peter at first felt Gentile Christians had to conform to Jewish dietary laws, or he could not fellowship with them." Paul, on the other hand, felt making Gentile believers conform to the law was adding works to salvation, and making grace of none effect. Galations 2:14-2, and 3:1-29.

Although we must be careful not to get caught up in the legality of literally physically keeping these Convocations, we ought to maintain a doctrinal understanding <u>as fulfilled in Christ</u>.

For example, studying The Tabernacle and its furnishings gives us a clear picture of the work and ministry of Christ and redemption, and most of us find this both illuminating and fascinating. But we have shied away from looking at The Feasts and Festivals because we are afraid of Judaizing the Church. We cannot Judaize by examining the doctrinal implications of these Feasts, any more than understanding the significance of the furnishings of The Tabernacle Judaizes the Church! The Feasts and Festivals are part of Scripture. Let's not close The Book on them! Why am I particularly zeroing in on the Feasts and Festivals? Because <u>The Feasts and Festivals reveal a complete prophetic sequence of The Revelation of The Lamb of God, Messiah</u>! Now <u>that</u> implication is something we all need to pay attention to in <u>understanding the unfolding of prophecy</u>.

Jesus' Discourses and explanations to His disciples were always given in the light of the fulfillment and understanding of the Scriptures of The Old Testament, and in accordance with the revealed truths that the Jews would have placed on their true culture and celebrations of The Feasts, <u>which were ordained by God Himself</u> through The Mosaic Law. Jesus, as a conscientious practicing Jew, would not step outside the boundaries of these already revealed truths when delivering His Discourses, because that would be akin to denying truth already revealed, so would be considered idolatrous and heretical. And to <u>add to the revelations of The Old Testament</u> beyond the context of already revealed Scripture given to the Jews would be akin to blasphemy, and to denying Himself. As God in the flesh, The Emanuel, The Incarnate Word, The Lamb of God, He could not, and of course would not digress. <u>Jesus came to fulfill all The Law and The Prophets, not to replace them with a new set of truths.</u> God's truth is <u>eternal, so cannot be replaced</u>.

Therefore, the entire Olivet Discourse given by Jesus to His disciples on The Mount of Olives will indeed unfold, and this fulfillment will be in accordance with what The Old Testament prophets prophesied. All will be fulfilled according to the prophetic time-table of The Feasts and Festivals which are God's Divine Appointments with mankind.

With this in mind, we are now able to begin to decipher the prophecies regarding The Church, and how The Covenant will be brought to completion for Israel.

CHAPTER 8
THE KEYS (CLUES)

I. Jesus Sends us on a Treasure Hunt:

Jesus points us to a key which serves to unlock his Olivet Discourse. He gets us started with this key, and in following His admonition to understand, we find there are further keys. In essence, He sends us on a treasure hunt which has the keys (clues) deposited along the way. These keys are interconnected with information given to Daniel regarding the end times, and from there we unlock a journey through the prophetic Scriptures.

When we look for signs, we must be careful to examine who the signs are directed toward in the passage. Daniel is obviously writing to the Jews, and in particular to the Israeli Nation in the end times. He is the prophet writing down what God has told him through Gabriel, the archangel heralding Messianic fulfillment, and also through dreams and visions. Daniel totally overwhelmed by the vision he received, and by what Gabriel told him. Daniel 8:26 -27. *"And the vision of the evening and the morning which was told is true: wherefore shut thou up the vision; for it shall be for many days. Verse 27. And I Daniel fainted, and was sick certain days; afterward I rose up, and did the king's business; and I was astonished at the vision, but none understood it."*

[54]Part of the prophecy indicates he will not be able to totally understand, because it is for those living at the time of the end to comprehend, so the meaning is sealed up until then. We are living in the time of the end, and Daniel is now beginning to make an awful lot of sense! The seal of the prophecy given to Daniel is now being removed, especially for the Christian, and very soon for the Israeli. Paul states, *"Blindness in part is happened to Israel until the fullness of the Gentiles be come in. And so all Israel shall be saved: as it is written, There shall come out of Zion the Deliverer, and shall turn away ungodliness from Jacob: for this is my covenant unto them, when I shall take away their sins."* Romans 11: 26-27. When The Gentile Age is officially over, Israel will finally understand and accept Christ. But this appears to be a process as well. Meanwhile, the Church is not to be ignorant! We are not to suffer from partial blindness.

Is the Church, then, able to understand Daniel? Yes! At least we will understand enough to realize approximately when the Rapture could

---

[54] Daniel 12:9.

take place. But the prophecy of Daniel is given in relation to the Jews. So who is to receive this revelation? In sequence, first of all the Church, but ultimately the Israelis who honestly have their spiritual and religious eyes opened to recognize the truth. So what are the signs that will begin to open their understanding and recognition, and at the same time give the Church clues as to where we are prophetically?

A. The Lifting of Israel's Blindness:

Paul states, "*Blindness <u>in part</u> has happened to Israel...*" That is important. Israel has always had access to the truth, but the majority of Jews seem to be somewhat blind as to its meaning, application, and significance. However, there have always been some who actually 'get it' as well. This blindness has never been totally complete, <u>but partial</u>. There will be some of Israel who are part of The Church-Bride because they have recognized Jesus as Messiah and Redeemer. These Christian Jews especially are a thorn in the side of most of world Jewry. The Messianic Jewish movement has picked up significantly since Israel became a Nation in 1948, and especially since the 1967 Six Day War when Jerusalem was briefly fully back in Israeli hands. There has been a revival of traditional Judaism at the same time. Many Jews are re-examining The Torah (The Book of Moses, also called The Pentateuch) and Tanach (the entire Old Testament), and some are even reading The New Testament as well. Their partial blindness is gradually lifting, because The Age of The Gentiles is now gradually ending.

The Rapture of the Church at, during, or near The Battle of Gog and Magog will be the next event to further clarification of the truth, and many of The Messianic Jews will be Raptured. This will wake-up many traditional Jews who are left behind, because they do believe in a sudden 'departure, or gathering' unto the LORD to take place in the end times in fulfillment of Rosh HaShanah.

Coinciding closely with the Rapture, the accompanying Gog -Magog Battle will be the theater of further phasing-out of The Age of The Gentiles, because Jerusalem and Judah will be placed totally into Israeli hands again as a result, although this will only be for a brief time. The Lord will seal 144,000 Jews as world Evangelists following this Battle and the Rapture. <u>It is obvious, these Jewish preachers must fully recognize the truth, or they will not qualify to be evangelists!</u> Blindness for them will be totally lifted! Untold millions will respond to their message, but neither they nor their converts will be part of the Church, but rather will be the Saints of The Days of Awe. Even the martyrdom of their converts will serve to help lift the blindness for the rest of Israel.

THE KEYS (CLUES)

The mid-70th Week (mid-Trib) Abomination of Desolation will further clarify to many Jews who Messiah really is, because obviously the impostor who desecrates their Temple cannot be Him. At this point, Daniel's prophecies will become pretty clear to the majority of Jews worldwide, because they will delve into the Scriptures in earnest to understand, realizing that much of what the Christians have said really is happening. They will cry out to the LORD, and plead with Him to come and deliver them as The Battle of Armageddon heats up. Very little blindness now! When Christ returns to Jerusalem at Yom Kippur, they will have 20/20 vision! And The Age of The Gentiles will be over.

Actually, the Rapture of the Church will probably be the chief sign to the Jews that prophetically indicates Rosh HaShanah now has been fulfilled. It would appear that the Rapture of the Church occurs approximately three years before the end of the 69th Week of Daniel, fulfilling the revealing of the identity of Messiah the Prince during the 69th Week of years. Jesus was revealed and hailed King at His Triumphal Entry into Jerusalem at 69 Weeks of years. He will again be revealed, but this time, not on the earth, but as He comes for His Bride and takes her to His Coronation at the sounding of The Last Trump, which also is a Coronation Trumpet, fulfilling the prophecies regarding the Coronation and Wedding of the KING in Heaven. Although those on the earth will not physically see Him at this time, the departure of the Bride will be a strong indication of the truth regarding Jesus Christ as Bridegroom and Messiah.

We must remember, Jesus fulfilled The Spring Feasts to the letter during His first coming. His birth, life, ministry, death, resurrection, and ascension are all pictured by The Spring Feasts. He will fulfill The Fall Feasts to the letter also during the count-down to taking His full position as KING of Kings, and the set-up of His rule and reign on earth from Jerusalem.

The prophetic sequence fits with the order and final curl of the prophetic spiral of The Fall Jewish Feasts, and allows three years time for the wrap-up of The Battle of Gog and Magog, the securing of Jerusalem and Judah by Israel, the building of The Third Temple with re-instituted Temple Worship expedited by The Raiser of Taxes, then the rise to prominence of the deceptive world-leader as the actual seven year Tribulation Week begins. Many Jews, following the Rapture and The Battle of Gog and Magog, will begin to realize that The Days of Awe have begun, and that Daniel's 70th Week of discipline for the Jews is soon to begin. The removal of the blindness for Israel will accelerate specifically during these days of spiritual self-evaluation, a practice in type that always takes place for the

Jews between Rosh Hashana and Yom Kippur, only this time, it will not be in type, but in the fulfillment of the Divine Appointments.

In regard to The Church, Paul states in 1 Corinthians 15:52, *"Behold I show you a mystery, we shall not all sleep. but we shall all be changed, in a moment, in the twinkling of an eye, at **the last trump**: for the trumpet shall sound, and the dead shall be raised incorruptible, and we shall be changed."* Bold mine.

Rosh HaShanah is also known as Yom HaDin, The Day of Judgment. An evaluation of mankind happens at this time, and judgment is brought down. Those who are totally righteous take part in a special gathering unto the LORD. This is pictured in the honoring of a significant New Moon Festival, Rosh HaChodesh (Head of the Month) that only occurs during Rosh HaShanah. This special Rosh HaChodesh is Yom HaKeseh, The Day of Concealment. This is exciting, because again we see a picture of the Rapture of the Church, the totally righteous Tzadikim! Psalm 81:3 states, *"Blow the <u>trumpet at the moon</u>, <u>at the time of the concealed moon</u>."* Also notice Psalm 27:5, *"For <u>in the time of trouble</u> (Jacob's Trouble) <u>He shall hide me in His pavilion</u>: <u>In the secret of His tabernacle (chupah) shall He hide me</u>: He shall set me upon a rock."* Underling mine. Since another name for the ten days from Rosh HaShanah to Yom Kippur is 'Jacob's Trouble,' this would mean the Church is hidden in the Heavenly secret Tabernacle for the ten years of 'Jacob's Trouble,' not just seven as we usually have believed. We will experience in The Father's House in Heaven, the equivalent of ten earthly years, participating in The Beama Judgment Seat of Christ, and The Marriage Supper of The Lamb, before returning to earth to rule and reign with Christ!

II. The Abomination Of Desolation is the Key Given by Jesus:

Jesus points us to The Book of Daniel, and specifically to The Abomination of Desolation, and tells us that we are to understand. In seeking to understand this specific event, we are strongly encouraged to examine the entire prophecy given to Daniel, and realize that Daniel's 70 Weeks of prophetic years determined upon *"thy people and thy holy city"* has much to offer in arriving at the important understanding Jesus obviously wants both Christians and Jews to acquire regarding these prophecies. Also, in examining Daniel, we quickly realize we must search throughout all of Scripture to arrive at a complete picture of the layers of the Prophetic Spiral. As we study further, it becomes obvious there are righteous individuals who do not remain on the earth to witness this sign when it actually takes place, and there are some folk who are affected directly by it. The Church is to understand this sign to pass along the truth to those who will need to face it. That will be the Jews and the Tribulation Saints who will actually witness the Abomination of Desolation six and one half years into The Days of Awe (mid-Trib.)

Following the Rapture of the Church, the period known as Jacob's Trouble, Yamim Nora'Im, The Days of Awe, also referred to as The High Holy Days, will take place. During this time there will be <u>further signs</u> given to the Jews which will serve to wake them up. The Rapture of the Church catches the attention of some of the Jews. The next major incident that should trigger their understanding is pointed out by Jesus, and refers to the Abomination spoken about in The Book of Daniel Chapter 11, verses 31-33. Gabriel explains that there are some Jews who will <u>begin to understand</u> following the fulfillment of this prophecy. *"And arms shall stand on his part, and they shall pollute the sanctuary of strength, and shall take away the daily sacrifice, and they shall place <u>the abomination that maketh desolate</u>. And such as do wickedly against the covenant shall he corrupt by flatteries: <u>but the people that do know their God shall be strong and do exploits.</u> And **they that understand among the people shall instruct many...**"* Emphases mine. This Scripture seems to indicate that when the AntiChrist finally is revealed for his true colors of flatteries and deception when the desecration of The Temple takes place, there will be some who recognize and accept who Messiah really is, and will become believers and true worshipers of God. They will have a strong faith, and do amazing exploits, teaching the truth to many others. So the recognition of the truth of Messiah will take place in stages. The Abomination of Desolation is one of the major keys that will unlock truth to Israel.

III. The Keys (clues) given by Gabriel:

Daniel is given a further set of keys to help us. Gabriel's explanation of these prophetic keys to understanding was very thorough and detailed, but left Daniel himself totally boggled. Gabriel makes a couple of statements that for Daniel must have frustrated him no end, but for us who live near the culmination of The Church Age, should give us goose bumps. Gabriel states, *"And the vision of the evening and the morning which was told is true; wherefore shut thou up the vision; <u>for it shall be for many days</u>."* Daniel 8:26. Also, Daniel 12: 8-10, *"And I heard, but I understood not: then said I, O my Lord, what shall be the end of these things? And he said, Go thy way, Daniel: <u>for the words are closed up and sealed till the time of the end. Many shall be purified, and made white, and tried</u>; but the wicked shall do wickedly: and none of the wicked shall understand; <u>but the wise shall understand</u>."* Underlining mine. These words read much like Jesus' explanation to His disciples! It is obvious that Jesus was stating in His Olivet Discourse that the time had now come to pay attention, because these prophecies given to Daniel, right down to

The Final Schedule Revealed

the ordered details, would begin their fulfillment throughout The Church Age, kicking into high gear particularly toward the end of this period, and in The Ten Days of Awe that would follow. Gabriel told Daniel that <u>those living at the time of the end of the coming Age (The Church Age) would actually be able to understand the prophecies</u>. Jesus also indicated the closer together and more intense these prophetic signs are in fulfillment, so the alert student of Bible prophecy will be able to discern what to Daniel was obviously a completely troubling mystery.

CHAPTER 9
SEVENTY WEEKS DETERMINED

If we look at Daniel 9: 24-27, we read, "*Seventy weeks are determined upon thy people and upon thy holy city, to finish the transgression, and to make an end of sins, and to make reconciliation for iniquity, and to bring in everlasting righteousness, and so seal up the vision and prophecy, and to anoint the most holy. Verse 25. Know therefore and understand, that from the going forth of the commandment to restore and to build Jerusalem unto the Messiah, the Prince, shall be <u>seven weeks, and threescore and two weeks</u>; **the street shall be built again, and the wall, even in troublous times**. Verse 26. And after <u>threescore and two weeks</u>, shall Messiah be cut off, but not for himself: and the people of the prince that shall come shall destroy the city and the sanctuary: and the end thereof shall be with a flood, and unto the end of the war desolations are determined. Verse 27. And he shall <u>confirm the covenant</u> **with many for one week**: and in the midst of the week he shall cause the sacrifices and the oblation to cease, and for the over-spreading of abominations he shall make it desolate, even until the consummation, and that determined shall be poured upon the desolate.*" KJV. Emphases mine.

In this passage we find that Daniel speaks of breaking down the 70 Weeks of years for the discipline of Judah (and ultimately for all Israel) and Jerusalem into segments of significance. The total 70 Weeks of years accomplishes several prophetic goals in regard to Redemption, the Jewish People, and the Holy City of Jerusalem::

    1. To finish the transgression.
    2. To make an end of sins.
    3. To make reconciliation for iniquity.
    4. To bring in everlasting righteousness.
    5. To seal up the vision and prophecy.
    6. To anoint the Most Holy.

According to the above, it will take the full 70 Weeks of years to accomplish all these goals. However this schedule of 70 Weeks of years has an agenda that takes some interesting twists, and hides some amazing surprises.

The full 70 Weeks of years determined equals 490 years. Gabriel tells Daniel there will be 69 Weeks of years from <u>the decree to allow the rebuilding of Jerusalem</u> until Messiah the Prince is revealed. That's 7 x 69 = 483 years. We know that Jesus entered Jerusalem through the Eastern Golden Gate on what we refer to as Palm Sunday exactly 483 years to the day after the decree was issued by Artaxerxes to allow the Jews to begin rebuilding the walls of Jerusalem. As Jesus proceeded through The Golden Gate riding upon the colt of a donkey, the common people shouted, *"Hosanna: Blessed is the King of Israel that cometh in the name of the Lord."* John 12:13.

"Hosanna" means "Save us," or "Deliver us." They honestly figured Jesus, who they correctly identified and hailed as King of Israel, would now save them from the oppression of the Romans, and set up The Kingdom of Israel. However, only a few days later, their religious and political leaders who were gathered in Pilot's Judgment Hall for Jesus' trial, were shouting, *"Crucify Him, crucify him."* Luke 23:21. So the fulfillment of these 69 Weeks was not total at that time. Although the common people hailed Him as King, the Jewish establishment, along with the Gentile Roman rulers, missed the truth of Who He really was, and is -- the Messiah. The Jews still must officially come to that realization. When they finally hail Him as their KING and true Messiah, He will not come riding on a lowly donkey of servitude, but on the white horse of the ultimate Victor and Royal Sovereign, riding through The Golden Gate to arise to His rightful Throne in His Temple on Mount Zion.

When we examine the further breakdown of Weeks given to Daniel, we quickly realize that the initial 69 Weeks until Messiah, The Prince, is a bit of a riddle, because Daniel is told by Gabriel that after the 62nd Week *"Messiah shall be cut-off,"* or in other words, be put to death, *"but not for Himself."* But we must note that in the sequence of events, Christ was crucified following His Triumphal Entry into Jerusalem. Logic tells us that since Messiah was revealed at exactly 69 Weeks at His Triumphal Entry, the crucifixion took place sequentially, then, at the beginning of the 70th Week just a few days later, not at the 62nd Week as Gabriel indicates. How can it be possible that He is *"cut-off"* at 62 Weeks, when His crucifixion really did take place a few days after His Triumphal Entry? Our sequentially thinking Westernized brains have a hard time wrapping around this one!

The answer lies in the little regarded rule we must keep in mind when we interpret Bible prophecy. We must not think only in terms of sequential, linear time and events, but according to the prophetic spiral. As already mentioned, the spiral allows for more than one fulfillment of a prophecy, accommodating what is termed The Law of Multiple Fulfillment. Many prophecies in Scripture regarding the descendants of Abraham, Isaac, and Jacob, have two to three fulfillments, but capitalize on varying circumstantial elements prophesied that are more completely fulfilled, or more literally fulfilled than the preceding or following fulfillment. Certainly some prophecies were only fulfilled once, but generally we are

SEVENTY WEEKS DETERMINED

able to look back at history and observe the fact that the Israelis were 'sent around the mountain again' on most of them. This spiral allows for more than one viable approach to understanding the unfolding of The 70 Weeks as recorded in Daniel.

Gabriel handles the prophetic spiral well by stating in Daniel 9 verse 24, *"Seventy weeks are determined upon thy people, and upon thy holy city..."* Who are the people he refers to? Ultimately, all the descendants of Israel, except it is possible to break this identity down without losing the truth of the prophecy, and thus allow for more than one fulfillment, and therefore expedite understanding and clarification.

Before Gabriel arrived to speak to him, Daniel was praying regarding his realization that The Babylonian Captivity was nearly complete. [55]The 70 years of captivity for Judah were nearly over, if what he read written by Jeremiah was true. But we must note that Jeremiah dealt only with those of The Babylonian Captivity, the two tribes of the Kingdom of Judah, not all Israel. Jeremiah's prophecy therefore, did not include the Ten Northern tribes of The House of Israel.

We know from history that the completion of the 70 years of captivity for The House of Judah was literal, and that they were allowed, by the decree of Cyrus, to return to Judah, and to begin rebuilding their Temple. Later, Artaxerxes' decree empowered them to repair the walls of the city of Jerusalem. But those of Judah who returned under these two Imperial decrees did not regain their independent Kingdom status. Rather, they were granted a limited degree of internal [56]self-governance.

The answer Daniel received via Gabriel therefore, was somewhat surprising. Daniel was wondering about the soon completion of the Seventy Year Babylonian Captivity for Judah, and Gabriel comes to him explaining something about 70 Weeks of discipline which will take place in the future. To make matters more complex, this prophecy regarding 70 Weeks appears to have more than one layer to its fulfillment.

---

[55]   Daniel 9:2. "In the first year of his reign I Daniel understood by books the number of the years, whereof the word of the LORD came to Jeremiah the prophet, that he would accomplish seventy years in the desolations of Jerusalem."

[56]   Pictoral Encyclopedia of the Bible, Volume 5, Merrill C. Tenney, Gen Ed., 1976, Regency Reference Library, p. 641, VI. Zerubbabel's Temple. Under the Persian kings, Judah was organized in the satrapy of Trans-Eupharatia, Ezra 4: 11, and was in the jurisdiction of the governor of Samaria in the days of Darius. Then, because of oppression from Samaria, the Jews in Jerusalem were allowed to have their own appointed governor.

The Final Schedule Revealed

Does this further prophecy apply at all to The Ten Northern Tribes of Israel? Yes it does, but not in initial concurrent sequence. In order to understand the fulfillment for all Israel, there are significant components of Gabriel's prophecy to consider. The heavenly messenger speaking with Daniel indicates a sequence of prophecies regarding the 70 Weeks determined for "*thy people and for thy holy city*" that are to be fulfilled up to and including 69 Weeks. The 69 Weeks are further broken down into 62 Weeks, and then an apparent leap to what appears to be the events of the 70th Week takes place. Strange! In the unfolding of the spiral of this prophecy, according to the explanation given by Gabriel, there are specified variables that allow for the insertion of other prophecies to be fulfilled. Also, all the prophecies to do with Daniel's 70 Weeks revolve around Judah, Jerusalem, and the Messiah, the total significance of which is also not at first readily apparent.

Notice verse 25 of Daniel chapter 9,. "*Know therefore and understand, that from the going forth of the commandment to restore and to build Jerusalem unto Messiah the Prince shall be seven weeks, and threescore and two weeks: ...*" [57]The revealing of Messiah at His Triumphal Entry took place, as I have already mentioned, 483 years exactly to the day after Artaxerxes decree to rebuild Jerusalem. But there was no fulfillment of the 70th Week immediately following the revealing of Messiah, unless one views the week following The Triumphal Entry as a tribulation week for Christ Himself. He certainly went through the greatest tribulation anyone ever has, or ever will, in enduring His betrayal, framed-trial, and crucifixion. But these events only lasted for a few days, not a full prophetic year, and certainly not a full seven years.

Notice, Gabriel's prophecy does not mention specifically, <u>at first</u>, anything regarding the rebuilding of The Temple, <u>only the holy city is mentioned</u> initially. But we know it will be necessary for The Temple to be rebuilt at some point, because the final reference Gabriel makes to the 70th Week requires The Temple, with Temple practices to be in place, in order for the Abomination to take place. "*And he shall confirm the covenant with many for one week: and in the midst of the week he shall cause the sacrifice and the oblation to cease, **and for the overspreading of abominations he shall make it desolate**, even until the consummation, and that determined shall be poured upon the desolate.*" Daniel 9:27. Emphases mine. What is made desolate because of abominations? The Temple. For how long? From the Abomination of Desolation mid 70th Week, perpetrated by AntiChrist

---

[57] The Triumphal Entry, The Prophet Daniel Foretells Jesus' Death, www.ida.net/users/rdk/ces/Lesson20.

SEVENTY WEEKS DETERMINED

and his cohorts, until all prophecy regarding the 70 Weeks is brought to culmination. So the Abomination will last for three and one-half years, the last half of the seven year Tribulation. The consummation of this time-period, bringing the Abominations to an end, will be the return of Messiah. He will pour our His judgment upon those who are desolate of the truth.

[58]The Second Temple was dedicated in 515 B.C.E., so had been in place for approximately 548 years by the time Jesus' ministry was complete. At the time of Jesus' Triumphal Entry, [59]Herod's Temple project (the enlargement and renovation of The Second Temple Complex) was taking place. Jesus and his disciples toured this facility, and it was during this inspection that Jesus indicated The Temple would be destroyed, then erected in three days, referring to His resurrection. Following this tour, Jesus gave his end-times Olivet Discourse. So the Second Temple in fact was in place when Messiah was revealed at the 69th Week. But this Second Temple was not The Tribulation Temple, because it was totally destroyed (not just desecrated) by the Romans under Titus in 70 C.E. Therefore, deduction tells us there must be a Third Temple in place before the 70th Week can begin to be fulfilled.

But let's back up to verse 25 of Daniel chapter 9, *"the street shall be built again, and the wall, even in troublous times."* This set of details has not yet been fulfilled. Reconstruction of The Temple has nothing to do with this statement, just a wall and a street. In other words, some degree of Israeli jurisdiction over Jerusalem, possibly in conjunction with a controversy over Mount Zion itself, is necessary for this wall and this street to be rebuilt. The Jews had very specific opposition to their reconstruction of Jerusalem

---

[58] Pictoral Encyclopedia of the Bible, Volume 5, Merrill C. Tenney, Gen Ed., 1976, Regency Reference Library, p. 643, History of the Temple. 1. In the era of Ezra and Nehemiah. The Ssecond Temple was completed in 516 -515 B.C.E. in the first month, Adar, (civil Calendar) during the 6th year of the reign of Darius. Ezra 6:15.

[59] Pictoral Encyclopedia of the Bible, Volume 5, Merrill C. Tenney, Gen Ed., 1976, Regency Reference Library, p.645, VII. Herod's Temple. The reason the Temple was renovated, according to Josephus who heard Herod's speech, was to provide the Jews an eternal remembrance of his name. (No wonder it was destroyed by the Romans in 70 C.E.! The Temple is supposed to be a remembrance of the Name of the LORD, and to the praise of His glory!) . Work on this facility began in the eighteenth year of Herod,The Great's reign, 20-19 B.C.E., but Herod did not live to see his renovations completed. He died in 4 B.C.E. The Second Temple complex renovations were never actually completed, so were still on-going during Jesus' life-time and ministry.

The Final Schedule Revealed

following their initial 70 years of captivity. They built with a sword in one hand, and their tools in the other. They fought an active war of opposition while they worked. However, the rebuilding of the wall and street, being in the singular in this passage, does not seem to fit with their time, as they would have been reconstructing walls and streets, plural. I will touch on the prophetic significance of the singular wall and street in a moment.

So what about the unfolding of the 69th Week at the time of Christ when Jerusalem was under Roman rule? Was there any major opposition taking place at that time? Any restoration or reconstruction of The Temple Mount and the city of Jerusalem during Christ's lifetime and ministry would have been under Roman supervision, but this was not particularly a problem. Certainly, at the beginning of the Roman occupation the Jews endured some opposition, but it was not specifically in regard to their Holy City, or The Temple Mount, or even to any restoration work. [60]"The Romans brought the "Pax Romana" (Roman Peace) to the region, even though this peace was tenuous at best. None of the above scenarios seem to really fit in with the reconstruction of a wall and a street, both singular, during a time of trouble. Actually, <u>the fact that this reconstruction is to occur during **"troublous times"** may in fact be key here</u>.

The final fulfillment of Daniel's prophecy is most intriguing and very complex, and yet it is, and will be, absolutely complete. This fulfillment takes place in two distinct parts, in two widely separated time-periods. It is explained in terms of increments that obviously must add up to 70 Weeks of years.

Notice the wording of verses 26 and 27: "*<u>After threescore and two weeks shall Messiah be cut off</u>, but not for himself: and the people of the prince that shall come shall destroy the city and the sanctuary: and the end thereof shall be with a flood, and unto the end of the war desolations are determined. Verse 27. And he shall confirm the covenant with many for one week: and in the midst of the week he shall cause the sacrifice and the oblation to cease, and for the overspreading of abominations he shall make it desolate, even until the consummation, and that determined shall be poured upon the desolate.*" KJV. Underlining mine.

The first thing that strikes us is that Messiah is *"cut off"* at the 62nd Week, and that this did not occur until <u>after His Triumphal Entry</u> which indeed was fulfilled at 69 Weeks. Now there's a conundrum! Obviously there must be an explanation, because the fulfillment actually occurred in that order. I have never read or heard anyone explain the reasoning

---

[60] Encyclopedia: Pax Romana, www.nationmaster.com/encyclopedia/Pax-romana, Latin: Roman Peace, 29 B.C.E. to 180 B.C.E. Time of relative peace throughout the Roman Empire.

here, but I would like to put forward an hypothesis, and show where the weeks of apparent discrepancy are possibly picked up again. The overall prophecy is regarding 70, not 69 Weeks until all the objectives of verse 24 are reached. None of the objectives have been completed, (except the third one which is, *"to make reconciliation for iniquity,"* because Christ completed Redemption on the cross.) The final fulfillment will complete them all! Obviously there is a key, or keys, by which we must unlock the sequence.

To further illustrate our puzzle, keep in mind the realization that we do not seem to have any obvious point from which to begin counting forward to the 62nd Week when Messiah was *"cut off."* This apparent lack of a starting point frustrates our Western mind-set even further. Where is the starting-block? Obviously we cannot begin counting from Artaxerxes' decree from which the 69 Weeks to The Triumphal Entry was calculated, because Christ cannot be cut-off before he is even born! So there must be another explanation.

We can in fact, as already observed, state that Messiah was revealed, although fleetingly as far as the Jewish religious and political hierarchy were concerned, at the 69th Week, exactly 483 years after the decree went forth. So why does Gabriel refer to Messiah being cut-off at the 62nd Week instead of just simply pointing out He would be put to death a few days after He was hailed King at 69 Weeks? Since He was indeed revealed at the 69th Week when The Triumphal entry occurred, He was then chronologically crucified in the following Week, the 70th Week. Indeed, <u>Jesus Christ tasted of the wrath of God on behalf of all mankind</u>, <u>fulfilling the requirement for wrath upon the sin of rejecting God</u>, <u>something which the 70th Week will be dealing with for those not accepting salvation now</u>, because at the end of the 70th Week, on Yom Kippur, everyone's eternal destiny will be sealed. He tasted of the Wrath of God upon sin for each of us <u>so we do not have to face God's wrath</u> on the nations of the earth, or endure the ultimate eternal wrath of God. However, Gabriel specifically states Messiah would be cut off at the 62nd Week. So logically, the beginning of the 70th Week at the time of the crucifixion, according to the prophetic spiral, is the same as Gabriel's 62nd Week. Interesting!

In essence, Jesus Christ has 'redeemed the time,' inserting the forgiveness, grace, and mercy of the Cross, so that all can now come to repentance and appropriate the perfect Atonement for sin, and have our names written into The Book of Life <u>before</u> the Wrath of God is poured out in full. <u>Mankind was brought to the brink of wrath</u>, <u>**then Christ took this punishment upon Himself**</u>, **resetting the time-table** to give mankind the avenue and the time to repent. Therefore, according to Gabriel, we must begin counting toward a future 69th Week during which Messiah will be again revealed, followed by the final 70th Week of wrath. Now we are able to do some logical calculative reasoning with this crucial piece of information in mind.

However, we first of all must realize that the Revelation of Jesus Christ in His fullness, to be crowned KING of Israel, ascending His earthly Throne, has not yet taken place. Many Jews became disillusioned about His role and identity when He was turned over to Pilot and Herod to be tried. As far as they were concerned, their true Messiah was not a common criminal! Their King was to be The Deliverer! Although most of the common folk accepted Jesus, the religious leaders never did recognize Him as their Messiah, and their bias has been taught to generations of Jews since. So there must be a further set of circumstances that will decisively reveal to the Jews, and to the world, His Messiahship.

In order for this revelation to take place, certain other circumstances must be in place that were not part of the scene at Messiah's first coming. It would be necessary for a sovereign Nation of Israel, not under the thumb of a foreign empire, to exist. After all, a Crown Prince must have a legitimate Kingdom in order to be crowned King. This scenario would, in God's prophetic time-table, only come to pass near the end of The Church Age, when Israel would again be a full-fledged nation. Israel again became a sovereign nation in 1948. Also, in order for a King to be placed on a throne, there must be a physical location for that throne to exist. Messiah will rule and reign from The Fourth Temple, Ezekiel's prophesied Temple which will be built by Messiah. Therefore, Mount Zion must be completely placed into Israeli hands. This will indeed take place, but only after much controversy, and what appears to be certain and complete loss.

Notice that Judah and Jerusalem, where The Temple Mount is located, are pivotal here. Jerusalem and The Territories (including Judea, which was the former Kingdom of Judah, as well as Samaria of the former Northern Kingdom) were placed into Israeli hands during The 1967 Six Day War, <u>so this date is significant to our calculations</u>, because the fulfillment has to do with Judah, Jerusalem, and the revealing of Messiah. So, **"*thy people*" and the "*holy city*" must figure conspicuously in our deliberations.**

And there must be <u>troublous times</u>, coupled with a controversy regarding reconstruction of a specific wall, and a specific street -- a helpful reference to the fact that this whole scenario develops under duress, and that even the relinquishment of control of The Temple Mount into the hands of Muslims following The 1967 Six Day War, followed eventually by the Intifada that has been taking place since September of 2000, may actually be part of the groundwork for this prophecy to be fulfilled. In essence, the flash-back that Christ and the cross brought about in the prophetic spiral, allowed The Age of Grace to be inserted. So the necessary elements to fulfill these prophecies were able to be laid toward the end of this Grace Dispensation, after Israel became a nation.

We do not have need of a starting point of imperial decree, then, for counting 62 Weeks until Messiah was *"cut-off."* Rather, we are told by Gabriel that in God's prophetic schedule, the beginning of the 70th Week when Messiah was crucified, initially was to be considered the same as the 62nd Week. **That places the Cross of Christ as the anchor of the final fulfillment of the 70 Weeks**, so it becomes possible for Christ to be revealed again during the 69th Week, and ascend His earthly Throne at the end of the 70th Week. But this is not sequentially chronological with the original 69 Weeks. Instead of a decree to begin counting again, we are pointed to an equation, which tells us to subtract the Cross, the new prophetic constant of our equation, from when Messiah will again be completely revealed. **Thus, 69 Weeks minus 62 Weeks (the constant of The Cross) equals 7 Weeks**, is our equation. Then the 70th Tribulation Week of Wrath will follow. This equation gives the prophetic time-table the ability to insert The Church Age of Grace, without upsetting the prophetic time-clock. So since the Cross of the 62nd Week, we have waited again for the revealing of Messiah, The Prince.

But when can we begin counting these 49 years leading up to the final 70th Week? Now obviously, there have been more than 7 weeks of years since The Crucifixion. Could there be an event that allows us to resume the prophetic time-clock? The explanations in Daniel and the other prophets reveal some clues.

First of all, *"thy people"* and *"the holy city"* are key. Now *"thy people"* are no longer just the two tribes of The House of Judah who went into captivity under Babylon, or those Jews who were the citizens of The Land of Palestine at the time of the Romans. They must include The House of Israel (The Northern Tribes) who were taken into captivity by the Assyrians in order for all Israel to be saved. [61]And they must include descendants of all those who were exiled into Egypt at the time of Jeremiah, and those dispersed by the Roman persecutions in 70 C.E. and the years following. In other words, there must be the return of a remnant from among all who

---

[61] Jeremiah 43: 4-8. The migration of the remnant of Judah to escape from the Chaldean Invasion, so that they would not also be carried away into Babylon, was against the Word of the LORD given by Jeremiah. But they went ahead and fled into Egypt anyway. It is interesting to note that Jeremiah went with them, to dwell in Egypt.

The Final Schedule Revealed

have been scattered among the nations, The Diaspora. In fact, we are able to narrow the prophetic identity regarding this fulfillment.

Captivity and Dispersion are not the same thing. Although ultimately all Israel will be saved, Judah still plays a key role. The Diaspora actually is not applicable to The House of Israel, because they were not officially 'dispersed.' They were taken into captivity by the Assyrians, but were never decreed to return. They just simply, for the most part, remained scattered. The House of Israel never returned from captivity in large numbers. In fact, Isaiah refers to those of The House of Israel as being *"outcasts,"* not *"dispersed."* However, Judah officially was given permission to return by the decree of Cyrus, ending their prophesied 70 year captivity. Therefore, The Diaspora refers specifically to those of Judah who were dispersed after their official return. They were taken into captivity, decreed to return, and subsequently were scattered among the nations. Ultimately Messiah will *"recover the remnant of his people, which shall be left, from Assyria, and from Egypt, and from Pathros, and from Cush, and from Elam, and from Shinar, and from Hamath, and from the islands of the sea. Verse 12. And he shall set up an ensign for the nations, and shall assemble **the outcasts of Israel**, and gather together the **dispersed of Judah** from the four corners of the earth."* Isaiah 11: 11-12. Emphasis mine.

So our present day Israel is made up of remnants of the assembled outcasts of The House of Israel, and the gathered of the dispersed of Judah. Essentially, God's discipline of captivity for The House of Judah lasted for 70 years, fulfilling Jeremiah's prophecy. They returned by decree, then they were scattered. So Judah was not a sovereign nation for approximately 2,534 years. In 1948 they began to officially return from Diaspora. But the captivity and scattering of The House of Israel lasted for approximately 2,670 years -- a very long time indeed to be outcast from their homeland!

Now, all of either group do not have to be physically living in Israel again for the 69 Weeks to be complete, or even for the 70th Week to unfold. Just a remnant is necessary. In fact, it will be after the 70 Weeks are fulfilled completely that Messiah will gather all of them back to their homeland. However at least representatives of all the dispersed and outcasts must be living in Israel for the remaining 7 weeks of years plus the Tribulation 70th Week to take place.

Part of the key was fulfilled when Ben Gurion officiated at the rebirth of the Israeli nation. Officially, all Jews, with no differentiation between the descendants of the two former Kingdoms of Israel and Judah, were invited to come home during the inauguration ceremony of the modern State of Israel on May 14, 1948. This fulfilled the prophecy found in Ezekiel 37:12-22. *"Thus saith the Lord God; Behold, O my people, I will open your graves,*

SEVENTY WEEKS DETERMINED

and cause you to come up out of your graves, and bring you into the land of Israel. Verse 13. *And ye shall know that I am the LORD when I have opened your graves, O my people, and brought you up out of your graves.* Verse 14. *And I shall put my spirit in you, and ye shall live, and I shall place you in your own land: then shall ye know that I the LORD have spoken it, and performed it, saith the LORD.* Verse 15. *The word of the LORD came again unto me, saying,* Verse 16. *Moreover, thou son of man, take thee one stick, and write upon it, For Judah, and for the children of Israel his companions: then take another stick, and write upon it, For Joseph, the stick of Ephraim, and for all the house of Israel his companions;* Verse 17. *And join them one to another into one stick; and they shall become one in thine hand.* Verse 18. *And when the children of thy people shall speak unto thee, saying, Wilt thou not show us what thou meanest by these?* Verse 19. *Say unto them, Thus saith the Lord God; Behold, I will take the stick of Joseph, which is in the hand of Ephraim, <u>and the tribes of Israel</u> his fellows, and will put them with him, <u>even with the stick of Judah</u>, and make them one stick, and they shall be one in mine hand.* Verse 20. *And the sticks whereon thou writest shall be in thine hand before their eyes.* Verse 21. *And say unto them, Thus saith the Lord God; Behold, I will take the children of Israel from among the heathen, whither they be gone, and will gather them on every side, and bring them into their own land:* Verse 22. *<u>And I will make them one nation in the land upon the mountains of Israel; and one king shall be king to them all; and they shall be no more two nations, neither shall they be divided into two kingdoms any more at all</u>:"* KJV. Underlining mine.

Israel, which now includes both Houses, will never again totally cease to be a nation, although under AntiChrist they will <u>almost</u> be wiped out. However, this is only part of the key to finding where we start counting again.

The other part of the key has to do with the city of Jerusalem itself, The Holy City. The Israelis of necessity must have jurisdiction over Jerusalem, and this control of Jerusalem must be a point of contention while they set about to try to re-build a wall and a street. Up until the 1967 Six Day War when Israel regained total control of Jerusalem and The Temple Mount, Jerusalem was not specifically up for grabs. Actually Jerusalem before this time was divided into four jurisdictional parts, and this division continued even after Israel was reinstated as a nation in 1948. One part was under the protectoracy of Britain, one part under Russia, one under the USA, and one sector under the UN. And, the Arabs lay claim to much of Jerusalem, especially in what is generally referred to as the Arab Sector, including most of The Old City. Israel, although a nation, had no real control over Jerusalem itself. [62]The United Nations still does not officially recognize Jerusalem as Capitol of Israel. The Israelis moved the Knesset from Tel Aviv to Jerusalem in 1949. <u>As a result, the contention for the city of Jerusalem has intensified.</u> [63]The international community would still prefer it to be administered by the UN. [64]The Muslims want it in the hands of the Palestinians who have vowed to re-take Jerusalem for themselves, and their desire is backed by almost all of the Arab world.

[65]<u>The Temple Mount remains controversial</u>, because after Israel gained control of it as a result of The 1967 Six Day War, Moshe Dayan handed the jurisdiction <u>of the top surface</u> of The Mount to the Jordanians, who in turn gave it over to the Palestinians, because the Muslim Mosques are there.

---

[62] The Temple Mount Faithful Newsletter, *The Beginning of the End-Time Gog and Magog War Against Israel and Jerusalem.* ,www.templemountfaithful.org/Newsletters/2001/5761-2.htm. "The UN has repeatedly made anti-Israeli resolutions declaring that Jerusalem is not the capitol of Israel and does not belong to her, and that Judea, Samaria, and Gaza, and the Golan Heights, are not a part of the land of Israel."

[63] Jerusalem Center for Public Affairs, www.jcpa.org/art/knesset4.htm. The Constituent Assembly First Knesset 1949-1951, Prime Minister's Statement Concerning Jerusalem and the Holy Places, Sitting 96 – 5 December, 1949, Debate on the Prime minister's Statement. "J. Riftin (Mapam): Two dangers threaten Jerusalem today, that of being sundered from the State of Israel through the pretext of internationalization under the UN, and that of partition by granting a legal-political status to the Transjordanian army which inveded part of jerusalem. The State of Israel must fight both those dangers."

[64] The Temple Mount Faithful Newsletter, www.templemountfaithful.org/Newsletters/2001/5761-2.htm. *The Beginning of the End-Time Gog and Magog War Against Israel and Against Jerusalem,* "Arafat has stated this war will not stop until he comes to Jerusalem. The Arab countries have decided to stand behind Arafat in his war against Israel." "They intend to destroy and burn the State of Israel, and occupy Jerusalem."

[65] Ruth Matar's Women in Green Radio Program, September 18,2002, E-mail transcript. <www.wfit2@womeningreen.org> *TEMPLE MOUNT OUTRAGE,* "Motta Gur, IDF Division commander shouted, "The Temple Mount is in our hands!" And on the fourth day of the war, for twelve glorious hours, the Israeli flag waved proudly over the temple Mount as confirmation of the miracle just experienced by the Jewish people." "...But Defense minister Moshe Dayan ordered the Israeli flag taken down. He handed over the administration of the Temple Mount to the Arabs,...." "Extraordinary! In victory, we left our holiest place in the hands of our enemies. Moshe Dayan's motivation is thought to have been that to do otherwise would lead to unending strife with the entire, enormous Muslim world."

Hence the travesty of the Intifada which was sparked by Arial Sharon visiting The Mount in September of 2000. But Daniel's prophecy does not necessarily hinge on the Israelis having a Temple on The Temple Mount, but rather <u>having full jurisdiction over The Holy City, which includes Mount Zion</u>.

And, Gabriel's prophecy does indicate that along with issues over The Holy City, the restoration of the wall and the street is pivotal. Again I wish to point out the grammatical structure of the sentence here. It does not say "walls" and "streets" but, "*<u>the street</u> shall be built again, and <u>the wall</u>, even in <u>troublous times</u>.*" Daniel 9:25b. Could this singularity and troublesome timing be significant?

When we take a look at Jerusalem today, we realize that the majority of the city actually lies outside the original city walls. The original walled portion of Jerusalem is referred to as The Old City. Most of the walls of The Old City have been repeatedly destroyed and then repaired by various empires, organizations, and governments over the past 2,700 years as Jerusalem has been conquered and re-conquered. So there has always been an on-going necessity for a great deal of repair work regarding The Old City walls. Certainly there is some restorative work still to be accomplished regarding these walls, but they are not the controversy. The Old City portion, also referred to as the *"holy city,"* contains The Temple Mount where The Wailing Wall, The Kotel, is located. <u>This portion of the Western Wall is the only holy site of The Temple Mount area consistently accessible for Jews and Christians</u>. The Mount itself is opened, then closed, then opened at the whim of the Muslim Palestinian caretakers who control when, and how many Jews and Christians are allowed to visit. And they often use varying degrees of intimidation against all non-Muslims who desire to make pilgrimage to The Wailing Wall or The Temple Mount. It was from the top of The Wailing Wall that Palestinian gunmen of the Al Aqsa Martyr's Brigade fired on worshipers at the beginning of the Intifada, and started the current round of unrest, suicide bombings and other terrorist attacks on Israelis, out of which has come the international cry for the formation of a Palestinian State. Troublous times? Yes!

⁶⁶"The Muslims were given official jurisdiction over the surface of The Temple Mount where the Mosques are located, but they have exerted their authority far beyond their boundaries, and have taken liberties to do their own excavating; destroying centuries of archeological and geological history by trucking loads of 'debris' from under The Temple Mount to make way

---

⁶⁶ The Voice of the Temple Mount Faithful: Newsletter, Summer 2001. *The Arabs Continue to Destroy the Remains on the Temple Mount.*

for Mosque complex expansion into the area known as Solomon's Stables. (Calling this area Solomon's Stables is a misnomer, because according to the archeologists working with The Israeli Department of Antiquities, these rooms under The Mount were used as places of prayer during the tenure of The Second Temple.) [67]The Palestinian Muslim activities under The Mount are without Israeli Government official approval, but no-one is doing much about it for fear of starting more terrorism, or sparking a war confrontation with the Islamic world.

[68]Now there is weakening of the southern and eastern walls, and the south portion of the Western Wall of The Temple Mount, because of the Palestinian unethical proceedings, and because the water-table under The Mount is rising. This rise in the water-table indicates that pressure has been released by their excavations, allowing the water seepage to occur. At last report, the bulge of the south wall was ninety-eight feet in length, and measurably increasing daily as it heads toward inevitable collapse, and some of the huge rocks forming the south wall are beginning to dangerously slide out of alignment with the rest of the wall, but the Palestinians are only half-heartedly addressing the problem. Actually, the stones of this wall are such that it is unlikely anyone can do anything to permanently fix the damage anyway. [69]The damage is of such great concern that there is fear the southeastern, and southwestern sections of the south wall could collapse at any time, and Muslim worshipers are in grave danger. If it collapses, the Al Aqsa Mosque, along with at least one other smaller mosque, will be totally destroyed.

[70]No one really knows how to address this issue, because if the Israelis dare to go in to collapse the damaged wall under controlled engineering

---

[67] The Voice of the Temple Mount Faithful: Newsletter, Spring 2000. *The Tragedy of the Destruction on the Temple Mount and the Weakness of the Israeli Government to Stop it Continues.*

[68] Prophecy in the News, J.R. Church, May 11, 2002. *Articles List: The Southern Wall is About to Fall!*

[69] Israelinsider, Israel's Daily Magazine, August 27, 2002, Ellis Shuman. "Mayer Ehud Olmert: "...the southern wall is indeed in danger of collapse" PM Sharon is warned by citizen's watchdog committee of the, ".clear and present danger that the southern part of the Western Wall and the Temple Mount might collapse" because of illegal construction work.

[70] One Jerusalem NEWSFLASH, <news@onejerusalem.org.> , September 12, 2002, *Save the Temple Mount.* "Years of construction work by the Muslim Wakf, which administers the site, has jeopardized the structural integrity of the ancient walls, and they are now on the brink of collapse, threatening the Temple Mount..." "For years, Israel Antiquities Authority officials have tried to

SEVENTY WEEKS DETERMINED

conditions, the Palestinians will take affront to their presence, thus causing an escalation of tensions. The wall cannot be repaired properly without first collapsing it totally. The Jordanians have sent in crews of engineers to determine the degree and source of the damage, and at least try to stabilize the wall, and perhaps fix part of the problem. But their efforts are kind of like trying to stop a slow moving loaded freight train with a toy pick-up truck. [71]If they collapse the wall, the Mosques will be destroyed along with the collapse. [72]If they do nothing, and the wall gives way on its own, killing and injuring Muslims and destroying the Al Aqsa Mosque and the expanded underground facility, Israel will still be blamed for not having done something about it, and the result will be the same tensions or worse. It appears the mosques are going to be destroyed when the wall does collapse.

[73]There is a roadway that runs fairly close to the southern wall of The Temple Mount area. It is amazing to note that in August 2001, on the Ninth of Av, which is the same day in history that both the First and Second Temples were destroyed, The Temple Mount Faithful, which is a group dedicated to the building of The Third Temple, gathered on the street below the southern wall for a prayer meeting. This gathering is not unusual. The Temple Mount Faithful gather annually below The Temple Mount on this important historical date. They also have two huge stones in their possession, which they have indicated will be the cornerstones used to construct a new Temple Complex. Their annual peaceful demonstration is done under strict police surveillance, with properly obtained permits, so it is not an ad hoc happening. What was significant about this particular prayer demonstration on the Ninth of Av 2001, is that **it was during this prayer meeting that a high portion of the south wall began to move**

---

gain access to the site to halt the deterioration wrought by Wakf construction, but Muslim Wakf officials ... have blocked all efforts by engineers to survey the damage and implement stopgap measures."

[71] One Jerusalem NEWSFLASH, <news@onejerusalem.org.> , September 12, 2002, *Save the Temple Mount.* "The wall will collapse," one Israeli official said recently. "The central issue at present is whether it will collapse on the heads of thousands of people who are praying there, or whether it will be done in a controlled manner."

[72] IsraelInsider, Israel's Daily Magazine, September 30, 2002. Ellis Shuman, *Israel Fears Temple Mount may Collapse due to Ramadan Crowds.*

[73] The Voice of the Temple Mount Faithful: Newsletter, Summer 2001. *A Cornerstone for the Third Temple Causes an "Earthquake" in the Middle East and all over the World in Tisha B'Av 2001.*

The Final Schedule Revealed

noticeably. While they were simply standing and praying, the wall began to move!

Gershon Saloman, the Chairman of The Temple Mount Faithful, immediately wrote a [74]letter to Ariel Sharon, the Israeli Prime Minister, requesting that the Israeli Government simply let the wall collapse without any interference. In this particular letter he also stated, quote: "The reason for the bulge and the danger of the wall collapsing is the hand of the G_d of Israel. The bulge and probable collapse is no accident, but the commencement of a godly move for the collapse of all the strange, pagan Arab presence on the Temple Mount, which is the most holy site of the Temple. <u>This is the fulfillment of the prophecies of the prophets of Israel for the redemption of the Temple Mount. We are now standing at the threshold of a new and decisive stage in the major historical prophetic godly move for the redemption of the Temple Mount, and the people of Israel, and of all the world.</u> We are now witnessing the final death throes of the cruel, foreign, and vandalistic occupation of the Temple Mount. If the Israeli Government will not immediately stop the enemy's occupation, as G_d expects it to do, then <u>G d Himself will very soon stop it, which He already has started to do</u>." End of Quote. Underlining mine for emphasis.

If the southern wall collapses, and actually it is not merely a case of 'if,' but inevitably 'when,' the street that runs along the wall perimeter will be severely damaged as well. [75]Any attempt to subsequently repair both **the wall and the street**, which both obviously will be severely damaged, will be done under duress, opposition, misunderstanding, and accusation by both sides! [76] Is this the situation Gabriel's prophecy in Daniel was referring to? It very well may be! Therefore, we have in place a real set of physical circumstances that may allow us to further identify where we possibly are in the unfolding of the final Weeks of prophecy as explained to Daniel.

---

[74] Prophecy In The News, Gary Stearman, JR Church,, May 2002 *The Southern Wall is About to Fall.*

[75] israelinsider, Israel's Daily Magazine, August 27, 2002. Ellis Shuman, *Southern Temple Mount wall reportedly in imminent danger of collapse.* Shuka Dorfman, Israeli Antiquities Authority: " The necessary cooperation needed with the Waqf is nonexistent,"

[76] One Jerusalem, <news@onejerusalem.org>, September 12, 2002, *Save the Temple Mount,* "The walls of Jerusalem's Temple Mount are in danger of collapse..." " "The wall will collapse, " one Israeli official said recently. "The central issue at present is whether it will collapse on the heads of thousands of people who are praying there, or whether it will be done in a controlled manner." "

SEVENTY WEEKS DETERMINED

[77](By the way, the recent sloughing of a small portion of the Western Wall in September 2003, [78]and again near the Mughrabi Gate of the Western Wall Plaza in February of 2004, are not the fulfillment of this prophecy regarding the wall and the street. No street area near these sloughs was severely damaged in these incidents. The recent slough, [79]along with the earthquake which caused most of Jerusalem and surrounding area to tremble, are a warning of what is to soon come!)

In essence, the Israelis do have the right to say what goes on around, near, and inside The Mount, but apparently they do not have the governmental mechanism, or decisive will, to make their wishes stick. It's just the surface of The Mount that is supposed to be administered by the Waqf, and these Muslim Palestinians live in Israel, so theoretically Israel controls their activities also. Israel has the right to override The Palestinian Authority since it is not a government of a sovereign state (yet!) but a ruling body within the Nation of Israel. So in essence, the Israelis do have say over The Temple Mount, but not the mechanism to enforce their wishes without having everyone in the Muslim world, and international opinion, down her neck.

This realization is a factor in the whole controversy that is keeping the entire world community boiling, with most nations and the UN calling for the formation of a Palestinian State. Now that eventuality really would upset the apple-cart for Jerusalem and The Temple Mount! If there is any situation other than The 1967 Six Day War from which to begin our count-down, the formation of a Palestinian State would be it! So the 'when' of the beginning of the count-down is open to interpretation. I lean toward The 1967 Six Day War, simply because it was the result of this war that allowed the Jews to have sovereign governmental jurisdiction over Jerusalem after

---

[77] Temple Mount Faithful, Gershon Saloman, Another Wall Collapses on the Temple Mount Near the Western Wall, Feb.14,2004. Partially result of the recent earthquake of February 11,2004.

[78] IsraelInsider, Israel's Daily Newsmagazine, www.israelinsider.com February 16, 2004. Ellis Shuman, *Collapse of embankment near Western Wall shows danger facing Temple Mount.* "A stone embankment under a walkway leading up to the Temple Mount's Mughrabi Gate collapsed on Saturday nicht, sending rocks tumbling into the women's section of the Western Wall plaza, but causing no injuries."

[79] Haaretz News Service, www.haaeretz.com, February 11, 2004, *Quake rocks Israel, neighbor countries.* "Housing and Construction Minister Effi Eitam convened a meeting Wednesday evening after an earthquake measuring 5 on the richter scale rattled Israel and its Middle East neighbors."

The Final Schedule Revealed

2,500 years, and to have any say at all regarding The Temple Mount and The Old City.

In summary, we have the presence in the Land of *'thy people,"* and tensions regarding *"the holy city."* We have *"the wall"* in great need of repair, and *"the street"* which will be severely damaged when this wall collapses. And we have factions laying some kind of claim to Jerusalem itself. That sounds pretty much like Daniel to me! So can the count-down begin again? I would say it already has. From when? I would suggest from The 1967 Six Day War. I will not be absolutely dogmatic here, but there must be a starting-point somewhere, and it must line up with Gabriel's explanation to Daniel.

So <u>tentatively</u>, where would the final 7 Weeks, the 49 years prior to the 70th Tribulation Week, end? If we were to use the June 5, 1967 Six Day War as a beginning date, and count forward 49 years, we would arrive in the year 2016. Except we must remember that a prophetic year has 360 days rather than 365.25 days. So there are 49 x 5.25 =257.25 days that we must subtract. That is approximately 8 3/4 months, which would place the end of the 49th year, (the end of the 69th Week) approximately in the Fall of 2015 in our calendar.

What does this <u>possibly</u> mean in regard to the Rapture? If we back up to the beginning of this 69th Week of years, we arrive at the year 2008. (15 - 7 = 8) But the Days of Awe are ten years, not just the seven years of the Tribulation. Therefore, the Church need only account for four of the seven years of the 69th Week, meaning the Rapture likely will take place three years before the end of the 69th Week, bringing us to approximately the year 2011.

Is this a dogmatic time-frame? <u>NO!!</u> There are other variables which may allow this prophetic sequence to transpire even sooner, or conversely, the entire sequence could be put on hold for another few years. But the fulfillment of the 49 years (7 Weeks) before the onset of the 70th Week Tribulation, appears to be well under way even now, and from what Jesus seems to indicate, once the prophetic signs begin toward the end of the Church Age, their unfolding becomes progressively more intense and rapid until they are all fulfilled -- much like the birth-pains leading to the delivery of a child.

But, the Church is not present for the full, intense time of travail, because the travail brings forth Messiah on the earth. So, the time of intense travail is actually The Days of Awe. Therefore, the birth-pangs are the High Holy Days from Rosh HaShanah to Yom Kippur. In essence, the Church, observes the somewhat hazy, slightly unsure time of <u>pre-labor pains</u>, an indication that full-blown travail may be imminent. A woman experiencing pre-labor contractions is not absolutely sure whether the contractions will develop into full-blown labor or not. This uncertain period of mild contractions is often termed <u>false labor</u>, because the contractions may actually stop again for a brief time. But she does know that because the contractions are noticeable, she will very soon go into <u>real labor</u>. The 'false labor' has purpose, because it prepares the woman's body for the real intense contractions of true labor, so her systems are not totally, and suddenly, overwhelmed.

However, it is not the Church that is having these contractions! Rather, it is Israel who awaits the time of birth. The woman to bring forth her Child is not the Church, but Israel! So, the Church is to direct her focus <u>toward Israel</u> in order to comprehend the approach of the end of this Age. For a short, but indeterminate time, the signs of imminent travail may be evident, then they may even appear to slow or subside, but the signs none-the-less are very real, and will soon pick up again in intensity. At the point of the onset of true travail for Israel, the Church is removed (Rosh HaShanah), and Israel is left to go through the time of intense travail until Messiah arrives at Yom Kippur.

The Church does not know <u>the day or hour</u> of the onset of true travail, which will be heralded by Rosh HaShanah. Also, the calendar has been tampered with sufficiently that we really do not know for certain what actual year we are in. When the Rosh HaShanah ingathering Rapture occurs, the calendar time-table will then be pegged for certain for all left on the earth. Then the Jews will have no excuse not to know what is going to transpire. The Rapture should reveal to the Israelis who are up on their eschatology regarding The Fall Feasts, that Jesus Christ is indeed The Redeemer and KING, and The Bridegroom. Of course most Israelis will not concede to this even though the evidence will be right in front of them. But 144,000 of them will understand, because they at least must have their doctrinal theology correct to be the sealed Evangelists who will take the truth to the people of all nations during The Days of Awe. So the countdown is ticking, but it's calculation in years is still somewhat hazy, and will remain so until the Rapture.

This approximate time has some ability to be flexible, because we are told we will not know the day or the hour of Christ's appearing for the Church. Jesus says in Mark 13:32, *"But of that day and that hour knoweth no man, no, not the angels which are in heaven, neither the Son, but the Father."* Matthew 24:36 states the same. *"But of that day and hour knoweth no man, no, not the angels of heaven, but my Father only."* However, Jesus states *"the day or hour"* not the *"month or year."* If we keep our eyes open, we will certainly have the ability to know at least the approximate <u>time and the</u>

season. Just not the day or hour. Paul states in 1 Thessalonians 5:1-4, *"But of the times and the seasons, brethren, you have no need that I write unto you. For yourselves know perfectly that the day of the Lord so cometh as a thief in the night. For when they shall say, Peace and safety; then sudden destruction cometh upon them, as travail upon a woman with child; and they shall not escape. But you brethren are not in darkness, that that day should overtake you as a thief."* And in verse 9 of the same chapter he states, *"For God has not appointed us to wrath, but to obtain salvation by the Lord Jesus Christ."*

III. The Key of "Peace and Safety."

One other clue Paul eludes to is the fact that the cry of 'Peace and Safety" will be heard around the time of the Rapture. So when we hear this slogan battered around in such a manner that peace and safety in The Middle East may become a reality in the eyes of the international community, we will know that *"sudden destruction"* is pretty much imminent! The scenario of setting up a Palestinian State certainly has the ability to bring this sequence about, and it may be sooner rather than later. The sudden destruction to follow would be The Battle of Gog and Magog that ensues over Israel's Covenant rights to her God-ordained borders, and over the fact that the Palestinians may not achieve what they want, namely incorporation of all of The West Bank into their Palestinian State, with the city of Jerusalem as their Capitol.

Russia tends particularly to side with the Palestinians, so it would not be inconceivable for Russia to lead the charge, even though she has helped broker the Palestinian State. If the Palestinians are not pleased with the interim settlement, they too may utter 'Peace and Safety,' but will also quickly set about to define the changes they want in place for entrenched borders of a Palestinian State that they will be willing to actually accept by the [80]year 2005, because Arafat has indicated they will not ratify anything less than the pre-1967 borders for Israel. The Palestinians want all of the West Bank including Jerusalem. Like most disputes, this will take time to go through the usual channels of the UN, the EU, etc. trying to persuade the nations to accept their view. But ultimately, it will result in war. The Palestinians may grudgingly accept the interim agreement, but it will all fall apart when the entrenchment date approaches. We therefore could be faced with a Middle East war by 2005 to 2008, or it could be sooner. This war could escalate quickly into The Battle of Gog and Magog where God deals with the nations over Israel's borders!

So if the southern wall of The Temple Mount collapses around the same time as The Battle of Gog and Magog, and well it might, the restoration of *"the wall and the street"* indeed will take place during *"troublous times,"* quite possibly during the lead-up to, or at the inauguration of the time of Jacob's Trouble following the Rapture. The southern wall of Mount Zion certainly could collapse before the Rapture, fulfilling this prophecy, but not long before. In fact, the wall already has crumbled in several places, particularly along the south-western corner. This certainly would qualify as one of the pre-birth pangs leading to full travail!

We therefore are already living during the final 7 Week lead-up to the fulfillment of the 69th Week, and then the final 70th Week will unfold. The Church will remain until approximately mid-69th Week (probably the fourth year of the 69th Week.) The Days of Awe will be the last three years of the 69th Week, plus the 70th Week. That's Ten Years of Yamim Nora'Im from Rosh HaShanah to Yom Kippur.

CHAPTER 10
THE CONTROVERSY REGARDING THE ABRAHAMIC COVENANT

Lets examine why The Covenant regarding The Land is so important to everyone, both Israeli and Muslim Arabs. [81]I say Muslim Arabs, because it is their belief that they have the right to control all of what they refer to as 'Palestine' including Jerusalem. The Palestinians are pawns in the Muslim Arab agenda to achieve this goal.

Jerusalem is the Holy City of the Jews, and it is their's by reason of the fact that it <u>lies in the territory that God gave to Abraham by Covenant</u>, and God declared He would place His presence and His Name there. However, this Covenant is the sticking point for the Palestinians and the rest of the Arab world, because they claim that they also are descendants of Abraham. It is their belief that when Israel sinned, and was taken into captivity by the Assyrians (the captivity and scattering of The House of Israel), and subsequently by the Babylonians (captivity of The House of Judah), Israel's right to The Abrahamic Covenant was broken. [82]So the Arabs believe that in order for The Land Covenant to be fulfilled, the descendants of Ishmael

---

[81] The Jerusalem Post, Internet Edition, Translated by Shira Guttgold. www.jpost.com/servlet/Satellite?pagename=JPost/A/JPArticl... Regional Media, Editorials From The Arab Press: *To annihilate the infidels is a divine decree.* "I would like to stress that annihilating the infidels is an inarguable fact, as this is the decree of fate."
"When the Koran places these tortures [to be inflicted on the infidels] in the solid framework of reward and punishment,...it seeks to root this predestined fact in the consciousness of Muslim society, asserting that the infidels will be annihilated so as to open a window of hope to Muslim society."
"The belief in "annihilating the country of heresy" therefore opens up for us a window of the possible. But it does not annihilate the infidel country for us!"
"This [annihilation] is merely a belief which, if unaccompanied by the words, "at our hands" that appear in the Koranic verse, will remain in the wonderful realm of ideas, like beautiful dreams that arouse conscientious emotions."
[82] A Short Summary of Islamic Beliefs and Eschatology www.templemount.org/islam.htm Collected by Lambert Dolphin. "Islam's claim as far as Israel is concerned is to assume (without any Biblical basis of course) that Ishmael, not Isaac, is the legitimate heir to whom the Abrahamic promises were passed."
"Although not commonly appreciated by most Christians and Jews, the various

and Esau must now be considered the rightful heirs of the Land. They are willing to fight to the death to bring about their understanding of the fulfillment of The Abrahamic Covenant, because they believe it is the will of Allah. <u>So what really is in dispute is The Abrahamic Covenant</u>.

What the Arabs, and particularly the Palestinians, fail to understand, is the mercy of God toward Israel, and the fact that the keeping of the terms of a covenant are not even contingent specifically on forgiveness, or on the need of forgiveness, but on the terms of the covenant itself. Yes, Israel sinned and broke faith with The Covenant of Promise, but that does not mean The Covenant was annulled. When God enters into Covenant, He does not ever go back on it. It is a fact that God's Covenant was specifically given to Abraham, then to Isaac, then to Jacob, and confirmed to Moses and the Prophets, so that it became part and parcel with The Mosaic Covenant, <u>making Israel only The People of The Covenant</u>. [83]In fact, the [84]Muslims have substituted Ishmael for Isaac, and the twelve sons of Esau as the patriarchs of the promises in place of the twelve sons of Jacob. So what essentially is going on here is a family feud over the understanding and interpretation of The Abrahamic Covenant.

This feud has roots in the blessings that Isaac gave to Jacob and Esau. We see Isaac's blessing to Jacob in Genesis 27:27-29. *"And he came near, and kissed hem: and he smelled the smell of his raiment, and blessed him, and said, See, the smell of my son is as the smell of a field which the LORD hath blessed:* Verse 28. *Therefore God give thee of the dew of heaven, and the fatness of the earth, and plenty of corn and wine:* Verse 29. <u>*Let people serve thee, and nations bow down to thee: and be lord over thy brethren, and let thy mother's sons bow down to thee: cursed be every one that curseth thee,*</u> *and blessed be he that blesseth thee."* Underlining mine.

Let's honestly observe reality. The descendants of Esau have much more land than the descendants of Jacob! Even the descendants of

---

sects of Islam, in their oral tradition, and from the Koran, maintain a complex and intricate eschatology dealing with the end of the age and the coming of a great world leader, or Mahdi. The center of these events at the end of the age is Jerusalem,..."

[83] A Short Summary of Islamic Beliefs and Eschatology www.templemount.org/islam.htm Collected by Lambert Dolphin." ... Muslin tradition substitutes Ishmael for Isaac as the son whom Abraham nearly sacrificed..."

[84] World Net Daily ExclusiveCommentary, Hal Lindsey, July 10, 2002, *Participating with Pagans.* The Koran says that the Jews changed their Scriptures to steal the Abrahamic Covenant so that the blessing would flow through Isaac, rather than Ishmael.

THE CONTROVERSY REGARDING THE ABRAHAMIC COVENANT

Ishmael have more territory than the Israelis. The Arab descendants of Abraham live in most of the geographical area surrounding Israel. But they are jealous of Jacob, and want to take over his tiny bit of real estate for themselves, thus pulling the entire blessing out from under Jacob.

Then we have Isaac's blessing to Esau recorded in Genesis 27:38-41a. *"And Esau said unto his father, Hast thou but one blessing, my father? bless me, even me also, O my father. And Esau lifted up his voice, and wept. Verse 39. And Isaac his father answered and said unto him, Behold thy dwelling shall be the fatness of the earth, and of the dew of heaven from above;* Verse 40. <u>*and by thy sword shalt thou live,*</u> *<u>and shalt serve thy brother</u>: and it shall come to pass when thou shalt have the dominion, that thou shalt break his yoke from off thy neck.* Verse 41. <u>*And Esau hated Jacob because of the blessing wherewith his father blessed him.*</u>*"* Underlining mine for emphasis.

Esau gave up his birthright, being tricked by Jacob. Even Isaac, their father, was deceived by Jacob. Ever since, the descendants of Esau have lived in an attitude of resentment, and have looked for ways to destroy Jacob, and lay claim to the birthright. According to the blessing bestowed upon Esau after Isaac blessed Jacob, Esau would indeed have both the fatness of the earth and the dew of heaven, indicating his descendants would have much land with resources. So Esau does have very great blessings! But notice, Jacob was already blessed in the same manner-- with fatness of the land, the dew of heaven, and plenty of corn and wine. So they both have promised blessings requiring the necessity for real-estate.

But the Arabs have capitalized on setting about to throw off the yoke of Jacob to obtain dominion. They certainly do not want to bow to, or serve Jacob in compliance with the terms of Jacob's blessing. Esau's blessing states that when he has dominion, the yolk of Jacob will be broken from off his neck. This is something Esau cannot manipulate, but which only can come about in God's timing! But the Arabs have capitalized on trying to manipulate Jacob's yolk of dominion, with one objective - namely to destroy Jacob, and take the birthright. What they fail to realize in their hatred and jealousy, is that in order for Jacob's yolk to be removed from off their necks, it does not necessitate Jacob's birthright must be usurped. In fact, <u>Jacob's Covenant blessing cannot be usurped!</u> The Arabs just don't 'get it!'

Isaac must have recognized the animosities that would be passed down, because he indicated that <u>the sword would be Esau's legacy to live by</u>, <u>and this sword has come down to the present as The Jihad Sword of Islam</u>. Unfortunately, along with this Sword the descendants of both Ishmael and Esau have <u>vowed curses against Israel</u>. What they fail to remember is that in so doing, <u>they are themselves being cursed by God exactly according to</u>

The Final Schedule Revealed

the terms of Isaac's blessing for Jacob. This Jihad Sword very well could bring about several scenarios: the formation of a Palestinian State in direct violation of God's Covenant, The Battle of Gog and Magog at the transition of the Age of Grace to The Ten Days of Awe, and be a factor in the build-up to The Battle of Armageddon at the end of the Tribulation. All the nations will be judged according to Isaac's blessing for Jacob. In fact, all nations will be either blessed or cursed according to whether they have blessed or cursed Jacob. So this is not merely a contest between brothers. There is a much wider scope. In fact, all nations of the world, along with Ishmael's and Esau's descendants, will have to face God regarding Jacob and The Abrahamic Covenant.

Also, I would like to point out the fact that it is the borders of Israel that are in dispute according to the international community, and are front and center as the cause of the unrest in The Middle East, and are, and will be, the sticking point in the formation of a Palestinian State, and any Peace Process attempted. The truth is, neither the Palestinians nor the Arab world want Israel to continue to exist, and many of their leaders, both religious and political, have stated so. The formation of a Palestinian State to co-exist alongside Israel is merely window-dressing for a desire to wipe-out Israel completely. In this regard, any 'peace' brokered will be tenuous and short-lived at best, Palestinian State or not.

And what about the final borders of Israel and Palestine as sovereign nations? Who will finally decide where they should be? The USA? Britain? France? The UN? Russia? The EU? China? The Arab League? Iran? Iraq? The Palestinians? Saudi Arabia? Jordan? Egypt? Israel? The Quartet? Have we forgotten anyone? YES! What about God's input into these deliberations?

According to the international community in general, including Israel strangely enough, The West Bank and Gaza, also inaccurately referred to as 'the disputed occupied territories' since The Six Day War of 1967, and recently designated as 'the illegally occupied territories,' since Camp David, are Lands open to negotiation. And according to the UN, the EU, the President of the USA (but not all his Congress), and the Arab World, Jerusalem is therefore up for grabs as well, because it lies right in the middle of this 'disputable' area.

When we look at a map of The Middle East, we clearly see that the back-bone of the region is a range of mountains extending from The Golan to The Red Sea. It is these mountains, with Jerusalem perched about mid-way in the range, that are the major contention, and along with Gaza, are referred to as 'the illegally occupied territories.' Judea, Samaria, and Gaza (together called 'Yesha') are considered open to negotiation by The

THE CONTROVERSY REGARDING THE ABRAHAMIC COVENANT

Quartet. But God has decreed, by Covenant, that these lands, <u>along with the sovereign territory Israel already decisively held before 1967, belong to the Israelis</u>. Anyone messing with The Covenant Lands will run headlong into The LORD of Hosts, and will definitely come out on the short end of that encounter! He literally gave these 'disputed' lands to Israel in The 1967 Six Day War. But Israel has been pressured into playing games over them ever since, refusing to lay decisive claim to them, yet not willing to give them up either.

For example, her mistake of returning The Temple Mount to the Jordanians, who gave it into the hands of the Palestinians, certainly has back-fired royally! <u>God will take Israel to task for this ambivalence, and will trounce the nations and peoples who are keeping this dispute going</u>. It is these 'disputed' Lands that the Palestinians are insisting be within the borders of a Palestinian State, and as such, they feel they will also gain Jerusalem! If Jerusalem is not to be fully theirs, they will consider accepting an agreement to make Jerusalem an international city controlled by the United Nations, just so long as Israel no longer controls it. In other words, they want to oust Jacob from The Covenanted Lands, and from Israel's Holy City inheritance! There's no doubt in my mind that this will result in all-out war! Not just once, but twice!

Lets look at a couple of prophetic Scriptures in regard to The Land Covenant, and to the borders of Israel in the end times.

Psalm 105:4-15. *"Seek the LORD, and his strength: seek his face evermore.* Verse 5. *Remember his marvelous works that he hath done; his wonders, and the judgments of his mouth;* Verse 6. *O ye <u>seed of Abraham</u> his servant, ye children of <u>Jacob his chosen</u>.* Verse 7. *He is the LORD our God: his judgments are in all the earth.* Verse 8. <u>*He hath remembered his covenant for ever, the word which he commanded to a thousand generations*</u>. Verse 9. <u>*Which covenant he made with Abraham, and his oath unto Isaac:*</u> Verse 10. <u>*and confirmed the same unto Jacob for a law, and to Israel for an everlasting covenant*</u>: Verse 11. <u>*saying, Unto thee will I give the land of Canaan, the lot of your inheritance*</u>. Verse 12. *When they were <u>but a few men in number: yea, very few, and strangers in it</u>;* Verse 13. *when they went from one nation to another, from one kingdom to another people;* Verse 14. *he suffered no man to do them wrong: yea he reproved kings for their sakes;* Verse 15. *saying, <u>Touch not mine anointed, and do my prophets no harm</u>."* KJV. Underlining mine for emphasis.

First of all, the exhortation is to seek the LORD, and seek His strength, and His Face forever. <u>The LORD is to be consulted</u>, because He has already done many wonderful things, and we are to remember this fact. <u>He ultimately is in control!</u> The seed of Abraham, and particularly the descendants of Jacob, are to seek Him. Seek Him about what? <u>His

Everlasting Covenant that He has made with them. This Covenant is very specific. It is regarding the Land of Canaan, and it is to last forever. It is non-negotiable!

The seed of Abraham refers to all the descendants of Abraham, so includes most of the Arab nations and Israel, so yes, they **all** really ought to pay attention here, because these verses spell out which of Abraham's offspring inherits The Covenant. The Covenant is not to be fulfilled by the Abrahamic offspring in general. **It is a specific group** of Abraham's descendants who inherit The Covenant. The Arabs MUST be brought to recognize WHO the beneficiaries of The Land Covenant REALLY are. So must Israel. Neither apparently understands as yet, but they really have no excuse not to understand.

The Land is neither the Arab's nor Israel's per se' to fight about. The Land belongs to The LORD, and as such, He has already, by incontestable Covenant, given it to the specified Abrahamic descendants of Isaac, of the lineage of Jacob. It is entrenched by God's Law, and no man has the right to challenge this legally binding Covenant, whether Arab or Jew, or anyone else. The above Psalm emphasizes this fact. The LORD "*confirmed the same unto **Jacob** for a law, and to **Israel** for an everlasting covenant, saying, Unto thee will I give the land of Canaan, the lot of your inheritance.*" And, this is an everlasting Covenant which cannot ever be changed, annulled, or contested successfully.

Jacob is Israel, and just in case anyone wants to challenge otherwise, both his names are used here. The first name, "Jacob," meaning "deceiver or supplanter," refers to Jacob's cunning deceit in taking the birthright from Esau, but his trickery cannot be used as an excuse to have the birthright revoked. The Muslims believe that because Jacob obtained the birthright through trickery, God ultimately will judge Jacob for it, and give the birthright to Esau anyway. God knew this reasoning would be a factor in the future, so to indicate that their argument would hold no water, He also uses the name 'Israel' in this passage. Remember, the LORD changed Jacob's name to Israel, meaning "*...for as a prince hast thou power with God and with men, and hast prevailed.*" Genesis 32:28.

The prince inherits the kingdom (the land with all its occupants and resources) of his father, the King. He really has no say in the matter. Its a done deal. This is not a birthday present which the prince can then do whatever he wants with, like give away again if he chooses, or share with another, or trade for something else, or even refuse to accept. This is his legally binding inheritance. He gets it whether he wants it or not! That is why The LORD has a controversy over The Land even with Israel. Israel cannot concede 'land for peace' in the dividing up of the inheritance without God's permission, and He isn't giving any permission! So much for the idea of a permanent Palestinian State!

Notice the implications. Because Israel is a prince, he has the authority of his position as the chosen, blessed son of the King to exercise his authority and rights in regard to The Covenant, and thus prevail. Obviously, Israel has not comprehended this powerful position yet! It is time for Israel to recognize the princely position held, and to begin exercising this position with authority. How dare anyone challenge the God-ordained Covenant! Israel does not fight for The Land alone. Anyone thinking they can negotiate or fight for all or any portion of The Covenant Land, fights God Himself! Israel has the right to stand up to her enemies and jealous neighbors, and claim The Land with all the authority of God backing him up! Now that is power with God and with men! Israel does not know it, but because of who God is, and what He has ordained, Israel already has prevailed! They just don't 'get it' yet. Wake-up, Israel!

When is this Covenant to be brought to fulfillment? According to Psalm 105: 11-13, when there are very few of them in the land, and strangers still live among these few, and most of the Jews are still scattered among the nations and kingdoms of the earth. That sounds pretty much like a description of the current Israeli nation! Although many Jews have returned to Israel, the vast majority are still in Diaspora, and there are 'strangers,'ie. Arabs and others, living among those few who do occupy the land. It is while this demographic is still in place that The Covenant will be fulfilled. The process of fulfillment of God's Land Covenant began when Israel became a nation again in 1948, and it expanded as a result of The 1967 Six Day War, and The 1973 Yom Kippur War, and ultimately will be complete under Messiah. Unfortunately, it will not come about without set-backs.

Allow me to point out one more observation regarding Psalm 105. Notice verses 14 & 15. *"he suffered no man to do them wrong: yea, he reproved kings for their sakes; saying, Touch not mine anointed, and do my prophets no harm."* Underlining mine. Certainly this passage is regarding the righteous, but the context of the entire Psalm is specific to God's Covenant people, because the reference is plural. No one is to do them wrong! God has reproved kings on their behalf in the past. The strong implication is that He will do so again if He must! God will not tolerate anyone touching His anointed or doing His prophets any harm. The anointed in context here are the children of God, and His prophets those who uphold the truth of God's prophetic Word. This reference to *"mine anointed"* and *"my prophets"* would include both the Church and Israel, because the Church is given the mandate to uphold the truth of the Gospel, and to warn of the wrath of God on those who are disobedient.

But more precisely, <u>the anointed is Israel</u>, the anointed inheritor of The Covenant, and the nation through which God's prophets spoke. This statement is emphatic, so it is a strong command -- not an optional directive. This command has ominous overtones for anyone disobeying. **Don't touch God's anointed! Or else!!** Perhaps the Palestinians, the terrorist Muslim jihadists, and the Quartet trying to 'divide the land,' and even the Israeli government, should have this riot act read to them! Because if the leaders of Israel, and the leaders of the other nations of the world, think they can ignore all that The Law and the Prophets have said, <u>then they will have to endure all that The Law and the Prophets have said</u>!

Isaiah 54:10, "For the mountains shall depart, and the hills be removed; but my kindness shall not depart from thee, <u>neither shall the covenant of my peace be removed</u>, saith the LORD that hath mercy on thee." Underlining mine. God's Covenant with Israel cannot be revoked by Israel, or by anyone else. This is God's Covenant with them, and He will not go back on it for any reason.

Actually, God will restore Israel, then He will make a New Covenant with them. Notice *Jeremiah 31: 31-33, "Behold, the days come, saith the LORD, that I will make <u>a new</u> <u>covenant</u> with <u>the house of Israel</u>, and with <u>the house of Judah</u>: Verse 32. Not according to the covenant that I made with their fathers in the day that I took them by the hand to bring them out of the land of Egypt; which my covenant they brake, although I <u>was</u> a husband unto them, saith the LORD: Verse 33. But this shall be the covenant that I will make with the house of Israel; After those days, saith the LORD, I will put the law in their inward parts, and write it in their hearts; and will be their God, and they shall be my people."* KJV. Underlining mine.

Isaiah 61:7-9, "<u>For your shame ye shall have double; and for confusion they shall rejoice in their portion: therefore in their land they shall possess the double</u>: everlasting joy shall be unto them. Verse 8. For I the LORD love judgment, I hate robbery for burnt offering: and I will direct their work in truth, and I will make an everlasting covenant with them. Verse 9. And their seed shall be known among the Gentiles, and their offspring among the people: **all that see them shall acknowledge them, that they are the seed which the LORD hath blessed."** KJV. Emphases mine.

<u>God promises He will return double blessing, even in response to the measure of their shame and confusion, which He forgives</u>. This is the LORD's judgment which He loves! Now this 'double' blessing has overtones that fit in with the sequence of end time events that are unfolding. It appears The Land, including Jerusalem,<u> will be given over to the Israelis twice more</u>. This happened once in 1967, but Israel

basically rejected a most important part of it, The Temple Mount. How could any Jew in their right mind reject the location of the heart of Judaic belief, worship, and heritage? So, since Israel gave up this blessing, God has to start again. Jerusalem and Judah will be given decisively to Israel as a result of The Battle of Gog and Magog (once) according to Joel and Ezekiel. They will lose their jurisdiction over Jerusalem and The Temple Mount during the time of Jacob's Trouble, when they are taken over by a despotic ruler, according to Daniel. Then God will return Jerusalem and The Temple Mount to Israel the second time, through His involvement in The Battle of Armageddon. It is His mercy and His proclamation to keep His Covenant, <u>even if it must involve a piece-by-piece time-table</u>. In fact, all of The West Bank, and more, will eventually be Israeli, but the total picture will not be complete until Messiah comes.

No one can deny that Israel is confused, and is being trapped into a position of being coerced regarding The Middle East Peace Process. It is as if she is being allowed no real say over her own sovereign jurisdiction, but is being told what to do by foreigners. Israel lives with a shameful reputation among the nations of the world <u>because of the way she is forced to handle the situations she faces</u>. Apparently, Israel cannot do anything right in the eyes of the international community, or the international press. For a prime example, <u>she acted in fear and confusion when she gave up The Temple Mount in 1967, and has been living with the fall-out of that decision ever since</u>. The Intifada was sparked, because in September of 2000 Ariel Sharon made a pilgrimage to The Temple Mount. The Muslim Aqsa Martyr's Brigade (Arafat's personal 'terrorist' arm of Fatah, who are <u>supposed to be keeping peace</u> on and around The Temple Mount) took exception to this visit of an Israeli Government official to The Mount, (Sharon was a Knesset member, but not yet Prime Minister at the time), and the atrocities have not stopped since then. But God is in control. He will turn the whole situation around so that all nations are going to have to acknowledge that Israel is the nation that is blessed of God by Covenant.

Notice Jeremiah 32: 37-41. *"Behold, I will gather them out of all countries, whither I have driven them in mine anger, and in my fury, and in great wrath; and I will bring them again unto this place, and I will cause them to dwell safely: Verse 38. And they shall be my people, and I will be their God: Verse 39. And I will give them one heart, and one way, that they may fear me for ever, for the good of them, and of their children after them: Verse 40. And I will make an everlasting covenant with them, that I will not turn away from them, to do them good; but I will put my fear in their hearts, that they shall not depart from me. Verse 41. Yea, I will rejoice over them to do them good, and <u>I will plant them in this land assuredly with my whole heart and with my whole soul</u>."* Emphasis mine.

This promise of a New Covenant will not be complete until after the Tribulation, when the LORD will gather Israel totally from all nations. The ingathering we see taking place now is partial. He will bring about a complete ingathering when He returns. Until that time, Israel will not be complete either in her Land, or in her worship, or in any lasting degree of peace. There still is much to be accomplished in establishing Israel, and it will be with wars and tribulations until Messiah comes.

Isaiah 62: 1-12. "**For Zion's sake will I not hold my peace, and for Jerusalem's sake I will not rest,** *until the righteousness thereof go forth as brightness, and the salvation thereof as a lamp that burneth.* Verse 2. **And the Gentiles shall see thy righteousness, and all kings thy glory:** *and thou shalt be called by a new name, which the mouth of the LORD shall name.* Verse 3. *Thou shalt also be a crown of glory in the hand of the LORD, and a royal diadem in the hand of thy God.* Verse 4. *Thou shalt be no more termed Forsaken;* **neither shall thy land any more be termed Desolate: but thou shalt be called Hephsibah, and thy land Beulah**: *for the LORD delighteth in thee, and thy land shall be married.* Verse 5. *For as a young man marrieth a virgin, so shall thy sons marry thee: and as the bridegroom rejoiceth over the bride, so shall thy God rejoice over thee.* Verse 6. **I have set watchmen upon thy walls, O Jerusalem, which shall never hold their peace day nor night**: *ye that make mention of the LORD, keep not silence,* **And give him no rest, till he establish, and till he make Jerusalem a praise in the earth.** Verse 7. *The LORD hath sworn by his right hand, and by the arm of his strength, Surely I will no more give thy corn to be meat for thine enemies; and the sons of the stranger shall not drink thy wine, for the which thou hast laboured:* Verse 8. *But they that have gathered it shall eat it, and praise the LORD; and they that have brought it together shall drink it in the courts of my holiness.* Verse 10. *Go through, go through the gates;* **prepare ye the way of the people**; *cast up, cast up the highway; gather out the stones;* **lift up a standard for the people.** Verse 11. *Behold, the LORD hath proclaimed unto the ends of the world,* **Say to the daughter of Zion, Behold, thy salvation cometh;** *behold, his reward is with him, and his work before him.* Verse 12. *And they shall call them, The holy people, The redeemed of the LORD; and thou shalt be called, Sought out,* **A city not forsaken.**" KJV. Bold emphases mine.

One gets the strong impression from this passage, that no one messes with the LORD's blessings for Jerusalem! Those who understand the will of the LORD for Jerusalem and Mount Zion are not to remain silent! The Daughter of Zion is the restored Old City of Jerusalem, and in particular, The Temple Mount. He is going to free this area, and give it back into the hands of His people, Israel, through battle. Notice this passage says. "<u>go through, go through the gates</u>; prepare ye the way of the people, <u>cast up, cast up the highway</u>, gather the stones; lift up a standard for the people." These are the cries of battle! The <u>action</u> is twice emphasized, indicating <u>double</u> prophetic fulfillment at <u>two</u> battles. Who is going to have to concede to the outcome of both these wars over Israel, Jerusalem, and The Temple Mount? The Gentiles! The Arabs. The UN. The EU. <u>Everyone who is trying to tear Israel apart</u>. And ultimately, all the nations of the earth.

Isaiah 63: 17-19, and Isaiah 64:1, *"O LORD, why hast thou made us to err from thy ways, and hardened our heart from thy fear? Return for thy servant's sake, the tribes of thine inheritance.* Verse 18. **The people of thy holiness have possessed it but a little while; our adversaries have trodden down the sanctuary.** Verse 19. **We are thine: thou never barest rule over them; they were not called by thy name.** Chapter 64:1 <u>Oh that thou wouldst rend the heavens, that thou wouldst come down</u>, *that the mountains might flow down at thy presence, as when the melting fire burneth, the fire causing waters to boil, to make thy name known to thine adversaries, that the nations may tremble at thy presence!"* KJV. Emphases mine.

This is a cry to the LORD to revive them, because they have erred and hardened their hearts from fearing God. This cry of repentance has been part of the cry of the Diaspora down through the centuries. They have desired earnestly to be restored to their Land and to their Temple Worship, and to their Holy City. Now they are in their Land <u>for a little while</u>, <u>since 1948</u>, <u>they still do not have their Temple</u>, and <u>The Temple Mount is still trodden down by their enemies</u>. Some Israelis are beginning to recognize they are God's chosen people, and also that <u>He never was</u>, <u>and is not</u>, <u>the God of their enemies who occupy their holiest site</u>. Allah is NOT Jehovah God! The LORD God of Israel never has been recognized as ruler over these who stand in their way of full worship on The Temple Mount. There is a cry for the LORD *"to rend the heavens and come down,"* and fight against their enemies, so the nations will tremble at His presence! Israel awaits her Messiah, The One Who will give her complete deliverance and freedom. But she is going to be deceived, and must go through a time of Jacob's Trouble first, then all will be totally restored to her. Yes, the LORD will rend the heavens and come down. Only not in the way they are expecting, but in Battle against the nations of the whole earth.

CHAPTER 11
TENTS OF JUDAH, and GOG AND MAGOG

Now we have an understanding of the seriousness of The Covenant, let's return to Daniel's 70 Weeks for a few moments.

According to Daniel 9:24, the focus of the 70 Weeks of discipline is in regard to *"thy people, and upon thy holy city."* Allow me to point out something that we may inadvertently miss, but which sheds more light on how events will transpire, and what the motives for these events are. The House of Israel went into captivity under the Assyrians in 722 B.C.E. The House of Judah, of which Daniel was part, was taken captive by the Babylonians in 586 B.C.E. When this prophecy was first delivered to him, Daniel's initial thought would automatically be that the prophecies would be regarding his own people, Judah, as well as for the city of Jerusalem. **"Thy people" for Daniel was Judah. "The holy city" for Daniel was Jerusalem.**

The fulfillment of 70 years of captivity under Babylon did come to an end for The House of Judah. But this 70 year discipline was not for The House of Israel who were not of the Babylonian Captivity, and never really officially began returning to The Land until 1948 and onward. In actual fact, the 70 Years of Captivity did not have anything directly to do with The House of Israel, The Ten Northern Tribes, but was only for The House of Judah, the two tribes. However, the prophetic word given to Daniel regarding the 70 Weeks of years will ultimately play out to include both The House of Israel and The House of Judah together. So the 70 Years of Captivity, and the 70 Weeks of Discipline are not the same thing. The 70 Years Captivity for Judah was indeed 70 actual years, whereas, the 70 Weeks of Discipline is 490 years, and will ultimately be regarding all Israel, both The House of Judah and The House of Israel.

I. The Tents of Judah:

The fact that Daniel would have considered the prophecy to be in regard to his own people and the Holy City, <u>namely Judah and Jerusalem</u>, is interesting in the light of Zechariah 12:7 which states, *"The LORD also shall save the tents of Judah first..."* This prophecy was fulfilled once already when those of The House of Judah returned from The Babylonian Captivity. But it was incomplete, because Judah remained a puppet of succeeding empires, without full sovereignty, so it will have to be fulfilled again <u>exactly as stated</u>. It would appear that the area referred to as former Judah, that includes Jerusalem and all of Judea, will be totally given into the hands of the Israelis first. And notice, this reference in Zechariah states, *"<u>tents</u> of Judah first."* Tents are not usually considered to be permanent dwellings. This indicates that this *"first"* saving in regard to Judah will have a degree of lack of stability or permanency to it. We already see this scenario unfolding in Israel where Judah and Samaria are currently part of the so-called 'Disputed Occupied Territories' of The West Bank so much in controversy today. Just as with the ending of The Times of The Gentiles being a process, so too will be the saving of the Tents of Judah. In fact, the two are interconnected, and <u>the Tents of Judah are key to understanding the prophetic sequence</u>.

Joel 2:32b to Joel 3:1-2. *"...in mount Zion and in Jerusalem shall be deliverance, as the LORD hath said, and <u>in the remnant whom the LORD shall call</u>. For behold, in those days, and in that time, when I shall bring again the captivity of Judah and Jerusalem, I will also gather all nations, and will bring them down into the valley of Jehosephat, and will plead with them there for my people and for my heritage Israel, whom they have scattered among the nations, and parted my land."* Emphases mine.

Notice, this passage in Joel is directly subsequent to where Peter ends his quote mid-sentence. Joel gives us the rest of the sentence of verse 32, explaining events immediately following the darkening of the sun and the blood-red moon. God will gather the nations into The Valley of Jehosephat to plead with them regarding the division of The Covenant Heritage Land, and the scattering of His Covenant people. The first battle regarding these issues will be The Gog-Magog Battle. The LORD states He will *"bring again the Captivity of Judah and Jerusalem."* The ingathering of this Remnant has been taking place since 1948. The coming controversy will be regarding recognition by the nations of Israel's right to The Land of the Covenant. Most nations at the moment do not fully accept Israel's Land rights. But the outcome of this first controversy will bring deliverance. Joel's passage indicates <u>deliverance for</u> **Jerusalem,** and **Mount Zion**. These are located in **Judah**. Daniel's 70 Weeks are in regard to **Judah** (his own people) **and Jerusalem** (the Holy City.) Therefore, **Judah, Jerusalem,** and **Mount Zion** are key to understanding the order of the fulfillment of these prophecies as God deals with Israel and the nations. <u>Once we are aware of the Jerusalem / Judah / Mount Zion connection</u>, we begin to see this theme popping up repeatedly throughout the prophecies regarding present-day Israel. **Judah, Jerusalem,** and **Mount Zion** <u>are key to understanding</u> the current events unfolding in Israel.

II. 'Land for Peace' May in fact Play a Role!

In light of the current situation concerning the formation of a Palestinian State on 'occupied lands,' we may begin to see a glimmer of why the so-called 'occupied territories,' including Jerusalem, have remained in controversy, and why the Israeli Government leadership, along with 'The Quartet', are willing to negotiate 'land for peace.' We also may understand why, to bring about the order of prophecy, The Battle of Gog and Magog will become necessary to decisively give the area of <u>Judah and Jerusalem first</u> into Israeli sovereign jurisdiction.

Jerusalem poses as a bone of contention throughout the whole process, even after Israel controls the entire city. Zechariah 12:2. *"Behold I will make Jerusalem a cup of trembling unto all the people round about, <u>when they shall be in the siege both against Judah and against Jerusalem</u>. Verse 3. And in that day I will make Jerusalem a burdensome stone for all people: all that burden themselves with it shall be cut in pieces, though all the people of the earth be gathered together against it. Verse 4. In that day, saith the LORD, I will smite every horse with astonishment, and his rider with madness: and I will open mine eyes upon the house of Judah, and will smite every horse of the people with blindness. Verse 5. And the governors of Judah shall say in their heart, the inhabitants of Jerusalem shall be my strength in the LORD of hosts their God. Verse 6. In that day will I make the governors of Judah like a hearth of fire among the wood, and like a torch of fire in a sheaf; and they shall devour all the people round about, on the right hand and on the left: and Jerusalem shall be inhabited again in her own place, even in Jerusalem. Verse 7. <u>The LORD shall save the tents of Judah first, that the glory of the house of David and the glory of the inhabitants of Jerusalem do not magnify themselves against Judah</u>.*" KJV. Underlining mine.

Notice the type of warfare used according to verse 6. *"The governors of Judah will be like a hearth of fire among the wood, and like a torch in a sheaf."* This sounds like Israeli IDF ground-troops moving among the hills of Judah, and the use of short-range missiles (*"torch in a sheaf."*) The result of this battle is obvious. **Judah will be delivered. Jerusalem becomes secure**. The tents of Judah (mountainous area of The West Bank settlements) are the focus during this war, and are <u>delivered first</u>. The issues driving the battle are: who controls Judah, and who gains jurisdiction over all of Jerusalem. So the conflict is regarding placement of the borders of Israel, and whether a Palestinian State will be permanently entrenched. The Palestinian State is supposedly to be carved out of the ' illegally occupied territories' of The West Bank and Gaza. Also, the question is whether Russia and her allies will get away with invading the mountains of Israel (this refers to The West Bank.) Jerusalem is not specifically attacked during this first conflict, but becomes entrenched as Israeli occupied. As a result, Israeli development of Jerusalem will be able to expand, enabling the building of The Temple on Mount Zion. Even so, Jerusalem will remain controversial.

This situation will continue to remain in flux until Messiah returns, because the next verses indicate that ultimately the LORD will have to intervene directly, especially on behalf of Jerusalem, because Jerusalem itself will eventually come directly under attack by many nations. This scenario occurs at Armageddon, the second Battle. Verse 8. *"In that day shall the LORD defend the inhabitants of Jerusalem, and he that is feeble among them at that day shall be as David; and the house of David shall be as God, as the angel of the LORD before them. Verse 9. And it shall come to pass in that day, that I will seek to destroy all the nations that come against Jerusalem."* So we must keep our eyes particularly on how prophecy is being played out for **Judah** (The Judean portion of the West Bank,) **and Jerusalem**, including **Mount Zion.**

III. The Battle of Gog and Magog: Ezekiel Chapter 38.

"And the word of the LORD came unto me, saying, Verse 2. *Son of man, set thy face against Gog, the land of Magog, the chief prince of Mesech and Tubal, and prophesy against him,* Verse 3. *And say, Thus saith the Lord God;* <u>Behold, I am against thee, O Gog, the chief prince of Meshech and Tubal:</u> Verse 4. *And I will turn thee back, and put hooks into thy jaws, and I will bring thee forth, and all thine army, horses and horsemen, all of them clothed with all sorts of armor, even a great company with bucklers and shields, all of them handling swords:* Verse 5. *Persia, Ethiopia, and Lybia with them; all of them with shield and helmut:* Verse 6. *Gomer, and all his bands; the house of Togarmah of the north quarters, and all his bands: and many people with thee.* Verse 7. *Be thou prepared, and prepare thyself, thou, and all thy company that are assembled unto thee, and be thou guard unto them.* Verse 8. <u>*After many days thou shalt be visited in the latter years*</u> *thou shalt come into the land that is brought back from the sword,* <u>*and is gathered out of many people, against the mountains of Israel, which have been always waste: but it is brought forth out of the nations, and they shall dwell safely all of them.*</u> Verse 9. *Thou shalt ascend and come like a storm, thou shalt be like a cloud to cover the land, thou, and all thy bands, and many people with thee.* Verse 10. *Thus saith the Lord God; It shall also come to pass, that* <u>*at the same time*</u> *shall things come into thy mind, and thou shalt think an evil thought:* Verse 11. *And thou shalt say, I will go up to the land of unwalled villages; I will go to them that are at rest, that dwell safely, all of them dwelling without walls, and having neither bars not gates,* Verse 12. *To take a spoil, and to take a prey; to turn thine hand upon the desolate places that are now inhabited,* <u>*and upon the people that are gathered out of the nations, which have gotten cattle and goods, that dwell in the midst of the*</u>

TENTS OF JUDAH, and GOG AND MAGOG

land. Verse 13. *Sheba, and Dedan, and the merchants of Tarshish, with all the young lions thereof, shall say unto thee, Art thou come to take a spoil? Hast thou gathered thy company to take a prey? to carry away silver and gold, to take away cattle and goods, to take a great spoil? Verse 14. Therefore, son of man, prophesy and say unto Gog, Thus saith the Lord God: <u>In that day when my people of Israel dwelleth safely,</u> <u>shalt thou not know it</u>? Verse 15. And thou shalt come from thy place out of the north parts, thou, and many people with thee, all of them riding upon horses, a great company, and a mighty army: Verse 16. And thou shalt come up against my people of Israel, as a cloud to cover the land, that: <u>it shall be in the latter days</u>, and I will bring thee against my land, that the heathen may know me, when I shall be sanctified in thee, O Gog, before their eyes. Verse 17. Thus saith the Lord God; Art thou he of whom I have spoken in old time by my servants the prophets of Israel, which prophesied in those days many years that I would bring thee against them? Verse 18. <u>And it shall come to pass at the same time when Gog shall come against the land of Israel, saith the Lord God, that my fury shall come up in my face.</u> Verse 19. <u>For in my jealousy and in the fire of my wrath have I spoken, Surely in that day there shall be a great shaking in the land of Israel</u>; Verse 20. So that the fishes of the sea, and the fowls of the heaven, and the beasts of the field, and all creeping things that creep upon the earth, and all the men that are upon the face of the earth, shall shake at my presence, and the mountains shall be thrown down, and the steep places shall fall, and every wall shall fall to the ground. Verse 21. And I will call for a sword against him with pestilence and with blood; and I will rain upon him, and upon his bands, and upon the many people that are with him, an overflowing rain, and great hailstones, fire, and brimstone. Thus will I magnify myself; and I will be known in the eyes of many nations, and they shall know that I am the LORD."* KJV. Underlining Mine.

Reading on into chapter 39. *" Therefore, thou son of man, prophesy against Gog, and say, Thus saith the Lord God; Behold, I am against thee, O Gog, the chief prince of Meshech and Tubal: Verse 2. And I will turn thee back, and leave but the sixth part of thee, and will cause thee to come up from the north parts, and will bring thee upon the mountains of Israel: Verse 3. And I will smite thy bow out of thy left hand, and will cause thine arrows to fall out of the right hand. Verse 4. Thou shalt fall upon the mountains of Israel, thou, and all thy bands, and the people that is with thee: I will give thee unto the ravenous birds of every sort, and to the beasts of the field to be devoured. Verse 5. Thou shalt fall upon the open field: for I have spoken it, saith the Lord God. Verse 6. <u>And I will send a fire on Magog, and among them that dwell carelessly in the isles, and they shall know that I am the Lord.</u> Verse7. So will I make my holy name known in the midst of my people Israel; and I will not let them pollute my holy name any more: and <u>the heathen shall know that I am the Lord, the Holy One of Israel</u>. Verse 8. <u>Behold, it is come, and it is done, saith the Lord God; this is the day whereof I have spoken.</u>*

Verse 9. *And they that dwell in the cities of Israel shall go forth, and shall set on fire and burn the weapons, both the shields and the bucklers, the bows and the arrows, and the handstaves, and the spears, and they shall burn them with fire seven years:* Verse 10. *So that they shall take no wood out of the field, neither cut down any out of the forests; for they shall burn the weapons with fire: and they shall spoil those that spoiled them, and rob those that robbed them, saith the Lord God.* Verse 11. *And it shall come to pass in that day, that I will give unto Gog a place there of graves in Israel, the valley of the passengers on the east of the sea: and it shall stop the noses of the passengers: and there shall they bury Gog and all his multitude; and they shall call it The valley of Hamongog.* Verse 12. *And seven months shall the house of Israel be burying of them, that they may cleanse the land."* KJV. Underlining mine.

The remainder of the chapter explains God's position in regard to forgiving Jacob, and calling them from all the nations, so His name is glorified. Notice some particulars regarding this battle, which serve to identify both the antagonists and the prophetic timing.

A. The Antagonists:

First of all, the antagonists appear to include: Gog, Meshech and Tubal, Persia, Ethiopia, and Libya, along with Gomer and Togarmah, and many other national people groups on the one side. These are opposed by Sheba, Dedan, the merchants of Tarshish, and the Young Lions, siding with Israel. Who are these nations today?

1) Those Opposing Israel:

The first antagonistic group includes Russia and most of the Islamic World: Persia (which is now Iran, Iraq), Syria, and Ethiopia (meaning the nations of the former Ethiopian Empire in Northern Africa), and Libya who has always remained somewhat of a renegade within all occupying empires. This group of aggressors will also include nations who were part of what was formerly the Eastern leg of The Roman Empire, including Gomer and Togarmah, who have been identified with areas of Eastern Europe, particularly East Germany and the Ukraine Balkins - Turkey area. This alliance includes the nations surrounding the Black and Caspian Seas. All the people-groups are not specifically mentioned by name, but are referred to as *"a great many people with thee."*

2) Israel's Defenders:

The nations defending tiny Israel from these aggressors predominantly belong to the West, either in geographic location, or in democratic ideology, and adhere generally to an alignment with the Judeo-Christian mind-set, even though this has been watered down and severely undermined in the past few years. Many of these allied nations appear to have the advantage of possessing both domestic and military naval capability, being referred to as *"merchants of Tarshish"* and *"Isles of the sea."* The prime movers of this group who appear to lead the charge against Gog and Magog are referred to as *"young lions."* This is a rather interesting designation, because the USA, South Africa, Canada, Australia, New Zealand, India, and even some of the far-Eastern nations, and some of South America, are either former colonies of The British Empire, or direct offspring. Britain has a Royal Lion as her symbol. So the Young Lions would be her offspring nations, also referred to in Scripture as The Lion's Whelps. It is these Young Lions, particularly the USA, Canada, and Australia, along with the Mother Lion of Britain, who currently align themselves as being strongly sympathetic toward Israel. Israel is going to be in need of the whole Pride of Lions to come to her defense!

Also, it is ironic that it is the current shenanigans of these same Young Lions that actually sets the stage for The Battle of Gog and Magog! Acting in concert with the Russian Bear, and with the support of Britain, the Mother Lion, they are pushing for the formation of a Palestinian State to co-exist along-side Israel in order to procure peace. Even though all the Lions defend Israel, they certainly have a direct hand in what transpires to bring about war! These cats get caught in their own game of Cat and Mouse.

Notice who appears to be kind of missing from this line-up. Egypt! Now that is interesting, because Egypt currently cannot seem to make up her mind who she really is! I say "kind of missing" for good reason, because she is involved - sort of. On the one hand, she has signed friendly agreements and treaties with Israel, and tries to think of herself as an ally of the USA because of the need for economic stability and aid. On the other hand, she aligns herself against Israel ideologically, religiously, and even politically. Egypt also has been hosting talks among the terrorist groups such as Hamas, Hizbullah, Fatah, Islamic Jihad, etc. in order to facilitate a measure of order within the Islamic world. In essence, Egypt is trying to sit on the fence, while placating the Islamic world, making all kinds of accusations against Israel along with the Palestinians, dismantling the agreed-upon friendly cultural exchange body that was set up in Egypt to

The Final Schedule Revealed

represent Israel, and allowing anti-Semitic presentations by the Egyptian media, inflaming the anti-Israel mind-set of the Islamic public.

[85]Egypt allowed the media to air during Ramadan, November, 2002, the forty-one episode dramatic series of "The Rider Without a Horse" which depicts Israeli Rabbis as promoting an ideological and political take-over of the entire world. This blatant anti-Semitism can hardly be overlooked. This series is based on the <u>Protocols of the Elders of Zion</u>, which is a vitriolic anti-Semitic set of forged writings which have fanned the flames of Jew-hatred throughout the last century, and particularly fueled the holocaust of Hitler's Nazi Germany. Apparently the Islamic extremists have picked up on it. The United States has strongly opposed the airing of this series, but Egypt is allowing it anyway in the name of 'free speech' and 'freedom of artistic expression.' So Egypt may not involve herself militarily in The Battle of Gog and Magog, but she certainly will have a direct hand in inflaming the aggression through supporting and abetting negative propaganda.

B. The Battle of Gog and Magog will occur in the latter years;

Ezekiel gives us a pretty clear indication of when this Battle will occur. *"After many days, and in the latter years."* These phrases sound pretty similar to Gabriel's statement to Daniel as to when the prophecies <u>will begin to be understood</u>. I would suggest then, that Ezekiel and Daniel refer to the same time-frame. So when will that time be? It appears that the latter days spoken of here, and in other prophecies, refer to the latter days of the Church Age before the Rapture, and before the Days of Awe begin. They are the final days of the period referred to by Joel and Peter as the 'last days' which is the Church Age of the Spirit's fullness. In order for there to be the final days of a time-frame, there must be a longer period of time that has already occurred, and that is about to wrap-up. This then must be referring to the Church Age that essentially has lasted for approximately 2000 years. Jesus indicated that prophetic signs would speed up dramatically toward the end of this dispensation, much as the pains of child-birth increase in intensity

---

[85]   The Jerusalem Post Internet, www.jpost.com/servlet/ Satellite?pagename=JPost/AJP/Artivcle... November 5, 2002, Adam Sharon, Washington. *US Jews protest 'Protocols' mini-series outside Egyptian embassy.* "The American Jewish Committee, the Jewish Community Council of Greater Washington, and the Jewish Federation of Greater Washington organized the lunchtime demonstration in response to Egypt's decision to air Knight without a Horse, a 41 episode series partly based on the Protocols of the Elders of Zion."

TENTS OF JUDAH, and GOG AND MAGOG

and become closer together indicating a child is soon to be born. The latter days of the Church Age are dramatic with the speed and intensity of all the signs being fulfilled almost simultaneously, and with the tiny new nation of Israel, and especially Jerusalem and the West Bank, becoming the center of world attention and controversy that all nations are perplexed about. <u>It is in the final days of this era that The Battle of Gog and Magog will occur</u>. So it appears the Church will still be here to witness much of this Battle. Then, very possibly as a result of nuclear warheads exchange, we will see the sun darkened and the moon turned blood-red, and the Rapture of the Church will take place.

1. The Weapons:

How do we know this battle could possibly make use of nuclear capabilities? Notice the devastation that falls upon the nations fighting this war. Verse 6 of Ezekiel 39 states, "*And I will send <u>a fire on Magog, and among them that dwell carelessly in the isles</u>, and they shall know that I am the LORD.*" <u>This is an exchange.</u> Both sides suffer the same type of fire! Also, this exchange may include chemical and biological weapons, because chapter 38, verse 21 states, "*I will call for a sword against him with pestilence (pollution) and with blood.*" And, God throws in his own arsenal of missiles from the heavens. This verse continues; "*and I will rain upon him, and upon his bands, and upon the many people that are with him, an overflowing rain, and <u>great hailstones, fire, and brimstone</u>.*"

We are able to understand that it will be feasible for the sun to be darkened and the moon to appear the color of blood with all the dust and debris, not just from bombs and military missiles, but from cosmic rain, and burning hail and brimstone as well. I think the Church will be very glad to have an escape at this juncture! It is quite apparent which side God is going to fight against, and who will come out on the short end of the stick! But also take note. God is not overly pleased with either side in this war. <u>He sends fire on both sides so they know Who He really is</u>, and have to recognize Him! Sure, the Gog and Magog forces are defeated, but the Isles and Young Lions are trounced as well, and Israel is disciplined as The Ten Days of Awe are ushered in.

But why does the LORD apparently have a bone to pick with the defenders of Israel? The answer to this question explains the timing of the Battle of Gog and Magog. Ezekiel's passage sheds more light here, as does Jeremiah chapters 4, 8 and 11 which also outline the deceptive peace that will come to The Middle East region. <u>It appears there may be</u>, <u>prior to this war</u>, <u>either a peace settlement that causes everyone to relax</u>, **or the promise**

of a settlement that could allow everyone to breathe easier. But about the time everyone feels safety is assured, destruction falls. Ezekiel 38:8 states, "After many days thou shalt be *visited in the latter years*, thou shalt come into the land that is brought back from the sword, and is gathered out of many people, *against the mountains of Israel*, which have been always waste: but it is brought forth out of the nations, *and they shall dwell safely all of them*." Verse 14 states, "Therefore, thou son of man, prophesy and say unto Gog, Thus saith the Lord God: *In that day when my people of Israel dwelleth safely, shalt thou not know it*?" Underlining mine.

What transpires? The Middle East has been in a constant state of unrest and controversy ever since Israel became a nation in 1948. The Palestinians and Islamic terrorist groups have kept the controversy going in hopes of tiring Israel out, to create a situation which will result in the annihilation of Israel. Then they will benefit from the Abrahamic Covenant, and inherit the Land. The majority of the nations of the world have sided with one aspect of this controversy or the other, and their alignments have become pretty clear especially since Sept. 11, 2001.

Now the 'Quartet' is attempting to follow a 'Road-Map to Peace' in The Middle East that will allow for the formation of a sovereign Palestinian State to co-exist along-side Israel, possibly pushing Israel's official borders back to the territory she controlled before the 1967 Six Day War, and giving the 'occupied territories' of Judea, Samaria, and Gaza to the Palestinians. Neither Israel nor the Palestinians are overly happy with this proposal, but Israel is tired of the terrorism and lack of security for her citizens. Therefore, the Israeli Government reluctantly is allowing this plan to proceed so that peace and safety can be attained. However, God is not pleased with this arrangement. He gave Israel all the land she now controls during The War of Independence fought in 1948, and subsequently in the [86]1967 Six Day War, including The Temple Mount in Jerusalem, and The West Bank. He will eventually give them much more. [87]But meanwhile,[88] Israel and the

---

[86] Jerusalem Post Internet Edition, <www.jpost.com/App/cs/ComtentServer?pagename+JPost...> Jun.12, 2002. *Stop Apologizing for 1967*. Michael Freund, Deputy Director of Communications & Policy Planning in the Prime Minister's Office from 1996 to 1999. "Israel did not occupy Judea, Samaria, and Gaza – we won them fair and square in an act of self-defense. The war of 1967 was one that Israel neither asked for nor initiated. And the time has come for us to stop apologizing for winning it."

[87] Israel's Prime Minister is appearing to be deceptive toward his own fellow citizens. He always supported the Yesha Settlements. In fact, he initiated many of them! Women in Green Hour, November 27, 2002. Ruth Matar. Before elections, Sharon stated in reference to Arafat, Sept, 3, 1993, "You can't dance

other nations are playing games with God's Covenant Lands. They are all hedging to one another about the outcome, and about the reasons they are even taking part in the negotiations. Every now and then someone actually states the case truthfully, and they are quickly denounced or ignored by both sides. So this game is being played by those on both sides.

Out of all this deception, there will emerge an agreement that will allow Israel to exist as a nation, and <u>probably there will at least be an interim Palestinian State as well</u>. All the nations who have had anything to do with this whole scenario will then feel they have accomplished a momentous feat. <u>They will have achieved peace in The Middle East</u>! NOT! All nations will have to recognize this accomplishment, both those allied with, and those against Israel, because the 'Quartet' which is the UN, the EU, the USA, and Russia, who all have been partner architects, will have to concede to the terms, and will require ratification and compliance. Israel will set about to bring some normalcy and a sense of security within her borders. The Palestinian State, because of its newness, also will revel in a degree of peacefulness, but they will nonetheless be disgruntled, because <u>they will not have the entire West Bank</u>, or absolute control of Jerusalem. So not everyone will be ecstatic about this arrangement! As a result, the "*Peace and Safety*" will be bogus.

Because Russia, along with all nations, must ratify this solution to what was a very difficult world problem, she should be able to sit back and relish her accomplishment. But she doesn't. <u>It suddenly occurs to her</u> that perhaps the Palestinians still do not have what they want, and anyway, there are resources to be had in the region. The people of The Middle East are secure. They have the possibility to become wealthy and contented. Why not get in on it? Or better yet, why not take over and obtain all the Land and the wealth for herself, or for her allies? She therefore sidles up to the Islamic world, who she has always had sympathetic alignment with anyway, and talks them into joining her in a rather aggressive plan to take

---

with a murderer." August 14, 1994, Sharon stated that Jerusalem is the capitol of Israell, because of the Temple Mount. November, 2, 1994,That "Jordan is the existing Palestinian State, there should be no other." But now PM Sharon supports the formation of a Palestinian State carved out of Gaza and West BankIsraeli land. The voters feel betrayed.
[88] Arutz-Sheva <IsraelNationalNews.com>, Women In Green Hour, May 7, 2003, Some recent quotes by PM Sharon: "I am ready to make painful concessions." "I know we will have to part with some of these places." "Eventually there will be a Palestinian State." " I will definitely say we will have to take steps that will be painful for the Jews."

over The Middle East. Now this plan sits very well with the Islamic mindset, since this is actually what they have been wanting all along. They accept Russia's plan of action, knowing it will further their own agenda of world Islamic domination, and particularly of annihilating Israel.

Or, this same result may be arrived at by the Islamic nations sidling up to Russia for major leadership and support in invading Israel to wipe her out. Russia agrees, then realizes this could really be very much to her benefit.

Either way, the West is left out of these deliberations, and is duped into believing all is finally well in The Middle East. Israel is secure, and the Palestinians apparently are happy. But are they? The Palestinians actually do not like the presence of Israel. They do not want any long-term co-existence. They would rather have Israel a footnote to history. But catching wind of the Russian/ Islamic Arab League Plan, they manage to remain calm and collected, hoping to take Israel by surprise. Now, calm and collected is very difficult when your mandate is Jihad! Russia and all the hoards of her diabolical scheme proceed to put together a military machine that is remarkable in strength, expertise, and armaments, and swoop down quickly, and unexpectedly, upon the mountains of The West Bank.

Now the democratic West is fully awake! What is Russia doing? Russia is one of the architects of the Peace! <u>She already knows Israel is supposed to be at peace because she helped to orchestrate it</u>! That is why verse 14 of Ezekiel chapter 12 states, "*...<u>In that day when my people of Israel dwell safely, shalt thou not know it</u>?*" This verse is not a question so much as it is a statement of fact and incredulity! Of course she knows it! So what is she doing? The only thing the West can think of is that she has become a turncoat. So the nations of the West ask, verse 13, "*Art thou come to take a spoil? Hast thou gathered thy company to take a prey? to carry away silver and gold, to take away cattle and goods, to take a great spoil?*" This series of honest questions indicates the nations of the West cannot believe what they see happening! Since the fall of Communism, Russia has taken a non-aggressive stand. So it will appear out of character for Russia and her allies to purposely break the international agreement that gives recognition of the right for <u>Palestine and Israel to co-exist safely within secure borders</u>.

What the West at first does not realize, is just how close to the truth this accusation really is! According to Ezekiel 38 verse 10, Gog <u>does</u> have a sudden thought! "*Thus saith the Lord God, It shall come to pass, that <u>at the same time shall things come into thy mind</u>, and <u>thou shalt think an evil thought</u>.*" Emphasis mine. At the same time as what? When Israel finally dwells safely, and many are returning to the land out of many peoples, in the latter years according to verse 8. But what is the evil thought? Verses 11 and 12. *"And thou shalt say, I will go up to the land of unwalled villages; I will go to them that are at rest, that dwell safely, all of them dwelling without walls, and having neither bars nor gates, to take a spoil, and to take a prey; to turn thine hand upon the desolate places that are now inhabited, and upon the people that are gathered out of the nations, which have gotten cattle and goods, that dwell in the midst of the land."*

What part of The Land is Gog particularly interested in? The mountains of Israel! Where are the mountains of Israel? They are the backbone of The Middle East region running along the Jordan rift. In other words, The West Bank! The Hill Country of Judea and Samaria! Just when the problem of the 'occupied territories' and the Palestinians has finally been resolved, Russia opens up the whole can of worms again!

It would appear then, that if there does happen to be a Palestinian State formed, the interim negotiated land settlement may actually end up being Gaza and possibly only the Samaria part of the West Bank, where most of the Palestinians live anyway. Israel, according to this passage, still has jurisdiction over much of The West Bank, because Ezekiel refers to the mountains as belonging to Israel, and even occupied by those who have been gathered out of many nations. (So, the halting of expansion of the settlements by Israel, being one of the negotiated conditions required by 'The Road Map,' somehow never does result in total dismantlement of these settlements, at least in Judea.) Now, to open up the controversy again won't be overly difficult for the Palestinians, because they will not be at all happy with their lot. So the whole powder keg will go off again! Only this time, no one, not Israel, or the West, or even Russia and her allies, has any understanding of the extent of the explosion this will cause world-wide!

All the nations up to this juncture have ignored God's plans for The Middle East, and particularly for Israel. But, they will all have to face Him. He will not be pleased with the divisive agreement that the nations reach regarding His Covenant Land. The nations of the world, including Israel, are seeking to carve it up, thinking that in doing so, they will achieve a wonderful thing, namely peace. But it all is being accomplished using deceit, and not according to God's Covenant. God has a vested interest in His Covenant with Israel, and His wishes cannot be pre-empted. So He will allow the whole situation to blow up in order to bring all nations into The Middle East to discuss this controversy with Him. Only, His manner of discussion will be through the discipline of war. His patience by this time will have pretty much run out with the nations, and with Israel. He will gather them all, then proceed to mete out a harsh lesson.

Meanwhile, the LORD does not want His Bride, the Church, to have to face His wrath, so He orchestrates a plan that will draw the nations up short, and at the same time provide a cover for removing the Church to safety. At the Rosh HaShanah judgment, all people of the earth are judged according to whether they are Rashim (wicked), or Tzadikim (wholly righteous), or intermediately secular and nominal. The sounding of The Last Trump of Rosh HaShanah separates the Tzadikim out from the other two groups, and removes them to a place of safety and blessing. Those left behind live through the judgments and wrath of God upon the earth. But the process begins with the call to battle. The Ten Days of Awe are ushered in immediately following the Rapture and The Battle of Gog and Magog which begins pre-Rapture. In a sense, The Battle is a transition from the Dispensation of Grace to the Dispensation of Awe.

The Holy Spirit's role in His fullness, power, and restraint of evil, will be removed along with the Church. But there will be one last chance for nations and individuals to examine their hearts and repent during the ten year span of The High Holy Days. Many people from among the nations of the world will repent during this time, so God seals the 144,000 Jewish Evangelists to preach and teach throughout the world. He pours out the severity of His wrath during the final seven years of The Ten Days of Awe, known as the Tribulation, or Daniel's 70th Week. This 70th Week is intended to discipline the nations, and in particular Israel, and turn the hearts of the Israelis fully back to Himself.

So what is the purpose of The Battle of Gog and Magog? To set the world stage for the Rapture of the Church, to prepare the world to receive one final concentrated evangelistic campaign, and to bring all nations under God's wrath and discipline, and give Israel jurisdiction over the 'Tents of Judah." The LORD has a controversy with those who attempt to divide up His Covenant Land, Israeli or otherwise, and who wish to scatter His Covenant people. That is essentially what The Battle of Gog and Magog is really all about! God uses this controversy to set the world stage for the Dispensation of Wrath.

2. The Location of the Battle of Gog and Magog:

Notice where The Battle of Gog and Magog takes place. <u>Upon the mountains of Israel, among the settlements that are not walled</u>. The King of the North states, "*I will go up to the land of unwalled villages.*" Ezekiel 38: 11. Daniel describes this invasion as well, and sheds some light on these unwalled villages. Daniel 11:15. "*So the king of the north shall come, and cast up a mount, and take the <u>most fenced cities</u>: and the arms of the south shall* not withstand, neither his chosen people, neither shall there be any strength to withstand." How do we know this is the same invasion? Daniel indicates this king also turns his face toward the Isles, and destroys many in the process. Daniel 11:18-19. *"After this shall he turn his face unto the isles, and shall take many; but a prince on his own behalf shall cause the reproach offered by him to cease; without his own reproach he shall cause it to turn upon him. Then he shall turn his face toward the fort of his own land: but he shall stumble and fall, and not be found."*

It appears there will be another leader, called a *"prince,"* who manages to turn this whole scenario around. A ruling-class Prince of Saudi Arabia? The ruling Prince of Kuwait? These are very possible princes who could definitely turn against a Russian/Arab alliance. The Arab world is not as consolidated and co-operative among themselves as some think. The Isles, the USA, Britain etc. are among the alliance that Ezekiel states are against the king who comes out of the north. When it suits their purposes, some of the smaller Arab nations will co-operate with the West. We certainly see this configuration as it has developed in dealing with Saddam Hussein. So the alignment of antagonists certainly does seem to suggest we are headed toward Gog and Magog shortly.

Russia, who can be identified as a major leader and provider in The Gog-Magog War, appears to be the catalyst to undertake this campaign. Thus this coming war has been referred to as The Russian Invasion of Israel. Russia at the moment is siding strongly with the Palestinians in regard to the formation of the Palestinian State, taking a much harder line on it than the USA or any other members of the Quartet. It would be easy to see how she will be swayed into the Arab Muslim camp, and have Persia (Iran and Iraq), Syria, Ethiopia and Libya, Gomer (Eastern Europe), and Togarmah (Turkey and the nations surrounding the Black and Caspian Seas), the South and Western countries of the former Communist Bloc, all join together with her in this war. They all basically are of the same mind-set against Israel.

On the other hand, the United States, the European Union, and the United Nations, although also negotiating for the formation of a Palestinian State, have a softer stance in regard to Israel. They are trying to broker a peace deal that will satisfy everyone, so as to bring atrocities and animosities permanently to an end in The Middle East. This is the stance of all the Young Lions, the offspring of The British Empire. They generally view themselves as friends of Israel, but in all fairness, are trying to be friends of the Palestinians as well. But this stance, borne from a strong belief in human rights, and the right to secure self-determination of both the Israelis and Palestinians, will not be enough to stop the aggression of those who actually desire to annihilate Israel and take The Land of Covenant for themselves and for their own gain. Sheba and Dedan, and the merchants of Tarshish, The Isles, and the Young Lions, in other words, most of what we refer to as the Western World, will not be in favor of the invasion of Israel, no matter what the apparent provocation.

God also will not be pleased with this military effort to force Israel to give up jurisdiction over any part of The Land of Covenant. Five-sixths of the invading army will be destroyed on the mountains of Israel, and the King of the North, and all who are with him, are going to be turned back, severely whipped. Meanwhile, this northern army will be further frustrated and decimated by news behind and to the East that will require immediate military intervention. This could be threats from China, or North Korea; or quite possibly from the uprising of any of the former Soviet Bloc Muslim provinces and states along Russia's southern borders. Georgia, Chechnia, or even Afghanistan or Kashmir could upset the balance of power. For Russia and her allies, the timing will not be good! Certainly the tension between India and Pakistan over Kashmir has proven to be a very real threat with the saber-rattling threat of erupting into all-out nuclear war. Everyone will want to keep a lid on that situation as long as possible, but can the impasse last for long? Is it possible that God is keeping the situations developing in the East as a trump card to play, preventing The Battle of Gog and Magog from achieving the desire to wipe out Israel, His People and Covenant Land?

C. The Raiser of Taxes:

Immediately following Gog and Magog, and the defeat of the King of the North, there is a brief rise to power of a leader who raises taxes, but his regime stumbles and falls quickly. Daniel 11:20. *"Then shall stand up in his estate a raiser of taxes in the glory of the kingdom: but within few days he shall be destroyed, neither in anger, nor in battle."* I will expand on the significance of this leader later in the book. Following this brief interlude, the AntiChrist rises to power.

D. Unwalled Villages and Fenced Cities:

In ancient times, most of the larger cities of The Middle East region had thick stone walls surrounding them. But the smaller communities in Canaan were encompassed with what is described as stone fences that brought some protection, but were not generally as thick or secure as the walls surrounding the major cities. When Israel entered the Land of

TENTS OF JUDAH, and GOG AND MAGOG

Canaan the first time, she was told to conquer all the cities and towns, and most of them are referred to in Scripture as being 'fenced' or 'walled'.

But The Battle of Gog and Magog, when the King of the North comes against Israel, does not take place in ancient times. Ezekiel and Daniel speak regarding The Gog-Magog Battle taking place during a time when there are <u>fenced cities and unwalled villages</u>. The question is, does Israel currently have fenced cities as well as unwalled communities? Yes! [89] And they are definitely controversial. The timing of when these fences are an issue indicates how close we are to the end of this Age. They are a bone of contention when the *"great Day of the LORD <u>is near, it is near, and hasteth greatly</u>."* Zephaniah 1:14a. The term 'the Day of The LORD' denotes The Day of Judgment, Yom HaDin, also called The Day of Wrath, Rosh HaShanah. This Day of Judgment ushers in Yamim Nora'im, The Days of Awe.

[90]The contention over[91] fences and small settlement communities is currently raging. The wording in Zephaniah regarding the approach of

---

[89] Arutz-7, February 11, 2004, *PROFS: "DISPENSE WITH THE FENCE!"*, "As Israel prepares to defend itself at The Hague in the upcoming deliberations about the alleged illegality of the counter-terrorism fence it is building aside heavily Arab-populated areas, there are those within Israel who wish to remind the public that even within Israel the partition is a matter of intense debate. In a lengthy statement to the media, "Professors for a Strong Israel" explains why it is "Time to Dispense with the Fence." Excerpts:
"Given the anticipated complications at the Israeli High Court of Justice and at the International Court at the Hague regarding the fence and its placement;
"Given the extraordinarily high cost of the fence and its uncertain cost-effectiveness...
"Given the alternate uses to which this money could be put, by investing both in more effective deterrents against [terrorists], and in the sorely needed social programs that are suffering cutbacks in the current social and economic crisis;
"Given the suffering endured by [both Arabs and Jews]...
"Given the undoubted future 'sacrifices to the fence' among soldiers who will need to patrol and secure it in order for it to be functional at all;
"Given the ability to circumvent the fence by tunneling under or by shooting over...
"Given the damage to the environment incurred by the fence's construction and maintenance;
"Given the unfortunate message of weakness and capitulation that the fence's construction broadcasts to the enemy -
"Professors for a Strong Israel strongly advises the Government of Israel to dispense with the fence of the absurd, and to move from the defensive to the offensive."
[90] The Washington Post Foreign Service, February 10, 2004, John Ward

The Final Schedule Revealed

The Day of The LORD is urgent, repeating itself for emphasis. This is a warning to be heeded! The Day of the LORD is imminent. The Day of The LORD is coming, and it is coming with haste! No more waiting for some day far off in the nebulous future.

Notice Zephaniah 1:14-16. "<u>The great day of the LORD is near, it is near, and hasteth greatly, even the voice of the day of the LORD</u>: the mighty man shall cry there bitterly. Verse 15. <u>That day is a day of wrath</u>, a <u>day of trouble and distress</u>, a day of wasteness and desolation, a day of clouds and thick darkness, Verse 16. <u>A day of the trumpet</u> and <u>alarm against the fenced cities</u>, and against the high towers." Underlining mine. The fenced cities mentioned here are in context with <u>the voice of The Day of The LORD</u>, the <u>Day of Wrath</u>, the <u>Day of Trouble and Distress</u>, <u>a day of clouds and thick darkness</u>, and <u>the Day of the Trumpet</u>! All these taken together describe the scenario of The Battle

---

Anderson, *Israel Hems In a Sacred City, Encircling of Jerusalem Complicates Prospects for Peace,* JERUSALEM -- "Israel is close to finishing a decades-long effort to surround Jerusalem with Jewish settlements, walls, fences and roads that will severely restrict Palestinian access to the city and could reduce the chance of its becoming the capital of a Palestinian state, according to documents, maps and interviews with Israelis, Palestinians and foreign diplomats. At the same time, a new barrier combining trenches, walls, electronic sensors and steel fences is being built around Jerusalem. The project, part of a large fence that is designed to cordon off the West Bank, has split some Palestinian neighborhoods and separated many Palestinians from their schools, jobs, families and lands."
"Israeli officials say that several of the measures are designed to deter the movement of Palestinian terrorists from the West Bank into Israel and that others are aimed at increasing the proportion of Jews in Jerusalem. Palestinians describe the measures as an attempt to break their religious, economic, political and cultural ties to the city and preempt negotiations over its final status."
[91] Israelinsider magazine, February 13, 2004. Ellis Shuman *Israel won't participate in Hague court hearings on fence,* "Israel will not participate in the oral hearings on the legality of the security fence at the International Court of Justice (ICJ) in The Hague this month, a ministerial committee headed by Prime Minister Ariel Sharon decided yesterday. The committee said the court has no authority to discuss the fence; Israel will suffice with its already submitted written affidavit. The Palestinians called Israel's decision an admission of guilt."
"The ICJ has no authority to discuss the terrorism prevention fence since it concerns Israel's basic right of self-defense," a statement issued by the Prime Minister's Media Adviser said. The ministers made their decision based on recommendations from officials in the Foreign and Justice Ministries, and after consideration of the positions of other countries, including the United States, Great Britain, Germany and Australia, which have also determined the court has no jurisdiction in the case."

of Gog and Magog, following which God will pour out His wrath during the coming Days of Awe. They particularly describe Rosh HaShanah. The mention of the clouds and thick darkness pretty much ties it up. When the sun is darkened and the moon turned to blood as a result of this Battle, the day will certainly be dark!

Accompanying this war scenario will be the sounding of a Trumpet, and the Voice of the LORD. That sounds very much like The Last Trump of Rosh Hashanah! I Thessalonians 4: 15 -17. "...*we which are alive and remain unto the coming of the Lord shall not prevent (precede) them which are asleep. For the Lord himself shall descend from heaven with a shout, with the voice of the archangel, and with the tromp of God: and the dead in Christ shall rise first, Then we which are alive and remaining shall be caught up together with them, to meet the Lord in the air...*"The Rapture, therefore, may occur while these fenced communities are under attack during the Russian Invasion, The Battle of Gog and Magog.

What does this mean? There is a current phenomenon in Israel. Due to the terrorist attacks that have mushroomed since the Intifada began in 2000, and especially since September 11, 2001, the Ariel Sharon government has, as part of its security measures, mandated the Israeli Defense Forces to contract massive lengths of barbed wire and concrete fences, cordoning off much of The West Bank, and parts of Gaza. These fences are supposedly being erected to protect the smaller Israeli communities by not allowing terrorists to be able to move about easily. They also are to facilitate the screening of people entering and leaving Israel. [92]They are particularly supposed to act as protection for Jerusalem and the surrounding settlements in Judea and Samaria.

There are many Israeli settlements and so-called 'out-posts' in The West Bank and Gaza, together known as Yesha. Palestinian towns exist there as well. [93]Yesha is under controversy, because the Arab Muslims

---

[92] Washington Post Foreign Service, www.washingtonpost.com , February 10, 2004, John Ward Anderson, *Israel hems In a Sacred City*. "Israel is close to finishing a decades-long effort to surround Jerusalem with Jewish settlements, walls, fences and roads that will severely restrict Palestinian access to the city, and could reduce the chance of its becoming the capital of a Palestinian state, according to documents, maps, and interviews with Israelis, Palestinians, and foreign diplimats."

[93] Arutz-7News Service, <www.IsraelNationalNews.com> March 3. 2004, Daniel Pipes, Director of the Middle East forum. *The Legality of the Yesha Settlements, Article for Israel national News*. "The director of the Middle East Forum explains that such a position "assumes that Palestinians seek only to gain control over the West Bank and Gaza, whereas overwhelming evidence points

The Final Schedule Revealed

want to secure these regions for themselves as a spoil, to oust Israel from the Territories, and form a Palestinian State. They want the agriculture, the towns, the land, and all the wealth that Israel has managed to produce in these areas.

[94]Fencing these communities is extremely controversial, especially for the Arabs, and also because many Jews do not see any benefit. They feel the fencing is becoming a barrier of animosity, and actually increasing attempted violence against innocent citizens. They cannot understand why the Israeli government is fencing in the 'good guys,' making its own citizens prisoners in their own communities, and leaving the 'bad guys' outside the fences to do whatever they want! They feel the fences will give people a sense of false security, and allow terrorists to approach with impunity to within reach of homes and businesses, and simply lob their terrorist grenades and missiles over the fence. Also, considering the

---

to their also aspiring to go further and control Israel proper. Therefore, pulling Israelis from the territories does no good. In fact, it probably does harm. Imagine that Israelis were uprooted and the Israel Defense Forces pulled back to the 1967 boundaries... Palestinians will see a pullback signaling that Israel is weak, appeasing and vulnerable. Far from showing gratitude, they will make greater demands. With Jenin and Ramallah in the maw, Jerusalem will be next on the agenda, followed by Tel Aviv and Haifa."″

[94] Jerusalem Post, Internet Edition, February, 23, 2004, Khaled Abu Toameh, *Arafat: Fence prevents PA State; Rage day declared.* "The wall that Israel is constructing is meant to prevent the establishment of an independent Palestinian State, with Jerusalem as its capital," Arafat said."
"An hour before the opening of the hearings at the International Court of Justice at The Hague, the Palestinian leader said, "We announce today to the whole world: The apartheid wall turns our towns into jails, our people to prisoners."
"Calling on Israelis to join the international objection to the fence, Arafat warned, "the 'settlement wall' will not bring security nor peace to the region,"
"Arafat also accused Israel of preventing Palestinians - Muslim and Christians - from visiting their respective holy sites. "Jerusalem is being separated from us, the holy city were Christ lived and died, where the prophet Mohammad ascended to heaven for his famous night journey.
"Hebron as well is being separated by the wall, so we cannot reach the holy Abraham mosque," Arafat added.
"Arafat spoke of the international objection to the security fence, mentioning Pope John Paul II condemnation of the fence. "This is not the way to achieve true peace between Palestinians and Israelis," he concluded.
"In his speech, broadcast from his West Bank headquarters, Arafat urged his people to "make their voices heard against this wall of expansion and annexation."

jihad mind-set of the Palestinian terrorist groups, those living in these communities suspect these fences will be viewed as barriers to challenge and breach, giving provocation for the terrorists to destroy those inside the fences. Also, many Palestinians are certainly being discriminated against as a result of this fence. Many have had their lands or farms carved up, or their routes to get easily to and from their businesses and jobs cut-off. So it is not a stretch to understand why these controversial barriers could play a part in encouraging Israel's enemies to attack and destroy!

These fences are not being erected without international attention. In fact, the Palestinians, along with several other Arab States, have filed a case against Israel at The Hague, claiming the fence is a violation of international law. [95]This hearing is taking place now at The Hague International Court of Justice. Israel has chosen to merely send a written declaration of her rightful position to defend her citizens against terrorists, and that the International Court of Justice has no real jurisdiction to rule on the matter. Major protest delegations on both sides of the issue have held demonstrations outside The Hague, and a mock-up trial has been staged to air the views for the international public to hear.

The King of the North may just look at the fences, and realize they could be a great asset to be used for his purposes, because they provide no real honest defense capability for Israel. Fences are not a barrier for planes and missiles. Ground troops can breach them relatively easily. So why not attack?

The fenced areas contain groups of smaller settlements and out-posts that are not fenced at all. In fact, it is the purpose of the fencing to eliminate the need to individually fence off each of the smaller communities. The security fencing also does not fit the true definition of the ancient fences, which were actual walls, and although they may be up to twelve feet or more in height, (some near Jerusalem are 24 feet high!) hardly fit the defense capabilities the ancient walls afforded. [96]War is not fought in the same manner, or with the same weapons as were used in ancient times. Therefore, essentially all the smaller communities and neighborhoods

---

[95] The Jerusalem Post Internet Edition, www.jpost.com February 2, 2004, Khalid Abu Toameh, *Arafat: The Hague must discuss fence*.

[96] Arutz Sheva News Service, www.israelnationalnews.com. February 25, 2004, *GSS CHIEF: P.A. TERRORISTS WORKING ON MISSILES TO BYPASS FENCE.*, "The Arabs of the Palestinian Authority, Dichter told the Foreign Affairs and Defense Committee yesterday, "are investing heavily in making weapons to get around the partition, such as long-range artillery." Neither the fence nor Sharon's planned disengagement would have any affect on such weapons, he said."

these fences are supposed to protect can be defined as *'unwalled villages!'* It's amazing how Scripture is so descriptively accurate!

Many feel that the placement of the security fences (which run close to, but not necessarily specifically along The Green Line) will act as a demarcation which will actually cause Israel to be unable to maintain a lasting grip on her right to the Territories. In essence, Israel is erecting a false border by putting the fences up, and this realization is feeding the Palestinian cause, because they see its presence as capitulation, and recognition by Israel that in essence the lands outside the fences are indeed Palestinian, not Israeli. So not only will the fences play into the hands of the enemy by possibly demarcating a division of The Land, but they could conceivably be a point of concession in the deliberations of the placing of the borders for the proposed Palestinian State! Of course this reasoning is totally against the Covenant of God. Even so, the Israeli government is insisting that the security fencing contracts continue. The people of Israel recognize that the fences represent a danger to Israeli sovereignty. Their government obviously does not, or if they do recognize the danger, they are willing to live with it if it means peace and safety may eventually result.

The security fences are scheduled to be complete within the next few months. The target date for the implementation of an interim Palestinian State originally was to be accomplished in 2003, but now the target is some time during 2004. So the pieces are all in place for the fulfillment of Scripture, right down to the fences, which will play a major role in the lead up to The Battle of Gog and Magog!

Let me interject an example of how the fenced cities and the unwalled settlements may indeed play a major role in the provocation for the King of the North to march on the mountains of Israel. When the Intifida was at the height of terrorism last year, and Jenine and Ramallah were under curfew to allow the Israeli Defense Force surveillance to search for terrorists, Ariel Sharon indicated to Arafat and the terrorist factions that if they did not cease their atrocities, Israel would step up and expand their settlement activities in the Territories. They have since adopted a stance of possible unilateral withdrawal from Gaza and some of the West Bank instead. But why would either move be a threat to the Palestinians?

In order to understand, we need to know something about how these settlements come about. They are sanctioned, and even orchestrated by the Israeli Government. However, these are not military installations and spy centers, as some have tried to tell us. Rather, they are legitimate settlements of Israeli immigrants, allowing expansion of Israel's agricultural base, and the building of peaceful family communities. The settlements also do increase security by bringing stability to a region. ⁹⁷However, the Palestinians and the international media have billed these settlements as illegal. ⁹⁸They are not at all illegal. In order for anyone to settle, they must obtain a permit issued by the Israeli government.

Also, the so-called 'illegal outposts' are not actually illegal either, even though permits are not always necessarily issued. ⁹⁹The Israeli Government has sanctioned, and even encouraged these outposts, sending settlers in to either occupy, or to use outpost sheds and caravans for storage or fuel supply. Many of the outposts lie within already permitted settlement areas, so do not require any further permits. The rest have been set up under government sanction for security reasons.

¹⁰⁰The Israeli government has made it a policy to settle families in areas where no one previously owned the land. No Palestinian, or

---

⁹⁷ Arutz Sheva English Program, www.IsraelNationalNews.com, Women in Green Hour with Ruth Matar, June 25, 2003. *Are Settlements in Judea and Samaria Legal?* "Keeping up with the policies of recent American presidents with regard to Jewish settlement in Judea, Samaria, and Gaza is like riding a roller coeaster. Former President Jimmy Carter decreed that Jewish settlements were illegal, Former President Ronald Reagan, on the other hand, always maintained that Jewish settlements in Judea, Samaria, and Gaza Strip were perfectly legal. The Bush Senior administration seemed to consider the West Bank and Gaza Strip to be 'foreign' territory to which Israel has no claim. Bill Clinton's Secretary of State, Madeleine Albright, had to reluctantly admit that Jews had a perfect right to settle in Judea, Samaria, and Gaza, but thought that this did not promote peace. President George W. Bush follows in his fathers footsteps..."
"... Palestine has never existed as an autonomous state. Palestinians are Arabs, indistinguishable from Jordanians, Syrians, Lebanese, Iraqis, etc."
"The President of the United States and the Prime Minister of Great Britain, and the leaders of Russia and Germany and France and the EU and the UN, none have the right to endorse the creation of a Palestinian state in Israel, nor should they demand that Israel violate G_d's covenant. Who put you all on the throne of G_d and gave you the right to violate G_d's covenant?"

⁹⁸ Arutz-7. <www.IsraelNationalNews.com> March 3, 2004, Quoted in the article, *The Legality of the Yesha Settlements* :Eugene Rostow, Distinguished Fellow at the United States Institute of Peace, has written the following (The New Republic, October 21, 1991):
"United Nations Resolution 242, which as undersecretary of state for political affairs between 1966 and 1969 I helped produce, calls on the parties to make peace and allows Israel to administer the territories it occupied in 1967 until "a just and lasting peace in the Middle East" is achieved. When such a peace is made, Israel is required to withdraw its armed forces "from territories" it

anyone else in recent history, has held legal title-deed to any of the lands occupied by these settlements or outposts. Neither were these lands used for agriculture, or any form of development, until the Israelis regained these areas fair and square as a result of the 1967 Six Day War. But the Palestinians are accusing Israel and the settlers of taking their lands from them as if they actually formerly lived in and owned these areas. Israel has never ousted legal Palestinian Arab land-owners to replace them with Israeli families. Homes and parcels of land have been bought and sold, Arab to Israeli, but these have all been totally legal, and at the wishes of the parties involved.

The land parcels designated for settlement are large. When Israelis are given permits to settle, they usually group themselves into small villages, both for protection as well as for convenience. They cannot expand so quickly as to settle families on the full extent of a permitted area all at once, so there is already permitted land for growth. The Palestinians have been sending illegal squatters into these legally-permitted lands to make life difficult for the Israeli settlers, and to deceive the rest of the world

---

occupied during the Six-Day War--not from "the" territories nor from "all" the territories, but from some of the territories, which included the Sinai Desert, the West Bank, the Golan Heights, East Jerusalem, and the Gaza Strip...

"The British Mandate recognized the right of the Jewish people to "close settlement" in the whole of the Mandated territory. It was provided that local conditions might require Great Britain to "postpone" or "withhold" Jewish settlement in what is now Jordan... But the Jewish right of settlement in Palestine west of the Jordan river, that is, in Israel, the West Bank, Jerusalem, and the Gaza Strip, was made unassailable. That right has never been terminated and cannot be terminated except by a recognized peace between Israel and its neighbors. And perhaps not even then, in view of Article 80 of the U.N. Charter, "the Palestine article," which provides that "nothing in the Charter shall be construed ... to alter in any manner the rights whatsoever of any states or any peoples or the terms of existing international instruments...."

[99] Women In Green Hour, Israel National News, October 23, 2002, www.I isralenetionalnews.com. *What Does the Bible Have to Say About Jewish Settlers?* Outposts are approved by the government.

[100] Arutz-7 Ruth Matar Radio Show, September 11, 2002, *Morality in the Israeli Defense Forces*, < michaele@netvision.net.il>, September 11. 2002. From an open letter to Dr. Sacks by Robert Miller. "You know, (or at least your should) better than anyone that the vast majority of the land Israelis now live on in Judea and Samaria, including East Jerusalem, was either vacant or legally owned by Jews and purchased by the Jewish National Fund, and only became "Arab" after the Jordanians committed ethnic cleansing against the Jewish population there in 1948."

into believing they own tracts of land there. When the Israeli government comes in to dismantle the illegal buildings, the rest of the Arab world and the international media accuse Israel of trashing Palestinian homes and lands. We have all seen news clippings where Israeli bulldozers have been sent to settlements to destroy Palestinian housing. But these have been illegal homes, which have been proven to be breeding grounds for terrorist organization activity, and they have been constructed illegally on Israeli Settlement land. They must be removed!

Certainly there have been Palestinians who were evacuated from specified areas because of war. But these evacuations were not orchestrated by the Israelis, but were carried out by the intervention of Arab League nations. There are only a few former Palestinian villages where the residents were evacuated and have since not been allowed to return for security reasons, to protect the Palestinians themselves. Actually, most Palestinian communities have been re-occupied by Palestinians.

Also, the so-called 'Right of Return' is a half-truth. The Arab League forced many Palestinians to leave during the 1948 War of Independence. And many more emigrated of their own accord to Jordan and other Arab States. Now Israel is being blamed for uprooting them. Also, the numbers who wish to 'return' have been severely inflated. The Palestinians talk of multiplied thousands, whereas the evacuations actually affected only a few thousand. The inflated numbers come from Palestinians who chose to emigrate and now want to return, or who have immigrated to Israel since 1948 and 1967, and who are now wanting other family members to join them.

Along with the controversy over settlements and outposts, many Palestinians have made a point of trying to tell the world that Israel is keeping them in refugee camps. Certainly some still live in communities that originally were set up as refugee camps, but it is by their own choice that they remain there. In fact, the Israelis can't seem to get them to move out! Why? These camps are useful for Palestinian propaganda, and are proven breeding grounds to plan terrorist activity. So if they live in squalid conditions, it is by their own choice. As long as they refuse to respond as full citizens, and as long as terrorist groups hide among them, they will continue to inherit the heavy hand of curfews, restrictions, and IDF monitoring.

Does the media make us aware of all this? No! They cause the masses to believe lies. Does the Israeli Government attempt to correct the media bias? No! They are afraid to speak up too dogmatically on these land issues for fear of reprisals from the Palestinian terrorists and the surrounding Arab countries. Why haven't the Palestinians really pushed their so-called claims legally? Because legally they have no leg to stand on, and they are afraid the international community will discover the truth so that they will have no place to live at all. As long as they can make everyone believe they are being treated badly, they have leverage to twist the sympathetic arm of the international community.

[101]As one of the terms of the 'Roadmap to Peace' under negotiation by the 'Quartet,' Israel is being told to dismantle the settlements in the territories. This is totally unfair, but Ariel Sharon, the Israeli Prime Minister, has indicated he is willing to do so unilaterally, even if the Palestinians will not stop all atrocities. The United States and the European Union are not totally favorable toward the unilateral approach. The settlements have been placed in jeopardy, and all the Israelis who legally occupy these settlements are in danger of losing their land and their livelihoods. Many are farmers, or make their living in support of agriculture. Also, most settlers believe the land they occupy actually does belong to Israel by Covenant according to Torah. According to them, [102]<u>The Covenant God made with Israel is ultimately the only title-deed any Israeli needs to occupy The Land.</u> [103]They have declared they will not be moved.

[101] ArutzSheva English Program, Women In Green Hour, www.IsraelNationalNews.com, June, 26, 2003. Ruth Matar, Transcript, *Are Settlements in Judea and Samaria Legal?* "Last Sunday night, 400 rabbis from all over the country met in Jerusalem to protest against the plan to give up parts of the Land of Israel to foreign rule. Former Chief Rabbi, Mordechai Eliyahu said: "No one, from the simplest person to even the Prime Minister, has the right to cede even one granule of the Land of Israel! The Holy One, Blessed be He, gave it to us! To us alone He gave it!"
Rabbi Dov Lior of Kiryat Arba said: "We will not make our security and safety dependent on conceding our rights to pieces of our Holy Land."
Rabbi Shlolom Gold, "We warned that the PLO had not given up its plan to defeat Israel in 'stages', and we pleaded with the government not to give them guns, and we warned that Jewish blood would flow in the Holy Land. What was the reaction? 'Rabbis, go back to your synagogues and yeshivas, and leave these issues to the people who really know – leave it to the military men, and the politicians, and the poets, and the talk-show hosts, and the other opinion-makers.' But we all now see the truth! We know how right we were, and how wrong we were! I say to the press: Read all the garbage that you wrote in the last ten years, and realize that the rabbis were right!"
"Mr. President Bush, you earned well-deserved admiration for your courageous and just actions in Iraq – but here in Israel, you have faltered. Deep down in your heart of hearts, you know there is absolutely no difference between ben Laden and Saddam Hussein, and Yasser Arafat! Only all-out war can crush what you called the 'axis of evil.' We call on you: Don't become the George Washington of a terrorist state alongside Israel! Please, listen to t he words of

Israel already has dismantled some of the outposts, (which are legal in that, although not settlements per se,' are generally on permitted tracts of land so do not need separate permit-deeds) and by doing so, is in essence conceding 'land for peace' already. Needless to say, this is not popular among the rural settlement folk who cry,[104] "Eretz Ysrael L'Am Ysrael." "The land of Israel belongs to the people of Israel." But the Government is not listening for fear of the Arabs. If this dismantlement does not appear to be happening fast enough, it is conceivable Russia could take exception, and use this issue as provocation to march against the settlements to force the Israelis out of The West Bank, and thus *"go up against the land of unwalled villages."* Or Russia could assist the Arab community under the same provocation.

E. The Outcome of The Gog-Magog Battle:

It would appear that the outcome of The Battle of Gog and Magog will be that Judah and Jerusalem will finally be given decisively into Israeli

---

the rabbis. Don't repeat the same mistakes of the last ten years.
Mr. Prime Minister Sharon: Don't do it! We're not occupiers – this is our very own land! Tell the world the Land is ours! Open a Bible and read it to them – they'll respect you for it! No one has the right to give away this Land, as it is ours in the past, present, and future. Mr. Prime Minister, Don't travel that road!" Emanuel Winston, Mid-East analyst, "Any leader of a country working with a foreign government to subvert that nation's plsitions would be considered treasonous. If Sharon has with malice aforethought stated that Israel's position in the territories is not 'in dispute', but tather, 'occupoed' to assist foreign governments, that is high treason in any language."
[102] Genesis 17:7-8. "I will establish my covenant between me and thee and thy seed after thee in their generation for an everlasting covenant, to be a God unto thee, and to tlhy seed after thee, And I will give unto thee, and to thy seed after thee, the land wherein thou art a stranger, all the land of Canaan, for an everlasting possession; and I will be their God."
[103] Arutz-7. <www.IsraelNationalNews.com>March 3, 2004, *Outposts Again in Danger*. Pinchas Wallerstein of Benjamin Regional Council."Let no one think that we should allow the Prime Minister to get away with his plan to take down the outposts. We will fight for each and every site. If we once thought that sacrificing an outpost would help save a community elsewhere in Yesha, let it be clear that there is no dialogue between us and the Prime Minister, and he is doing this only to prove to the Americans that he can take down all of Yesha - and this is what it will lead to."
[104] Women in Green, <wfit2@womeningreen.org> September 26,2002. *"We are fighting to retain possession of our Biblical Homeland."* Banners spread throughout Israel.

hands. But because Scripture indicates this deliverance is for the "<u>tents of Judah first</u>," <u>Jerusalem and her borders will also remain in contention until the end of the Tribulation</u>. Recall, tents are not necessarily permanent dwellings, so this deliverance will not be totally without controversy.

But since God has promised the *"tents of Judah"* will be saved first, Israel will be able to rebuild the Temple. Israel cannot, (nor will she even consider) build a Temple as long as she does not have full jurisdiction over The Temple Mount area. This cannot happen until something momentous enough occurs that will oust the Muslims from The Temple Mount, or at least take away the jurisdiction of the Palestinian Authority from overseeing the area of Mount Zion. It would take a war, or a major natural disaster (such as an earthquake, or even the collapse of the south wall of The Mount,) or a combination of both, to accomplish such a feat, because Muslims do not give up territory easily, especially territory they feel they have right to under Allah!

But notice that the nations are gathered purposely by the LORD to this battle to *"plead with them for my people and for **my heritage Israel**, whom they have scattered among the nations, and **parted my land**."* Bold emphasis mine. Joel 3:2. God considers Israel, <u>meaning all the descendants of Jacob</u>, His people and heritage. Why does He speak of them as His heritage? Because of the Covenant He made with Abraham, Isaac, Jacob, and with Moses regarding His relationship with Israel as His people by Covenant, and The Land as belonging to Israel by Covenant. Therefore, not only are they His heritage people, but The Land is His Covenant Land, and the nations have parted it and scattered its inhabitants several times, and will seek to do so again! Now that really does spell trouble for anyone attempting to divide The Land He gave by Covenant to Israel. The formation of a Palestinian State within The Covenanted Lands of Israel, which includes the 'disputed territories' will result in running into dispute with God Himself, and He will assemble the nations who attempt it into The Middle East to deal with them there about it! Thus, we have God's reasons for The Battle of Gog and Magog.

The result of this Battle does not mean that all of The West Bank disputed territories will be given into Israel's hands. Just <u>Judah</u> (which is Judea, the land occupied by the former Kingdom of The House of Judah) and <u>Jerusalem</u>, will be totally secured at this juncture. Zechariah chapter 12 indicates an interesting sequence. Verse 2: *"<u>Behold I will make Jerusalem a cup of trembling</u> unto **all the people round about**, <u>when they shall be in siege both against Judah and against Jerusalem</u>."* Underlining and bold mine. Notice, according to this verse, <u>Jerusalem and Judah are the major factors in the contention</u>. The Palestinians are wanting Jerusalem specifically to

TENTS OF JUDAH, and GOG AND MAGOG

be the capitol of their Palestinian State. Ariel Sharon, although working along with the Quartet's 'Road Map,' has stated Jerusalem is not on the table for negotiation. He is not in favor of any Palestinian government presence taking up headquarters in any sector of Jerusalem. This is a stand-off position he is taking, [105]because Arafat has also indicated that any Palestinian State will have Jerusalem as its seat of government. Jerusalem is indeed a burdensome stone! So it is pretty much a given that the Palestinians will not inherit the city of Jerusalem through negotiations. They will not control Jerusalem, <u>at least not for any extended length of time</u>. Thus the Palestinian disgruntlement when their own State is set up, and they don't get the full prize they are hoping 'The Road Map' will bring them.

And notice <u>who</u> is contentious, *"...all the people round about."* That would be the Arab nations. Iraq, Iran, Syria, Lebanon, Saudi Arabia, Egypt (it is unclear whether Egypt actually takes a military stand against Israel during The Gog-Magog Battle that follows. It would appear she is not a direct military contender at this juncture. But she may be a supplier and back-room coach.) Jordan, and of course the Palestinians, qualify also as being part of the *"people round about."* The Arabs! And therefore most interestingly, the Arab Muslims. This verse indicates which people are in contention regarding Jerusalem and Judah. Those nations surrounding her that want Jerusalem and Judah for themselves, and for their own agenda. All of the Arabs want the Palestinians to have a homeland called Palestine, with Jerusalem as its capitol.

Actually, they want all of the Land of Israel, including the 'occupied territories,' but Jerusalem and Judah are the plumb they are after at the moment. Their intention is like the camel and the tent. Once his nose is in the tent, no one can turn him around, or oust him, but he will obviously take over completely! We are witnessing the development of this scenario of contention right now. The controversy is over Israel's jurisdiction and borders, and the territory to be occupied by a Palestinian State.

---

[105] One Jerusalem News, <news@onejerusalem.org> January 22, 2002. Related News. *"Yasser Arafar wants a Palestinian state with Jerusalem as its capitol.* Arafat told a group of visitors to his headquarters in Ramallah yesterday, "I swear to god, I will see (the Palestinian State), whether as a martyr or alive. Please, god, give me the honor of becoming a martyr in the fight for Jerusalem."

The Final Schedule Revealed

IV. The 'Plan of Stages:'

[106]Notice the following. Moshe Ayalon, Chief of General Staff, Lt-Gen., speaking to an assembly of Rabbis in Jerusalem on August 25, 2002., "The PLO has never sought anything besides Israel's destruction, and is still trying to implement its "plan of stages" to annihilate Israel. The goal of the current Palestinian leadership is not a "two-state solution," but a Palestinian State as a stepping-stone toward the elimination of Israel as a Jewish state." Arutz SHEVA, Israeli National News.com. Opinion. Ruth Matar (Radio Show) September 1, 2002. Underlining mine.

[107]Also, from Nadia Matar, "Women for Israel's Tomorrow (Women in Green), Monday, August 26, 2002, "Quoted in HaAretz Aug 26, 2002, Ayalon says, among other things: that Palestinian violence threatens to contaminate and infect Israeli Arabs; that the PLO is still trying to implement its "plan of stages" leading to Israel's destruction; that the failure to supress Palestinian terror is leading to the radicalization of Israeli Arabs and their enlisting in terrorism; that the capitulation by Ehud Barak to Syria in Lebanon was a fiasco that led to escalated violence and terror by the Palestinians and made it impossible for Israel to get to negotiations with Syria because Barak proved to Syria that violence pays and is the best path; that the capitulation in Lebanon signaled to the Arabs that Israel is destructible; and that the PLO has never sought anything besides Israel's destruction."

Ruth Matar's Women in Green Hour on Arutz Sheva English Radio, August 28, 2002. "Iran, after the Khomeini revolution of 1979, is a state which openly advocates the destruction of Israel. The Iranians are also acting to support Palestinian terrorist organizations wherever they are -- Hamas, Islamic Jihad, the Popular Front, and even the Palestinian Authority itself."

---

[106] Women in Green, August 26, 2002. Chief of General Staff, Lt-Gen. Moshe Ya'alon, speaking to an assembly of Rabbis in Jerusalem, Aug. 25, 2002. "The current Palestinian leadership does not recognize the State of Israel's right to exist as a Jewish state, and is trying to realize its" doctrine of stages." "...the PLO is still trying to implement its "plan of stages" leading to Israel's destruction..."

[107] Ruth Matar's Women in Green Hour, August, 28, 2002, Arutz Sheva English Radio, Internet transcript. "Women in Green" <wfit2@womeningreen.org> *Is there any Difference Between Israeli Arabs and Arabs Under the Palestinian Authority?* "The PLO has never sought anything besides Israel's destruction, and is still trying to implement its"plan of stages" to annihilate Israel." "Shimon Peres: Stop living in your "New Middle East" fantasyland. Stop pretending that Yasser Arafat has renounced violence and is a valid peace partner for Israel."

Take note of the cry of Nadia Matar in her speech at the Tisha B'Av (ninth of Av) march around the walls of the Old City held 2002. "Today, the majority of the people is loyal to the heritage and to the Land. <u>Most of the people want a Zionist-Jewish state at whose center will stand</u>, <u>not the Western Wall, but The Temple Mount</u>. But, today, we unlike the desert generation, are stuck with a weak political leadership that does not understand that whoever controls the Temple Mount, controls all of Eretz Israel."

"Our tikkun (corrective measure) must consist of our proclaiming to the entire world that <u>the Temple Mount is the heart of the people of Israel, its physical and spiritual heart</u>. And we, the people, demand that we will have Jewish-Zionist leadership, "Zionist" named after Mount Zion. <u>Leadership that will not fear to open for us the gates of the Temple Mount</u>, and that <u>will not fear to clean up and expel from there the Arab contamination</u>, and that will not be afraid to assert: <u>the entire Land of Israel belongs to the people of Israel, in accordance with The Torah of Israel</u>."

"...<u>May it be His will that after so much mourning and tears, the people of Israel will act in such a manner that we merit the coming of the Messiah and the rebuilding of Jerusalem, speedily in our days. Amen</u>." End of quote. Underlining mine

Israel will survive. Israel will again control the whole of Jerusalem and Judah, including The Temple Mount, but at what cost?

Everyone becomes involved in this dispute, and Jerusalem is the most contentious part of the whole drama. Notice verse 3 of Zechariah 12 *"And in that day will I make Jerusalem a burdensome stone for all people: all that burden themselves with it shall be cut in pieces, though all people of the earth be gathered against it."* The result of this Battle over Jerusalem will be verse 7, *"The LORD also shall save the tents of Judah first, that the glory of the house of David and the glory of the inhabitants of Jerusalem do not magnify themselves against Judah."* Emphasis mine. In other words, Judah is placed into the hands of Israel first.

Since Jerusalem is in the center of Judah, and The Temple Mount is part of The Old City of Jerusalem, this means that Jerusalem, including Mount Zion, will finally again be in Israel's hands following this war. The ramifications here are significant. If Jerusalem were to be undisputedly given into Israeli total jurisdiction <u>before the whole of Judah, the area of Judah could be viewed as less important to the security and sovereignty of Israel</u>. However, Jerusalem will remain as a burdensome stone of contention, and the dispute will cause major consternation and liability for everyone who dares to try to solve the issues regarding Jerusalem. Eventually, Jerusalem is going to be a catalyst to draw all the people of the earth against it. But the LORD saves *"the tents of Judah first"* so that the *"glory of the house of David and the glory of the inhabitants of Jerusalem do not magnify themselves against Judah."* In other words, <u>Judah (The West Bank Judean territories) is not to be used as a bargaining chip as 'land for peace' just to ensure Jerusalem is secured</u>. The LORD knew this bargaining possibility would be a very real temptation for Israel. Although Israel seems to be traveling down this 'Road' as part of the negotiations for the implementation of the Palestinian State, through promises to halt and/or withdraw settlements from the region, and by cordoning off much of Judea with the presence of security fences, the LORD is not going to allow Judah to be bargained away and given to those not of The Covenant to solve the issues regarding Jerusalem. <u>He is not going to allow Israel to take the view that Judah is less important than Jerusalem</u>.

So there are forces, both political and religious, at work in The Middle East, and in the world at large, which influence the current status quo, and will have a major say in the outcome of the negotiations of the formation of a Palestinian State, and therefore over the sovereign borders of Israel, as well as in the subsequent outcome of The Battle of Gog and Magog. However, the controversy will not be completely settled by this Battle, because Daniel 9:27 and 11:31-33 indicate that there will be forces that still do not accept the Land of Israel, and particularly Judah, Jerusalem, and The Temple Mount, as being rightfully Israel's. Notice, Daniel 11:32, *" And such as do wickedly **against the covenant shall he corrupt by flatteries**:"* Who is this referring to? First of all, it refers to *"such as do wickedly,"* and these, a deceiving world leader, will be able to *"corrupt by flatteries."* Why?

What group of people are there who take wicked action against the Covenant? If we look at the situation in Israel and the surrounding nations today, we find who these people are, and we certainly see them taking wicked action against the Covenant even now! It is not hard to conclude that the Palestinians are against the true Covenant. It is not hard to see that the Muslim terrorist organizations are doing wicked things in Israel, and that their motive is against the Covenant God made with Abraham, Isaac, and Jacob regarding the Land and Jerusalem! It is not hard to see that the surrounding Arab League nations are applauding the plot to form a Palestinian State, thus dividing the Covenant Land, and have an eventual wish to annihilate Israel, the people of the Covenant and God's inheritance. And, it is not even hard to conceive that the nations of the world, and even Israel itself, are in such controversy that they will concede to and accept the flatteries of promises agreed to by negotiation, to put an end to the apparent impasse' and concede to the formation of a Palestinian

State in order to allow a measure of peace and safety. And, it is not hard to see that this will all result in the opposite of peace and safety!

Notice this quote taken from the Jerusalem Post, September 17, 2002 entitled, **Sharon: Israel cannot trust its neighbors to carry out agreements,** by the Associated Press. "Prime Minister Ariel Sharon said Tuesday that Israel cannot trust its neighbors to carry out agreements. ...Speaking at a memorial service for soldiers killed in the 1973 Mideast war, Sharon said: "We can't take anything for granted. We can't accept any promise blindly. We must be prepared for anything and depend largely on ourselves. The Arab world has still not accepted our existence and still has not accepted our birthright to build a Jewish state in our birthplace." Ariel Sharon still believes in this statement he made back in 1973, but he has succumbed to the pressures to agree to following "The Road Map to Peace' presented by 'The Quartet' anyway! Why? He is more interested in international acceptance for Israel, and Peace and Security, than in hanging onto what is now perceived as an impossible ideal. He would rather give up territory than face what appears to be an unthinkable alternative in his own mind. He feels he has no choice. He has become convinced that the existence of Israel depends on bowing to the very real outside pressures of the Palestinians and the international community. He has forgotten the Covenant is backed up by the LORD. It is this very lack of faith in the God of Israel that will lead Israel into Battle where they really will be fighting for their very existence!

Also notice this inflammatory statement given by Sheik Kamal Khatib, the deputy head of the Islamic Movement's northern branch, from a sermon he delivered to a massive Islamic Movement gathering at The Temple Mount on August 24, 2002. Quote taken from The Jerusalem Post, November 8, 2002, article written by Etgar Lefkovitz entitled, "Islamic Movement leader questioned." Quote, "El Aksa Mosque, the Western Wall, and all of Palestine belongs to the Muslims exclusively, and no one else has the right of ownership over them." While Jerusalem police questioned him on Monday November 7, 2002, investigating allegations of incitement against Israel, Khatib informed them that his speech was "nothing more than commentary on the Koran," so was therefore "in no way inciting." When asked to consider retracting his comments, he stated,"we will not relinquish our rights for the Temple Mount, not even in negotiations." So if negotiation won't cause the Muslim community to relinquish their so-called 'rights' to the Temple Mount, then war will be inevitable, and the LORD will <u>make them</u> relinquish.

So will there be a Palestinian State, and will it include Jerusalem and The Temple Mount as the Palestinians and other Muslims want? It is a very real possibility an interim Palestinian State may be formed. But any portion of Jerusalem, including The Temple Mount, will be contentious, because God will not be pleased about what everyone is attempting to pull-off! God says He has a controversy with those who seek to divide His Land, and are against His Covenant. We will see war. Since this war will result in Jerusalem and the Judean area of The West Bank being placed into Israeli hands, obviously Jerusalem, including The Temple Mount, and the surrounding area of Judea, will not be part of this Palestinian State <u>for any length of time</u>, if at all. Gaza and the rest of the 'occupied territories,' except for Judea, may be part of it, at least temporarily. There is supposed to be an interim Palestinian State in place by the end of 2004, with entrenched borders by 2005. Somehow I do not think any of this will happen according to 'The Road Map' plan! And only one war won't be enough to wrap it all up either!

After The Battle of Gog and Magog, those who lose their jurisdiction over The Temple Mount, and lose their prize of Jerusalem and Judea, will not be pleased. Who would that be? The Arab Muslims, and in particular, the Palestinians! These are the ones who are going to keep the pot seething until it all boils over again after The Abomination of Desolation half way through The Tribulation, which will ultimately result in another world war regarding Jerusalem and Israel. These are the ones who are against The Covenant God made with Israel regarding The Land, and feel they have right to it. Thus we have the seeds for the deception regarding The Covenant by the coming powerful leader know as The AntiChrist.

CHAPTER 12
CONFIRMATION OF THE COVENANT

Daniel 9:27 sheds more light on this Covenant controversy that only now is beginning to make an awful lot of sense. "*And he* (a flattering world leader who very well may be who we refer to as the AntiChrist) <u>shall confirm the covenant with many for one week</u>: *and in the midst of the week shall he cause the sacrifice and the oblation to cease, and for the overspreading of abominations he shall make it desolate, even until the consummation, and that determined shall be poured upon the desolate."* KJV. Parentheses and underlining mine.

This verse usually has been interpreted to mean the Antichrist will make a seven year covenant or treaty with Israel. But the verse does **not state** that there is a treaty **specifically with Israel**, but that he **confirms the Covenant with many for one week**. This agreement, then, is not a treaty signed with Israel per se', **but a confirmation of who has rights to The Covenant**. And "*many*" is not Israel, <u>but the many peoples who are negotiating, and who want the rights to The Covenant. Part of this leader's plan appears to concede Israel's right to The Covenant for seven years,</u> albeit with deceit. He even goes so far as to confirm The Covenant by flattering **many other nations** into ratifying it, perhaps through negotiations expedited through the EU particularly, and recognized by the UN and The Arab League, into allowing Israel to operate her rights for seven years. Then he will see to it (confirm) that within seven years he will give The Covenant Lands into the hands of the "*many*." This is an agreement he confirms he has the power to deliver on. **Could this actually be part of the 'plan of stages?'** that Moshe Ayalon, Chief of General Staff of the Israeli Defense Forces has warned us about?

<u>So the 'real' confirmation of 'Covenant rights' is an under-the-table agreement that after these seven years have transpired, the deceitful world leader will see to it that the Muslim Arab world, and the Palestinians, have the final rights to The Covenanted Lands.</u> **In other words, he uses deceit to trick Israel and her allies! Treachery!** Daniel chapter 11 indicates he operates with deception and flatteries. This charade very possibly could be carried out partially because of the groundwork now being laid in the setting up of the Palestinian State, which already has earmarks of being a process that is to take place in 'stages' over a period of a monitored timeframe. Although the 'Road' calls for ratification of entrenched sovereign borders for Israel and a Palestinian State by 2005, this process will not be

smooth. I doubt that they will reach their scheduled deadlines, and thus the process will undoubtedly include war. However, there will arise a world leader who will manage to put a lid on the situation after The Gog-Magog Battle -- at least for a while. Meanwhile, the many people surrounding Israel who feel they have rights to The Covenant Lands, are being primed to believe they ultimately will force Israel out of The Middle East. <u>AntiChrist will facilitate the confirmation of The Covenant with these nations</u>.

This will be quite a feat he will manage to pull off in light of Islamic belief that Israel lost all rights to The Covenant when Jacob sinned, so they now consider themselves the rightful Abrahamic descendants who inherit The Covenant. <u>What **really** is occurring here is a diabolical scheme</u>.

The AntiChrist is a sneaky, deceitful, lying world leader, who will operate and control a repressive world ideological religious, economic, and political system. All the world appears to be looking for a world leader who will be able to work both with the West, as well as with the ideology of the Islamic world, and somehow broker a lasting peace in The Middle East. We must remember that Jihad takes many forms, but ultimately it is war against anyone who Islam considers dhimmies and infidels, and especially the infidels of the Jews, the USA, and the Christianized West. According to Islam: terrorism, suicide bombers, murders, war, lies, and complete deception, are all legitimate weapons in this 'jihad.' AntiChrist will use this Islamic mind set for his own ends, confirming the Islamic understanding of The Covenant.

I. Weary Israel:

The context of Jeremiah chapters 4 through 8 appears to be describing the coming Battle of Gog and Magog. Notice Jeremiah 4:30 and 31 regarding Israel during this whole process, and how the description seems to have earmarks of Islamic jihad tactics. *"And when thou art spoiled, what wilt thou do? Though thou clothest thyself with crimson, though thou deckest thee with ornaments of gold, though thou rentest thy face with painting, in vain shalt thou make thyself fair; thy lovers will despise thee, <u>they shall seek thy life</u>. For I have heard a voice as of a woman in travail, and the anguish as of her that bringeth forth her first child, the voice of the daughter of Zion, that bewaileth herself, that spreadeth her hands, saying, Woe is me now! <u>for my soul is wearied because of murderers</u>."* Emphasis mine.

According to these verses, Israel will be *"spoiled."* The spoils of war. The spoils of jihad! Her land will be taken and divided up to form a Palestinian State, and she even will be invaded by Russia and all her allies, who she thought were honestly trying to create a peace for her, but as soon as it is

CONFIRMATION OF THE COVENANT

achieved, will take advantage of her anyway. No matter how hard she tries, even going along with 'The Road Map' for peace, and doing whatever she can to make herself accepted within the international community, she finds nothing will make her desirable among the nations. She is a nation despised. She thinks Russia, the UN, and the other members of The Quartet, are on her side at least in providing some safety and security. But it will not last. Instead, she will find herself in anguish, like a woman in travail. She longs to bring forth her Messiah who she knows will bring true peace and safety. But instead, she will find herself in the situation again where her enemies, who she thought could finally be her friends, are back at their same opposition and terrorism tactics. She is weary with having to put up with suicide bombers, terrorism, and murderers. Obviously, the tactics of the PLO-backed Islamic Jihad, Hamas, Fatah, and other terrorist groups, will kick into gear once again, and Israel will tire of it all!

How do we know these verses refer to present-day Israel? This passage identifies the woman in travail and anguish as *"the Daughter of Zion,"* not ancient Israel, but her descendant. And, much of the dissent will center on issues regarding jurisdiction over Jerusalem and The Temple Mount, because Zion actually is more correctly a name for The Old City, and particularly, Mount Zion. The Daughter of Zion would be more precisely then, the current city of Jerusalem, dealing specifically with issues regarding The Old City and The Temple Mount.

A. The Battered Woman Syndrome:

The above reverence from Jeremiah reads very much like the description of a battered woman! The unfortunate thing about battered women is that they lose their perspective regarding who to really trust. They make judgments and decisions that are intended to better their situation, but inevitably they only manage to endear themselves to those who will take advantage. The weariness of rejection, enduring violence, verbal and emotional abuse and misunderstanding, makes them vulnerable. Israel is much like this. After all she has been through, she will still be vulnerable to deception, and will be a sitting-duck for the flatteries and false promises of the AntiChrist, who will promise to take good care of her, but will sell her to her abusers through deception.

B. Is Armageddon another Name for Gog and Magog as Some Believe?

Gog and Magog is not the only Battle fought regarding Israeli jurisdiction and sovereignty. To accomplish all His purposes, the LORD will have to assemble the nations a second time into The Middle East <u>toward the end of The Days of Awe</u>. The basic controversy will still be in regard to the existence of Israel and her borders. Mankind simply will not let this go! But neither will the LORD, until Israel is fully in control of all The Land He gave by Covenant to Abraham, Isaac, and Jacob, and until He rules and reigns from The Throne of David in Jerusalem

The antagonists of The Battle of Armageddon appear to be very similar (but not entirely the same) to the line-up as for Gog and Magog -- only at that time literally every nation on earth will participate. Very little seems to have changed, except that mankind is now bent on not only annihilating Israel, but unknown to even themselves, the nations if left to their own devices would ultimately annihilate themselves! But God cannot, nor will not, allow this to happen, because there really is no such a thing as eternal annihilation, and the time for final reckoning of all mankind is not yet. Mankind, whether righteous or unrighteous, is an eternal being. So for any to be saved from this juncture of mankind's existence at The Battle of Armageddon, the LORD will step into the picture, not unseen this time, but seen, and very prominently a participator in battle. He comes back to earth with His Saints, appearing in The Clouds of Glory. Yom Kippur! The Great Shofar will be sounded! Every eye will see Him descend from the heavens in power and great glory accompanied by His Bride, The Church! He will quickly end the war, and set up His Kingdom, ruling from Jerusalem. The fulfillment of The Feast of Tabernacles, Sukkot, will follow, and Israel will be secured in The Land of Covenant once and for all, and will turn their hearts totally toward Him, realizing He is their Messiah and KING. All nations will come under His control. All governments will annually report to Him during Sukkot by sending ambassadors to take part, or suffer drought, and plagues in their lands as discipline. All law will proceed from Jerusalem, and the world will feel the iron rule of justice and righteousness whether they like it or not! Satan will be bound for 1000 years in The Bottomless Pit, and the Law of Peace will become absolute.

We will look more closely at The Battle of Armageddon in the second section of the book.

II. The "Plight" of the Palestinians:

Many world leaders are sympathetic to the 'plight' of the Palestinians, and believe Israel occupies The West Bank and Gaza illegally. The media has been hoodwinked thoroughly into promoting this thinking. They are very vocal, and extremely effective in spreading this propaganda. The general understanding is that the impoverished Palestinian Arabs have been displaced from their Country, their homes, and their lands, and have been placed into 'refugee camps' by the Israelis.

In actual fact, the 'Palestinian' Arabs did not have a recognized geographical nation called Palestine before the Israelis received nationhood. Before the Nation of Israel was brought into existence again in 1948, The Holy Land, which was an unorganized wasteland, often referred to as 'Palestine,' was sparsely populated by a mixture of a few Arabs scattered among a much larger population of Jews. The majority of so-called 'Palestinian' Arabs have moved into Israel from Jordan, Lebanon, Syria, and other Arab states <u>since</u> 1948, so were not indigenous to The Holy Land at all! But do the international media make the general public aware of this? NO! Why? Because they have swallowed the propaganda fed to them. [108]

---

[108] Women in Green, <wfit2@womeningreen.org> February 26, 2004, Letter From Ruth Matar, *Whose Land Grab?* "There was never such a thing as Palestinian people or a political entity called Palestine. The PLO was founded in 1964, three years before Israel's 1967 defensive war, when Israel had to withstand the attack by five well-armed States – Egypt, Iraq, syria, Lebanon, and Jordan, with their large armies and arsenals. At the end of the Six Day War, the Biblical Heartland of Judea and Samaria was liberated by Israel from Jordan. Jordan occupied Judea and Samaria between 1948 and 1967. King Hussein of Jordan, during this illegal occupation, renamed Judea and Samaria the "West Bank", i.e. the west bank of the River Jordan."

"Yes, there is an attempted land grab – not by Jews– but by Arabs who have come to the Holy Land from srrounding Arab countries during the last hundred years for work opportunities and a less repressive life style. Since 1967, the Arabs have established almost twice as many settlements than the Jews in the liberated territory of Judea and Samaria! This land grab has been heavily funded by Saudi Arabia. Sadly enough, the world does not find the frantic Arab building activities in the Holy Land an obstacle to peace."

" The Hebrew word, "Mitnachalim" has been translated as "Settlers." The correct translation is "Inheritors." The Jewish people are the Inheritors of the Land which the Almighty promised to their Forefathers as an everlasting inheritance."

The Final Schedule Revealed

The so-called 'Palestinians' have come to Israel to escape prejudice, to get jobs, and to have access to education and medical services. Very little of this infrastructure existed in The Holy Land until Israel became a nation. Agriculture on a large and profitable scale did not exist either. So what has been taken from the Palestinian Arabs? Very little. [109] In fact, they have benefitted!

Yes, there were some Arab communities that were relocated, and some Palestinians do not dwell where they formerly lived. This does amount to an injustice that needs to be addressed. But to be fair, Israel did not in fact bring about these relocations. Lebanon, Syria, Jordan, and other Arab League nations are the ones at fault. Israel has not necessarily done everything without making some mistakes along the way, and not all the injustices have been corrected, but they were not all her injustices! However, as already pointed out, the land has not been populated by Israelis without due legal process.

And, we also must realize that many Palestinian enclaves have proven to be breeding grounds for terrorists. Are all Palestinians terrorists? No! But in a conflict where the enemy hides himself among the innocent, steps must be taken to try to protect the innocent, even if it means relocating them to weed out the radicals. So if there are Palestinians who suffer under curfews and travel restrictions, it is because there are among them those who have placed themselves in opposition to Israel, and threaten Israeli security, including the security of innocent Arabs.

Who are these 'Palestinians?' One thing for certain, they are not, and never have been, a particular ethnic people. Contrary to what the media would have us believe, the majority are displaced, and/or immigrant Arab workers from surrounding Arab countries, so have no distinctive ethnicity of their own. [110] Even Arafat is from Egypt. Most have come to Israel from

---

[109] Women in Green, <wfit2@womeningreen.org> December 23, 2002. Joseph Farah, *The Settlement's Issue*. "If Israel's policies make life so intolerable for Arabs, why do they continue to flock to the Jewish state? Why aren't they leaving in droves if conditions are as bad as they say?
The truth? There is more freedom under Israeli rule then there is in any Arab country."

[110] Women in Green, <wfit2@womeningreen.org>December 23, 2002.Joseph Farah, *The Settlements' Issue*. "Arafat himself was born in Egypt. He later moved to Jerusalem. If at the moment, he is living in the West Bank, he is a "settler' there, not a native. Indeed, most of the Arabs living within the borders of Israel today have come from some other Arab country at some time in their life. ...They have come from Jordan, Egypt, and indirectly, from every other Arab country you can name – and many non-Arab countries as well. These surely aren't "Palestinians."

somewhere else, so are not indigenous to The Land at all. There is no language, currency, successive Arab-Palestinian government, or history of a sovereign <u>Arab</u> nation called 'Palestine.' [111]<u>In fact, the 'Palestine' of both Roman and Ottoman history was considered to be Jewish</u>, not Arab! Therefore, Israel has not been carved-out of any pre-existent self-determined Arabic Palestinian nation. They are infringing on no-one. So if anyone could claim the right to be called 'Palestinian,' it would be the Jews who were living in The Land before 1948!

Even the so-called 'Right of Return' that the Palestinians are trying to have implemented is a misnomer. The few Arabs who became refugees were relocated because of war, and the Arab Nations around them forced this movement. In fact, they initiated it. According to Emile Ghoury, Secretary of the Palestinian Arab Higher Committee, "The fact that there are these refugees is the direct consequence of the act of the Arab states in opposing partition and the Jewish state." Beirut Telegraph, September 6, 1948. The whole 'plight' thing is a ploy of lies perpetrated to discredit and dishonor Israel.

Jerusalem for many centuries was a recycled heap of ruins under the control of various peoples and religious groups. The 'Palestinians' were not even remotely interested in forming a nation with Jerusalem as capitol until Israel became a nation in 1948. Now that Israel has made Jerusalem into a progressive bustling center, and The West Bank into a world-class agricultural success, they want it. And most of the world seems to side with the Palestinians! They will not prosper in their quest though, because God has decreed Israel to have full rights to both The Land and Jerusalem by Covenant.

A. Why Must Israel control Jerusalem?

Once Israel gains total control over all of Jerusalem, The Times of The Gentiles will again cease -- temporarily. This development will be of great significance, because it will set the stage for Israel to finally be able

---

[111] Jerusalem Post, Internet Edition. Www.jpost.com/servlet/Sattilite?pagename=JPost/A/JPArticle... March 10, 2003. Evelyn Gordon, *The real double standard*, "...Palestinians began thinking of themselves as a separate nation only after Israel was created in 1948. Before 1948, the only people known as 'Palestinians' were the Jews who lived under the British Mandate. The region's Arabs called themselves 'Arabs', not 'Palestinians', they called the area "southern Syria", not "Palestine," and they considered themselves not a separate nation, but part of the larger Arab nation that covers the Middle East."
" Nor is there a distinct Palestinian language. The Palestinians speak Arabic."

to build The Third Temple on Mount Zion. There must be a Temple in place, complete with full priestly ritual and daily sacrifices, in order for the scenario of The Abomination that makes Desolate to take place, and for the sacrifices and the oblation to cease, as indicated by Daniel 9:27. Joel's description of The Battle of Gog and Magog, when the sun is darkened and the moon is turned to blood according to chapter 2:31-32, indicates the deliverance of Mount Zion and Jerusalem. *"...for in mount Zion and in Jerusalem shall be deliverance, as the LORD hath said, and in the remnant whom the LORD shall call."* Joel 2:32. It is not specifically the presence of The Temple itself that is important here, but the control of all of Jerusalem, including Mount Zion, and this lines up with the prophecy in Daniel that indicates *"thy people"* (Judah) and the *"holy city"* (Jerusalem) must completely be in Israeli hands in order for the 70 Weeks to be fulfilled. Daniel 9:24. But just because this control over all of Jerusalem comes to pass, it does not mean the countdown of the final 70th Week of discipline begins immediately, but only that the elements necessary are finally in place.

III. God Deals with Israel Predictably:

When we examine Scripture, we see that God deals with Israel in predictable ways. The Israelis are a chosen people, not because they are any better than anyone else, but because God has chosen them as the people through whom He would send the Redeemer, and through whom also He would reveal His time-table, making them an object lesson or illustration to keep our eyes upon, to find out what He has done, what He is doing, what He will do, and why. In order for this to be understandable, God set out a distinct plan given through The Law and Prophets, which would be predictably fulfilled in and through Christ, and through the Israeli nation. Therefore, we are able to look at Israel and read what God is doing according to that prophetic plan, and know where we are in the scheme of things.

When Israel was finally poised to enter The Promised Land after their deliverance from Egypt, God had already told them to possess Canaan, and that He would be with them. But they exhibited a lack of faith in God's promises, and sent in the twelve spies. Ten spies brought back a negative report, so they did not proceed to conquer the Canaanites, even though two spies gave a very positive, faith-filled report. God had already stated they were victorious, but because of fear of the nations residing in Canaan, <u>they developed a devastating case of cold feet</u> that, because of their lack of faith, kept them wandering in the desert another 40 years, and <u>a whole generation passed</u> before they finally entered The Promised Land. Well what does this historic situation have to do with Israel today?

IV. The 1967 Six Day War:

Some feel that when Israel took Jerusalem in the June 5th to10th 1967 Six Day War, that because Israel finally gained total **control of all of Jerusalem** after 2500 years (their measure of sovereignty has always been tempered by the presence of Babylon, Media-Persia, Greece, or Rome keeping them under their thumbs,) that now The Times of The Gentiles has ended. However as already mentioned, an interesting scenario occurred in 1967. The day after Jerusalem, including The Temple Mount area, was finally in their jurisdiction, the Israelis government handed The Temple Mount back to Jordan. Subsequently, Jordan handed it over to the newly formed Palestinian Authority, so **Israel gave up total sovereignty over The Temple Mount.** Why?

The Israeli government developed a severe case of cold feet because of the pagan Islamic presence of the mosques that currently sit on The Temple Mount. They did not want to risk the possibility of all-out war with the Arab Muslim Nations by exercising absolute jurisdiction over The Mount. Apparently within only twelve hours, Israel forgot what God had just done for them! Over the previous six days, obviously with God's Divine help, they had just fought against the Arab nations surrounding them, and had come out victorious, gaining The Temple Mount and The West Bank! Hello!! What was their problem? The intimidation of other nations, and already present strong, pagan religious beliefs, caused them to back out of what God had decisively handed to them! So in an effort to avoid further war, they are ultimately going to run headlong into it!

Question. Could it be that God **planned initially for The Age of The Gentiles to cease in 1967**, but He will assist Israel in bringing Gentile domination over every part of Jerusalem to an end **40 years later, giving the privilege to the next generation of Israelis?** I am not being absolutely dogmatic here, but it is an interesting possibility to consider!

If we do a little speculative calculating, we find that 40 years after 1967 brings us to 2007. The year 2007 has some significance in the deliberations currently on-going regarding the formation of a Palestinian State. The year 2007 initially was the target date for the finalization of Palestinian State borders. This target date has since been moved to sometime between 2004 (the American target date) and 2007 (Arafat's target date.). The United States, The United Nations, Russia, and The European Union (referred to as 'The Quartet') are actively working out a 'Road Map to Peace' to bring about an interim Palestinian State by 2004, to be entrenched by 2005 or 2007. Is this a coincidence? I don't think so!

The Final Schedule Revealed

I wonder if we will see The Battle of Gog and Magog underway by 2007 instead, with Israel gaining absolute control over Judah, and The Temple Mount placed decisively into Israeli hands again by late 2007 to 2008. <u>The LORD may drag this process out for several more years beyond this time-sequence</u>, but somehow it seems too many scenarios are beginning to come together for this to stretch a great deal further. He could extend it to 2011-2012 (possible mid-69th week) as already mentioned regarding the 'lost' Seven Weeks of Daniel, with the count beginning from 1948, following which The Days of Awe would occur. Or, He could wait again for another complete generation to pass.

One more thought. This is purely speculation, so please do not jump on me here. There is one other comparative sequence to consider, which also points out if nothing else, just how close we may be to The Battle of Gog and Magog regarding Judah and The Temple Mount, and therefore also indicates an approximation of when the Rapture could occur. Teshuvah is 40 days, with 30 days being Elul, followed by The Ten Tishrei Teshuvah Days of Awe. If The Last Trump of Rosh HaShanah calls the righteous who are pure and holy, having their names inscribed in The Book of Life according to the greeting during Elul, then we do have another possible clue to break down prophetic fulfillment.

The criteria given is that one must have remained righteous since the previous Yom Kippur Day of Atonement until Rosh HaShanah. There was a war in 1973 called The Yom Kippur War. Taking a prophetic year for a day, 30 Teshuvah Days corresponding to Elul would then take us to the year 2003, with The Ten final Tishrei Days of Teshuvah following. Since 2003 was the <u>initial</u> target date for the formation of an interim Palestinian State, but is now passed, I would then also suggest we may be very close to the end of The Dispensation of Grace!

I will not dogmatically state the Rapture will occur immediately, but only that <u>this is a startling warning</u>, and ought to make us examine our hearts seriously, because Teshuvah does come eventually to the end of its 30 day Elul, and the Tishrei Rosh HaShanah harvest-call will then take place, following which the entire world will face the judgment of God! It is also interesting to note that counting 40 years (a 40 year discipline period for Israel regarding The Land) from 1967 (because they rejected The Temple Mount), and counting 30 years from the 1973 Yom Kippur War (a prophetic Elul Teshuvah), both bring us to a similar time-frame within only four years of each other. I hardly think this is coincidental, and it also illustrates the fact that until the Rapture takes place, it is indeed possible God has some room for flexibility, showing His grace. But once the

Rapture takes place, the final Tishrei Teshuvah Ten Day (year) countdown will be irreversible and sequentially decisive.

So we certainly cannot know the day or hour of Christ's return for His Bride, but we definitely are able to recognize the Times and Seasons in relation to Israel that we are living in, and therefore be ready when The Last Trump sounds! And when it does, Israel will be on the 'Road' to the absolute fulfillment of The Covenant, and the LORD Himself will undermine the AntiChrist's attempt at the confirmation of the covenant with the nations who surround Israel.

PART 2: THE REVELATION EXPLANATION

THE PURPOSE OF THE BOOK OF REVELATION

The Book of Revelation reveals the identity, position, and ministerial office of Jesus Christ, in relation to individuals, to the Church, to Israel, and to the nations. It also takes us beyond the limitations of the earthly realm, and allows us to have a glimpse into the interaction and intervention of the heavenly dimension in the workings of the universe, and in the affairs of mankind, bringing about God's Plan of The Ages.

The full name for this prophetic Book, written by John the Apostle, states its purpose. <u>The Revelation of Jesus Christ</u> -- an interesting name for a book, since the purpose of the Feasts and Festivals also is to reveal Messiah. So one would expect The Book of Revelation to make obvious reference to The Convocations, and in particular to The Fall Feasts and Festivals, which it definitely does. This Revelation therefore includes a great deal of prophetic information that is expedited in and through the Person, work, and position of Jesus Christ. Revelation is not just a Book about end-time events per se', but draws from pertinent information that is historical, contemporary in John's day, as well as futuristic in nature. In other words, Revelation truly is a Book of Prophecy, telling forth the truth of the plan and purpose of redemption and reconciliation with God, procured through the completed work of Jesus Christ, The Lamb of God.

The first chapter gives us a physical description of the Holy and Awesome Person of Jesus Christ, from eternal existence before Creation and time, to eternal existence without end. It shows His perfect Deity. Isaiah had a similar revelation and encounter with this Eternal One, Who has inserted Himself into human affairs in order to procure for mankind what man could not do for himself, namely redemption from sin and death through The Atonement, and reconciliation with God. Jesus is portrayed in Revelation as: The Creator, The Ancient of Days, The Alpha and Omega, The Beginning and The End, The First and Last, The Firstfruits of the Dead, The Son of Man, The Redeemer, The Sovereign KING, The Messiah, The Lamb, The Lion of the Tribe of Judah, and The Bridegroom. The Book of Revelation depicts Him in all His majesty, glory and power. He is the One who was, and is, and is to come, The Almighty. He is the One that lives, and was dead, and is alive forevermore, and He holds the Keys of Hell and of Death.

Much could be written about Him from the first chapter alone. But we see Christ most clearly as He moves among the Candlesticks, which are The Church redeemed and empowered by the Holy Spirit. Seven is used throughout this passage to describe the Candlesticks, the Holy Spirit, and The Angels of The Seven Churches; indicating this is the fullness and perfection of each. The complete Person and Office of the Holy Spirit is depicted as The Seven Spirits of God. Christ carries The Seven Stars, which are the Angels (Ministers) of The Seven Churches, in His right hand. He speaks by His Spirit to The Seven Churches in chapters two and three.

John is invited into the Heavenlies for a glimpse of The Glory of The Throne of God, and of things that are beyond the dimension of the earthly. John is taken on an incredible journey more exciting than any science-fiction movie. He observes reality which has, is, and will be fulfilled according to God's will, both in Heaven and on the earth.

CHAPTER 13
THE SEVEN CHURCHES

As Christ moves among The Seven Candlesticks, He gives a pertinent and personal message to each. He points out their strengths and weaknesses, and pronounces blessings and warnings. These messages are multifaceted in their application <u>to several layers</u> of the prophetic Dispensation of The Age of Grace, The Church Age. So the prophetic spiral in several intertwined layers is definitely in play. Each Church is addressed according to the name of the original City that existed in Asia (Turkey- Greece area) at the time of John's writing, so is indicative of what each Church was like at that time, and the message needed. However, down through the centuries of The Age of Grace, there have been seven distinct eras of Church influence in the world, and these have occurred in exactly the same order as the Churches mentioned. Therefore, Jesus Christ addressed the Church of each era, including our own. Also, we are able to identify contemporary denominations, as well as individual congregations, which show earmarks of these Seven Churches, and therefore need the same messages from the LORD. Finally, when we examine individuals within The Body of Christ, we again see the same pattern. Many have tried to promote one or another of these prophetic applications as the only possible interpretation. However all are applicable, and in fact all are absolutely necessary in understanding the mission, message, and mandate of the Church, and of how The LORD perceives His Church. Jesus Christ explains His plans and purposes for each Church in the past, in the present, for the end of this Age, and for what will follow for the Righteous both in Heaven, and during The Ten Days of Awe.

The Church holds a unique position in relationship with Christ. We often refer to the Church as The Bride of Christ. But there also is a broader identification. Those who are born-again believers during The Church Age are The Betrothed Bride, and await the coming of The Bridegroom. But in finality, are all who are 'members' of The Seven Churches taken into Heaven for The Wedding? When we examine this concept more closely, we must come to the realization that not all who apparently align themselves with these Churches are ultimately The Wedded Bride. This means that there will be <u>some</u> who are 'members' of these Churches who will not be taken in The Rapture, but will have to remain on the earth to go through The Days of Awe along with the unbelievers.

Does this mean they lose their salvation? No! In fact, it appears they may become <u>part</u> of the group we refer to as The Tribulation Saints, <u>along with</u> many who also come to belief in Christ during the Jacob's Trouble era. So when 'The Church' is addressed or mentioned, we must take note of the context and message to understand the implications of the term.

Jesus told a parable of Ten Virgins. Matthew 25:1-13. *"Then shall the kingdom of heaven be likened unto ten virgins, which took their lamps, and went forth to meet the bridegroom. Verse 2. And five of them were wise, and five were foolish. Verse 3. They that were foolish took their lamps, and took no oil with them: Verse 4. But the wise took oil in their vessels with their lamps. Verse 5. While the bridegroom tarried, they all slumbered and slept. Verse 6. And at midnight there was a cry made, Behold the bridegroom cometh; go ye out to meet him. Verse 7. Then, all those virgins arose, and trimmed their lamps. Verse 8. And the foolish said unto the wise, Give us of your oil: for our lamps are gone out. Verse 9. But the wise answered, saying, Not so; lest there be not enough for us and you; but go ye rather to them that sell, and buy for yourselves. Verse 10. And while they went to buy, the bridegroom came; and they that were ready went in with him to the marriage: and the door was shut. Verse 11. Afterward came also the other virgins saying, Lord, Lord, open to us. Verse 12. But he answered and said, Verily I say unto you, I know you not. Verse 13. Watch therefore, for ye know neither the day nor the hour wherein the Son of man cometh."*

All ten were virgins, meaning they were all without imputed sin. But only five of them were allowed in to the wedding. Why? It appears they all had lamps that had gone out, and they all were sleeping. The difference between those who were wise and those who were foolish, was that five had oil in their vessels with their lamps, so were able to trim their lamps. Five had no oil with them, therefore were not able to trim their lamps. The foolish had to go out to obtain oil, because the wise were unable to share with them, or there would not have been enough oil for all. While they were out, the Bridegroom came. Those who had gone to buy, must have been able to obtain oil, because eventually they returned. But they found the wise had gone in to the wedding while they were out, and the door was now shut. They were not able to go in.

What does the oil refer to? Oil is a symbol of the Holy Spirit. The factor that separates the wise from the foolish, is their position in regard to the Holy Spirit. Those who were wise may have let their lamps go out, and they also may have drifted to sleep, but they were equipped with the ability to access the resources provided by the presence of the Holy Spirit, so they were able to trim their lamps immediately when the cry signaling the Bridegroom's approach was uttered. In other words, they were not defeated by the unfortunate circumstance that their lamps had gone out,

THE SEVEN CHURCHES

because they had immediate access to the One who is able to provide, and they knew how to listen to His voice and leading. They had made careful preparation according to the Holy Spirit's directives. Those who were foolish obviously had no sense of the necessity to have the resources of the Holy Spirit directly available in their lives (they had no oil with them), but quickly realized their own foolishness, and immediately set about to correct their lack of accessible resource. But they woke up to what they needed too late to access the wedding.

What does this mean? Is the anointing enablement of the Holy Spirit upon the Church only operational for a specified time-period? Yes! The Holy Spirit's mandate as Friend of The Bridegroom, to assist The Bride, does come to an end. Those who have heeded His voice and leading have oil in their vessels, so are able to trim their lamps, and go prepared to meet The Bridegroom when He returns. Those who have ignored the Holy Spirit's prompting are obviously not equipped with the appropriate preparations for the Bride to make. Only those who willingly prepare during the Age of the Holy Spirit's full ministry to the Church will be able to participate in the Wedding Procession leading to The Father's House. After The Bride is safely presented to The Bridegroom, and is ushered into the Father's presence, the Holy Spirit's role as Friend of the Bridegroom, <u>to prepare The Bride</u> is complete. Does this mean the Holy Spirit is totally removed from the earth? No! Just His role in regard to the Bride is complete. He no longer needs to be The Restrainer of Evil, because He no longer must protect the Bride. After The Friend of the Bridegroom safely delivers the Bride to The Groom in traditional rendezvous ceremony, God's wrath will then be poured out on the disobedient on the earth during the Days of Awe.

Does the unfortunate position the foolish find themselves in mean they now are no longer considered virgins? No. They still are virgins, only very contrite, sad virgins. They are too late to participate with the wise virgins as The Bride. The message Jesus is portraying in this illustrative parable, is that some foolish believers do not recognize the preparatory role of the Holy Spirit during the Elul Days of Teshuvah, so remain on the earth after the Rosh HaShanah Cry and Last Trump are uttered. They must go to purchase oil. They go to pay the price of not preparing properly, of not recognizing Christ's wishes, and of not yielding to the Holy Spirit's leading and empowerment.

It is obvious that they must be able to find oil, because they do return. But they return to a shut door. They cannot enter The Wedding. They are able to trim their lamps, but not at the appropriate time. This does not mean they eternally lose out. It just means they are not able to be part of

The Bride, because they were not ready when The Bridegroom came. The cry of *"Behold the Bridegroom cometh, go ye out to Meet Him."* caught them totally off guard. None of the Ten Virgins know for sure when this cry will be uttered, but that does not leave room for lack of preparation. In the traditional Jewish wedding, the bride does not know for certain the timing of the return of the bridegroom to receive her to himself. This aspect of the bride not knowing when the groom is to return, is totally typical. She knows she must be prepared at any time, as expedited and directed by The Friend of The Bridegroom. If she chooses to not prepare, that is her own foolishness.

What was the accusation against these? *"I know you not."* Does this mean these are not born-again? No! It means they do not <u>know</u> the Bridegroom intimately enough to take heed to the Holy Spirit's leading (keep oil with their lamps), and thus do what they know the Bridegroom desires, so they are not prepared. In other words, <u>this lack of listening to the Holy Spirit is **an affront** to the Bridegroom, because they obviously do not respect their own Betrothed enough to honor His wishes, or love Him enough to want to know His desires</u>. Just because He is not physically present does not mean they cannot get to know one another through communication! In not listening to the Holy Spirit, these miss out on the one avenue <u>to really get to know the Bridegroom, and for Him to really get to know His Bride</u>. He may be physically absent, but He is very much present by His Spirit, and He wants a living, loving relationship. He wants to plumb the depths of His relationship with His Beloved, and get to really know her! But the foolish did not pursue this provided avenue to carry on the relationship in intimate communication, so the Bridegroom says, *"I know you not."*

Can we blame Him? All communication via The Friend, the Holy Spirit, was ignored. His desires were ignored. No wonder these are not allowed in, but the door is shut! Jesus, the LORD of Heaven and earth, cannot be faulted for wanting to marry someone Who He knows, and who knows Him. This is not a blind marriage of arrangement, but is based on the intimate relationship of love and communion by His Spirit!

Jesus, in the parables of Matthew chapter 25, is not addressing unbelievers, but those who will be part of The Kingdom. The question here is not about being born-again, but of commitment, and ultimately what this commitment will mean pertaining to the Believer's role and position in The Kingdom. This discussion is specifically with His followers, not with the large crowds. We must keep the context in perspective. Jesus is still giving His Olivet Discourse in Matthew 25, so is addressing the ramifications of the end-times sequence. The importance of Teshuvah, which the disciples would have been totally aware of, is pivotal. And obviously, along with the Season of Teshuvah, The Fall Feasts are integral. Rosh HaShanah is the call to the Marriage. Those who have heeded the Holy Spirit during the Elul Days of Teshuvah, the courtship days of the Bride and Bridegroom, will be taken. Those not prepared for the Wedding simply will not be taken, but will remain to go through the final Ten Days of Teshuvah, to try and purify them, so that they have opportunity to be ready for Yom Kippur when Christ returns with His Bride, and ultimately will still enter The Kingdom.

Bringing this message forward into the lives of members of the Church today, we see the oil of the Holy Spirit is available for all these virgins, but only five of them give Him recognition, and yield to Him. Only five understand the anointing gifts of empowerment He gives, and allow the fruit He is able to produce in their lives to make them overcomers and effective ministers until Christ, their Bridegroom, comes for them. The other five know the Holy Spirit is present in the world, but do not access His gifts or empowerment until it is too late for participation in the Wedding. What does this tell us? Apparently, not all who claim to be believers will make the Wedding! In fact, Jesus seems to divide the wise and the foolish about fifty-fifty. Half are wise. Half are foolish. Hey! I didn't give this ratio! Jesus did! Does this mean that about half of those who consider themselves members of the Church will be raptured, and half won't? It is a sobering thought worth contemplating! Will those left behind cease to be believers? No. But they will certainly be very sorrowful believers, and will have to face all that comes on the world while The Wedding takes place in Heaven. But it goes without saying, these also will be very sincere believers, under no illusions from now on! They will still have opportunity to repent of their foolishness, and obtain the oil of the Spirit.

During the Church Age of Grace, the Church is The Betrothed Bride of Christ, and in Jesus' messages to The Seven Churches, He sets out His observations, His admiration, and what is necessary for His Bride's well-being. Just like any Bridegroom, Jesus Christ has certain expectations of His Bride. He knows what He expects her to accomplish, and what her ultimate position and role will be. He also, like any betrothed suitor, desires an ongoing, rightful, loving relationship with His Betrothed, even while He is Himself preparing for their Wedding, so cannot be physically present. He loves His Betrothed Bride, and certainly it is not unreasonable for Him to expect His love to be reciprocated. The Holy Spirit's role in the life of The Bride is therefore very important to Him!

Also, in order for the Wedding to take place, there are preparations which must be made by both The Bride and The Groom. The Betrothed Bride does not simply sit and wait for her Bridegroom to show up and whisk her away. In essence, the words of Jesus to the Seven Churches in Revelation chapters 2 and 3, are directed to His Beloved as messages of His love and concern, and as such should not only be heeded, but deeply appreciated by The Bride, who desires to prepare in such a way as to please her Bridegroom, and thus be prepared when He returns for her at the Rapture. He is sharing His heart with her.

For the purposes of this book, I have chosen to briefly examine what Jesus stated to the Churches from the perspective of our own era, and particularly as applicable to each of us as individual members of The Church. The reason I am taking this approach is because there is absolutely nothing we can change about the historical Church of John's day, nor about past eras of religious impact and influence. What has been, is past. Certainly the past sets the tone for the present, but in the final analysis, we cannot rest upon the achievements or the mistakes of the past. We must accept full responsibility in the here and now. We therefore must evaluate our own Church era, and particularly examine our individual lives in the light of these messages Jesus give to us.

There is a passage in Revelation chapter 19 verses 7-8 which indicates the readiness of the Bride to wed her Bridegroom. " *Let us be glad and rejoice, and give honor to him: for the marriage of the Lamb is come, <u>and his wife hath made herself ready</u>.* Verse 8. *And to her was granted that she should be arrayed in fine linen, clean and white: for the fine linen is the righteousness of saints."* Underlining mine. The term *"wife"* is obviously in comparative context to a Jewish Betrothed Bride who is about to enter into Marriage Covenant. Recall that a betrothed couple are often referred to with the terminology 'husband' and 'wife.' Our western culture only uses these designations after the wedding vows have been taken.

According to verse 7, His Wife (Betrothed) has made herself ready. Because she has done so, she is given raiment of fine linen, clean and white, to wear. These linen garments, which are her wedding dress, are the righteousness of the saints. But she does not provide them herself. Rather, the Bridegroom provides them. In other words, the making of herself ready, although involving righteousness in her life, does not specifically require her own ability to provide clothing herself, but hinges directly on her worthiness to be given her wedding garments. She has prepared herself to wear these robes in purity, holiness, and love. So how does The Bride prepare, and make herself ready to receive this honor?

We have overtones of the traditional Jewish wedding preparations portrayed here. When the betrothal takes place, the young man who intends to marry, gives his chosen Bride-to-be gifts of raiment, wine to seal the betrothal, the Shitre Erusin document of His intentions (His Word),

THE SEVEN CHURCHES

and he assigns a knowledgeable trusted Friend to help the Bride prepare herself according to his wishes before the wedding takes place. In order for the Bride to know his wishes, he must also communicate to her what his expectations are. That is only honest and fair. Otherwise, how will she know his desires? Then he takes his leave, promising to return for her when his preparations are complete in his own Father's house.

The assigned Friend of the Bridegroom quickly enters the picture to represent him, and to assist the Bride in achieving the goals that have been, and will subsequently be, clearly set out. In other words, while the betrothed Groom is gone to make his own preparations, the Friend becomes the spokesman through whom he communicates with his Bride-to-be, and through whom the Bride communicates with him. The Groom is able to share his concerns and any pertinent or helpful information through this Friend until he sees the Bride face to face again when he comes for her. It is absolutely imperative that the Bride listen carefully to this special Friend, and follows his leading and instructions, so she is prepared for when her Bridegroom returns for her. She does not do this out of fear of getting it wrong, but as a result of her loving intimate relationship with The Bridegroom, kept alive and expedited by the Friend. Obviously, this Friend is the coordinator of the wedding preparations, specifically helping The Bride, and fanning the flames of love for her Groom.

When Jesus was about to leave, He promised His disciples He would send the Comforter who would lead them into all truth. This Paraclete (one who comes alongside) would abide (live directly) with them, and assist them. The Holy Spirit comes alongside us, and helps us understand, not just Scriptural interpretation of truth, but also the application resulting in change in our lives and in our activities while on earth waiting for our Bridegroom to return. The outpouring of the Holy Spirit on The Day of Pentecost was the manifested arrival of this Friend of The Bridegroom to The Church. In other words, His complete seven-fold ministry is available to empower and anoint us, both as individuals, as well as members of the corporate Church. He also has in His possession all the gifts needed to assist us, and is the Giver of strength to help us grow and to manifest fruitfulness in our lives and ministry. He is the One who draws men to Christ for salvation, thus assisting in bringing The Bride to completion. He is The Convictor, pointing out our sin and weaknesses, so we can deal with issues, and thus be able to grow in holiness and righteousness, bringing us to maturity. He is the One who leads and guides in our lives, setting out the path each of us is to take. He also is The Protector and Restrainer, prompting us to shun evil, and to cling to that which is good. And, He is the One who keeps reminding us of the great love of our Bridegroom, guiding us in ways that will allow us to show our love for Christ. It is imperative then, that we listen to the Holy Spirit! That is why Jesus stated to each of The Seven Churches, *"He that hath an ear, let him hear what the Spirit saith unto the Churches."*

The messages the LORD gives to the Churches set out what we, as His chosen Bride, are to be, what we are to avoid, what we are to correct, and what He expects us to accomplish. In essence, Jesus gives messages to His Bride, stating very serious considerations that He shares directly from His heart. This is not unlike a betrothed couple discussing what they appreciate and commend in one another, what they see needs changing, and what their future plans and aspirations are, and whether they are even compatible to live up to these aspirations. We know these important issues must be addressed long before the final Covenant Wedding Vows are entered into. This is the period of courtship which allows each of them to examine who they really are, who the other really is, and if in the long run their lives will mesh into a life-long marriage that fulfills each of them separately, and yet melts them together as a united entity. Their goals, and how they are to be achieved, must be discussed. Their attitudes must be allowed to become evident, and also their expectations of one another. That is why most Pastors will not perform a wedding unless times of counseling are first completed. A couple cannot simply marry, then ride off happily into the sunset as Hollywood and the entertainment media portray. Preparation for marriage takes concerted effort, adjustment, and honest evaluation. A great many terrible situations leading to divorce could be avoided if we would only follow the example Christ not only gives, but rightfully expects in our very real relationship with Him.

Of course we know that Jesus Christ, because He is God Incarnate, is totally sinless and holy, so has no attitudes or faults that need to be addressed. He is absolutely perfect. However, He has chosen an obviously imperfect Bride. Her weaknesses and imperfections cannot be allowed to come between them, so these must be addressed. In essence, the messages to The Seven Churches do just that. Jesus sets out to His Bride what He appreciates, and what He is proud of about her; and He gives commendations accordingly. However, He has no illusions about her faults, and in all fairness and concern, He bravely points out these shortcomings. He is absolutely transparent here, sharing His disappointments, and even going so far as to indicate that if she is unwilling to address these issues, He will have to take punitive measures. It appears that those who do not address His very real concerns, will ultimately be rejected as being worthy to remain as part of The Bride. That realization certainly is sobering! But those who take repentant action will be received, and have place in The Kingdom at His side. The important thing for the Churches, and particularly for the individual members, is to listen carefully to the Holy Spirit, and respond accordingly. None of the issues raised by Christ to The Churches is impossible to be addressed if we listen to the Spirit, and appropriate the Spirit's help and leading, and particularly pursue the loving relationship. So how does The Bride prepare and make herself ready for The Wedding? By taking Christ's admonitions seriously, and by listening to the Holy Spirit, and responding accordingly! It's that simple, and it ought to be a joy, because we know our Bridegroom's desires, and we have help to achieve His wishes. If we truly love Him, none of His admonitions will be a burden to address!

So what has Jesus Christ indicated to us, His Betrothed Bride? What is our preparation? Let's look briefly at some of the things The Bride must address. There are many in-depth studies regarding each of these messages to the Seven Churches, but the emphasis I am taking in this book is that there are issues we as The Bride must address, with the help of the Holy Spirit, to prepare for our Wedding, and thus be ready when Jesus Christ comes for us.

A. The Ephesian Church:

Revelation 2:1-7. Jesus states to the Church in Ephesus, *"Unto the angel of the church of Ephesus write: These things saith he that holdeth the seven stars in his right hand, who walketh in the midst of the seven golden candlesticks; Verse 2. I know thy works, and thy labor, and thy patience, and how thou canst not bear them which are evil: and thou hast tried them which say they are apostles, and are not, and hast found them liars: Verse 3. And hast borne, and hast patience, and for my name's sake hast labored, and hast not fainted. Verse 4. Nevertheless, I have somewhat against thee, because thou hast left thy first love. Verse 5. Remember therefore from whence thou are fallen, and repent, and do the first works: or else I will come unto thee quickly, and will remove thy candlestick out of his place, except thou repent. Verse 6. But this thou hast, that thou hatest the deeds of the Nicolaitans, which I also hate. Verse 7. He that hath an ear, let him hear what the Spirit saith unto the churches; To him that overcometh will I give to eat of the tree of life, which is in the midst of the paradise of God."*

The Ephesian type of individual and congregation in The Body of Christ has a lot going for him/her. Jesus commends this person and congregation as being willing to work tirelessly, with great patience and endurance. He commends her for her aversion to evil, and for the ability to see through those who pose as apostles, but really are not. So she is obviously doctrinally and spiritually perceptive. His one real issue with

The Final Schedule Revealed

this Church is that despite all her ministry, sincerity, and pursuit of truth, she has lost her first love for her Bridegroom.

Let's put ourselves in His shoes for a moment. How do we think it makes Him feel, knowing the one He loves really does not share passionate love for Him anymore? That must hurt! In other words, she has set about to do everything right, but has become so caught up in her ministries and identification of falsehood and evil, she has forgotten they are betrothed, and that she is supposed to be in love with her Bridegroom who will soon quickly come to take her to their Wedding. When He does come, if she has not repented of this apathy toward Him, He will have to remove her Candlestick from its place. In other words, the one who has not re-fanned the flame of love for Him will not be part of the Bride. He loves her, but He cannot marry someone who does not love Him back! He desperately wants this Church to recognize what has transpired, and to turn this situation around!

Jesus commends her again, pointing out that He is aware that she hates the activities of the [112]Nicoliatans (a group of misguided individuals who tried to incorporate the philosophies, fleshly indulgences, and ideals of the world into the Church, in order to control, and to steer policies, doctrines, and ministries accordingly. They were elitist, power hungry, and pluralistic.) He hates the Nicolaitans too! So He points to the truth that they really do still have something in common! It's sad though. They should have love in common, but at the moment mutual hate for ungodliness is all that seems to be holding them together.

How can this problematic lack of love that has sidetracked this Church be overcome? Through repentance, and by listening to the Holy Spirit! Pay attention to the Friend of the Bridegroom! Listen to Him and do as He says, because He knows the Bridegroom intimately, and will assist in restoring the love relationship. The one who overcomes this fault in preparation for the Marriage, will have the privilege of eating of The Tree of Life which is in the midst of The Paradise of God.

I have a hunch Paradise is the location of some of the Wedding preparations Jesus has been making in His Father's Estate in Heaven, and

---

[112] Merrill C. Tenney, General Editor, The Zondervan Pictorial Encyclodedia of the Bible, Volume Four, 1976, The Zondervan Corporation, Grand Rapids, Michigan, p. 435-436. "...have forsaken true Christian doctrine; ...lived in unrestrained indulgence as to what a man ate and as to how he lived." "*The Apostolic Constitutions* described them "shameless in uncleaness." "...the Nicolaitans abandoned themselves to pleasures like goats in a life of shameless self-indulgence." "In the letter to the church at Pergamum The Nicolaitans were associated closely with those people who held the teachings of Balaam."

where He plans to take His Bride when He comes for her. The Tree of Life was present in The Garden of Eden. But after the Fall it was carefully guarded. Mankind was banished from The Garden, so no longer was able to eat of it. According to the above passage, it appears the Bride will have unlimited access to partake again of this Tree. What a privilege! Christ and His Bride will stroll in loving communion through The Garden of Paradise where The Tree of Life has been transplanted, and the Bride will freely partake of its fruit -- no longer barred or forbidden. The Tree of Life also is going to be present in The New Jerusalem, the permanent dwelling of the Bride. Whether The New Jerusalem is currently located in Paradise, or is a separate location to which The Tree of Life again must be transplanted, is open to speculation. I tend to think it is separate, because the Jewish wedding generally takes place in the Father's House, in facilities prepared specifically for that occasion. But the married couple eventually have their own home.

What expectations does The Bridegroom have in order for this Church to be prepared? It would appear from examining the message given to the Church of Ephesus, Jesus is pleased with her commitment, faithfulness, purity of doctrine, and her ability to identify impostors and false-doctrinal infiltrators. He is pleased with her patience and forbearance, and commends her willing labor. He is glad she has not shirked her message or mission. She has not fainted. But along with all of these commendable attributes, <u>He also really does want to be loved</u>! Hello! He wants that relationship any honest Bridegroom wants. Will all of this Church be part of The Bride? In finality, only the individuals of this Church who heed this message from The Bridegroom, and listen to the Holy Spirit Who is ready to assist in restoring the love-relationship, will qualify!

B. The Church of Smyrna.

Next He addresses the Church of Smyrna. Revelation 2:8 -11. *"And unto the angel of the church in Smyrna write. These things saith the first and the last, which was dead, and is alive :* Verse 9. *I know thy works, and tribulation, and poverty, (but thou art rich) and I know the blasphemy of them that say they are Jews, and are not, but are the synagogue of Satan.* Verse 10. *Fear none of those things which thou shalt suffer: behold, the devil shall cast **some of you** into prison, that ye may be tried; and <u>ye shall have tribulation ten days</u>: be thou faithful unto death, and I will give thee a crown of life.* Verse 11. *He that hath an ear, let him hear what the Spirit saith unto the churches: He that overcometh shall not be hurt of the second death."* Bold and underlining mine.

The Final Schedule Revealed

This Church is The Suffering Church, having overtones of those who are imprisoned and/or martyred for their faith. Jesus has only encouragement for this persecuted, impoverished Church. She does not have much of this world, and lives in need, but He reminds her that she is rich because she belongs to Him. He lets her know He understands, and is taking note of all the injustices being done to her. He is aware of those who are Jews (believers) outwardly, but actually are of the Synagogue of Satan.

It is here we realize the term 'Church' takes on a broader meaning, referring to all committed born-again believers. Notice, Jesus appears to be addressing persecution against true believers in two eras. One group is persecuted and martyred during The Church Age. The other significant group appears to be of The Ten Days of Awe, because He specifically mentions <u>persecution for ten days</u>. So He also is addressing The Tribulation Saints who will be put to death for their faith. The word of comfort He has for them all (from either Age) is that they will receive a Crown of Life, and The Second Death will have no ability to hurt them. He points out the comforting fact that He understands, because He is The First and The Last, and He also experienced unjust death Himself -- a death of persecution and misunderstanding, but He overcame death, and is alive forevermore. He can relate! The only difference is, He laid down His life Himself, willingly. No man took it from Him. He allowed it. The martyrs also lay down their lives willingly for their faith in Christ, but others have, and will, take their physical lives from them. But they will be resurrected in victory!

The martyrs and persecuted of The Church Age are all resurrected and raptured at Rosh HaShanah, along with all other Bride-ready believers of The Church Age. Those who will be martyred during The Ten Days of Awe, will be resurrected at Yom Kippur at His Return, and will be given the honor to rule and reign with Christ alongside The Bride. These all are referred to as The Church of Smyrna. Some are of The Church Age who fit into this persecuted category, so are of The Bride. It would appear then, that all betrothed Smyrna-type individuals of The Church Age will be included as part of The Bride. None of The Persecuted Church will be left behind at the Rapture. The Tribulation Saints who suffer the ten days, are either new believers during The Days of Awe, or are repentant believers who were not of The Persecuted Church, but were not ready until after the Rapture. Although not specifically of The Bride, they will have special recognition in The Kingdom.

This message to the Smyrna Church highlights those persecuted for their faith, pointing out the dichotomy of those who are true believers, and those who are not. But the reference to those of the Synagogue of Satan

THE SEVEN CHURCHES

has overtones of those who will be deceived by AntiChrist during The Ten Days of Awe, so this message cannot be taken only from an historical perspective, or as only referring to those of The Age of Grace. Although He addresses all persecuted suffering believers, it appears Jesus takes pains to particularly single out Christians of Jewish orientation. Over the course of The Church Age most believers have been Gentile, with only a few Jewish believers as part of their number. Separating out true Jews from impostors, within the framework of synagogue attendance, has not particularly been a problem for Gentile believers. It will be The Tribulation Saints who will be differentiated <u>as separate from those who claim</u> to be true Jewish believers, but in reality are of the synagogue of Satan. This suggest that the LORD is also addressing the converts of the 144,000 Jewish Evangelists during The Ten Days of Awe, coupled with those believers of The Church Age who will not have been taken in the Rapture, but have remained to be tried and purified <u>ten days</u>.

Are all these believers part of the Bride? <u>The persecuted and martyred Saints of the Church Age definitely are.</u> Those of The Days of Awe obviously are not able to attend the Wedding which takes place in Heaven during The Ten Days of Awe. They cannot be in two places at once! They may not be The Bride, but definitely will be included in the Household of The KING alongside The Bride when He returns at Yom Kippur. So this message to the Smyrna Church addresses both Ages of those persecuted for Christ's sake.

Notice, Jesus does not have anything negative to say regarding this Church. He loves them, and He knows they love Him. They have enough to deal with already without any heavies being placed upon them. But He does remind them that they do have the Holy Spirit alongside to help. The Holy Spirit is The Comforter for both groups. This message would seem to indicate then, that those who become honest committed believers during The Ten Days of Awe are also born of The Spirit unto salvation. There is no other way to be born-again except by the wooing of the Holy Spirit. Even though the office of the Holy Spirit as <u>The Friend of The Bridegroom and The Restrainer of Evil</u> is ended when the Spirit-filled believers of The Church Age are Raptured, this removal of <u>the restraint</u> does not mean the Holy Spirit no longer has any role on earth during The Ten Days of Awe, but that He takes a more limited, somewhat differently defined role among believers at that time. So the message for the Smyrna Church is one of encouragement and commendation, but as far as Bridal readiness is concerned, <u>only those persecuted Smyrna</u> believers of The Age of Grace will be part of The Bride.

C. The Pergamos Church:

The next message is to The Church of Pergamos. Revelation 2:12-17. *"And to the angel of the church in Pergamos write, These things saith <u>he which hath the sharp sword with two edges</u>. Verse 13. I know thy works, and where thou dwellest, even where Satan's seat is: and thou holdest fast my name, and hast not denied my faith, even in those days wherein Antipas was my faithful martyr, who was slain among you, where Satan dwelleth. Verse 14. But I have a few things against thee, because thou hast there them that hold the doctrine of Balaam, who taught Balak to cast a stumbling block before the children of Israel, to eat things sacrificed unto idols, and to commit fornication. Verse 15. So hast thou also them that hold the doctrine of the Nicolaitans, which thing I hate. Verse 16. Repent: or else <u>I will come unto thee quickly, and will fight against them with the sword of my mouth</u>. Verse 17. He that hath an ear, let him hear what the Spirit saith unto the churches; To him that overcometh will I give to eat of the hidden manna, and will give him a white stone, and in the stone a new name written, which no man knoweth saving he that receiveth it."* Underlining mine.

In this message, Jesus reveals His authority against pagan philosophies and occult practices. The Pergamos Church was situated where paganism was rampant.[113] He particularly identifies Baal worship, a type of Satanism which was <u>the very trap that led Israel to commit spiritual fornication</u>. It is no wonder Christ is jealous over this Church, and gives these admonitions! He admires their stand in holding fast to His Name, and in not denying their faith, even in the face of obvious opposition and persecution. He gives an example of what He means by mentioning Antipas who was martyred because of his faithfulness to the LORD. Somehow this incident that personally happened to one of their own members, served to strengthen them, and He is pleased about that.

But He also has a few concerns. They harbor some who actually are beginning to tolerate, and even entertain, the doctrines of Balaam. These pagan philosophies were the precise stumbling-block that caused Israel

---

[113] Merrill C. Tenney, General Editor, The Zondervan Pictorial Encyclodedia of the Bible, Volume Four, 1976, The Zondervan Corporation, Grand Rapids, Michigan, p. 435-436. "A story is recorded of the seduction of the Israelites into immoral and idolatrous unions with the women of Moab (Num 25:1-5). Had this situation not been checked, Israel would have been destroyed as a nation. Numbers 31:16 attributed the success of this seduction of God's people to the evil influence of a prophet named Balaam. ... Balaam became, therefore, in Heb. History a symbol of an evil man who led God's people into immorality and sin." "It may be that the doctrine of the Nicolaitans was dualistic. They prob. Reasoned that the human body was evil anyway and only the spirit was good."

to sin through idolatry! They may not actually be participating in these practices, but are exhibiting a tolerant attitude toward those who do. Such tolerance is dangerous! He also is concerned for the presence of the Nicolaitans which he tells them He hates. Basically, the Nicolaitan doctrines were rooted in self-aggrandizement, and control through vain philosophy. These things will only serve to drag them down. They must repent of their tolerance of these pagan ways, or He will come quickly, and fight against them with The Sword of His mouth.

We see a sorting of the harvest here. Those who repent immediately will be blessed, and will not be taken by surprise when He comes for them at Rosh HaShanah. Those who do not repent will not be ready, so His sudden coming will be like a thief to them, therefore they will remain to be part of the scene when Christ must return to fight with a Sword proceeding out of His mouth. When does He fight in such a manner? When He returns at Yom Kippur to fight against the AntiChrist and the nations at the end of The Days of Awe. Revelation 18:14-15. *"And the armies which were in heaven followed him upon white horses, clothed in fine linen, white and clean* Verse 15. *And out of his mouth goeth a sharp sword, that with it he should smite the nations:...."* If none of those who have this Pergamos attitude toward the false philosophies and religions of the world are going to have to face this scenario when He returns at Yom Kippur, then He would have no need to give warning. So some of this Church mind set will be left behind at the Rapture if they do not repent first.

But there is a blessing for those who repent of the sin of allowing tolerance of false, compromising teachings into the Church before Christ comes to take His Bride. They will eat of the hidden manna, and will receive a white stone with a new name inscribed. This will be exclusively special, so will be most precious, because only those who receive the stone know the new name that He bestows on them. A name in the Hebrew culture has great significance. Therefore, receiving a new name will mean He changes their name to represent His acceptance of them, showing His admiration, and undying love written in stone.

So what is the focus of the Bridegroom's message for the Bride to pay attention to in her preparations? Do not tolerate false doctrines and pagan philosophies, because these will only serve to drag down the believer, and water down the message of salvation and holiness. We need to focus our attention on Jesus Christ, and on His truth, rather than develop a compromising attitude toward the false philosophies in our society and in our world. This message certainly flies in the face of our western ideals of synchronism and multi-culturalism, which is defined as absolute tolerance to any and all religions and beliefs at the expense of the Gospel of Jesus

Christ. These may exist in our society, but we do not have to give the impression we receive everyone's choice of beliefs with open arms, when we know their religions and pagan practices are ultimately leading them to eternal damnation. We must accept people, but we must also seek to win them to Christ, and not simply 'live and let live' when it comes to eternal destinies. Christianity is not just another world religion in a line-up of choices. The Church has the message of salvation. Christianity is a relationship with God based in repentance, bought by the blood of Christ, and turning away from the philosophies and destructive things of this world. Jesus did not come to introduce a new religious system, but to bring man into reconciliation with God. We cannot fall into the trap of 'tolerance.' In fact, He does not want His Bride to take a wishy-washy stance, because the enemy is not satisfied with mere tolerance, but ultimately seeks honor and respect. Then he will slide in and begin corrupting even the Church. The Bride of Christ is not to be corrupted, but she is to keep herself unspotted from the world! Listen to, and heed the Spirit's Voice!

D. The Church of Thyatira:

Next, Jesus sends a message to the Church in Thyatira. Revelation 2: 18- 29. *"And unto the angel of the church in Thyatira write; these things saith the Son of God, who hath his eyes like unto a flame of fire, and his feet are like fine brass; Verse 19. I know thy works, and charity, and service, and faith, and thy patience, and thy works; and the last to be more than the first. Verse 20. Notwithstanding I have a few things against thee, because thou sufferest that woman Jezabel, which calleh herself a prophetess, to teach and to seduce my servants to commit fornication, and to eat things sacrificed unto idols. Verse21. And I gave her space to repent of her fornication; and she repented not. Verse 22. Behold, I will cast her into a bed, and them that commit adultery with her into <u>great tribulation, except they repent of their deeds</u>. Verse 23. And I will kill her children with death: and all the churches shall know that I am he which searcheth the reins and hearts: and I will give unto every one of you according to your works. Verse 24. But unto you I say, and unto the rest in Thyatira, as many as have not this doctrine, and which have not known the depths of Satan, as they speak; I will put upon you no other burden. Verse 25. But that which ye have already hold fast till I come. Verse 26. And he that overcometh, and keepth my works unto the end, to him will I give power over the nations: Verse 27 And he shall rule them with a rod of iron: as the vessels of a potter shall they be broken to shivers: even as I received of my Father. Verse 28. And I will give him the morning star. Verse 29. He that hath an ear, let him hear what the Spirit saith unto the churches."* Underlining mine.

Again, Jesus commends this Church for their compassionate works, their faith, and their patience. They have made significant progress in these areas, because their works are now greater than at the first. This Church has a lot going for it! But in His introductory statement, Christ reminds them He is The Son of God, and His eyes are like flames of fire, and His feet like fine brass. In other words, as The Son of God, He holds a position of absolute authority, power, and justice. He sees what is going on in their midst, and His eyes are flaming, showing His anger and indignation. His feet of brass speak of His position as The Righteous Judge who will certainly bring forth judgment. So in the middle of all that is right with this Church, there are serious issues which must be addressed, or judgment will be forthcoming.

The Church of Thyatira went one step beyond that of Pergamos. They allowed false teachings and fornication right into the Church; not just to sit in the pew, but to take up position to be heard and heeded. Perhaps they took the stance we so often hear today, that one benefits from truth wherever one finds it. This teaching is absolutely a form of spiritual adultery, because even if doctrinal truth can be gleaned from the teachings of spiritual sources outside of God's revealed Word, we must ignore the source. If truth is taught, it already is taught in Scripture. Why go outside of Scripture to false religions, pagan philosophies, and doctrines of men to glean truth, even if the truth we are looking for appears viable? We must remember, even Satan in tempting Eve stated 99% truth, but the 1% error made everything he stated into absolute falsity, and his deception has led all mankind down the path of destruction and separation from God ever since. Truth tainted is truth corrupted. In fact, it does not qualify as truth in God's eyes.

Jezebel was caught up in pagan practices, yet she was allowed to teach in the Church! In so doing, she created a following that caused many to commit fornication and adultery with her. Yet she still not only remained, but obviously was allowed to be in a position where she was considered a person to be listened to. What a travesty! She was given time to repent, but she obviously did not, yet she was not removed from a position of influence within the Thyatira Church. Unfortunately, she led many astray as a result. The Lord is so incensed with her and her following, He will cast her and her followers into a bed together, so they will have to go through <u>great tribulation</u>. That certainly sounds like they will have to face the wrath of God during The Days of Awe! And He will kill her children (offspring of false pagan teachings and practices,) <u>putting them to death</u> <u>through His wrath</u>. This message is a strong admonition to all the

Churches, both of The Church Age, as well as to those who must remain during The Days of Awe.

Does He mete out discipline even now on those who are so obviously non-repentant? Yes. Only during this Age of Grace, we often do not recognize His discipline as readily as we should. Unrepentant sin always leads to judgment in one form or another for those who insist on remaining in it, and especially on those who teach others with the intent to lead them astray. It is certain Jesus Christ will not want any of these deceivers, or deceived, to be part of His Bride at His Wedding in Heaven! He will not marry unrepentant fornicators and adulterers! But He does offer time to repent now, and also during the final Ten Days of Teshuvah. The question is, will any caught up in these practices and mind-sets take Him up on His admonition to repent, either now, or then?

For those of Thyatira not involved in this blatant sin within the ranks of the Church, He places no other burden. Those not involved obviously are appalled at what is going on, because it really is a concern to them, but the LORD is not holding them accountable. It is also obvious the leadership of this Church is taken-in by those involved, to allow the sin to continue, and to even provide avenues for those following paganism to teach their practices and ideologies. So those not involved cannot seem to do anything about the situation, even though they may honestly have tried. When we see false practices and pagan philosophies creeping into the Church, we must speak out about them to expose those involved, and to uphold the truth to protect the Church, even if the leadership or majority do not listen. All that is required is that we hold fast to our faith until Christ comes. Those who contend for purity and truth will be taken as part of the Bride when Christ comes at the Rapture. If there are some who repent following the Rapture, and certainly there will be, these also will eventually be blessed, but will not be of the Bride.

What will be the reward for faithfulness and repentance? Those who remain faithful to Christ will be given power to rule over the nations. This is fitting, because those who were unrepentant will have to listen and obey! Those who were taken at the Rapture will rule and reign as the Bride at Christ's side. Those who repent during The Days of Awe will also be privileged to rule alongside the Bride. Therefore, it is important to listen to the Holy Spirit, and understand what He is saying to the Churches! Heeding what He says will determine whether we are part of the Bride, or if we lay aside His counsel until we wake up to find we must become Tribulation Saints, when it will be much more difficult, but absolutely necessary to heed. It certainly is better to respond to the Spirit during the Elul days of Teshuvah before Rosh HaShanah, than to have to face the Ten

Days of Awe, the last ten days of Teshuvah! Better yet, <u>don't entertain false, pagan, idolatrous philosophies and fornication at all</u>. Listen to the Spirit and stay pure. The LORD is looking for a pure Bride!

E. The Sardis Church:

The Sardis Church is next on the list. Revelation 3:1-6. "*And unto the church of Sardis write; These things saith he that hath the seven spirits of God, and the seven stars; I know thy works, that thou hast a name that thou livest, and art dead. Verse 2. Be watchful, and strengthen the things which remain, that are ready to die: for I have not found thy works perfect before God. Verse 3. Remember therefore how thou hast received and heard, and hold fast, and repent. If therefore thou shalt not watch, <u>I will come on thee as a thief, and thou shalt not know what hour I will come upon thee</u>. Verse 4. Thou hast a few names even in Sardis which have not defiled their garments; and they shall walk with me in white: for they are worthy. Verse 6. He that overcometh, the same shall be clothed in white raiment; <u>and I will not blot out his name out of the book of life</u>, but I will confess his name before my Father, and before his angels. Verse 6. He that hath an ear, let him hear what the Spirit saith unto the churches.*" Underlining mine.

This is the strongest, most sobering message Jesus gives yet! This admonition does not begin with commendations. In fact, the introduction refers to the fact that He has the Seven Spirits of God, and the Seven Stars. In other words, He is the giver of the Holy Spirit in fullness, and holds dear the completion and perfection of the entire Church expedited through the work and ministry of the Spirit. So the Church is able, by listening to the Holy Spirit, able to become all that is mature in ministry and in life. Jesus is pointing out the fact that His words and wishes as represented by the Holy Spirit's total role and presence, are to be absolutely heeded by His entire Church. He is incensed that this Church has apparently entirely ignored the fullness of the Holy Spirit, and His intended role among them! This means they completely discount the perfecting work of the Holy Spirit. Now that is indeed dangerous for the Bride!

The Seven Stars refer to the intended perfect ministry of leadership as given by the LORD through the Holy Spirit to the Churches, and directed specifically by Jesus Christ through the Holy Spirit's empowerment, enablement, gifting, and directives. It is obvious this Sardis Church does not recognize, give credence to, or even seek any input by the Holy Spirit, or any anointing from God for teaching or ministry!

Are they even a Church? Well, at least in man-made organization and affiliation they are. As far as Christ is concerned, they have a name that they are alive, but in fact are dead. What an indictment! They are dead!

How would any of us like to marry a corpse? No love, no warmth. No willingness to even consider what the Spirit, The Friend of the Bridegroom states or suggests. No communication then with Christ, because this must be expedited through the Holy Spirit. Nothing! He mentions that their works are not perfect (neither holy, nor wholly acceptable) before God. What they are doing apparently gives absolutely no glory to God. They have their own agenda, and God and His Word, and especially any Holy Spirit anointing, are not part of it.

Is there any hope for this Church? It appears that Christ is taking a long shot that He may be able to appeal to their reason, if nothing else. Obviously in the past there was a genuine relationship, or Christ would not even refer to the fact that there may be something left to revive. He appeals to their intelligence and ability to remember. What are they to recall? They are to remember what they received and heard, and grab tenaciously onto those things, and repent. Jesus gives a solemn warning. If they do not watch, He will come on them like a Thief, and they won't know what hour He will come upon them. What is being stated here?

Both Jesus and Paul refer to the coming of Christ for His Church as that of a Thief in the night. But this Sardis Church is being warned that if they do not remember their salvation and the things they received, and are caught not watching, they will be in danger of being lumped together with the unbelievers of the world who will not be looking for, nor even expecting Christ to come. They will be caught totally off guard at The Last Trump of Rosh HaShanah. In fact they will have no clue, because they will not even perhaps believe in the Rapture of the Church. Do any of us know Christians who take this stance, who also do not believe in the work of the Holy Spirit in our day? They give no credence to the power of God! These will be left behind to definitely have to face the same wrath that will be poured out on the ungodly during The Days of Awe.

Now comes a statement by Christ given more as an observation rather than as a commendation. The fact that this statement is couched in the negative comparison shows just how far the general member of this Church has fallen from truth. This declaration compares a handful of folk with the position of the whole. There are a few names even in Sardis who have not soiled their garments. A few names indicates there are very, very few. Paraphrased, this means in our vernacular, "I can count, as if on one hand, those who have not become tainted with the Sardis mind-set." But these will walk with Christ in white because they are worthy. This means only these few who have remained fervent for the LORD will be part of the spotless Bride, worthy to wear the wedding dress He provides, and walk with Him in Wedding Procession.

Those who overcome are promised they will be clothed in white raiment, and their names will not be blotted out of The Book of Life. Here is direct reference to The Books being opened on Rosh HaShanah, and again at Yom Kippur. Those who are worthy will be raptured because their names are already written in The Book of the Wholly Righteous, which is The Book of Life. Those who repent during The Days of Awe, and renew their faith and fervent love for the LORD, will not have their names blotted out of The Book of Life.

This obvious reference to Yom Kippur is a very sobering statement, indicating that there are those who had their names written in The Book of Life at one time, but they have sinned, and have refused to recognize their need for repentance. So their names will be eternally blotted out, and they will be assigned their portion along with the wicked (Rashim) to await eternal punishment and separation from God. They may have accepted Christ at one time, and even remained nominally attached to a 'church' organization, but lived a life devoid of faith, giving lip-service to the doctrines of Scripture, but not really believing any of it to the point of application in true life-changing devotion. So they will miss the Rapture, and ultimately if remaining non-repentant, miss the final sealing of the righteous on Yom Kippur, and their names will be blotted out of The Book of Life instead. Those who repent will have their names lifted up before The Father and all the holy angels. In other words, Christ proudly will vouch for them before The Father and all the holy angels.

Again, we are able to see this Church has hope. Christ loves them, and really wants them to be a part of His Bride, or at least have place in His Kingdom, but they must do a couple of key things. Remember their past commitment and belief, repent, and listen to the Holy Spirit. For anyone in love with their Bridegroom in preparation for their own wedding, doing these simple things should not be too much to be expected!

F. The Philadelphia Church:

In contrast to the Ephesian, Pergamos, Thyatira, and Sardis Churches who all had issues that needed addressing, (but not the suffering Smyrna Church), Philadelphia is a breath of fresh air! Here is a Church that really is in love with the Bridegroom, and they let the LORD and others know it. In other words, Philadelphia is thinking and acting like a betrothed Bride!

Revelation 3:7-13. *"And to the angel of the church in Philadelphia write: These things saith he that is holy, he that is true, he that hath the key of David, he that openeth, and no man shutteth, and shutteth, and no man openeth;* Verse 8. *I know thy works; behold, I have set before thee an open door, and no man can shut it: for thou hast a little strength, and has kept my word, and has not denied my name. Verse 9. Behold, I will make them of the synagogue of Satan, which say they are Jews, and are not, but do lie; behold, I will make them to come and worship before thy feet, and to know that I have loved thee. Verse 10. Because thou hast kept the word of my patience, I also will keep thee from the hour of temptation, which shall come upon all the world, to try them that dwell upon the earth. Verse 11. Behold, I come quickly: hold that fast which thou hast, that no man take thy crown. Verse 12. Him that overcometh will I make a pillar in the temple of my God, and he shall go no more out: and I will write upon him the name of my God, and the name of the city of my God, which is new Jerusalem, which cometh down out of heaven from my God: and I will write upon him my new name. Verse 13. He that hath an ear, let him hear what the Spirit saith unto the churches."*

Jesus introduces this message by stating He is holy and true, and has the key of David, meaning He is the rightful, righteous KING of The Kingdom. Let that truth sink-in! Our Bridegroom is The Ruler of Heaven and Earth! He is the One who opens and no man can shut, and shuts and no man can open, referring to the fact that He controls everything. What He says ultimately is how it is, and will be. He is all powerful, and is in absolute, complete control. His Word is Law! His influence is absolute! His love is perfect! If He opens a door regarding an issue, no one can usurp His wishes and close it. If He opens or closes a door, no one else has the power to open or close it. He really is The KING! There especially is one door that the Bride should be very happy He has control over. He will open the door in Heaven and invite His Bride into His prepared chambers, and no one can shut that door against her. But He also shuts the door to those wedding chambers, and no one can open.

<u>This Church is totally taken at the time of the Rapture of Rosh HaShanah</u>. Even though they have only a little strength, they have kept His Word, and not denied His name. They have been honored to name The Name of Christ in this world. He will make them of the synagogue of Satan, who say they are Jews but are not, to come and worship before their feet, and know that Christ has loved them. In other words, when the Rapture takes place, the unbelievers will have to concede Christ really loved these Christians, and they are His Bride. The Jews who will be left behind especially will have a hard time with this during The Days of Awe, and particularly those who will worship at the synagogue of Satan, meaning those who will align themselves with AntiChrist who will require their worship. At Yom Kippur, those same unbelievers will have to bow down before these Christians, because Christ will require obeisance and honor be extended toward His Bride who rules at His side.

Jesus states <u>He will keep this Church from the hour of testing that will come upon the entire world</u>. This is a specific reference to the hiding of His Bride during The Days of Awe. <u>She does not have to experience this time of wrath that comes upon all the earth</u>. He reminds this Church that He is coming quickly, and to hold securely onto her position and loyalty, so no man can take her crown. He that overcomes will be made to be a pillar in God's house, and will never leave this honorable position; and will receive the Name of God, and the name of the City of God, meaning she will be identified with God and with the City of the New Jerusalem, as His wife. Jesus states He will give this totally righteous Church His own New Name. A wedded Bride takes on the name and identification of her Husband. This Church will definitely be His wife! All she needs to do is continue to listen to the voice of the Holy Spirit until He comes for her.

G. The Laodicean Church:

Revelation 3:14-22. " *And unto the angel of the church of the Laodiceans write: These things saith the Amen, the faithful and true witness, the beginning of the creation of God:* Verse 15. *I know thy works, that thou art neither cold nor hot: I would thou wert cold or hot.* Verse 16. *So, then because thou are likewarm, and neither cold nor hot, I will spew thee out of my mouth.* Verse 17. *Because thou sayest, I am rich, and increased with goods, and have need of nothing; and knowest not that thou art wretched, and miserable, and poor, and blind, and naked:* Verse 18. *I counsel thee to buy of me gold tried in the fire, that thou mayest be rich; and white raiment, that thou mayest be clothed and that the shame of thy nakedness do not appear; and anoint thine eyes with eyesalve, that thou mayest see.* Verse 19 *As many as I love, I rebuke and chasten: be zealous therefore, and repent.* Verse 20. *Behold, I stand at the door and knock: if any man hear my voice, and open the door, I will come in to him, and will sup with him, and he with me.* Verse 21. *To him that overcometh will I grant to sit with me in my throne, even as I also overcame, and am set down with my Father in his throne.* Verse 22. *He that hath an ear, let him hear what the Spirit saith unto the churches.*"

Here we see the heartfelt passionate love and longing of the LORD for His Bride. He is the true and faithful One that will bring all to pass. He is the Creator. In other words, He is reminding this Church that the One she is betrothed to is, in fact, the Creator of the whole universe, and He is true to His own Word. But He does not want her to be in love <u>just with His position</u>, but to be totally sold out in committed love <u>to Him -- for Himself</u>.

He is not overly pleased with the attitude of this Church, because He finds her neither cold nor hot, but lukewarm in her relationship with Him.

The Final Schedule Revealed

He is not inclined to want to marry someone who is lukewarm at best, and we certainly cannot blame Him for that. Her lukewarmness leaves Him revolted. He will spit her out unless she repents. He has no intention of marrying a tepid dishrag!

Not only is she lukewarm in her feelings toward Him, she is also conceited! She feels she is rich, and does not need anything. She does not really need Him -- just the affiliation of being betrothed to His position, and what that will mean in feeding her own pride. But in fact, she is poor and wretched, and totally blind to her need, and naked of any righteousness. So she is certainly not ready, nor worthy, to have the honor of putting on the wedding raiment! But there is really no need for her attitude. Its all in her own head. She needs to develop a new perspective, and a new devotion. She needs to see everything differently, and acknowledge what He sees. He states He will rebuke and chastise her, because He really does love her. His desire is not just to be harsh with her, but to hopefully talk some sense into her, and jolt her back to reality!

He stands at the entrance and knocks, waiting to be let back into the relationship. He lingers at the door, asking whether there may be a slight chance of any intimate communication. This is an offer of Himself, but He is being the perfect gentleman. He will not intrude where He is not really, and fervently, wanted! But if she desires Him to, He will come in immediately. If she will just open the door of her heart and invite Him in, He will commune with her over an intimate romantic dinner. All He expects is some consideration, and the chance to spend some loving time with the One He is betrothed to, but she has shut Him out, and is playing a game of hard to get. She is giving the impression she has no need of anything, least of all from Him! But in reality, she has nothing herself of any worth. He is trying to convey His concern and love for her, but finds Himself in an awkward position. It is becoming obvious He will have to soon make a difficult decision as to whether He will be able to remain committed to accepting her as His future wedded Bride.

He reminds this Church that those who overcome this ambivalence, and self-seeking haughtiness and pride, will have the honor of sitting with Him in His throne, just like He overcame, and has position with His Father in His throne. He is telling her that if she will only drop her attitude, and again recognize His love for her, and respond to Him passionately, she will receive the honor of royal position by His side! After all, she is betrothed by the KING! Christ overcame the temptations of this world, and was victorious, so has received the honor of sitting upon The Father's Throne. All she needs to do is wipe the false perspectives from her eyes with His healing perception, and overcome her own lukewarmness toward Him.

She needs to clothe herself, and cover her nakedness with the white raiment and gold finery He will provide for her, if she will only ask. Then she will have the honorable privilege to rule alongside Him! He pleads with her to listen to the counsel of the Holy Spirit, the Friend He has been trying to communicate through, and the Voice who is telling her to smarten-up! The Holy Spirit is not just getting on her case here, but is the Counselor to be heeded by all the Churches in preparation to be the Bride.

This Laodicean Church is perhaps in the most vulnerable and dangerous position of all the Churches He has addressed, because she apparently does not acknowledge her real need and shortcomings. One of the signs of reaching maturity is the ability to own up to faults, and to address them. Christ is not about to marry someone who is immature and full of pride. He does not want a spoiled brat for a wife!

H. In summary of the Seven Churches:

Let's summarize what the Bridegroom, Who has addressed these Seven Churches, is expecting the Church-Bride to do to be ready when He comes for her. Certainly she must continue to do the things He admires in her, shunning evil and paganism, standing up for truth, taking part in benevolence, and spreading the Gospel. She is a very capable and talented Church, but in all her busyness, He simply does not want her to overlook His passion and great love for her. A Bride should be in love with her Bridegroom, and have a passionate desire to please and serve Him, to commune with Him, and to share with Him. She should be excited and honored that He loves her, has chosen her as His Betrothed, and desires the best for her, and that He has provided all she needs.

All she has to do is show Him her love and respect, and prepare carefully for the Wedding, waiting for Him in an honorable manner, and taking vigilant steps to be sure she is ready according to His desires when He comes for her. With all the promises He states will be in store for the Bride, and everything He has provided, it is a real mystery how anyone would not love Him. The only thing the Bride must really do is listen to the Holy Spirit, the Friend of the Bridegroom, and act accordingly. Those who abide by His guidelines of love and purity will be accounted worthy to be whisked away to the Wedding. Those who do not, will be left behind, and will have a further ten years to repent and come to terms with Christ before it is forever too late, but they will not be His Bride. His desire though, is that the Seven Churches will listen to the Holy Spirit's directives and prompting, and assure their place at His side as the Bride. As with any courtship leading to wedded covenant, everything is based

The Final Schedule Revealed

upon the love of the Bridegroom for the Bride, and the love of the Bride for the Bridegroom, which is all proper, true, and honorable.

CHAPTER 14
THE THRONE ROOM, and THE SEALED BOOK

Many of us have considered anything mentioned beyond the first few verses of Revelation chapter 4 to be referring to events that take place during the Tribulation, once the Church, as represented by John the Revelator, is called to *"come up hither."* However, this explanation does have some complications. So let's keep the prophetic spiral in mind as we travel through The Book of Revelation, and we shall see whether this general perception is totally valid, or whether there is room for the spiral to circle- back around with any significance regarding The Church Age, as well as for pre-Days of Awe Israel and the nations, beyond Revelation chapter 4.

I. The Throne Room:

John is invited by a voice saying, *"Come up hither, and I will show thee things which must be hereafter."* Revelation 4: 1. He is taken by the Spirit into Heaven, where he is given a glimpse of what awaits. He sees a door opened, and hears the sound of a trumpet giving him a message. The trumpet he hears is the Last Trump of Rosh HaShanah calling the wholly Righteous into the Courts of Heaven. There John is given a glimpse of the majesty of The Throne Room of God. The One sitting upon The Throne is described in terms of precious stones. Jasper and a sardine stone show His precious and priceless, pure stature, and office. An emerald rainbow surrounds The Throne. In front of The Throne is what appears to be a sea of glass that is absolutely clear like crystal. About The Throne are seated twenty-four elders all clothed in white, and having gold crowns upon their heads. Lightening, thunders and voices emanate from The Throne. There are Seven Lamps of fire burning before The Throne, which are the Seven Spirits of God. Seven speaks of complete perfection, so this is a picture of the Christ in absolute majesty and glory.

Surrounding The Throne itself are four creatures full of eyes all around. John describes these creatures as if he is standing facing them, so he tells us what he sees. The first appears to have the face of a lion, the second that of a calf, the third that of a man, and the fourth, the face of an eagle. These are the Cherubim which minister to the One seated upon The Throne in Heaven. Ezekiel and Daniel saw these same creatures, and describe these beings, not simply as four creatures each having a different face, but indeed each having these four faces. The Cherubim are not just visionary, symbolic, metaphorical creatures, but are very real.

Whenever the Cherubim are mentioned, the Shekinah Glory of the presence of the LORD seated upon The Throne of God is indicated, because the Cherubim accompany the Glory of God. There were Cherubim made of gold attached to the Mercy Seat of The Ark of the Covenant in The Holy of Holies in the wilderness Tabernacle, and later in The Temple on Mount Zion. The Glory of God dwelt between the Cherubim. But the earthly Holy of Holies represented the far greater reality of the Tabernacle and Throne in the Heavenlies.

Day and night these Cherubim cry, *"Holy, holy, holy, Lord God Almighty, which was, and is, and is to come."* Revelation 4: 8. Whenever these four beings give glory unto the LORD, and give Him thanks, the twenty-four elders fall down before Him, and worship Him that lives forever and ever, casting their crowns at His feet, saying, *"Thou art worthy, O Lord, to receive glory and honor, and power, for thou hast created all things, and for thy pleasure they are and were created.* Verse 11. The twenty-four elders represent the leaders of the twelve tribes of Israel, and the twelve apostles. Only those who are worthy are allowed to sit or stand in the presence of Him Who sits on The Throne.

Other beings obviously come and go from this presence of The Glory of The LORD. There are multitudes of angels and redeemed saints who stand at varying times, either before The Throne, or under the altar that is present in the heavenly Tabernacle of The Throne Room. Vapors of incense arise from off the altar before The Throne, and represent the prayers of the saints. The tears of intercession, remorse, and repentance offered unto the LORD by the children of God, are carefully collected in vials, and held precious. We could go on and describe the significance of all that is pictured and represented in the presence of the LORD, and of The Throne of God, but the focus of this book is to dwell on the convocational events orchestrated from this Throne Room.

Whenever we see The Throne mentioned in Scripture, it is this scene described by John that should come to mind. Just as Ezekiel on several occasions saw the Cloud of The Glory of The LORD, and the Cherubim that surround The Throne hovering above or settling upon the earth, John is given the privilege of viewing this Glorious Throne scene in Heaven. This is the Heavenly Control Center from which all things are orchestrated for the entire universe. John is given a glimpse of how operations and decisions made by The LORD are expedited by the creatures who come and go from this Control Center, and how these affect all that takes place in Heaven, and on the earth.

II. John's Prophetic Journey:

As John is taken on a journey revealing what has, is, and will come to pass through Christ, we see the prophetic spiral is definitely at work in The Book of Revelation. Flash-back, overlap, and transition are being used by Christ, the angels, and by John as he writes what is revealed to him. John, under the inspiration of the Holy Spirit, incorporates a 'back to the future' approach. You will see what I mean as we progress.

The orientation of our generation allows some ability to relate to this approach and its significance, because we have a mind-set that is not foreign to the type of reasoning needed to follow the techniques John uses. The veil has been slowly dropped as we now have scientific evidence for the possibilities of parallel, interactive dimensions. We are now aware that there are many more dimensions than just three. For example, the existence of an actual dimension called Heaven may not really be such a difficult concept to embrace, and yet many people still dismiss its reality. Eternity, although difficult for our finite minds to totally grasp because we are limited by our senses to time and space in the realm of earth, does not seem so far-out anymore. We are exposed to such concepts as the possibility that time itself perhaps has variables. The fact that light does not always travel at a constant rate of speed, but is subject to other factors within the universe, no longer is beyond our ability to at least consider, even if we do not totally understand. Eternity is the reality. Time, that God spoke into existence as part of His Creation, is the 'warp' wrapped within, yet permeated by, eternity. God dwells within the dimension of eternity, so has the ability to know the end from the beginning as relative to time, all at once. This concept up until now has been difficult for us finite humans to conceptualize, but we are beginning to understand in a very small measure.

Following the Millennium there will be a new Heavens and a new Earth that will allow us to relate to time and space from an eternal perspective, taking us full circle to the perfection and stability of original Creation. Revelation reveals the One who is able to bring this about! The LORD God, The Almighty, The Creator Himself revealed in all His Glory!

The Book of Revelation has been considered primarily from a metaphorical perspective by most Christians. Certainly metaphor is used, but the root of the symbolism is not merely literary, but has foundation in historical actuality, and fulfillment in prophetic fact. The symbolisms in all instances can be identified as those already used in The Old Testament, so we have a built-in reference to identify what is metaphorical, along with the intended interpretation, and what is actual in and of itself. Also, our ability to understand and interpret has been heightened because of many scientific breakthroughs that have been rapidly taking place -- a fulfillment itself of the Daniel 12:24 that *"knowledge shall be on the increase"* just before the return of Christ. Also, world events are shedding much light on prophecy, and we now are living much of Revelation, Daniel, Isaiah, Ezekiel, and all the Prophets, as their prophecies are being fulfilled right before our eyes, and are directly affecting our lives.

The challenge in interpreting The Book of Revelation is to differentiate between what is concurrent, what is sequential; what is historical, and what is still future. John, by the Spirit's revelation, takes us on a trip that reveals much that is both beyond, as well as within time and space, and that affects all who have lived, and will live, of beings eternal and temporal, righteous and unrighteous, holy and unholy, earthly and celestial. John's prophetic glimpse is the revelation of reality as facilitated through Jesus Christ.

III. An Example from The Sixth Seal:

For example, notice Revelation 6:12, <u>because this is important for the Church as well as for Israel</u>, and sheds light on what Joel stated, and Peter quoted in The Book of Acts regarding the duration of the Age of the Holy Spirit's power and fullness. *"And I beheld when he had opened the sixth seal, and lo, there was a great earthquake; and the <u>sun became black as sackcloth of hair, and the moon became as blood</u>."* There is still light being given off by the sun, but it appears as though looking at it through a woven sheet of sackcloth, much like looking through a blanket. The moon is shining, but its appearance is blood-red. This cosmic situation suggests there is a great deal of atmospheric haze and disturbance, possibly as would occur if there were a massive disaster causing cloudiness.

Many have probably, at one time or another, viewed these phenomena in a small localized fashion if we have looked at the sun and moon through the smoky haze of a forest fire. It's pretty awesome, and somewhat scary -- appearing surreal. Those of us who have lived through the forest fires and fire-storms of this past summer understand this analogy! The night of the fire-storm, the angry red-orange sky, against a threatening back-drop of enormous flames, was described by most of us using such terms as 'apocalyptic,' or 'nuclear winter.' The atmosphere looked, and felt, like it was literally going to ignite above our heads, even though the fire itself for most of us, was still two to three kilometers away. Needless to say, we did not question being evacuated!

THE THRONE ROOM, and THE SEALED BOOK

What if this atmospheric phenomenon were to take place over a good portion of the earth's surface? The interesting thing is, the cause of the cosmic appearance John describes regarding the sun and moon need not necessarily be world-wide for all on earth to view, and/or be affected. After all, the Trade Center pillars of blood, fire, and smoke were not world-wide, but certainly were viewed world-wide, and have since affected, and continue to affect people world-wide. If war is the cause of the sun being darkened, and the moon appearing as blood, and the stars not appearing to shine, we can be sure the play-by-play of the war will be filmed, documented, and broadcast visually world-wide.

Also, the fear of nuclear fall-out, coupled with the devastation wreaked by a shower of fiery meteorites, will send everyone into a frenzy trying to find a way to hide from the effects. Many will long for an underground bunker or stone hide-out, and fear will drive many to cry out, desiring to hide themselves from God, Who they will blame for the situation. They will recognize these disasters as 'Acts of God.'

Somehow Israel will inevitably become front and center as always, so the war itself will include Israel. Gog and Magog may begin as the result of a conflict with Iraq, or even with Syria, followed by a direct invasion of Israel by Russia and her allies, but however it begins, it will ultimately be about Israeli jurisdiction. If we think this is far-fetched, we need only to look back at Desert Storm, and see that Israel neither started, nor even officially entered the fray, but war-heads were lobbed in her direction anyway. If Israel is not in the thick of it to begin with, she will be placed there. The Battle of Gog and Magog will be waged over issues regarding Israel, and this scenario is shaping up even now.

We've heard from the New Age about collective consciousness, but the devastation this war and the simultaneous disasters and cosmic changes that accompany it will cause, will result in something akin to collective guilt and fear! What we read in Revelation 6:17 is shortly to become reality. We must realize The Days of Awe are soon to unfold, and there will be great fear because of what is to transpire upon the earth. *"For the great day of his wrath is come; and who shall be able to stand?"* Jesus also indicated the same in Luke 21:26. *"Men's hearts failing them for fear, and for looking after those things <u>which are coming on the earth</u>: for the powers of heaven shall be shaken."* Therefore this war and its effects are pre-Days of Awe - **a sign that God's wrath is about to be** poured out in earnest <u>in the near future</u>. But is this the beginning of the Tribulation? Not quite.

Also, the Rapture of the Church will take place around this time, because these changes appearing in the sun and moon are the final sign given by Joel and Peter for the Church Age. So yes, the Seals show flash-back, and this means that Seals one through five, and the events occurring at the opening of the Sixth Seal, are all pre-Days of Awe.

The reason I am beginning with the example of some of the Sixth Seal idiosyncrasies, is because they are foundational to unlocking end-time events that are now beginning to take place, and also serve to help identify the key players involved as we progress through The Book of Revelation in light of the coming Divine Appointments, The Fall Feasts.

IV. FIGS:

Before delving into an explanation of each of the Seals, I want to draw on one more metaphor that is used. One of the events that occurs when the Sixth Seal is opened, is the shaking of the Fig Tree, indicating our current Nation of Israel has particular significance. We are able to observe then, the transition that Joel mentions. There must be a re-focusing on Judah and Jerusalem just prior to, and after the Rapture of the Church, bringing in the deliverance for this particular geographical area. But why are figs mentioned?

Jesus says some things about figs. (He even had a controversy with a fig tree when he was hungry, and the fig tree lost! Mark 11:12-14, and 11: 20-22.) But Revelation 6:13 speaks of the stars of heaven falling unto the earth just like a fig tree dropping untimely figs when shaken in a mighty wind. A meteorite shower? Perhaps. But the overtone would seem to indicate that some of these objects could be man-made, like missiles or bombs. Perhaps it means both meteorites and bombs at the same time. That's not unlike when God rained fiery meteorites on the Assyrian army to end a war. He seems inclined to do that occasionally when a war, which of course is fought by imperfect people, is not quite accomplishing what He intends. So it would stand to reason He may mix His own cosmic missiles in with our man-made ones. But what does this have to do with figs?

Figs in Scripture indicate people -- specifically the people of Judah. So here's Judah again! Jeremiah had a vision of two baskets of figs. One basket had very good figs, and the other very bad figs. Jeremiah 24:5 -10 states, *"Thus saith the LORD, the God of Israel; Like these good figs, so will I acknowledge them that are carried away captive of Judah, whom I have sent out of this place into the land of the Chaldeans for their good. Verse 6. For I will set mine eyes upon them for good, and I will bring them again to this land: and I will build them, and not pull them down; and I will plant them, and not pluck them up. Verse 7. And I will give them a heart to know me, that I am the LORD; and they shall be my people, and I will be their God; for they shall return unto me with their whole heart. Verse 8. And as the evil figs which cannot be eaten, they are so evil; surely thus saith the LORD, So will I give Zedekiah the king of Judah, and his princes, and the residue of Jerusalem, that remain in this land, and them that dwell in the land of Egypt:* Verse 9. *And I will deliver them to be removed into all the kingdoms of the earth for their hurt, to be a reproach and a proverb, a taunt and a curse, in all places whither I shall drive them.* Verse 10. *And I will send the sword , the famine, and the pestilence among them, till they be consumed from off the land that I gave unto them and to their fathers."* KJV. Underlining mine.

This passage indicates the good figs (Judah) were taken captive by the Babylonians for their own good. God removed them from The Land so He could bring judgment to The Land, because they had not been keeping the Sabbath of The Land. They were removed both for discipline as well as for safety. Exactly 70 years later, they were given Cyrus' royal decree permission to return to The Land formerly occupied by The Kingdom of Judah. However, this return has never been complete.

The evil figs (also of Judah) that remained in The Land at the time of the Babylonian Captivity, experienced God's judgment in the form of famine, sword, and pestilence. They ultimately were further dispersed into Egypt and other kingdoms. These also have never fully returned.

But since Israel became a nation in 1948, many have now begun to return from all the countries where they were scattered following the Babylonian Captivity and subsequent dispersions. The Jews in these countries are referred to as living in 'Diaspora,' the Dispersion. The dispersion was not the Babylonian captivity per se', but came about as a result of many situations that have occurred since that time. Also, the Diaspora has more directly to do with The House of Judah than The House of Israel, because the House of Israel never officially returned following The Assyrian Captivity, so was never dispersed again from The Land, but remained outcasts. They were not issued any official royal decree to return by the Assyrians, as those of Judah received under Cyrus of the Medio-Persian administration. But because there still are those of the Kingdom of Israel who can be identified by tribe, these also are referred to, somewhat erroneously, as living in Diaspora. Some of both Houses have ultimately returned since 1948. Some to blessing; some to hardship. The return will not be complete until Messiah. <u>Until then, the figs</u>, specifically <u>Judah</u>, but ultimately all Israel, <u>will be shaken</u>. When all the shaking is done, only the good figs will remain to inherit The Land.

Now the figs can be identified as representing Judah directly. But they also represent all Israel, because the LORD prefaces His explanation regarding the figs with a statement that He is the God of Israel. **Therefore, fulfillment will have its roots in the fact that Israel must exist as a Nation, because the LORD is the God of Israel**. The people of Israel today include both the House of Israel and the House of Judah. In fact, we do not differentiate between these two Houses any longer. **However, Judah and Jerusalem are highlighted, indicating much of end time prophecy is unfolded around what happens to Judah (the original figs) and Jerusalem.**

Therefore, the mighty wind that shakes the tree so that the untimely figs fall, must have something to do with a **controversy over Judah and Jerusalem**. Revelation 6:13 does not indicate the tree is uprooted, just shaken, so that the untimely figs fall. In other words, Judah and Jerusalem may be secured, but at the price of loss of life and limb of people who live there. It is even possible that there may be one more dispersion of some of them. This shaking of the Fig Tree, indicated by the meteorite shower and exchange of nuclear and conventional weapons of war, along with an earthquake, will usher in the dispensation known as The Wrath of God, The Day of the LORD, The Days of Awe. According to Revelation 6:13, this shaking of the fig tree occurs at the time of the opening of the Sixth Seal, around the same time-frame as the sun being darkened and the moon being turned to the color of blood, and accompanies war. This war is The Battle of Gog and Magog.

But Jesus states something else in conjunction with the Fig Tree in Luke 21:29-32. *"And he spake unto them a parable; Behold the fig tree, and all the trees; When they now shoot forth, ye know that summer is nigh at hand. So likewise ye, when ye see these things come to pass, know ye that the kingdom of God is nigh at hand. Verily I say unto you, this generation shall not pass away, till all be fulfilled."* If the Fig Tree refers to Jerusalem and Judah, and yes, ultimately all Israel, then who are the other trees? They are the rest of the nations. When God is about to bring His discipline to bear on Israel, specifically in regard to Judah and Jerusalem, He also will bring His wrath upon all nations who gather into The Middle East because of controversy regarding Judah and Jerusalem. When we see these things begin to come to pass, we are to realize that the end result of all that will transpire just prior to, at the beginning of, and during The Days of Awe, will ultimately result in the set up of the Kingdom of Messiah on earth. In other words, the opening of the Sixth Seal begins the final process.

A. "This Generation shall not Pass..."

Jesus states that the generation that sees and experiences the onset of these events, will not pass until all is fulfilled. Some take the view that the word 'generation' refers to 'this ethnic nation' meaning Israel as an ethnic entity. Although this is a shade of the meaning of the word 'generation,' it is not the intended meaning here. Rather, the primary meaning in this context must refer to the generation of people living at the time. To assign the secondary ethnic meaning would infer that there will eventually come a time when ethnic Israel will ultimately cease to exist, either nationally, or as a people, after all is fulfilled. But that is not what Jesus is saying. **The ultimate goal of all that is to be fulfilled is to establish Israel both as an ethnic entity, and as a permanent national entity!** So in this context, 'generation' must refer to those who are alive to understand and see these goals brought to fruition. This generation of people will not pass away until all these things are fulfilled. All will occur during their adult lifetime, and they will see the Kingdom of Messiah established on the earth, with Jesus Christ ruling and reigning from Jerusalem and Judah, and all the borders of The Land of Covenant, Israel, will be unquestionably secure. I feel we are that generation, because we are seeing much of what Jesus spoke coming to pass right in front of our eyes.

CHAPTER 15
THE SEALS

If we look carefully at the Seals opened by The Lamb as explained in Revelation chapters 6 and 7, we are able to come to an understanding of: the schedule of events leading up to The Battle of Gog and Magog, the approximate time of the Rapture, the ushering-in of the entire period of Jacob's Trouble, and ultimately, The Second Coming of Christ to the earth. In explanation, it is impossible to separate each Seal out totally from all the others, because they are all interconnected, revealing concurrent and overlapping information. In the explanation regarding these Seals, you will notice we must often refer to The Sixth Seal to understand their significance. The Sixth Seal is the 'key' Seal.

Also, in order to understand the Seals in conjunction with the remainder of The Book of Revelation, relative to the rest of prophetic Scripture, we must observe several layers of the prophetic spiral. These layers explain many concurrent elements, i.e. specific cosmic events, identification of ideologies, empires and alliances, and world leaders and their affiliations. All of these important elements have context in the past, in the present world in which we live, and in the future, so are not merely historical or metaphorical. So to explain the Seals, we must round out our understanding of several issues at once.

Who opens these Seals? To answer this question we must back up into Revelation chapter 5 for a moment. Verse 1."*And I saw in the right hand of him that sat on the throne a book written within and on the backside, sealed with seven seals. Verse 2. And I saw a strong angel proclaiming with a loud voice, Who is worthy to open the book, and to loose the seals thereof? Verse 3. And no man in heaven, nor in earth, neither under the earth, was able to open the book, neither to look thereon. Verse 4. And I wept much, because no man was found worthy to open and read the book, neither to look thereon. Verse 5. And one of the elders saith unto me, Weep not: behold, the Lion of the tribe of Judah, the Root of David, hath prevailed to open the book, and to loose the seven seals thereof. Verse 6. And I beheld, and, lo, in the midst of the throne and of the four beasts, and in the midst of the elders, stood a Lamb as it had been slain, having seven horns and seven eyes, which are the seven Spirits of God sent forth into all the earth. Verse 7. And he came and took the book out of the right hand of him that sat upon the throne. Verse 8. And when he had taken the book, the four beasts and four and twenty elders fell down before the Lamb, having every one of them harps, and golden vials full of odors, which are the prayers of the saints. Verse 9. And they sang a new*

The Final Schedule Revealed

song, saying, Thou art worthy to take the book, and to open the seals thereof: for thou wast slain, and hast redeemed us to God by thy blood out of every kindred, and tongue, and people, and nation. Verse 10. *And hast made us unto our God kings and priests: and we shall reign on the earth."*

Who is able to open The Seven Seals? No one is found in Heaven, on earth, or under the earth who is worthy to open The Seven-Sealed Book. John is devastated and weeps. But Jesus, The Lamb of God Who was slain, yet Who lives, prevails to open the Book. He is The Lion of The Tribe of Judah, The Root of David. He takes the Book out of the hand of Him who sits on The Throne. Now the entire world is about to have unveiled a side of The Lamb of God that here-to-fore has been hidden. We are about to come to an understanding of the meaning behind the titles, 'Lion of The Tribe of Judah,' and 'Root of David.' In simply opening the Book, and cracking open the Seals, Jesus Christ is revealed in triumph and majesty, and great power.

The opening of these Seven Seals inaugurates and orchestrates the drama of the final Days of Awe, until He rules and reigns upon the earth. The breaking of The Seven Seals unleashes the final curl of the spiral of end-time prophecy as revealed and orchestrated by Christ Himself. These Seven Seals bring all to completion. He is worthy of all the praise and glory of all creatures in Heaven and earth, and under the earth. Just as He fulfilled The Spring Feasts completely at His First Coming at the Times Appointed, The Fall Convocations are now to be fulfilled -- fulfilled at the Times Appointed, and Jesus Christ is ultimately to be revealed in all His awesome glory and power.

The question for us is this. John saw the awesome vision as a glimpse of what was to unfold, and what it would mean. But are we the ones, in this generation, who are now to see these prophecies come to fruition? Are we ready for these fulfillments? Is this world ready for what is about to take place? Is Israel ready?

The Times Appointed (mo'ed) have arrived! We have Seals, Trumpets, Thunders, Vials, and Sickles. There are props and there is music. But there are also participants. The Church, the nations, Israel, the righteous and unrighteous, angels and demons, Satan, and above all Jesus Christ, are all to take part. The final days of The Age of Grace are here, soon to be followed by The Days of Awe. Rosh HaShanah, Ha Teruah, Rosh HaChodesh -Yom HaKeseh, Yamim Nora'im, Yom Kippur, Tekiah HaGadol, Sukkot, Shemini Atzeret - Simchat Torah. Read your programs, because here we go! No more preparatory rehearsals. And no one gets to sit-out and watch from the side-lines. There are no side-lines, and there is no passive audience. All of us are involved.

THE SEALS

The only choice we have is the decision we make regarding our own souls. This decision will determine not just our role as individuals, but the ultimate eternal destiny of each and every one of us. Those who are righteous have the best role along with Christ. All others have a difficult part with absolutely no glory attached. It is imperative to repent and accept Jesus Christ as Savior and LORD before it is too late, and most preferably before Rosh HaShanah. The Elul Days of Teshuvah are soon to be over. The final Tishrei Ten Days of Teshuvah, The Days of Awe, are about to be unleashed upon the world.

A. The First Seal: Revelation 6:1-2.

"And I saw when the Lamb opened one of the seals, and I heard, as it were the noise of thunder, one of the four beasts saying, Come and see. And I saw, and behold a white horse: and he that sat on him had a bow; and a crown was given unto him: and he went forth conquering, and to conquer." KJV.

The rider on the white horse carries a bow, and wears a crown, indicating he is a world recognized political leader, and he goes out conquering with the purpose to conquer and control completely. He has phenomenal success as he rides. This rider is a world leader who intends to take control of the nations for his own posterity and purposes, but this person's true identity is not revealed when he begins his ruthless quest. The Church may wonder about this rider, because we may see earmarks of AntiChrist in the actions and policies of this leader. But The Church will not be able to be decisively certain as to his identity, because AntiChrist won't be fully revealed until after the restraint of the Holy Spirit is removed, and therefore until after the Rapture.

This rider is mounted on a white horse at the opening of the First Seal. White horses historically, and as indicated in Scripture, were meant for Kings and celebrated military heroes to ride. But this leader is neither a King by birth, nor by family ascension, because the crown he wears is more accurately translated as a cap of authority, rather than the diadem of inherent ascension. As a matter of fact, Scripture indicates he will not be honored as a king, particularly by Israel.

Daniel 11:21. *"And in his estate shall stand up a vile person, to whom they shall not give the honor of the kingdom: but he shall come in peaceably, and obtain the kingdom by flatteries."* Also, his ascent to prominence will not arise out of a personal military career. Rather, he will ride to power on the back of political and ideological scenarios that shape the world. There will be a need for someone to take command, and to sort things out. So he will begin his ride at the opening of the First Seal, <u>but take up his position as</u>

AntiChrist well into the unfolding of the Sixth Seal. Therefore, he is not in total control immediately following The Battle of Gog and Magog as we generally have believed. Let me explain.

Look at Daniel 11: 20, which is a verse many seem to leave out when explaining the rise to power of AntiChrist. Notice the context of the entire passage, reading from verse 15 through to verse 21. "*So the king of the north shall come, and cast up a mount, and take the most fenced cities: and the arms of the south shall not withstand, neither his chosen people, neither shall there be any strength to withstand,* Verse 16. *But he that cometh against him shall do according to his own will, and none shall stand before him, and he shall stand in the glorious land, which by his hand shall be consumed.* Verse 17. *He shall also set his face to enter with the strength of his whole kingdom, and upright ones with him; thus shall he do: and he shall give him the daughter of women, corrupting her: but she shall not stand on his side, neither be for him.* Verse 18. *After this shall he turn his face unto the isles, and shall take many: but a prince for his own behalf shall cause the reproach offered by him to cease; without his own reproach he shall cause it to turn upon him.* Verse 19. *Then shall he turn his face toward the fort of his own land: but he shall stumble and fall, and not be found.*" At the opening of the Sixth Seal, the King of the North marches into The Middle East to fight The Battle of Gog and Magog, but is obviously defeated.

Then verse 20 states, "*Then shall stand up in his estate a raiser of taxes in the glory of the kingdom: but within few days he shall be destroyed, neither in anger, nor in battle.*" There is one more leader in Israel following The Gog-Magog Battle, before the rise of AntiChrist! This leader has a thing for collecting taxes, possibly to expedite repair of the ravages of the war. However, the above context appears to indicate there is a more focused reason. This Prime Minister's government begins the process of rebuilding the Temple, by purposely collecting taxes earmarked for that task, because he is "*a raiser of taxes in the glory of the kingdom*." What is Israel's kingdom glory? **The presence of The Temple on The Temple Mount**.

But his time in office is very brief, because within a few days of taking power, he passes from the scene. We are not told much about why, or how, his tenure is destroyed; only that it is not because anyone is angry with him, and no one makes war with him. So this Raiser of Taxes takes office very briefly in Israel, during a time of relative peace following The Battle of Gog and Magog. Many people miss the mention of this interim leader, but he is important because of what takes place immediately following the Gog-Magog War. We must, therefore, keep him in mind.

Then, following this Tax Raiser's demise, and entering peacefully through flatteries, the AntiChrist, who has been riding his white horse since the opening of the First Seal, arises. His personal ascent to prominence and position is from the basis of the need for a firm hand to bring in world stability. His strong point will initially be along the lines of persuasion and negotiation rooted in accepted ideology. Notice Daniel 11:21-26. "*And in his estate shall stand up a vile person, <u>to whom they shall not give the honor of the kingdom: but he shall come in peaceably, and obtain the kingdom by flatteries</u>*. Verse 22. *And with the arms of a flood shall they be overthrown from before him, and shall be broken; yea, also the prince of the covenant."* Underlining mine.

Who is The Prince of The Covenant? Jacob! Somehow this vile person will wrangle a situation where he will determine to break The Covenant with Jacob through threats of military action put forward against Israel by those nations surrounding that have the ability to take up arms, but <u>he brokers a solution of peaceful deception instead</u>. This technique is termed 'crisis control.' Create a crisis, then control the outcome.

Verse 23. *"And after the league made with him, he shall work deceitfully: for he shall come up, and shall become strong with a small people."* He does not arise from a particularly large or recognized nation, but works from within a relatively small identifiable group. Does he work along with the Palestinians?

Verse 24. *"<u>He shall enter peaceably</u> even upon the fattest places of the province; and he shall do that which his fathers have not done, nor his fathers' fathers; and he shall <u>scatter among them</u> the prey, and spoil, and riches."* AntiChrist infiltrates his own people and ideology among the citizens of The Land, viewing Israel as prey, a spoil, and a source of obtaining wealth This is use of manipulative gorilla-terrorist tactics, where both Israelis and Palestinians are 'prey.' Even the individual lives of Palestinians are expendable. Suicide bombers? By the way, this is the stance of the Palestinian leaders, and militant Islamic groups even now. Infiltrate the society, taking Israel for all you can get, and destroy them in the process! The Palestinian terrorists are already using this technique to break down Israeli sovereignty, but it appears AntiChrist will use these tactics extremely successfully, because he will use the jihad of deception, not just against Israel, but against other nations as well.

Verse 24b *"yea, and he shall forecast his devices against the strongholds, even for a time.* Verse 25. *And he shall stir up his power and his courage against the king of the south with a great army; and the king of the south shall be stirred up to battle with a very great and mighty army; but he shall not stand: for they shall forecast devices against him.* Verse 26. *Yea, they that feed of the portion of his meat shall destroy him, and his army shall overflow: and many shall fall down slain."* This leader will come in peaceably, but finish his tenure by being defeated at the time of another war. He will enter The Land (Israel) through a strategy of 'peace,' to take a prey and a spoil. He will have designs against other

The Final Schedule Revealed

strongholds (other nations and powers who fall willingly, or unwillingly, under his spell) and be successful. Eventually, he will use military action against the King of the South, and manage to thoroughly subjugate him for a time. The King of the South is Egypt. During The Gog-Magog Battle, Egypt does not appear to be a major combatant. At the moment, Egypt seems to be trying to take a stand that, although is not entirely neutral, is not in great favor of war either. But Egypt won't remain sitting on the fence during AntiChrist's tenure, because he will view Egypt as a renegade that must be militarily brought into line.

1. "The Portion of his Meat:"

The next verse is enlightening within the context of Daniel's experiences in Babylon, and may assist us in identifying the background ideology and support system of this rider on the white horse. Daniel 11:26. "*Yea, they that feed of the portion of his meat shall destroy him, and his army shall overflow...*" It would appear that there will be powers that share AntiChrist's ideology, who work together to destroy the King of the South. This sounds like a degree of cooperation from within the Arab League itself, which this leader will use to further his cause through deception, and ultimately through war. The seeds of this mechanism for subjugation are already in place in The Middle East among the Arab nations, and may have roots in Islamic ideology, as well as in political rivalry.

Also observe the phrase "*the portion of his meat.*" That is the terminology Daniel and his friends used to identify the fare that was offered to them to eat in Nebuchadnezzar's court. The Hebrew children did not partake of the Babylonian excesses, but chose to eat a simple diet of cereals and vegetables instead. However, at the time of the coming world scene, there are obviously those indicated by this verse who will choose to partake. Could this clue identify the source of the *"portion of his meat?"* Namely, could Iraq, which is the present day country occupying the territory of the seat of the former Babylonian Empire, play a role in the distribution of the ideology (*"meat"*) the conflicting forces represent? And could this *"meat"* already be the ideology which has served to shape the entire Middle East conflict ever since Israel again became a Nation, and has desired to contaminate the purity of Israel, weakening her national sovereignty in the eyes of those nations who do partake?

Notice Zechariah 2:7 which is an interesting verse to keep in mind. It states: "*Deliver thyself, O Zion, that dwellest with the daughter of Babylon.*" The daughter of Babylon in our day would be Iraq. Will Iraq play a role? I hardly think we need to ask this question, since even now we have a controversy with Iraq that has already erupted into war. Just speculation, but Saddam Hussein did present himself as a 'king' (which he obviously is not) and called himself the current Nebuchadnezzar. He even went so far as to try to re-build the ancient city of Babylon. I am NOT saying he is the AntiChrist, because too many leaders already saw through his self-deception, and as far as we are able to ascertain, he is now defeated and out of office, thanks to the actions of The Coalition Forces. But Iraq may represent the ideology, and the area of the world from which its ancient roots stem. Saddam Hussein has been toppled, but he may yet play a role of some nature. If not, then his successor surely will.

Arafat, who happens to be the leader of a very small people-group (the Palestinians), and of the same ideology as Saddam Hussein, is currently undergoing changes in his role as well. He is fighting to maintain his dictatorial dominance as he is now having to cope with a spokesman Prime Minister and cabinet making up a new governing body within the Palestinian Authority.

Do these role-changes mean their undergirding ideology is also toppled? NO! In fact, these two leader's demise could pave the way for the real deceivers to arise! And yes, there are two of them, namely AntiChrist and his False Prophet, who also appears to be a leader in his own right. This could be significant in light of Daniel 11:28 which states, *"And both these kings hearts shall be to do mischief, and they shall speak lies at one table; but it shall not prosper: for yet the end shall be at the time appointed."* (Time appointed, mo'ed.) So do two 'kings' presuppose the AntiChrist and the False Prophet in ideology? We could be seeing this situation developing even now.

But the rider on the white horse is going to eventually be the predominant leader, and although he is strong and powerful, he will not necessarily have all who are supposedly in his camp totally excited about all he sets out to pull off! Is AntiChrist specifically from Iraq? Not necessarily, but certainly he will adhere to an ideology that originated from the area of ancient Babylon, which has come down to the present through The Daughter of Babylon and her allies. What is this ideology? Islamic world domination.

2. Islam and Jihad:

The white horse represents position, strength, and authority. There is only one way this leader, who is not a King by inheritance, can receive his authority, and that is through a world recognized body such as a religious/political system. Islam has the ability to possibly provide such a system. <u>This leader may ride to power on the back of Islam</u>. In other words, he <u>may use Islam to legitimize his mandate to ride forth conquering and to conquer</u>. <u>Jihad!</u> Since deception is a legitimate form of Jihad, he may **appear** to be some type of moderate, or even a Jew, at first. The Church will not be able to figure out the personal identity of this leader, because he will not be revealed until after the Rapture. So we must put the interpretation regarding the recognition of this rider and his horse into the proper perspective according to when he will arise to prominence. To do so, we must look at some things Paul says, and that Daniel states.

Paul tells us in 2 Thessalonians 2:1-12, *"Now we beseech you, brethren,* ***by the coming of our Lord Jesus Christ, and by our gathering together unto him,*** *Verse 2. That ye be not soon shaken in mind, or be troubled, neither by spirit, nor by word, nor by letter as from us, as that* <u>*the day of Christ is at hand*</u>*. Verse 3. Let no man* <u>*deceive*</u> *you by any means; for that day shall not come,* ***except there come a falling away first***, *and* <u>*that man of sin*</u> *be revealed, the son of perdition: Verse 4. Who opposeth and exalteth himself above all that is called God, or that is worshipped; so that* <u>*he as God sitteth in the temple of God, showing himself that he is God.*</u> *Verse 5. Remember ye not, that, when I was yet with you, I told you these things? Verse 6.* ***And now ye know what withholdeth that he might be revealed in his time***. *Verse 7. For the mystery of iniquity doth already work:* ***only he who now letteth*** (prevents, or holds back) ***will let, until he be taken out of the way.*** *Verse 8. And* <u>***then shall that Wicked be revealed***</u>, <u>*whom the Lord shall consume with the spirit of his* mouth, *and shall destroy with the brightness of his coming:*</u> *Verse 9. even him,* <u>*whose coming is after the working of Satan with all power and signs and lying wonders*</u>, *Verse 10. And with* ***all deceivableness*** <u>*of unrighteousness in them that perish;*</u> *because they received not the love of the truth that they might be saved. Verse 11. And for this cause God shall send them strong delusion,* ***that they should believe a lie***: *Verse 12. That they all might be damned who believed not the truth, but had pleasure in unrighteousness."* KJV. Emphasis mine.

Verse 1 sets out the topic Paul is addressing to the Thessalonian Church, so indicates the context of all Paul is about to say in the next several verses, namely the coming of the Lord Jesus Christ and our gathering together unto Him, meaning the Rapture. He is not referring to The Second Coming, but the gathering together of the Church unto Christ. In using the terminology *"by our gathering together unto him"* we know Paul is referring to one of the harvests, so he is referring to a coming fulfillment of one of the Feasts, namely, Rosh HaShanah. Why Rosh HaShanah? He is clarifying the hope of the Church, and it is specifically The Church-Bride who is looking forward to Rosh HaShanah.

3. "A Falling Away First:"

Take note of the phrase, *"a falling away first"* in verse 3 regarding the revealing of the Man of Sin, The Son of Perdition, and the coming of The Day of Christ. (another terminology for The Day of The LORD, which always refers to His coming judgment on the unrighteous nations.) The *"falling away first"* generally has been presented as referring to a massive falling away from the truth of God's Word, a rampant apostasy or departure from doctrinal accuracy. This interpretation certainly has validity, because as we near the end of The Church Age, we are warned to be wary of false teachers who will propagate erroneous doctrines, and of folk growing cold in their faith, and even turning against Christ in the last days, fulfilling that shade of the meaning.

However, the context suggests a further emphasis which also is valid according to the meanings of the Greek words Paul uses. Paul is not specifically addressing the topic of false doctrine here, rather, he is answering concerns the Thessalonian Church had regarding when the Rapture would occur, (some were under the impression the Rapture may have already taken place, and that they had missed it), and when the AntiChrist would appear on the world scene. I would like to suggest a further meaning for this phrase that actually fits with the context of 2 Thessalonians chapter 2, and with Jesus' Olivet Discourse, and with the end-time schedule regarding the revealing of AntiChrist in relationship to the Seals of Revelation, and to the prophecies given to Israel in Daniel chapters 9 to11. It also makes sense in regard to the order and timing of the Rapture of the Church. Both shades of meaning may be implied concurrently, but the contextual overtones suggest the second alternate meaning is the more predominant.

Allow me to take a quote from Joseph Good's book, Rosh HaShanah and the Messianic Kingdom to Come, Chapter 10, page 135. Quote: "Kenneth Wuest, a noted Greek scholar, states in his word studies an interesting point that has much to do with the catching away of the living believers. He states that the phrase "falling away" is a mistranslation of the Greek word "apostasia" and should rather be translated "departure." The root verb "aphistemi" is found fifteen times in the New Testament. It is translated "depart" eleven times. Although it is often found translated in similar meanings, the predominant meaning of this verb in the New Testament is that of the act of a person departing from another person or place. Liddel and Scott in their classical lexicon give as the second meaning of "apostasia," "a departure, a disappearance." Dr. E. Schuyler English, to whom the author is deeply indebted for calling his attention to the word "departure" as the correct rendering of "apostasia" in this context, is authority for the fact that the Greek word (means) "a departure." Wuest further states that "apostasia was at times used to denote a defection or revolt; however, this meaning should not be imposed upon the word where the context does not qualify the word by these meanings." " End of Quote. Underlining mine.

So we are able to see from the Greek meanings that are possible for the phrase "*a falling away first*" in context with the Church being gathered together unto Christ at the Rapture, that there is a somewhat different meaning intended from what we usually associate this verse to be saying. If we use the meaning "a departure, a disappearance," we would read this verse, "*Let no man deceive you by any means; for that day shall not come, except there come a departure (disappearance) first, and that man of sin be revealed, the son of perdition.*" Now this makes much more sense in context with verses 6 and 7 of the same passage. If we were to take the usual apostasy meaning only, we could conceivably be around to see the AntiChrist actually revealed, and then the Rapture would occur, according to the wording of verse 3. But this possibility does not fit with what verses 6 and 7 indicate. Paul cannot give one intimation in verse 3, then contradict himself in verses 6 and 7!

According to verses 6 and 7, The Man of Sin cannot be revealed until the Holy Spirit's restraint of evil during The Church Age, is removed. The restraint must be taken away, then The Man of Sin can be revealed. If the Holy Spirit's role as The Restrainer of evil is removed, then the Church must be removed also, because the Church is never to have the protective role of the Holy Spirit removed until she is presented to Christ. Thus we must refer back to the original intended explanation for Paul's introduction to the chapter. This chapter is explaining our gathering together unto The Lord, the Rapture, and when it will take place, and that it must take place before The Wicked One can be revealed. So in this context, "*falling away first*" means "*departure or disappearance first.*" The Rapture will definitely be a great disappearing of millions of people from the earth, and it will take place before AntiChrist is revealed.

4. The AntiChrist needs a mechanism to obtain power:

After the Holy Spirit in His present protective role is removed, and the Church has been raptured, there will be no more restraint against evil. The AntiChrist will have the ability to deceive many of those who will be left behind. Verses 8 to 12 of this same chapter in 2 Thessalonians describe what AntiChrist will be like, and this passage lines up with Daniel 11:

36-39 which describes many of his activities, including: setting himself up in the Temple, declaring himself to be God. So the Rapture must take place shortly after the sun is darkened and the moon is turned to blood according to Acts chapter 2 and Joel chapter 2, but before the Man of Sin is revealed according to 2 Thessalonians chapter 2. Thus we have a pretty decisive and relatively narrow time-frame for the Rapture.

But does this mean that the Rapture occurs at the opening of the First Seal? No! The Rapture occurs near the time when the sun is darkened and the moon turned to blood at the opening of the Sixth Seal. Does this then mean the Man of Sin is revealed at the opening of the First Seal? Again, no! Paul states that AntiChrist will be revealed after the Rapture, so this revealing does not occur until after the opening of the Sixth Seal.

Also, The Wicked One does not necessarily immediately take control in Israel following The Battle of Gog and Magog, because we realize there is the short rule of the Leader who raises taxes with the purpose of rebuilding The Temple. Then after his demise, AntiChrist enters Israel. So how do we know it is AntiChrist who is riding on the white horse of the First Seal, and what does this mean?

A horseman can ride for quite a while before he is positively identified. We know that world leaders do not arise out of thin air. In other words, it takes some mechanism and some time for a leader to gain enough credibility for other world leaders to receive him, his policies, and his purposes. I would suggest this personage arises on the world scene quite legitimately, and will even provide answers to a number of the world's international problems both before, during, and after The Battle of Gog and Magog that transitions to the coming Days of Awe. Therefore, this rider may ride for quite a time-period before he is revealed as *"the man of sin."* He may be a leader or member of a ruling body right now. If so, there is a current political figure who is even now being deceptive, and has his eyes on more power than just being a political head of a nation or international organization. His ambition will drive him, and at the same time will cause him to remain mum regarding his true aspirations. He is waiting for the right moment, then he will seize control through lies and deceit, and will ride conquering those who agree with his policies, and to conquer all who oppose him. Thus he will eventually be positively identified by his aspirations, and through the deceptions he implements when he finally seizes the upper hand of power.

Meanwhile, he rides from the time of the opening of the First Seal! (Which, by the way, may actually be opened just prior to the opening of The Sixth Seal, because Seals One through Five appear to be opened in fairly rapid succession, so overlap pretty much simultaneously in the prophetic spiral. There may not be a lengthy time-period, therefore, between the opening of the First Seal and the opening of the Sixth.) Until he is revealed, he rides in the deception of peace, and even continues this charade for a fair while after he is revealed. He may take steps to surround himself with those who are easily swayed to his side before The Days of Awe begin. The question remains, has the First Seal been opened, so is this deceptive rider out there somewhere in the world scene even now? I believe the white horse may have already left the starting gate, and is gaining momentum, building toward a full gallop.

5. Meaning of the term, "The Man of Sin:"

[114] *"The man of sin"* is an interesting title that Paul the Apostle uses to describe this coming world leader, who he also refers to as *"this Wicked,"* and the *"son of perdition."* Recently, I was watching a videotape of an interview with an expert on Islam. The Video: <u>Islam: Fighting Israel and the West</u>, put out by Midnight Call Ministries, interviews Robert Morey who is a recognized authority on Islam. Robert Morey wrote a book entitled <u>The Islamic Invasion</u>, which exposes Islamic ideology. In the interview, he mentions a rather revealing piece of information regarding the identity of Allah. [115]He says that the name "Allah" actually is an Arabic

---

[114] Notes and References on Islam by Chuck Missler, <u>www.templemount.org/missler.html.</u>, (accompanying the briefing package "The Sword of Allah: The Rise of Islam") *Ur of the Chaldees is first mentioned in the account of Abraham's journey in Genesis 12:1. The spiritual ruler of Ur was the moon-god. This god would ultimately become the supreme deity of the entire Babylonian empire. The root names of many individuals in Babylon preserves links to the gods of the Babylonian pantheon:...."
"Senacherib, or "Sin Ech-erib" = "Sin multiplies his brothers."
"The god "Sin" was elevated to the top of the Babylonian pantheon by Nabu-na'id (Nabodnidus) in an effort to make Babylonian religion more acceptable to subjects like the Arabians and Aramaeans. The Arabians esteemed the moon god, but had more difficulty identifying with Marduk, the supreme Babylonian deity associated primarily with the city of Babylon."
"The god Sin, "The Controller of the Night," had the crescent moon as his emblem, and the lunar-based calendar, which became the primary religious symbols of Islam, was worshipped in Arabia as AI-Ilah. Mecca became the center of all pagan religions of Arabia before Mohammed. AI-Ilah, the Moon God, was the "Lord of the Ka'aba" ("cube") which was formerly the center of pagan worship, ruling over 360 idols. Lucrative trade routes resulted. The Ka'aba black cube in Mecca is of course the center of Islamic worship today."
[115] A Short Summary of Islamic Beliefs and Eschatology, Collected by Lambert Dolphin, <u>www.templemount.org/islam.html</u> "The pre-Islamic deities of Arabia

name for an ancient <u>pagan moon god</u> who had another name known on earth among his followers. <u>This other name is "SIN."</u> He points to the fact that the Israelites wandered for forty years in The Wilderness of Sin, named after the moon-god that was worshiped by the people occupying this wilderness. [116]"This moon god was married to the sun god, and had daughters, the stars. He had no sons. This information is found, not in the Koran, which is the Meccan revelations, but in the Hadith writings of the sayings of Muhammed. Most of the non-Muslim world do not know this history of Allah, so Muslim teachers deceive us by appearing to quote only from the Koran. To you and me, most Muslims will adamantly deny Allah had a wife or offspring. According to Robert Morey, many Islamic adherents are unaware of this information, so they also have been deceived!

This Ancient pagan deity, "SIN," was not unknown among the nations of the ancient world. Apparently the moon god, "SIN," was predominant long before Babylon, among those who lived in the area of Haran, and

---

which were most venerated were astral deities, especially the triad of the moon god, the sun goddess, and the god associated with the planet Venus. The moon god was the chief and was protector of the cities. These deities were given various names, however the moon god was evidently originally the Babylonian moon god Sin. To end division among his people in Mecca, Muhammad elevated the moon god Al Ilah to the chief and only god. (It is not widely known in Islam that Allah was a sexual being, having fathered three daughters--this is documented in the E.B.)."

[116] Notes and References on Islam by Chuck Missler, <u>www.templemount.org/islam.html</u> The Sabeans' Religion (pre-Muhammad) "Astral religion, which involves worshipping heavenly bodies ("the host of heaven") is strongly warned against in the Bible. In such idolatrous systems the Moon is often viewed as a male deity; and the Sun, a female deity; with the Stars their offspring. A Lunar cyclical calendar results. For example the practice of fasting from crescent moon to crescent moon. Derived from these forms of worship of the host of heaven are the practices of bowing and prayer toward Mecca; the requirement for a Holy Pilgrimage (hajj) to Mecca, in order to circle the Ka'aba, the site of the protective black stone. Al-Ilah was Lord of the Ka'aba; is to be circled 7 times and kissed. Pilgrims then run to the Wadi Mina to throw stones at the Devil. These rites are practiced in Islam today."

"Pagans who lived in Saudi Arabia before Muhammed was born worshipped toward Mecca because Mecca is where their idols were located. Because this pagan worship centered on Mecca was so widespread, a rapid acceptance of Muhammad's new religion was possible. Thus, Islam is a previously heathen religion modified into a monotheistic form by discarding all the other pagan gods except for Al-Ilah."

may have come down through the ancient Sumerans along with Marduk and Shamash, Istar, Adad, and Nabu, according to The Bible Almanac, J.I. Packer, Merrill C. Tenney, William White Jr., pages 136, 150. <u>Muhammed therefore did not found the Islamic religion</u>, as most of us have been led to believe, <u>but brought it forward to prominence</u> in a re-worked format from the ancient past.

[117]So the name "SIN" tells us two things. 1. Islamic roots did not begin with Muhammed in the seventh century C.E., but he literally revived an ancient, pagan moon-god-worship religious system, hence the dome and crescent moon that appear on almost all mosques. (Muhammed denied founding Islam. He was right about that!) And 2. Since "SIN" is an ancient earthly name for Allah, the coming *"Man of Sin"* could conceivably be a Muslim. I am not going to be dogmatic here, [118]but it is an interesting possibility, especially considering the Islam vs non-Islam stance currently being taken throughout the Islamic world, particularly concerning matters regarding Israel and the West who they label as satanic infidels.

Robert Morey also mentions that another designation for Allah is "god of gods," and that Muslim men are often referred to as "kings" among themselves. To put this in perspective, on October 22, 2002, The CBC Network aired "The Ottomans" which is the third part in the three-part video series entitled "Islam: Empire of Faith" put out by PBS. This well-documented presentation explains when, how and why The Ottoman Empire was created, and its influence and extent both religiously and geographically, as well as politically and economically. One startling revelation is the fact that the Ottoman ruler wore various titles according to the regions of his empire. For example, in the European sector he was to be called "Emperor" or "Caesar," and like the Caesars, <u>required ritualistic worship as if he were a god</u>. In other areas he would be referred to as "Sultan," "Ayatollah," or "Sheik." He also referred to himself as "King of kings," a rather blasphemous title in light of the fact there can only be one true KING of Kings, Jesus Christ, but revealing the acceptable practice of Islamic men being referred to as "kings." (Jews use the term 'king' for

---

[117] Notes and References on Islam by Chuck Missler, www.templemount.org/islam.html Archaeological and linguistic work done since the latter part of the 19th century has discovered overwhelming evidence that Muhammad constructed his religion and the Quran from pre- existing material in Arabian culture.

[118] Women in Green, March 12, 2003, wfit2@womeningreen.org. *Who "Invented" Iraq and the Modern Middle East?* "The great danger to the world today is that these Arab Islamic states have spawned a virulent hatred of the Free World against the Judeo-Christian civilization as a whole."

a man as well, in identifying a Bridegroom at his wedding.) Since an Islamic leader ruled over men, he would refer to himself then as the "King of kings." In other words, the ruler of The Ottoman Empire took on the highest title possible for each region of the Empire in order to rule over the souls of men, and demanded absolute allegiance and obeisance.

When the Ottomans finally conquered Constantinople, the Muslims took over the Byzantine Church, which was the largest Catholic Church of the region, and transformed it into a mosque. They also nick-named Constantinople "The New Rome." Therefore, Paul's title *"man of sin"* for the coming AntiChrist may not be so far-fetched, and neither is his indication that this leader will eventually set himself up in The Temple in Jerusalem to be worshiped as a god. None of this activity is outside the realm of Islam, either so-called 'moderate' or 'radical.'

The above sheds some light on the fact that the eastern leg of the former Roman Empire may have more to do with end-time prophecy than we have formerly considered. We have always tended to put all the prophetic marbles into the nations occupying the western leg of the former Roman Empire. The truth is, both legs, and feet, and toes of Nebuchadnezzar's Image may play key roles in the unfolding of prophecy, and where the AntiChrist may come from. He may be religiously affiliated with the Islamic East and Middle East, but raised and educated, and brought to power in the West, producing a multi-faceted individual who truly can flatter everyone according to their ideologies. A true deceiver!

"The Ottomans" video presentation also pointed out another Islamic tactic being used against the unsuspecting West. The Ottoman Empire expanded through both ideological and military means. They generally entered an area either as peaceful infiltrators, or militarily, then proceeded to set up their rule through a somewhat deceptive method. They would take the best of the existing hierarchy, who usually were Christian, and employ them as their civil servants to run the local seats of government, and keep the economy running smoothly. They would help government agencies and businessmen with finances, and provide any other resources they needed. They did not even try to convert them to Islam. Now think about it. That sounds very much like the 'moderate,' 'peace-loving' Islam we are told is the 'real' Islamic faith. They try to appear to be accepting, and even respectful of individuals who adhere to other religious beliefs. Fortunately, many rank and file Muslims really do take this peaceful stance, otherwise, the world would be an even more dangerous place than it is now.

But at the same time, those in charge would remove the children (boys) of the Christian families from their parents, and take them to the Islamic

The Final Schedule Revealed

palaces and mosques, where they were treated very well. Then they would indoctrinate these children into Islam, and proceed to educate and train them to be jihad fighters and fearless killers. These youth became radicals, willing to do anything in the name of Allah, and in the service of the Emperor, so they became a formidable fanatical army.

This has overtones of the child warriors and youth suicide bombers we hear about and see on television. That means the Islamic machine still operates the same way! Placate and subjugate the adults, then transform their own children into hate-filled fanatical terrorists. This tactic is even now being used among 'passivist' Islamic adherents. [119]The school textbooks printed by the Palestinian Authority, for example, and funded by the UN and other 'educational aid' organizations around the world, are filled with anti-Semitic and anti-Christian rhetoric, and praise the highest and deadliest forms of jihad in the service of Allah. It is no wonder The Middle East is filled with fearless suicide bombers and terrorists who have no concern for human life, even their own! These unfortunate young fanatics will do anything in the name of Allah, thinking they will receive the highest rewards in paradise.

The ideological goal is to attempt to transform the society within one generation. The Ottoman Empire pretty much managed to do this. They marched into Eastern Europe, and overturned the Orthodox Christian enclaves, then proceeded tp transform them into Islamic strongholds. Much of the unrest in Bosnia, Chechnya, etc. is obviously split along religious ideological lines between Christians and Muslims, arising directly

---

[119] The Jerusalem Post Newspaper: Online News from Israel, www.jpost.com/Editions/2002/02/06/Features/Features.42946... A portrait of enmity, Arieh O'Sullivan. "...a wide ranging report in which examples drawn from Islamic media, literature, textbooks and popular culture show mounting hatred for Jews, Israel, and the West."
"Each country expresses its incitement differently, Ehrlich says. In Syria and the Palestinian Authority it is mainly in schoolbooks. In Egypt and Iraq it is in the media, most particularly the caricatures and songs. In Iran it can be found mainly in sermons and leader's statements."
"Incitement comes in all forms, Ehrlich says, displaying Arabic translations of Adolf Hitler's Mein Kampf, and the Protocols of the Elders of Zion."
"...Some(Islamic) preachers refer to the Jews as "apes, pigs and worshipers of Satan." Others encourage suicide attacks and praise the attack on the World Trade Center."
Copies of Ehrlich's report are available from the Israeli Government Press Office.
[120] A Short Summary of Islamic Beliefs and Eschatology, www.templemount.org/islam.html., Collected by Lambert Dolphin," Islam,

from the Ottoman influence. [120]The Islamic purpose and goal is ultimately to obtain world dominance, destroying the Jews, Christians, and anyone else who does not profess Islam. It would appear they <u>may almost</u> be able to pull this off for a short time under AntiChrist.

6. The Temple Desecration:

The Temple desecration will ultimately positively identify this world leader who will have begun his quest riding the white horse at the opening of the First Seal. If there remains an Islamic presence on The Temple Mount following The Battle of Gog and Magog of the Sixth Seal, it is not inconceivable that some type of negotiated agreement may be reached which will allow the Israelis to build a Temple there, just so long as they do not interfere with the Muslims themselves. The question is whether the Israelis will go for a plan that will allow an Islamic presence to remain on The Mount. Personally, I do not believe the Israelis will build their Temple with Muslims still desecrating The Temple Mount, so I feel that somehow the Muslims will be totally ousted. But even so, once Israel again controls the Mount, it will take some type of negotiated deception for Muslims to be allowed near enough to The Temple Mount to carry out The Abomination of Desolation. But stranger things have happened! This may fit in with the 'plan of stages' that the Islamic nations currently are following, and therefore the flatteries and deception Daniel refers to. If so, it definitely will show how wicked and treacherous the Man of Sin's goals are!

But AntiChrist personally <u>may partially</u> also be of Jewish <u>ethnic</u> origin, even though he arises from without Israel. The descendants of Jacob have an ability that most of us do not. Because they have been outcast and dispersed among the nations for so long, they have had the opportunity to become registered, recognized citizens of a myriad of countries. Many of them therefore have assimilated to the point no-one really recognizes them as separate in ethnic origin from any other citizen. This could give them a

---

from its beginning, has been a religion of the sword (al Harb). The concept of Holy War (Jihad), mandated by Allah, requires Islam to completely subdue the earth through military conquest. The world is thus divided between Dar al-Islam ("House of Islam") and all areas yet unsubdued by Islam, Dar alHarb ("House of War"). All other religions and all other prophets after Mohammed are false, and all non-Muslims are infidels or dhimmi (tolerated minorities under Islamic rule-such as Jews and Christians). This controlling command eventually brought Islam to Israel, and is the reason for the Muslims' uncompromising control of the Temple Mount. ,"

great deal of leverage internationally if it were to suit their purposes. But they do not use this affiliated identity negatively, rather are proud to be accepted, productive citizens of the countries where they live.

However, <u>it is possible the emerging AntiChrist may choose to reveal his ethnic roots when it best suits his purposes</u>. Of course he would also have to make it appear he is 'converting' to Judaism at the same time, <u>an act of deceptive Jihad</u>, which is perfectly acceptable among Muslims to further their cause! <u>He is</u>, <u>after all</u>, <u>a deceiver</u>! He may appear and act, and even be registered as an Islamic Arab, and may arise to international recognition and power under this guise. Then deceptively 'convert' to Judaism for the purpose of desecrating The Temple, allowing him to ultimately proceed to take steps to set himself up to be worshiped.

But we must realize, he will also be misidentified by many Jews to be their 'Messiah.' Jews will not accept a non-Israeli ethnically, or religiously, as their Messiah. Some have thought he may personally be of the tribe of Dan, a particularly renegade group who were taken captive by the Assyrians, Dan being one of the Ten Tribes of The Northern House of Israel. That identification is certainly open to challenge though, because Messiah is ethnically of the tribe of Judah, being a direct descendant of David, which identifies Him as being of the House of Judah. But whether most Jews are aware of this fact is also debatable. Regardless, there are, strange as it may seem, people who consider themselves of the Tribes of Israel who are also Muslim. Very few of these live in Israel at the moment. But this ethnic deception, and perception, could explain how it will become possible for AntiChrist to approach The Temple Mount to place the Abomination, since after The Temple is built, it will be very difficult for anyone not ethnically Israeli to enter The Temple itself for any reason.

So the white horse may be the steed of Islam which philosophically inspires the jihad of deceit, allowing the rider carrying the bow to ideologically and politically be a deceptive Islamic world leader. But does this entire charade take place at the opening of the First Seal? No. AntiChrist merely <u>begins</u> his ride with the intent to conquer.

B. The Second Seal: Revelation 6:3-4:

"And when he had opened the second seal, I heard the second beast say, Come and see. And there went out another horse that was red: and power was given to him that sat thereon to take peace from the earth, and that they should kill one another; <u>and there was given unto him a great sword.</u>" KJV. Underlining mine.

THE SEALS

The Second Seal is the Red Horse who's rider has power to take peace from the earth, and he carries <u>a great sword</u>. Now this is most significant in the light of current world situations and ideological affiliations. The rider may be a world leader who also has strong affiliations with a particular philosophy. The horse is <u>red</u>, indicating <u>the philosophy is war</u>. **The underlying philosophy and motivation of Islam is Jihad**, meaning 'holy war.' [121]The rider on the red horse is given a great sword to take peace from the earth. [122]**This could very well be the Sword of Islam**, <u>the symbol of Jihad against all who are not Muslim.</u> [123]The Islamic Terrorists and Islamic leaders have indicated they will use the Islamic Sword against all who do not adhere to Islam, who they consider infidels. <u>They definitely have the power to take peace from the earth through their many faceted levels of Jihad!</u> So this rider and horse is currently riding also, representing active military and/or terrorist war, so is not specifically referring only to the AntiChrist. This rider and horse have the ability to bring about The Battle of Gog and Magog just prior to the Rapture of the Church, before The Days of Awe begin.

C. The Third Seal: Revelation 6:5-6:

"And when he had opened the third seal, I heard the third beast say, come and see, And I beheld, and lo a black horse; and he that sat on him had a pair of balances in his hand. And I heard a voice in the midst of the four beasts say, A measure of wheat for a penny, and three measures of barley for a penny; and see thou hurt not the oil and the wine." KJV.

The Third Seal is a Black Horse with a rider carrying a pair of balances. This rider has the ability to control international trade and commerce

---

[121] *A Short Summary of Islamic Beliefs and Eschatology* www.templemount.org/islam.htm Collected by Lambert Dolphin. "This dual religious and social character of Islam, expressing itself as a religious community commissioned by God to bring its own value system to the world through jihad (holy war or holy struggle)."

[122] *A Short Summary of Islamic Beliefs and Eschatology* www.templemount.org/islam.htm Collected by Lambert Dolphin. "Islam, from its beginning, has been a religion of the sword (al Harb). The concept of Holy War (Jihad), mandated by Allah, requires Islam to completely subdue the earth through military conquest."

[123] The Jerusalem Post, Internet Edition, September 12, 2002. www.jpost.com/servlet/Satellite?pagename=JPost/A/JPArticl... Regional Media, Translated by Shira Guttgold. Editorials From The Arab Press: *To annihilate the infidels is a divine decree.* "I would like to stress that annihilating the infidels is an inarguable fact, as this is the decree of fate."

through the manipulation of commodities. He is able to set the prices for grain, and exercises control of the consumption and distribution of oil and wine. The Arab world, which is predominantly Islamic, has the ability to control world prices and the flow of crude oil, and the distribution of goods through cartel and terror, <u>but they are not the only identification of this rider</u>. Of course along with war, whether Jihad or otherwise, comes scarcity of commodities and increased prices. Also, the fourth Pale Horse very well may accompany this horse, because a weather pattern that brings about famine and drought, especially in grain growing areas of the world, would be a major factor in determining world grain prices. [124]We certainly have seen the beginnings of this scenario where the USA, Canada, Russia, South Africa, and Australia, the chief providers of world grain, have been hit with the worst drought and infestations of locusts and grasshoppers on record.

There is much speculation circulating regarding why the USA and Britain went into Iraq. Some analysts are stating the war with Iraq was about oil, not about toppling Saddam Hussein because of His atrocities and non-compliance regarding Weapons of Mass Destruction (W. M. D.'s). This cry in itself is indicative of the importance oil has to the world economy, and especially to the Western industrialized nations. Somehow I do not agree that the Iraqi war is <u>only</u> about oil, <u>but oil is definitely part of the equation</u>. Even though oil already flows from Iraq to the USA, and the USA needs this oil, as well as Iraq needs the monetary benefit from the sale of oil, the people of Iraq have not benefitted. If oil shortage was the only problem, it certainly would not benefit the USA to create a situation which could deplete the supply of oil. It therefore could be argued that with a regime change in Iraq, the flow of oil can then be increased to the West, so the war in Iraq was about oil. If that is the case, then not hurting the oil or the wine will fit right in with Scripture.

Whatever transpires in Iraq, we can be certain the flow of oil will not be affected to any great degree. Perhaps this is part of the situation referred to by the voice heard as the black horse rides, stating, *"see thou hurt not the oil or the wine."* Revelation 6:6b. Wine represents the total wealth from strong economic exchange. The war against Iraq (which officially is over, but continues anyway) cannot permanently disrupt world economic activity, even though prices may fluctuate, and stock markets may remain unstable. Why? The world needs an economy still intact for Israel to be able to build The Temple! If the Raiser of Taxes is going to actually collect taxes for that

---

[124] C.B.C..CA News. <u>Www.cbc.ca/cgi bin/templates/print.cgi?/2001/07/19/ grasshopper.</u> *Plague of grasshoppers descends on Alberta.* July 19, 2001.

purpose following Gog and Magog, and no one is angry with him, Israelis themselves must have viable earning power. That means the world economy cannot totally collapse. Hence, *"hurt not the oil or the wine."*

So we cannot place all the blame for this Black Horse and his rider's activities directly on the Islamic plate. Some is weather, some purely economic, some political, some is war and terrorism, and some ideologic. Since September 11, 2001, we are able to observe hoof-prints of this horse, and hear the voice of prophecy telling us to pay attention to supply, and prices to come.

Notice where the voice of warning comes from. Not from the rider on the black horse, but <u>from the midst of the four beasts surrounding The Throne in Heaven</u>. Who are these four beasts? They are the Cherubim. So who's voice are we hearing? The One who sits upon The Throne utters this warning regarding the oil and the wine. The Voice is The LORD's, uttered in concern for the world's economy. Is He trying to get our attention? **911, an emergency is developing!?** Will He soon be pointing out the prices we will have to pay for our daily needs, and reminding us that He is allowing this situation to develop to draw the nations up short? In the past He often has used the weather and natural catastrophes to discipline nations. Withholding rain, allowing war, famine, earthquakes, floods, pests, shortages etc. Question is, are we going to ignore the black horse and rider, and are we going to pay attention to the Voice? Once this Black Horse sets out, there will not be a stop in his path until his quest is over, and it would appear this horse and rider are proceeding at full gallop even now!

D. The Fourth Seal: Revelation 6:7-8:

"And when he had opened the fourth seal, I heard the voice of the fourth beast say, Come and see. And I looked, and behold a pale horse: and his name that sat on him was Death, and Hell followed with him, And power was given unto them over the fourth part of the earth, to kill with sword, and with hunger, and with death, and with the beasts of the earth." KJV.

The fourth Pale Horse has a rider called Death, and a passenger riding with him named Hell. These have the power to kill with the sword, with hunger, with death, and with the beasts of the earth. The devastation they wreak is the result of war, famine, negative economic control of currencies and movement of goods and services, and pestilence (pollution, infestations, disease, etc.) Ultimately, these riders on the Pale Horse will manage to devastate one quarter of the earth's population. That's a pretty fair chunk of humanity! The combination of these two riders on this fourth horse has earmarks of the work and purposes of Satan to steal, to kill, and to destroy, and to ultimately ban as many people as he can to Hell. Satan is on a roll. He does not want mankind to obtain eternal life through repentance, so he does all he can to turn men's hearts away from God.

1. Summary of the Four Horsemen:

In summary, these four horsemen do not necessarily ride consecutively, but their horses gallop in parallel tracks. In other words, these first four Seals may be opened in such quick succession that their effects are evident cumulatively. We are seeing all these horses and their riders already having an impact in countries that have been, and are being devastated through wars, terrorism, famine, drought, floods, and other disasters. Not only are the third-world countries who do not have the economic industrial base and infrastructure to help themselves being hit, but the effects are beginning to become evident even in the more wealthy nations, especially since 911. We are already hearing the galloping hoof-beats of these four horses and their horsemen, and are beginning to witness their devastations.

E. The Fifth Seal: Revelation 6: 9-11:

"And when he had opened the fifth seal, I saw <u>under the altar</u> the souls of them that were slain for the word of God, and for the testimony which they held: and they cried with a loud voice, saying, How long, O Lord, holy and true, dost thou not judge and avenge our blood on them that dwell on the earth? And white robes were given unto every one of them; and it was said unto them, that they should rest yet for a little season, until their fellow servants also and their brethren, that should be killed as they were, should be fulfilled." KJV.

The Fifth Seal has interesting implications. Notice the wording and setting. *"I saw <u>under the altar</u> the souls of them that were slain for the word of God, and for the testimony which they held:"* Who are these? They are martyrs for the preaching of the Word of God, and for their testimony which they hold. But notice where they are. They are under the altar. What altar? The altar of The Mercy Seat in the Tabernacle in Heaven. Why are they there? They are pleading for avengement of their blood! What time-period are they from? They are the martyrs who have given their lives for the sake of the Gospel of Christ throughout The Church Age. These are not The Tribulation Saint Martyrs who are mentioned in chapter 7 of Revelation, but are of The Church. What happens to them? They are told to wait and rest a while longer, because there will yet be many more to join them.

THE SEALS

What dispensation will the martyrs who join them be from? I believe they also will be from The Church Age before the Rapture. But they are from a specific time-frame of this period -- a time of unprecedented religious persecution of Christians.

One of the signs Jesus mentioned that would indicate the nearing of the end of The Age, is that persecution will be rampant, and many Christians will be delivered up to be killed. This scenario has been picking up in intensity, until we now have an identification label of a specified group of Christians known as The Persecuted Church, or The Suffering Church.

Therefore, many of these martyrs will be of The Persecuted, Suffering Church, coupled with many more from the jihad and world war that is coming. These martyred Christians will <u>join with those under the altar</u> who have been told their rest is only <u>a little season more</u>.

The ten-forty window, the Islamic controlled areas of the world, seem especially to be growing in intensity of hatred toward Christians. Many Muslims are anti-Christian, exhibiting an 'AntiChrist spirit!' Christians are infidels according to Islam. We are seeing the atrocities they are committing against Christians (and Jews) in Indonesia, Sudan, Egypt, Nigeria, and other Islamic controlled nations even now. Extreme Muslims exercise jihad against Christians for, and in the name of "Allah!" What is their slogan? [125]"First the Saturday people, then the Sunday people!"

---

[125] Arutz-Sheva, www.israelnationalnews.com *First, the Saturday People*, by Jack Engelhard, September 15, 20'03.
"...As President Bush protests too much about their "peaceful religion," the New York Post, in its editorial upon the second anniversary of 9/11, tells it straight: "Much of Islam, with its billion plus adherents, and even many in the West — in countries like France and Germany – despise America, its freedoms, and particularly its success."
Ditto Israel, except that Israel comes first. As they say in their sermons – "First the Saturday people, then the Sunday people."
...Both Daniel Pipes and Bernard-Henri Levy say that Fanatical Islam is the problem. Moderate Islam is the answer. I hope they're right. But I am not so sure. For all I know, it was "moderate" Islam that gave us 9/11, and it is moderate Islam that continues to give Israel 9/11 every single day.
Fanatical Islam hasn't yet been heard from.
Those who think it's all about Israel are indeed hiding under the covers. As they slumber, another mosque grows in Brooklyn. (Certainly in Toronto and Paris.)
...That is not the Bill of Rights they pray to five times a day in their mosques.
Bush is pleased that the schools are running again over there, but does he have a clue as to what (besides hatred for the West) the imams are teaching those kids? By the way, that 87 billion dollar figure is nearly triple the amount the federal

The Final Schedule Revealed

First and foremost,[126] rid the world of Jews. [127]But along with this goal, concentrate also on eliminating as many Christians as possible!

This Fifth Seal also indicates that the time of avengement <u>is soon to come</u> on those who dwell on the earth, indicating this scene is pre-Days of Awe, so the martyrs to join them are also pre-Days of Awe. Will all these martyrs be resurrected and raptured? Yes. They are all members of the Smyrna-type suffering, persecuted Church. They will take part in the resurrection of The Last Trump of Rosh HaShanah. So the final days of The Church Age is the time-frame covered by the Fifth Seal. The Fifth Seal overlaps with the first four Seals, and transitions to the opening of the Sixth Seal.

F. The Sixth Seal: Revelation 6:12 to chapter 7:1-17.

I will not transcribe this entire passage, but will quote from it as the explanation unfolds. Also, it is impossible to properly explain this Sixth Seal without also turning to Daniel chapters 11 and 12. Please take the time to read these entire passages from both prophetic Books. Because it is impossible to explain the other previous Seals without reference to the Sixth Seal, we have already covered some of the explanation. As a result,

---

government spends on America's schools.
Maybe it's not the oil. Maybe it's something more sinister that prompts the world, and our State Department, to side with terror, as long as it is "only" Israelis who are dying.
Wait, now, and see what grows from the soil of Ishmael. Your churches are next. For Sunday is coming, Sunday bloody Sunday."
[126] The Israel Report, http://www.cdn-friends-icej.ca/isreport/feb02/horizon.htmlFebruaru 8, 2002, *The Rolling Horizon Into The Coming War* by Emanuel A. Winston, Middle East Analyst & Commentator.
"The war coming soon will truly display Islam's latent ambitions to dominate the world and be recognized as important beyond the oil under their feet. Since the Arab world has produced nothing in recent generations to advance civilization, there is little for which they can claim respect and high position in world affairs. Having said that, there is one thing that will bring them into international prominence and that is to engage in a massive war of Islam vs. Israel (first) and the West (second). "First the Saturday people; then the Sunday people."
[127] MIDDLE EAST DIGEST February 1998, www.cdn-friends-icej.ca/medigest/feb98/tragic.html ,Stan Goodenough "Christian ears have not yet become accustomed to Arafat's latest tune 'until the Palestinian flag is hoisted over all the walls, minarets and churches of Jerusalem' This follows another slogan: 'First the Saturday people - then the Sunday people'."

we realize the Sixth Seal is the transitional Seal. It begins in The Church Age, but most of it takes place during The Ten Days of Awe.

1. The Moon, Earthquake, and War:

Notice verse 12 of Revelation 6. *"And I beheld when he had opened the sixth seal, and, lo, there was a great earthquake; and **the sun became black as sackcloth of hair, and the moon became as blood:...**"* Now that sounds rather familiar! -- the fulfillment of Joel 2:31a, and Acts 2:20-22. This is the final sign given to the Church. So the Rapture may very well occur during the events surrounding the opening of the Sixth Seal. Such a conclusion would make sense in light of the events that have just been mentioned in regard to the riding of the horsemen of the first four Seals, who represent the devastation of war, famine, and pollution, economic woes, as well as the Fifth Seal martyrdom of many Christians. All we are awaiting now is the opening of this Sixth Seal.

Remember, it is possible for these Seals to be opened pretty much at once, or at least in rapid succession. The only reason we tend to consider sequence, is because in order for each Seal to be adequately described, they are presented as a list, but their effects are both cumulative and concurrent. Also, these Seals concurrently take time to unfold their devastation, so do layer and overlap each other. This understanding describes the lead-up we now observe in the world where diseases are out of control, super-bugs and antibiotic resistant bacteria that once responded to drug treatments are becoming more and more of a health concern, and famine threatens the entire world as we have witnessed drought and pests destroying crops, while other areas have had crops disappear because of massive flooding. World economics are very shaky, especially since September 11, 2001. The international stock markets and commodities trading have taken on an erratic pattern. Many folk are worried about the security of their investments. Millions are dying of AIDS in the Third World, particularly in Africa. SARS, West Nile Virus, Avian Flu, and Mad Cow Disease have reared their ugly heads, with no-one knowing exactly how to prevent their spread, or even how to properly and effectively treat them. The nations are perplexed and frustrated over many issues regarding international trade, the environment, the poor, the necessity for foreign aid, unrest in The Middle East, Afghanistan, Iraq, North Korea, Haiti, etc.

The nations are uneasy about stability in Iraq, Iran, and the threats being voiced by some Islamic regimes. Israel's situation with the Palestinians is debated unendingly, as world leaders try to hash out a lasting peace in The Middle East, and attempt to satisfy everyone in the process. A strong hand is needed, and the world is ready to accept anyone who appears to have real answers, opening the way for a charismatic world leader to step in. I would suggest we are now seeing these Seals being opened, and Gog-Magog is just around the corner. All four horses and their riders are not simply poised to ride, but have begun riding, and are headed into a full gallop since September 11, 2001! <u>911 has already been called</u>! Also, the Islamic threat to Christianity, the Jews, and the West, has definitely picked up in intensity, and in boldness. All this is in preparation for the fulfillment of the Sixth Seal.

But what about the great earthquake that accompanies the opening of the Sixth Seal? The earth has been overdue for massive earthquakes for quite some time now. As just one example, an earthquake to occur along The San Andreas Fault has been predicted for many years. Whether this fault will give-way when the sun is darkened and the moon turns the color of blood during The Gog-Magog Battle, we cannot necessarily say for sure. But it certainly is possible! The truth is, an earthquake of great magnitude that will affect much of the surface of the planet, will take place at the Sixth Seal opening. *"...every mountain and island were moved out of their places."* That sounds like a pretty fair global shakeup! Some of the debris in the air causing the color of the moon to turn red, and the sun to be darkened at the same time, could also be the result of this earthquake.

So several devastating situations will take place all at once, coming together to produce the effects described by the opening of the Sixth Seal just prior to the Rapture of the Church. There will be war(s) with possible nuclear and chemical - biological components. There will be cosmic meteorite showers of ice, rock, fire and brimstone, and there will be a massive earthquake. Also, if these will not be enough for the population and governments of the world to deal with at one time, shortly after the moon appears blood-red, the born-again Christians will disappear! All in all, the opening of the Sixth Seal will be pretty dramatic!

The opening of the Sixth Seal appears to be a description of The Gog-Magog Battle itself, and this war both precedes, and then leads into the period of The Ten Days of Awe. Revelation 6:13-17. *"And the stars of heaven fell unto the earth, even as a fig tree casteth her untimely figs, when she is shaken of a mighty wind.*" These stars could very well be meteorite and brimstone showers that fall on the armies fighting on the mountains of Israel. Coupled with what appears to be a nuclear exchange, this cosmic shower devastates the invading armies, and ends The Gog-Magog War, leaving Judah and Jerusalem in Israeli hands. Verse 14. *"And the heavens departed as a scroll when it is rolled together; and every mountain and island were moved out of their places."* This could result from the devastation of nuclear war and the great earthquake together.

Verse 15. *And the kings of the earth, and the great men, and the rich men, and the chief captains, and the mighty men, and every bondman, and every free man, hid themselves in the dens and in the rocks of the mountains;* Verse 16. *And said to the mountains and rocks, Fall on us, and hide us from the face of him that sitteth on the throne, and from the wrath of the Lamb."* The Sixth Seal sees the desire of all, whether of notable rank or common, to hide themselves in the dens and rocks of the mountains from *"him that sitteth on the throne, and from the wrath of the Lamb."*

The Sixth Seal is when men realize <u>The Wrath of God is now imminent</u>, and they wonder who will be able to stand (fight and/or survive.) At least they do acknowledge that God does exist, and that He may not be very pleased with mankind, and that The Lamb of God, Jesus Christ, has justification for His wrath against them. Even their accusation against God shows men still have a sense of God-consciousness and justice, even though they certainly do not repent! Verse 17 *"For the great day of his wrath is come; and who shall be able to stand?"* But the Wrath of God is not intended for the Church, so as soon as the sun is darkened and the moon turns blood-red, the Church is removed.

2. The Calm:

After this, we have the events of Revelation chapter 7, and we find an interesting occurrence. Following the Rapture of the Church, and after The Battle of Gog and Magog, and the devastation of the earthquake, <u>an uneasy calm settles over the earth</u>. The four angels that hold the four winds, who stand on the four corners of the earth, are commanded to not allow the wind to blow on the earth, sea, or on any tree. <u>This is indicating a short time of peace</u>. God allows mankind time to stop, regroup, rethink, and recover. The blowing of wind symbolizes the power, influence, and struggle of empires, rulers, religions, and ideologies which have controlled, and seek to control the sea of mankind. The sea symbolizes the nations of the whole earth, and the trees are the individual nations and their leaders. Four winds are mentioned here. The four winds refer to the influence that four major empires have exerted, and continue to exert, in shaping the world we now live in. Four ideologies, different from one another, but interconnected as well, have been allowed to blow over the earth, but their influence and progress is stopped for a short time. But it is only for a short time!

These influential winds are also represented by the Four Beasts mentioned in Daniel chapter 7. These empires have always desired control of world politics, economics and religion. The fourth beast, a diverse seven-headed, ten-horned, ten-crowned monster, having attributes of the three beasts who precede him, represents the power and mechanism out of which the AntiChrist (The Little Horn) arises. His full power is held in abeyance for a little while longer, by God not allowing any of these four winds to blow for a little season. The angels (fallen warring angelic beings who have influence over these empirical ideologies) are commanded in Revelation 7:1, " *And after these things, I saw four angels standing on the four corners of the earth, holding the four winds of the earth, that the wind should not blow on the earth, nor on the sea, nor on any tree.*" The angels in control of these winds are not allowed to blow on the earth, on the sea, or on any specific tree (nation.) They are not allowed to influence the nations for a short time.

Why are these winds not allowed to blow? Revelation 7:3-4 gives us the answer. *"Hurt not the earth, neither the sea, nor the trees, till we have sealed the servants of our God in their foreheads. And I heard the number of them which were sealed: and there were sealed a hundred and forty and four thousand of all the tribes of the children of Israel."*

Verses 5-8 indicate these specifically are of Israel who are sealed, namely twelve thousand from each tribe. After the Church is Raptured, the taking of the Gospel message of Salvation through Christ to the world must continue, so others may yet have a chance to be saved. The Church has had the anointing empowerment of the Holy Spirit without measure during The Church Age, to spread the Gospel to all nations, peoples, and individuals. But once the Church is removed, the spiritual mandate shifts totally back to Jews being the disseminator of truth to the world, and the fullness of the Holy Spirit is not evident. The hiatus of The Calm of peacefulness allows for 144,000 Jews to be chosen to carry out this mandate throughout the period of The Ten Days of Awe. God places His Seal upon their foreheads, designating them for ministry, and marking them for Divine protection, both from the coming persecutions of AntiChrist's regime, as well as from the devastations of The Wrath of God.

We know that The Days of Awe are ten days (prophetic years), but the Tribulation 70th Week of Daniel is seven years. <u>So there are three years prior to the Tribulation that appear to be The Sixth Seal Calm for the nations of the earth.</u> The 144,000 Israeli Evangelists are sealed, and the Gospel is preached throughout the entire world, with many accepting Jesus as Savior and Messiah. <u>This Calm is followed by the seven year Tribulation, The 70th Week of Daniel.</u> AntiChrist arises peacefully to his full position at the beginning of the Tribulation following The Calm, and he brings in a manipulated period of economic and political stability, deceiving the nations. The first three and one-half years of the Tribulation is therefore a troublesome period of false security, but mid-way through the Tribulation, his true colors abruptly show.

The period of Calm orchestrated by God at the beginning of The Ten Days of Awe, to be felt throughout the whole world before the Tribulation, also will allow the Temple to be built on Mount Zion, and Temple worship to be restored, so this period falls immediately after The Gog-Magog Battle, and will be the time of the tenure of the leader known as the Raiser of Taxes for The Glory of the Kingdom. Daniel 11:20. This Prime Minister in Israel may in fact be brought to power as the result of an Israeli election either during, or immediately following Gog and Magog.

Up until the present, Israel's Government has been dominated by secularists. However, the last election that took place in Israel, (January, 2003) has seen a resurgence of interest in the religious parties, and they actually gained in recognition according to the poles. Although this has not equated into a massive number of right-wingers in the Knesset, a ground-swell has begun.

Why? The majority of the common folk on the streets of Israel do not want anything to do with the formation of a Palestinian State, or in giving up any of the territories, or in dismantling the settlements. This stance is slowly being undermined, however, and many are becoming tired of all the terrorism, threats, and lack of being taken seriously by their Prime Minister. Israel's government, last time anyone checked, is still considered to be democratic, so is supposed to represent the general population in policy decisions. In fact, the vast majority of the population, and this includes taking into consideration the Arab citizens, feel that the formation of a Palestinian State would not bring peace, but would destabilize the region even further. The Jews do not want further destabilization and atrocities, whereas, the terrorist organizations are split on their position. Some are actually rather delighted with the prospect, because having a State of their own would allow them to arm, and conduct greater opposition to the viable presence of Israel as a nation . Others have stated they are opposed, because they would rather just eliminate Israel quickly and entirely, and set up their State, with the whole area then being Islamic Palestine.

Let me illustrate. Headline, THE OVERWHELMING MAJORITY OF THE JEWISH PEOPLE ARE AGAINST A PALESTINIAN STATE! Ruth Matar, Women in Green, November 13, 2002. Quote. "The "road map to peace" is a road map deeper into the hell of Oslo, a road map to the "peace of the grave" for the Jews and the Jewish State. According to this

The Final Schedule Revealed

road map, there will be a provisional Palestinian State, which is on land within Judea and Samaria, by the year 2003, and a full state by the year 2005. In addition, according to this road map, all Jewish "outposts"-- a purposefully deprecating term for small Jewish communities-- will be dismantled, and all construction in existing larger Jewish communities in Judea and Samaria will be frozen. Jewish communities, which interfere with territorial continguity of this planned Palestinian State will be uprooted and all its Jewish inhabitants will be transferred." This date sequence has been changed to a goal for a Palestinian State by 2004, and still to be entrenched by 2005.

Why is the current elected government turning their back on their own citizens, and on their Land? This absolutely makes no logical sense. God is not going to sit back and allow the dismantlement of Jewish communities and homes without repercussions. He especially won't let Judea be permanently negotiated away, because that is where Jerusalem and The Temple Mount are located. What about Samaria? Samaria was part of the former Kingdom of Israel. If the tents of Judah are to be saved first, then Samaria may be part of the interim Palestinian State along with Gaza, but this does not mean the Jews living in Samaria and Gaza now, or even in the rest of the West Bank, are going to allow this to happen without resistance.

In the same letter Ruth Matar asks, "Since the overwhelming majority of the Jewish People are against a Palestinian State, how come we are not screaming our objections from the rooftops?" She goes on to point out that Israel certainly could use help in getting the protests out. Ruth indicates that the media bias has a great deal to do with the cry of the people not making it to the news, and that even Sharon's Prime Minister's office seem to ignore all the petitions that are being sent. The people apparently have no voice in this matter!

Ruth then cries, "What right does Ariel Sharon have to agree to the establishment of a Palestinian State on Jewish land? How about if President George W. Bush would decide to support the creation of a foreign state for Mexicans in parts of Texas? Wouldn't he have to get the permission of Congress for that? Ariel Sharon has never brought the question of a Palestinian State for a vote by the Knesset. (the Israeli Parliament). In fact, his own Likud party, at its recent convention, voted overwhelmingly against such a Palestinian State. And he certainly seems not one bit concerned about the opinion of the majority of Israelis."

So, what we are seeing is a situation where many of those now elected from Likud and Labor, the two major parties, are actually out of touch with the man on the street. The only reason Sharon (Likud) was re-elected, is because the voters were more intent on keeping Mitzna (Labor) out, than running the risk of splitting the vote and allowing Labor to win by default. They know Mitzna would sell them out, and would totally dismantle all the settlements, causing Israel to withdraw to within pre-1967 borders, and the Palestinian State would be a reality almost before anyone had time to blink. At least Sharon takes a more moderate approach, even though he is co-operating with The Quartet in 'The Road Map for Peace,' which calls for the formation of a Palestinian State to be carved out of the so-called 'occupied territories' of Judea, Samaria, and Gaza, together called 'Yesha.' In fact, it appears only Ariel Sharon and Benjamin Netanyahu are supporting these negotiations. A handful of ministers have been threatened with dismissal from cabinet if they do not support this stance. The rest of the Likud Party membership is privately against the formation of a Palestinian State. But the PM carries the day whether his party agrees or not. Privately, neither Sharon nor Netanyahu apparently are in favor of the Palestinian State either, but are pursuing it anyway, because they see no other way to bring about stability in The Middle East.

Ariel Sharon is not totally in favor of the dismantlement of the settlements, but has agreed to a slow program of dismantlement if necessary. This has the settlers very worried. If the present Israeli Government can manage to drag things out, and it appears The Quartet is not in 'drag- your- feet' mode, they may in fact be able to put off the Palestinian State for a while yet. However, The Quartet (The United Nations, The European Union, The United States, and Russia) wants all deliberations completed in 2004 if possible, and at the most, 2005. If all does not go according to plan, we easily could see the Battle of Gog and Magog develop sooner than we think. If all goes according to plan, the result will still be the same, namely war, but it could take a year or two longer. And, if a Palestinian State becomes viable in any form, we all can count on the fact that the next election in Israel will not be too kind to either of the major political parties.

It is interesting to also note that Labor stated they would not partner with Likud to form the coalition needed to form a majority government. So, Sharon had to accept right-wingers into the coalition. As a result, the religious Right is now developing a true representative voice in the decision making process of the Israeli government! God is beginning to place His people for the next item on the agenda, namely, The Battle of Gog and Magog, and the rebuilding of The Temple. The next election very well could see one of the religious Right parties winning much more political

The Final Schedule Revealed

clout. The next election also could occur after The Battle of Gog and Magog, when Israel is tired of war, negotiation, and everything else.

And, this election could come about much sooner, if the Right Wing has their way. [128]They have already tried on several occasions to bring about a non-confidence vote within the Knesset in retaliation for [129]Sharon's Unilateral Withdrawal Plan, which he insists must be carried out in Gaza and parts of the West Bank, to separate the Palestinians from the Israelis, and to bring in more stability before preceding to implement 'The Road Map.' But, however this scenario unfolds, even with the eventual implementation of 'The Road Map', the result will ultimately be a great

---

[128] The Jerusalem Post, Internet Edition, www.jpost.com/servlet/Satellite?pagename=JPost/JPArticle/Printer&cid=107632529480Feb.9,2004. Gil Hoffman. *Sharon survives close no-confidence vote.*
"Prime Minister Ariel Sharon's government narrowly survived a vote of no-confidence for the second week in a row on Monday, defeating a motion protesting the diplomatic and economic situation by a vote of 47 to 45.
The entire National Union faction and National Religious Party MKs boycotted the vote to protest Sharon's plan to withdraw unilaterally from 17 settlements in the Gaza Strip. But NRP ministers Effi Eitam and Zevulun Orlev decided to vote against the motion to ensure that it would be defeated.
National Union MKs wrote Sharon a letter warning him that if he does not raise his plan in the next cabinet meeting, they will no longer consider themselves obligated by coalition discipline and government decisions. The letter said that if the plan passes in the government, the faction would quit the coalition.
"As loyal partners in the government so far, we want to make clear that you have no right to make us partners in your disengagement plan against our will," the faction wrote. "You cannot continue presenting this dangerous plan as prime minister without bringing it to a vote in the government. This misleads the public and it is contrary to the rules of good governance." "

[129] Arutz Sheva News Service, <http://www.IsraelNationalNews.com>Mar. 11, 2004 *DISENGAGEMENT PROPOSAL: RAZE JEWISH GAZA AND 4 SHOMRON TOWNS NOW, MORE LATER.*
"More than two months after Prime Minister Sharon first announced his plan to unilaterally withdraw from Gaza, Maariv reports its details today. The main points: All of the Jewish residents in Gaza are to be expelled, except those living in the three northern communities; another 15-20 communities in Judea and Samaria will be destroyed, if certain conditions are fulfilled; and the Philadelphi route along the Sinai-Gaza border will remain under Israeli control and will even be expanded.
Maariv's report was based on a document drawn up, at Prime Minister Sharon's request, by National Security Advisor Giora Eiland, with recommendations for the implementation of the disengagement plan. Sharon first outlined what he saw as the goals of the plan, including the following:

sense of loss for Israel, and the citizens will feel betrayed. Thus a shift to the right will follow.

[130]Unfortunately, there also will result a great sense of victory by the Palestinians. Sharon's Unilateral Withdrawal Plan already has many of them cheering! In their eyes, terrorism is certainly paying off big-time! The formation of the Palestinian State is just around the corner, and inevitably, so is The Gog - Magog Battle with Russia leading the way. [131] Israel, The United States, The United Nations, The European Union, Russia, and the whole international lobbying-crew, do not understand what they

---

* a long-term improvement of the security situation
* prevention of a split in the nation
* enlisting of international support
* maintaining the PA's obligation to fulfill its Road Map obligations
* causing the PA leadership to feel that it had lost something by not reaching an agreement
* reduction of the impression that Israel had retreated under fire
* reasonable long-term economic cost
* and more.

...A withdrawal from most of Yesha and the destruction of the communities there - what the report calls the "complete move" - is possible only if the Americans agree that this will create Israel's final and recognized borders.
As noted, the recommendation is to "present the Americans with the 'large but not complete' alternative as the goal, and to conduct negotiations to achieve formal international support for this move, with a commitment that there will be no further diplomatic demands on Israel until the PA state to be established implements the first stage of the Bush vision and the Road Map."

[130] Arutz-7 <http://www.IsraelNationalNews.com> March 11, 2004. *SAAR IS AGAINST, DEF IS IN FAVOR*. Master terrorist Muhammed Def, who heads the Hamas military command in Gaza, already sees the disengagement plan as a victory for terrorism - even before it has been approved by the Israeli government. "The criminal Sharon," Def is heard saying on a tape played on Channel Two television this week, "who... came to power [with the promise of] eliminating resistance [terrorism - ed. note] within 100 days, and whose campaign slogan was 'Netzarim and Tel Aviv are the same' - this same Sharon has now decided on a total evacuation and full withdrawal from Gaza, with nothing in return. This is one of the biggest signs of victory. Israel's fall is near..."

[131] Women in Green mailtomichael@womeningreen.org, March 11. 2004. *LEOPARDS DO NOT CHANGE SPOTS, ONLY TACTICS.*
Women in Green, mailto:michael@womeningreen.org , March 11, 2004. *A PALESTINIAN STATE - A U.S. BLUNDER* by Yoram Ettinger
"A Palestinian State would undermine U.S. VALUES AND INTERESTS. The 1976 Entebbe Operation and the 1981 bombing of Iraq's Ozirak Nuclear Reactor

are unleashing upon the entire world in pushing for the formation of a Palestinian State! If they really believe they will solve The Middle East situation, they are sadly mistaken! The first backlash very well could be the raised ire of threatened families being uprooted, which will bring about the next thing to a civil war within Israel. Then, when this fails to settle down, the entire world will become involved, and we will have World War Three, (Gog - Magog) on our hands.

Following the Gog - Magog War, the general population may well turn their hearts to the Right, and there may be a religious awakening when they realize they now have controlling access to The Temple Mount, <u>finally</u>, and Judah and Jerusalem has been kept within their jurisdiction. Certainly the majority will be excited to see The Temple re-built. This possibility in itself could sway the election following Gog and Magog, because the people will realize that if they are ever to build a Temple, they will have to elect a government who will support the project. That is why there will be a raise in taxes by a Prime Minister immediately after Gog and Magog, and no one will be overly upset by it.

It is unfortunate that this elected leader will remain in power for only a short time. We are not told why he loses power, only his demise is not because anyone is angry with him, and there is no war that brings him down. This lack of war tells us his tenure is during the three year Calm at the beginning of The Ten Days of Awe. Obviously there are other factors that cause his demise. Perhaps health. As soon as he is off the scene, AntiChrist takes over, and the 70th Tribulation Week begins.

I would like to point out one more observation regarding the period of Calm. In order for any government leader to feel confident to raise taxes, and not have everyone angry with him as a result (a miracle indeed!), the world economy cannot necessarily be completely devastated by The Gog-Magog War. A global economy still exists, and the people of Israel must be working in order to be able to pay taxes at all, let alone absorb an increase! In fact, the world economy may go through a recovery at this time, much like the economic recovery that occurred following World War Two, allowing everyone to get back on their feet -- not only as rebound from the war, but rectifying the economic devastation of the Great Depression of the

---

dealt a blow to global terrorism. The establishment of a Palestinian State would be perceived as a reward to the role model of terrorism, dealing a blow to the US war on global terrorism. It would condemn Jordan's Hashemite regime to oblivion, would recharge Saddam's and Taliban's allies in Iraq and Afghanistan, would bolster Iran and Syria and would facilitate the re-entry of Russia to the Mideast."

Dirty Thirties. This recovery since the end of WW II has virtually carried us until now, and has only recently been slowing down without the trend of lasting stability.

The demise of our strong world economic base has sped up since 911, as we have observed the galloping of the four apocalypse horsemen picking up. Gog-Magog may well slow them down, or at least the black horse anyway. The Calm God enforces indeed may allow for a short time of world-wide economic recovery, and for a very good reason. The time for The Third Temple to be built has arrived! In order for Israel's economy to rebound, the world economy must rebound also, because Israel depends on the world economies probably more than any other nation on earth! Also, the last concerted evangelistic campaign to reap the final harvest of souls is launched. This also will require funding.

In other words, the world does not come to an end following Gog and Magog! The entire world will be reeling from war, earthquakes, famine, disease, and even from the Rapture of the Church. But God in His wisdom and mercy allows breathing space, even as He prepares to pour out His wrath. So the period of Calm and economic recovery will allow the leader known as The Raiser of Taxes to have his brief time of rule to rebuild the Temple, allowing Temple worship to resume after approximately 2000 years!

3. AntiChrist's Rise:

Following the demise of The Raiser of Taxes, AntiChrist rises to prominence as Daniel's Tribulation 70th Week gets under way. He obtains his position peaceably, actually coming across as one who honestly desires to maintain world stability. He brokers an agreement of continued peace among the nations, even going so far as to recognize, at least on the surface, that Israel by Covenant, has rights to Jerusalem, and a right to exist. But as previously pointed out, this is all treachery! He actually believes The Covenant is meant for the Arabs, and agrees with them regarding bringing this understanding about. At the onset of the Tribulation, the last seven years of The Days of Awe, he consolidates his position as the dominant world leader.

4. Persecution of the Tribulation Saints:

Following The Calm and the rise of AntiChrist, there begins a time of intense persecution of those who receive the message of salvation as preached by the 144,000 Jewish Evangelists. The height of this persecution intensifies around the mid-Trib period of The Days of Awe, following the desecration of The Temple. AntiChrist requires that he alone be worshiped as god, so anyone practicing other beliefs will be put to death. Because of their testimony of the truth, there will be a great many who have accepted Christ who will be put to death. These are not the martyrs previously mentioned regarding the Fifth Seal. Rather, they are pictured as standing <u>before The Throne of The Lamb</u>, not under the altar. Revelation 7: 9-10 states, *"After this, I beheld, and, lo, a great multitude, which no man could number, of all nations, and kindreds, and people, and tongues, <u>stood before the throne, and before the Lamb</u>, clothed with white robes, and palms in their hands:* Verse 10. *And all the angels stood round about the throne, and about the elders and the four beasts, and fell before the throne on their faces, and worshipped God."* Who are these? Verse 14 states *"...<u>These are they which came out of great tribulation</u>, and have washed their robes, and made them white in the blood of the Lamb.* Verse 15. *Therefore are they before the throne of God, and serve him day and night in his temple, and he that sitteth on the throne shall dwell among them."* Underlining mine.

5. AntiChrist Confirms The Covenant for one Week, The Tribulation period of Seven Years:

Daniel 9:27 states *"And he shall **confirm the covenant <u>with many</u>** for one week,..."* Now, that does not mean he really wants to do this as a friendly gesture favoring Israel, <u>nor that he really believes</u> Israel has rights to The Covenant. Merely that he will *"confirm"* it for seven years <u>with the many nations that surround Israel</u>. <u>But his real intention</u> becomes clear sooner than everyone expects, because the verse goes on to state, *"and **in the midst of the week** shall he cause the sacrifice and the oblation to cease, and for the overspreading of abominations he shall make it desolate, even until the consummation, and that determined shall be poured upon the desolate."* Emphases mine.

So his <u>real intent</u> engages into gear half-way through the seven year Tribulation period, probably because of pressures from his Arab cohorts. Notice the wording of Daniel 11: 30-32 again, *"For the ships of Chittim shall come against him; therefore he shall be grieved, and return, and **have intelligence with them that forsake the holy covenant. And <u>arms</u>** shall stand on his part, and <u>**they shall pollute the sanctuary**</u> of strength, and shall <u>**take away the daily sacrifice**</u>, and <u>**they shall place the abomination that maketh desolate**</u>. And such as do wickedly <u>against the covenant</u> shall <u>he corrupt by flatteries</u>; but the people that do know their God shall be strong, and do exploits. <u>**And they that understand among the people shall instruct many**</u>; yet they* *shall fall by the sword, and by flame, by captivity, and by spoil, many days. Now when they shall fall, <u>they shall be holpen with a little help</u>; but many shall cleave to them with flatteries. And some of them of understanding shall fall, to try them, and to purge, and to make them white, even to the time of the end: because it is yet for a time appointed."* Emphases mine.

This world leader, who probably is Muslim officially and privately, but also deceptively, (because he may <u>pose publicly</u> as a Jewish sympathizer in order to deceive Israel especially), will flatter the other nations, and *"have intelligence with them that forsake the holy covenant."* The Islamic Arab Nations who are against the Holy Covenant, along with their allies, immediately begin plotting again to overthrow and annihilate Israel, so will provide the AntiChrist with the promise of armed military backup and international military intelligence. The wording in these verses has traditionally been used to point to the superior intelligence of AntiChrist, and he probably is a pretty brainy individual. But the context appears more in the military lingo of intelligence gathering and war strategy. So his 'peace' with Israel is not meant to last! That is part of his agreed upon deception brokered along with his Islamic allies against Israel.

6. AntiChrist's Con Job is only Partial

But not everyone is conned into his ideological camp, at least as far as The Middle East is concerned. Daniel 11:30. *"For the ships of Chittim shall come against him..."*

Chittim is somewhat nebulous to identify, and appears to have evolved in geographical identity over time. This progressive identity is traceable in Scripture. [132]Originally, it appeared to refer to the people of Kittim, which is now the island of Cyprus. Isaiah 23:1-2 *"The burden of Tyre. Howl, ye ships of Tarshish; for it is laid waste, so that there is no house, no entering in: from the land of Chittim it is revealed to them. Be still, ye inhabitants of the isle, thou whom the merchants of Zidon, that pass over the sea, have replenished."*

But, according to The New Bible Dictionary, the term has also been found in Phoenician inscriptions referring in a "more general way to the coastlands of the E. Mediterranean." Numbers 24: 24 indicates ships *"come from the coast of Chittim, and shall afflict Asshur, and shall afflict Eber, and he also shall perish forever."* And Jeremiah 2: 9-10 appears to be a prophecy which indicates an end-time scenario of discipline from the LORD toward

---

[132] J.D. Douglas, Organizing, Editor, The New Bible Dictionary, Wm. B. Eerdmans Publishing Co., Grand Rapids, Michigan. (1062 Copyright, Inter Varsity Fellowship,) p. 701-702.

renegade Israel, typified by Asshur. *"Wherefore I will yet plead with you, saith the LORD, and with your children's children will I plead. For pass over the isles of Chittim and see; and send unto Kedar, and consider diligently, and see if there be such a thing."* Chittim is described here as being *"isles'"* plural, not just as one island. Then Ezekiel further clarifies the plurality of Chittim in chapter 27 where the LORD speaks against Tyrus. Verse 4: *"thy borders are in the midst of the seas, thy builders have perfected thy beauty.* Verse 5. *They have made all thy ship boards of fir trees of Senir, they have taken cedars from Lebanon to make masts for thee.* Verse 6. *Of the oaks of Bashan have they made thine oars; the company of the Ashurites have made thy benches of ivory, brought out of the isles of Chittim."*

However, Scripture appears to align a group of ships possibly with some type of alliance that comes in the end against AntiChrist, according to Daniel's vision. Daniel 11:40. *" And at the time of the end shall the king of the south push at him: and the king of the north shall come against him like a whirlwind, with chariots, and with horsemen, and with many ships;..."* Psalm 104:26 also makes reference to ships coming.

The name, Chittim, appears to have developed into more of a descriptive designation referring to those who were seafarers in general, as opposed to a specific nation or country. Therefore, because seafarers often traveled both from beyond, as well as within the Mediterranean Sea, the term Chittim appears to include seafarers from the nations surrounding, as well as from the lands and continents that were beyond the shipping-lanes of the entrance to The Mediterranean. In other words, <u>Chittim in prophecy very likely refers to those nations who have major naval capability</u>. The nations who have most of the world's naval power are also designated in Scripture as "Isles of the sea."

It would appear then, that the USA and Britain, possibly along with Australia and South Africa, are against much of AntiChrist's policies particularly in regard to Israel. These nations have the largest and most advanced Navy fleets in the world, and are generally determined that Israel exist. They will fight for Middle East co-existence, <u>and will insist on honoring the entire seven year agreement that has been internationally reached in the name of Middle Eastern Peace</u>. In other words, they will not look too kindly on the Arab Islamic nations plotting and carrying out, along with the AntiChrist, the Abomination which pollutes Israel's new Temple facility, and threatens to divide Jerusalem. This desecration is carried out, not only by the AntiChrist, but is planned and <u>committed on purpose by all that are on his side, and in his philosophical and religious camp</u>. Notice Daniel 11:31 states *"**they** shall pollute the sanctuary, and **they** shall take away the daily sacrifice, and **they** shall place the abomination that* *makes desolate."* Whose diabolical plan is this? Basically it is the result of a common cause imbedded in an ideology that does not recognize the Israelis' right to The Land Covenant, or The Temple Mount and Jerusalem as Divinely belonging to Israel. The spokesman for this desecration is the AntiChrist, <u>but **many** plot together to carry it out</u>.

Verses 27 to 29 of Daniel 11 seem to indicate at least <u>two leaders</u> are acting together here, one of whom turns out to be the AntiChrist, but both of them very deceitful. This could refer to the symbiotic relationship that develops between the first and second Beasts of Revelation chapter 13, namely the first Beast who is the AntiChrist, and the second Beast who is the False Prophet. *"<u>And both these kings</u>* (Islamic men, and therefore their leaders, often refer to themselves as 'kings' or 'princes') <u>*hearts shall be to do mischief, and they shall speak lies at one table*</u>; *but it shall not prosper; for yet the end shall be for the time appointed. Then shall he return into his own land with great riches; and <u>his heart shall be against the holy covenant</u>; and he shall do exploits, and return to his own land. <u>At the time appointed he shall return</u> and come toward the south; but it shall not be as the former or as the latter."* Both these 'kings' apparently confer together to deceive the people and nations of the earth (tell lies at the table of negotiation.)

[133]Their underlying desire, and even belief, is to spoil Israel (take her Land and wealth,) and ultimately dominate the world. They achieve these goals at least partially, and AntiChrist, who apparently is the more dominant of these two leaders, returns to his own land with his spoils. So even though he eventually sets his headquarters in Jerusalem, he initially does have a homeland-base elsewhere. But he returns, and comes against those of the South (Egypt). But now his whole attitude and demeanor has changed. No more Mr. Nice Guy! However, God has a pre-scheduled Divine Appointment with him! Here is one of God's Appointments with the peoples of the earth -- a Feast of judgment. Yom Kippur.

---

[133] *A Short Summary of Islamic Beliefs and Eschatology*, <u>www.templemount.org/islam.</u> Collected by Lambert Dolphin, *Islamic Eschatology*.
"Although not commonly appreciated by most Christians and Jews, the various sects of Islam, in their oral tradition, and from the Koran, maintain a complex and intricate eschatology dealing with the end of the age and the coming of a great world leader, or Mahdi. The center of these events at the end of the age is Jerusalem, not Mecca, and Jesus is one of the principle participants in the coming great judgment, according to Muslim belief." Author's note: Their view of who Jesus is, is not the Christian view! But their Mahdi could very well be the AntiChrist.

7. Deceptions, Manipulations, and Flatteries:

Deceptions and manipulations have been part of the way kings and empires have handled The Middle East over the centuries, but a further fulfillment still is to come, because the final fulfillment is not as the former, or as the latter, indicating this passage has at least three specific separate incidences in the prophetic spiral where it was, and is to be fulfilled. The former would refer to the raping, domination, and destruction of The Land and people of Israel in the past by the first three Beasts of Daniel's vision. The fourth Beast appears to be the perpetrator of the latter two, but his final assault is far more drastic than his own previous attempt, referring to the fact that The Roman Empire influence plays twice in this prophecy. Once in ancient times, overlapping with Christ's first coming in which He fulfilled The Spring Feasts, and once more during The Days of Awe before Christ's Second Coming, during which tenure The Fall Feasts will be fulfilled by Christ.

Daniel 9:26 and 27 makes the connection between the two assaults by this fourth Beast. *"...and the people of the prince that shall come shall destroy the city and the sanctuary; and the end thereof shall be with a flood, and unto the end of the war desolations are determined. Verse 27. And he shall confirm the covenant with many for one week: and in the midst of the week he shall cause the sacrifice and the oblation to cease, and for the overspreading of abominations he shall make it desolate, even until the consummation, and that determined shall be poured upon the desolate."* Verse 26 describes the Roman destruction of the Temple during a time of war in 68 to 70 C.E. under Titus. But at a specified time in the future, according to verse 27, a further travesty rooted in this same empirical background, will give rise to the Abomination of the Temple, and this Abomination will remain in place until the *"consummation,"* which means until it will be brought to an end at a specified time (mo'ed) when pre-determined judgments will be poured out upon those who operate outside of the truth. Who are those who are *"desolate of the truth"*? Those who will not concede to God's Word and Covenant! Interesting!

In the final assault of the fourth Beast, the Islamic Arab nations are conned into allowing the Israelis to have some kind of negotiated rights to The Covenant. There appears to be some type of seven year agreement among many nations, perhaps brokered through The European Union, likely in combination with the United Nations and the O.I.C. or The Arab League. While these negotiations are going on, a measure of politically manipulated peace does descend, which lasts until the middle of the Tribulation Week. But the AntiChrist, who himself is deceptive in this agreement that will be reached, sets about to align himself specifically with those who actually desire to *"do wickedly against the covenant,"* and he proceeds to corrupt them by *"flatteries,"* inducing them to join him in placing the Abomination of Desolation that causes Temple worship to cease.

It is interesting to note that the Abomination that makes Desolate is directed specifically toward the Temple worship of the Jews. Jesus states in His Olivet Discourse that understanding this incident explained in Daniel, and recognizing its ramifications, is pivotal, and will result in the need for some to actually flee from Judea into the mountains. Matthew 24:15 & 16. *"When ye therefore shall see the abomination of desolation, spoken of by Daniel the prophet, stand in the holy place, (whoso readeth, let him understand:)* [134]*Then let them which be in Judea flee unto the mountains."* If the desecration is carried out as a form of Islamic Jihad, it will be very momentous, rendering The Temple and The Temple Mount useless initially, even to the perpetrators, because Muslims are not in favor of certain desecrations either. Some feel this abomination will repeat the desecration of the sanctuary that was previously enacted by Antiochus Epiphanes, the sacrificing of swine offered on the altar, and filling The Temple with ceremonially unclean Gentiles and their pagan worship. If this is so, even some Muslims will be horrified! Those carrying it out will feel they are performing perfect Jihad, because no practicing Jew will now wish to enter The Temple, thus they will regain control of The Temple Mount through treachery. Brilliant move! Now all they need do is ceremonially 'cleanse' The Temple according to Islamic religious law, and they have successfully regained The Temple Mount in Jerusalem, and ousted the Jews. They have the camel's nose back inside the tent! From this regained vantage point, they will then be able to resume their plans to take over the entire Land of Covenant, and destroy Israel forever. This is why The Battle of Armageddon actually will have much the same issues, and a similar line-up of antagonists as The Battle of Gog and Magog. But all this will backfire, because they will have again forgotten The God of Israel in their deliberations and diabolical activities.

---

[134] Author's Note: Who are these who must flee Judea? They would obviously include the Temple Priests as well as many government leaders, because when the Desolation takes place, their lives very well may be in jeopardy. The exile of Israel's government takes place at this mid-trib juncture, and lasts for three and one-half years. They are protected in the mountains of Edom, at Bozra, which is likely the fortress of Petra.

8. AntiChrist the Anti-type of Messiah:

The AntiChrist will not stop merely at deception and negotiated flatteries. His true colors will emerge after this incident, because he will proclaim himself to be god. AntiChrist is an antitype of Messiah. Messiah is Immanuel, God incarnate, dwelling with man in human flesh. Could AntiChrist actually set himself up as incarnate Allah in the flesh? This would definitely antagonize both the Tribulation Saints and the Jews! But what he will not count on is the possibility his actions ultimately will alienate him from many of his Islamic supporters as well. Even though Islam has had this type of ruler-worship in the past, it may not necessarily be a popular concept to actually implement among many present-day Muslims. See Daniel 11:36-39. *"And the king* (he may view himself to be a king according to Islamic doctrine) *shall do according to his own will; and he shall exalt himself, and magnify himself above every god, and shall speak marvelous things against the God of gods, and shall prosper till the indignation be accomplished: for that, that is determined shall be done."* He will set himself up in The Temple for everyone to worship him as 'god.'

The terminology, *"God of gods"* can be interpreted two ways, and in this context both have validity. In fact, both may actually play a role in what transpires.

According to Robert Moyer, Suleymon The Great referred to himself both as 'King of kings,' and as the 'God of gods.' The 'King of kings' is relatively easy to interpret in light of the fact that in essence all Muslim men are referred to as 'kings.' To be the 'King' of an empire of 'kings' would then be a logical, if blasphemous title. The term 'God of gods' has even more blasphemous overtones. <u>It suggests the possibility that there is more than one God,</u> <u>so has implications of polytheism</u>. For the Christian, as well as for the Jew, this concept in and of itself is blasphemous enough, but for the Muslim, it produces a conundrum, because according to <u>publicly understood</u> Islamic doctrine, [135] Allah is sovereign and alone.

Privately, their clergy does recognize the Moon-god, Sun, offspring-stars concept as being part of their doctrinal past, although they certainly don't broadcast it among their own adherents as present doctrine. So all gods besides Allah are considered inferior. In other words, their <u>public</u> interpretation of who "god" is, is very similar to the definition of the Judeo-Christian God. They even allow their own adherents, as well as Jews and

---

[135] *A Short Summary of Islamic Beliefs and Eschatology*, Collected by Lambert Dolphin, *Arabic Inscriptions in The Dome of The Rock in Jerusalem*, "There is no God but Allah alone"

Christians, to believe that Allah is simply another name for the God of the Bible. However, in actual fact, they believe Allah is greater than the God of the Hebrew Scriptures.

Now this is not readily known by most Muslims. Neither is it known by most Christians and Jews. Why? Because Muslim prayers and writings are meant only for their clerics to understand and interpret. Their Imams will deny these things to anyone who they consider to be an infidel, making it appear [136] Allah is just another name for the same God the Christians and Jews worship, pointing out that they include The Torah in the Koran, [137] so they worship the God of Abraham. But digging deeper into both their history and their own writings, one begins to realize Allah cannot be, so therefore <u>is not Yahweh,</u> according to Robert Moyer, an expert on Islamic practices and beliefs.

Also, because AntiChrist will speak against the God of gods, his interpretation of who God is will be brought into question. Since the Islamic god is not the Hebrew God, his understanding will be to speak against the Hebrew God. Now, he may, or may not actually totally comprehend his own stance here, because he is himself deceived. He feels he is able to set himself up above any god, by undermining even his own false-doctrinal background with another false doctrine of his own making, thus taking a stance that is against all other gods including the true God.

9. "Allah is God; Allah is Greater:"

[138] Islamic teachers control the beliefs of their own adherents and others, through deception. [139] Most Muslims believe they are monotheistic, and their god is beyond understanding, and is even remote from interfering directly

---

[136] *Notes and References on Islam*, by Chuck Missler, " Allah = Al-Ilah. Arabic for "the god." pre-Islamic name, corresponding to the Babylonian Bel."... "The Moon-god; crescent moon. One God? (at a time) is a concept found in other pagan derivitive religions:"... "Islam is a previously heathen religion modified into a monotheistic form by discarding all the other pagan gods except for Al-Ilah."

[137] *Short Summary of Islamic Beliefs and Eschatology*, Collected by Lambert "Islam's god Allah is not the same as the God of Judaism or Christianity. Neither are its accounts of figures from the Jewish and Christian Bibles the same."

[138] *Where Did Allah Come From?*, Robert A. Morey, 1996 Research and Education Foundation. "Does the average Muslim know that he is worshipping a moon god? No. Does he know why the crescent moon symbol sits on top of his mosque? No. Is he shocked and perhaps angered at these facts of history? Yes. But can mere denial or angry threats refute the fact that Islam is nothing more

in mankind's affairs, but requires absolute, unquestioned, and detailed ritualistic worship. They proclaim, "Allah is god, Allah is greater," when they demonstrate or set out to perform an act of Jihad. Most often, this is translated from Arabic to English as "Allah is god, Allah is great." But this is not a true English translation. [140]The comparative should be translated "greater." If their god is the only god, then why state that Allah is greater? Greater than whom? Hence, Allah would be considered to be the 'god of gods,' the greatest of them all. [141]Allah, also known in the ancient past by the name "SIN," was held in highest honor from among a line-up of ancient [142]Sumeran pagan gods, and Ur of the Chaldees, out of which Abraham was called, was a city dedicated in honor of the god SIN. The prophetic ramifications for the Abrahamic descendants are obvious! The final showdown will take place between the descendants of Abraham who have

---

than a modern version of the ancient religion of the moon god Allah? No. The average Muslim has been kept in the dark by the Mullahs and Imams who would lose their power if the truth ever got out."

[139] *Notes and References on Islam*, by Chuck Missler,"Islamic "Allah" implies a God who is unknowable, impersonal, capricious (untrustworthy)."

[140] Women in Green, www.womeningreen.org. March 30, 2004, Jan Willem van der Hoeven, Director, International Christian Zionist Center, *Allah is not God*, "This Allah has nothing, nothing to do with the God of the Bible. And no matter how many times the muezzins shout out that Allah hu ahbar - 'our Allah is greater' - the God of Israel remains infinitely greater and is the only true and living God and Creator, a God of love to be worshiped as the Creator of us all."

[141] *A Short Summary of Islamic Beliefs and Eschatology*, Collected by Lambert Dolphin.
"The Encyclopedia Britannica is a good resource for understanding the roots of Islam. Mecca at the time the prophet was born was inhabited by the tribe of Quraysh (Koreish) to which the clan of Hasim belonged. The city was a mercantile center with shrines to many gods, chief of whom was Ilah. The Ka'bah sanctuary in the city square guaranteed the safety of those who came to trade. The pre-Islamic deities of Arabia which were most venerated were astral deities, especially the triad of the moon god, the sun goddess, and the god associated with the planet Venus. The moon god was the chief and was protector of the cities. These deities were given various names, however the moon god was evidently originally the Babylonian moon god Sin. To end division among his people in Mecca, Muhammad elevated the moon god Al Ilah to the chief and only god. (It is not widely known in Islam that Allah was a sexual being, having fathered three daughters--this is documented in the E.B.)."

[142] The Bible Almanac, J. I. Packer, Merrill C. Tenney, William White Jr., Thomas Nelson Publishers, 1980, New York. p.130. "One of the foremost cities of Sumer was Ur. ... Ur was an important trading post dedicated to the god Sin,

refused to give up their pagan worship that Abraham was told to leave behind, and those who worship The LORD God of Israel. The paganism of Ur has followed Abraham's descendants right into Jerusalem, and is presently occupying The Temple Mount, the very location from which Messiah will rule and reign! No wonder the LORD is jealous over Zion and over His Land and chosen people! There is only one realm where the false doctrine of Islam has its roots, and that is with Lucifer, who aspired to be able to dethrone God, and set himself up as the supreme deity, thus ruling over God and all other beings. This realization sheds much light on what transpires next in the saga of AntiChrist.

10. There is only One True God:

We (Christians and Jews) know that Yahweh is the only true God, and <u>all other identities are not gods at all</u>. There is no possibility of any form of polytheism, because no other gods exist. Period! Any other being or identity referred to as a god then, would be a false, or bogus god. Not a god at all! That is why God states in The Law of Moses, *"Thou shalt have no other gods before me."* Exodus 20:3. And Isaiah the prophet writes, *"Thus saith the LORD, the King of Israel, and his Redeemer the LORD of hosts: I am the first, and I am the last: and <u>beside me there is no God</u>."* Isaiah 44:6. His powers allow Him to be omnipresent, omniscient, and omnipotent. He has no beginning, and no end. He is the eternal God. Therefore, He is able to present Himself to mankind in whatever form He chooses. So for Him to become incarnate in human flesh, and become The Son, is entirely within His ability. So, the God of the Bible deals with mankind by presenting Himself in His fullness as three distinct personage roles: The Father, The Son, and The Holy Spirit.

This is not unlike our own ability to 'wear more than one hat.' Neither is it difficult to understand when we remember man himself is a triune, total identity of body, soul, and spirit. Also, a man can be a father, a son, and a husband all at once. In fact, we all operate positionally and occupationally in multiple role-identities. Does this make each of us a god? NO! But it does illustrate something about God. We have been created in His image. We have the ability to mirror some of His attributes. However, at no time can a man, or any created being, actually attain to the reality

---

and the goddess Ningal." p. 136. "The Babylonians modified the Sumerian religion. Besides Marduk, their important gods were Ea (god of wisdom, spells, and incantations), Sin (moon god), Shamash (sun god and god of justice), Ishtar (goddess of love and war), Adad (god of wind, storm, and flood), and Marduk's son, Nabu (scribe and herald of gods.)

of the infinite majesty and power, and unfathomable depths of God. The only man who has that ability is God Himself incarnate in human flesh, Jesus, The Messiah, Redeemer, and KING. Therefore, for any man other than Jesus Christ to proclaim himself a god, his claim is blasphemy. So for the AntiChrist to set himself up as a god to be worshiped in The Temple on Mount Zion in Jerusalem, is not only pagan, it is blasphemy!

Are we now finished with the Sixth Seal? Sort of. We will refer back to it as we continue.

CHAPTER 16:
THE SEVENTH SEAL

I. The Seal of the Seven Trumpets:

Revelation chapter 8 explains the Seventh Seal. Seven is the number indicating perfection and completion, so always refers to the fulfillment of anything God inaugurates, and orchestrates. This Seal is also known as The Seal of the Seven Trumpets. The prophetic basis of the sounding of these Seven Trumpets has implication both in what has been inaugurated, as well as in how all will come to completion, so we are able to see that their sounding involves process, not simply incident. The Seventh Seal then, definitely shows the prophetic spiral at work.

These trumpets, when we begin to examine them, actually clarify for us more detail regarding the purposes of the Seals, and particularly reveal God's input into all that transpires from The Battle of Gog and Magog through to the end of The Days of Awe. Therefore, The Seventh Seal is God's jurisdictional Seal, and the Trumpets are His clarion calls heralding what is to unfold. The first five Seals are earthly in implication, being allowed of God to be orchestrated and initiated according to His prophetic plan. The Seventh Seal is His sovereign coordination and input into the affairs of mankind, and becomes most obvious and significant beginning with The Battle of Gog and Magog, and the Rapture of the Church at the opening of the Sixth Seal. The Seven Trumpets then, sound in the lead-up to The Last Trump of Rosh HaShanah, throughout The Ten Days of Awe, culminating with The Great Shofar of Yom Kippur.

When this Seventh Seal is opened, there is silence in Heaven for about half an hour while the seven angels who stand before God are given their trumpets. Notice, the explanation begins in Heaven, indicating the origin of the trumpets is directly from God Himself, and the angels who sound them are marshaled, then sent from the presence of Him Who sits on The Throne. Another angel comes and stands beside the altar before The Throne, and he carries a golden censer containing much incense to be offered on the altar with the prayers of all saints. Because verse 3 specifically states *"the prayers of all saints"* there is some grounds to interpret the opening of this Seventh Seal as actually concurrent with the opening of the Sixth Seal just prior to the Rapture, just before the sun is darkened and the moon turned to blood. (This is not unlike the first five Seals being opened pretty much all at once.) The smoke of the incense, which represents the prayers of the saints, ascends before God out of the angel's hand. Then the angel takes the censer and fills it with fire from off the altar, and casts it into the earth, producing voices, thunderings, lightning, and an earthquake.

I will not go into detail regarding each of these Seven Trumpets of the Seventh Seal, but here is a quick overview.

Notice, this is the <u>Seventh</u> Seal, seven being the number of God's completeness and perfection, so the trumpets of the Seventh Seal are orchestrated by God, and have a definite pre-ordained culmination in and through Christ, The Lamb of God. The first four of these trumpets originate outside the jurisdiction of anything man can either generate without God's enablement, or even prevent, and the last three trumpets are the "Woe" Trumpets which appear to include acts of God, negative input from mankind, and input by angelic and demonic beings. I will explain further as we examine each trumpet.

The first four trumpets have basis within the time-clock of God's physical Creation of the universe, and therefore, are cosmic signs of the prophetic count-down originating from the Creation itself - the earth and all He brought forth upon it, and the heavens - the sun, moon, and stars. So with the sounding of the first trumpet of the Seventh Seal of Revelation, mankind has a reminder of who God is, what His will is, and that He is in total control.

These trumpets also indicate that God brings His judgment and justice to bear, and that He keeps The Books. Rosh HaShanah is a judgment of the individual people of the earth, whether they are righteous, wicked, or simply nominal and need to be jolted awake. HaTeruah blast of Rosh HaShanah is God's <u>final warning</u> of impending eternal judgment upon mankind. The Book of Life is opened, and the Wholly Righteous are accounted for and Raptured. This trumpet also is the promise of coming judgment on the wicked, and heralds one last short period in which mankind has a chance to examine their hearts before the Yom Kippur judgment when The Great Shofar is sounded. When Tekiah HaGadol is sounded at the end of The Ten Days of Awe, The Book of Life is again opened, and those whose names are found written there are invited into The Kingdom of the reign of Christ, and the destinies of all up to that juncture are eternally sealed. (Don't confuse these openings of The Book of Life at Rosh HaShanah and Yom Kippur with the opening of The Book of Life at The Great White Throne judgment following the Millennium. At that time The Book of Life will be opened to prove the unrighteous wicked are <u>not</u> entered there.) These Seven Trumpets are God's final call during The Ten Days of Awe, The High Holy Days, when mankind has a last chance to honestly examine their hearts before God, and decide their eternal destinies. They also highlight the culminated outworking of the redemptive plan God set in motion, and judgment upon all that is evil.

The Seven Trumpets point out the result of the corruption, contamination, and desecration brought upon all of Creation through the Fall of man, and therefore the result of the curse on God's Creation. But God reminds mankind also of the promise of restorative reconciliation through the blood of The Lamb slain on the cross as the perfect atonement. Mankind must repent and receive this provision, or suffer eternal judgment. That is the message of these trumpets! The truly amazing thing is, God orchestrated the time-clock of the universe to co-ordinate with man's activities. The Seven Trumpets are the sounding of the acts and orchestrations of God as He brings to completion The Mystery of The Ages.

I know this is hard to picture. Perhaps a brief explanation regarding the sounding of the trumpets would clarify our understanding. All the Feasts and Festivals have trumpets blown. There are trumpets blown on each day of these Feasts, as well as at specified times during The Days of Awe. The Feast of Trumpets, Rosh HaShanah, has many trumpet blasts, and these may be blown both concurrently, as well as <u>with many blasts on each trumpet, much like an orchestra made up of trumpeters</u>. Also, there are trumpet blasts during The Ten Days of Awe leading up to the final trumpet blast on Yom Kippur.

The Seventh Trumpet, and all the trumpets, <u>are not just consecutive instruments playing solos</u>, but play their music <u>whenever it appears</u> on their interactive scores. <u>That is why the first four trumpets, along with The Seventh Trumpet, can join in with one another until they are all sounding at the same time, and they begin playing when the Sixth Seal is opened</u>. The drama has music, and this music is provided by the Seventh Seal!

The Seventh Trumpet can be described much as we would designate a first violin of an orchestra. <u>It is a lead voice, and plays at designated times throughout the presentation.</u> So <u>The Seventh Trumpet is a positional trumpet</u>, not just another instrument in a consecutive line-up of instruments. As such, it is <u>a special voice played on more than one occasion</u>, at different times within the prophetic presentation. This is much like the fact that there can be two or more movements in a symphony presentation where the lead violin plays a prominent sound. The Seventh Trumpet then, <u>plays a lead</u> part in prominent addition to the Trumpet Quartet, and later is the <u>predominant voice</u> of the final trio of Woe Trumpets.

The Seventh Trumpet relates directly to **the two horns of the ram** that was caught by its horns in the thicket, and that became the substitute sacrifice in place of Isaac. This ram was representative of Jesus Christ,

THE DAYS OF THE SEVENTH TRUMPET

ROSH HASHANAH   **YOM KIPPUR**

Tishrei 1-10
Yamim Nora'Im
The Days of Awe
The High Holy Days
Jacob's Trouble

HA TERUAH SHOFAR   **TEKIAH HAGADOL**

The Akeida Lamb, representing The Lamb of God.

FIRST HORN   **OTHER HORN**
The Lamb revealed   **The Lamb revealed**
to the righteous.   **To the whole world.**

**"In <u>the days</u> of the voice of the seventh angel
when he shall begin to sound
The mystery of God
should be finished
as he hath declared to
his servants, the prophets."
Revelation 10:7.**

THE SEVENTH SEAL

who fulfilled the prophecy given by Abraham to Isaac, when Isaac asked, *"Behold the fire and the wood: but where is the lamb for a burnt offering?"* Abraham answered, *"God will provide <u>himself a lamb</u> for a burnt offering."* Genesis 22: 7-8. The Jews refer to this entire incident of Abraham, Isaac, and the substitute ram, as the Akeida. Jesus, God in the flesh, is The Akeida Lamb of God. He became the substitute Sacrificial Lamb offered for our sin. Thus, **the ram's two horns represent Christ**, and when blown **<u>reveal Christ The Lamb of God</u>**. So **<u>The Seventh Trumpet</u>**, as typified by **one of the ram's horns**, is sounded as **HaTeruah**, The Last Trump of Rosh HaShanah when **Christ The Lamb upon The Throne is revealed in glory to the Wholly Righteous Bride at the ingathering Rapture**, and indicates the separational judgment of Rosh HaShanah, and ushers in The Days of Awe. The final sounding of **<u>The Seventh Trumpet</u>** typifies **the other horn of the same ram**, and is sounded at Yom Kippur as **Tekiah Ha Gadol**, The Great Shofar, **revealing Christ The Victorious Lamb of God to the whole world**, <u>and signals the Yom Kippur judgment, the resurrection of the Tribulation Saints, and the ingathering of the Elect at the end of The Days of Awe.</u> **The Seventh Trumpet position is then defined as the Trumpet of The Revealing of Christ, The Perfect Lamb of God.** The blasts and their meaning are what is significant <u>whenever</u> this Seventh Trumpet is blown.

I trust this explanation helps in placing when these trumpets are blown, and what they indicate, and how it is possible for the Seventh Seal Trumpets to layer, beginning their blasts when the Sixth Seal is opened. <u>The Sixth Seal is a very dramatic Seal, so the drama is accompanied by the startling blasts of the first four Trumpets, already sounding, joined by the lead voice of the Seventh Trumpet</u> revealing The Lamb to the Righteous. (Five trumpets joining-in with one another until they are playing together.) Then there is a dramatic <u>Calm</u>, followed by a build-up in the presentation. At mid-Tribulation, the final three trumpets begin to sound. This final Woe Trumpet Trio, <u>of which The Seventh is again the most startling voice</u>, wraps up the drama during the final three and one half years of the seven year Tribulation period of The Ten Days (years) of Awe, <u>culminating in Yom Kippur</u>, **and Christ, The Victorious Lamb of God, is totally revealed** to the whole world, and **<u>The Mystery of Christ is complete</u>**.

A. The First Trumpet Sounds:

Revelation 8:7. *"The first angel sounded, and there followed hail and fire mingled with blood, and they were cast upon the earth: and the third part of trees was burnt up, and all green grass was burnt up."* KJV.

The first trumpet is one of four cosmic trumpets, showing God's direct involvement in The Battle of Gog and Magog. Here we have God's cosmic weapons (a massive meteorite shower) added to the arsenal of man's weapons exchange. These God-sent missiles cause much damage to the earth's plant life, burning up one-third of earth's trees, and all green grass. Obviously, these missiles from space impact on a wide area of the earth's land masses to cause forest fires, and to eliminate all grass. The burning up of the grass means famine will follow, because food-grain crops, which are cultivated grasses, will be eliminated along with all other grass, and much of the fruit crop (trees) will be devastated also. This trumpet is a 'one-third' warning of further judgment to come.

B. The Second Trumpet Sounds:

Revelation 8:8-9. *"And the second angel sounded, and as it were a great mountain burning with fire was cast into the sea: and the third part of the sea became blood:* Verse 9. *And the third part of the creatures which were in the sea, and had life, died; and the third part of the ships were destroyed."* KJV.

This is a description of the devastation that could possibly result from the impact of a huge meteorite hitting the earth. Stray meteorites (of both asteroid and comet origin) have been coming fairly close to the earth in the past few years. Although this in itself is not unusual, the frequency and size is. One meteorite of repute this past year was apparently about the size of a football field. Perhaps you recall seeing this meteorite on the news. It looked like a huge tumbling potato. Fortunately it was deflected off its impact course with earth.

[143] At the same time this meteor was sighted, there was some concern regarding another larger meteor that appears to be headed this way, and if it does not stray, is estimated to possibly collide with earth in 2017. Actually,

---

[143] Reuters, Peter Bond, spokesman for The Royal Astronomical Society. Dr. Benny Pheiser, asteroid expert at Liverpool John Moore's University, Northern England. A huge asteroid appears to be headed straight for us. It apparently measures approximately one to two miles in width. It is estimated that its impact could cause such massive upset to the earth's eco-systems, that economic activity could retrogress to resemble The Dark Age. This asteroid is identified as 2002NT7. It's possible collision with earth could take place in 17 years, February 1, 2017, according to the U.S. Linear Sky Survey Program astronomers. The actual chance of a direct hit is currently rated as one in one million, since it easily could change its course, as many do. "This thing is the highest threat that has been cataloged, but the scale in terms of the threat keeps changing."

because of its size, if it does come close to the earth, the gravitational pull of the earth itself could speed up the approach of this large meteor/asteroid. So it is possible it could arrive much sooner than anyone expects, if it does not become deflected. Scientist have been trying to down-play the danger by stating this meteor really is a great way off, and could change course, so there really is nothing much to worry about. Most meteors never really make it to the earth's surface anyway, but are burnt up in the atmosphere. But the size of this one gives it a chance to be more dangerous. It's weight and mass would make it more difficult to deflect, and chances are it may not completely vaporize if it enters the atmosphere. It may burn on the outside, but it could impact as a huge fiery ball if it does not vaporize.

This cosmic threat will not be without precedent, because God has rained down fiery meteorites in the past. Brimstone and hot hail have been known to pelt the earth, and the earth's surface shows craters where meteorites have impacted. The missiles that God adds to The Battle of Gog and Magog certainly could lend one to realize it is possible that a huge meteorite could fall into one of the oceans around the same time. The impact would certainly cause great pollution in the sea, the death of fish and other marine creatures, and could destroy one-third of ocean-going vessels if it impacted a busy shipping-lane.

Whether this fiery mountain that falls into the sea is the meteorite currently under surveillance on a collision course with earth, remains to be seen. The one that threatened to collide with earth last year managed to sneak up on us by surprise. Literally no one was expecting it! It seemed to come out of nowhere. With all the observatories and scientist constantly monitoring space, it really is a wonder how something that huge could 'sneak' anywhere! But apparently it is possible. The explanation given is that it's approach was masked by the brightness of the sun, so no-one actually saw it until it was almost past the earth's outer atmospheric circle. By that time, the danger was already over! What else is 'sneaking' through our solar system, and will anyone be able to give any warning? It is therefore very possible this Second Trumpet scenario could conceivably occur much sooner than we anticipate.

C. The Third Trumpet Sounds:

Revelation 8:10-11. *"And the third angel sounded, and there fell a great star from heaven, burning as it were a lamp, and it fell upon the third part of the rivers, and upon the fountains of waters; Verse 11. And the name of the star is called Wormwood: and the third part of the waters became wormwood; and many men died because of the waters, because they were made bitter."* KJV.

Another huge meteor! Only this one does manage to break-up in the atmosphere, disintegrating into a fine, dust fall-out that settles over land, polluting a third of earth's rivers, lakes, and streams, so that a third of earth's fresh water supply is contaminated, causing many people to die after drinking it. It is known now that some meteorites are composed of ice, gases, and cosmic debris. The tails of comets apparently often contain this type of meteorite formation. So it is not difficult to understand that a large meteor of such a composite nature could burn up upon entry, and then disintegrate into a poisonous powder. This meteor could be part of the same meteorite shower as the last two Trumpets, this one also being a 'one-third' warning.

If there are any scientists able to observe this meteorite shower that impacts the earth because of these first three Trumpets, they certainly will have a front-row seat to observe what a massive meteorite shower can do to the earth's surface. This will not be merely speculative, but the conclusions of observed and experienced reality! The question is, will they live to tell the tale?

D. The Fourth Trumpet:

Revelation 8:12-13. *"And the fourth angel sounded, and the third part of the sun was smitten, and the third part of the moon, and the third part of the stars; so as the third part of them was darkened, and the day shone not for a third part of it, and the night likewise.* Verse 13. *And I beheld, and heard an angel flying through the midst of heaven, saying with a loud voice, Woe, woe, woe, to the inhabiters of the earth by reason of the other voices of the trumpet of the three angels yet to sound."* KJV.

There are changes in the amount of light that will be visible from the sun, moon, and stars, so the day and night will be darker by about one-third as much light as normal. The darkening of the sun and moon takes place during The Gog-Magog Battle. Since that is the case, the Rapture may take place at this time. This Fourth Trumpet comes with a sober warning. Three Woes are yet to come as the next three angels sound their Trumpets.

The first four Trumpets appear to play as a quartet, sounding almost simultaneously rather than merely consecutively, and are warnings, the fourth indicating the worst is yet to come. People will wish for the rocks and the mountains to hide them from the *"things that are coming on the earth, and from the face of him that sits on the throne, and from the wrath of the Lamb."* Revelation 6:16. They will realize The Day of God's Wrath is imminent, and wonder if anyone will be able to survive. The Seventh Seal opens as a

THE SEVENTH SEAL

Sixth Seal overlap, and transitions at Rosh HaShanah to The Days of Awe period, then continues until Yom Kippur. Therefore, it would appear these first four Seventh Seal Trumpets <u>layer</u> and <u>overlap</u> with the opening of the Sixth Seal, sounding during The Battle of Gog and Magog. The cosmic manifestations of the first four Trumpets are the *'stars'* that fall on the earth, described as the result of the shaking of The Fig Tree, so occur when issues over Judah and Jerusalem are the reason for battle.

The first four of the seven Trumpets are Elul Teshuvah Trumpets announcing the wrap-up of Elul. The onset of Tishrei is heralded by the <u>joining-in</u> of The Seventh Trumpet, so all five are also Rosh HaShanah trumpets. Thus we have the Trumpet quartet building in crescendo until the joining- in of The Seventh Trumpet lead voice, Ha Teurah Shofar, The Last Trump of Rosh HaShanah. These then continue to play together until the Gog and Magog Battle is over. They appear to stop sounding at the onset of The Calm.

II. The Woe Trumpets:

The last three Tishrei Teshuvah Trumpets of the Seventh Seal are sounded several years after the Rapture of Rosh HaShanah, during the seven year Tribulation segment of The Ten Days of Awe, culminating in Yom Kippur. More precisely, <u>they begin to sound during the last three and one-half years of The Seventieth Week</u>. This is not a hard concept to wrap our brains around when we keep in mind the fact that God orchestrates the three year period of Calm following The Gog-Magog Battle. Then, subsequent to this three year Calm, the first three and one-half years of the seven year Tribulation are relatively devastation free as AntiChrist consolidates his position and power. (Total 6 1/2 years.) <u>It's the last three and one-half years of the Daniel's 70th Week that is referred to as The Great Tribulation, when the full impact of God's Wrath is poured out</u>. The fifth, sixth, and <u>Seventh</u> Trumpets, The Woe Trumpets, appear to include some input by mankind, some influence by both angelic and demonic beings, along with input from God Himself, as He orchestrates the drama until Yom Kippur.

A. The Fifth Trumpet Sounds, The First Woe:

Let's examine the Fifth Trumpet of the Seventh Seal, The First Woe. Revelation 9: 1-12. *"And the fifth angel sounded, and I saw a star fall from heaven unto the earth: and to him was given the key of the bottomless pit. Verse 2. And he opened the bottomless pit; and there arose a smoke out of the pit, as the smoke of a great furnace; and the sun and the air were darkened by reason of* the smoke of the pit. Verse 3. *And there came out of the smoke locusts upon the earth: and unto them was given power, as the scorpions of the earth have power. Verse 4. And it was commanded them that they should not hurt the grass of the earth, neither any green thing, neither any tree; but only those men which have not the seal of God in their foreheads. Verse 5. And to them it was given that they should not kill them, but that they should be tormented five months: and their torment was as the torment of a scorpion when he striketh a man. Verse 6. And in those days shall men seek death, and shall not find it; and shall desire to die, and death shall flee them. Verse 7. And the shapes of the locusts were like unto horses prepared unto battle; and on their heads as it were crowns like gold, and their faces were as the faces of men. Verse 8. And they had hair as the hair of women, and their teeth were as the teeth of lions. Verse 9. And they had breasplates as it were breastplates of iron; and the sound of their wings was as the sound of chariots of many horses running to battle. Verse 10. And they had tails like unto scorpions, and there were stings in their tails: and their power was to hurt men five months. Verse 11. And they had a king over them, which is the angel of the bottomless pit, whose name in the Hebrew tongue is Abaddon, but in the Greek tongue hath his name Apollyon. Verse 12. One woe is past; and, behold, there come two more hereafter."* KJV.

There is some debate as to the identification of the locusts described here. Some feel they are mutated insects, some feel they describe war machinery, and some think they are demonic manifestations. I somewhat tend toward a hybrid of all camps, because what is described seems outside the normal, but certainly not outside the possible! The description leaves room for some speculation. Probably no one will know for certain what these locusts <u>really</u> are until the event described actually takes place. <u>I will not be absolutely dogmatic about the locust's identification, but will put forward a couple of possibilities to consider.</u>

What John describes <u>could be</u> a swarm of genetically engineered locusts, designed with biological capabilities beyond normal; but they may be about normal locust size, allowing them to be released as a massive cloud such as is indicated in verse 2. These would be 'programmed' to target only mankind -- not grass, or trees, or any greenery like normal locusts do.

They could, then, be a type of DNA altered insect. How altered is described in verses 7 to 10. Their bodies are shaped like horses, they have tails as scorpions, their heads appear to be gold-crowned, and they have hair similar to a woman's hair. Their faces appear almost human. The overall shape of a normal locust does seem to appear with some of these physical attributes already. They do appear to have a stylized horse-shaped profile to their bodies, and to wear a 'cap,' and do have somewhat humanoid facial features. The hair is added, and a scorpion-like tail containing a sting certainly may be genetically bred from foreign DNA, along with the fact that their personality type and appetite preference is altered from herbivore to carnivore!

Fortunately, they only have the ability to attack for five months, <u>about one locust season</u>, so they hurt mankind only for five months, and then die out. This five months is mentioned twice in the Revelation chapter 9 passage, indicating five months is key to understanding how long the plague lasts, and that five months is indeed five months. It would appear that this plague ends through natural causes -- the death of the altered insects themselves.

This possibility of genetic manipulation is not really far-out for us to consider. Great strides are being made in cloning, and in the entire array of genetic engineering technologies. Governments are trying to slow this research down, but it is taking place in illegal laboratories around the world anyway, as scientists are looking for ways to deliver 'medications' and 'treatments' etc. It is not a real leap to realize it may be possible to produce an insect exhibiting the physical description, that could deliver a 'sting' such as is described in Revelation chapter 9 verses 4-6. So the technology for developing such a biological, living weapon is already scientifically feasible.

But it will take coupling this technology with the intelligence and inspiration of the demonic to produce, and to release. Thus we can identify the brand of 'star' that falls from heaven unto the earth when this Fifth Trumpet is blown. Angelic beings, both holy and fallen, are often referred to in Scripture as 'stars.' This one *'fell'* unto the earth, so he is of the fallen variety. His destination is The Bottomless Pit, which he opens with the key that has been given to him, and he releases what appears to be 'smoke' as from a burning furnace. The amount of 'smoke' is so great it dims the sun, and the air is darkened by it. What this fallen angel appears to be doing is releasing the cloud of locusts.

It is interesting to note that these locusts will only be able to hurt those who have <u>not been sealed by God in their foreheads</u>. The only protection to attack then, is having God's protective 'Mark.' So it would appear these 'locusts' will only be able to hurt those who are not the 144,000. Everyone else is fair game. This in itself shows there are alternate spiritual forces at work here, beyond the realm of mankind's abilities. This attack on mankind is part of the direct conflict between Satan's realm and God's realm, and it will literally be played-out in preying on God's crowning Creation, mankind, but can only hurt those who are not under God's protective seal upon their lives. The fact that the 'locusts' arise out of

The Bottomless Pit shows they are inspired by intelligence that is of the demonic underworld. Proof of demonic involvement in producing these 'locusts' is the identification of the head fallen angel in charge of this project. It would appear this attack on mankind could be a combination of scientific genetic engineering on the part of mankind, inspired, controlled, directed, and delivered by a spirit-being, Abaddon in the Hebrew, or Apollyon in the Greek.

Question. Is it possible such research is being carried out successfully in hidden underground labs in Iraq or Iran, or in other remote locations? If so, no UN Inspector, or Coalition Forces Team, will be able to find them. They certainly won't be looking for this type of biological and chemical weaponry delivery system. And since Apollyon is involved, unknown even to the researchers themselves, he will see to it no one finds the location!

I find it interesting to note this passage is dogmatic in making sure mankind has access to the name of the fallen angel in charge. It gives us his name in <u>both</u> Hebrew and Greek. Why? Perhaps <u>the code name</u> of this project may be either, or both. I feel this named identification of the fallen angel in charge of this project, is somehow given as a clue and warning of what is about to take place. It may be that those searching the Scriptures will be able to recognize the true situation. If that is the case, probably only the 144,000 will pick up on it, but it will give them a further motivation to win as many to Christ as possible during these five months of torment, and perhaps give men the encouragement they will be needing to remain alive, because most who are attacked will wish to die. The locust's stings are not fatal, but are very painful.

Some interpret these locusts to be massive swarms of military helicopters equipped with chemical and biological weapons. This may also be a valid interpretation, however it has some logistical difficulties attached. First of all, it would be economically exorbitant for any nation, or group of nations, to manufacture enough of these aircraft to swarm in such a manner as the sun is obscured because of the number of them, and to sustain the intensity of attack for five months world-wide. A localized region such as only The Middle East could be targeted, but the cost of producing such a massive swarm to obscure the sun, even from only a small geographical area, would be prohibitive.

Secondly, the release of these locusts does not necessarily seem to be in direct conjunction with a specified international war effort, but rather appears to be <u>an attack on all of mankind itself</u>. It could be an international terrorist-type attack designed to subjugate total populations, but the use of swarms of military aircraft would be outside the capabilities of terrorist groups.

Thirdly, military hardware generally is deployed to seek out, to kill, and to destroy enemies. The locusts are sent out only to torment, suggesting the delivery of the swarm is not through use of aircraft, missiles, or bombs. And fourthly, the fact that within five months the torment comes to an end, indicates there may be some built-in time-clock which limits the effects of this attack, other than merely a cease-fire. The written context of this passage in Revelation chapter 9 does not necessarily give one the feeling of being a war-zone scenario, but more an attack on mankind in general, inspired by the demonic underworld.

So, from man's point of view, and economic practicality, I must confess I still lean toward these locusts being a genetic engineering research program gone wrong. Or, there could be a more focused, deliberate purpose involved for such a project.

Who could possibly wish to use such a form of attack against mankind? Obviously Satan, but more definitively, the AntiChrist, who by this juncture of the Tribulation is possessed by Satan. Also, whatever these weapons are, whether genetic, biological, or hardware, or a combination, they must be sanctioned, funded, and produced somewhere. Saddam Hussein has shown us that radical Islamic ideology is not above using biological and chemical weapons. He has used chemical agents against certain pockets of his own population. So it is possible AntiChrist, who may have a similar mind set, may be behind this attack on mankind. He may desire to intimidate those who are not falling willingly into his camp, and he may even realize his own people are vulnerable, but carry it out anyway, (not at all unlike the jihad mind-set that encourages suicide bombers.) The fact is, everyone world-wide is targeted. Except he does not count on one result. The 144,000 who have Divine protection are not affected. Worse yet from his perspective, these are Jews! Now if AntiChrist has Islamic roots, he won't be too thrilled about that!

Just a note of explanation regarding the Satanic possession of AntiChrist, because this does have some bearing on the perpetrator behind this locust attack. Satan has finally obtained a position of authority in the world by this juncture, so proceeds to govern demons and men accordingly. AntiChrist appears to be possessed by Satan after his mortal wound is healed. Genetic engineering may also play a role in the healing of his wound, giving legitimate entrance, allowing Satan to take over the body and thinking of AntiChrist.

We have often debated regarding the cloning of a human being, and wondered if the clone is essentially the same person as the original, and thus what eternal significance this will ultimately have for the clone. Most of us have come to the conclusion that the spirit and soul of the clone cannot be that of the original God-formed individual, so must be demonic in origin. Well, it would appear Revelation may give us a clue regarding the answer to this debate, because the world will come face to face with the consequences of operating outside the God-ordained reproductive cycle, both of tissue cells, and the propagation of species. Even AntiChrist, although not a full clone, may be healed of his mortal wound through the cloning of human cells. Genetically, these cloned cells may be 'human,' but the spirit-life-force indwelling these cells will be anything but! The same then would be true for genetically engineered locusts. So genetic engineering may play a role in the unfolding of this First Woe Trumpet.

B. The Sixth Trumpet Sounds, The Second Woe:

The Sixth Trumpet of The Seventh Seal involves input by empires and angels, but Jesus Christ is the One who wins the victory. Revelation 9:13 to 11:14 explains this Second Woe. The passage is a lot to transcribe, so please read it from your own Bible before proceeding.

Notice, when the sixth angel sounds, John hears a voice emanating *"from the four horns of the golden altar which is before God, saying to the sixth angel which had the trumpet, Loose the four angels which are bound in the river Euphrates. And the four angels were loosed, which were prepared for an hour, and a day, and a month, and a year, for to slay the third part of men."* Verses 13 to15 of Revelation chapter 9. Four angelic beings that have been bound, are now loosed. Their location is interesting. They have been bound in The River Euphrates. This is not coincidental. We see ties to the geographic area of the former Empires of the Babylonians, Medio-Persians, Greeks, and the Eastern leg of the ancient Roman Empire, who all controlled The Middle Eastern area at one time or another in history. The four angelic being's purpose is to wage war, and that war will last for an hour, a day, and month longer than a year. Now, that is a very specific time-frame! Once this war starts, if anyone is reading The Book of Revelation at that time, the date of the end of this war will then be calculable.

The description of the army and their horses <u>does indicate modern tanks this time</u>. But the war, which is The Battle of Armageddon, will be devastating, because one-third of mankind will be wiped-out by what appears to be the use of massive fire-power, some of which may be nuclear, and some neutron. The tanks appear to be able to deploy their weapons from both the front (mouth) and the back (scorpion-like tails.)

THE SEVENTH SEAL

Why does this battle come to an abrupt end? Yom Kippur. Jesus Christ returns! But just because Christ returns and ends this battle before mankind annihilates himself, does not mean everyone suddenly, and willingly, turns their hearts to the LORD. There seems to be an antagonistic haughtiness rampant among the two-thirds who are left of the earth's population following this battle. Revelation chapter 9:20-21. *"And the rest of the men which were not killed by these plagues yet repented not of the works of their hands, that they should not worship devils, and idols of gold, and silver, and brass, and stone, and of wood: which neither can see, nor hear, nor walk: Neither repented they of their murders, nor of their sorceries, nor of their fornication, nor of their thefts."* Mankind, even after all that he has been through, is still not yet ready to repent and turn to God. Amazing!

1. The "Mighty Angel:"

[144]A Mighty Angel, <u>this is not a created angelic creature</u>, comes down out of heaven, clothed with a cloud, a rainbow surrounding his head, his face shining as the sun, and his feet appearing as pillars of fire. He carries in his hand a little Open Book, and sets his right foot upon the sea, and his left foot on the land. He cries out with a loud voice, and Seven Thunders are heard.

Who is this "Mighty Angel?" This is Christ Himself. [145]No-one but The Lion of the Tribe of Judah, the Root of David, The Lamb Who was slain, is able to break open the Seals of the Book. No one else appears out of Heaven in Clouds of Glory, a rainbow surrounding His head, His face shining as the sun, and His feet as pillars of fire. Ezekiel, Isaiah, and John saw the LORD, and described Him in this manner on more than one occasion. So what is being described here? The Glory of the LORD! The Shekinah Glory that accompanies The Lamb and surrounds The Throne, descends upon the earth. Yom Kippur! The Second Coming of Christ.

But he is called a *'mighty angel'* in this passage. The term, 'angel' is a word simply meaning 'messenger.' In this instance, <u>Christ is His own messenger delivering and expediting His message Himself</u>.

Now, this is where we begin to realize that The Book of Revelation definitely is not a western-minded chronological sequence, but has multiple layers of explanation covering prophetic fulfillment during a specified time-frame. All of what transpires during The Days of Awe, as well as what follows after, cannot be described in chronological sequence,

---

[144] Revelation 10:1-3.
[145] Revelation 5: 6-7.

so the techniques of flash-back and layering must be incorporated. This is where we realize that these Seals, Trumpets, and Woes overlap, and/or layer-up significantly.

The Mighty Angel, who in this case is Christ Himself, (the term 'angel' simply meaning a heavenly messenger or ministering heavenly being, so The Son of God can deliver His own message, and Himself minister), utters a loud Voice like the roaring of a Lion. A descriptive metaphor for the LORD is that of being The Lion of The Tribe of Judah. A lion never roars unless there is something to roar about. Unlike most cats, lions are much more predictable creatures. A lion generally does not roar unless he is either disturbed about something, or is victorious. The roar of The Lion of The Tribe of Judah must then be most significant. And Judah must have something to do with it, since He is The Lion of The Tribe of Judah, and He is roaring. What is He roaring about? Let's continue so we may find out.

2. The Seven Thunders:

Revelation 10:1-7. "*And I saw another mighty angel came down from heaven, clothed with a cloud: and a rainbow was upon his head, and his face was as it were the sun, and his feet as pillars of fire:* Verse 2. *And he had in his hand a little book open: and he set his right foot upon the sea, and his left foot on the earth,* Verse 3. *And cried with a loud voice, as when a lion roareth: and when he had cried, seven thunders uttered their voices.* Verse 4. *And when the seven thunders had uttered their voices, I was about to write: and I heard a voice from heaven saying unto me, Seal up those things which the seven thunders uttered, and write them not.* Verse 5. *And the angel which I saw stand upon the sea and upon the earth lifted up his hand to heaven,* Verse 6. *And sware by him that liveth for ever and ever, who created heaven, and the things that therein are, and the earth, and the things that therein are, and the sea, and the things which are therein, that there should be time no longer:* Verse 7. <u>*But in the days* of the voice of *the seventh angel, when he shall begin to sound, the mystery of God should be finished,*</u> *as he hath declared to his servants the prophets.*" KJV. Emphasis mine.

The number seven is the number of perfection and completion, meaning these Thunders indicate finality and absolute perfect culmination. They are uttered by God The Father. How can we verify this?

First of all, the sounding of the Seven Thunders is not an isolated incident without precedent. Thunders, lightnings, and voices are uttered when the angel from The Throne casts the censer filled with fire from off the altar into the earth. Revelation 8:5. Also, thunders, fire, lightnings, and a trumpet were uttered at Mount Sinai as Moses was given The Torah, and the people were warned not to go near the mountain, or they would surely die. The awesome holy presence of God rested upon the mount in the sight of the people, and God declared to Moses He would descend upon the mount in a thick cloud. *"And it came to pass on the third day in the morning, that there were thunders and lightnings, and a thick cloud upon the mount, and the voice of the trumpet exceeding loud; so that all the people that was in the camp trembled."* Exodus 19:16. Unregenerate man could not approach the holy presence of God without coming under condemnation and judgment, even though the people had been sanctified according to the command of the LORD. <u>But they all heard the trumpet and the thunders</u>.

It is interesting to note that many Jews believe this trumpet was a Tekiah blast. The Jews believe that while Moses was upon the mount, He was not merely given The Law, but <u>the entire Torah</u>, taking mankind back to Creation, and the awesome power of God. He was also given the truth and ramifications of original sin, and the promise of redemption through the Atonement, and reconciliation for mankind to ultimately be brought back into full fellowship with God. Whenever thunders, accompanied by the sound of a trumpet, are mentioned in Scripture, the Voice of God The Father is speaking, and momentous things are about to happen.

The Voice of The Father uttered from the Heavens, along with thunders, were not new to John. [146]He was exposed to the Voice of God the Father uttered in the presence of Christ at Jesus' baptism, and also on the Mount of Transfiguration, and [147]later again just before Jesus went to the cross. On these occasions, The Father was glorified, and Jesus was glorified by The Father. So when we combine The Old Testament utterances of the thunders with The New Testament utterances of the Voice of the Father, we always see the majesty, holiness, power, and glory of God, and the fulfillment of His purposes prophetically in and through Jesus Christ.

Just before Jesus went to the cross, He was talking to His followers, and told them, John 12:23-31. *"The hour is come that the son of man should be glorified.* Verse 24. *Verily, verily, I say unto you, <u>Except a corn</u>* (kernal) *<u>of wheat fall into the ground and die, it abideth alone: but if it die, it bringeth forth much fruit</u>.* Verse 25. *<u>He that loveth his life shall lose it: and he that hateth his life in this world shall keep it unto life eternal</u>.* Verse 26. *If any man serve me, let him follow me; and where I am, there also will my servant be: if any man serve me, him will my father honor.* Verse 27. *Now my soul is troubled; and what shall I say? Father, save me from this hour:<u> but for this cause came I unto this hour</u>.* Verse 28. *<u>Father, glorify thy name</u>.* Then came there <u>a voice from heaven</u>, saying, <u>I have both glorified it, and will glorify it again</u>. Verse 29. *The people therefore,*

---

[146] Matthew 3:13-17, Mark 1: 9-11, Luke 3:21-22, Matthew 17: 1-8, Mark 9:1-8.
[147] John 12:23-33.

that stood by, and heard it, <u>said that it thundered</u>: *others said, an angel spake to him*. Verse 30. *Jesus answered and said*, <u>This voice came not because of me, but for your sakes</u>. Verse 31. **<u>Now is the judgment of this world: now shall the prince of this world be cast out.</u>**" KJV. Emphasis mine. There are some interesting parallels and prophecies in Revelation chapter 10:1-7 which coincide with this passage in John. So let's examine these two passages for a few moments.

The Seven Thunders in Revelation chapter 10 are the Voice of God The Father. <u>What The Father actually stated remains concealed</u>, because John was told <u>not to write down</u> what the Seven Thunders uttered, but he was "*to seal up those things which the seven thunders uttered, and write them not.*" Revelation 10: 4. So we cannot speculate <u>directly</u> on what the Thunders said, <u>but we are able to notice some things about the fact that the Thunders were uttered at all</u>, and <u>John heard them</u>, <u>and was at least allowed to record that fact</u>.

When the Voice of Thunder spoke before Jesus went to the cross, it was uttered to specifically glorify The Name of The Father, and it is obvious this glorification was to be expedited through Christ. The people standing by were not able to hear the words uttered, but heard only the sound of Thunder. <u>But Jesus knew what was uttered</u>. The people obviously knew that this was not just a regular thunder-clap, but was a heavenly message. Jesus states that the Thunder did not come for His benefit, but "***for your sakes**. <u>Now is the judgment of this world: now shall the prince of this world be cast out</u>.*" John 12: 30-31. Jesus was stating that it was important for the people who were His followers to recognize that the time had now arrived <u>to initiate the countdown toward the judgment of this world, and now the prince of this world,</u> Satan, <u>shall be defeated, and will ultimately be cast out</u>. So even though the people standing there did not actually understand the words spoken, **Jesus gave them the reason why the Thunder was uttered**. It was for their sakes. And it was because "*the hour is come, that the Son of man should be glorified,*" so Jesus prayed "*Father, glorify thy name.*" God's judgment was to fall on the world, and Satan cast out, and the kingdoms of this world given permanently into the hands of Christ, The KING of Kings. So we at least know the utterance of the Thunders glorifies The Name of The Father, indicates ultimate judgment, heralds the dismissal of Satan from input into the affairs of the nations, and exalts the victory of Christ as The Eternal Sovereign over all nations. Thunders then, indicate the absolute fulfillment of God's Redemptive Plan, expedited through the Sovereign Victory of Christ over the works of Satan.

Jesus' death and resurrection gained this victory. He became the "*kernal of wheat*" that died, was buried, and arose victorious to multiply into much

THE SEVENTH SEAL

fruit. He did not come to save His life, *"**but to lay it down**,"* because *"he that loveth his life shall lose it, but he that hateth his life in this world shall save it unto eternal life."* Jesus not only was giving a principle of selfless commitment for us to follow, but was stating that this was exactly what He was about to carry out, both by example for us to follow, and in the <u>reality of what was to be fulfilled prophetically</u>. <u>What He was about to do in going to the cross was the beginning of a whole series of events that would culminate in the end of Satan's jurisdictional claim on mankind</u>, and result in the absolute transfer of the kingdoms of this world from Satan's stranglehold, into The Kingdom of God.

Anyone in the course of the outworking of this process who loves his life in this world, will ultimately lose it. Anyone who hates his life in this world, will ultimately save it unto eternal life. This statement is not simply a lofty principle, or even an admonition to dedication of one's life unto the LORD rather than following one's own personal agenda. Although that is a valid interpretation and application, <u>the prophetic implications are much more than that</u>, and for those living during the tenure of the AntiChrist, this statement by Jesus Christ will take on a very physical, as well as spiritual, dimension. Those who love this life, and accept The Mark of The Beast as a way to preserve their life, will ultimately lose their life eternally. Those who are willing to give up their physical life to preserve their eternal destiny, will pay by martyrdom. This test of commitment will be very stark, and real, for the Tribulation Saints. Notice, Jesus made this prophetic statement within the context of His explanation for the reasons why The Thunders were uttered, and that they were uttered for the sake of those listening.

So has Satan been cast out? He is defeated, but still must be cast out of this world. His ultimate defeat <u>began with the cross</u>, <u>and the victorious resurrection of Jesus Christ</u>, <u>but is still to be brought to complete fruition</u>.

The Seven Thunders uttered in Revelation chapter 10 carry the same implications, because even though John is not allowed to write down what actually was uttered, <u>Jesus Christ</u>, <u>again acting as His own heavenly messenger</u>, <u>gives us an explanation</u>, just as He did for His disciples in John chapter 12. <u>His message is not an interpretation of the exact words uttered by The Father</u>, <u>but an explanation of what will result</u> when Christ is totally glorified in the earth.

Revelation 10:5-7. *"And the angel* (who in this case is Christ Himself) *which I saw stand upon the sea and upon the earth lifted up his hand to heaven, Verse 6. and sware by him that liveth for ever and ever, who created heaven, and the things that therein are, and the sea, and the things which are therein, <u>that there should be time no longer</u>:* Verse 7. **But in the days of the voice of the seventh** *angel, when he shall begin to sound, the mystery of God shall be finished, as he hath declared to his servants the prophets."* KJV. Emphases mine.

In the course of **the days** when The Seventh Trumpet voice begins to sound (at the opening of the Sixth Seal at Rosh HaShanah, until the same Seventh Trumpet sounds as the predominant voice of the Woe Trumpet trio, culminating in Yom Kippur), in the **Days**, plural, of the sounding of this **Seventh Trumpet**, The Mystery of God will be brought to completion. This refers to the Ten Day Fall Feast drama when The Seventh Trumpet is The Last Trump, Ha Teurah Shofar of Rosh HaShanah, and is Tekiah HaGadol, The Great Shofar of Yom Kippur, and Christ is revealed as total Victor. These **days** of the sounding of this Seventh Trumpet **are The Ten Days of Awe.** These Days of Awe will wrap-up all righteousness, bind Satan, and usher-in The Kingdom of God on Earth. (See chart, page 284.)

Christ is standing astride the sea, and the land. In other words, He now is LORD of all nations (sea), and of all the earth (physical Kingdoms, and the earth itself). He holds the open Book -- His fulfilled title-deed. His stance is that of ownership, all authority, and of Government. Satan has no more authority to mess any longer with any aspect of Creation, which was created by *"Him that liveth forever and ever."* Again, this speaks of Christ Himself, because He not only is eternal, but procured Eternal Life for us all. But He is the only One who was able to atone for sin, and overcome eternal death and wrath once and for all. This is what Jesus meant when in His explanation of the Thunder of God's Voice in John chapter 12, he stated, *"for this cause came I into the world."* He was not merely referring to His victory over sin at the cross, or His victory over death through the resurrection, but He was proclaiming that His death and resurrection would now bring about the spiritual, and even the physical mechanism whereby Satan is defeated and cast out, and now Christ has an open path to ascend to His rightful position as LORD over all Creation for all eternity, totally reversing and eliminating the curse. He is the One who created the heavens and the earth. The *"prince of this world,"* no longer can hang onto any title or authority, but now is cast out. This victory will finitely become evident during The Days of Awe, beginning when the seventh angel who holds The Seventh Trumpet begins to sound at Rosh HaShanah, culminating in absolute triumphal blast at Yom Kippur.

So, let's put this together time-wise. Revelation 10:6b -7. *"...that there should be time no longer,* **but in the days** *of the voice of the seventh angel, when he shall begin to sound, the mystery of God shall be finished, as he hath declared to his servants the prophets."* When the seventh angel sounds, *"there should be time no longer"* and the *"mystery of God"* will be finished, just as the prophets prophesied. Time's up for Satan!

THE SEVENTH SEAL

Some interpret *"there should be time no longer"* to mean time itself ends. This is unrealistic, because after Satan is defeated, the earthly reign of Christ occurs for a thousand years. So time itself does continue! <u>The context ultimately of the uttering of the Thunders, is the transfer of the Kingdoms of this world from the oppressive domination of Satan, to the dominion of Christ,</u> just as Jesus Himself stated in John chapter 12. **The days of the countdown <u>for time</u> remaining <u>for Satan</u>**, and for his hold over the nations, begins at Rosh HaShanah when the seventh angel <u>begins to sound</u> the Seventh Trumpet voice known as The Last Trump, Ha Teruah. This time-countdown begins with this Seventh Trumpet, indicating there are only ten more *"days"* to go, and these *"days"* end with Tekiah HaGadol, The Great Shofar blast of The Seventh Trumpet voice (blown by the same seventh angel) at Yom Kippur.

We are familiar with this type of countdown reasoning, especially when it begins with the number ten. We use this countdown ourselves. Ten, nine, eight, seven, ... **In the days (The Ten Days of Awe) of the voice of the seventh angel, when he begins to sound, the Mystery of God will be finished**. There will be <u>no more time required</u> to complete what has been shown to the prophets regarding the Mystery of the Revealing of Christ, and the Kingdoms of this world belonging to Christ. It is amazing how our understanding of The Feasts, and the accompanying Trumpets, allows us to unravel these prophecies, and place their application into proper perspective! *"There should be time no longer"* is not the same as saying, "time itself no longer exists," and Christ here is not saying time no longer exists, but "<u>Time's up. Enough! That's it! I'm taking over completely now, and everyone, especially Satan, will have to recognize this reality</u>."

So what are The Seven Thunders indicating? They are glorifying The Father, and heralding the fact that judgment now is to be brought to completion, and Satan's position as being prince of this world is ended. <u>Jesus now has all authority in heaven and in earth</u>. <u>The Mystery of the saving, authoritative power of redemption and reconciliation through Christ, to bring all Creation back into fellowship with God for eternity, now is complete</u>.

Will we ever be told what The Seven Thunders, the Voice of God The Father, actually said? I don't know, but we know that The Father is glorified through the finished work of The Son. Jesus Christ is The Victor! He stands on the sea and on the land, and He raises the open Book. The open Book indicates righteousness has won, not through man's own deeds, but because the blood of Jesus Christ, through the atonement, has defeated sin and death, and all that has been written in the Law and the Prophets regarding righteousness and The Kingdom, is now complete. Jesus Christ,

The Final Schedule Revealed

<u>The Lamb of God</u>, has completed the *"mystery of godliness."* He is KING of Kings, and LORD of Lords, over all in Heaven, or in earth, or under the earth. The battle is finished! Yom Kippur! Jesus Christ, The KING, The Redeemer, reigns!

So now is the Sixth Trumpet and the Second Woe over? Not yet! There is an agenda that must be fulfilled during the count-down of The Ten Days of Awe, to bring all that the prophets have said to completion. The victory has already been won at the cross, but Satan did not roll over and play dead! The Seventh Seal is not yet complete, and therefore The Seventh Trumpet is not finished sounding. In fact, the Second Woe of the Sixth Trumpet, and the Third Woe of the Seventh, still must be prophetically fulfilled. The Seven Thunders simply are telling us that the victory that is already won, is imminently to become evident. So, we have been given explanation and insight into the ultimate purpose of what is transpiring during The Ten Days of Awe, <u>parenthesized</u> and <u>announced</u> by the two significant utterances of the voice of The Seventh Trumpet, revealing the triumph of The Perfect, Risen Lamb of God, accompanied by The Seven Thunders revealing His absolute victory, glorifying The Father.

CHAPTER 17
MEASUREMENTS, WITNESSES, and AN EARTHQUAKE

I. The Measuring of The Temple Complex:

The Temple, the altar, and even the people who worship in The Temple, are to be measured. John is given a measuring rod to do this. <u>He is not to measure the court outside The Temple, because it is to be given to the Gentiles, who will occupy the Holy City for forty-two months</u>. This gives us insight into what will transpire regarding jurisdiction over Jerusalem during the last three and one-half years of the Tribulation. Even though Jerusalem and Judah will be placed into the hands of the Israelis as a result of The Gog-Magog Battle, Jerusalem remains a *"burdensome stone and cup of trembling."* So Jerusalem becomes the stronghold of AntiChrist domination during the final throes of the Tribulation, after the Abomination of Desolation that takes place mid-70th Week. Jerusalem becomes the seat of AntiChrist's government after The Temple is desecrated, and he sets up his headquarters there. So the Times of the Gentiles resumes mid-Trib, because all of Jerusalem is again not directly under Israeli jurisdiction.[148] In fact, the Israeli Government, and the Temple Priests, must be removed from Jerusalem temporarily, and relocated elsewhere, just to preserve the Israeli national identity.

---

[148] Author's Note: Jesus states in Matthew 24: 15-22 that following the Abomination of the Temple, folk will have to flee from Jerusalem. Do all Jews flee? No. Who will be fleeing? Logic tells us that it will not be safe for the Temple Priests to remain in Jerusalem. The Temple Priests especially will be in danger of being put to death because they will certainly not be allowed in the Temple, or on the Mount, and absolutely will not comply with AntiChrist's immediately imposed rules of pagan worship. Also, the Knesset members, the Prime Minister, and the President, would obviously have to flee from Jerusalem. They definitely will be in mortal danger, because AntiChrist will not recognize Israel's government. Jesus states those fleeing are to go to the mountains, not even returning home for their belongings, and pray that their flight does not take place in the Winter, or on the Sabbath, because if they must vacate during Winter, they will have to endure great hardship. The ramifications of a Winter flight without benefit of extra clothing or blankets, under great duress, we can readily understand. But why not flee on the Sabbath? The Sabbath has Jewish travel restrictions, and some priests, and Torah observant dignitaries, may be sorely tempted to not flee immediately, putting themselves and their

II. The Two Witnesses:

But the AntiChrist does not have a free ride in Jerusalem. There is opposition, and some of it does not come from where he, or any other world leaders expect. Revelation 11:3 - 6. *"And I will give power unto my two witnesses, and they shall prophesy a thousand two hundred and threescore days, clothed in sackcloth. Verse 4. These are the two olive trees, and the two candlesticks standing before the God of the earth. Verse 5. And if any man hurt them, fire proceedeth out of their mouth, and devoureth their enemies: and if any man will hurt them, he must in this manner be killed. Verse 6. These have power to shut heaven, that it rain not in the days of their prophecy: and have power over waters to turn them to blood, and to smite the earth with all plagues, as often as they will."*

Within the AntiChrist dominated city of Jerusalem, perhaps taking up a post at The Wailing Wall, (we are not told necessarily where they will station themselves, but at the site of The Wailing Wall would be easy for everyone to find them, and would be a logical location from which to stage a protest by Jews, because again they will have lost access to The Temple Mount because of the Abomination), we find two God-ordained Witnesses. Their purpose appears to be neither political, nor specifically religious, <u>but rather to proclaim judgments against the enemies of God by prophesying, and by exercising signs and</u> <u>wonders to get people's attention,</u> <u>and to kill the enemies of Israel</u> <u>and of God</u> <u>with fire proceeding out of their mouths.</u>

It would appear their identities are at once Jewish Prophets, and Messengers of Messiah, because verse 4 of Revelation chapter 11 describes them as *"the two olive trees, and the two candlesticks"* that stand before God. The two Olive Trees represent all Israel. Probably one Witness will be from a tribe of The House of Judah, and one from a tribe of The House of Israel. However, Zechariah also sheds some light on who these Two Olive Trees are <u>in their ministry role</u>. Zechariah was shown a Seven-Branched Menorah, and on each side stood an Olive Tree. The angel speaking with Zechariah identified their purpose, saying, *"This is the word of the LORD unto Zerubbabel, saying, Not by might, nor by power, but by my spirit, saith the LORD of hosts."* Zechariah 4:6. Therefore, these Two Olive Trees will be

---

families in even greater danger. They will be forced to flee under self-imposed condemnation. Also, AntiChrist may persecute them particularly on the Sabbath. Muslims do not give any regard to the Jewish Sabbath, and in fact, may mock it with violence, particularly targeting all Israeli dignitaries at that time. Israeli Law, and its enforcement, either religious, or secular, will suddenly be useless in protecting the Jews immediately following AntiChrist's take-over.

filled with, and anointed by the Holy Spirit, to carry out their mandate just before Christ returns. The angel further identified these Olive Trees by stating, *"These are the two anointed ones, that stand by the Lord of the whole earth."* Zechariah 4:14. In other words, these Spirit anointed Witnesses stand in prophetic affirmative ministry before the LORD Who made Heaven and earth, proclaiming His absolute sovereignty.

Also, the Witnesses are identified as two Candlesticks. The lights burning on the branches of the Menorah were oil-lamps. The oil was fed to the branches of the Menorah from one reservoir of oil called The Servant Lamp. The Servant Lamp represents Jesus Christ, The Light of the World, and also shows He is the Giver of the oil of the Holy Spirit. So we see the presence of the Holy Spirit in full anointing fills the Two Candlesticks, empowering them for their ministry in accordance with the prophetic plans and purposes of Jesus Christ. Therefore, the role of the Spirit's anointing is not entirely removed from the earth at the time of the Rapture, but will be very active in anointing the lives and ministry of these Two Witnesses! We must conclude then, that these Two Candlesticks carry the prophetic mantle of Prophets, in like manner as the anointing that rested upon Moses and Elijah.

Are they Moses and Elijah as some have declared? [149]Elijah did not die, but was translated (raptured.) [150]Moses did die, and God buried him in a secret place. Whether Elijah returns, and Moses is resurrected so that <u>they are</u> these Two Witnesses is somewhat debatable, but we do know these Witnesses operate under the <u>same Holy Spirit anointing</u>; performing signs and wonders patterned in type by those performed by Moses and Elijah. Thus the Spirit of God is their anointing for the same ministry mandate as rested upon Moses and Elijah.

The Elijah anointing would be patterned along the same model as the Spirit of Elijah that rested upon John the Baptist. John was not Elijah re-incarnated. [151]He was born the son of named earthly parents, and was contemporary with Christ, being six months older; and he was Jesus' second cousin. Reincarnation is not a Scriptural concept. [152]John the Baptist was anointed by the Holy Spirit from the time of his conception, and operated in ministry in like manner as the same Spirit anointing that rested upon Elijah. Jesus acknowledged this anointing was upon John. John the Baptist was anointed to fulfill *"the voice of one crying in the wilderness, Prepare ye the*

---

[149] 2 Kings 2: 11.
[150] Deuteronomy 34: 1-8. Jude 9.
[151] Luke 1: 36- 41.
[152] Luke 1: 12- 17.

way of the Lord, make straight in the desert a highway for our God." Isaiah 40: 3. [153]The anointing of the Holy Spirit that rested upon John the Baptist in fulfillment of the prophecies given to the prophet Isaiah, was specifically to empower him to prepare the way of the LORD, announcing the imminent onset of the ministry of Christ during His First Coming. Matthew 17: 11-12 shows Jesus' Identity of the Spirit anointing upon John the Baptist as that of Elias (Elijah.) *"But I say unto you, That Elijah is come already, and they know him not, but have done unto him whatsoever they listed. Likewise shall also the Son of man suffer of them. Then the disciples understood that he spake unto them of John the Baptist."*

[154]John's mandate was to prepare the hearts and minds of the people to receive Jesus, the Messiah. [155]He identified Jesus as The Lamb of God who takes away the sin of the world. In like manner, the Two Witnesses will prepare the way of the LORD just before He returns the Second time.

The Two Witnesses take up their post in Jerusalem halfway through Daniel's 70th Week, and minister for one thousand two hundred and sixty days. That's a few days short of three and one-half years. Revelation 11: 3. *"And I will give power unto my two witnesses, and they shall prophesy a thousand two hundred and threescore days, clothed in sackcloth."* Why is their mandate described for a specified number of days? God has a time-table, and He operates within this schedule in predictable ways, especially in regard to the nation of Israel, His Covenant heritage people, and regarding His Covenant Land, and the restoration of The Kingdom to Israel, and His arrival as sovereign LORD, KING, and Righteous Judge. He has revealed His time-table to His prophets, and will fulfill what the prophets have said, right down to the exact number of days. The 1260 days indicate <u>the exact</u> number of days these Two Witnesses will have given to them to complete their testimony.

AntiChrist and his regime will not be happy about the mandate of the Two Witnesses, just as Pharaoh was not inclined to co-operate willingly with Moses, but hardened his heart. Every day will be a hassle regarding these two end-time prophets who will be looked upon with disdain, fear, and awe. They will stir up hatred world wide, because the people of the earth will be fearful, as well as fascinated by them and their message. And, they will be horrified.

---

[153] Isaiah 40: 3, Matthew 3:1- 3, Matthew 11: 7- 15. Matthew 17: 11- 12, Mark 9: 11- 13,
[154] John 1: 6- 23.
[155] John 1: 29.

[156] These two will exercise specific powers because of their prophetic anointed position. They will have the ability to destroy anyone who tries to harm them, by dry-roasting them with fire blown out of their mouths. They will have power to stop the rain from falling during the days of their mandate. They also will have the ability to turn water into blood, a similar power Moses exercised in Pharaoh's presence before the Exodus. They will have the power to discipline nations by smiting the earth with plagues as often as they wish. We therefore observe prophetic fulfillment and typical repeat in their activities and mandate. The Children of Israel were set free from bondage following the plagues of Egypt, and were ultimately led into The Covenant Land of Promise. Israel will again be set free by The LORD God of Israel, Who will establish them in The Land of Covenant following the completion of the mandate of these two prophets of God, who will have the Spirit-anointed power to perform many of the same signs and wonders as Moses.

At the completion of their mandate, God will allow the *"beast that ascends out of the bottomless pit"* to make war against them, and overcome them, so that they are murdered. Revelation 11:7. Who is the Beast that ascends out of The Bottomless Pit? This is Satan, who by this juncture will have taken up bodily residence in the form and possession of AntiChrist. He will make war against the Two Witnesses. Everyone up to this point will have been rather stumped as to how to silence the Two Witnesses, since no enemy will be able to get close to them without being killed by fire. In fact, no-one, not even Satan, would be able to harm them at all, except God allows it.

AntiChrist will think he has pulled off a real victory when the Two Witnesses are assassinated. [157]Everyone world-wide will celebrate, and send gifts to each other. A real macabre celebration! They will gloat by not immediately burying the two bodies. This in itself shows that the Israelis will be either subjugated, or definitely ignored in dealing with the funeral preparations, because in Israel, bodies must be prepared for burial before sundown. The lack of immediate burial will not be an oversight by AntiChrist's authorities. Rather, the bodies will be left lying, to make these guys who have troubled everyone for so long into objects of derision, indicating what will happen to anyone opposing the regime. For three and one-half days, their bodies will lie in the street where they were murdered, and everyone world-wide will view them. The Satanically possessed

---

[156] Revelation 11: 4 - 6.
[157] Revelation 11: 7 - 10.

The Final Schedule Revealed

AntiChrist will gloat, because Satan will be gloating. The proclaimers of conscience, righteousness, and opposition, have been silenced!

[158]But God is not finished with the Two Witnesses! Even though the 1260 days of their testimony comes to an end, they will have one final drama to perform. Through what happens next, God reminds Satan that he is defeated. After three and one-half days, the Witnesses are resurrected, and the whole world watches as they stand up, very much alive! This unexpected development causes everyone to become extremely fearful! This is not a TV sci-fi sit-com, or a movie with special effects. This is reality! (And we thought 911 was strangely movie-like! But God is the master of special effects. Only His are reality, not staged, and they come with pointed, prophetic messages and results as well!) <u>This is a resurrection that takes place before everyone's eyes</u>!

A voice from heaven speaks audibly, <u>so everyone can hear it</u>, and commands the two resurrected men to *"Come up hither."* In the sight of everyone watching from all nations and peoples, they ascend into heaven, just as Jesus ascended; and a Cloud receives them. This Cloud is not just a weather cloud, but rather the presence of the Shekinah Glory -- the same Cloud that received Jesus at His ascension, and in which He will return to earth. The Witnesses are received into the presence of The LORD, and to The Throne of The Lamb. Their resurrection and ascension re-enacts the truth of the resurrection and ascension of Christ, and the resurrection and Rapture of the Church, which many have, and will have dismissed with alternate explanations. Now no-one will be able to deny the truth. The enemies of the Witnesses watch, aghast. God shows the entire world that He has the upper hand. In fact, He always has, but now is when He crushes any vestige of deceptive authority Satan thought he may have had. From here on in, God calls all the shots directly.

III. The Earthquake:

As if the dramatic events involving the Two Witnesses are not enough to unnerve everyone, [159]a massive earthquake will strike the earth within the hour. A tenth part of Jerusalem will be flattened, and seven thousand men will perish. The reason for the great number killed all at once may indicate that these may have gathered near The Temple Mount area to worship AntiChrist. Or they may be spectators at The Wailing Wall, observing the events regarding The Witnesses; or a combination of the above. This earthquake apparently splits Old Jerusalem into three sections.

[158]   Revelation 11: 11 - 12.
[159]   Revelation 11: 13.

MEASUREMENTS, WITNESSES, and AN EARTHQUAKE

The earthquake is not without geological basis. There is a fault-line running under The Temple Mount, extending from The Mount of Olives into The Old City. There is concern over the seismic activity this fault-line is even now displaying. Actually, there are two separate geological weaknesses regarding The Temple Mount, and both may play significant roles in how prophecy will unfold for Mount Zion, and for Jerusalem.

Engineers from Jordan recently were sent in to assess the on-going damage to the south-eastern wall of The Temple Mount area, and have taken note that the fault-line that runs under The Mount has also been acting up. [160]The south-eastern section of the wall of The Mount is bulging, and in danger of collapsing. [161]These two problems apparently are not necessarily geologically connected, according to the engineers. The bulge in the south wall is the result of destabilizing and weakening brought

---

[160] Author's Note: Isaiah 30: 9-14 sheds much light on this bulge in the wall. Because of Israel's iniquity in listening to the advice of others, and looking to Egypt to help protect them, (when they pull out of Gaza unilaterally) rather than trusting in God, their waywardness is likened to the bulge in a wall that suddenly gives way. This illustration will take on a very real dimension, which will be both a blessing (because it will be part of freeing the Temple Mount, and a trouncing from the LORD, because it will result in much tension and consternation between Israel and the Islamic world when the wall does collapse. It is even now bulging!

[161] The Temple Mount Faithful, Gershon Salomon, February 16, 2004, *Another Wall Collapse on the Temple Mount Near the Western Wall*. Archeologist and Scientists Say, It Was As a Result of The Earthquake in Israel on February 11, 2004. Quote: " On Saturday 22 Shevat 5764, 14th February 2004, another wall on the Temple Mount collapsed in the area of the Western Wall. The wall was the continuation of the Western Wall and which contained the western (Mugrabe) gate leading to the Temple Mount. Stones from the collapsed wall fell in the women's prayer area at the Western Wall while women were praying in the area. It was a miracle that none were hurt."

"As stated above, it happened on Saturday while Jerusalem was being covered with snow. The collapse occurred 4 days after the earthquake which shook all of Israel, including Jerusalem. The earthquake was stronger in the Jerusalem area than in other areas as Jerusalem is closer to the epicentre which was north of the Dead Sea. Archaeologists and scientists stated that the collapse of the wall was as a result of the quake as well as the snow. The archaeologist, Dr. Eilat Mazal, from the committee for the prevention of the destruction of the antiques on the Temple Mount said that "the occurrence of another much bigger collapse is only a question of time and it will cause a major disaster". Other archaeologists and scientists stated that the collapse is just a forerunner of further collapses on the Temple Mount."

about by Palestinian excavations taking place inside The Mount to allow an underground mosque to be built. The Palestinians have hauled away tons of material, with no permission from the Israeli authorities to do so. Not only is a great deal of archeological evidence of Israeli history on, around, and under The Mount now lost, but the damage and weakening of the south wall is irreversible. So we have an unstable fault-line, and a weakened south wall.

[162]This whole situation has caused much consternation, because the entire southern area of The Mount is considered unstable, and indeed a portion of the south-western wall recently sloughed this past September (2003), and another section in the same vicinity collapsed in February 2004, as a result of an earthquake following a snowfall. No major damage to structures resulted, so these recent incidents are not the fulfillment of Gabriel's prophecy regarding the wall and street in Daniel, but warning bells should be going off in everyone's minds! Couple the man-generated damage of the coming major wall-collapse, with the fact that there also is measurable seismic activity occurring along the fault-line, and we are able to see that we may indeed be very close to the end of this Age!

The fact that the south-eastern portion of The Temple Mount wall, where the major bulging has become apparent, has not yet collapsed, indicates God could be keeping His hand on this structural situation to unleash as part of the strategy to bring about the deliverance of Mount Zion into the hands of the Israelis following The Gog -Magog Battle and Joel's blood-red moon. The seismic activity of the fault-line, which will inevitably lead to an earthquake, is being held in abeyance until after The Two Witnesses have done their thing. So God will use these two weaknesses that have been identified under The Temple Mount to accomplish two important, but separate prophetic fulfillments. The collapse of the wall, and extensive damage to the street below, could destroy the Al Aqsa Mosque, along with the underground mosque expansion, bringing about the removal of the Muslims from The Mount, and thus pave the way for the building of The Third Temple during The Calm at the beginning of The Days of Awe. But the fault-line which will result in the earthquake definitely will have impact in the fulfillment of the Sixth Trumpet, Second Woe, following the ascension of The Two Witnesses.

There is one other consequence of this earthquake that will be especially significant. Because it will split The Mount of Olives, pass under The Temple Mount, and extend into the Old City of Jerusalem, it will wreak God's judgment on the seat of AntiChrist's regime and pagan worship. Because AntiChrist will have set his headquarters in the desecrated Temple on The Temple Mount, the earthquake will physically oust him from Mount Zion, because his facilities will be severely damaged. He will have to vacate the premises, and set up shop elsewhere, or immediately take time-out to repair enough of the damage to allow his headquarters to function. The earthquake will play an integral physical role in the disruption of his control, because even his computerized image-worship system will be severely damaged, immediately putting him out of contact with, and therefore out of control of most people world-wide, and particularly out of command of his forces that will be fighting The Battle of Armageddon, which will also be in full theater at that juncture. Couple this natural earthquake disaster, and its ramifications, with the plague of darkness of the Fifth Vial that will be poured out *"upon the seat of the beast; and his kingdom was full of darkness; and they gnawed their tongues for pain,"* Revelation 16:10, and we are able to ascertain why AntiChrist will lose his position and power quickly. This earthquake, and the accompanying darkness that falls on his Temple Mount headquarters, will be devastating for his technologically dependent regime, and will prove to many the fact that he is not infallible.

Notice the shift of who is in control. The First Woe, which is the Fifth Trumpet, is the last time Satan has any direct controlling input. Whereas with the Sixth Trumpet, the Second Woe, God takes absolute control. However, all is not yet complete, and the prophetic spiral continues.

CHAPTER 18
TEKIAH HA GADOL, THE SEVENTH TRUMPET, THIRD WOE

Let's take a look at Revelation chapter 11, starting at verse 15. *"And the seventh angel sounded; and there were great voices in heaven, saying, <u>The kingdoms of this world are become the kingdoms of our Lord, and of his Christ; and he shall reign for ever and ever.</u> Verse 16. And the four and twenty elders which sat before God on their seats, fell upon their faces, and worshiped God, Verse 17. Saying, We give thee thanks, O Lord God Almighty, which art, and wast, and art to come: because thou hast taken to thee thy great power, and hast reigned. Verse 18. And the nations were angry, and thy wrath is come, and the time of the dead, that they should be judged, and that thou shouldest give reward unto thy servants the prophets, and to the saints, and them that fear thy name, small and great: and shouldest destroy them which destroy the earth. Verse 19. And the temple of God was opened in heaven, and there was seen in his temple the ark of his testament: and there were lightnings, and voices, and thunderings, and an earthquake, and great hail."* KJV. Underlining mine.

The sounding of The Seventh Trumpet as <u>the predominant voice</u> in the trio of Woe Trumpets, explains <u>the culmination</u> of all that takes place during the last half of the seven year Tribulation portion of The Ten Days of Awe. So again we observe a concurrent layering, and sequential overlap in the explanation given. The sounding of Tekiah HaGadol, The Great Shofar of Yom Kippur, wraps up the Revelation of Jesus Christ, The Lamb. In fact, to understand the significance of what transpires, John gives us a flash-back to the birth of Christ, then projects forward. Was this Seventh Trumpet sounded at Christ's birth? Very possibly! After all, He was born The Lamb of God, and The Seventh Trumpet voices, sounded first as HaTeurah Shofar, then as HaTekiah Shofar, reveal The Lamb. The soundings of The Seventh Trumpet are the predominant Messianic Trumpet Blasts of The Holy High Days from Rosh HaShanah to Yom Kippur. Therefore, <u>The Seventh Trumpet of The Seventh Seal is the Trumpet of the completion of the revelation of The Mystery of The Lamb of God, the fulfillment of the theme of The Book of The Revelation of Jesus Christ</u>. Most of the remainder of The Book of Revelation explains HaTekiah of this Seventh Trumpet, the Third Woe.

By now, we all have come to the conclusion that The Book of Revelation is the revealed script of the entire Mystery of God's Plan of the Ages, to reveal Christ in all His glory and victory. The LORD Himself delivered the script to John, so we could read it ahead of time. Why would He do that? To allow us to follow along, and know where we are as participant players, and to prepare us to be ready on cue! The next participants who will be needing this script are the 144,000 and the Israeli nation. All nations of the entire world need it, but probably won't even pick it up. However, that will not exempt them from taking part!

I. The Woman Clothed with the Sun, and the Moon at Her Feet:

In order to understand all that is culminated, in Revelation chapter 12 we read that John is taken through the main events of the travail of the woman clothed with the sun, with the moon under her feet, and a crown of twelve stars on her head. She is in pain to deliver her child. A great red dragon having seven heads, ten horns, and seven crowns upon his heads, appears. His tail drags with him a third of the stars (angelic hosts) of heaven, and casts them to the earth. This dragon stands before the woman, ready to devour her child as soon as it is born. She delivers a man child, whose right and destiny it is to rule all nations with a rod of iron; and her child is caught up to The Throne of God. The man-child is Jesus Christ, The Lamb of God, Messiah, Redeemer, and KING of Kings. Satan thought he could devour Him at His birth. When that did not work out, he tried to destroy Him at the cross, but Jesus arose, victorious over sin and death, then ascended to The Throne to take up His rightful position at the right hand of the Father. He will return as Sovereign. Satan is trying to prevent this as well.

A. The Sustaining of the Woman:

[163]The woman flees to a wilderness place prepared by God, where she is sustained for 1260 days. Interesting number! <u>This is the same number of days that the Two Witnesses have to deliver their testimony</u>. In other words, this woman who is identified as Israel, is hidden in protective safety while the Two Witnesses plead the case for her and her Child. We become aware that their testimony ultimately, albeit reluctantly, is received by some folk, because of what subsequently takes place among the nations. This reception of the truth by some may be partly why AntiChrist eventually has the Two Witnesses assassinated -- a murder that could not take place without God's allowance, because God has a greater purpose and plan.

---

[163] Revelation 12: 6.

TEKIAH HA GADOL, THE SEVENTH TRUMPET, THIRD WOE

Why must Israel's government (her internationally recognized governing entity) be given protective custody during the tenure of the ministry of the Two Witnesses? This particular time period is also the final 42 months of Gentile control over Jerusalem. *"But the court which is without the temple leave out, and measure it not; for it is given unto the Gentiles: <u>and the holy city shall they tread under foot forty and two months</u>, Verse 3. And I will give power unto my two witnesses, and they shall prophesy a thousand two hundred and threescore days, clothed in sackcloth."* Revelation 11:2-3. Emphasis mine.

When AntiChrist and his henchmen carry out the Abomination of Desolation, desecrating The Temple, they also gain control over the city of Jerusalem. AntiChrist moves his headquarters into The Temple, then proceeds to set himself up to be worshiped as god, and becomes the uncontested sovereign over The Land. That means Jerusalem cannot remain the seat of the Israeli national Government, because AntiChrist does not recognize Israel's own sovereignty, or Jerusalem as Israel's capitol. Hmm! <u>Sounds like some form of the goals of Palestinian Statehood, with Jerusalem as capitol, may eventually be temporarily reached</u> under AntiChrist! The Arabs want all Israel to be Palestine, with Jerusalem as the capitol. It makes one wonder if AntiChrist may be able to manage to temporarily achieve this goal!

At first glance, it appears Israel has been overrun. But Israel does not cease to exist, because God will not allow the nation to be totally dismantled again. One of the main reasons The Battle of Armageddon is fought, is regarding the sovereign borders of Israel, just as that will have been the main reason for The Battle of Gog and Magog. We have the issue raised again, only this time Israel appears to really have no chance of gaining the victory, with AntiChrist entrenched in The Temple and ruling from Jerusalem. So AntiChrist manages to pull off what no one before him has done. <u>He successfully divides up The Land, with the inclusion of Jerusalem</u>! Daniel 11: 39 states, *"Thus shall he do in the most strongholds with a strange god, whom he shall acknowledge and increase with glory: and he shall cause them to rule over many, and <u>shall divide the land for gain</u>."* Since God has a controversy with those who divide His Covenant Land, <u>this also is the beginning of the downfall of AntiChrist</u> and his forces. At the height of his success his destiny is sealed, and <u>his demise begins because he is in direct conflict with God Himself</u>. Therefore Israel is protected. But with Jerusalem under Gentile domination again, and The Land divided, how are they protected?

Israel's government leaders and dignitaries are taken from Jerusalem to a stronghold, probably to the mountain fortress of Petra which is in Jordan,

The Final Schedule Revealed

and from there Israel is able to maintain her identity as a nation. Israel's government becomes a legitimate government in exile. Revelation 12:14 states, "*And to the woman (Israel) were given <u>two wings of a great eagle</u>, that she might fly into the wilderness, into her place, where she is <u>nourished for a time, and times, and half a time, from the face of the serpent</u>.*" She is saved by an eagle's wings. Who is this eagle? Most likely the wings of the American Eagle will whisk them to safety. The United States is not only a Young Lion by reason of lineage from Britain, but in taking on a stance of sovereign independence from the Mother Lion, chose to represent himself by the national symbol of an Eagle. So there is no discrepancy in the identification of who this Eagle could be.

The United States of America has always been the greatest supporter of Israel. They also have a vested interest in Israeli sovereignty. Israel's sovereign territorial jurisdiction will have already been challenged once at The Battle of Gog and Magog, with Jerusalem along with the area of the former Kingdom of Judah entrenched as Israeli territory, internationally recognized by all as a result. To see The Temple and Jerusalem taken over, and Israel's borders being again questioned, will understandably raise the ire of the United States. In the cause of world peace and safety, the USA will not tolerate these issues being raised again in such a way that they have no say in the deliberations and outcome. It would stand to reason that they will take steps to preserve Israel's government, even if they must whisk her dignitaries away to another location from which to operate.

Why will the USA take this drastic protective action on behalf of Israel? They will realize that the Israelis have been done a great injustice by the AntiChrist taking over and desecrating the Jews most holy sight, The Temple Mount. They will balk at the coerced pagan repressive religious/economic system AntiChrist will enforce world-wide from Jerusalem. The American Young Lion/Eagle will begin to wake-up to what really is transpiring! Israel will be hidden and nourished (sustained) for forty-two months, the last three and one-half years of the Tribulation; during the same period as the testimony of the Two Witnesses, and the Gentile occupation of The Temple Mount and Jerusalem.

But why will Jordan go along with this protection plan, and give sanctuary to Israel's leaders? Jordan is an interesting anomaly. The policies of Jordan have always been somewhat ambivalent toward Israel. At times Jordan has been an avowed enemy. At other times, Jordan has embraced Israel, and even taken evasive interceptive action to protect Israel from attack by other Arab countries and Islamic terrorists. Therefore, Jordan appears to have a love-hate relationship with Israel. Jordan is Israel's main trading partner in The Middle East, and many of the Palestinian Arabs who live in the West Bank are former Jordanian citizens, and have relatives living in Jordan.

Because the Hashemite Kingdom of Jordan borders on Israel, Iraq, Syria, and Saudi Arabia, she is forced to be somewhat of a moderate voice in many situations that arise in The Middle East. After all, Jordan does want to survive! It is certain though, Jordan will not relish Israel being totally dismantled at this juncture, because that would upset her economy and relative wealth, which definitely comes of her interaction with Israel.

It is not a stretch to understand why Jordan will seek to protect Israel when AntiChrist shows his true colors, because his repressive regime and far-out views will eclipse the more moderate position Jordan normally takes, and she will not wish to be coerced. Israel actually may stand up for Jordan's sovereignty, desiring Jordan be protected from AntiChrist's tactics, so Jordan will view Israel as an immediate asset. Throughout their recent brief history together, Israel always seems to manage to surface from adversity in victory, so Jordan may simply decide it would be in her best interests to preserve Israel's identity. Therefore, Jordan's motivation may be borne of self-preservation rather than out of any great love for Israel. This does not mean Jordan will suddenly accept Israel's unchallenged existence, but merely that Israel may be her best bet to allow them both to avoid being totally overwhelmed by AntiChrist's radical regime. At least it will be worth the try. So Jordan offers sanctuary to Israel's leaders, in cooperation with the Eagle.

B. AntiChrist has Enemies:

Also, it appears Egypt and Russia may suddenly wake up at this juncture, because Daniel 11:40 says, "*And at the time of the end shall <u>the king of the south push at him</u>: and <u>the king of the north shall come against him like a whirlwind, with chariots, and with horsemen, and with many ships</u>.*" At The Battle of Armageddon, Egypt becomes directly involved. Russia, having been defeated at The Gog-Magog Battle, appears to have learned a lesson, and joins forces with Egypt, along with the military and navel power of the West, against AntiChrist. But the outcome does not seem to go in favor of this alliance to save The Middle East from the clutches of AntiChrist and his forces, because the same passage continues, "*and he (AntiChrist) shall enter into the countries, and shall overflow and pass over. Verse 41. He shall enter also into the glorious land, <u>and many countries shall be overthrown</u>: <u>but these shall escape out of his hand, even Edom, Moab, and the chief of the children of Ammon</u>.*" AntiChrist is more powerful, and overthrows many.

But Edom, Moab, and Ammon escape from his domination. These three ancient national areas make up most of the existing nation of Jordan. Jordan does not become overrun, but escapes. Why? Bozrah (this ancient city may be near the former mountain fortress city of Petra) is in the southern Jordanian mountains of former Edom. So, in fulfillment of Jesus' prophetic word, immediately following the Abomination, Israel's dignitaries literally flee to the mountains into exile, and they are helped by Jordan and the United States. Jordan protects and sustains the Israeli Government in conjunction with the Eagle. So it appears the AntiChrist and his crew actually do have some enemies among the nations, and Israel has some allies!

Verse 42 of Daniel 11. " *He shall stretch forth his hand also upon the countries: and the <u>land of Egypt shall not escape</u>.*" Egypt is not a friend of AntiChrist at this juncture, but becomes subdued militarily, and subjugated by AntiChrist's economic system. Verse 43. *"But he shall have power over the treasures of gold and silver, and over all the precious things of Egypt: and the Libyans and the Ethiopians shall be at his steps."* So AntiChrist takes whatever he wants, especially in Egypt, Libya, and Ethiopia. He takes over their wealth and economies, subjugating them by his economic system of the super-computer image that the False Prophet sets up. Verse 44. *"But <u>tidings out of the east and out of the north shall trouble him</u>: therefore he shall go forth with great fury to destroy, and utterly to make away many.* Verse 45. *And he shall plant the tabernacles of his palace between the seas in the glorious holy mountain; <u>yet he shall come to his end, and none shall help him</u>."* KJV. Underlining mine.

It appears that the dragon, Satan, who tries to bring the entire world under his direct rule through the AntiChrist, actually finds that he is without many friends in the world. When his true colors show, as he transports his control center to The Temple in Jerusalem, many nations begin to turn against him. As he progresses toward the end of the Tribulation, he finds himself more and more hemmed in. He may control world economics and religion, and have the ability to kill almost everyone not taking the 'mark,' <u>but that does not mean the nations appreciate him</u>! The tidings out of the East could be the advancement of the two million man army from China. The tidings out of the North very well could be advancement by Russia. He will not be expecting either to turn on him. Russia especially will be a surprise, since up until this juncture, Russia has been on his side, and in his confederacy, along with the Arab Islamic strongholds.

C. Michael Stands Up For Israel:

Now the LORD's forces become directly involved. Daniel 12:1-13. "*And at that time shall Michael stand up, the great prince which standeth for the children of thy people: and there shall be **a time of trouble**, such as never was since there was a nation even to that same time: and at that time thy people shall be delivered, every one that shall be found written in the book.* Verse 2 *And many of them that sleep in the dust of the earth shall awake, some to everlasting life, and some to shame, and everlasting contempt.* Verse 3. *And they that be wise shall shine as the brightness of the firmament; and they that turn many to righteousness as the stars for ever and ever.* Verse 4 *But thou, O Daniel, shut up the words, and seal the book, even to the time of the end: many shall run to and fro, and knowledge shall be increased. Verse 5. Then I, Daniel looked, and, behold, there stood other two, the one on this side of the bank of the river, and the other on that side of the bank of the river. Verse 6. And one said to the man clothed in linen, which was upon the waters of the river, How long shall it be to the end of these wonders? Verse 7 And I heard the man clothed in linen, which was upon the waters of the river, when he held up his right hand and his left hand unto heaven, and sware by him that liveth for ever that it shall be for a time, times, and a half; and when he shall have accomplished to scatter the power of the holy people, all these things shall be finished. Verse 8. And I heard, but I understood not: then said I, O my Lord, what shall be the end of these things? Verse 9. And he said, Go thy way, Daniel: for the words are closed up and sealed till the time of the end. Verse 10. Many shall be purified, and made white, and tried; but the wicked shall do wickedly: and none of the wicked shall understand; but the wise shall understand. Verse 11. And from the time that the daily sacrifice shall be taken away, and the abomination that maketh desolate set up, there shall be a thousand two hundred and ninety days. Verse 12. Blessed is he that waiteth, and cometh to the thousand three hundred and five and thirty days. Verse 13. But go thou thy way till the end be: for thou shalt rest, and stand in thy lot at the end of the days.*" KJV. Underlining mine.

This passage gives us much insight into the Seventh Seal of Revelation, and Jesus' Olivet Discourse on the end times, and the final blast of The Seventh Trumpet. The fulfillment of this passage takes place during the last three and one half years of Daniel's 70th Week. So we are looking at the same time period that begins with: The Abomination of Desolation, the oppressive rule of AntiChrist from the desecrated Temple in Jerusalem, the testimony of The Two Witnesses, The Battle of Armageddon, and ends with The Second Coming of Christ, and the set up of Christ's rule and reign on the earth.

The Final Schedule Revealed

Notice the time-frame of the mandate of The Two Witnesses is described as lasting for 1260 days, and the Abomination of Desolation when the sacrifices are stopped lasts for 1290 days. That means AntiChrist <u>will only have a 30 day month left of his tenure after The Two Witnesses have completed their testimony</u>. Also, Israel's protective custody is over, having lasted 1260 days. So, the completion of The Witnesses' testimony heralds the end of the power of the AntiChrist, and the shift of power back to Israel who he thought he had managed to subdue and scatter. God is then glorified among the nations, and they witness God's power and majesty in the resurrection and ascension of The Two Witnesses three and one-half days later! AntiChrist does not realize it, but he now has only 26 1/2 days remaining in office.

D. Resurrection of Two:

It has been almost two thousand years since Christ was resurrected and ascended to Heaven. Many peoples and nations will no longer recognize the truth of the events of the first coming of Messiah, so for most of them, it will take the above events to make them realize the truth regarding Jesus Christ. Also, many will still not believe in the Scriptural explanation for the resurrection and rapture of the Christians, because they will have swallowed alternate explanations for their disappearance. Cosmic convergence, aliens, etc. Therefore, since the majority of Christians will have been either raptured, or martyred by AntiChrist, there will be only one group of righteous left in the world. These will be those who have the Seal of God in their foreheads, the 144,000. AntiChrist wages war with them and their converts throughout the entire seven years of the Tribulation Week, and for the most part will prevail against them, particularly during the last three and one-half years. He will not be able to do much to the 144,000 themselves, because they are Sealed by God for protection, but he will manage to murder The Two Witnesses, and pretty much all of their converts. So, Satan will think he has won!

But instead of the resurrection and ascension of One (Jesus Christ), or the resurrection and Rapture of many (the Church), there will be the resurrection <u>of two</u>, and they also will ascend with the whole world watching. This will be a resurrection and Rapture occurring within The Days of Awe. Now the whole world will witness double the truth.

AntiChrist's days will now be definitely numbered, but how will he be brought down? Again there is process, and to understand we must look at the victory of Christ's takeover first, then back-track to the events bringing about AntiChrist's defeat.

E. Heavenly Coronation:

Messiah takes up His full position at the 1335th day, 45 days after the defeat of AntiChrist, according to Gabriel's explanation to Daniel. Obviously it will take approximately six weeks for Christ to calm the nations from battle, and become the <u>recognized</u> Ruler in Israel, and return Israel's Government to Jerusalem. Not that He does not have everyone's attention, or that He could not do all this immediately, but <u>it will take time</u>, <u>because the nations fight against Him</u>, and because even with the end of Armageddon, most nations of the earth are still haughty against God according to Revelation 16:11. So does Sukkot happen on the 45th day? No, Sukkot is 5 days following the Yom Kippur Second Coming. The first Sukkot following Christ's return will indeed take place 5 days later, <u>but the entire world will not be ready for a major celebration and acceptance of Christ at that juncture</u>. Rather, He will arise to take His position, and begin to restore The Kingdom to Israel, and then He will set matters straight among the nations. Order must be restored first. So 45 days after His Second Coming, restoration of the entire world will begin.

Sequentially, Christ's Coronation will take place in Heaven at His Wedding. Jesus Christ is the Bridegroom/KING according to Jewish wedding tradition. At the same time, Rosh HaShanah, announced by The Seventh Trumpet blast of Ha Teruah, The Last Trump, representing the first Ram's Horn, signals the inauguration of The Ten Days of Awe on earth. While the Wedding and Coronation occur in Heaven, The Ten Days of Awe take place on the earth. His return to earth with His Bride at His side to end The Battle of Armageddon, and wrap up judgment, occurs on Yom Kippur. He takes matters immediately in hand in Israel, restoring Jacob to The Land of Covenant. His ascension to The Throne of David begins on Succot five days following Yom Kippur, but it takes forty more days for any degree of international recognition to <u>begin</u> to occur. Daniel 12:12 states *"Blessed is he that waiteth, and cometh to the thousand three hundred and five and thirty days."*

II. YOM KIPPUR!

Yom Kippur! The Day of Atonement. The final Day of Redemption. The sounding of Tekiah HaGadol, The Great Shophar! Tekiah HaGadol is a special Seventh Trumpet blast. Ha Tekiah was blown at Creation, announced the giving of The Law to Moses on Mount Sinai, and is represented by the second horn of the Ram caught in the thicket. Now it is also blown as a Shevarim blast. The Shevarim announced the beginning and ending of Battle. Tekiah HaGadol will announce to all Creation that all that The Law and The Prophets have said is now fulfilled. This Great Shofar will announce to the entire world that the kingdoms of this world no longer belong to Satan, but now belong to The LORD, The Messiah, and He will reign forever. The Battle of Armageddon is won. The blast of this trumpet will take place at the 1290 days.

AntiChrist is finished! Satan is defeated! The Voice of the Father will Thunder. Revelation 11:15-19 now is fulfilled. "*<u>The kingdoms of this world are become the kingdoms of our LORD, and of his Christ; and he shall reign for ever and ever</u>. Verse 16. And the four and twenty elders which sat before God on their seats, fell upon their faces, and worshiped God, Verse 17. Saying. We give thee thanks, O Lord God Almighty: because thou hast taken to thee thy great power, and hast reigned. Verse 18. And the nations were angry, and thy wrath is come, and the time of the dead that they should be judged, and that thou shouldest give reward unto thy servants the prophets, and to the saints, and them that fear thy name, small and great: and shouldest destroy them which destroy the earth. Verse 19. And the temple of God was opened in heaven, and there was seen in his temple the ark of his testament: and there were lightnings, and voices, and thunderings, and an earthquake, and great hail.*" Underlining mine.

The Book of Life will once more be opened, and everyone who lived or died during The Days of Awe will be finally sealed. A great resurrection will take place at this time. This will be the resurrection of The Tribulation Saints. Those who have been made white and purified through repentance during The Days of Awe will be found written in The Book of Life. Those who chose to remain totally wicked during The Days of Awe, the Rashim, will be sealed also, to await the resurrection of the unrighteous. Some of these Rashim were sealed when The Books were opened on Rosh HaShanah, but were mercifully allowed to live through The Days of Awe. They were, in God's mercy, given one last chance to repent before death. On Yom Kippur none of the wicked are found entered in The Book of Life of The Lamb whose blood has been sprinkled on The Mercy Seat in Heaven. They have not appropriated The Atonement. The Rashim are sealed to await their sentencing at The Great White Throne Judgment.

The AntiChrist and the False Prophet are cast alive into The Lake of Fire on the 1290th day. Satan and his fallen angels are permanently cast out of Heaven upon the earth. Then they are bound and cast into The Bottomless Pit for a thousand years during The Millennial Reign of Christ. At the end of the thousand years, Satan and the these fallen angels will be loosed once more, and allowed to try the hearts of men for a short time. Then will come a final Battle and the destruction of the earth as we know it, and of the heavens. Following this will be The Great White Throne Judgment where all the unrighteous will be sentenced, and cast, along with Satan and his fallen angels, into The Lake of Fire where the AntiChrist and False Prophet already are. Then there will be a New Heavens and a New Earth where only righteousness dwells. But let's not get ahead of ourselves here.

III. Michael, The Archangel, Israel's Heavenly Military Defender:

Notice, Michael, the Archangel who oversees the forces of God in regard to Israel, commands the forces in the Heavenly realm at the end of The Days of Awe. Revelation 12:7-9. *"And there was war in heaven: Michael and his angels fought against the dragon; and the dragon fought his angels. Verse 8. And prevailed not; neither was their place found any more in heaven. Verse 9 And the great dragon was cast out, that old serpent, called the Devil, and Satan, which deceiveth the whole world: he was cast out into the earth, and his angels were cast out with him."* This war between God's heavenly angelic forces under the command of Michael, and Satan forces of evil, has been taking place for a great while. Daniel was exposed to the fact that this conflict was already ongoing in his own day. When Daniel prayed, it took Michael twenty-one days to fight his way through the war raging in the heavenlies to deliver God's answer to Daniel's petitions. There is good reason why some prayers take time to be answered!

According to this passage in Daniel 12, Michael, the military Archangel protector for Israel, will *"stand up"* during the time of unprecedented trouble. He will fight for Israel during these final three and one-half years of the Tribulation when AntiChrist is doing his worst, and while God is pouring out the full Vials of His Wrath. And just when it appears Israel is totally lost, there will be deliverance.

This victory is brought about when Jesus Christ returns. Revelation 19:15 says of Christ, *"And out of his mouth goeth a sharp sword, that with it he should smite the nations: and he shall rule them with a rod of iron: and he treadeth the winepress of the fierceness and wrath of Almighty God."* Michael does not procure the victory here, but musters the forces in the heavenlies for the final onslought. Christ Himself, wielding the Sharp Sword of His Word, is The Victor!

Notice Daniel 12:1 states in regard to Israel, *"...and at that time thy people shall be delivered, every one that shall be found written in the book."* Again we see the overtones of the victory that is achieved at Yom Kippur, proclaimed by the sounding of The Great Shofar. The end of the Battle will culminate in the forces of Heaven fighting against the forces of evil that have deceived the nations of the earth, and against Satan, the False Prophet, and AntiChrist (the unholy trinity.) Some feel this battle mentioned in Daniel is only symbolic of the war between the forces of good and the forces of evil. Although the battle is between good and evil, this battle is very real! Christ comes back as Victor and Sovereign, riding on a white horse, leading His Saints in royal battle array. He is The LORD of Hosts, and He will come to deliver those found *"written in the Book."*

A. The Battle of the Ages:

Armageddon is the final Battle in regard to Israel and the nations, of a war that began long before the Tribulation. According to Revelation 12, we realize the man-child the woman brought forth is Jesus Christ, Who has ascended into the Heavens unto The Throne of God. The dragon is Satan who sought to devour this Child at His birth. He still is seeking to devour this Child. In fact, Satan has been at war against God since The Garden of Eden. This war really became intense once Israel, the chosen people of God, became a nation under Moses, and entered The Land of the Abrahamic Covenant under Joshua. Thus, we have a description of the mechanism of world empires and authorities Satan has used to try to: undermine the Nation of Israel, derail the Plan of Redemption, prevent reconciliation of mankind with God, and pre-empt the rule and reign of Christ. The predominant world empires that have existed in the past give us an insight into how this struggle has unfolded, and what will ultimately transpire.

The Dragon has had his identifying features displayed through these empires, but we also have seen the Hand and Voice of God ultimately dictating the final outcome. In order to understand, we must take a look at these empires as revealed to us by the prophets, and particularly through the encounters, experiences, dreams, and visions of Daniel, and John the Revelator.

B. The Mutations of the Dragon:

The Dragon has exhibited the ability to trans-mutate (adapt) according to the ruling empires of each period throughout history. In Daniel 7:6 this Beast has four heads, ten horns, and ten crowns. He also presents himself successively diverse as a Lion with Eagles wings, a Bear with three ribs between its teeth, a four-winged Leopard with four heads and ten horns, and will finally mutate himself into a dreadful hybrid of all the above. At the time of the birth of Christ, the dragon was depicted as having seven heads, ten horns, and seven crowns upon his heads, and he drags with him one third of the angels of heaven, and casts them to the earth. Revelation 12:3. But during the time of the end, he will mutate into a beast with seven heads, ten horns, ten crowns upon his heads, with the names of blasphemy written on all his heads. Revelation 13:1.

Notice, no matter how many heads or crowns he has had throughout history, he always has had ten horns. No matter how he tries to disguise himself, his horns just keep giving him away! Therefore, he figures he had better do something about these confounded horns to disguise himself for his last and final attack during the Tribulation. So he takes the best of all his disguises, keeps all his heads and crowns, then applies a little 'selective genetic engineering,' and mutates his horns. From among his ten horns he grows another Little Horn having a man's eyes, and uproots three of his other horns. The new Little Horn is quite a character though, because not only is it able to see a great deal, but it also has a mouth that speaks blasphemies. Now somehow in the whole process of growing the Little upstart of a Horn, the genetic information of all the heads becomes mutated as well, because they all end up with blasphemies written across their foreheads. So much for the disguise! With his nosy Little Horn having a big mouth, and with nasty neon signs on all his heads, the dragon's cover is blown out the window! Oh well, it all kind of suits his ego.

The Little Horn is the strongest, and exerts the most authority and dreadfulness, but only for a short time -- the final seven year period of The Ten Days of Awe, called Daniel's 70th Week. Truth be known though, the Dragon still has horns. Disguise or no disguise, he is doomed before he starts! He may fool man for awhile, but he cannot fool God. But before we go into describing the four 'Beasts' the Dragon presents himself as, and his side-kick Beast, the False Prophet, we need to examine a little more regarding the AntiChrist's rise to power, so we understand how he actually becomes the above 'Little Horn.'

C. Is AntiChrist a Muslim?

"Neither shall he regard the God of his fathers, nor the desire of women, nor regard any god: for he shall magnify himself above all. But in his estate shall he honor the god of forces: and a god whom his fathers knew not shall he honor with gold, and silver, and with precious stones, and pleasant things. Thus shall he do in the most strongholds with a strange god, whom he shall acknowledge and increase with glory: and he shall cause them to rule over many, and shall divide the land for gain." Daniel 11:37-39. Notice, the dividing of The Land of Israel for gain is a major factor in the motivation of what this leader sets out to accomplish. He seeks to divide it for some form of profit. Sounds familiar! Who has been seeking division of The Land for their own gain? The Palestinian Muslims, and other Islamic Arab States. Could this be an identifying factor

of who AntiChrist will be, and where he will arise from? Let's continue. But keep in mind, God takes exception to anyone carving-up His Covenant Land of Israel.

1. Self-seeking Pride, Greed, and Not Desiring Women:

These verses in Daniel chapter 11 shed light into several areas. AntiChrist's mind-set is self-seeking pride. He will step outside the accepted framework of traditional religious ritual and worship, going out on a self-made limb which even his fathers would not be able to recognize. He will set himself up as the ultimate sovereign deity, and require everyone to worship him as 'god.' Some feel he may perhaps be celibate, not desiring women. Others believe he may be secretly homosexual. However, this stance would not sit well with most Muslims according to Koranic teaching. The Koran does contain the essence of the Torah, along with other writings sacred to Islam, so is <u>officially</u> against homosexuality in this life. Rather, <u>he may not give women any honor or equality,</u> <u>a stance which is well within the practice of Islamic belief</u>, even though it is also not supported by The Koran. Women are not considered on an equal playing-field with men in Islam. They do not <u>fully</u> participate in the life of the community the same way women of Christian and Judaic practices do. Also, the status of women in Islamic nations varies from country to country. Consequently, there is no real agreement or consistency regarding Islamic women, or their role in society. It should not be a stretch then, to see that AntiChrist will not have much public respect for women, and take this stance to a new height beyond what even most Muslims would go.

2. The 'God of his Fathers:'

Now here is the real crux of his identification, and ultimately of his downfall. He eventually will not give regard to any god but himself. Notice the phrase, *"the God of his fathers."* The capitalization of the word 'God' here, leads some to suggest the AntiChrist could personally be at least partially of Israeli <u>ethnic</u> origin. There is a chance this has some merit. He may not be a full-blooded Arab at all, but rather a member of one of the tribes of Jacob who has turned his back on God, and has become a Muslim, but at first may pose as a Judaic proselyte. This is not without precedent, because there have been Jews found living in the Diaspora who have outwardly 'converted' to Islam as a cover for their identities, just as there were Jews who became 'Christians' to hide their identities during the holocaust of World War Two. An outward conversion of a Muslim to

Judaism, and converting back again when the time is advantageous to his agenda, is not a real reach. Allah certainly is not the God of his fathers if he *is* of Jewish descent! But then, because of his desire to divide The Land for gain, he may be of Arabic ethnicity, or at least <u>an Arab - Palestinian sympathizer</u>. Or he could be from Christian lineage, but has turned his back on his roots, converted to Islam, then become a radical. However, it is possible there may be more of an explanation regardless of his ethnic or religious origin, which compels him to engage in activities that cannot be described any other way than the worship of *"a strange god."*

3. The "god of forces," The Mechanism of his Pagan Idolatry:

AntiChrist will worship a strange pagan deity Daniel identifies as the *"god of forces."* He will not be alone in worshiping this *"strange god."* The manner of this worship will be accommodated by the offerings of gold, silver, and precious stones, and allow the adherent unimpeded access to pleasant things. It appears this worship will also take place from his estate (position) and from many strongholds, or locations, both physical and possibly political. The wording in Daniel 11: 36-39 is interesting, because it seems to indicate a <u>system whereby he will be able to consolidate political, economic, and religious power</u>, *"in his estate,"* that will perpetuate this false worship. Until recently, these verses were often interpreted to be simply indicative of offerings made to a false, pagan god, and an idolatry with a huge, although coerced, following. While this is certainly so, <u>it will also be accommodated by a mechanism, a system</u>.

Many computers operate using gold and silver circuitry, and chips of silica. The most advanced chips and circuitry also now contain carefully engineered crystal components made of precious stones, which are able to exponentially multiply the processing and retention of information, and enhance functional application. These allow for efficient wireless interaction through connection via satellite, so can be used anywhere in the world. I would suggest then, that the *"god of forces"* could easily be the 'god of scientific technological advancements in computer generated communications.' A *"strange god"* indeed! It is certain his fathers would never have been familiar with this 'god.'

The advancements in the field of computer technology and communications are staggering, and are developing so quickly, it seems to be a field that has generated a life and intelligence of its own. (No pun intended.) Super-computers able to 'think and reason' for themselves are on the drawing board. Telepathic interaction through electromagnetic-neuromuscular processing, facilitated by implanted chips is now being

The Final Schedule Revealed

studied, and has tremendous possibilities. [164]Chip technology research companies have made remarkable breakthroughs in this area, and the US military is seriously following this technology, realizing its application for use in unmanned military aircraft, tracking personnel and equipment, etc. It appears AntiChrist and his False Prophet will not only be fascinated by this stuff, but will make use of it for manipulation, control, and power over all who tie-in to it. As the one at the control center of political, economic, and religious power, AntiChrist will be 'worshiped.' But scientific technology is not the only 'strange pagan force' driving these advancements so they can be exploited.

4. The Personal Tragedy Factor:

Around the time of the Abomination of Desolation, which takes place mid-Tribulation (mid-70th Week,) a personal tragedy befalls the AntiChrist. He experiences a mishap (it would seem this is an attempt on his life) whereby he has inflicted upon him a deadly wound. But this wound is miraculously 'healed.' One of the metaphorical descriptions of the AntiChrist is that he is called "The Beast." Now this terminology is descriptive not only for his personal traits and ruthlessness, but more specifically for his position and seat of power supported by both his origins that have brought him to power, as well as his positional representative leadership as head of 'The Beast' of nations. We see this aptly described in Revelation 13:1-18. This passage describes the manner in which he exercises his powers, and gives a clear depiction of who is really driving him following his mortal injury. He becomes Satanically possessed following this injury, so his mind-set is altered. Satan has always sought to usurp the worship of God, and claim all the accolades for himself. Thus we find the AntiChrist develops an insatiable desire for everyone to worship him. The result is described in Revelation chapter 13.

[164] WorldNetDaily.com November 1, 2000. *Digital Angel unveiledHuman-tracking subdermal implant technology makes debut,* "... in addition to locating missing persons and monitoring physiological data, Digital Angel will be marketed as a means of verifying online consumer identity for the burgeoning e-commerce world. ...in an interview last March, the chief scientist, Zhou, told WorldNetDaily he believes the implant will be as popular as cell phones and vaccines.
Digital Angel "will be a connection from yourself to the electronic world. It will be your guardian, protector. It will bring good things to you," said Zhou. "We will be a hybrid of electronic intelligence and our own soul," he added.
WorldNetDaily.com , *YOUR PAPERS, PLEASE* ...March 20,2000. *Big Brother gets under your skin.* Julie Foster, Ultimate ID badge, transceiver implanted in humans monitored by GPS satellites.

CHAPTER 19
THE TWO BEASTS OF REVELATION 13

There are two Beasts mentioned in this chapter. The first describes AntiChrist's identity, and the second is a supportive leader and system who causes the people of the world to fall in line and worship the first 'Beast.' This second Beast is identified as the False Prophet. So let's examine these two Beasts.

I. The Beast Arising from the Sea:

"And I stood upon the sea, and saw a beast rise up out of the sea, having seven heads and ten horns, and upon his horns ten crowns, and upon his head the name of blasphemy. Verse 2. And the beast which I saw was like unto a leopard, and his feet were the feet of a bear, and his mouth as the mouth of a lion: and the dragon gave him his power, and his seat, and great authority." The sea symbolizes the nations and peoples of the earth. It is this sea that often is troubled and stormy. It is the same sea that has produced the nations and empires of the world. Out of this sea, a Beast arises, having seven heads and ten horns, wearing ten crowns. 'Heads' refer to powerful heads of state of ethnic, political, and ideological origins. 'Horns' speak of current authority and power. 'Crowns' speak of sanctioned, recognized political position and leadership. Generally we have identified the first Beast of Revelation 13 as being associated with the nations of the revived Roman Empire of Western Europe; possibly the confederacy of The European Union. The philosophy behind the rule and authority of this Beast is blasphemy against the true God, so it also is a religious system that attempts to set itself up as the truth, replacing God with it's own ideology.

But verse 2 tells us the origin of this Beast, by explaining from where its powers historically arose. This Beast is like <u>a Leopard</u>, with the <u>feet of a Bear</u>, and the <u>mouth of a Lion</u>. Now that is a revealing combination! Who is this strange hybrid animal? To identify these hybrid characteristics, we must look at the animal symbols Scripture gives to the four 'Beast' Empires. We find these four Beasts described in the interpretation of a prophetic dream God gave to Daniel.

It is interesting to note that the four winds that are controlled by four angelic beings are also mentioned by Daniel. In Revelation chapter 6 they are commanded at the opening of the Sixth Seal not to blow on, or hurt the earth, or any tree. The four winds are the influence and aggression that has blown over the whole world in the past, and also which continue to influence nations and leaders today. These influences are what is driving the unrest in our world, and Satan and his forces have been the inspiration behind these entities. It is no surprise that Satan eventually finds a way to take over the body of the leader of the fourth Beast, which is AntiChrist. But before he begins his final onslaught, the nations are given a very short period of 'rest' from the expanding influence of these four 'beastly winds' or ideologies, when the four winds are not allowed to blow. Then the restraint is removed as Daniel's 70th Week begins. By this time, the angels holding the four winds have changed location from the four corners of the earth to the river Euphrates. The ramifications of this move are significant, revealing the empirical roots of the past, evolved into an empire with international control during The Tribulation.

A. The Origin of the Hybrid Beast:

Daniel 7:1-14. *"In the first year of Belshazzar king of Babylon, Daniel had a dream and visions of his head upon his bed: then he wrote the dream, and told the sum of the matters. Verse 2. Daniel spake and said, I saw in my vision by night, and, behold, the <u>four winds of the heaven strove upon the great sea</u>. Verse 3. <u>And four great beasts came up from the sea, diverse one from another</u>. Verse 4. The <u>first was like a lion</u>, and <u>had eagle's wings</u>: I beheld till the wings thereof were plucked and it was lifted up from the earth, and made stand upon the feet as a man, and a man's heart was given to it. Verse 5. And behold another beast, <u>a second</u>, <u>like to a bear</u>, and it raised up itself on one side, and it had three ribs in the mouth of it between the teeth of it: and they said thus unto it, Arise, devour much flesh. Verse 6. After this I beheld, and lo another, <u>like a leopard</u>, which had upon the back of it four wings of a fowl: the beast had also four heads; and dominion was given to it. Verse 7. After this I saw in the night visions, and behold a <u>fourth beast</u>, dreadful and terrible, and strong exceedingly; and it had great iron teeth; it devoured and brake in pieces, and stamped the residue with the feet of it; and it was <u>diverse from all the beasts that were before it</u>; and <u>it had ten horns</u>. Verse 8. I considered the horns, and, behold, <u>there came up among them another little horn</u>, <u>before whom there were three of the first horns plucked up by the roots</u>; and, behold, <u>in this horn were eyes like the eyes of man, and a mouth speaking great things</u>. Verse 9. I beheld till the thrones were cast down, and <u>the Ancient of days did sit</u>, whose garment was white as snow, and the hair of his head like the pure wool: his throne was like the fiery flame, and his wheels as burning fire. Verse 10. A fiery stream issued and came forth from before him: thousand thousands ministered unto him, and ten thousand times ten thousand stood before him: the judgment seat was set,* *and the books were opened.* Verse 11. *I beheld then because of the voice of the great words which the horn spake: I beheld even till the beast was slain, and his body destroyed, and given to the burning flame.* Verse 12. *As concerning <u>the rest of the beasts, they had their dominion taken away: yet their lives were prolonged for a season and time</u>.* Verse 13. *I saw in the night visions, and, behold, <u>one like the Son of man came with the clouds of heaven</u>, and came to the Ancient of days, and they brought him near before him.* Verse 14. <u>*And there was given him dominion, and glory, and a kingdom,*</u> *that* <u>*all people, nations, and languages, should serve him; his dominion is an everlasting dominion*</u>, *which shall not pass away, and* <u>*his kingdom that which shall not be destroyed.*</u>" KJV. Emphasis mine.

I have fully written out this passage because it has much to tell us. When we put it into the context of the Revelation 13 passage, and keep the sequence and implications of the Fall Feasts in mind, we begin to have a clear picture of what is about to transpire. Also we must remember, previous to this, Daniel interpreted Nebuchadnezzar's prophetic dream regarding an image. When we place the interpretation of Daniel's own dream together with Nebuchadnezzar's image, we are able to observe that the Beasts in Daniel's dream are parallel to the body sections of Nebuchadnezzar's image. So we are able to interpret these Beasts as representative of four great world Empires and ideologies which have influenced the nations of the entire earth. These Empires all have had fallen angelic powers behind them, and their winds of influence will again be released during the final Beast's tenure.

1. The Winged Lion.[165] The Babylonian Empire: 606 - 536 B.C.E.

[166]The head of Nebuchadnezzar's image, and the Winged Lion of Daniel's dream, represent The Babylonian Empire, which had great power and influence world-wide. Babylonian culture was polytheistically pagan, being steeped and rooted in Chaldean occultism. Its military might was feared for its aggression, and [167]Babylon swallowed up many peoples, cultures and languages, becoming one of the largest and most influential

---

[165] The Zondervan Pictoral Encyclopedia of the Bible, Vol. 1, 2. Merrill C. Tenney,Ph D, General Editor, The Zondervan Corporation, Grand Rapids, Michigan, Vol. 1. p. 439 - 449, Vol. 2. P. 423 - 438.

[166] Halley's Bible Handbook, New Revised Ed. Henry H. Halley, Zondervan Publishing House, Grand Rapids, Michigan, 24th Edition, 1965. P. 212, 336 - 340.

[167] Great People of the Bible and How They Lived, Earnest C. Wright, Principal Advisor and Editorial Consultant. The Readers Digest Association of Canada, 1974. P. 222 - 274.

Empires this world has ever known. Because of its vast influence and cosmopolitan approach, it incorporated many of the practices of subjugated groups into law and tradition. So although totalitarian in many ways, the Babylonian Empire also exhibited a limited degree of tolerance toward the nations it conquered. For example, following the Babylonian Captivity of Judah in 586 BCE, the Jews who were left in Judah were given a measure of local autonomy over their own affairs, just so long as they realized they were under the thumb of the Babylonian monarchial system. However, Babylon did have its repressive aspects subject to the whims of its ruling King(s). The Babylonian Empire also exhibited an unprecedented ability to control and manipulate wealth.

2. The Bear. The Medes, who act in alliance with the Persians: 536 B.C.E. - 331 B.C.

The second Beast is depicted by the chest and two arms of Nebuchadnezzar's image, and in Daniel's dream as a Bear lying down on it's side chewing on three ribs. This Bear still exists. The Empire of the Medes and Persians took over the Babylonian Empire, defeating Belshazzar. Their influence and administration covered the countries that we now identify as Iran, Iraq, the southern provinces of Russia, extended into The Middle East as far as Syria, and included the original Kingdom of Judah. [168]The Medes themselves were a warlike group of tribes that originated from the geographical area surrounding The Caspian and Black Seas. Historically, we can trace a gradual northern migration and infiltration of the tribes of the Medes into what we now recognize as the Russian stronghold of the Eurasian continent. So both history, as well as Scripture, give us a revealing insight into where the Russian Bear originated, and its prophetic influence in the past, as well as in the future. The fact that this Bear is now the official mascot symbol of Russia, indicates that the prophetic influence of the Medes has come down to the present. The Medes were powerful, and were of non-Arabic ethnic origin. Whereas the Persians who formed an alliance with the Medes, and took over the Babylonian Empire as contemporary allies, were Arabic Assyrian -Persians. [169]Darius was a Mede. Cyrus was a Persian, but had sealed alliance ties with the Medes possibly through marriage. His

---

[168] The Zondervan Pictoral Encyclopedia of the Bible, Vol. 4, Merrill C. Tenney,Ph D, General Editor, The Zondervan Corporation, Grand Rapids, Michigan, 1076. p. 148 - 150. 710 - 720.

[169] Halley's Bible Handbook, New Revised Ed. Henry H. Halley, Zondervan Publishing House, Grand Rapids, Michigan, 24th Edition, 1965. p. 345.

Father-in-Law may have been Darius, which would explain the peaceful transition from the Medes to the Persians. This alliance between the Medes and Persians has come down to the present as the tendency toward co-operation and understanding between the Russians and the 'Arabs'. This Medio-Persian Bear alliance will again have influence in the days ahead!

Daniel lived through the reigns of all the successive rulers of these first two Beasts, the Lion(Babylon), and the Bear (Medio-Persia.) It was under Cyrus The Great that The House of Judah, by official decree, was allowed to return to the area of Judah, indicating the 70 years of their prophesied captivity were over. However, Judah did not arise as a recognized nation under her own sovereignty at that time, but the returned of Judah remained a puppet to the Empire, and under subsequent administrative empirical changes, became dispersed -- The Diaspora.

3. The Leopard. The Greek Empire: 331B.C.E. - 167 B.C.E.

[170]The Medio-Persian Empire was taken over by the Greeks, the Leopard, represented by the abdomen of Nebuchadnezzar's image. Alexander The Great accomplished his conquest in only six years, hence the four <u>wings</u> showing swiftness, and the extent of his campaigns. He extended the influence of The Greek Empire to include areas as far east as Afghanistan, Pakistan, and the other 'stans' of the area, down into northern India; also into Arabia, Northern Africa including Egypt, and portions of Southern and Eastern Europe. Alexander died as a burnt-out young man in the city of Babylon. The Greek Empire after Alexander's death, splintered administratively into 1. Asia the Great under Seleucus, 2. Asia the Less under Perdiccas, 3. Macedonia under Cassander, and 4. Egypt (including most of Northern Africa and The Middle East) under Ptolemeus. Hence the four heads, along with the <u>four</u> wings of this original Leopard. The Greek influence was particularly evident in the disciplines of philosophy, education, arts, and polytheism.

The Roman Takeover. A Mixture.

I am not giving this paragraph a successive number for our outline, because in essence, what is described <u>historically</u>, was <u>not a fully grown</u> fourth Beast. <u>The fourth Beast, in maturity, is yet to come</u>. Follow me here.

---

[170] The Zondervan Pictoral Encyclopedia of the Bible, Vol. 2, Merrill C. Tenney, Ph D, General Editor, The Zondervan Corporation, Grand Rapids, Michigan. 1076. P. 812 - 850.

This fourth Beast is depicted by the legs and feet of Nebuchadnezzar's image, and the multi-headed Beast in Daniel's dream. It is not pictured <u>as a particular species of animal</u> such as describes the previous three Empires. Rather, it is referred to as a collection of diverse animal parts -- iron teeth, the mouth of a Lion, an Eagle-like influence, varying numbers of heads with horns, all attached to a Leopard body with Bear's feet. The Ancient Roman Empire represented an immature pre-cursor of this fourth Beast. The strength of this Beast is evidenced in that its influence has also never been totally removed from the world, but is again rising. It is interesting to note the symbols of The Roman Empire were derived from the Babylonian Eagle and Lion, and also from iron, showing its strength. The Roman take-over of the splintered Greek Empire was neither swift nor total, and although the Romans methodically campaigned militarily, which was their strong suit, there were other alternate influences at work in bringing an end to the Greek Empirical dominance.

The Middle East was wrested from the Greeks primarily through the Maccabean uprisings. Of particular significance in the region was the dethronement of the Greek Antiochus Epiphanes, who himself was a pre-type of AntiChrist. Then a series of Helenistic Hasmonean Kings briefly took over in The Holy Land, and it was into this setting that the Romans, following the Maccabean Uprisings, invaded and conquered The Middle East, maintaining the existing monarchical system as a puppet, just changing occasionally who occupied the puppet's throne. Jesus Christ was born, ministered, was crucified on a Roman cross, was buried, arose, and ascended during the cosmopolitan 'Pax Romana' period.

So the fall of the Greek Leopard was piecemeal, and The Roman Empire did not extend as far East as the Greeks, but did include the greater portion of both Eastern and Western Europe, Egypt and pretty much all of North Africa, The Middle East, and Asia The Less around the Caspian and Black Seas. It barely extended into the area we now identify as Iraq, but its influence extended much further. It also eventually split administratively, and religiously, into two distinct parts -- hence the two legs of Nebuchadnezzar's image. These legs, over the course of the last 2000 years, have further broken down into nations which are variously governed by democracies (clay) and kingdoms (monarchies or dictatorships represented by iron.) Hence the feet and ten toes of the image. The toes are not so much identifiable countries, as they are ethnic and political groups that have given rise to the countries we have today. Therefore, when we begin to apply the principle of ten nations to the revived Roman Empire, we must be careful that we do not become distracted by the number and

THE TWO BEASTS OF REVELATION 13

names of the nations themselves -- which is obviously more than ten, or limit their identity to only the western European theater.

Just as The Roman Empire expanded relatively slowly, so too The Roman Empire also gradually <u>seemed</u> to disintegrate. It never really was conquered by another great Empire. <u>In essence, The Roman Empire has never actually ceased to exist</u>, but has remained as an influence in how the European nations in particular have developed. It has remained as a vestige political entity through the Vatican, and the influence of the Roman Catholic Church. In essence, the Pope as head of the Vatican, which has its own sovereign national status, is a Caesar successive chronologically through religious/political succession from Constantine, who was a successive Caesar himself. The Pope is still considered to be a force to be reckoned with, particularly in the so-called Christian nations. Everyone wants to know what the Pope thinks, or does not think, regarding certain issues. But the Roman Church is not from where the ultimate impact of the fourth Beast will arise.

The Roman empirical spirit of co-operation economically and politically has slowly been revived, and is again becoming a high profile force of reckoning in the form of The European Union, having its own international currency, and policy-law making Parliament, which has the clout of enforcement for all its members. The Roman Empire all but died out, but has been revived in a form that recognizes the national sovereignty of its members, while influencing the politics, laws, and economic growth within each for the mutual benefit of all. Thus we have heads, crowns, and horns, and a mixture of iron and clay. And whether we like it or not, The European Union is beginning to exercise 'iron teeth' when it comes to international issues -- gnawing the world into a new shape.

4. The Fourth Beast: Not just Europe, but an Evolved World Order.

Now let's examine our hybrid monster - the fourth Beast. This Beast has not yet had its time of absolute dominance. It is a Beast that incorporates <u>characteristics of all the former Beasts</u>, as well as having the heads, horns, and crowns of the Roman influence. Its overall body-shape is that of the Leopard, showing it is rooted in the geographical and ideological underpinnings of the original Greek Empire. Its feet are the paws of a Bear, indicating The Medio-Persian Empire influence, and connection with Russia. It has the mouth of a Lion, revealing a philosophical, pagan occult influence, and the monetary clout and authority taken from the arena of The Babylonian Empire. It has multiple heads, four at one time (from the four-way split of The Greek Empire), then seven heads with iron teeth, ten horns and ten crowns, indicating a revived Roman Empire. It sprouts a Little Horn that uproots three of the others. This Little Horn has the eyes of a man, and a mouth that speaks blasphemies. It would appear then, that the Roman characteristics give this Beast its eyes, voice, and cerebral profile, and the political mechanism whereby the AntiChrist (The Little Horn) is able to emerge as the predominant world leader. But the body gives it its philosophy and terrible clout, and the Bear's paws its momentum.

Since all these animalistic features appear to be rooted in all the former Empires, lets examine their significance. The Babylonians have given it the mouth of a Lion -- the Lion of Babylon. It roars in an intimidating manner. Is that an assumption? No. That's one of the things lions do best! They roar. They can also devour. The roaring of this Lion's mouth is probably what should be considered first. What is it roaring about? The implication is that it has an outspoken authority and ideology that intimidates, and is counterfeit to Christ. (Christ, as The Lion of The Tribe of Judah, roars, so this impostor Beast is counterfeit.) Could there be an ideology in our end-time world that is currently intimidating the nations, and speaks particularly in threatening terms against Israel and the Christian West, and has a stronghold base in the geographical area formerly occupied by The Babylonian Empire? Yes! Islam. To Islam, Israel and the West are infidels. They call the USA the 'Great Satan,' and Israel, 'the Little Satan.' This Lion's mouth utters threats against all who are not Islamic, referring to them as infidels and dhimmies. The Beast roars!

And it has teeth, indicating it has the very real ability to influence policy and bring about implementation. The iron teeth in the Lion's mouth indicate one of several connections to The Roman Empire root, and shows that this Beast has the ability to chew up anyone not coming into agreement.

The Leopard body of this Beast suggests it also is rooted in the former Greek Empire that extended over most of the area of the former Medio-Persian Empire, suggesting the main body of this Beast arises out of the area The Greek Empire covered. In other words, it is descendent from the geographical area that the Eastern European, Middle Eastern, and Islamic-Arab nations now occupy. It is sleek, and cat-like. It can be deceptive and swift, pouncing when one leasts expects. A Leopard can run very fast. It also cannot be trusted, nor totally tamed. A Leopard is a cat, after all. Who owns a cat? It decides who it owns! It also is uncannily smart, stalking with a stealth that even the one watching often mistakes for playful observation or interest. But watch out! It will use its powers of deceptive intelligence against you! Is there an area of the world we cannot seem to totally trust or tame? Yes, and it just so happens it also lies in the area of the former Greek Empire that now is predominantly Islamic! Amazing!

Notice, this Beast has the feet of a Bear. Now this is interesting! The Medio-Persian Empire was depicted as a Bear. The paws of this Bear would geographically be on it's southern aspect, indicating its connection to the Caspian and Black Seas area -- the republics and provinces along Russia's southern borders from which the Medes and Persians originally arose. Of course we know Russia's mascot identification is the Bear. One cannot have the Bear's paws without having something to do with the rest of him! But only the feet are specifically mentioned. These paws are attached somehow to the Leopard body. This must be somewhat of a frustration for a cat! If it has ideas to pounce, it will naturally want to be able to do so efficiently and swiftly, counting on its feet to propel it and land effectively. But Bear's paws are somewhat cumbersome and big! They don't 'pounce' well. But they can run, grab, and tear-apart. It would appear then, that <u>Russia may in fact provide 'feet' to the program for this Beast</u>. Russia may be the source of military armaments and expertise, and provide man-power <u>to allow this Beast to reach its objectives</u>.

But the Bear's paws also provide much more. These Bear paws have the ability to <u>pace the progress of the hybrid Beast</u>. The predominant mood of the Islamic provinces of Southern Russia is toward independence from Russia. <u>They would actually feel much better aligning themselves with the Islamic world</u>. Thus they may actually <u>desire to detach from the Bear</u>, and <u>attach to the Leopard</u>. Ideologically, they already have! Therefore, they have the ability to connect the whole Bear with the Islamic/Arab objectives, one of which is to march against Israel and annihilate her. Now the Russian Bear at this juncture has no such intention of annihilating Israel, or permanently detaching its paws, (granting independence to the southern provinces) but merely working along with the UN, the USA, and the EU in bringing about peace in The Middle East.

However, Russia does have a problem. She could really use a Mediterranean sea-port, and she certainly could use the wealth and resources of The Middle East. She therefore may begin to shift her mind-set to being more aggressive against Israel, and this would certainly sit well with the Islamic desire to wipe Israel off the world map. Russia tends to be sympathetic toward Iran, Iraq, and Syria anyway, providing them with scientific, monetary, and military expertise from time to time, thus arming them. So the Bear's paws may play a major role in The Battle of Gog and Magog, as well as in the other shenanigans of the fourth Beast throughout most of The Days of Awe. However, the total Bear does not necessarily <u>always</u> agree with where the Bear-paws want to take it.

The Final Schedule Revealed

So what about the heads, horns, and crowns of this abominable critter? Because The Roman Empire took over from the Greeks, it managed to insert its influence into both Eastern and Western Europe, and eventually into The Middle East. Under Constantine, The Roman Empire officially became Christian in both East and West. We have the Roman Catholics in the West, followed along by the Protestant Reformation; and the Eastern Orthodox, the Russian Orthodox, and Ukrainian Orthodox in the East. Both these so-called Christian enclaves were, and often still are at odds with each other; as well as both have in varying degrees, and at different times, despised the Jews. So we see that the religious climate has produced the geographical arrangement of the two branches of Catholic Churches, and along with the Crusades, brought about much of the animosities we still deal with even today.

Islam has taken advantage of this dichotomy, and come up the middle of the religious, political, ideological scene. Islam views Christianity as being imperialistic, trying to spread its ideology through atrocity and deception, colonization, and even war. Unfortunately, they do have a point! According to Jesus and Paul, the Church was never given a military sword, but The Sword of The Spirit, The Word of God. The Church was not called to take over the world militarily, nor to physically subjugate others, but to spread the Gospel peacefully, persuading man everywhere of the truth of Salvation through Christ. It is unfortunate that Christianity did not always adhere to its true mandate! Salvation does not come at the edge of a bloody sword! So if the nations of the West, and particularly the Church, think we are operating under a handicap, we are! And this is partially of our own making. (The Sword of Islam is a counterfeit of the Sword of the Spirit. It is unfortunate the Christian Sword has more often than not been wielded inappropriately in Church history, in a threatening manner similar to The Sword of Islam, particularly during The Crusades! Shame on us!)

But generally, the Church of late, together with the Western nations, has adopted a more humanitarian/democratic look at life -- a 'live and let live' philosophy. The pendulum has swung the opposite direction to a position of humanistic error and blindness. The so-called Christian world does not understand the totalitarian mind-set often displayed by the nations of the East, and certainly cannot understand The Islamic Sword. They think they can negotiate anyone into their 'freedom' way of thinking. They also tend to take what people say as being what they mean. That especially will get the whole world into trouble! So, the current vestiges of The Roman Empire are based in secularism and in watered-down Christianity, neither of which are helping to solve world unrest. Pluralism is one of the West's watchwords, but this existential approach that preaches a freedom more closely resembling anarchy, espouses human rights, and even seeks the tolerance and inclusion of faiths not of Christianity, is the fertile ground from which the Little Horn will be able to grow and thrive.

But at the same time, the horns (contemporary, political governing authorities) of this Beast are more progressive when it comes to economics and education. These leaders are showing a willingness to work together with the desire to benefit all. Allowing for freedom of thought, research, and political and philosophical posturing, they have the ability to bring to the scene of the tenure of the fourth Beast, a system whereby he can operate with impunity. So The Roman Empire heads, horns, and crowns will accommodate his aspirations and ambitions. The fourth Beast's iron teeth indicate the Roman strength to put 'teeth' into whatever policies are put forward.

Another interesting feature is noticeable about the heads, horns, and crowns of this fourth Beast. Most agree that the heads, horns, and crowns are representative of the revived Roman Empire. So the revived Roman Empire has <u>the cerebral characteristics of the fourth Beast</u>. But there is diversity here. Western Europe remains fairly strongly in the combined ideological camp of Judeo-Christianity and humanism, whereas the Eastern European areas are a mix, with atheistic Marxism being partially displaced by equally hard-line ideologies. Islam is fitting into this vacuum rather handily in much of Eastern Europe, especially since the fall of Communism. Fed by the presence of vestiges of the Ottoman Empire influence, Islam also is having a fair bit of success infiltrating the West. Most of the member nations of The European Union are from Western Europe, but there are Islamic leaning members from the Eastern European sector as well. [171]

Turkey just had elections this past year, and now has an Islamic government, and Turkey is currently under consideration for entrance into The European Union. Interesting, considering the fact that [172]Israel

---

[171] The Jerusalem Post Internet Edition, Nov. 5, 2002, www.jpost.com/servlet/Satellite?pagename+JPost/AJPArticle... *Islamist party works to calm fears of jittery world after victory*, Herb Keinon in Ankara. Israel is concerned about the victory of the AKP pro-Islamic Justice and Development Party in Turkey elections. The leader, of the party, Tayyip Erdogan, is attempting "to calm world fears that he will radically change the country's secular character or foreign policy." His priority is the issue of acceptance into the EU, which is to be discussed in Copenhagen.

[172] The Jerusalem Post InternetEdition, November 11, 2002. www.jpost.comservlet/Satellite:pagename=A/JPArticle... *Netanyahu pledges to*

The Final Schedule Revealed

is now being recommended for EU Membership as well. Drawing up a confirmation of The Covenant by AntiChrist may in fact have a ruling law-making body through which to be implemented already, especially if Israel becomes an accepted member! With some members having Islamic influence, this agreement may not be so far-fetched for AntiChrist to manage to pull-off! We see the dichotomy in the struggles of Chezchnia, Bosnia, Serbia, Albania, etc. Even France now has an appointed Muslim representative in government to deal with Islamic issues. So we see the 'cat-like hybrid Beast' creeping!

The seven heads, ten horns, and ten crowns of the fourth Beast, have arisen out of the ethnic backgrounds related to the former Greek and Roman Empires. The Leopard did have a time when it only had four heads. Originally these were the split of the Greek Empire into four distinct geographical regions under rulership of four administrative governments. So the four heads mentioned by Daniel refer to the geographical four-way split that occurred after Alexander the Great's death, from the era of the original Leopard. Revelation's seven heads obviously refer to seven politically administrative countries or regions that have arisen from within the former jurisdiction of the Greek Empire (four heads), as well as the Roman Empire (three more heads,) but which will be relevant during the reign of AntiChrist. So this hybrid Beast has both ancient roots and future fulfillment. Daniel states that one head of this Beast has a mouth with iron teeth, revealing the vocal Roman Empire influence, and the fact that The European Union will play a major role in developing policy that affects the entire world during the reign of AntiChrist. These iron teeth are in the mouth, so can rip, devour, and intimidate.

At this point, Daniel's depiction of this Beast switches from ancient to end-times, revealing the ten horns. Then the Little Horn full of eyes grows up, displacing three horns. All that this Beast accomplishes from this point onward in Daniel chapter 7 is in the same prophetic time-frame as Revelation chapter 13. The Little Horn is AntiChrist. He has the political clout to uproot three of the other horns. Whether these three horns are of Western ideology, or Eastern, or a mixture of both, is not clear. But I would tend to think he manages to usurp the authority of Western thinking, especially since he would appear to be Islamic himself, so would tend to use flatteries, deception (possibly outwardly appearing

---

stick by US Mideast 'road map.' Herb Keinon," Netanyahu, in his conversation with Berlusconi, asked him to look into thepossibility to Israel joining the European Union. This idea has been on the table by some members of the European Parliament, and has gained a degree of support in Italy."

THE TWO BEASTS OF REVELATION 13

to be a Judaic adherent to hide his true Islamic affiliation) and persuasion to spread Islamic ideology. Jihad takes many forms. He then eventually speaks terrible things against God's people and The Temple, throwing off his deceptive cover, which is not surprising for a Muslim. But his time in power fortunately is going to be short.

In summary then, this hybrid Beast has Bear's paws, likely indicating particularly the ideology of the southern Russian provinces, which seem to align themselves with Islamic sentiments, and also shows a propensity for Russia to be sympathetic to the Arab Nations. Therefore Russia has the ability to take this Beast wherever it needs to go. The momentum then is provided from military, scientific, and monetary backing from Russia, along with perhaps some influence in bargaining. The mouth is that of a Lion. If we read Daniel's description of this Beast, we find the Lion once had four wings which were plucked off. The winged Lion originally was Babylon, which now is Iraq and Iran, and surrounding peoples. The heads, horns, crowns, and iron teeth show the Greek and Roman influence of The European Union. The organization of The European Union may very well provide the political mechanism for this Beast to arise. But the main body is that of the Leopard, identifiable as the former area occupied by The Greek Empire. I would tend toward feeling this Beast's philosophical and religious motivation arises from that area of the world. This Beast arises out of an ideology of blasphemy, which is infiltrated into, and processed by the heads and the Little Horn. These horns, then, arise out of the former Roman Empire. And finally, the current predominant ideology from the former Persian/Babylonian/Greek Empires, which is spreading into the Eastern, then Western legs and feet of the former Roman Empire areas, is now Islam, which is directly opposed to, and wishes to dominate, and particularly displace Christianity and Judaism.

This Beast is not just from Western Europe as we have often thought, but from the entire root of all these Empires. It is from this Hybrid Fourth Beast Empire (world scene) that the AntiChrist will arise.

B. Beast Worship:

Let's continue. Revelation 13:3. "*And I saw <u>one of his heads as it were wounded to death; and his deadly would was healed</u>: and all the world wondered after the beast.* Verse 4. *<u>And they worshipped the dragon which gave power to the beast,</u> saying, Who is like unto the beast? Who is able to make war with him?* Verse 5. *And <u>there was given unto him a mouth speaking great things and blasphemies; and power was given unto him to continue forty and two months.</u>* Verse 6. *And he opened his mouth in blasphemy against God, to blaspheme his* name, and his tabernacle, and them that dwell in heaven. Verse 7. *And it was given unto him to make war with the saints, and to overcome them; and power was given him over all kindred's, and tongues, and nations.* Verse 8. *And all that dwell upon the earth shall worship him, whose names are not written in the book of life of the Lamb slain from the foundation of the world.* Verse 9. *If any man have an ear, let him hear.* Verse 10. *He that leadeth into captivity shall go into captivity; he that killeth with the sword must be killed with the sword. Here is the patience and the faith of the saints."*

Verse 3 mentions the tragedy that befalls The Beast, the Leader of The Fourth Beast Empire. One of his heads suffers a deadly wound, and this deadly wound is miraculously healed. Everyone is amazed! The specific circumstances of this tragedy are not explained. Perhaps it is an assassination attempt. Revelation 13:14 indicates the deadly wound is inflicted by a sword. This sword may have overtones of Islamic in-fighting that could result from inside treachery, so may be inflicted by The Sword of Islam. Such is not unknown, or uncommon, among differing factions and individuals within their ranks, if they feel the act of jealous Jihad is justified. Sunnis and Shiites, for example, are not particularly friendly toward one another. Or animosity could originate from among the Jews by someone who is justifiably upset with the deception and rumors of the abominable desecration and subsequent blasphemous takeover of their Temple. Or, a terrorist or assassin could act on his own. I tend to lean toward The Islamic Sword explanation, because its use in such a manner definitely fits within Islamic ideology.

This leader, according to normal medical science, should not survive. But he does, and his mortal would is healed. This healing may be facilitated through the use of breakthrough genetic engineering medical technology, so all the world will be interested in the amazing positive result. But the overtones of the above passage indicate that there is an incredulousness regarding his survival and healing, suggesting there is more at work here than just medical science, because it appears from the above Scripture, at this juncture in his career, this leader becomes Satanically possessed.

Now the whole picture begins to take on a pretty bazaar twist. Has Satan finally found a willing host person in the leadership of world politics and religion, who he can indwell, thus becoming an 'incarnate god,' and therefore having the ability to cause men to worship him? AntiChrist becomes the Counterfeit Messiah! His powers increase significantly. The above verses from Revelation 13 have one phrase repeated several times. *"He is given power..."* Verse 4 tells us who gives this power to him. The Dragon. In other words, his powers of control, authority, and even of speech, come from Satan, and he exercises these over all nations and peoples, touching every aspect of their lives.

Anyone who becomes a Christian (Tribulation Saint) he has the power to execute, and all who do not have their names written in The Book of Life worship him. This phenomenon is not just Middle Eastern, or European, but takes place all around the world. Who is really being worshiped here? It is the Dragon (Satan) who causes everyone to worship him. Everyone becomes intimidated by him, and the general consensus is that no one can fight him successfully. He opens his mouth and speaks blasphemies against God, and against his tabernacle (Judaic Temple worship), and <u>against those who now are dwelling in Heaven</u>.

Now <u>that</u> is a revelation regarding what is really transpiring! Not only is he against God Himself, and the people on earth who worship God in truth, <u>but he is against those who are in Heaven with God</u>. <u>Why would that 'get his goat?'</u> The Raptured Christians, who's disappearance has become a great testimony to the truth of God's Word, has resulted in many becoming believers in Christ. He is afraid of this testimony undermining his authority and imposed self-worship, so attempts to strongly oppose the truth of the Raptured Church. Obviously, to be so vehemently driven against those now living in Heaven, he realizes they were absolutely right, meaning Scripture is right, and Christ is the Victor, so he is angry about it. His persecution reaches new and powerful heights, especially against those who accept Christ. His victims are the Tribulation Saints mentioned in Revelation chapter 7: 9. These give their lives for their faith, and stand before The Throne of The Lamb, clothed in white robes. These are not part of the Bride, who were Raptured. Revelation 7:13 -17 identifies them, and declares what happens to them. *"And one of the elders answered, saying unto me. What are these which are arrayed in white robes? and whence came they? Verse 14. And I said unto him, Sir, thou knowest. And he said to me, <u>These are they which came out of great tribulation, and have washed their robes, and made them white in the blood of the Lamb</u>. Verse 15. Therefore are they before the throne of God, and serve him day and night in his temple: and he that sitteth on the throne shall dwell among them. Verse 16. They shall hunger no more, neither thirst any more; neither shall the sun light on them, nor any heat. Verse 17. For the Lamb which is in the midst of the throne shall feed them, and shall lead them unto living fountains of waters: and God shall wipe all tears from their eyes."*

It seems both the raptured who have slipped from beyond his reach, as well as the Tribulation Saints, really serve to produce in him a hatred far beyond anything the world has ever experienced. Under Satan's (the Dragon's) inspiration and possession, AntiChrist sets up a world system whereby only those who worship him are intended to survive. Fortunately for everyone, he will only have 42 months tenure left *("power is given unto him for forty and two months.")* During this last half of The Tribulation, he will set about to harness any and every resource available to do his dirty work. The Second Beast of Revelation chapter 13 expedites the manner in which he is worshiped and obeyed, and provides the system whereby he either subjugates, or annihilates.

II. The Second Beast of Revelation 13:

Verse 11. *"And I beheld another beast coming up out of the earth; and he had <u>two horns like a lamb</u>, and he spake as a dragon.* Verse 12. *And <u>he exerciseth all the power of the first beast before him, and causeth the earth and them which dwell therein to worship the first beast, whose deadly wound was healed</u>.* Verse 13. *And he doeth great wonders, so that he maketh fire come down from heaven in the sight of men,* Verse 14. *And deceiveth them that dwell on the earth by means of those miracles which he had power to do in the sight of the beast; saying to them that dwell on the earth, that they should make an image to the beast, which had the wound by a sword, and did live.* Verse 15<u>. And he had power to give life unto the image of the beast, that the image of the beast should both speak, and cause that as many as would not worship the image of the beast should be killed.</u> Verse 16. <u>And he causeth all, both small and great, rich and poor, free and bond, to receive a mark in their right hand, or in their foreheads:</u> Verse 17. *And that no man might buy or sell, save he that had the mark, or the name of the beast, or the number of his name.* Verse 18. *Here is wisdom, Let him that hath understanding count the number of the beast: for it is the number of a man; and his number is six hundred threescore and six."* KJV. Underlining mine.

Who is this other Beast mentioned in Revelation chapter 13? He is the support Beast, the False Prophet. His description and activities further identify the AntiChrist's aspirations, and reveal how he implements his world domination of economics, strange-god worship, and persecution of the Tribulation Christians, and of anyone who is not compliant. His activities line up perfectly with Daniel 11:36 -39, showing the mechanism of AntiChrist worship, using gold, silver and precious stones.

This second Beast is described as having *"two horns like a lamb,"* meaning there are <u>two world leaders</u> working closely together here, but The False Prophet himself becomes the more predominant. The False Prophet works with the direct support of the second horn. These leaders (horns) may appear to be benevolent moderates, thus like a lamb. <u>We have a counterfeit of The Lamb, and of The Seventh Trumpet which is pictured by the two horns of the Ram!</u> The False Prophet himself then, arises from within a support system. The resources to accomplish his mandate come from affiliations within this system, giving him access to scientific

THE TWO BEASTS OF REVELATION 13

technology, and the funding to do the research and development necessary to produce the 'intelligent, living image' of the AntiChrist. In all likelihood then, the False Prophet arises from within the progressive entity of The European Union. It is The European Union nations that already have the scientific base of easily accessible education and skills, being able to draw from around the world, along with the monetary resources necessary to co-ordinate the technology he requires.

But this second Beast speaks like a Dragon, indicating he is doing Satan's bidding. Revelation 13:11. *"...he had two horns like a lamb, and he spake as a dragon."* This second Beast does all the up-front public relations for the first Beast. He acts as a type of Prime Minister for AntiChrist's regime. He is given the authority and power to do everything he does by the first Beast; and he causes the whole world to bow down and worship the first Beast whose deadly wound was healed. He causes fire to fall from heaven in the sight of men. He is given power to counterfeit this miracle the Two Witnesses perform, much like the wise men of Egypt were able to simulate some of God's miraculous signs exhibited through Moses before the Exodus. So this second Beast seeks authority and recognition through being a 'copy-cat,' thus deceiving many who do not have the ability to realize he is not empowered by God, but by Satan. Revelation 13:14. *"And deceiveth them that dwell on the earth, by means of those miracles which he had power to do in the sight of the beast:"* So everyone pretty much stands back in awe, and tends to give him the benefit of the doubt by obeying him! In order to deceive, one must actually have knowledge of truth, but choose to pull the wool over the eyes of others anyway. He uses his 'miracles' to deceive.

A. The Image of The Beast:

But what really takes the limelight is the image he produces of the first Beast, and everything this image is capable of. This image is the working 'living idol' of the AntiChrist - worship system. The False Prophet proposes a rather technologically advanced project -- the building of an intelligent computer system which will incorporate the personality of the first Beast. Verse 14 indicates that because of the 'miracles' he is capable of producing in the sight of the first Beast (at the bidding of the first Beast,) he is able to suggest to the nations that dwell on the earth, *"that they should make an image to the beast, which had the wound by a sword and did live."* What he appears to be doing and saying, is that the 'miracles' demonstrate the fact that such an image is indeed possible. Therefore he already is using the technology to perform these 'miracles.' Now it's just one step further to produce an image that contains the personality and abilities of the first Beast, AntiChrist. Thus he involves many people from around the world in order to receive the necessary funding and resources, and to staff the project with trained scientists and technicians, and to put in place the technological net which will allow this 'image' to perform world-wide. Once complete, the second Beast has the <u>ability to give life unto (program with **'real-life qualities'**) this image, so that it speaks</u>. He is able to apply the technology to program this super-computer so that it 'thinks' and 'interacts' using the personality and intelligence of the first Beast. Thus he will be able to cause everyone to worship the image of The Beast, or be killed.

Revelation 13:15. "<u>And he had power to give life unto the image of the beast, that the image of the beast should both speak, and cause that as many as would not worship the image of the beast should be killed</u>. Verse 16. And he causeth all, both small and great, rich and poor, free and bond, <u>to receive a mark in their right hand, or in their foreheads</u>: Verse 17. And that no man might buy of sell, save he that had the mark, or the name of the beast, or the number of his name. Verse18. <u>Here is wisdom. Let him that hath understanding count the number of the beast: for it is the number of a man: and his number is Six hundred threescore and six</u>."

Notice, I did not say 'life-like,' but 'real-life qualities.' Is it actually possible for someone to channel 'life' and 'intelligence' into an inanimate collection of electronic parts, and transmit this force around the globe? The image of the first Beast appears to be a supercomputer system that is capable of processing logic and function in a manner that is more than just 'information-in / information-out.' The technological sciences have been researching ways to build computers that can actually 'think' and 'reason,' and which humans can control through thought processes. They know this is possible, and there are scientists and technicians currently testing the technology. It is now possible to implant a micro-chip into one individual, and through satellite pick-up, have that person communicate with another micro-chip-implanted individual, both using thought processes only! No keyboard. No Internet connection through a server system of wires. Not even voice activation! This technology uses the electro-neuromuscular-chemical exchange of information that naturally occurs within the brain and nervous system during thought processes. All that is needed is an implanted circuit to direct thoughts to the area of the programmed receiver one wants to communicate with, and the other connected bio-chip(s) will receive the information, and have the ability to respond and interact. The amount of information transmitted and received is thus limitless, because no memory-bank, other than the programmed connection itself, is necessarily required. In essence, these bio-chips <u>become an extension</u> of the persons

THE TWO BEASTS OF REVELATION 13

using the system. <u>It seems it really will be possible to *"give life unto the image of the beast*</u>!" By using electro-neurochemical-muscular-transmission technology, this 'life' will not be simulated, <u>but an actual projected brain circuitry extension of AntiChrist himself</u>, and of anyone else who ties in with his image! Thus this image will, through such technology, be able to control the thoughts, transactions, and actions of anyone accepting the bio-circuitry 'mark' in their hand or forehead. This system will become the manner in which all economic transaction will be carried out, so it will become mandatory for everyone world-wide to be connected, no matter where they live or work, and no matter their age, gender, or status.

[173]This technology will also be used for world-wide surveillance. Those who refuse to accept connection to the system will be eliminated by the same 'living' computerized system, because they will be hunted down by it! In essence, AntiChrist will be able to locate anyone he wants to track on the earth, and interact with that individual, thus controlling that person and his activities. Massive applied wireless G.P.S. technology! No wonder Christ must return! No one will be safe!

It is a good thing all this will only have a very short 3 1/2 years to be implemented. Otherwise no one would survive the Image of the Beast! If it can eliminate those who refuse the connective neuromuscular-electrochemical chip 'mark,' then what is it going to be able to do even to those who somehow slip-up while connected to the system? Technology is great, but this one will have the capability to truly take over and become a monster! No wonder Scripture states that there will be <u>wisdom in recognizing the number of The Beast,</u> <u>or the number of his name,</u> <u>or his name itself</u>. These codes are specific pathways that the False Prophet will use to channel AntiChrist's personality directly through the '<u>living</u>' <u>network</u>. These code-sequences will activate control of anyone taking the 'mark,' so will be the path to personal identification and use of the interactive system.

---

[173]   www.ABCNews.com, SCI/TECH , March 18, 2004. *I, Chip? Technology to Meld Chips into Humans Draws Closer*, Paul Eng. "Down the line, it could be used [as] credit cards and such," says Chris Hables Gray, a professor of cultural studies of science and technology at the University of Great Falls in Montana. "A lot of people won't have to carry wallets anymore," he says. "What the implications are [for this technology], in the long run, is profound."
"...Any technology of this kind is easily abusive of personal privacy," says Lee Tien, senior staff attorney for the Electronic Frontier Foundation. "If a kid is track-able, do you want other people to be able to track your kid? It's a double-edged sword."

The Final Schedule Revealed

The number 666 is the foundational example given in Scripture of what to look for in identifying this path. The sequence <u>666 could very well be the coded path that initially is used by the AntiChrist to connect and program his own personality into the computerized system first, and from which all others must then interact</u>. There is nothing intrinsically evil about the number 666 itself. Some folk have tried to suggest that this number is somehow Satanic. Well, perhaps it becomes a tool for his use, but it is only a numerical presentation, just like 215 or 587 or any other numerical sequence identification. What will make this particular 666 number significantly 'different' is what it will be used for! <u>This number is the computer ID of a man</u>, AntiChrist. It appears there actually will be <u>three computer pathways</u> AntiChrist will use to program himself into this neurological system. The number 666, the number of his name, and his name itself. Revelation 13:15 -18. So it will be wise to take note of these three identification/access pathway codes. The person receiving the 'mark' allowing communication to take place, will connect directly with these pathway options once 'logged-in.' Problem is, once a person is logged into the system, they cannot ever log-out. The 'mark' is permanent. If they try to disconnect, they will be killed in the trying, so in essence, they lose their personal identity, free will, and the ability to choose their own eternal destiny.

Warning! If you have not accepted Christ, so are not taken in the rapture of the Church, and you are offered a bionic implant to tie-in with a world super-computer system that has the programmed ability to reason and think, don't take it! Run! Why? It is only technology. **Yes. But it is applied technology in the wrong hands**! This will be mis-applied technology that will be <u>designed and manipulated to control everyone world-wide, and that will be controlled by the Satanically possessed AntiChrist and his False Prophet.   Anyone accepting access to this Satanically controlled computerized system will lose their eternal soul, because Satan will literally control them</u>. In essence, Satan will have found a method to project himself in a counterfeit of the omnipresence, and omniscience of the Holy Spirit. But Satan's purpose will not be to operate in love, protection, and respect for the free-will of his victims!

If you don't accept the computer 'mark,' <u>make sure you do accept salvation through the blood of Christ</u>, because this intelligent computerized image of The Beast will also be able to track you down as <u>not being tied-in</u> to the system, and you will not be able to buy or sell, and neither will you be able to hide. Most likely you will be liquidated by the same computer system, which will interpret anyone who <u>does not have encoded access</u> as an enemy. AntiChrist's network will have the ability to activate a system

THE TWO BEASTS OF REVELATION 13

to eliminate you. This possibility is no longer so far-fetched either. All it need do is scan a particular area of the earth's surface. <u>If it detects a person who's body is **not** emitting a signal for the network to recognize, it automatically could set a tracking system in motion.</u> Scripture does indicate the second Beast will be able to cause fire to come down out of heaven. The ammunition source could be an armed satellite, or originate from a computerized space-station, or activate via satellite a series of strategically placed delivery systems on the earth's surface to do the same. It could alert teams of security police to track down the errant individual, and have them beheaded. This seems to be the execution of choice, especially for The Tribulation Saints. Whether this beheading is strictly physical, or accomplished by electronically destroying one's brains, it will accomplish the same end.

The technology is already being developed by those trying to make computers and micro-chips wireless, and strategically interactive. It just needs a team to refine all the pieces into an integrated system. And we think science fiction is far out! Perhaps not!

But for those who accepts Christ, and refuse the 'mark,' this will not be the end. Even though beheaded, they will find themselves standing before The Throne in Heaven. They will have an eternal future in The Kingdom of God. Those who accept the 'mark' will not have any place in Heaven or in The Kingdom of God. So at this juncture, those who lose their physical life, will save their souls and gain eternal life if they accept Christ. The choice is pretty clear! This will be the literal fulfillment of what Jesus referred to when He stated, *"he that loveth his life shall lose it; and he that hateth his life in this world shall keep it unto life eternal."* John 12:25. But recall, this statement by Jesus was made in context with His explanation regarding the Voice heard from heaven sounding as Thunder, and Jesus stating that the circumstance was because *"now shall the prince of this world be cast out."* John 12:31. Jesus is ultimate Victor! Satan will be cast out! This victory process began at the cross, and will be brought to absolute fruition at The Second Coming of Messiah.

CHAPTER 20
THE OFFICIAL WELCOMING DIGNITARIES

Revelation chapter 14 gives us an explanation of what transpires immediately as Christ returns to the earth, and explains The Second Coming from the perspective of those who will officially be on hand to welcome Him.

Verse 1. *"And I looked, and, lo, a Lamb stood on mount Zion, and with him a hundred and forty and four thousand, having his Father's name written in their foreheads."* We are given an insight into the position the 144,000 Evangelists hold in ministry. They are Divinely protected during The Days of Awe. The 'mark of protection' placed upon them during The Calm of the Sixth Seal, is not just a number that keeps them from being zapped by AntiChrist. <u>It is The Name of God The Father.</u> So they have the 'mark' of The Father. (Therefore, we must conclude that <u>anyone taking the 'mark' of AntiChrist</u> <u>receives the counterfeit 'mark' of a false god</u>!) The 144,000 Jews are chosen, and marked for a very great honor.

The 144,000 stand on Mount Zion with The Lamb, indicating that when The Second Coming of Christ occurs, they are the welcoming dignitaries on hand when Christ returns in clouds of glory to The Mount of Olives. They will stand on Mount Zion, facing The Mount of Olives, and have the 'front row seat' to observe The Second Coming of The KING of Kings, The Messiah, Jesus Christ! Jesus ascended from The Mount of Olives, and will return to The Mount of Olives. Then He will proceed to Mount Zion, and He will stand in victory with the 144,000 after defeating AntiChrist and his forces, when He takes up His position as KING.

I. Explanation at the Time of The Ascension:

Notice the implications of Acts 1:1-12 regarding Christ's Second Coming. When Jesus ascended, there was a group of His followers who stood on The Mount of Olives, and watched as *"he was taken up; and a cloud received him out of their sight. Verse 10. And while they looked steadfastly toward heaven as he went up, behold, two men stood by them in white apparel: Verse 11. Which also said, Ye men of Galilee, why stand ye gazing up into heaven? This same Jesus, which is taken up from you into heaven, shall come in like manner as ye have seen him go into heaven."* KJV.

The Final Schedule Revealed

This is the promise of The Second Coming. But it also is much more than that. The disciples <u>at that time</u> did not know when Jesus would return, but Jesus did give them some clues regarding the timing. These clues would be prophetically significant <u>for those disciples who are alive</u> on the earth, <u>and watching for His return</u>. These promises have a context that will make prophetic sense at the end of The Days of Awe, particularly for the 144,000 Jewish Evangelists who will know their Bibles, and are the disciples of Christ, and who will also realize that Jesus is The Messiah, The KING of Kings, and that He will return to The Mount of Olives. He will touch-down upon the very location He ascended from. Therefore, they will monitor The Mount of Olives expecting His return.

Prior to ascending, Jesus had spent forty days giving proof of Who He is, and giving His followers directives they were to follow, *"Until the day in which he was taken up, after that he through the Holy Ghost had given commandments unto the apostles whom he had chosen: Verse 3. To whom also he showed himself alive after his passion by many infallible proofs, being seen of them forty days, and <u>speaking of the things pertaining to the kingdom of God</u>: Verse 4. And being assembled together with them, commanded them that thy should not depart from Jerusalem, but wait for the promise of the Father, which , saith he, ye have heard of me. Verse 5. For John truly baptized with water; but ye shall be baptized with the Holy Ghost not many days hence."* Acts 1: 2 - 5. Underlining mine.

One of the main objectives Jesus accomplished during the forty days before He ascended, was to give ample proof of His resurrection, and speak about many things regarding The Kingdom of God. Why would He speak of The Kingdom of God to the disciples at that time? Is 'The Kingdom of God' the same as saying 'the restored Kingdom of Israel?' No! Jesus indicated The Kingdom of God is within you. Luke 17:20-21. *"And when he was demanded of the Pharisees, when the kingdom of God should come, he answered them and said, The kingdom of God cometh not with observation: Verse 21. Neither shall they say, Lo here! or, lo there! for, behold, the kingdom of God is within you."* The Kingdom of God is not founded upon political and geographical jurisdiction or succession, but is built from the repentant hearts of regenerated mankind entering into The Kingdom through the atonement blood of Christ. Will this Kingdom of God have anything to do with the coming restored Kingdom of Israel? Yes! Those who are of The Kingdom of God will rule and reign with Christ when The Kingdom is restored to Israel.

Verse 6 of Acts chapter 1 sheds some light here. *"When they therefore were come together, they asked of him, saying, Lord, wilt thou<u> at this time restore again the kingdom to Israel</u>?"* Notice Jesus' answer. Verse 7. *"<u>It is</u>*

THE OFFICIAL WELCOMING DIGNITARIES

not for you to know the times or the seasons which the Father hath put in his own power..." Emphases mine. In other words, the followers of Christ at that time were not to concern themselves regarding when The Kingdom would be restored to Israel. Rather, they were to focus on the mandate of the next verse, because The Church Age of the spreading of the Gospel, empowered by the Holy Spirit, was to take place before the restoration of The Kingdom to Israel. Verse 8. *"but ye shall receive power after that the* Holy Ghost is come upon you; and ye shall be witnesses unto me both in Jerusalem, *and in all Judea, and in Samaria, and unto the uttermost part of the earth."* Immediately following this explanation, Jesus ascended.

In other words, the building of The Kingdom of God in the hearts of mankind world-wide was to take precedence over the political restoration of The Kingdom of Israel, and they would need the empowerment of the Holy Spirit to accomplish this mandate. Christ was not calling His followers to political activism, or to use their energies to ensure His rise to The Throne of David, but to be activists for The Kingdom of God among all nations, beginning at Jerusalem, then extending to Judea, Samaria, and to the far reaches of all the earth. However, they did not fully understand at this juncture.

The order Jesus explained in Acts chapter 1 is exactly the sequence that has, and will, take place before the restoration of The Kingdom of Israel on the earth. Jesus did not ignore their question, but answered it succinctly! The disciples were Jews. They knew The Kingdom was to be the restored to Israel, and Messiah would ascend to The Throne of David on earth. Had the time now arrived, now that He had finished the work of redemption, and indeed was alive forevermore? Logical question. After forty days, his followers would have realized Jesus walked among them in super-human form, now possessing a resurrected eternal body. Would He now ascend The Throne of David to reign for ever and ever?

Jesus pointed out that the timing of the set up of His earthly Kingdom was in The Father's hands. They, as first century Jews, would not understand the Times or the Seasons regarding His ascension to The Throne of Israel and restoring The Kingdom, because the timing is in The Father's own power. They did not understand the fact that The Age of The Church, and the empowerment of the Holy Spirit for a time of spreading the Gospel, must first take place. In fact, it was not necessary for them to understand, but to be obedient. Their mandate would not involve helping to free Israel to set up The Kingdom. Rather, their commission was to await the empowerment of the Holy Spirit, then take the Gospel to Jerusalem, Judea, Samaria, and to the uttermost parts of the earth. They did not know 2000 years would pass before Christ's promised return. Having answered their question, Jesus ascended into Heaven. This took them by surprise! They had expected Messiah to ascend The Throne of David, but they watched as He ascended into Heaven instead! Why would He leave now? What could it mean?

They must have stood gazing into heaven for quite a while. After a time, two men dressed in white robes interrupted their surprised gazing, and gave the rest of the explanation. Jesus would return the same way He left!

How does this tie-in with the 144,000 of Revelation chapter 14? To understand, we must back up and take a glimpse into the minds and hearts of the Jews who witnessed the Ascension. These disciples who watched Jesus Christ ascend, would ultimately be the group who founded the Church after the Holy Spirit was poured out. They were also Jews. Their mandate began in Jerusalem, and was to expand to reach the whole earth. These disciples were specifically then, not called to be citizens of an earthly Kingdom called Israel, but they were to be ambassadors for The Kingdom of God, manifested in the world as the Church. The Church has the mandate of the Gospel of Messiah, including, but not focusing solely upon, the coming reign of Messiah. The Church is not concerned with the set up of the earthly Kingdom of Israel. Our concern is not merely of Messianic political power, but of the redemptive power of Christ reconciling man to God.

The two men dressed in white completed the explanation. They revealed the fact that there will come a day when Christ will return to The Mount of Olives by descending from the clouds of Glory, in the same manner as He left. Their explanation was not just an add-on to put the disciples' minds at ease. Their explanation would then have caused the disciples to realize that at the time of the return of Christ The Kingdom will be restored to Israel, completing the Messianic prophecies.

How do we know that? The disciples are standing on The Mount of Olives discussing their concern regarding The Kingdom being restored. Christ tells them not to be focused on that fulfillment, because The Father has the timing in His own hands. Then it appears Jesus ignores their questions, apparently changing the subject by telling them to go to Jerusalem to await the anointing of the Holy Spirit Who will empower them to spread the Gospel. Then they must carry out their mandate in a specified order.

They have no way of knowing that He is about to ascend at this juncture, until they realize He is literally rising off the ground right in front of them. Whoa!! The shock of watching someone arise off the ground without so much as an explanatory warning, or apparent mechanical assistance, must have rendered their minds numb for several moments. For sure, they did not have the benefit of knowing that the phenomenon of air or space-travel was possible, let alone without any protection. They didn't even have the advantage of a Sci-fi "Beam me up Scotty!" to relate to. The accounts of Enoch and Elijah doing much the same routine was, after all, certainly true. But that was then. It just simply is not normal for anyone to suddenly, bodily, take off into the wild blue yonder, heading up into the clouds!

Once the initial shock of what they had just witnessed and experienced settled down, a multitude of questions must have begun swirling through their minds as they continued to gaze upward. "What just happened?" "Why did He do that?" "How did He do that?" "That cloud into which He has disappeared --there's something different about it!" "Where has He gone?" "Is He about to come back? In the next five minutes? In the next hour? Perhaps tomorrow?" "What does all this mean?"

They very well could have been gazing up into the heavens for a fair while, perhaps expecting Him to tumble down out of the sky, or at least descend in some unexplainable controlled reverse order of what they had just witnessed. After all, Messiah is to ascend The Throne of David. He won't leave them permanently! Their minds are still pretty much hung up on the restoration of The Kingdom to Israel thing, and this ascension of The One who by now they fully understand is to take The Throne, just does not seem to fit They need an explanation!

While still standing and gazing incredulously up into the sky, expecting they aren't sure what next, they become aware of two men standing near them, both dressed in white. These men have an explanation for them. Jesus Christ definitely will return in the same manner as He left! This is an "Aha!" moment for these boggled disciples, causing them to realize that at <u>that time</u>, <u>when He returns</u>, The Kingdom of Israel will be restored! OK! After that sinks in for a moment, they realize, "We already knew that!" For a brief moment they feel somewhat let-down.

Then understanding jolts them. The real "Aha!" hits them! They are not supposed to be spending the next six months puzzling over what just occurred, or when The Kingdom will come to fruition. They are to get on with the directive Jesus gave them! As they slowly make their way down the mountain-side toward Jerusalem, their pragmatism returns. They even begin to get excited! What is going to transpire when they receive power from on High? How will they know when this power comes upon them? What does it mean to be baptized with the Holy Spirit and with fire? Now they are on the right track, with the appropriate mind set and questions!

Notice, the two men dressed in white did not state that the specific individuals who watched Christ ascend would be the same ones who would witness His return. Their explanation was only that Christ would return in like-manner as they saw Him go. The truth is, those who saw Him ascend from The Mount of Olives that day, will return <u>with</u> Him from Heaven! Their position will be participation as members of the Bride, the Church, returning with Christ; not from the vantage of an Israeli waiting for Messiah, standing watching from the ground!

The Israeli's on the ground who will witness Christ descend from Heaven, will in fact be the 144,000 Evangelists who will have been sealed with The Father's Name in their foreheads, according to Revelation 14:1. But they will not wait specifically on The Mount of Olives, but on Mount Zion. And, these won't be the only ones to see His return. Every eye shall see Him! Yom Kippur! <u>So, The Father does have in His own power the Times and Seasons which will bring to fruition the earthly restoration of The Kingdom to Israel</u>!

So does this mean we cannot know when His return is supposed to occur? Some folk use Acts chapter 1:7 to discourage people from thinking they can even hazard an educated approximation of when Christ will come at the Rapture, or when He will return to set up The Kingdom Yom Kippur, because after all, Jesus stated it was not for them to know the Times and Seasons which are in the Father's hands. However, we have in our possession an explanation of the fulfillment of The Messianic Kingdom. These prophecies are all explained in both The Old and New Testaments. In fact, the prophecies regarding Messiah and His earthly reign, when He sits upon The Throne of David, are so obvious, the Jews accept these prophecies even today, and are awaiting their fulfillment. The prophecies regarding the first coming of Christ as The Suffering Messiah, The Redeemer and Lamb of God, fulfilled through Jesus Who is Messiah, is lost on most of them. They don't understand.

However, Jesus' prophetic Discourse, coupled with John's prophecies in The Book of Revelation, in conjunction with The Old Testament prophecies, <u>make it entirely possible to track the sequence of fulfillment</u>. The key to unlocking the time-table is not so much the Church, <u>but what happens to Israel as a nation</u>, and in particular, what happens to Judah, Jerusalem, and Mount Zion. In fact, **Paul states we are able to know the Times and the Seasons!** Was Paul contradicting Jesus? Absolutely not! Jesus was merely explaining <u>to the disciples who were gathered on The Mount of Olives</u>, that <u>their mandate</u> was not to be worried over the Times and Seasons that God already has in His power, because <u>they won't be able to piece it all together;</u> and besides, they have a more immediate, important mandate.

But we must recall, Jesus also stated in His Olivet Discourse regarding the end times, Luke 21:28. *"And when these things begin to come to pass, then look up, and lift up your heads; for your redemption draweth nigh."* In other words, there will come a time in God's time-table when it will be expedient to understand, and to discern the Times and Seasons. Who is to understand? The disciples who will be living near the time of the end when these prophecies begin to unfold. So we, living at the time of the end of this Age, ought to be able to know, according to the signs taking place in the world around us, approximately when the Rapture will take place, and those left behind will then have a pretty succinct time-table. *"Now learn a parable of the fig tree; When his branch is yet tender, and putteth forth leaves, ye know that summer is nigh: So likewise ye, when ye shall see all these things, know that it is near, even at the doors."* Matthew 24: 32-33. According to Jesus' words in Matthew, the disciples who are able to track what is unfolding for The Fig Tree (Judah being the prophetic focus, but because God is The God of Israel, this ultimately means Israel as a whole) will have a pretty good idea when these prophecies will be fulfilled. And more particularly, Jewish believers (the 144,000) will be able to finally understand. These are the saints who will have to live through all that Jesus and the prophets indicated during the lead up to The Messianic Kingdom of Israel on earth.

The 144,000 sealed of Israel will have this privilege. They are of Israel, and represent Israel. Even though they are believers in Jesus Christ, and also have the mandate to take the Gospel to all the earth during The Days of Awe, they are not of The Church Age of the Holy Spirit. Rather, the 144,000 are Jews who must understand when these things will take place, and The Father will bring about the necessary circumstances which will result in assembling them in Jerusalem on Mount Zion, to welcome The Messiah when He returns to restore The Kingdom to Israel.

We must remember, Israel still is looking for Messiah to come. Messiah will come! Jesus was right. It all is a matter of timing, and for the Jews, the sequence should become clear following The Church Age when the focus of prophecy shifts back to revolve around Judah, Jerusalem, and Mount Zion, because the countdown to the restored Kingdom of Israel resumes in earnest at the onset of The Ten Days of Awe. So it is the 144,000 Sealed Jewish Evangelists who will be on hand to witness the fulfillment of the answer to the first century disciples' questions!

We know that the Two Witnesses who give their mandated testimony to the world, will be murdered in Jerusalem, and their bodies will lie in the street without burial for three and one-half days. This incident may draw the 144,000 from around the world to Jerusalem to show respect. While they and the whole world watch, the Two Witnesses will be raised back to life, and will ascend into Heaven. Couple this remarkable incident with the massive earthquake that subsequently takes place in Jerusalem an hour later, and we can perhaps begin to see why everyone world-wide will be mesmerized by the events taking place in Jerusalem! We must keep in mind, The Battle of Armageddon will also be in full theater during this same time period. The presence of the 144,000 Evangelists in Jerusalem will not be outlandish in anyone's mind. In fact, they just may be left alone out of fear, because everyone will be abuzz about the drama surrounding the Two Witnesses. AntiChrist will likely leave them alone, because to have that many murdered, only to see them raised back to life, then disappear while the whole world watches, would not be especially good PR for him! He has no way of knowing that what happened to the Two Witnesses won't happen to these guys also! Something beyond his understanding and power is at work, and he certainly would not want it to multiply!

Meanwhile, because of the war, the Israelis will be concerned for their very existence as a nation. Their government at this juncture will have been in protective seclusion for almost three and one-half years. Collectively the Jews they will cry out for deliverance, and for their Messiah to come. The 144,000 who know the truth, realize from Scripture <u>that the next immediate item on the prophetic program is for Messiah to descend,</u> to <u>stand upon The Mount of Olives.</u> **Yom Kippur!** The 144,000 assemble themselves on Mount Zion to pray, and to watch across the valley toward The Mount of Olives, waiting anxiously for His promised return. They will be gazing up into Heaven, just as the first century disciples did! Only this time, they won't have long to wait. Jesus, Messiah, will descend!

II. Besides being Jews, Who are the 144,000?

Revelation chapter 14 explains some interesting details regarding these 144,000 Jews who are sealed with The Father's Name in their foreheads during The Calm of the Sixth Seal, and who will witness the Coming of Messiah at the wrap up of the Seventh Seal, when Tekiah HaGadol is sounded at Yom Kippur. This passage explains their mandate for the entire period of The Ten Days of Awe, and gives some identifying characteristics. Verse 2: *"And I heard a voice from heaven, as the voice of many waters, and as the voice of a great thunder: and I heard the voice of harpers harping with their harps:* Verse 3. *And they sung as it were a new song before the throne, and before the four beasts, and the elders: <u>and no man could learn that song, but the hundred and forty and four thousand, which were redeemed from the earth</u>.* Verse 4. <u>*These are they which were not defiled with women; for they are virgins*</u>. *These are they which <u>follow the Lamb</u> withersoever he goeth. These were redeemed from among men, <u>being the first fruits unto God and to the Lamb</u>.* Verse 5. *And in their mouth* *was found no guile: for they are without fault before the throne of God. Verse 6. And I saw another angel fly in the midst of heaven, having the everlasting gospel to preach unto them that dwell on the earth, and to every nation, and kindred, and tongue, and people, Verse 7. Saying with a loud voice, Fear God, and give glory to him; <u>for the hour of his judgment is come</u>: and worship him that made heaven and earth, and the sea, and the fountains of waters."* KJV. Underlining mine.

A. The 144,000 are The Firstfruits of a Massive Harvest.

According to Revelation 14:2, a voice cries-out from Heaven sounding like the voice of many waters. This is the Voice of The LORD in all His glory and victory, spoken over the nations of the earth. The rumblings of Great Thunder, The Voice of God The Father uttered in finality, are heard. The Mystery of the Ages is now to be wrapped up. The Son is glorified, and The Father is glorified. The kingdoms of this world now belong to Christ.

Many are gathered who play harps. These sing a New Song before The Throne, and before the four Cherubim, and the elders. They sing a Song that only can be learned by the 144,000. Interesting. They have a Song that is different from that sung by the Church. <u>Their position is that they are The Firstfruits of the descendants of Jacob, and The Firstfruits of The Tribulation Saints.</u> So, these 144,000 Jewish young people <u>are The Firstfruits unto the LORD of The Dispensation of The Days of Awe</u>.

The Firstfruits of a crop are always presented unto the LORD <u>at the beginning of a harvest</u>, indicating a full and final harvest will be brought in from around the world at the harvest ingathering of Yom Kippur. So these 144,000 who have completed their mandate, will stand on Mount Zion. Jesus will descend upon The Mount of Olives in The Shekinah Glory Cloud, the same Cloud into which the disciples witnessed His Ascension. Riding upon a white horse through The Eastern Gate, Messiah will proceed to The Temple Mount. There the singing 144,000 Israeli Evangelists will greet Him.

So these 144,000 Firstfruits of the Sons of Jacob will be present when the LORD returns to Mount Zion, fulfilling <u>the promise</u> of the prophetic Scriptures, indicating the time for the complete redemption harvest of all Israel, and of the Tribulation Saints has come. This harvest will not have need to be taken (caught away) anywhere, because the LORD Himself will be present with them, and they will stand in His presence without having to leave the earth. Christ will descend, to restore The Kingdom to Israel!

B. Virgins:

Now we are given a flash-back to the beginning of The Days of Awe, revealing further insight into who the 144,000 Sealed Jewish Rabbis are, along with their message and mandate while in ministry. These 144,000 are virgins, indicating they have not been caught up in the sin and corruption of the world. They are not deceitful in any way. They have not committed fornication, either spiritually or physically. Their position of purity is prophetically important from the standpoint of the Israelis. It was the sin of committing fornication with the false gods of the heathen nations surrounding them that brought about God's discipline upon Israel and Judah in the first place, with The House of Israel being Outcast from their homeland, followed by the Seventy Years of captivity for The House of Judah, and their subsequent Diaspora. God <u>still seeks a pure people for Himself on the earth</u>. He still desires Judah and Jerusalem to be presented to Him in holiness. His desire is that <u>all Israel be saved</u>, <u>and brought back into complete restoration of purity and communion with Himself</u>. He chooses these 144.000 virgin Israeli young people to illustrate that it is possible to be holy before Him, but only through Christ's redemptive atonement, and by living lives set apart, sanctified in His service.

These 144,000 representing all the tribes of Israel, hold a position of honor. Revelation 14:4-5. *"These are they which were not defiled with women; for they are virgins. These are they which follow the Lamb whithersoever he goeth. These were redeemed from among men, being the first fruits unto God and to the Lamb. And in their mouth was found no quile: for they are without fault before the throne of God."* They are redeemed, meaning they have been regenerated by the blood of The Lamb. They are The Firstfruits unto God and to The Lamb of The Dispensation of The Days of Awe, which will culminate in the Yom Kippur harvest. These are then, The Firstfruits not only of Israel, but of all that will be the harvest of righteous from among all nations. They will represent all who become righteous during The Days of Awe time-frame, and so will be The Firstfruits Wave-Offering of all nations before The LORD, The Lamb, The KING, when He returns to Mount Zion.

III. The Three Angel's Messages:
A. "Last Call!"

Verse 6 of Revelation 14, which is a flash-back to the opening of the Sixth Seal, tells us an angel flies in the heavens, who has the *"everlasting gospel to preach unto them that dwell on the earth, and to every nation, and kindred, and tongue, and people."* The message will be Verse 7, *"Fear God, and give glory to him, for the hour of the judgment is come: and worship him that made heaven, and earth, and the sea, and the fountains of waters."* This is a message of exhortation and hope, as well as a warning. The judgment of God upon the earth is now to be poured out. This judgment is The Days of Awe wrath of God, to be poured out upon the earth, and upon all who reject Christ and His finished work. This is <u>the Last Call to repentance and reconciliation</u> -- the message of the final Ten Days of Teshuvah.

B. "Babylon is Fallen:"

Another angel follows the first, stating, *"Babylon is fallen, is fallen, that great city, because she made all nations drink of the wine of the wrath of her fornication."* Notice the contrast between Babylon and the purity of the 144,000 virgins. Babylon represents the idolatry and adultery of the world system, and its pagan practices. It also represents the basis of AntiChrist's Beastly roots, originating from The Empire of Babylon.

The city of Babylon, which was the seat of the government of the original Babylonian Empire, fell because of corruption, so was destroyed. However the influence of The Babylonian Empire has extended even to our time, and has literally corrupted all nations, resulting in the coming wrath of God. All nations have drunk of the fornications of Babylon, and have participated in the debaucheries of her pagan practices and evil desires. This angel proclaims the demise of Babylon -- not simply a city, although the site of the ancient city of Babylon has been partially revived and may again play a role, but a pervading debauchery that has corrupted all nations since the days of Ancient Babylon. Corrupt Babylon is fallen! There is victory and justice in that statement!

C. Angelic Warning Re: The Mark of The Beast:

A third angel follows along with the other two, stating in a very loud voice, *"If any man worship the beast and his image, and receive his mark in his forehead, or in his hand,* Verse 10. *The same shall drink of the wine of the wrath of God, which is poured out without mixture into the cup of his indignation; and he shall be tormented with fire and brimstone in the presence of the holy angels, and in the presence of the Lamb.* Verse 11. *And the smoke of their torment ascendeth up for ever and ever: and they have no rest day nor night, who worship the beast, and his image, and whosoever receiveth the mark of his name."* Revelation 14: 9-11.

This is a pretty strong and clear message the third angel presents. It will be impossible to refute or ignore! Obviously this message is a warning not to accept The Mark of The Beast, and a declaration of what will happen to those who do accept it. This warning message goes out just prior to, as well as during the period when AntiChrist and The False Prophet seek to subjugate all mankind through their system of The Image of The Beast. All who receive the ability to interact with the intelligent super-computer system will ultimately be lost, with no hope to escape eternal torment. All the holy angels and The Lamb will be present to pour out judgment on them. This message is so clear, no-one will be able to say they either did not hear it, or understand it.

Verses 12-13 of Revelation 14 indicate that there will be martyrs for the sake of the LORD during The Days of Awe, and what will become of them. *"Here is the patience of the saints: here are they that keep the commandments of God, and the faith of Jesus. And I heard a voice from heaven saying unto me, Write, <u>Blessed are the dead which die in the Lord from henceforth</u>: <u>Yea</u>, <u>saith the Spirit</u>, <u>that they may rest from their labors; and their works do follow them</u>."* Obviously there will be many who become Saints, keeping the commandments of God, because they exercise faith in Jesus, the Savior and Redeemer. But these also will pay for their faith with their physical lives. Anyone not worshiping The Beast, or taking his Mark, will die a martyr's death. So all the folk who accept Christ during The Days of Awe, (except for the 144,000 who have the protective Seal of God) will be included. According to the above verse, these are blessed, even though they also physically die for their faith. They will rest from their labors, and their works will be judged later at the Yom Kippur judgment when they will be resurrected.

IV. The Ingathering of The Harvests:

Following the initial Firstfruits of any harvest, there is the reaping and ingathering of the entire crop. Let's take a moment to explain this further, because we have had heated debates over something we have had only partial understanding of in regard to the timing of the harvests. The Fall Feasts, just like The Spring Feasts, are celebrations of ingathering of harvests, <u>plural</u>. The Spring Harvests have already been fulfilled in Christ. But when Christ arose on The Feast of Firstfruits following Passover, His resurrection indicated a further <u>series of Fall Harvests</u> were to follow. The Firstfruits, followed by the harvested crop of each Fall Feast, sheds light on: the Rapture of The Church, the resurrection and ascension of The Two Witnesses, the Firstfruits identification of the 144,000, the resurrection and ingathering of The Tribulation Saints, the complete ingathering of Israel, and ultimately judgment of all nations.

Christ indicated He became The Firstfruits of all the wholly righteous of the coming harvest of souls, -- harvests where Jesus indicated *"the fields are white already to harvest."* John 4:35b. The cultivation of the crop for the harvest of The Age of Grace has been taking place over the last 2000 years since Christ ascended, being enabled by the Holy Spirit's anointing of labourers to work in the fields. However there is coming a Day when the LORD of The Harvest will come to collect all His bounty. At that time, the Holy Spirit will have completed His empowerment and anointing, and the entire harvest for The Church Age will be garnered unto the LORD.

Christ will come at Rosh HaShanah in Clouds of Glory, and He will receive this harvest in the air above the earth. The wholly righteous of The Church Age will be resurrected and/or changed, and rise to meet Him in the air, then will remain with Him, going wherever He goes from then on. This is the Rapture of The Church-Bride at the end of The Age of Grace. It is heralded by the sounding of The Seventh Trumpet as Ha Teruah, The Last Trump of Rosh HaShanah, (the first horn of The Ram revealing The Lamb to the righteous), which also announces the onset of The Days of Awe, the final Ten Days of Teshuvah.

Then a new Dispensation -- a time of further harvests of crops, begins. During The Calm of The Sixth Seal, the 144,000 Israeli young men will be Sealed by God to anoint them for a great harvest that will take place during The Ten High Holy Tishrei Teshuvah Days of Awe, and to lay the groundwork for the ingathering of The Tribulation Saints, and for Israel. The 144,000 then, are The Firstfruits of the harvests of The Days of Awe.

Near the end of the last 3 1/2 years of The Tribulation Week, at 1263 1/2 actual days after the mid-Trib point, The Two Witnesses will be resurrected and ascend. This is not an ingathering of the total harvest of The Days of Awe, but is a testimony indicating all that the prophets have said regarding Messiah, The KING, is true, and will now be brought to completion. So they are gathered to their reward. It is very likely they will return to the earth with Christ and The Church only 26 1/2 days later, so they will be included in the harvest at Yom Kippur.

At Yom Kippur there will be a resurrection harvest of The Tribulation Saints, calling them into the presence of the LORD when Christ returns in Clouds of Glory, <u>this time setting His feet upon the earth</u>. There will be no need for a Rapture here. Tekiah HaGadol, the Seventh Trumpet blast revealing The Lamb to the whole world on Yom Kippur, (the other horn of The Ram) is a resurrection blast of the ingathering harvest of the righteous Tribulation Saints from The Days of Awe, and also calls all Israel to their homeland. Five Days (both a literal five days, and ultimately five years) later, the Sukkot harvest of the nations will take place.

Christians are often confused as to the timing of the Rapture, many feeling it takes place at The Second Coming, while others dogmatically state the Rapture is pre-Trib. Some place it mid-Trib, while others totally deny the need for a Rapture at all, and we all point to Scriptures to prove our positions. Actually, all of us have shades of truth here, but we apply it in partial accuracy, <u>because most of us do not understand the Convocation Appointed sequence of The Fall Feasts</u>, coupled with the ramifications of The Trumpets, and that the <u>total Fall Harvest sequence</u> actually takes place over Fifteen Prophetic Days, not just the seven years of The Tribulation. When we understand The Feasts and The Seventh Trumpet blasts taking place at <u>both</u> Rosh HaShanah (the catching away ingathering of the risen and/or physically changed righteous believers,) and again at Yom Kippur Ten Days (years) later (the resurrection and ingathering of The Tribulation Saints, but not caught away because the LORD of the Harvest has already descended), <u>followed five Days (years) later</u> by the separation harvest judgment of The Nations at Sukkot, this becomes clarified.

Terminology is important. 'To be gathered unto,' 'gathered,' 'ingathered' 'reaped,' 'reaping,' 'caught up,' 'departure,' 'ingathering,' are agricultural terminologies most often used in Scripture regarding these harvests. If the LORD Who is to collect His harvest is not physically present on the earth at the time of an ingathering Seventh Trumpet blast, the gathering will of necessity require the harvest to be taken to where He is. Hence the explanations given in 1 and 2 Thessalonians, and 1 Corinthians, where Paul speaks of the Church being caught up to meet the LORD in the clouds of Glory in the air. Such is Rosh HaShanah, the ingathering of the harvest from The Church Age, which also is described as a 'catching away' or 'snatch;' also referred to as 'a great departure.' At that time, Christ will come for His Elect Chosen Bride, to take her to The Father's House for their Wedding and His Coronation, so the Bride is called to her participation in The Wedding Procession. She *"goes out to meet Him"* in the air, because she is ready.

If the LORD, Messiah, is to be present <u>on the earth at the time of an ingathering of a harvest</u>, the gathering of His Elect will of necessity be <u>on the earth</u>, <u>because that is where He will bodily be</u>. It is absolutely logical then for Jesus to state in Matthew 24:29-31 *"Immediately <u>after the tribulation of those days</u> shall the sun be darkened, and the moon shall not give her light, and the stars shall fall from heaven, and the powers of the heavens shall be shaken: Verse 30. And then shall appear the sign of the Son of man in heaven: and then shall all the tribes of the earth mourn, and they shall see the Son of man coming in the clouds of heaven with power and great glory. Verse 31. And he shall send his angels with <u>a great sound of a trumpet</u>, <u>and they shall gather together his elect from the four winds, from one end of heaven to the other</u>."*

THE OFFICIAL WELCOMING DIGNITARIES

After the Tribulation, He will send His angels to gather His elect *"from the four winds,"* (the ingathering of Israel from the far reaches of the earth) and *"from one end of heaven to the other,"* (referring to the resurrection of The Tribulation Saints.) Notice this is accomplished along with the sounding of <u>a Great Trumpet</u>, The Great Shofar, Tekiah HaGadol, of the harvest of Yom Kippur. This ingathering harvest takes place when Christ returns in power and great glory at His Second Coming. The Tribulation Saints are raised <u>to meet Him on the earth</u>, and Israel awaits to greet Him, represented by the 144,000 who are the Firstfruits of all the tribes of Israel, and of those who have received salvation during The Days of Awe. So at Yom Kippur there will be an ingathering resurrection harvest of The Tribulation Saints, and an ingathering harvest-call to collect Israel.

Therefore, all of us have had correct shades of interpretation, but we just have not necessarily applied the Scriptures we use to the appropriate Fall Harvests. Most of us have not been aware that there even <u>is</u> more than one harvest and ingathering!

To summarize, the ingathering <u>appointed harvests</u> of The Fall Feasts, <u>which occur in specified order</u>, begin with the resurrection and catching-away Rapture of The Bride at Rosh HaShanah, followed Ten Days (years) later with the ingathering harvest of the resurrection of The Tribulation Saints, and the ingathering call to Israel, when Christ sets His feet upon The Mount of Olives at Yom Kippur. Then at Sukkot, five Days (years) later, all Nations will be called to account. This is all totally logical when placed into context with the harvest sequence of The Fall Feasts! All told, there will be fifteen Days (years) of Harvest, culminating with the first day of the Sukkot Week. Following Sukkot, Shemini Atzeret - Simchat Torah will then become reality, and the Word of the LORD as given by the Sovereign LORD and KING , and Righteous Judge over all nations, will proceed from Jerusalem.

Micah 4:2 - 9. " *And many nations shall come, and say, Come and let us go up to the mountain of the LORD, and to the house of the God of Jacob; and he will teach us of his ways, and we will walk in his paths; for the law shall go forth of Zion, and the word of the LORD from Jerusalem,* Verse 3. *And he shall judge among many people, and rebuke strong nations afar off; and they shall beat their swords into plowshares, and their spears into pruning hooks: nation shall not lift up a sword against nation, neither shall they learn war any more.* Verse 4. *But they shall sit every man under his vine and under his fig tree; and none shall make them afraid: for the mouth of the LORD hath spoken it.* Verse 5. *For all people will walk every one in the name of his god, and we will walk in the name of the LORD our God for ever and ever.* Verse 7. *In that day, saith the LORD, will I assemble her that halteth, and I will gather her that is driven out, and her that I have afflicted;* Verse 8. *And I will make her that halted a remnant, and her that was cast far off a strong nation: and the LORD shall reign over them in mount Zion from henceforth even for ever.* Verse 9. *And thou, O tower of the flock, the stronghold of the daughter of Zion, unto thee will I come, even the first dominion; the kingdom shall come to the daughter of Jerusalem."* KJV.

As an aside, notice one more interesting observation regarding this prophecy given by Micah. Verse 5 seems to indicate a phenomenon which will take place during the reign of Christ. Not all people will necessarily embrace The LORD as their Redeemer and God, even though they will be under His world system of righteous rule. Apparently, during this period there will still be those who worship false gods, even though they literally have The God of Israel, the only true God, ruling over them. *"For all people will walk every one in the name of his god,* (small 'g')." But all Israel will worship Him. *"and we will walk in the name of the LORD our God* (Capitol 'G') *for ever and ever."* Some would argue that the ancient Hebrew did not have the ability to differentiate between upper and lower case, so this entire verse refers to the same 'God.' But the wording of this verse is written as a converse comparison, so that the first clause appears to indicate a pagan pluralism of *"all people"* to *"walk in the name of their god,"* as opposed to *"we will walk in the name of the LORD our God for ever and ever."* At the end of The Millennium, Satan and his fallen angels will again be released from The Bottomless Pit to try the hearts of mankind, and one more battle will take place before the final Great White Throne Judgment. Satan would not be able to entice anyone into battle against the LORD if everyone of all nations accepted Christ. If all readily turned to the LORD as God in truth, there would be no-one from the Millennial period who would have any reason to rebel, even under enticement and temptation. So the seeds of disobedience and rebellion against truth, and against God Himself, will still exist, even under Christ's righteous reign. That is why He will have to rule over the nations with the heaviness of an iron rod during the Millennium, and require annual accounting every Sukkot!

IV. "The First Resurrection," and "The Second Death:"

"The First Resurrection" is a rather interesting term. There appears to be several resurrections mentioned in Scripture. Christ was raised as the Firstfruits of all the Righteous. [174]At His resurrection many were raised along with Him as the wave-offering of the coming harvests. This was the resurrection of The Firstfruits of the Righteous of The Age of Grace, and

---

[174]   Matthew 27:52 - 53.

subsequently of The Age of Awe, promising the coming great Fall Harvests, plural, of Righteous souls. The resurrection of Tzaddikim (Righteous) at the Natzal (ingathering deliverance) when Ha Teruah (The Last Trump) of Rosh HaShanah sounds before The Ten Days of Awe, is the total harvest of The Age of Grace. Toward the end of the Tribulation period, the Two Witnesses will be resurrected, followed 26 1/2 days later by a further full harvest resurrection of The Tribulation Saints, when Tekiah HaGadol (The Great Shofar) of Yom Kippur is sounded at the end of The Days of Awe. Finally, there will be a resurrection of all the Wicked (Rashim) after the last great Battle with Satan following The Millennium. The resurrection of the Wicked has no Firstfruits, because the Wicked are not offered in thanksgiving onto the LORD, but are separated out during the harvests, and are bundled to be burned.

"The First Resurrection," is a term that is <u>positional</u> rather than specifically chronological, although it contains within it both order and chronology. It is a term used to designate the resurrection of those who have <u>a spiritual position of righteousness and favor before God</u>. Therefore, "The First Resurrection" refers to the resurrection of the Righteous, no matter which dispensation they are from. These are blessed, and will reign with Christ. Revelation 20:6 states, *"Blessed and holy is he that hath part in <u>the first resurrection</u>: on such <u>the second death</u> hath no power, but they shall be priests of God and of Christ, and shall reign with him a thousand years."*

"The Second Death" is also a positional term, but follows chronologically after the entire order of The First Resurrection. The term "Second Death" is applied to the resurrection of the Wicked to eternal judgment. Paul states there is a resurrection of the just, and of the unjust. Acts 24:15. *"...And have hope toward God, which they themselves also allow, that there shall be a resurrection of the dead, <u>both of the just and unjust</u>."* So what is described in the term "The Second Death" is a contrasting term to "The First Resurrection," indicating there really is no such thing as eternal physical death, even for the Wicked. All, whether Righteous or Wicked, will be resurrected to Eternal Life, but the difference is where and how that Eternal Life will be spent. "The Second Death" indicates the reality that even the Wicked will exist eternally, forever separated from God, existing in eternal horror. "The Second Death" has no power over those who participate in the order of "The First Resurrection." So the term "First Resurrection" refers to the eternal living destiny of the Righteous, and the term "Second Death" refers to the eternal living destiny of the Wicked.

The fact that the resurrection of the Righteous takes place in stages, does not take away from the fact that all Righteous are participant in The First Resurrection. It appears that God in His mercy provides venues whereby the Righteous are taken to their blessings of eternal incorruption <u>in specific order</u>. This order falls into line with the sequence of The Feasts and Festivals as orchestrated and fulfilled by the LORD, The Redeemer, Jesus Christ. These Convocations relate specifically to the Harvests of grain(s) and fruit(s). <u>Christ is The Firstfruits of all who are Righteous</u>, being raised on The Feast of Firstfruits, which is The First Day of The Week following The Spring Feast of Passover. Then The Counting of The Omer, the days between Passover and Shavuot, takes place. Shavuot is fifty days after Passover. Jesus, after being raised spent forty days upon the earth. On the day He ascended, He told His disciples they would receive the Spirit's anointing and power to spread the Gospel to the entire world. This anointing took place on Shavuot, ten days after His ascension. Thus Shavuot in fulfillment, inaugurated The Age of Grace. This has been a time of planting, and of cultivating the crops for the final series of Harvests. These Harvests will take place during the fulfillment of The Fall Feasts. Each Fall Harvest necessitates a resurrection of Righteous, <u>each in specified order</u> according to when the grain(s) or fruit(s) are ready for harvest.

    By the way, Sunday, which is The First Day of The Week in our calendar, <u>is not a Christian substitute for the Weekly Jewish Sabbath</u>, but is a weekly commemoration in honour of the resurrection of Christ which took place on The Feast of Firstfruits. Originally, the early Church disciples met together on <u>both</u> The Weekly Sabbath, <u>as well as</u> on The First Day of The Week, <u>in honor and recognition of The Risen Christ</u>. Thus it was known as The LORD's Day. John received his Revelation of The LORD while on the Isle of Patmos <u>on The LORD's Day</u>. Revelation 1:9. Most Christians do not meet on The Weekly Sabbath any longer, but we do continue to meet together weekly on The LORD's Day. Unfortunately, most Christians do not understand why, and erroneously call Sunday the Sabbath. What we are celebrating in meeting on The LORD's Day, is Christ's resurrection, and the promise that we too will be resurrected, and/or changed to receive an incorruptible body like unto Christ's risen body, and that we will ultimately be taken to be with Him where He is! Now that's worth celebrating!

    The prophetic sequential order aspect of The First Resurrection is what Paul was referring to in 1 Corinthians 15:20-26. *"But now is Christ risen from the dead, , and became the first fruits of them that slept. Verse 21. For since by man came death, by man came also the resurrection of the dead. Verse 22. For as in Adam all die, even so in Christ shall all be made alive. Verse 23.* **But every man in his own order***: Christ the first fruits; and afterward* <u>*they that are Christ's*</u> *at his coming.* (His Coming at the Rapture, and the resurrection of the Righteous at Rosh HaShanah.) Verse 24. *Then cometh the end, when he* *shall have delivered up the kingdom to God, even the Father; when he shall have put down all rule and all authority and power."* Emphases mine.

Yom Kippur is Christ's Second Coming and the earthly beginning of His rule and reign, at which time there will be a final ingathering and resurrection of Righteous from The Ten Days Of Awe. Verse 25. *For he must reign, till be hath put all enemies under his feet."* Verse 26. <u>*The last enemy that shall be destroyed is death.*</u>*"* This last clause often is interpreted to mean Christ will destroy death through resurrection. Although that certainly is true, it carries a more specific connotation within the context of <u>the order of resurrections</u> Paul is speaking about in this passage. The Wicked are not resurrected until <u>the end of the order</u>, but are raised all at once for the final Great White Throne Judgment. Revelation 20:12 refers to them as *"The dead small and great"* who *"stand before God, and the books are opened..."* These are no longer physically dead, but are very much alive, having been raised to eternal life, fulfilling <u>the resurrection of the unjust</u>. But they are referred to as *"dead"* because of their eternal separation from God. This is The Second Death. Those appointed to The Second Death will be eternally punished in The Lake of Fire.

CHAPTER 21
THE SICKLE HARVESTS, and THE JUDGMENT OF THE NATIONS

A sickle is an agricultural tool used for reaping a mature crop that is ready to be harvested. The remainder of Revelation chapter 14 gives us the account of the Sickles that are thrust in to reap the earth. They describe the reaping of two diverse types of Fall crops -- grains, and the fruit of the vine. Again, the time-span covered indicates another layer of explanation regarding the prophetic spiral, using overlap, backtrack, and progressing forward techniques to give emphasis, and to explain more detail. This time we begin at the in-gathering of Rosh HaShanah, then progress through The Battle of Armageddon to The Second Coming of Christ, the harvest of Yom Kippur, following which there are resultant ramifications beyond the reaping of the Second Sickle which will allow us to gain a further degree of understanding regarding the annual accounting of the nations during Sukkot.

Revelation 14:14-20. *"And I looked, and behold a white cloud, and upon the cloud one sat like unto the Son of man, having on his head a golden crown, and in his hand a sharp sickle. Verse 15. And another angel came out of the Temple, crying with a loud voice to him that sat on the cloud, Thrust in thy sickle, and reap: for the time is come for thee to reap; for the harvest of the earth is ripe. Verse 16. And he that sat on the cloud thrust in his sickle on the earth, and the earth was reaped. Verse 17. And another angel came out of the temple which is in heaven, he also having a sharp sickle. Verse 18. And another angel came out from the altar, which had power over fire; and cried with a loud cry to him that had the sickle, saying, Thrust in thy sharp sickle, and gather the clusters of the vine. Verse 19. And the angel thrust in his sickle into the earth, and gathered the vine of the earth, and cast it into the great winepress of the wrath of God. Verse 20. And the winepress was trodden without the city, and blood came out of the winepress, even unto the horse bridles, by the space of a thousand and six hundred furlongs."* KJV.

There are four individuals, and two Sickles mentioned here.

I. The First Sickle: The Ingathering of The Sheaves of Grain:

The first individual is The Son of Man, Jesus Christ, and He is sitting on a cloud. The cloud is The Shekinah Glory surrounding The Throne. Jesus wears a golden crown, indicating His sovereignty as LORD of Lords,

His royal position as KING of Kings, and His authority as The Righteous Judge. He is the One who holds the first sharp Sickle in His hand. An angel comes out of the heavenly Temple, and calls out with a loud voice to the One who sits on The Cloud of Glory, telling Him to thrust in His Sickle to reap, because the harvest of the earth is ripe. So He thrusts in His Sickle and reaps.

Why does Christ wield the Sickle that reaps? This Sickle is used to reap the sheaves of grain. Grain is symbolic of the people of the earth. This reaping is the gathering-in of the righteous from the earth to blessing, and the judgment separation of the unrighteous to coming wrath. Jesus, Messiah, is the only One with the authority to do the reaping of the souls of men, because He alone is The Righteous Judge. As The Redeemer, The Lamb of God, He alone became the victorious, sufficient Atonement for the sins of mankind.

This reaping of His Sickle indicates <u>He is dealing with the eternal destinies of individual people</u>. His field is the earth. He is The Husbandman, so He is the only One who has the right to decide on the fate of the harvest. The Church has been invited by Him to participate in the planting, sowing, and watering of His fields during The Church Age. But when Jesus gave His great commission to the disciples, He also pointed out that the fields *"are white already to harvest,"* John 4: 35, indicating the urgency of their labors in preparing for the coming harvests. However, this wielding of His sharp Sickle suggests He <u>personally does the gathering and sorting of His harvests</u>. The fact that there are tares also gathered, indicates <u>He exercises separational judgment of the gathered harvests</u>. Recall, Jesus stated the tares (Wicked) were to be allowed to grow alongside the wheat (Righteous) until the harvest, <u>at which time the separation would take place</u>. The wheat would be gathered into barns, and the tares (Rashim) bundled by the angels to be burned.

The <u>reaping of the first Sickle</u> takes place in two phases, at two separate reapings of grain crops. The first reaping takes place at the resurrection and Rapture when Christ gathers-in the righteous unto Himself to take them to the place He has prepared for them in Heaven. This reaping and gathering is for all those who have their names written in The Book of Life before Rosh HaShanah, when the sealing of the eternal destinies of the wholly righteous from The Church Age takes place. All others are left together on the earth to await further reaping and sorting of the next grain crop at Yom Kippur.

Ten Days (years) later there is the reaping of the second grain harvest of The Tribulation Saints who were put to death for their testimony and faith during The Days of Awe. The ingathering of this next phase of the harvest of grain takes place at Yom Kippur. Again, Christ Himself wields the same first sharp Sickle, and reaps both the good wheat along with the tares. He separates the wheat from the tares at the judgment of The Day of Atonement on Yom Kippur, when those who have repented during The Days of Awe are found written in The Book of life. Those whose names are not found written in The Book of Life are tares (Rashim), and are sealed and bundled for eternal punishment. So the first Sharp Sickle is used twice by The LORD, for two separate <u>Fall Harvests of grain</u>. A sickle is an agricultural implement. It can be used more than once by the same Husbandman to reap His own crops, so both Harvests of the Righteous qualify as being part of this first Sickle harvest. The term 'First' here is not used in reference to chronology, but rather as describing crop-type, and also fits with the description regarding the terminologies used for the 'order' of the 'First Resurrection."

II. The Second Sickle: The Sickle of Wrath Upon the Clusters of Grapes:

An angel holds the second Sickle, and a fourth tells him to thrust in his Sickle and gather <u>the clusters of the vine</u>. This Sickle describes the Wrath of God upon <u>the clusters of grapes</u> (nations) who are upon the earth. The LORD pours out His wrath on all nations, who He gathers into The Middle East, because He has a controversy with them, specifically regarding His Covenant Land and His Heritage people, Israel. The clusters of grapes are cast into the winepress of God's Wrath. This winepress is to be trodden outside Jerusalem, and the blood that flows at this Battle (Armageddon) covers the horses bridles. The fact that this Sickle is wielded by an angelic-being suggests this could be referring to Michael who *"stands up"* to do battle for Israel, according to Daniel chapter 12.

While the reaping and sorting of the harvests of grain of the first Sickle begins at the Rapture of Rosh HaShanah, and is completed at Yom Kippur, both done personally by the LORD, the reaping of the grapes (nations) of the second Sickle takes place beginning with The Battle of Armageddon, and culminates at Yom Kippur. Although Michael wields the second Sickle at Armageddon, he does so in concert with the culmination of the pre-ordained out-pouring of the Vials of Wrath proclaimed against the nations by the LORD. So the wrath upon, and eventual victory over the Nations, is a process that takes place over a time period (the final three and one-half years of the Tribulation 70th Week) culminating with Yom Kippur at The Second Coming Christ. But the second Sickle harvest of nations begins at Yom Kippur, and culminates during Sukkot. So again we see typical overlap, but beginning with Armageddon and Yom Kippur.

The subsequent judicial hearings which will take place for the nations will take place in the Temple Courts of the LORD as He officiates as The Righteous Judge and KING of Kings during Sukkot. It appears the first actual Sukkot after Christ's return may be somewhat of an international write-off as far as official celebrations are concerned. But eventually the nations will realize they cannot continue in an antagonistic stance against the LORD. Therefore, the Sukkot judgment of the Nations will take place annually. So the reaping of the second Sickle gathers-in the nations as they are thrown into the winepress of God's Wrath at The Battle of the Great Day of the LORD at Yom Kippur, following which the accounting judgment of the nations will take place during Sukkot.

III. The Judgment of the Nations, Sukkot:

Sukkot is like a Thanksgiving Feast, and it is a celebration of goodness and peace in the presence of The KING, the LORD of all Creation, Who has chosen to make His will and authority known among men. This Feast initially will be of particular relevance to Israel as a nation, and subsequently to all nations, because it celebrates the presence of The Wind, The Living Water, The Wine, and The Light, and all will have particular significance as these will be celebrated in The Fourth Temple. A complete celebration of Sukkot has not taken place since the destruction of The Second Temple under the Romans in 70 C.E. The First and Second Temples were dedicated on Sukkot, The Feast of Dedication, so it is possible Sukkot will again be celebrated when The Tribulation Temple is dedicated. How many subsequent annual Third Temple Sukkot celebrations will take place, will depend on how long it takes for this Third Temple to be constructed, and how long the Jews will have to practice their Temple worship in this new facility before AntiChrist desecrates it. For sure, they will not have full Temple worship during the Days of Awe for any great length of time. It is possible their full freedom of Temple rituals will only be for perhaps three and one-half years before they are ousted by AntiChrist's abominable desecration take-over of The Temple Mount. So the Sukkot celebrations dedicating the Fourth Temple under Messiah, The KING, will have particular significance for the Israelis, and especially for those who up until His return were not living in Israel.

However, The Feast of Tabernacles also will be the one Feast that will be a requirement for every nation to celebrate by sending ambassadors to Jerusalem each year, or suffer severe consequences. For this reason, we realize Sukkot is also a Feast of Judgment, not of individuals, but of Nations. It is at this Feast we find the separation of the Sheep Nations from the Goat Nations. Matthew 25:31-34. *"When the Son of man shall come*

THE SICKLE HARVESTS, and THE JUDGMENT OF THE NATIONS

in his glory, and all the holy angels with him, <u>*then shall he sit upon the throne of his glory*</u>*: Verse 32.* **And before him shall be gathered all nations**: <u>*and he shall separate them one from another,*</u> *as a shepherd divideth his sheep from the goats: Verse 33. And he shall set the sheep on his right hand, but the goats on the left: Verse 34. Then shall the King say unto them on his right hand, Come, ye blessed of my Father,* **inherit the kingdom prepared for you from the foundation of the world**:" Emphases mine.

How do we know this passage is Sukkot? Sukkot is when The KING's ascension to The Throne of David is celebrated. He will gather all nations before Him to call them to account for their policies, separating the Sheep Nations from the Goat Nations, and this accounting will continue to be held annually at Sukkot throughout the Millennium.

This passage in Matthew chapter 25 goes on to list several solemn categories of judgment that will be brought to bare regarding the nations. These statutes will clarify where their policies, loyalties, and sympathies lay. Although these criteria have valid application for the individual, the context of this passage, which still is Jesus' Olivet Discourse regarding the unfolding of end-time prophecy, shows He is addressing the topic of nations, and He is explaining the terms of the Sukkot judgments.

So what will the statutes of judgment be for the nations? Matthew 35: 35-46. *"For I was ahungered, and ye gave me meat: I was thirsty, and ye gave me drink: I was a stranger, and ye took me in: Verse 36. Naked, and ye clothed me: I was sick, and ye visited me: I was in prison, and ye came unto me. Verse 37. Then shall the righteous answer him, saying, Lord, when was we thee ahungered, and fed thee: or thirsty, and gave thee drink? Verse 38. When saw we thee a stranger, and took thee in? or naked, and clothed thee? Verse 39. Or when saw we thee sick, or in prison, and came unto thee? Verse 40. Then the King shall answer and say unto them, Verily I say unto you, inasmuch as ye have done it unto one of the least of these my brethren, ye have done it unto me. Verse 41. Then shall he say also unto them on the left hand, Depart from me, ye cursed, unto everlasting fire, prepared for the devil and his angels: Verse 42. For I was ahungered, and ye gave me no meat: I was thirsty and ye gave me no drink: Verse 43. I was a stranger, and ye took me not in: naked, and ye clothed me not: sick, and in prison, and ye visited me not. Verse 44. Then shall they also answer him, saying, Lord, when saw we thee ahungered, or athirst, or a stranger, or naked, or sick, or in prison, and did not minister unto thee? Verse 45. Then shall he answer them, saying, Verily I say unto you, Inasmuch as ye did it not unto the least of these, ye did it not to me. Verse 46. And these shall go away into everlasting punishment: but the righteous unto life eternal."* KJV.

It appears the criteria of judgment will be directly related to how each nation has treated the impoverished, their policies in regard to immigration and treatment of refugees, the way they have treated the sick, their treatment of their prisoners, and the manner in which they have addressed poverty. These are policy issues on the part of every nation, be they domestic, or regarding foreign international affairs. Have they been involved in foreign aid? Have they welcomed and housed those who are fleeing war or persecution, or protected those facing issues such as genocide? How much have they publicly given toward medical care of their citizens, and toward medical aid for those who have suffered disasters at home and abroad? In particular, how have they treated the Jews, and other ethnic groups? This set of criteria will be harsh, but also just, and will definitely separate the sheep from the goats! Those who have had policies that have benefitted others in their need, will be blessed and welcomed into the family of nations in His Kingdom. Those who have been harsh toward those in need, both domestically and internationally, will be cursed, and assigned to await eternal punishment. As the nations gather before Him, Jesus, the Messiah, will already know the score. He assembles the nations and separates them, <u>then</u> lets them know His reasons and the ensuing sentence. This Sukkot judgment of the nations will be integral to His reorganization of The World Order, and the authoritative inauguration of His just rule over the nations. But as pointed out earlier, <u>it may indeed take five years to totally organize these official Sukkot ceremonies</u> and international judicial hearings.

The day following the week-long Feast of Sukkot will be Shemini Atzaret - Simchat Torah, The Eighth Day, and the honoring of God's revealed Word. This will first of all be the local Israeli ceremonies, celebrating Messiah's Royal reign of righteousness, peace, and <u>daily administrative government</u> from The Throne of David in The Kingdom of Israel, according to His Own Word. Secondly, it will celebrate Messiah's Sovereignty as KING of Kings over all nations, and the <u>proclaiming of His Word unto all nations</u> from Mount Zion in Jerusalem.

Isaiah 2: 1-4. *"The word that Isaiah the son of Amoz saw concerning Judah and Jerusalem. Verse 2. And it shall come to pass in the last days, that the mountain of the LORD's house shall be established in the top of the mountains, and shall be exalted in the top of the hills; and all nations shall flow unto it. Verse 3. And many people shall go and say, come and let us go up to the mountain of the LORD, to the house of the God of Jacob; and he will teach us of his ways, and we will walk in his paths: for out of Zion shall go forth the law, and the word of the LORD from Jerusalem. Verse 4. And he shall judge among the nations, and shall rebuke many people: and they shall beat their swords into plowshares, and their spears into pruninghooks: nation shall not lift up sword against nation, neither shall they learn war any more."* KJV.

CHAPTER 22
THE VIALS OF WRATH

Revelation chapters 15 and 16 explain the Vial judgments that are poured out during the last three and one-half years of the seven year Tribulation period of The Ten Days (years) of Awe. We again observe a flash-back, but only to the mid-Trib position. This final three and one-half years is often referred to as The Great Tribulation, being the period when God pours out His fiercest wrath upon the earth. It is the period the AntiChrist and the False Prophet also do their worst deeds. Revelation 15:1 states, *"And I saw another sign in heaven, great and marvelous, seven angels having the seven last plagues; for in them is filled up the wrath of God."* The pouring out of these seven last plagues onto the earth fulfills (brings to completion) God's Days of Awe judgments on the peoples and nations of the earth, and ultimately brings about the repentance of all Israel, and the establishment of Israel as a nation of righteousness in The Land of Covenant.

As we proceed through these seven Vials, notice how they remind us of The Ten Plagues of Egypt that God orchestrated through Moses, to persuade Pharaoh to set the people free at the time of the Exodus. There is a plague of sores, the turning of water into blood, thick darkness, frogs, burning hailstones. There is massive heat from the sun which obviously causes crop failures, death of livestock and famine, as well as heat exhaustion, sunburns, skin cancers, etc. What we do not see listed is the death of all the firstborn. God does not desire death for mankind. Rather, His finished work on the cross has atoned for the sin of mankind. He, the Firstborn of the Father, tasted death for every man. But it is up to mankind to appropriate this atonement. So even in His wrath, God proclaims and exercises His love and mercy. But do the majority of men repent and turn to God? No! They blaspheme Him instead!

Also, just as with the plagues of Egypt, the Vial judgments expose the idolatry of the worship of pagan gods. For example, the Egyptians worshiped a false deity that had the image of a frog. The plague of frogs undermined this false deity orientation. Also, the plaque of darkness strikes against the worship of the sun, moon, and stars. Therefore, those today who worship the environment, astrology, the occult, the sun, moon and stars, will be made to realize these are not gods at all, but merely nature. These Vials, which magnify against mankind's pagan loyalties and achievements, are 'acts of God,' sending nature out of control, bringing devastation, destruction, and death. So much for those of the

New Age who worship the environment, the cosmos, and 'mother nature!' Therefore, what we observe as the Vials are poured out, is a decisive swipe at everything mankind without God considers important for life and sustenance, economics, self-esteem, and spirituality.

The result of the out-pouring of these Vials of Wrath will be a parallel reflection of the deliverance of the Children of Israel from Egypt. Israel will be delivered again, not from the Land of Egypt, but from the 'Egypt' of all her sworn enemies and their pagan orientations. Only this time, Israel will be completely restored to The Land of Promise under Messiah, because Satan's stranglehold upon the kingdoms and nations of this world will be utterly broken. Christ will rule over the nations with absolute justice, and with a rod of iron.

Before the Vials are poured out, Revelation 15: verses 2 to 4 describe the setting, and indicate what happens to The Tribulation Saints who are killed by the AntiChrist because of their testimony. *"And I saw as it were a sea of glass mingled with fire: and <u>them that had gotten the victory over the beast, and over his image, and over his mark, and over the number of his name</u>, stand on the sea of glass, having the harps of God. Verse 3. And they sang the song of Moses, the servant of God, and the song of the Lamb, saying, Great and marvelous are thy works, Lord God Almighty; just and true are thy ways, thou King of saints. Verse 4. Who shall not fear thee, O Lord, and glorify thy name? For thou only art holy: for all nations shall come and worship before thee; for thy judgments are made manifest."*

The Tribulation Saints stand in Heaven before The Throne, on a sea of glass mingled with fire, which speaks of clarity and purity. They have harps of God, and sing two songs: <u>The Song of Moses</u>, and <u>The Song of The Lamb</u>. The Song of The Lamb we can readily understand. But why do they also sing The Song of Moses? The Tribulation Saints are not of The Age of Grace, but come out of The Days of Awe period where The Mosaic Law of the Israelis again becomes the uppermost doctrinal frame of reference. It is the period when Temple sacrifice and worship will have been re-instituted, but which will be abruptly stopped when AntiChrist and his henchmen desecrate The Temple. However, The Days of Awe period is also when the truth of Jesus, Who is the Redeemer and Messiah, will be preached by the 144,000 world wide. So these Tribulation Saints know their righteousness is not of The Law per se,' but of The Lamb of God who became the perfect atonement for sin, fulfilling all the requirements of The Law. These will have washed their robes in the blood of The Lamb, so will stand pure before Him. That is why they have two songs to sing, bringing Law and Grace together as one through Christ.

THE VIALS OF WRATH

The Song of Moses also contains a prophetic significance we may easily overlook. The Song of Moses celebrated the deliverance of the Children of Israel from Egypt at the time of the Exodus. However, The Song of Moses contains a prophecy that has not yet been fulfilled, but will be brought to fruition because of the miraculous deliverance which will become evident under Messiah when He returns. This absolute, final, prophetic fulfillment of The Song of Moses is what these Tribulation Saints will be singing about! I will point out the nature of this prophecy later.

One would think, humanly speaking, that the Tribulation Saints gain no victory at all, since they will be put to death for not complying with AntiChrist's system. But it is their very non-compliance with the diabolical system of AntiChrist, and their faith in the atonement of the blood of Jesus Christ, that will make them overcomers, and therefore victorious. They refuse to fall into the AntiChrist's trap! They heed the third angel's warnings concerning what will become of all who accept the Mark of The Beast, or worship the Beast, or bow to his image. They are victorious over the fleshly desire to physically live for the satisfactions of this world. They are victorious over sin. Even though they will have been martyred, they are victorious over death, because Christ has obtained the victory over death and hell for them. They recognize Who truly is The Holy One, The Lord God Almighty, and that all nations will have to bow before Him Who makes His judgments known to all. They will endure much, but will be victorious over all through Christ. Revelation 12:11. *"And they overcame him by the blood of the Lamb, and by the word of their testimony; and they loved not their lives unto the death."* They are Overcomers!

I. The Seven Angels Pour Out The Seven Vials of Wrath:

The Tabernacle of The Testimony in Heaven is opened, and out of it come seven angels who are to pour out the seven last plagues. One of the four beasts that surround The Throne gives these angels the Seven Golden Vials full of the wrath of the eternal God, Who lives for ever and ever. The Temple in Heaven is filled with the smoke of The Shekinah Glory presence and power of God. No man is able to enter into The Temple until the seven plagues are fulfilled. Revelation chapter 16 begins with the utterance of a great Voice emanating from The Temple, commanding the seven angels to, *"Go your ways, and pour out the vials of the wrath of God upon the earth."* As with the Seals and Trumpets, these Vials layer and overlap, rather than simply follow consecutively, because they are of the closing sequence of notes played by the Seventh Trumpet, which is of the Seventh Seal.

The Final Schedule Revealed

A. The First Vial: Revelation 16:2. *"And the first went, and poured out his vial upon the earth; and there fell a noisome and grievous sore upon the men which had the mark of the beast, and upon them which worshiped his image."* The taking of The Mark of The Beast in order to interact with the super-computer network, will be very harmful to the physiology of human body systems. The bionic neuromuscular, physio-electronic connection will upset all the body systems of those who have The Mark, and the most easily observed symptom will be that they will break out in skin sores that are very painful and itchy. Anyone experiencing the pain of shingles may have some idea of what these people will go through. The sores could possibly be indicative of massive systemic interference of the immune system, a physiological response not unlike Hodgkins or similar lymphomas, or AIDS, causing the patient to be susceptible to conditions and imbalances which erupt into symptomatic skin lesions. Mankind will be tampering with the physiological balance God placed within the human body. Notice, this Vial does not have any adverse effect on those who do not take The Mark of the Beast, and do not worship his image.

B. The Second Vial: Revelation 16:3. *"And the second angel poured out his vial upon the sea; and it became as the blood of a dead man: and every living soul died in the sea."* Every living thing in the sea dies from the effects of the pollution of the oceans, not just a third, as was evident when the second Trumpet was sounded. Now this will be pretty devastating, considering many people world-wide depend on the sea for food and employment. The fishing industry will not only be devastated, but completely wiped out. The first four Trumpets were warnings, but these Vials are the full impact of the wrath of God poured out during the final three and one-half years of the Tribulation, so are of The Woe Trumpet trio, and specifically of The Seventh Trumpet, which is the predominant instrumental voice, building in intensity to the Tekiah HaGadol blast.

C. The Third Vial: Revelation 16:4-7.*"And the third angel poured out his vial upon the rivers and fountains of waters; and they became as blood. And I heard the angel of the waters say, Thou art righteous, O Lord, which art, and wast, and shall be, because thou hast judged thus. For they have shed the blood of saints and prophets, and thou hast given them blood to drink; for they are worthy. And I heard another out of the altar say, Even so, Lord God Almighty, true and righteous are thy judgments."* The third angel pours out his Vial upon the rivers and fountains of waters, the fresh water supply, and they become as blood. The angel who pours out this Vial speaks, and another angel also comments. Even the angels see the justice in this judgment on the fresh water sources, because innocent righteous blood has been shed by those who are being judged. Again, this appears to be a world-wide judgment, as opposed to the one-third judgment of the third Trumpet that was sounded at the onset of The Days of Awe. This vial may be similar in origin to the Third trumpet, in that it very well also may be from a cosmic meteorite encounter. Only this time, the poisonous powder of the burning up of the meteorites in the atmosphere, settles out on all the world's fresh water supply, not just on the supply of a limited portion of the earth's fresh, surface water.

D. The Fourth Vial: Revelation 16:8-9. *"And the fourth angel poured out his vial upon the sun; and power was given unto him to scorch men with fire. And men were scorched with great heat, and blasphemed the name of God, which hath power over these plagues: and they repented not to give him glory."* Mankind apparently understands these plagues are orchestrated by God, so chooses to blaspheme His Name rather than turn to Him in repentance. Notice this particular judgment is the <u>fourth</u> Vial. The sun, moon, and stars were spoken into being on the <u>fourth</u> day of Creation. God ordained these heavenly lights to be blessings.

However, God's prophetic time-table is written in the cosmic heavens, and this judgment affects all mankind on the earth. There is absolutely nothing anyone can do to stop a cosmic judgment ordained by God. Many of the judgments of The entire Days of Awe period appear to originate from within the cosmos. All the cosmic judgments are outside the realm of man's ability to manipulate, except for some of the atmospheric changes which may result from the air pollution of warfare. (First of all the sun and moon were darkened by one-third at The Battle of Gog and Magog. There were meteorite showers resulting in devastations as the first four Trumpets were blown.) <u>Several years later, during the last half of the Tribulation, the sun seems to go into an exaggerated nova, scorching men with great heat at the pouring out of this fourth Vial</u>. The fourth Vial will be particularly difficult for mankind to cope with, because it will produce great famines, as well as result in the physical symptoms of heat exhaustion. But, as pointed out by the two angels, God's judgments are just.

E. The Fifth Vial: Another cosmic judgment. The sun, moon, and stars will be completely hidden as the kingdom of the Beast is plunged into thick darkness. Revelation 16:10-11. *"And the fifth angel poured out his vial upon the seat of the beast; and his kingdom was full of darkness; and they gnawed their tongues for pain. And blasphemed the God of heaven because of their pains and their sores, and repented not of their deeds."* The fifth angel pours his Vial upon the headquarters of The Beast, so that his kingdom is filled with darkness. This plague particularly seems to strike at what could be the heart of AntiChrist's pagan roots -- Islam. Islam is historically based in ancient moon-god worship. Darkness, and especially not being able to see the moon or stars, along with the sun being darkened at the same time, will be devastating for AntiChrist, just as the Plague of Darkness was devastating for Pharaoh.

This fifth Vial is poured out in a specific geographical location. AntiChrist's headquarters. Where are AntiChrist's headquarters at this juncture? Jerusalem. God will bring judgment against AntiChrist's pagan, oppressive rule and practices that will be based in His Holy City! People will gnaw their tongues for pain, and blaspheme the God of Heaven because of their pains and sores. How does their reaction tie-in with this darkness? It would appear the darkness may actually upset the network of the communication system, and those who have The Mark will experience a painful physiological response because the bionic pathways (satellite connections) are interrupted. Thus, the darkness will help expedite the downfall of AntiChrist by putting him out of direct communication with his world. This darkness will coincide with the final days of The Battle of Armageddon when the sun is darkened, and moon and stars do not give off any light, thus bringing about devastating chaos to AntiChrist's forces. But people still will not repent of their deeds.

F. The Sixth Vial: Revelation 16:12 to 15. *"And the sixth angel poured out his vial upon the great river Euphrates; and the water thereof was dried up, that the way of the kings of the east might be prepared. And I saw three unclean spirits like frogs come out of the mouth of the dragon, and out of the mouth of the beast, and out of the mouth of the false prophet. for they are the spirits of devils, working miracles, which go forth unto the kings of the earth and of the whole world, to gather them to the battle of that great day of God Almighty."* The sixth angel pours out his Vial on the Euphrates river, so that the waters dry up making way for the kings of the East. This is the path taken by the two million man army from the far East to march to The Middle East. This sixth Vial represents preparations and engagement for war on a massive scale that this world has never seen.

During the judgment of the sixth Vial, three evil spirits like frogs come out of the mouth of the Dragon, out of the mouth of The Beast, and out of the mouth of the False Prophet. These are miracle working demons, and they go to the kings of the earth to co-ordinate them all to fight <u>The Battle of the Great Day of God Almighty</u>, the Battle which takes place when the focus of Armageddon shifts from the nations and alliances already fighting each other, to militarily face Christ and His heavenly forces. It is obvious that the Dragon (Satan), the Beast (AntiChrist), and the False Prophet, realize they are now up against a formidable Foe that requires more than just human input and expertise. They now are facing God Himself, Jesus Christ, The LORD of Hosts, Who has returned to take up His rightful sovereign, victorious position on the earth. So three demons are commissioned to pull-off a miracle -- to shift the focus of the animosities of the leaders of the nations from their own agendas against one another, to agree to band together against Christ.

Satan has been trying to prevent the LORD from taking up His rightful sovereignty ever since The Garden of Eden. Now the Dragon's rebellion has finally come to this show-down. Needless to say, Satan, AntiChrist, and the False Prophet are not thrilled about this development! When Christ bursts upon the world scene, obviously prepared with all the hosts of Heaven riding in awesome battle array upon white horses, the nations will stop fighting each other, and marshal together to fight against Him. Demonic activity always attempts to thwart the purposes of God. The armies who are lured into this final onslaught are enemies of each other, just as much as they are against Christ, producing a powder-keg which will result in devastations beyond anything man has ever before perpetrated. Without the LORD's direct intervention into this demonically orchestrated Satanic act of rebellion against Christ, no one would survive. Yet God allows this gathering of all nations to teach them His judgments, and ultimately to show His absolute sovereignty over all rulers and powers, both of the earthly, as well as of the Spiritual realm.

1. An Invitation Inserted by Christ Himself:

An invitation and warning, dictated by Christ Himself, is inserted at this point into the prophetic written narrative. He cries, "*Behold I come as a thief.* (When no-one is expecting Him, referring back to when He comes as a Thief at Rosh HaShanah.) *Blessed is he that watcheth, and keepeth his garments, lest he walk naked, and they see his shame.*" Verse 15 of Revelation 16. This statement by Jesus Christ reminds those who read this Revelation explanation, that there is hope, and they do not need to face these judgments. There is no need to have to go through all this! It is possible to be clothed in righteousness, to be watching, and to be removed to safety before any of this begins to transpire, and so be blessed. He reminds us He is coming to take the righteous from the world before the judgment and wrath of God is poured out. So this is a warning and invitation given by Christ Himself, stating that it is possible to be taken when He comes as a

The Final Schedule Revealed

Thief to remove the righteous to safety, rather than have to endure all that is going to take place on the earth. Those who remain will be exposed, and their shame will become obvious for all to see.

Why would Jesus insert this cry of warning and mercy? He really loves all people, and does not want anyone to have to end up enduring His judgments of wrath during The Days of Awe, -- especially the Vials of Wrath which, like it or not, those left behind will have to face. This is the cry of His heart! Following this plea, dictated personally to John by Christ Himself, the prophetic saga continues.

G. The Seventh Vial: *Revelation 16:17-21. " And the seventh angel poured out his vial into the air; and there came a great voice out of the temple of heaven, from the throne, saying,* <u>*It is done*</u>*. Verse 18. And there were voices, and thunders, and lightnings; and there was a great earthquake, such as was not since men were upon the earth, so mighty an earthquake, and so great. Verse 19. And the great city was divided into three parts, and the cities of he nations fell: and great Babylon came in remembrance before God, to give unto her the cup of the wine of the fierceness of his wrath. Verse 20. And every island fled away, and the mountains were not found. Verse 21. And there fell upon men a great hail out of heaven, and every stone about the weight of a talent: and men blasphemed God because of the plaque of hail; for the plaque was exceeding great."*

The seventh angel pours out his Vial into the air. A Voice from The Throne utters a cry of victory! Accompanying this Voice are other voices, Thunders, and lightnings; and an earthquake greater than any earthquake ever before in the history of the earth. Jerusalem is divided by the earthquake into three parts, and the great cities of the nations fall. It is this earthquake that kills the 7,000 men in Jerusalem an hour after the Witnesses are resurrected and ascend. Babylon (the corrupt economic ideological system that has undergirded all Empires represented by the four Beasts) comes to remembrance before God, so He can pour out on her the wine of the fierceness of His wrath. Babylon, the corrupt world system, is brought to judgment.

Verse 20. *"Every island fled away, and the mountains were not found."* Now for the islands to disappear, and all mountains to not be found, this earthquake obviously has a devastating effect on the topography of all the land masses of the earth. Can you imagine not being able to find The Canadian Rockies? Or The Swiss Alps? Or The Himalayas? Truth is, all these ranges do lie along known fault lines. If the fault-lines give-way, these mountain ranges could disappear! Along with the earthquake, there appears to be a massive hailstone shower. According to verse 21, most of these hailstones will weigh approximately 96 lbs (one talent) each. It is this massive hailstone shower that really gets to the people on the earth at this time, so that they blaspheme God. These hailstones may be either ice or hot brimstone, or a mixture of both, indicating another massive cosmic meteorite shower, possibly caused by the earth passing through a comet's tail.

H. Summery of These Vials:

The pouring out of the Seven Vials is <u>the culmination of the curse placed on all of God's Creation after Adam and Eve's fall</u>. These judgments therefore, <u>are totally just</u>! The Seven Vials are poured out quickly, so are progressively overlapping, rather than strictly sequential. Their devastations take place during the final three and one-half years of the seven year Tribulation portion of The Ten Days of Awe, and most of them have direct impact during The Battle of Armageddon time-frame, so are aimed at the unrighteous nations and peoples of the earth, and specifically at the AntiChrist and his oppressive system, and at the Dragon, Satan.

1. There is a Place of Safety:

<u>Appointed Times of reckoning</u> for all mankind are scheduled. What was set in motion from The Fall of mankind, is a time-clock of prophecy that will <u>all</u> be fulfilled. God has revealed the details in Scripture -- like a well-prepared schedule. All we need do is read it, then pay attention to the signs occurring around us in order to see how God's prophetic schedule is being played out until the end. We do not need to walk blindly. Faith is not closing our eyes and taking a blind leap. Faith is walking according to what God has said and revealed, and accepting His redemption so we are brought out from under the curse. The prophetic clock cannot be stopped, but we can access the ultimate place of safety in and through Christ. The perfect sinless Lamb of God provided a pathway whereby man is able to be completely restored to his pre-Fall spiritual purity, and thus attain intimate fellowship with God, to eternally enjoy both His physical, as well as His spiritual Creation, and dwell in His loving Presence eternally.

If it were possible for mankind to be annihilated -- to cease to exist eternally -- there really would have been no need for Redemption, or even for judgment! Mortal, unregenerate man would simply cease to exist at death, and that would be that. There would be no hereafter for the unrighteous, and therefore no need for eternal punishment. Thus there would be no deterrent against sin either. If this life is all there is, then what is the big deal?

But man IS eternal, <u>both</u> the righteous and the unrighteous! It is a big deal! The only way we can overcome the ultimate eternal living death of separation from God is through the shed blood of The Lamb, Jesus Christ. This is a mystery, but this mystery is not beyond the ability of mankind to understand so that we can grasp and accept it. In fact, we MUST accept it! There is no other way! *"Neither is there salvation in any other: for there is none other name under heaven given among men whereby we must be saved."* Acts 4:12. Everyone will one day bow before Him, and acknowledge He is LORD.

"Wherefore God also hath highly exalted him, and given him a name which is above every name: That at the name of Jesus every knee should bow, of things in heaven, and things in earth, and things under the earth; and that every tongue should confess that Jesus Christ is Lord, to the glory of God the Father." Philippians 2: 9-11.

CHAPTER 23
THE FALL OF THE WHORE, BABYLON

Chapters 17 and 18 of Revelation explain the fall of Babylon that transpires as a result of God pouring out His wrath on the nations of the earth. One of the seven angels which has the seven Vials comes to John, and states, *"Come hither; I will show unto thee the judgment of the great whore that sitteth upon many waters*: Verse 2. *With whom the kings of the earth have committed fornication, and the inhabitants of the earth have been made drunk with the wine of her fornication."* Revelation 17:1-2. John is carried by the Spirit into the wilderness, and he sees a woman sitting upon a scarlet-colored Beast that is full of the names of blasphemy, and having seven heads and ten horns. Where have we met this Beast before?!

I. The Whore, Babylon: Revelation Chapter 17.

It appears <u>The Whore rides the fourth Beast</u>, the final world Empire-scene which is made up of components of all the major Empires that have preceded it. This is the coming Empire of AntiChrist and his henchmen. The focus in this passage is on this woman riding the Beast. She is dressed in purple and scarlet, and is decked with gold, pearls, and precious stones. She is wearing a golden belt, and is carrying a golden goblet in her hand. The goblet is filled with abominations and filthiness of her fornication. She has a name written on her forehead, *"Mystery, Babylon the Great, The Mother of Harlots and Abominations of the Earth."* She is drunk with the blood of the saints, and with the martyrs of Jesus.

Who is this woman? <u>She is a corrupt religious, economic, and political philosophical system</u>. Some say she is the Roman Catholic Church which has become corrupt, and has subjugated many world-wide. But this woman has a larger, more pervasive identity and role. <u>She represents all the corruption that the rulers of the nations of the earth have drawn upon to rise to their height of power and wealth</u>. Her origins are firmly rooted in the background ideology of ancient Babylon, which was ruthless, and was steeped in the occult. She also has roots in the thinking of the Medes and Persians, who were haughty and considered themselves invincible. She has a major root in the world-view arising out of the education, philosophical reasoning, and scientific thinking of the Greeks. She hails from the justice system, economics, and crushing military iron-might of the Romans. She has the influence and resources of all these Empires at her disposal.

Her lineage is both wealth and royalty, indicated by her purple robes and golden belt. Her ruthlessness is portrayed by the scarlet color of her robes. The golden goblet she carries portrays and betrays her idolatry. She drinks from the goblet of wealthy exalted position and religious piety, but what she drinks is anything but holy! Her drink is abominations and fornication. And not only is she drinking it, but she has lured the rulers and kings of all nations to partake with her, because she is a seductress. She has offered them much, and they have fallen for her and her seductions. There is much more portrayed here than just the corruption of the Roman Catholic Church! In fact, I would suggest the Roman Catholic Church <u>has been corrupted by her seductions</u>, along with all other nations and empires. So what is described in Revelation regarding this Whore cannot be just the Roman Catholic Church. In fact, connection with, and to, what has been perceived to be a Christian organization and political system, no matter how corrupt, will not be considered politically correct either by AntiChrist or his False Prophet during the Tribulation. I would suggest then, <u>that The Whore represents the extreme,</u> and <u>obviously corrupt excesses of all avenues of wealth,</u> <u>power,</u> <u>and manipulation,</u> <u>that has,</u> <u>or ever will be used to subjugate the nations of the earth</u>. She represents all that has allowed, or will ever allow any empire or regime to control the souls of men.

She obviously has been, is, and will be against the Church and The Tribulation Saints, inspiring their persecution and murder, because she is drunk with their blood. This in itself shows she is not a specific religious organization such as the Catholic Church. Many who become Tribulation Saints will likely be Catholics who wake up to the truth after the Rapture of the born-again Christians. They may leave the organized Church (Catholic or otherwise) because they realize the whole truth has not been taught. Some have suggested the martyrdom that takes place during the Tribulation may be a restoration of the atrocities of the Inquisition. That may be part of it, <u>but this Whore is more than just that</u>. She drinks abominations and filthiness of her fornication, indicating she is actually one who knows the truth, but has chosen to live and act otherwise, refusing the truth. Her fornication under AntiChrist's regime will include all those who show a willingness to act in concert to rid the world of all vestiges of Christianity. Why would the Roman Catholic Church want to take a position that ultimately would wipe itself out? This Whore is broader based in ideology beyond the scope of apostate Christianity.

<u>She is riding the seven-headed,</u> <u>ten-horned Beast</u> which we already have discovered produces the AntiChrist system, and is itself rooted in

THE FALL OF THE WHORE, BABYLON

ancient Babylon, Medio-Persia, Greece, and Rome. All these give her inspiration for her momentum. She rides with purpose. She is active, and is a force to be reckoned with. She has the ability to deceive all nations into her line of thinking and action. She is rich and powerful, and ruthless. <u>She holds the reigns of The Beast</u>.

II. The Beast with Seven Heads and Ten Horns:

The remainder of the chapter describes the Whore and the Beast she rides. Revelation 17:7. *"And the angel said unto me, Wherefore didst thou marvel? I will tell thee the mystery of the woman, and of the beast that carrieth her, which hath the seven heads and ten horns."* KJV.

Notice the explanation begins with this Beast having seven heads and ten horns. Initially, <u>The Beast has not as yet grown the Little Horn</u>, indicating the relationship of this Whore with this Beast Empire has already become established long before The Days of Awe begin, while the world scene still is 'normal.' In fact, from ancient times until pre-Tribulation is when this Whore appears to have done the most damage! Her allegiances and loyalties are entrenched, and <u>her influence steers the course for the rise of AntiChrist to power</u>.

Generally we look upon a rider as the one in control of the animal being ridden. The Whore rides, so holds the reigns of The Beast. <u>Therefore, The Beast does not control her, rather she controls it</u>! She holds the reigns of international political and economic policy -- not just religious identification and wealth, although these are definite factors also within her ability to manipulate. But as the rider of The Beast, she is directing where it goes, and ultimately how, and when it achieves maximum control of the world scene. She has a hand in what this Beast ultimately does, and therefore in what it becomes.

A. The Succession of Rulers:

Revelation 17: verse 8. *"The beast that thou sawest was, and is not; and shall ascend out of the bottomless pit, and go into perdition: and they that dwell on the earth shall wonder, whose names were not written in the book of life from the foundation of the world, when they behold the beast that was , and is not, and yet is.* Verse 9. *And here is the mind which hath wisdom. The seven heads are seven mountains, on which the woman sitteth.* Verse 10. *And there are seven kings: five are fallen, and one is, and the other is not yet come; and when he cometh, he must continue a short space."*

This passage portrays an evolving description of The Beast the Whore rides. Verse 10 suggests there is a succession of rulers who precede the coming AntiChrist. Five of these rulers have previously had their time in authority, referring to the prominent rulers of the former empirical systems. One of them currently reigns, meaning one ruler was in power at the time John wrote The Book of Revelation. One is still to come, meaning there will arise another ruler who will have great power and influence world-wide. Seven rulers.

Verse 11. *And the beast that was, and is not, even he is <u>the eighth</u>, and is of the seven, and goeth into perdition.* The AntiChrist arises through a successive mechanism. He has connection with the seven previous empirical rulers, because **he is one of these seven himself** (is from their root) but **he becomes the eighth**. He will receive recognition beyond his position as one of the seven, in other words, his final position will become a form of governance of his own making, so he actually is the eighth arising out of the seven. He is Satanically possessed, indicated by the fact that he arises out of The Bottomless Pit, and his ultimate destiny is perdition -- eternal living punishment in The Lake of Fire.

The seven heads are also depicted as seven mountains where The Whore sits. Some have identified the seven mountains as being the seven hills of Rome. Another explanation given is that these mountains represent the hills of Jerusalem. I tend to lean toward the possibility that both explanations have credence, but at varying times, and in different roles as prophecy unfolds. In fact, since the seven heads from which succession or order the eighth arises, are seven mountains, I would suggest these mountains are successively representative of the centers (cities) of the seats of these governing rulers and their systems, both political and economic. A mountain then, represents both a governing ruler, and whatever center the dominant empirical control issues from. We have therefore, the possibility of several heads of state, and cities, taking up the identification of being a 'mountain.'

B. Ten Concurrent Kings:

Verse 12. *" And the ten horns which thou sawest are ten kings, which have received no kingdom as yet; but receive power as kings one hour with the beast."* Unlike the heads described above, <u>the horns are rulers that are all contemporary, and concurrently become involved in world politics along with The Beast for a short period of time</u>. Now don't fault me here, but it appears every animal I have ever seen sporting horns, has had their horns growing out of their heads. Right? We are able to safely conclude then, that these ten horns also grow out of the heads of this Beast. In other words, let's place the horns where they belong. On the seven heads. That

THE FALL OF THE WHORE, BABYLON

alone should help us identify these leaders who will rule concurrently with the AntiChrist, and where they will hail from. The heads grow out of the Beast that has a body like a Leopard, the feet of a Bear, and the mouth of a Lion. These horns then, arise out of the succession of the former world Empires, so must be rulers of countries that now occupy the areas formerly covered by the Empires represented by these animal characteristics. It is noteworthy that many countries arising from within these former Empires are, in our day, Islamic (but not all.)

C. Iron Teeth:

The mouth of this Beast has iron teeth. Keeping the above reasoning intact, most of us realize that teeth are found in a mouth, which anatomically is part of a head. So we become aware of two things. The passage is speaking anatomically of a mouth with teeth; NOT the part of the head that produces horns. This observation allows us to conclude that this head with the mouth and iron teeth is perhaps not really a definable country, but rather a political body such as The European Union, which has the ability to speak with one voice on behalf of its members, and the power (iron teeth) to implement policy.

D. Heads and Horns:

All seven heads grow horns, (become current nations with representative leaders.) At least two, and possibly more, of the seven heads which arise out of the geographical region of the former empires, become members of the revised Roman Empire (iron.) This could very well be the European connection. But some of the heads also represent other areas of the former empires, because the entire hybrid beast with its seven heads is being considered here. So why do at least two heads need to be European?

The discrepancy in the number of heads (seven) verses horns (ten) may shed some light here. If we look at the usual configuration of two horns per head, there are either two heads who do not grow any horns at all, (which makes little sense, since every nation has a government), or there is a configuration where one head has three horns to begin with, and another head has two. The other five heads have one horn each. Now that distribution does seems to line up with what apparently happens to these horns.

The head with three horns (these may represent three countries agreeing together) has these uprooted, and one nasty opinionated Little Horn with the ability to exercise authority over all the others, grows up in their place. So AntiChrist comes to power when ten world leaders (horns) that are geographically and ideologically rooted in the jurisdictional areas of the seven heads of the former world empires, also are in power. Then he uproots three of these rulers (horns) and takes most of their <u>international influential power</u> from them. <u>They are uprooted,</u> <u>but not necessarily destroyed</u>. It is possible to detach horns from a head without totally destroying the horns themselves. In fact, we know horns indeed can be 'harvested,' and then used for the purposes of the one harvesting them. It appears AntiChrist does exactly that. The uprooting of these three horns represents the demotion of the influence of three governing leaders, making them subservient, <u>while they still hold on to a reduced national leadership role</u>. I would suggest this is what occurs here, because we subsequently see <u>these ten horns</u> **all** <u>have power along with The Beast</u> for a short time, and later, <u>they</u> **all** <u>make war with The Lamb</u>, and **all ten** <u>hate</u> <u>The Whore</u>. So none of them cease to exist as horns.

Also, the other European connection may stem from the head with two horns (two countries, or leaders working together.) This would represent the two horns of The False Prophet as mentioned in Revelation 13:11. (The Counterfeit Lamb.) But then again, because of the activities of The False Prophet, promoting the pagan worship of AntiChrist, these two horns may represent one nation from Western Europe, and one from the East, indicating co-operation. The False Prophet himself becomes the stronger of the two in this relationship.

Keep in mind, <u>the ten horns do not include the Little Horn</u> who has a mouth speaking blasphemies. Because of its strange anatomy and abilities, we find the Little Horn indeed has powers that the ten horns do not. This Little Horn is the AntiChrist who uproots three of the ten horns. He is not one of the ten horns per se,' but is still rooted in the seven heads, becoming the eighth. He arises from the head that has the deadly wound which heals.

Verse 13. *"These have one mind,* (co-operate together) *<u>and shall give their power and strength unto the beast</u>.* Verse 14. *<u>These shall make war with the Lamb, and the Lamb shall overcome them</u>: for he is Lord of lords, and King of kings: and they that are with him are called, and chosen, and faithful.* Verse 15. *And he saith unto me, The waters which thou sawest, where the whore sitteth, are peoples, and multitudes, and nations, and tongues.* Verse 16. *<u>And the ten horns</u> which thou sawest upon the beast, <u>these shall hate the whore</u>, <u>and shall make her desolate and naked</u>, <u>and shall eat her flesh</u>, <u>and burn her with fire</u>.* Verse 17. *For God hath put in their hearts to fulfill his will, and to agree, and give their kingdom unto the beast; until the words of God are fulfilled.* Verse 18. *And the woman*

THE FALL OF THE WHORE, BABYLON

which thou sawest is that great city, which reigns over the kings of the earth." KJV. Emphases mine.

Most of us have placed this description solely in the geographical location of The European Union, and in the countries that make it up. I would suggest that it presents itself as The European Union, <u>but has a much broader base</u>, both historically, and in the actual unfolding of the end-time prophecies. Since the horns' origins are all rooted in the heads of the former world empires, all these empires, and the countries that have emerged from their jurisdictions, have an influence in this description. However, the seat of powerful clout may be <u>brought to fruition through what essentially is The European Theater</u>, which is the financial powerhouse, and <u>the political vocal representation of that part of the world</u>. We have then, a blend of East and West portrayed; an international powerful governmental and financial, ideological, conglomerate Beast.

The ten leaders (horns) are not controlled <u>totally</u> by AntiChrist. Their roles are <u>orchestrated by God Himself to do His will</u>. Notice verse 17 of Revelation chapter 17. *"<u>For God hath put in their hearts to fulfill his will, and to agree and give their kingdom unto the beast; until the words of God are fulfilled</u>."* From our perspective, they appear to be manipulated by AntiChrist, however, this could not even occur except God allows it. Why is this important? <u>Ultimately, these leaders, **all ten of them**, are used by God to set the stage for **the fall** of AntiChrist, which is not necessarily their first intent</u>, and the destruction of The Whore, **which is their intent**. Now there's a dichotomy!

E. "The Beast:"

But what, or who, is the 'Beast?' This Beast *"was, and is not, and yet is, and goes on to perdition,"* according to Revelation 17:8b. What is being described is a three-layered prophecy, all layers having interactive validity of interpretation, so all must be considered to fully understand. First of all, *"which was."* The origins of The Beast are not easily discerned, because <u>the original</u> empires exist only in vestige form at the time of the final fulfillment. <u>But their powerful influence is very much alive and active</u>. The Babylonian Empire no longer exists. The Medio-Persian Empire does not exist. The Greek Empire no longer exists. But the influences of these former empires have shaped the world we now live in. So the 'empire' roots of this Beast are here indicated.

However, there is one more empire to consider, which adds depth to the above influences. It is also valid to interpret this clause as indicative of The Roman Empire, <u>which was</u> in the past, gradually fell, and <u>yet is</u>

revived, and ultimately produces the AntiChrist. This interpretation is not exclusive as an either/or scenario, but rather as <u>along with</u> the above interpretation. <u>The fourth 'Beast' Empire is a hybrid.</u>

Thirdly, since this prophecy has layers of concurrent fulfillment, the term 'Beast' <u>refers also to the personage who rises to the helm,</u> The AntiChrist. So the fact that this Beast *"was, is not, and yet is,"* also is reflected in the personal unfolding of AntiChrist's rise to power-- his apparent 'death' from the mortal wound he receives, his astounding healing, and his subsequent Satanically inspired power and repressive control over the world scene. In fact, this aspect of interpretation and fulfillment is the ultimate focus, because the same verse narrows it down. It states, *"The beast that thou sawest was, and is not; and shall ascend out of the bottomless pit, and go on to perdition,"* indicating AntiChrist, following his deadly wound and miraculous healing, becomes the actual physical embodiment of the one who ascends out of The Bottomless Pit. He becomes possessed by Satan, and will ultimately go on to perdition. So although the re-emergence of The Roman Empirical dominance through The European Union does play a role, this verse pretty much identifies <u>who this is ultimately</u> speaking about. The Beast who *"goes on to perdition."* The Beast goes to his eternal terrible living judgment, because ultimately this 'Beast,' the AntiChrist, along with The False Prophet, is cast alive into The Lake of Fire.

What we have portrayed in this passage is a coming world Empire rooted in past empires, that is a conglomerate <u>fourth hybrid Beast</u>, AND a prominent Satanically possessed Ruler of this fourth Beast who is referred to as "<u>The Beast</u>," who goes on to perdition. The ones who apparently will really wonder about the power and influence of this Beast, will be the wicked who do not have their names written in The Book of Life. Revelation 17:8. *"The beast that thou sawest was, and is not, and shall ascend out of the bottomless pit, and go into perdition: and <u>they that dwell on the earth shall wonder, whose names were not written in the book of life from the foundation of the world</u>, when they shall behold the beast that was, and is not, and yet is."* The unrighteous Rashim will be fascinated by, and therefore deceived by this Beast.

F. The Woman Sits upon Seven Mountains:

Revelation 17:9b. *"And the seven heads are seven mountains where the woman sits."* As already mentioned, some have identified these seven mountains with the city of Rome, and with the Roman Catholic Church. I am not throwing out the possible involvement of the apostate Roman Catholic Church <u>in helping to set the stage</u> for the deception to happen, and

THE FALL OF THE WHORE, BABYLON

possibly even providing some credence to the rise of AntiChrist, his False Prophet, and his repressive regime. But I do not believe either AntiChrist or his False Prophet are Catholic, so they will not be supported directly by any form of 'Christian' financing and/or ideology. Also, the False prophet cannot be any brand of 'Christian," since he will have no problem setting up the image-system used for Beast worship. I believe AntiChrist could very well be a 'moderate' Muslim to begin with, but becomes a radical, using the jihad of deception, even possibly posing as a Jew. There is a strong tendency for certain pockets of humanistic thinking to accept Muslims in the name of peace, progress, and understanding. This is all part of the deception AntiChrist will manipulate to gain credibility, and to advance the purposes of his corrupt beastly empire. But, he definitely is against Christianity in any form!

So where, and what, are these seven mountains? The seven mountains represent the location from which The Whore has the most ability to provide the greatest affective influence. These mountains could represent various locations from which The Whore has particularly had financial, political, and ideological influence down through the ages.

"*And upon her forehead was a name written, MYSTERY, BABYLON THE GREAT, THE MOTHER OF HARLOTS AND ABOMINATIONS OF THE EARTH.*" Revelation 17:5. Scripture states that the idolatrous Whore is named, among her other revealing titles, Babylon the Great. So her origins, as well as her influence, are Babylonian, and this fact would place her stemming from the ideology coming from that part of the world. She has been around a long time, seducing all empires up to the present. Her current Babylonian ideological influence has both humanistic and Islamic connections in the day in which we live, and also is extremely wealthy. But that is not her only seductive stance, or root of influence. Notice, she '*sits on the seven mountains*' according to verse 9 of this chapter, meaning she has acceptance and influential powers, financially and politically. She is not the empire per se', rather <u>she is the driving force undergirding, and therefore influencing all empires and nations through corruption</u>. That allows the mountains she sits on to have whatever location is necessary for her influence to remain the strongest, whether from Babylon (Iraq, and possibly the revived ancient city itself,) Rome (representing the political-religious arm of the former Roman Empire,) or Athens (representing the Greek influence,) or Moscow (representing the Medes and Persians,) or from New York (The United Nations and The World Trade Center,) or Brussels (The European Union,) or Jerusalem (the eventual seat of AntiChrist's power) which also is built on seven hills. Notice these are seven centers (mountains of political and economic clout.) This is one obvious application of interpretation.

Along with, but not in exclusion of the above, the seven mountains also are the seven heads according to verse 9. These seven heads produce the ten horns, and the Little Horn, which together will be the final corrupt empire -- the hybrid Empire of The Beast. Every empire and nation must operate a fiscal system. This Whore has ideologically seduced and bank-rolled every one of them since The Babylonian Empire. Even so, there must be a financial and political center located somewhere, so both explanations of who The Whore is, and where the seven mountains are, have merit. They are not mutually exclusive interpretations, but actually work together.

G. The Rise of AntiChrist:

The <u>seven kings (heads)</u> are representative of the heads of governments that have held power over a major period of time <u>in history</u> before AntiChrist comes on the scene. He is the eighth, and rises to prominence from among the seven during the seven year Tribulation period of The Ten Days of Awe. Notice he is considered one of them by orientation. In other words, the former ideological and philosophical forms of these governments definitely will provide him with the background clout and mechanism for his debut onto the world scene.

But <u>ten concurrent world leaders (horns)</u> provide <u>the immediate end-time scene</u>. AntiChrist may be a well-placed, well-liked, and well-respected leader who rises to the top because of them. He is not specifically one of these ten horns, but sprouts from one head to take power <u>along with them</u>. His ambitions allow him to particularly usurp the representative power of three horns, but he does not totally destroy them. They still exist. (I will explain this more in a moment.) When he reaches the pinnacle of his influence, he continues in his position and authority for a short time of seven years (The Tribulation 70th Week.) Then he is removed at the return of Christ, and is cast alive into The Lake of Fire along with his False Prophet.

G. Ten World Leaders:

The ten horns indicate there will be ten world leaders from the areas that were occupied by the former empires of the preceding Beasts, who appear to form the ideological and political body through which AntiChrist reaches his position. We must remember, The Roman Empire, the last empire which is not itself a definable Beast until it becomes the Lion's

THE FALL OF THE WHORE, BABYLON

mouth and iron teeth of the fourth hybrid Beast Empire, is represented by the two legs and feet of Nebuchadnezzar's image. <u>Both these legs</u> are described as having feet and toes of iron mixed with clay, meaning they have administrative diversity. The legs of the image therefore are two identifiable regions of geographical, political, and ideological diversities, arising from a common origin. The legs and feet are similar in appearance, but are also mirror opposites, just like the two legs and feet of a person appear to be the same, but are in fact opposites. They form <u>a matched opposing pair</u>. So these ten leaders are from both legs and feet, but their philosophy arises pretty much from the same root, indicating some of them may consider themselves democratic secular humanists ideologically (Greek and Roman influence), but are also sympathetic toward the legitimacy of other political/religious ideologies; and some could be Muslim, Marxist, or totalitarian in orientation (Babylonian and Medio-Persian influence). None will bill themselves publicly as being 'Christian' by the time AntiChrist arises on the scene. They certainly would not want to 'lose their heads!'

In identifying The European Union as the political body from which AntiChrist arises, some feel the number of membership nations must be reduced back to ten. This is not necessary, because The European Union has a ruling parliamentary body which operates <u>similar</u>ly to the Security Council of the United Nations. This representative body speaks and acts on behalf of all member European Union nations. It is not difficult therefore to understand how <u>ten horns</u>, plus <u>the Little Horn</u>, may arise from within this international body, regardless of the number of member nations there are.

The ten horns are given power <u>along with The Beast</u> for one hour according to Revelation 17:12. *"And the ten horns which thou sawest are ten kings, which have received no kingdom as yet; but receive power as kings one hour with the beast."* In other words, <u>all eleven leaders</u> operate together <u>as equals</u> as the representative ruling council within The European Union -- for a short time -- one hour. Whether this hour is literal, or prophetically figurative, is somewhat unclear. I would tend toward giving this hour a prophetic numerical time-value translated into days. One prophetic year for a day. Each prophetic year has 360 days. Each day has 24 hours. So 360 divided by 24 = 15 prophetic days for each prophetic hour. That's half a month. These ten representative international leaders have equal power along with <u>one other representative</u> for approximately 15 days.

Then something momentous occurs. <u>This other member</u>, who turns out to be the Little Horn, somehow manages to consolidate all the power of the council into his own hands. He becomes the undisputed Leader within

The Final Schedule Revealed

this ruling body. In the course of this one-man take-over, the other ten give him their support. But this does not occur without some controversy. In order to consolidate his position, he must have everyone on-side. But three leaders (horns) are not so sure his power-grab is necessary. However, he manages to override the stance of these three. They are uprooted. They may give their support reluctantly, or with hesitation, but are non-the-less coerced into a unanimous position to be on-side, so that he usurps their wishes (they are out-voted), and he becomes the predominant leader over the ruling council. The three still exist, (he may have to put up with their presence because they were originally appointed by due process into their positions, so constitutionally cannot be removed), but he makes certain they hold no major portfolio of power within the council. The other seven may simply hand over their allegiance and support willingly. He accomplishes this feat so slickly, that when the *"hour"* of equal power is up, he is in absolute control. Such a consolidation of power is not necessarily outlandish. Some coups have taken place in less time!

<u>How do we know all ten horns still exist</u> even after AntiChrist's uprooting' of three of them? [175]<u>The ten of them</u> hate The Whore, and they all make war against The Lamb. [176]This war against The Lamb is The Battle of The Great Day of God Almighty, the closing skirmish of The Battle of Armageddon, according to the sixth Vial. It is obvious then, that they all ten still hold on to their leadership, <u>particularly within their own nations</u>, right up until Christ returns. So because these leaders ultimately do go along with the AntiChrist in making war against The Lamb, <u>they all still exist</u>. All these leaders and nations take an active part in AntiChrist's persecution of The Tribulation Saints, so are against Christ, and they remain in the anti-

---

[175] Revelation 17: 12-14. "And the ten horns which thou sawest are ten kings, which have received no kingdom as yet; but receive power as kings one hour with the beast. These have one mind, and shall give their power and strength unto the beast. These shall make war with the Lamb, and the Lamb shall overcome them,...."
Revelation 17: 16-17. "And the ten horns which thou sawest upon the Beast, these shall hate the whore, and shall make her desolate, and naked, and shall eat her flesh, and burn her with fire, For God hath put in their hearts to fulfill his will, and to agree, and give their kingdom unto the beast, until the words of God shall be fulfilled."
[176] Revelation 16: 13-14. "And I saw three unclean spirits like frogs come out of the mouth of the dragon, and out of the mouth of the beast, and out of the mouth of the false prophet. For they are the spirits of devils, working miracles, which go forth unto the kings of the earth and of the whole world, to gather them to the battle of that great day of God Almighty."

THE FALL OF THE WHORE, BABYLON

Christian camp right up to the end of The Battle of Armageddon, until they literally fight against Christ Himself. For this reason, I believe some of these leaders may be Islamic, and some humanistically oriented. They are obviously deceived by AntiChrist at any rate, be they either from the Western, or from the Eastern ideological spectrum, and all are from the geographical areas of the former empires. Ultimately, Jesus, the Messiah, will overcome them all, including AntiChrist.

However, The Beast's methods as orchestrated by the False Prophet fall into a disputable position as far as these ten horns are concerned. Although they give AntiChrist their allegiance, and do so from a stance of unanimity, either willingly or coerced, something happens to partially change their thinking regarding his methodology, and this becomes evident in their attitude toward the Whore.

I. The Woman sits upon The Waters:

The place where the woman sits is described as [177]'waters,' indicating the global vastness of her influence. [178]She continues to spread her fornications throughout many peoples, multitudes, nations, and tongues. In this regard, she does resemble **the resource network that The False Prophet draws upon to facilitate promotion of the AntiChrist**. She may represent the flow of the resources, but she does not represent The False Prophet himself. [179]Her adornment of gold, precious stones, and pearls, indicates her stock of wealth, and speaks of the influence of her economy in the setup of the pagan idolatrous worship-system of the super-computer image, which likely uses gold, silver, and precious stone circuitry to operate. She is the source of the provision of the finances necessary to build and operate this system world-wide. She will accommodate the false

---

[177] Revelation 17:1b. "...I will show unto thee the judgment of the great whore that sitteth upon many waters."

[178] Revelation 17:2. "With whom the kings of the earth have committed fornication, and the inhabitants of the earth have been made drunk with the wine of her fornication."
Revelation 18:3. For all nations have drunk of the wine of the wrath of her fornication, and the kings of the earth have committed fornication with her, and the merchants of the earth are waxed rich through the abundance of her delicacies.

[179] Revelation 17:4-5. " And the woman was arrayed in purple and scarlet color, and decked with gold and precious stones and pearls, having a golden cup in her hand full of abominations and filthiness of her fornication: And upon her forehead was a name written, MYSTERY, BABYLON THE GREAT, THE MOTHER OF HARLOTS AND ABOMINATIONS OF THE EARTH."

worship (spiritual fornication) of AntiChrist by providing the necessary monetary and material resources for the False Prophet to use. This system certainly will affect everyone world-wide of all nations, peoples, and tongues, and will seek to seduce multitudes astray to their doom. So just as she has bank-rolled all the former empires, she will bank-roll the empire and influence of the fourth Beast and the Little Horn as well.

But all is not clear sailing for this Whore. <u>The ten horns of the fourth Beast Empire hate The Whore</u>. Notice <u>Scripture does not say the Little Horn hates The Whore</u>, just the ten horns. So <u>AntiChrist's regime develops a flaw</u>. These leaders, who apparently are in the AntiChrist's camp ideologically, *"shall hate the whore, and shall make her desolate, and naked, and shall eat her flesh, and burn her with fire."* Revelation 17:16. But they still remain firmly within AntiChrist's camp at the same time. As soon as they realize that The False Prophet's system is beginning to undermine their own sovereignty and ability to operate with impunity within their own countries, they recoil, and they react. Verse 17. *"For God hath put in their hearts to fulfill his will, and to agree, and give their kingdom unto the beast, until the words of God shall be fulfilled."* Therefore, even though they give their support to AntiChrist, they begin to realize the implications of the repressive economic pagan base that undergirds the mechanism through which he works, and they begin to withdraw their support <u>for the system. So they hate The Whore for providing the means by which The False Prophet is able to set up AntiChrist's absolute control system, and they plot to dismantle and destroy her!</u>

The woman is a whore, meaning she has committed seductive fornication with many, none of whom she is under covenant of marriage to. In fact, whoredom is her intended occupation. She is a prostitute. She therefore ought not to be having <u>any</u> intimate relations with The False Prophet, AntiChrist, or the ten horns, or any of the world's nations. She prostitutes herself because she is gain, power, and wealth. The ten horns *'devour her,'* meaning they oppose her to the point of chewing her up to annihilation. They burn her with fire. Thus, the resulting Battle of Armageddon where it appears there is nuclear exchange. This exchange literally burns the network of resources required to keep the computerized operating systems of the international economic order operational. Without the back-up resources (the Whore), the system itself is threatened with collapse.

The war is pretty bizarre. These ten horns support AntiChrist's ideologies and policies, but apparently not The False Prophet's tactics that are supported by the resource system called The Whore. So they set out to destroy The Whore. Although the ten horns are against The Lamb also,

THE FALL OF THE WHORE, BABYLON

and certainly as such, are against Israel and The Tribulation Saints, they do not agree with the methods emerging. The result will be a house divided against itself, and it will be brought down, but not only from within. The LORD Himself does not allow this scenario to develop completely, because mankind ultimately would be destroyed in the process. Christ returns, and brings an end to the whole mess.

IV. The Crack in AntiChrist's Armor:

Although the ten horns remain in AntiChrist's camp, there is a crack in his armor. This crack allows The King of the South, and The King of the North *'to push at him,'* and to come against him with ships and chariots, and the military. See Daniel 11:40-45. "And <u>at the time of the end</u> shall <u>the king of the south</u> *push at him: and the* <u>king of the north</u> *shall come against him like a whirlwind, with chariots, and with horsemen, and with many ships; and he shall enter into the countries, and shall overflow and pass over.* (They come against AntiChrist, but he overpowers them.) Verse 41. *"He shall enter also into the glorious land, and many countries shall be overthrown; but these shall escape out of his hand, even Edom, and Moab, and the chief of the children of Ammon.* Verse 42. *He shall stretch forth his hand also upon the countries: and the land of Egypt shall not escape.* Verse 43. *But he shall have power over the treasures of gold and of silver, and over all the precious things of Egypt: and the Libyans and the Ethiopians shall be at his steps.* Verse 44. *But tidings out of the east and out of the north shall trouble him: therefore he shall go forth with great fury to destroy and utterly to make away many.* Verse 45. *And he shall plant the tabernacles of his palace between the seas in the glorious holy mountain: yet he shall come to his end, and none shall help him."* KJV.

The King of the South, Egypt, along with Ethiopia and The King of the North (the Russian alliance) seize the opportunity to come against AntiChrist and his forces at the time of the end. Jordan sides with the West, and Israel's government is whisked away for protection by the wings of The Eagle, to a rock fortress within Jordan, probably Petra. Thus we observe the beginnings of the battle-lines of The Battle of Armageddon.

If everyone was securely in AntiChrist's camp, there would be no earthly reason to assemble for battle! But there will be several sides and motivations to this war. There will be forces pro-AntiChrist, and forces against. There will be forces pro-False Prophet, and forces against him. There will be forces against the misuse of the world's economic and technological resources (The Whore) as well. Then there will be forces which actually wish to protect Israel and reverse the division of The Land of Covenant. And almost all of them will be against Christ, except Israel, who by this juncture will be crying out to God for deliverance, and to send

Messiah. So we see the development of an intricate web of hostilities, where undercurrents of ideologies and loyalties begin to wear down the world's nations into fragile affiliations and deceptions. No one will truly trust anyone else. The resulting war will be fought as much brother against brother, the Whore, AntiChrist, the False Prophet, and Israel, as it will ultimately be fought against Christ.

Israel will become front and center in this war. Along with the fact that many nations begin to resent AntiChrist's coerced worship-system, (his *'strange god'* that he will promote in most *'strongholds,'*) <u>Israel's borders (the Land-rights of The Covenant) will be used as the provocation</u> to entice them all into The Middle East, <u>as AntiChrist manages to divide up The Land, according to Daniel 11:39</u>. But unlike the situation that took place at The Gog-Magog Battle, he may actually pull-off a greater subversion of The Covenant! *'Thus shall he do in the most strongholds with a strange god, whom he shall acknowledge and increase with glory: and he shall cause them to rule over many, <u>and he shall divide the land for gain</u>."* Is this an attempt at the expansion of the Palestinian Islamic State, as one of the 'stages' in annihilating Israel completely? Possibly. If so, AntiChrist is using the Palestinian situation to reach his own ends, and to entrench the strange-god worship of himself and his image, subjugating many. It would appear he is attempting to carve out a geographical national area <u>for himself</u>, trampling on all vestiges of Israel, <u>thus destroying Israel as a nation for good</u>. After all, he is the antithesis of Christ, and Satan would prefer to take over The Messianic Heritage (The Covenant and Land,) and become the world ruler whose seat of government is Jerusalem and The Temple on Mount Zion. <u>For Satan, this would be the ultimate victory over Jesus Christ -- over God Himself. Israel will be used as the bait</u>. The only 'friends' Israel may have on earth will be The United States and her allies, and possibly Jordan. But AntiChrist is already a defeated foe, only he doesn't realize it yet.

Satan, AntiChrist, The False Prophet, The Whore, and all who support them, are totally defeated. Do the plagues of God's wrath defeat them? No, but they certainly make waging war difficult! Is their defeat ideological? No. Is their defeat simply because of economic collapse? No. Do the armies of the nations friendly to Israel defeat them? No! None of these things deter AntiChrist from his quest for absolute domination and control.

If deliverance depended solely on all these factors, even collectively, they would not be enough to defeat the enemy. Why? Because the real battle is not specifically for world domination politically, economically, or even ideologically. <u>The real battle is for the eternal souls of mankind, and to thwart the purposes and promises of God</u>. The real war is between the

THE FALL OF THE WHORE, BABYLON

forces of darkness and the Kingdom of Light. This is where the battle has always been waged since Lucifer fell. <u>The real issue is who is in control, not just of earth,</u> <u>but of Heaven as well.</u> Who sits on The Glorious Throne?

V. The Fall of Babylon:

Before we deal with what becomes of AntiChrist, The False Prophet, and their henchmen, we need to examine what takes place specifically in regard to The Whore. The downfall of Babylon, the system of corruption represented by The Whore, will take place at the end of the Tribulation, [180]when the ten horns do the LORD's bidding against The Whore, and Christ Himself ultimately brings the corrupt system to an end. Along with her demise, AntiChrist's hold on the world will crumble.

Revelation Chapter 18 goes into more detail regarding the Fall of Babylon. Another powerful angel comes from Heaven to John, and the earth is illumined with his glory. Revelation 18:2. *"And he cried mightly with a strong voice, saying, Babylon the great is fallen, is fallen, and is become the habitation of devils, and the hold of every foul spirit, and a cage of every unclean and hateful bird. Verse 3. For all nations have drunk of the wine of the wrath of her fornication, and the kings of the earth have committed fornication with her, and the merchants of the earth are waxed rich through the abundance of her delicacies."* This speaks of the fact that Babylon is not just a location, but a world system of financial influence and economics. The root of this corrupt economic system arose out of The Babylonian Empire, with the fiscal policies originating from the ancient city of Babylon. All nations of the whole earth have partaken with her in her corruption and fornication. The ancient city of Babylon was destroyed, but Saddam Hussein began rebuilding the site into a modern facility, so it may again briefly become a financial and cultural center with world influence, and it will ultimately be destroyed, never to be inhabited by man again. But the economic system we currently operate under in world-trade and control came from Babylon originally. This corrupt system, which AntiChrist will build upon for his own ends, will be destroyed.

Revelation 18:4. *"And I heard another voice from heaven, saying, Come out of her, my people, that ye be not partakers of her sins, and that ye receive not of her plagues. Verse 5. For her sins have reached unto heaven, and God hath remembered her iniquities. Verse 6. Reward her even as she rewarded you, and double unto her double according to her works: in the cup which she hath filled fill to her double."* These verses incorporate flash-back to the time of the Rapture of the Church. The Babylonian-based world system has corrupted

---

[180] Revelation 17:16-17.

the entire world long enough. God is going to pour out His wrath on her <u>double</u> for all her iniquities. But before He does, He calls out His people so they will not have to endure the worst of Babylon's sins that take place under AntiChrist, or endure the plagues that come on the earth as a result of her fornications. The righteous are removed before The Ten Days of Awe begin.

Verse 7. *"How much she hath glorified herself, and lived deliciously, so much torment and sorrow give her: for she saith in her heart, I sit a queen, and am no widow, and shall see no sorrow. Verse 8. Therefore shall her plagues come in one day, death, and mourning, and famine; and she shall be utterly burned with fire: for strong is the Lord God who judgeth her. Verse 9. And the kings of the earth , who have committed fornication and lived deliciously with her, shall bewail her, and lament for her, when they shall see the smoke of her burning."* The rest of the chapter describes the destruction of Babylon, the ungodly world economic and cultural-pagan system that has been so corrupt. We have seen shades and warning of these verses in the attacks on The World Trade Center as the prophetic spiral has already gone around at least once in fulfillment of these verses. But this prophecy will be totally fulfilled at the end of The Days of Awe.

So let's summarize and clarify the physical city location of The Whore who is to be destroyed. We must realize it is possible to define Babylon as the re-built city of Babylon in Iraq. This city indeed has been rebuilt partially already by Saddam Hussein, and it still may become a nerve-center for world economics and the spread of ideologies, and of course it will be destroyed again. So yes, these verses <u>will apply</u> to the actual revived city of Babylon. But the center of world economics and international politics, wherever that may be headquartered, is also <u>a type</u> of the Whore of Babylon. Thus, as far as an actual city is concerned, as already mentioned, several cities of the world, including New York, have already filled this position in our time. New York, being the location of The World Trade Center, as well as the location of the headquarters of The United Nations, has been the latest most celebrated example. But at least two prominent locations will take up this identity, one of which will certainly be the revived city of Babylon itself for a period of time during the Tribulation segment of The Days of Awe.

Ultimately, when the seat of AntiChrist's governance and surveillance, and total control of all buying and selling through The Mark of The Beast becomes centered in Jerusalem, even Jerusalem will take on the identifiable location of where The Whore sits, because Jerusalem will be the city from which AntiChrist will set about to rule over the nations of the earth through coercion. It is here, during The Battle of Armageddon, with all

THE FALL OF THE WHORE, BABYLON

the nations gathered, that Christ will appear, and terminate the corruption of The Whore, and end the careers of AntiChrist and The False Prophet, pouring out His wrath upon them.

So wherever the control of world economics, pagan religious practice, and political policy stems from, this city can be prophetically referred to as the seat of The Whore, and will be judged accordingly. The actual physical Babylon being built now in Iraq may play a small part in showing the object lesson of judgment to the world, by becoming once again totally desolate forever according to Revelation 18:21-23. *"And a mighty angel took up a stone like a great millstone, and cast it into the sea, saying, thus with violence shall that great city Babylon be thrown down, and shall be found no more at all. Verse 22. And the voice of harpers, and musicians, and of pipers, and trumpeters, shall be heard no more at all in thee; and no craftsman, of whatsoever craft he be, shall be found any more in thee; and the sound of a millstone shall be heard no more at all in thee; Verse 23. And the light of a candle shall shine no more at all in thee; and the voice of the bridegroom and of the bride shall be heard no more at all in thee: for thy merchants were the great men of the earth; for by thy sorceries were all nations deceived."* The destruction of this city of Babylon will be complete and permanent.

But when we continue reading, we find that verse 24 has overtones of Jerusalem representing the false religious, repressive political, and corrupt economic system of The Whore, because it says, *"And in her was found the blood of prophets, and of saints, and of all that were slain upon the earth."* It is from Jerusalem the AntiChrist will exile Israel's government, will attempt to control the souls of men, will orchestrate his persecution of The Tribulation Saints, and will give the order to kill many righteous people on the earth. It is also from Jerusalem that the blood of the prophets of old still speak. So Babylon, the system, will definitely fall, and all cities that take up the administrative center for The Whore's Babylonian system will be judged.

But unlike the revived city of Babylon which will never again be inhabited following Armageddon, Jerusalem will survive and become glorious under the rule and reign of Jesus Christ.

CHAPTER 24
THE BRIDE, ISRAEL, AND THE TIMES AND SEASONS

In Revelation chapter 19, John records his glimpse of the celebrations taking place in Heaven around The Throne. Verses 1-3 state: *"And after these things, I heard a great voice of much people in heaven, saying, Alleluia, Salvation, and glory, and honor; and power, unto the Lord our God: Verse 2. For true and righteous are his judgments; for he hath judged the great whore, which did corrupt the earth with her fornication, and hath avenged the blood of his servants at her hand. Verse 3. And again they said, Alleluia, And her smoke rose up for ever and ever. Verse 4. And the four and twenty elders and the four beasts fell down and worshiped God that sat on the throne, saying, Amen; Alleluia. Verse 5. And a voice came out of the throne, saying, Praise our God, all ye his servants, and ye that fear him, both small and great."* KJV.

After the destruction of The Whore on earth, those gathered around The Throne in Heaven rejoice, giving praise and honor unto the LORD because of His awesome power and deliverance. These acknowledge the fact that God has brought about due justice against the corrupt world system that has held men hostage and in bondage throughout the centuries, and has committed atrocities and murders against the righteous.

Remember the saints who stand before the Throne in Revelation chapter 7? These were martyrs for the sake of Christ during the Tribulation. Also, recall that the Church Age martyrs of the Fifth Seal of Revelation chapter 6, asked when God would avenge their blood on those who dwell on the earth. In these verses in Revelation chapter 19, all of those who were martyred from both eras, stand before The Throne in Heaven. With the unfolding of The Days of Awe judgments, their desire for justice is brought to fulfillment. Their blood is avenged, and they finally are able to have the satisfaction that God's timing and ways are just, and their tormentors have been dealt with. They are most grateful, and offer worship and praise to God for His power and justice. The twenty-four Elders and the four Cherubim who surround The Throne, bow down in agreement, saying, "Amen; Allelujah!"

Then we are given a flash-back.

What has been taking place in Heaven while The Days of Awe judgment's have been meted out on those who remain on the earth? Not only have the raptured saints been protected and hidden from God's wrath, but they have been gainfully involved as well. Verses 6-10 of

The Final Schedule Revealed

Revelation chapter 19 give us a glimpse into their heavenly activities. Verse 6. *"And I heard as it were the voice of a great multitude, and as the voice of many waters, and as the voice of mighty thunderings, saying, Alleluia, for the Lord God omnipotent reigneth.* Verse 7. *Let us be glad and rejoice, and give honor to him: for the marriage of the Lamb is come, and his wife hath made herself ready.* Verse 8. *And to her was granted that she should be arrayed in fine linen, clean and white: for the fine linen is the righteousness of saints.* Verse 9. *And he saith unto me, Write, Blessed are they which are called unto the marriage supper of the Lamb. And he saith unto me, These are the true sayings of God.* Verse 10. *And I fell at his feet to worship him. And he saith unto me, See thou do it not: I am thy fellow servant, and of thy brethren that have the testimony of Jesus: worship God: for the testimony of Jesus is the spirit of prophecy."* KJV. This is Rosh HaShanah fulfilled in Heaven! The Church, The Bride of Christ, stands in great honor with her Bridegroom, clothed in fine white linen, representing the righteousness of the saints. She is worthy, and has made herself ready according to the prompting voice and assistance of the Holy Spirit.

Notice several important prophetic observations John makes us aware of regarding the marriage of Christ and the Church. John is in awe of the proceedings taking place surrounding The Throne, which involve the multitudes who are gathered, and who are thunderously, as the *"voice of many waters,"* giving honor, worship, and praise to God, the omnipotent sovereign Ruler. Why are these gathered? *"The marriage of the Lamb is come, and his wife hath made herself ready."* John is told by the angel who is showing him these things, to write, *"Blessed are they which are called unto the marriage supper of the Lamb."* Who are those <u>called</u> unto the Marriage Supper of The Lamb? The righteous. <u>The Tzadikim who are called at Rosh HaShanah.</u> These are indeed blessed, because they are already prepared, having repented and accepted the Atonement offered for their sin, and have maintained righteousness through the sustaining power and anointing of the Holy Spirit. They are the Bride!

John is told to note, *"These are the true sayings of God."* Why would he specifically be told what must be quite obvious already? The truth of what is taking place is being underlined, not just for John, but so that <u>what he is to record</u> is emphasized. <u>What is told him is the true Word of God Himself, and actually will take place</u>! John is overwhelmed at what he sees and hears, and falls at the feet of the angel that is showing him these things. The angel's response is most intriguing, because first of all, he adamantly instructs John not to worship him, because he is a fellow-servant doing God's will. *"Worship God."*

Then the angel states, verse 10 of Revelation 19, *"the testimony of Jesus is the spirit of prophecy."* In other words, Jesus' <u>testimony</u>, the <u>Shitre Erusin</u>

THE BRIDE, ISRAEL, AND THE TIMES AND SEASONS

of betrothal, which is legally binding regarding what He has promised, will come to pass exactly as He has stated both through the written Law and Prophets, and His verbal Word. His promised Word to His Betrothed Bride will become fulfilled wedded reality! We know all that the LORD has said will come to pass, so this statement does indicate the LORD's sovereign prophetic position. He is Prophet, Priest, and KING. As such, all prophecy will be fulfilled according to His Word. But this statement specifically states, *"the testimony of Jesus is the spirit of prophecy."* Most Jews do not believe Jesus is the Emanuel, God incarnate in human flesh. They do not yet accept Him as LORD, absolutely equal with, therefore God Himself incarnate in human flesh. This statement proclaims the fact that Jesus is God, because His testimony is the unalterable prophetic Word. That is indeed a revelation of who Jesus is! Jesus is LORD! Also, in context with the Marriage Supper of The Lamb, this statement proves Jesus is The Lamb. Therefore, since His testimony is not only the fulfillment, but the essence of prophecy, He is the Prophet, Priest, and KING, and He is the Bridegroom.

One must recall the Jewish marriage traditions to understand the full import of what is being stated here. When a Jewish young man betroths to himself a bride, she is sanctified, set apart, unto him only. He is also set apart only unto her. She drinks the wine which he has provided, sealing the betrothal. He pays the bride-price, and gives her both written documentation as well as his verbal word, that all he promises will in fact come to pass. In other words, all that he claims to be, and all that He has said He will do, is being set on the line for her. This is the Shitre Erusin. In our very real relationship with Jesus Christ, this is the acid test that *"The testimony of Jesus is the spirit of prophecy."* This testimony is therefore not only about Him and His Bride, but includes everything He has stated will occur in the unfolding fulfillment of His Prophetic Word, revealing the Times and Seasons that the Bride must also be aware of, indicating to her when He will return for her. So, the Shitre Erusin of Jesus incorporates all Prophecy!

Along with his Father's blessing, he provides her with all she needs to prepare herself for their wedding. All the provision is therefore made by the groom. Jesus has provided all that is necessary for His Bride to be prepared. He offered the wine, His shed blood, and payed the bride-price by laying down His own life, and has provided the robes of righteousness, and has given His prophetic Word. All the Bride must do is partake of the wine in order to be set apart, sanctified only unto Him. She is cleansed by His blood and made pure. She has made herself ready by partaking of salvation, putting on the robes of righteousness He has provided, and by living a life of holiness, lead by the Holy Spirit, sanctified, set-apart, knowing she is betrothed, and that he will return in great wedding procession to call her unto Himself.

She has <u>been chosen, and will be called</u> to the marriage. When a groom takes his bride, he comes for her with much fanfare of trumpets, pomp and ceremony, and with much shouting. She does not know for sure what day, or hour of the day he will come, so she must be ready at all times for him to arrive. But, he does not come all the way to her home. Rather, <u>he calls out to her to come meet him</u>. She must be prepared to do so, dressed in the garments he has provided. The Bride of Christ, through the Bridegroom's provision of atonement at the cross, has made herself ready for when He will come for her. She wears the robes of righteousness He has provided. He will descend from Heaven with a great shout, and with the Archangel's voice, and with the sound of The Last Trump of Rosh HaShanah. He will receive His Bride, not at her place of residence on the earth, but will <u>call her out to be where He is</u>. She will be called to meet Him in The Clouds of Glory in the air, then He will take her in great ceremonial procession to His Father's House in Heaven. She will be thus honored and blessed. Then the Bride will be given her <u>ceremonial wedding garments</u>, pure and white, that the Bridegroom will provide specifically for the wedding, because she is worthy. All who are called (gathered unto) The Marriage Supper of The Lamb will be thus blessed.

1 Corinthians 15:51-52. *"Behold I show you a mystery; We shall not all sleep,* (die physically) *but we shall all be changed,* Verse 52. *In a moment, in the twinkling of an eye, at <u>the last trump</u>: for the trumpet shall sound, and the dead shall be raised incorruptible, and we shall be changed."* Paul mentions The Last Trump of Rosh HaShanah, Ha Teruah, the Trumpet Blast that will be sounded to raise the righteous dead to life, and change the living believer's mortal bodies to immortal, incorruptible bodies.

Paul states in 2 Thessalonians chapter 4:13-17. *"But I would not have you to be ignorant, brethren, concerning them which are asleep, that ye sorrow not, even as others which have no hope.* Verse 14. *For if we believe that Jesus died and rose again, even so them also which sleep in Jesus will God bring with him.* Verse 15. *For this we say unto you by the word of the Lord, that we which are alive and remain unto the coming of the Lord shall not prevent* (precede) *them which are asleep.* Verse 16. *For the Lord himself shall descend from heaven <u>with a shout</u>, <u>with the voice of the archangel</u>, and <u>with the trump of God</u>: and the dead in Christ shall rise first:* Verse 17. *Then we which are alive and remain shall be caught up together with them in the clouds, to meet the Lord in the air, and so shall we ever be with the Lord.* Verse 18. *Wherefore comfort one another with these words."* Then he continues on into chapter 5. Verse 1. *But of the times and the seasons,* brethren, ye have no need that I write unto you. Verse 2. For yourselves know perfectly that the day of the Lord so cometh as a thief in the night. Verse 3. For when they shall say, <u>Peace and Safety</u>; then sudden destruction cometh upon them, as travail upon a woman with child; and they shall not escape. Verse 4. <u>But ye, brethren, are not in darkness, that, that day should overtake you as a thief.</u> Verse 5. Ye are all the children of light, and the children of the day: we are not of the night, nor of darkness. Verse 6. Therefore let us not sleep, as do others; but let us watch and be sober. Verse 7. For they that sleep sleep in the night; and they that be drunken are drunken in the night. Verse 8. But let us, who are of the day, be sober, putting on the breastplate of faith and love; and for a helmut, the hope of salvation. Verse 8. <u>For God hath not appointed us to wrath</u>, but to obtain salvation by our Lord Jesus Christ, Verse 10. Who died for us, that whether we wake or sleep, we should live together with him." KJV. Underlining mine.

Since we are not appointed to wrath, we are to be concealed and protected from The Day of The LORD -- The Day of His judgments on those who dwell on the earth. The LORD will not stand for His chosen Bride to be exposed to the devastations that His wrath will produce. He is not angry with His own Bride! Rather He will protect her. This deliverance will take place on the Day in which He will come as a Thief in the night, when the world will not be expecting Him, when they will rather be concerned with "Peace and Safety!" The LORD will come for us in Shekinah Clouds of Glory. He will utter a shout of joy! Finally, He is able to come for His Bride! The Archangel's voice will also be heard, and the trumpet (Ha Teruah, The Last Trumpet Blast of Rosh HaShanah) will sound. In the twinkling of an eye, we who are still alive will experience a body-change from corruptible to incorruptible. The born-again Christians who have died throughout The Church Age will be resurrected first, then together we will be <u>caught up to meet the LORD in the air</u>. We will then be taken into The Father's House in Heaven for The Coronation-Wedding. Although we do not know the day or hour of His coming for us, we certainly should not be caught by absolute surprise, because we should be expecting Him, and be ready and excitedly waiting as a Bride, <u>prepared to be called</u>.

Who is this passage written to? Verse 15. "..<u>we which are alive and remain unto the coming of the Lord</u>." **That's us!** And notice what Paul says <u>to us</u> about <u>when to expect these events to occur</u>. According to I Thessalonians 5:1, we ought to know <u>the Times and the Seasons</u>, and <u>he states he really has no need to write to us about this timing</u>. The Shitre Erusin document is already in the Bride's possession! Jesus already has spelled it out! What does this mean? Firstly, Paul's letter is addressed to us, sent across the centuries to prepare us. Secondly, *"The testimony of Jesus is the spirit of* *prophecy,"* we ought to be aware of the Times and the Seasons taking place in the world around us in relation to The Prophetic Time-Table.

At first glance Paul seems to be contradicting what Jesus stated before He ascended from The Mount of Olives. *"It is not for you to know the times or the seasons, which the Father hath in his own power."* Acts 1: 7. Jesus was addressing the disciples gathered with Him on The Mount of Olives before He ascended, so His remarks were specific to them -- for their time. But Paul states to us who are alive when Christ returns, *"But of the times and the seasons, brethren, ye have no need that I write unto you..."* What has changed?

The disciples of the early Church would not recognize the Times and the Seasons which would fulfill these prophecies, because the prophecies would not unfold within their life-time. But we do need to know, and have no excuse not to know, because the schedule leading up to the Appointed Time of Christ's return should now become understandable, because the pre-scheduled Fall Appointments with mankind (His Convocations, Fall Feasts) are now about to unfold. Therefore we have no excuse to say we are not aware of the Times and Seasons that we are living in. Although these Appointed Times and Seasons are in the Father's power, we are now at the point in His scheduled program of dealing with mankind, and in the wedding preparations, when we should be fully aware that the very next Appointment is the Rapture of The Church. Rosh HaShanah! How can we know that? By being awake, and understanding the very real prophetic fulfillments that are taking place around us, especially in regard to Israel. The Days of Awe are just around the corner, so Rosh HaShanah of necessity must take place soon! Certainly we will not be able to know the day or hour, just as the Jewish bride does not know the day or hour of when her bridegroom will come for her, but we can, and must, know the Times and the Seasons.

CHAPTER 25
THE TIMES AND SEASONS EXPLAINED IN THE PSALMS

According to JR Church and Gary Stearman of Prophecy In The News, the Psalms, beginning with Psalm 48, contain references to prophecies that have been fulfilled <u>within each year since Israel became a Nation in 1948</u>. Many of the Psalms hark all the way back to Creation, then progress forward through the main events of how God has dealt with mankind, and especially with the Israeli people. Prophecy In The News is offering a book on this subject which I have not as yet had opportunity to read, but I decided to attempt to check into this postulation for myself.

My observation is that they indeed are onto something of prophetic significance revealed in the Psalms. The keys to spotting the prophecies lie within the metaphorical symbolisms that the Psalmist(s) draw upon, mostly from creation and the beauty of the natural world. These symbols, coupled with the celebrations, are not unique to The Psalms, but are able to be interpreted from their symbolic application as revealed in the rest of Scripture. So when we travel through the Psalms of Ascent, we realize they are not only songs of worship, praise, encouragement, and admonishment, but have been arranged in <u>prophetic order</u>, revealing the gradual unfolding of the prophetic spiral. In fact, each Psalm is not an entity only unto itself, but rather is part of a prophetic whole, revealing The Plan of The Ages, unfolding in <u>the exact spiral order</u> as the messages given by the Prophets, as stated within Jesus' Olivet Discourse, and as portrayed through The books of Daniel and Revelation. Once we realize this phenomenon, the Psalms takes on an added dimension.

One may wonder if it is possible to discern prophecies which will likely be fulfilled within a certain year, or perhaps in the next, etc. <u>We must approach such an exercise with a great deal of caution</u>, because one cannot necessarily be exact or dogmatic in relating to specific years regarding prophecies not yet fulfilled. Each Psalm contains historical, current, and future prophecies beyond the year in which we live. Also, many prophecies, as we have already discovered, have multiple applications, or may unfold over a period of several, or even many, years. However, we certainly are able to identify the major prophecies which are <u>in the works to be fulfilled</u> according to the <u>Times and the Seasons</u> we live in.

With this in mind, let's take a brief look at Psalms 103 through 105, because these numerically coincide with our current time-frame in

The Final Schedule Revealed

calendar years. According to Gary Stearman and JR Church, Psalms 103 and 104 contain a major theme, *"Bless The LORD,"* and as such, they are seamlessly tied together within the spiral of prophecy, addressing the fact that the soul is to *"Bless The LORD,"* pointing out His wondrous works within Creation, in our world, and in our daily lives. The LORD's awesome character is most evident in these Psalms, and should encourage each of us to come into His presence with worship and praise, to bless Him, because He indeed is worthy! For us, The Bride, these Psalms describe our awesome Bridegroom in His majesty, power, and sovereignty. That alone should make these Psalms significant! But Psalm 105 shifts dramatically to a decidedly different prophetic focus.

I. Psalm 103:

Psalm 103 begins by pointing out the awesome fact that the LORD meets our every need. Then beginning with verse 6, we are reminded that the LORD is The Righteous Judge, particularly in regard to the oppressed. What Nation is under great oppression from her neighbors, and from those who dwell within her borders? Israel! We are taken back to the fact that His ways were made known unto Moses, and His *"acts unto the children of Israel."* Verse 7. This is a reference to The Law of Moses, and The Prophets (testimonies of God's intervention on behalf of Israel and all nations,) which have been, are, and will be brought to fulfillment through the grace, mercy, and justice of Jesus Christ. The LORD's great love, mercy, and grace are most evident in this Age of Grace in which we live, and certainly have been in evidence among the nations since Israel has again become a Nation.

A. A Prophetic Teshuvah Warning:

Verse 8 of Psalm 103 highlights a prophetic invitation and warning. I believe this message is indeed going out into the world by the Holy Spirit's anointing upon the Church, calling all to take heed. What is this warning? It is important to repent NOW, because The Age of Grace will not last forever! *"The LORD is merciful and gracious, slow to anger, and plenteous in mercy.* Verse 9. *He will not always chide:* neither will he keep his anger for ever.*"* The patience, grace, and mercy of the LORD is certainly evident as His disciplinary warnings (chiding) have been proclaimed by His Spirit through the Church. But this Age will soon come to an end, and Elul Teshuvah, the Age of Grace calling all to repent and return to God, will be over, because he *"will not keep* (hold back) *his anger for ever."* Verse 10 states that up to this point, *"He has not dealt with us after our sins; nor rewarded us after our iniquities.* Verse 11. *For as the heaven is high above the earth, so great is his mercy toward them that fear him.* Verse 12. *As far as the east is from the west, so far hath he removed our transgressions from us.* Verse 13. *Like as a father pitieth his children, so the LORD pitieth them that fear him.* Verse 14. *For he knoweth our frame; he remembereth that we are dust."* The grace and mercy of the LORD are evident throughout The Church Age as the invitation to come to Him for forgiveness has gone forth. He certainly has not treated us according to our sins, but has offered mercy and forgiveness.

But there is urgency to this message. Verse 15. *"As for man, his days are as grass; as a flower of the field, so he flourisheth."* Verse 16. *For the wind passeth over it, and it is gone; and the place thereof shall know it no more."* Wind, in Scripture, often is used in reference to the Holy Spirit. The Wind of the Holy Spirit is blowing over the fields that are ready to harvest during this Day of Grace. But soon the anointing and wooing of this Wind will pass. The life of a man is also soon gone, and the memory of who he was in this world is quickly forgotten. Man's life is short, but so too is the time left for the Wind of the Holy Spirit to blow freely to draw men to Christ! <u>The LORD will not withhold His anger forever</u>! Because this is a warning, we know these verses refer to the imminent drawing to a close of The Age of Grace. If we were to use the premise that each Psalm in this series does contain at least one or more prophecy(s) as related to each year of fulfillment, these verses in Psalm 103, for example, do appear to indicate the year 2003 was still within The Age of Grace. And of course we know this is true, because The Church is still here! But, because the wrath of the LORD will not be withheld forever, how many more years of His grace and mercy are there remaining?

B. His Covenant, and His Commandments:

A transitional prophetic message occurs within Psalm 103. When this transition is to be brought to completion is as yet unclear. However, the warning signs regarding what is soon to come to pass are evident.

Verse 17 begins the shift, pointing to an eternal attribute of the LORD. *"But the mercy of the LORD is from everlasting to everlasting..."* Although His mercy is everlasting, this verse continues, *"... upon them that fear him, and his righteousness unto children's children;* Verse 18. <u>*to such as keep his covenant*</u>, *and* <u>*to those that remember his commandments to do them*</u>*."* Underlining mine. These verses are prophetically transitional, and are qualified!

Although the current Age of Grace is a dispensation during which the Holy Spirit has full wooing ability to draw mankind's hearts to the LORD by empowering The Church to take the Gospel to every creature, there is coming a Day when the everlasting mercy of God will take on an application toward a more specific group. Verses 17 and 18 appear to indicate that at that time, only those who <u>fear the LORD</u> and <u>keep His Covenant</u> and <u>His Commandments</u> will taste of His everlasting mercy! Certainly those who accept Jesus as LORD and Savior do fear the LORD, and keep The New Covenant through The Blood of The Lamb, and fulfill all The Law and The Prophets through Christ, so these verses <u>definitely apply</u> to Church Age believers.

<u>But there is a further fulfillment in the spiral</u>. Why are The Commandments and The Covenant mentioned, since The Age of Grace does not fall under the legalism of The Mosaic Law? And what Covenant is being ultimately referred to, since verse 18 actually <u>does not state</u> The <u>New</u> Covenant? <u>Is</u> this verse then ultimately referring to The New Covenant? When indeed is this prophetic word to take place, and why is the everlasting mercy of the LORD thus qualified?

Verse 17 begins to narrow down prophetically <u>the identity</u> of who will keep His Covenant and His Commandments. *"His righteousness will be unto children's children."* Who are these?

C. Times and Seasons of Transition:

Israel became a nation in 1948. The children of the founders of the current Israeli Nation were the <u>next generation</u> (*children*), and generally are presently Israel's mature adults. It is a remnant of the <u>grandchildren (*children's children*) of the founders of the current nation of Israel, who will turn wholly to the LORD in righteousness, and will keep The Commandments, and honor The Covenant God made with Abraham, Isaac, and Jacob</u>! But we must keep in mind that <u>many</u> of this third generation will also choose <u>not</u> to serve the LORD! Therefore, <u>this third generation is marked by great polarization</u>. In fact, these grandchildren of the founders of the Nation of Israel are the <u>Days of Awe generation</u>, and many of them will be deceived by AntiChrist, and <u>all of them will reap the judgments and discipline of the LORD</u>. By the way, these grandchildren are now entering young-adulthood, and are beginning to make their presence and thoughts known within Israel. So sometime within the time-frame covered by verses 17 and 18, this transition will occur, <u>and the prophetic focus will shift entirely back to Israel</u>!

The focus of world attention is even now turning toward The Middle East, so the transition has already begun. This phenomenon has picked up in intensity especially since 9/11. There is an increase in activity in the unfolding of prophecy in regard to The Land of The Covenant, with many Israelis taking <u>obvious diverse positions</u>. Some are turning to God, while many are denying or questioning whether He is to be recognized as having any direct input into what is currently transpiring within the Nation of Israel. While Israel's government is taking a humanistic stance, and claiming their prideful self-sufficiency, yet appearing inept and confused, there is a strong revival of Torah significance (a desire to return to The Mosaic Law) growing among many young Israelis and Jewish youth organizations. There also is a rising cry regarding The Land Covenant. Many of the young families who occupy the Settlements are of <u>the third generation</u>. Unfortunately, before turning wholly to the LORD, many will also fall under deception.

D. Heavenly Preparations:

At the same time, we are given insight into what is probably the most significant prophecy in Psalm 103 regarding the unfolding of the Times and Seasons, and this is described in relation to the heavenly preparations for the fulfillment of The Days of Awe. Our gathering unto the LORD is the heavenly hope of The Church. At the Season of earthly transition, we must look toward Heaven, and as the Bride, be encouraged that all is now ready in Heaven. Psalm 103, verses 19 to 21 state, *"<u>The LORD hath prepared his throne in the heavens</u>: and his kingdom ruleth over all. Verse 20. Bless the LORD, ye his angels, that excel in strength, and do his commandments, hearkening unto the voice of his word. Verse 21. Bless ye the LORD, all ye his hosts; ye ministers of his, that do his pleasure. Verse 22. Bless the LORD, all his works in all places of his dominion: bless the LORD, O my soul."*

The focus shifts from Israel in verses 17 and 18, to the heavenly realm in verses 19 to 22. The LORD is seated upon His Throne in the Heavens, surrounded by all His angelic hosts. We are able to parallel these verses with what John saw and described in the Book of Revelation. Through a visionary invitation, he was able to witness this heavenly scene, and was told to write down what he saw, so we would be prepared for what was to become a reality.

John saw what would take place far into the future. But there <u>comes a time when the future becomes the NOW</u>. The Throne is now prepared! Putting it into our vernacular, <u>The Heavenly Control Center is NOW ready</u>, and the LORD Himself is seated as the Commander! All is now ready to begin the countdown to Rosh HaShanah, for the calling of The Bride unto The Wedding and Coronation of The KING, and the subsequent carrying out of the judgments of God's discipline and wrath during The Days of Awe on the earth until Yom Kippur. All is in readiness for the unfolding of the prophetic Appointments! The LORD has marshaled His heavenly hosts around His Throne, equipped them, and given them His instructions. Those gathered around The Throne *"Bless the LORD!"*

The Psalmist, from his earthly position, now totally aware of the heavenly reality, admonishes his own soul to *"Bless the LORD!"* He is now aware of both the Times and the Seasons on the earth, and the Times and the Seasons in Heaven. In this regard, the Psalmist represents the righteous Bride, The Church. We will soon be taken in wedding procession into The Shekinah Glory of The Throne Room, and be able to stand before the LORD, our Bridegroom, to bless Him face to face! The transition for the Bride, Rosh HaShanah, is imminent. The transition from Grace to Awe for those who will remain on earth is also set to begin. So Psalm 103 prophetically is a Psalm making us aware of the Times and Seasons we now live in!

II. Psalm 104:

Let's proceed now to Psalm 104 which also is a *"Bless the LORD"* Psalm, so must be taken together with Psalm 103 in significance. Recall, some of the prophecies mentioned in each Psalm are now historical, some current, and some still future. This Psalm appears to begin where Psalm 103 left off, but also does flash back in reference to Creation, and then spirals forward again. The *"Bless the LORD"* of verse 1 is uttered from the heart of the Psalmist, meaning Psalm 104 begins from the position of the righteous in the earthly realm. There does not appear to be a gap of time between the *"Bless the LORD"* of the angelic hosts surrounding The Throne, and the Psalmist's *"Bless the LORD, O my soul,"* of Psalm 103 verse 22, and the opening *"Bless the LORD, O my soul"* of Psalm 104:1. Rather, the blessing may be in concert with verse 22 of Psalm 103, meaning there are heavenly as well as earthly beings blessing the LORD, much within the same contemporary time-frame.

A. The LORD is Seated In His Chariot:

Notice the Psalmist's description of the LORD in Psalm 103, then take note of His appearance, attributes, and location as described in Psalm 104. The Psalmist's description reads much as John, Isaiah, and Ezekiel describe the LORD. They saw Him in the Clouds of Glory, clothed in brightness, seated upon His Throne. Obviously He is stationed in the heavenly realm, but now He is described as Sovereign over all His Creation. *"Bless the LORD, O my soul. O LORD my God, thou art very great; thou art clothed with honor and majesty: Verse 2. Who coverest thyself with light as with a garment: who stretchest out the heavens like a curtain: Verse 3. Who layeth the beams of*

THE TIMES AND SEASONS EXPLAINED IN THE PSALMS

his chambers in the waters: who maketh the clouds his chariot: who walketh upon the wings of the wind: Verse 4. *Who maketh his angels ministering spirits; his ministers a flaming fire:"* The LORD is not just seated on The Throne, but He and The Throne, although in the heavenly realm, are hovering above the earth, indicated by the fact that He lays His chambers in the waters.

Where are the waters? The waters are above the earth. The Psalmist describes the Heavens as stretched out like a curtain, suggesting the level of the Heavens which is the air-canopy surrounding the earth, not the level of the cosmic Heavens containing the sun, moon, and stars. The support-beams of His chambers rest within this air-canopy, upon the waters the air contains, suggesting water-vapor and clouds -- real water-clouds.

But appearing along with these air-borne, water-vapor clouds (beams), there is <u>a specific Cloud</u> (singular.) This is not a water-cloud. Rather, it is The Shekinah Glory Cloud which accompanies the presence of the LORD. The LORD is riding within this Cloud, which is described as <u>His Chariot</u>. A chariot suggests a mode or vehicle of transport. Isaiah, Ezekiel, and John saw the LORD in this Cloud-Chariot that has obviously entered air-space in the past, surrounded by angelic-Cherubim (Seraphim) beings. [181]Ezekiel saw this Chariot settle upon the earth, and fill The Temple in Jerusalem. [182]Moses and all the Israelites saw it as a Pillar of Cloud by day, and a Pillar of Fire by night, leading, and protecting the Children of Israel from their enemies at the time of The Exodus. [183]Moses encountered this Cloud on Mount Sinai, and many times in The Tent of Meeting as he communed directly with the LORD. [184]This Glory Cloud stood above the Wilderness Tabernacle, and later filled The Temple in Jerusalem, so that the LORD's presence was so overwhelming no-one could even enter. [185]This Cloud was encountered by three of Christ's disciples at His Transfiguration before He went to the cross. [186]And 40 days after His resurrection, those standing on The Mount of Olives watched as this same Cloud received Christ at His Ascension. Isaiah, Ezekiel, and John described The LORD as appearing

---

[181] Ezekiel 1:1-28. Continuing to read on through chapters 2 and 3, we find The One seated on the throne in this vision of the Glory of the LORD, speaks to Ezekiel, and lifts him up from the earth to show himl what must come to pass . Ezekiel's encounter parallels John's in the book of Revelation. Ezekiel 10:1-22 describes the Glory of the LORD entering over the threshold of the Temple. The Glory of the LORD fills the re-built Temple, Ezekiel 43:1-5.

[182] Exodus 13: 17-22 .

[183] Exodus 19: 16, Exodus 24: 16-18, Exodus 33: 7-10.

[184] Exodus 40: 34-38, I Kings 8: 10-11.

[185] Matthew 17:1-8, Mark 9: 2-8.

[186] Acts 1: 9.

within this Cloud, clothed with brightness and with fire, seated upon a Throne, surrounded by a rainbow, with what appeared to be a pavement of clear crystal under His feet. So the epiphany of the LORD's presence within this vehicle of Glory has apparently come within close proximity to the earth on many occasions, and will do so again. It actually does exist!

What will be the LORD's reason for again entering the earth's airspace in this manner, especially since He is able to be omnipresent, so does not really need to limit Himself to location, time, or space? As with all previous occasions when He chose to reveal Himself in these Clouds of Glory, He will be on a tremendously significant mission! The LORD is to come into the air-canopy above the earth, riding His Shekinah Glory Cloud - Chariot, <u>to receive His Bride</u>! In other words, since all is prepared in Heaven according to Psalm 103, He is now seated in His Chariot in Psalm 104, so is ready to come in The Cloud of Shekinah Glory to receive His Beloved, and take her to be forever with Him. The Bridegroom is Coming! We will be taken at the Rapture to meet Him in the Shekinah Glory, which will rest within the air-canopy above the earth. Rosh HaChodesh -Yom HaKeseh. Rosh HaShanah!

The question is, are we ready and prepared to meet our Bridegroom? Paul tells us we will be changed, and together with the resurrected righteous from throughout the entire Church Age, will rise to meet Him <u>in the air</u>. We sing about going to meet the LORD in the air, but somehow we have an "In The Sweet By and By" attitude toward this event. Sure, we do believe it will unfold, someday, in the unknown nebulous future, on a Day known only to the LORD, at His whim. First of all, this event cannot come to pass on His whim. There is no 'whim' decision involved. If anyone has control regarding timing, it is The Father in accordance with Jewish wedding tradition! But more importantly, has it actually really registered that the nebulous future is no longer so nebulous, or unendingly future, but that the Time and Season is now upon us? If all is <u>now ready</u> in Heaven for Christ to receive His Bride, is anything standing in the way of His return?

Will the Rapture then take place in 2004, since Psalm 104 describes this readiness of the LORD, and that He is excitedly seated in His Chariot, prepared to ride upon the waters in the air-canopy? Perhaps. Since our resident Friend of The Bridegroom, the Holy Spirit, has indicated through the Psalmist that all is now ready, the waiting-game won't last much longer for the Bride! What we do know for sure is that the Rapture will take place according to God's Divine Appointment Calendar!

B. Creator and Righteous Judge: The Voice of Thunder:

Verses 5 to 9 of Psalm 104 describes the LORD as the Creator, who judges in righteousness. Verse 5. *"Who laid the foundations of the earth, that it should not be removed for ever, Verse 6. Thou coverest it with the deep as with a garment; the waters stood above the mountains."* Verse 6 appears to refer, as a flash-back, to the judgment of The Flood of Noah which covered the entire surface of the earth to a water-level above the mountains. Verse 7. *At thy rebuke they fled; at the voice of thy thunder they hasted away."* The waters receded when they were rebuked, and The Voice of Thunder was uttered, a reference to the fact that God's judgment was thorough and complete, and righteousness prevailed in accordance with God's plan of dealing with the sinfulness of mankind at that juncture. The receding of the waters at the utterance of <u>The Voice of Thunder</u> was a prophetic <u>pre-type of The Thunders of Revelation</u>, picturing The Father's Voice announcing the complete victory of Christ over the controlling works of Satan. So The Thunder ordering the receding Flood Waters spoke of a full redemption to come for mankind, for the nations, and for all Creation.

Verse 8. *" They go up by the mountains; they go down by the valleys unto the place which thou hast founded for them. Verse 9. thou hast set a bound that they may not pass over; that they turn not again to cover the earth."* The waters have a boundary set mercifully by God, so that they cannot ever again destroy mankind, or wipe-out all living creatures from the earth. Symbolically, waters also speak of the peoples and nations of the whole earth. God has a boundary set for the nations, and they will not be able to pass beyond that boundary to again destroy the earth with sin, prophetically pointing toward the coming Days of Awe, and The Seven Thunders which will announce the unfolding of Christ's Yom Kippur Victory, and the fact that He will rule over all nations, setting their boundaries in righteousness according to His own Word!

We are reminded that the LORD cares for His Creation. The Psalmist points out the natural systems which God has set in place to maintain balance within the physical world around us – the water-cycle, the food-chain, light, darkness, and even the esthetic value of His Creation to foster pleasure and appreciation, and inspire praise and worship to the One Who created it all.

But there also is a prophetic story being told which is easy to gloss over unless we dig a little below the surface.

Verse 10. *"He sendeth the springs into the valleys, which run among the hills. Verse 11. They give drink to every beast of the field; the wild asses quench their thirst. Verse 12. By them shall the fowls of the heaven have their habitation, which* sing among the branches. Verse 13. *He watereth the hills from his chambers: the earth is satisfied with the fruit of thy works.* Verse 14. *He causeth the grass to grow for the cattle, and herb for the service of man: that he may bring forth food out of the earth:* Verse 15. *and wine that maketh glad the heart of man, and oil to make his face shine, and bread which strengtheneth man's heart."* These verses not only describe the physical care the LORD provides for His Creation, but also speak of the very real spiritual blessings of His grace toward all during this Age of Grace we now enjoy. There are springs of refreshing in the valleys and among the hills of life, as we yield to Him, and to His Holy Spirit. Even the beasts and wild asses (the ungodly empires and their ofttimes ' wild' and stubborn rulers) are blessed by this outpouring of God's care and love. The wine and oil of the Holy Spirit are present in fulness to draw mankind to Christ, and to bless those who will respond with spiritual refreshing and anointing.

C. Trees, Birds, and Beasts:

Verse 16. *"The trees of the LORD are full of sap; the cedars of Lebanon, which he hath planted;* Verse 17. *where the birds make their nests: as for the stork, the fir trees are her house.* Verse 18. *The high hills are a refuge for the wild goats: and the rocks for the conies."* Trees symbolically represent nations and their leaders. The cedars of Lebanon and the fir trees, are wild evergreens which are strong, but represent idolatry and pagan roots. The Birds which lodge in the branches of these trees, are considered to be defiled or unclean. <u>Israel was not to partake of anything unclean</u>. Symbolically, trees and birds represent the ideologies and abominations of pagan practices within empires, nations, and peoples, that influence and control the lives of those who dwell upon the earth. All nations and peoples have nested within these trees, and still partake of their false sustenance and protection. Therefore, birds (people) and their nests (dwellings and governing systems) which are built within the wild trees, represent those who are embedding themselves within the ideologies that are counter to godliness and righteousness. For example. In our day, when we think of Lebanon, we immediately picture the people and government of that country. Most Arabs are Islamic. Islam's roots can be traced back to ancient Sumer, brought forward through Babylon and succeeding empires, then popularized, reworked, and renamed by Muhammed.

The cedar tree also speaks of Babylonian strength and idolatry. [187]Nebuchadnezzar had a dream of an enormous cedar tree, and all the

---

[187] Daniel 4: 1-37.

birds of the air lodged in its branches. The Babylonian Empire connection has influenced literally all empires and nations since his time down to the present.

The unclean stork is mentioned in Psalm 104, and it lodges in the fir tree, which was most often used in ancient paganism for occult practices and idolatry. Many idols were carved from the wood of the fir tree. But then again, wood of the same tree was gathered to burn in the fire, indicating mindless dichotomy, and lack of sound reasoning! Idolaters will burn!

High hills represent political, economic, and ideological strongholds, where wild goats (ungodly nations, and world influential movers and shakers) dwell. Whereas the rocks represent the hiding places of the weak who are oppressed and subjugated. The shy, defenseless conies hide among the rocks, but at the same time are easy pickings for wild beasts and birds of prey. It's amazing any of them manage to survive! If it wasn't for the rocks, they would become extinct. The conies represent the defenseless people of this world under the oppression of godless, totalitarian, and pagan regimes. The only protection they have is found among the rocks, the righteous who are salt and light in this world. The only eternal protection any of us have is found in The Rock of Christ, and we gain strength and encouragement from the living stones of the Body of Christ, the Church.

D. Significance of the Moon, and the Sun:

Thus far in Psalm 104, verses 10 to 18, we read a symbolic description of the empires, nations, and pagan scene out of which this present world has emerged. But Verse 19 presents a prophetic symbolism which causes us to focus upon the righteous, and upon the LORD, rooted, not in ancient, pagan empires and nations, but originating within the cosmic Creation of God that is beyond the direct control of man. *"He appointed the moon for seasons: the sun knoweth his going down."*

From what we have learned regarding The Feasts, the moon is a symbol of The Tzadikim, the Righteous, so symbolizes the Bride in this present dispensation, and the Tribulation Saints and the righteous of Israel during The Days of Awe. The moon's phases are appointed to represent the prophetic Seasons for the Righteous, so if we are to be able to interpret the Times and Seasons, we must understand what these symbolisms mean. We are not called to be in the dark regarding the Righteous, either figuratively or literally. The Bride certainly is not to participate in the darkness of The Days of Awe, but is to walk in the light of understanding,

The Final Schedule Revealed

and to be concealed from coming earthly judgments. Rosh HaChodesh -Yom HaKeseh! The New Moon Day of Concealment.

The Bride is to recognize the Full Moon, when the Holy Spirit's anointing upon the Church to fulfill the mandate to spread the Gospel is complete. At that time the physical moon will appear red. Also, the Church is to keep her focus on <u>the phases of the moon</u> as it progresses to the New Moon, Rosh HaChodesh, especially the New Moon Yom HaKeseh which is the Day of Concealment of Rosh HaShanah, indicating the Rapture. Subsequently, the moon will indicate a further cycle for the Righteous of The Days of Awe, when it will be darkened almost completely prior to the return of Christ, indicating faith on the earth will almost not be evident. I will not go into all the ramifications of the moon symbolism, since we have already covered this topic earlier in the first section of this book.

However, in conjunction with the moon's Appointed Seasons, this verse states, *"and the sun knoweth his going down."* Verse 19b. The sun symbolizes the Bridegroom, Jesus Christ, The Sun of Righteousness. According to true traditional marriage ceremonial procedure, the Bridegroom does not know for sure when He may go to collect His Bride. This is not His decision or call to make. However, He is not left forever in the state of not knowing when He may proceed, or the wedding would never take place! Since the Times and Seasons are in The Father's power, it rests upon The Father to give the "Go-ahead" signal. At that moment, the Bridegroom <u>knows</u> the Appointed Time when He is to go to receive His Bride! *"<u>The sun knoweth his going down</u>."* The Groom knows with certainty, but the Bride still has a latitude of awaited surprise. He is totally ready to *"go down,"* and <u>now knows when</u>. This mention of the sun knowing his going down in Psalm 104 would suggest, along with the fact the the LORD is personally prepared and already riding in His Chariot, that He has received His "Go-ahead!" from The Father.

Does this mean Messiah will come for His Bride in 2004? What is significant is the knowledge that He must already know <u>now</u> when He is to come, so could arrive at any time. Yes, it is a very real possibility He could come for His Bride this year. Or it is possible He may come several years down the prophetic road. The admonitions given by both Jesus and Paul are simply that we must be aware of the Times and Seasons which will herald our gathering unto Him. We are not promised that we will know the year, or even the month, and for sure we cannot know the day or the hour. Therefore, I would hesitate to be dogmatic regarding fulfillment during the 2004 year, because the LORD may in fact know now when He is coming according to Jewish tradition, but just because He knows, does not mean He necessarily will come immediately. The fact that He knows for sure, and is seated in His Chariot, should be a motivation for us to be absolutely ready! There is no reason for Him to be seated in His Chariot unless He is to come very shortly! I'm sure He wants to come, and is excitedly chafing to go for His Bride, but even He must wait until <u>The Appointed Time</u>.

E. The Transition to The Days of Awe:

Following the cosmic symbolism regarding the Bride and the Bridegroom, indicating the Times and Seasons, and the imminent Rapture, the Psalmist take us next to a metaphorical description of the transition to The Days of Awe period. He again uses symbols from nature, this time beginning with the cosmic night-day cycle -- a natural progression from the moon and sun of verse 19, because the sun and moon regulate the cycles of the Seasons, and the Times of Harvests, which at this juncture in the unfolding of prophecy is important for The Fall Feasts and The Days of Awe. It is interesting to note the order is night, then day, because just prior to the Rapture the world will be in darkness, followed by light; and this is not just symbolic, but will be observable cosmic reality as the prophecies unfold. The Rosh HaShanah Rapture will take place within the time-frame of when the sun is darkened by a third, and the moon's light is reduced by a third, appearing red. Then there will be a short time of Calm (three years) indicated by the light of day, followed by a great time of spiritual darkness over the entire world, The Tribulation, (Daniel's seven year 70th Week.) Together, these add up to ten years, The Ten Days of Awe. At the end of The Tribulation, the sun will be darkened again (the Fifth Vial Darkness), and the moon will not give off any light at all, following which The Second Coming of Christ will usher-in His great everlasting Light. Yom Kippur.

Psalm 104: 20. *"Thou makest darkness, and it is night: wherein all the beasts of the forest do creep forth.* Verse 21. *The young lions roar after their prey, and seek their meat from God.* Verse 22. *The sun ariseth, they gather themselves together; and lay them down in their dens.* Verse 23. *Man goeth forth unto his work, and to his labor until the evening."* During the stint of darkness which will take place during the duress of The Gog-Magog Battle, fought regarding Israel's borders, upon the mountains of The West Bank, " *the beasts of the forest"* will *"creep forth,"* meaning the influence of the beastly empires will begin to emerge from the *"forest."* A forest is made up of trees, which represent the nations, and the beasts represent both the empirical roots, as well as the leaders of these nations. These *"beasts"* creep forth under cover of darkness, meaning their orientation is from an ungodly root of spiritual darkness. These world leaders will coalesce to form a world ruling body. We see the beginnings of this world order of nations taking shape even now. This alignment of nations arising out of the former Beast Empires will produce the line-up of nations fighting over the problems of The Middle East, and will eventually result in the Ten Horns, and the Hybrid Beast Empire of The Little Horn. Their power-base begins to emerge before, and during, The Gog-Magog scenario, but does not come to full-blown power at that time.

"*The Young Lions*" who lead the charge against these 'beastly' enemies of Israel during Gog and Magog "*roar after their prey.*" They "*seek their meat from God.*" Verse 21. This means they have a desire to do God's will, and seek His counsel, indicating the Young Lions are the nations which have a Judeo-Christian base, and their seeking for wisdom likely does begin before the Church is removed. This does not mean these Young Lions necessarily understand the ramifications of all their decisions, but they are at least trying. Once the Church is removed, the godly influence will be greatly reduced in these Young Lion nations, but they will maintain a desire for some equitable character, so ultimately do later become antagonists of AntiChrist.

Following the darkness of The Gog-Magog Battle, and the Rapture of the Church, which is prophesied by Joel and Peter to take place near the time of the blood-red moon, [188]a Calm descends upon the world scene, and the evil winds of change which are controlled by four demonic angelic beings, are put on hold. The demonic influences are not allowed to blow on the earth, or on any existing tree (nation) for a short season. During this Season of Calm, which lasts for approximately the first three years of The Ten Days of Awe, <u>the sun again arises</u>. Psalm 104 verse 22. "*The sun ariseth, they gather themselves together, and lay them down in their dens.*" There is day! All the "Beasts" of darkness, and the Young Lions, retreat to lie down in their dens (within their own jurisdictional borders.) Israel is then able to build The Third Temple, and the 144,000 Jewish Evangelists are sealed and anointed to preach the Gospel of Christ world-wide. This period of The Calm of The Sixth Seal following The Battle of Gog and Magog, and the Rapture of Rosh HaShanah, appears to be a time of great evangelism as the Light of The Son shines forth. Mankind is allowed to recover and regroup, "*gather themselves together,*" and go about life in a relatively peaceful manner. <u>The Beasts and Lions return to their dens and lie down "until evening.</u>" But the "*evening*" eventually does come, and the Seventieth Week Tribulation darkness is ushered in when these Beasts, which then

---

[188] Revelation 6: 12-17 to 7: 1-3.

emerge as a formidable Hybrid Beast Empire of Darkness, again arise, and are allowed to exert their diabolical influence in the world.

The Psalmist takes time in the next few verses of Psalm 104 to marvel at the works of God, even in a sin-filled world. Verse 24. *"O LORD, how manifold are thy works! In wisdom hast thou made them all: the earth is full of thy riches.* Verse 25. *So is this great and wide sea, wherein are things creeping innumerable, both small and great beasts.* Verse 26. *There go the ships: there is that leviathan, whom thou hast made to play therein."* The earth is full of the blessings and wisdom of the LORD, and of great riches. These are available for the great and wide sea of humanity to enjoy. This *"sea"* contains the *"creeping"* things, the *"small and great beasts."* This speaks of the provision of the LORD, even for all nations of the earth.

But it is from these very nations the *"Beasts,"* the diabolical leaders arising from within the former world empires, who are both powerful, and not so powerful, emerge. Verse 26 indicates the naval powers, *"ships"* which are on one side, and Leviathan, Satan, on the other, which intimates there may be a skirmish planned, which is either short-lived, or averted in leading up to the Tribulation, which will result ultimately in the subjugation of the nations under AntiChrist. This fits well with the fact that AntiChrist appears to arise to his position from a position of negotiated flatteries as he consolidates his position among the nations. He *"plays"* among the nations, meaning he deceives them. His game is flatteries and deceptive promises in the name of 'Peace.' This coerced deception and control will ultimately produce The Battle of Armageddon, which begins with a series of uprisings for various reasons among the nations, and results in drawing all nations into The Middle East over issues which again rise to the surface in Israel, because AntiChrist divides up The Land.

Verses 27-30 enlarge on the mercy and provision of the LORD, even for these who obviously are antagonistic toward Him, indicating, even in judgment He shows mercy. *"These wait all upon thee; that thou mayest give them their meat in due season.* Verse 28. *That thou givest them they gather; thou openest thine hand, they are filled with good.* Verse 29. *Thou hidest thy face, they are troubled; thou takest away their breath, they die, and return to their dust.* Verse 30. *Thou sendest forth thy spirit, they are created: and thou renewest the face of the earth."* Again, we observe a spiral which covers the entire end-time sequence as the LORD deals with the nations of the earth. We see that even the Beasts and Leviathan are sustained by Him. Unless He allowed it, they would not be able to accomplish anything! If He opens His hand, they are nourished. If He hides His face, which He will during The Great Tribulation period, they will be brought to the Vial judgments and the sentence of eternal death. Ultimately, The LORD's Spirit will come forth again, and He will restore the earth to beauty, wholeness, and righteousness.

F. The Glory of the LORD will Endure in Righteousness:

Psalm 104: 31. *"The glory of the LORD shall endure for ever: the LORD shall rejoice in his works."* The LORD will rule and reign! Yom Kippur, followed by the joyous celebrations of Sukkot!

Verse 32. *" He looketh on the earth, and it trembleth. He toucheth the hills, and they smoke."* Again the prophetic spiral is in play. At the time of Gog and Magog, at the opening of The Sixth Seal, there will be a massive earthquake. Ten years later at the wrap-up of The Days of Awe, a great earthquake will take place an hour after the Two Witnesses are resurrected, a few days before Christ's Yom Kippur Second Coming .

Verse 33. *"I will sing praise to my God while I have my being."* This verse is symbolic in its order for the righteous who will sing praise to the LORD: 1. before The Throne of The Lamb at Rosh HaShanah, and 2. by the assembled Tribulation Saints before the Throne, singing The Song of The Lamb, and The Song of Moses, and 3. for the 144,000 who will greet Him, singing upon Mount Zion at Yom Kippur!

Verse 34. *"My meditation of him shall be sweet; I will be glad in the LORD."* The celebration and praise of the LORD will take place in His presence: 1. by the Bride in Heaven during the marriage festivities, and 2. during the Sukkot inauguration celebrations of His rule and reign, pictured in particular by the Beit HaShoevah ceremonies in The Temple. This will be a time of great, sweet, rejoicing and merriment as Christ's rule is officially ushered in.

Verse 35. *"Let the sinners be consumed out of the earth, and let the wicked be no more. Bless thou the LORD, O my soul. Praise ye the LORD."* This last verse of Psalm 104 encapsulates the triumph of the LORD over the wicked, casting out evil forever. At Yom Kippur, AntiChrist and the False Prophet will be cast into The Lake of Fire; and Satan, the Dragon, will be bound, and cast along with his fallen angels, into The Bottomless Pit. At that time the wicked (Rashim) will be sealed to their fate to await eternal punishment. All forces will be brought under Christ, and He will rule over all nations in righteousness. Sukkot, Beit HaShoevah, Shemini Atzeret - Simchat Torah. This verse is also a projected spiral forward to The Great White Throne when all the Rashim will be totally eliminated from the earth forever, and *"the wicked will be no more."*

G. Summarizing Psalms 103 and 104:

Notice how Psalms 103 and 104 parallel the unfolding of The Feasts and Festivals, and follow the course of The Book of Revelation, and The Book of Daniel. The Psalmist addresses these prophecies through the symbolisms used throughout Scripture. Once we are aware of the meanings of these symbols, it becomes relatively easy to spot the appropriate prophecies, and then to interpret the prophecies accordingly. The parallels are too obvious to say we are reading into these Psalms, because the order would break down quickly if one were to simply try to attach unintended prophetic interpretation. But the sequence and spiral is definitely there, indicating the inspiration of the Holy Spirit upon the Psalmist as he wrote, the same Holy Spirit who also inspired Moses, the Prophets, and John to reveal God's Appointment Time-Table. We therefore cannot turn a blind eye to these prophetic truths.

I find it especially interesting from the perspective of the Bride, to notice the references regarding the preparedness of The Throne, Christ's readiness to come in the Shekinah - Cloud Chariot, and that the *"moon is appointed for seasons,"* and the fact that *"the sun knoweth his going down."* These speak directly to the Bride, and ought to encourage us, spurring us on to readiness, because we soon will be caught up to meet our Bridegroom in the air-canopy. John's observation that the Bride has made herself ready takes on a clearer, more direct dimension when we read these Psalms, especially in light of the events in our world which are so quickly fulfilling prophecies regarding the end of this Age of Grace, and the obvious soon ushering in of The Days of Awe. The Rapture will occur very soon. We must keep our eyes on the signs around us, and particularly discern the Seasons of the Moon, which will declare to us where we are in the unfolding of God's Appointment with His Church-Bride. The cry of *"Behold the Bridegroom cometh, go ye out to meet Him"* is soon to be broadcast. Then Yom HaKeseh, The Day of Concealment, will take place! Rosh HaShanah!

III: Psalm 105:

Psalm 105 shifts to a very different emphasis, and although the Psalmist sets out to write it as a Song of Thanksgiving, verses 1 through 15 are worded rather strongly. In fact, the entire Psalm carries an authority of warning and admonishment which cannot be ignored. The focus in this Psalm is almost exclusively on Israel, a shift of emphasis which cannot be overlooked in light of the fact that following the blood-red moon and the Rapture, the prophetic focus shifts to deliverance for Judah, Jerusalem, and Mount Zion, according to Joel. I have already addressed the first 15 verses of this Psalm previously in the book, so will not again write out this passage. However I do wish to put Psalm 105 into prophetic perspective relative to Psalms 103 and 104.

A. The People Who are to Seek the LORD:

The Psalmist exhorts the people to remember the works of the LORD, and to glorify His Name in thanksgiving, praise, rejoicing, and singing. They are to seriously, earnestly, seek Him. Who are the people who are to thus seek the LORD? According to verses 1 through 6, the descendants of Abraham. This is a timely message for the nation of Israel in this day in which we live, because although some are serious in trying to understand and please the LORD, the overall spiritual condition of the Jews, both in Israel and world-wide, is still either apathy or legalism, neither of which helps them to grasp the mercy, and the promises of God in relation to everyday affairs in their lives, or in government, or in their existence as a nation. Separation of religion and state is rampant among them, so that the LORD and His Word are generally ignored by the majority of their political decision makers.

But what really is being emphasized is the fact that <u>all Abrahamic descendants</u> are to seek Him! They are to seek His will regarding <u>the very **issue** over which they are all currently making a point of ignoring Him</u>! And, this issue is primary, not only to procuring peace in The Middle East, but to bringing in lasting peace throughout the entire world. It is foundational to the unfolding of God's prophetic will for Israel, and ultimately for all nations. This primary issue is the single issue all nations must now grapple with, because it is intertwined with the principal players behind the terrorism and violence which is spreading and multiplying around the world.

Who are the people promoting and carrying out terrorism, not just in Israel, but throughout the world, taking nations hostage to achieve their goals? Answer. The radical Muslim Arab groups arising from among the descendants of Abraham, who feel they have a superior understanding of how world issues should be handled. Are all Arabs Muslims terrorists? Fortunately, no! But there is a significant Islamic Arab terrorist sub-culture, and we must take their threats very seriously!

Psalm 5 verse 6 cries out, "*O ye seed of Abraham his servant, ye children of Jacob his chosen.*" Who are the seed of Abraham? Both the Jews and the Arabs. But who has been chosen? The seed of Abraham who are the children of Jacob. It is certain the Arab descendants of Abraham through

Ishmael, and Isaac through Esau, are definitely ignoring this important Word of the LORD!

B. The Major Issue:

What is the primary issue? The major issue is The Covenant God made with Abraham, Isaac, and Jacob regarding The Land of Promise. The powerful nations of the world (particularly 'The Quartet') are using this issue to coerce Israel into an untenable situation against the obvious will of God. As such, the nations, including Israel, are all marching straight toward the wrath of the LORD, because they are taking a willingly blind, prideful stance against The Word of the LORD. Unfortunately, the Children of Jacob are just as much at fault as the Arabs and the other nations, because they are not being obedient to The LORD's Word either!

In light of the observation that each Psalm does appear to address at least one prophecy which is to be fulfilled in the equivalent year since Israel became a nation, the year 2005 could very well be the year The Covenant issue of The Land reaches its zenith. 2005 could be the year "Peace and Safety" may become a definite reachable reality as far as the nations are concerned, and they may actually broker such a Peace in the near future. But The Covenant is the key prophetic issue regarding the unfolding of The Prophetic Calendar, so 2005 may be the year the LORD will make His Voice most loudly heard in warning regarding tampering with His Covenant!

Does this mean the Rapture will take place before or during 2005? Not necessarily, but the speed of prophetic fulfillment and significance for Israel will definitely rise several notches, as the nations continue to coerce Israel into dividing up The Covenant Land to form a Palestinian State. What we may in fact observe, is the unfolding of the final lead-up to Gog and Magog taking shape as this controversy unfolds. It appears the Church may still be here for the onset of Gog and Magog, so it certainly is possible we will not yet have been raptured. Just because all is in readiness for the catching away of the Church-Bride, does not necessarily mean it takes place absolutely immediately. This Battle over The Land does appear to take place within the same time-frame as the sun being darkened and the moon turned to blood, according to the opening of the Sixth Seal, and according to Peter's quote from Joel regarding the duration of The Age of the fullness of the Holy Spirit. Therefore, because The Covenant of The Land controversy is even now heating up, this entire sequence of prophetic fulfillment is already in its Time and Season! The Bride, symbolically represented by the moon, is to be looking for, and to be totally aware of the

The Final Schedule Revealed

Times and Seasons! Jesus Christ will come soon, very likely right in the middle of the fall-out over the nations ignoring the LORD's Covenant with Israel, after "Peace and Safety" have apparently been achieved, following which destruction will suddenly ensue!

C. "Moreover..."

The remainder of Psalm 105 takes us on a flash-back journey with the LORD, reminding us of His dealings and deliverance throughout Israel's history, showing both His judgment and His mercy. The prophetic parallels indicating how He will again deal with Israel, <u>beginning with The Land</u>, cannot be ignored, or glossed over easily as being just a history lesson showing God's power. We therefore cannot divorce the first 15 verses which deal with The Covenant, from the rest of Psalm 105.

In fact, verse 16 begins in the King James, with the word *"Moreover..."* Now this word is not merely a literary connector, but is a serious legal term. We most often see this word used when documents are drawn up. It is used to introduce the binding nitty-gritty terms of fine-print, and the clauses which are to be unerringly adhered to. "Moreover" is frequently used in drawing up the terms of a Constitution, a binding business transaction, or a Covenant. The "moreover" statements are legally binding. Since Psalm 105 is directed to *"the seed of Abraham, the chosen of the children of Jacob,"* it would do well for them all to pay serious attention to this legally binding *"Moreover"* of The Covenant!

So what are the *"Moreover"* terms of the LORD's Covenant with the seed of Abraham, the chosen children of Jacob?

1. Called-Out, and Called-To:

God called Abraham out of Ur of the Chaldees, interestingly, out of the occult paganism of Chaldean culture which was co-existent with The Sumeran Empire. The Sumerans and the Chaldeans, along with the worship of other pagan deities, popularized the worship of the moon-god SIN, the current ramifications of which we have already indicated. Abraham's roots, therefore, were pagan, but God <u>called him out</u>. He was to leave the land of his fathers behind, not just physically, but spiritually as well. God promised He would bless Abraham, and he would be the patriarch of many nations. From among his many descendant nations, the LORD said He would call out a people and Nation dedicated to Himself in righteousness. Through Abraham's seed would come The Seed, Jesus

Christ, The Deliverer, The Redeemer who would reconcile man to God. Through Abraham all the nations of the earth would be blessed.

But Abraham was not just called-out to leave his roots and traditions behind. He was called out of a defiled, pagan land, to be taken to a Land that God would show him -- a Land of Promise. This Land would belong to his righteous "Seed" forever. Abraham, when he arrived in The Land of Promise, was shown the extent of his inheritance. [189]He was promised all the land that his eyes could see. However, not all was clear sailing for Abraham, and he did not permanently settle in this Land, but traveled extensively, living in tents, sojourning among strangers and enemies. So he did not, during his own lifetime, fully claim his Covenant inheritance.

2. The Seed of Abraham:

Abraham's descendants do occupy The Land of Promise, but not all are of the chosen line through Isaac and Jacob. Also, most of the Arab descendants of Abraham have not set aside their paganism, but adhere fervently to <u>one particular pagan root</u> that was resurrected by Mohammed, and has come down to the present as Islam. They worship the ancient moon-god, Allah, SIN! So there are Abrahamic descendants who are obviously being disobedient to the admonition <u>to leave their pagan worship behind</u>, and it is these who are the source of most of the unrest and animosities Israel today faces in The Land of Promise! Israel, when first commissioned to occupy The Promised Land, was told by God to completely cleanse The Land of the pagan inhabitants. But because they were disobedient, God is going to make them face their enemies who obviously still embrace pagan beliefs. Most of the Palestinian Arabs who presently live in Israel are from other Arab countries, with their roots dating back to the Babylonian, Medio-Persian Empires, and surrounding peoples out of whom Abraham was called. These are all antagonistic toward Israel, and through their practices and violence, are still polluting The Land with their pagan worship, and much shed blood. But the LORD is going to take them to task, and Abraham's descendants, through the line

---

[189] Genesis 13: 14-17. "And the LORD said unto Abram, after tht Lot was separated from him, Lift up now thine eyes, and look from the place where thou art northward, and southward, and eastward, and westward: For all the land which thou seest, to thee will I give it, and to thy seed for ever. And I will make thy seed as the dust of the earth: so that if a man can number the dust of the earth, then shall thy seed also be numbered. And walk through the land in the length of it and in the breadth of it; for I wil give it unto thee."

of Isaac and Jacob, will inherit The Land, and The Seed, Jesus Christ, will reign in The Land forever.

3. Melchizedech:

Although Abraham did not receive the promised inheritance immediately during his own lifetime, he did tithe faithfully to the KING of SALEM, Melchizedech. Who was Melchizedech? Hebrews 6: 26 to 7:1-4. *"Whither the forerunner is for us entered, even Jesus, made a high priest for ever after the order of Melchisedek. Chapter 7:1. For this Melchizedeck, King of Salem, priest of the most high God, who met Abraham returning from the slaughter of the kings, and blessed him:* Verse 2. *To whom also Abraham gave a tenth part of all, first being by interpretation King of righteousness, and after that also King of Salem, which is King of Peace."* Who is The King of Righteousness? The King of Salem? The King of Peace? Jesus Christ!

Melchizedech was <u>an epiphany presence of the LORD in the days of Abraham</u>, and[190] He laid the foundations of the city of Salem (Peace), which is now Jerusalem. [191]The historical understanding among most Christians and Jews is that Jerusalem was built by the Hittites. The ancient Hittites did build the city which was captured from the Jebusites by the Israelis four centuries later. But what is not often remembered, is that the Hittites built their city on an existing foundation which was laid originally by Melchizedech. Jerusalem truly is The City of our God, The City of Peace! In fact, the LORD says He placed His presence and [192]His Name there. This is not merely a spiritual presence and association of Jerusalem with the God of Israel. <u>His Name really is there! Physically!</u>[193] If we look at a topographical map of Jerusalem, we see The Old City area is broken up and surrounded by valleys. If we trace these valleys with a pen, we easily recognize a letter of the Hebrew alphabet, the letter 'Shin.'

---

[190] Hebrews 11: 8-10.
[191] Ezekiel 16: 3, 45.
[192] 2 Chronicles 6:6.
[193] New Bible Atlas, D.R.W. Wood, M.A. Managing Editor, Inter-Varsity Press, Lion Publishing, Tyndale Publishing House, 1985. P. 104, Note the shape of the diagram of the City of Jerusalem. It forms the Hebrew letter 'Shin.' Also notice the inside front and back covers, depicting a topographical shading of the Jerusalem area of the Judean hills.
The Holy Bible, Authorized King James Version, New Encyclopedic Reference Edition, Zondervan Publishing House, Grand Rapids, Michigan, 1966, p. 1196. Note the topographical insert for Salem. The valleys form the Hebrew letter "Shin."

The Shin is the Hebrew letter used for the Name of the LORD, HaShem. HaShem, The LORD, chose a particular chunk of earthly real-estate for Himself, and <u>literally wrote His Name on it</u>! This real-estate is Jerusalem. We are actually able to view this phenomenon from satellite! We are told in Hebrews 11:8-10, *"By faith Abraham when he was called to go out unto a place which he should after receive for an inheritance, obeyed, and he went out, not knowing whither he went. Verse 9. By faith he sojourned in the land of promise, as in a strange country, dwelling in tabernacles with Isaac and Jacob, <u>the heirs with him of the same promise</u>: Verse 10. For he looked for <u>a city which hath foundations, whose builder and maker is God</u>."* Underlining mine. When Abraham looked out over the land to view his inheritance, he was looking at real-estate that already was claimed by, and inscribed with the Name of the LORD, etched in topographical writing!

[194]Melchizedech, The King of Righteousness, The King of Salem, was identified by the writer of Hebrews as being without father or mother, so He is eternal. Since Melchizedech is eternal, and He is The Eternal High Priest, His position cannot be taken up by another. Jesus <u>is</u> High Priest <u>forever</u> after the Order of Melchizedech! Forever means forever, both eternally past, and eternally future. The LORD was called Melchizedech in Abraham's time, and received tithes from Abraham. He still is LORD and Eternal High Priest in our time, and He is The KING of Righteousness who came to take away the sins of the world. Jesus Christ will come again as victorious KING and Eternal High Priest, and make His abode in His own City, the City for which He personally laid the foundations, Jerusalem. So, the LORD called Abraham out of the pagan culture of the Chaldees, and led him into The Land He had already prepared, to seek for a city which would be of eternal significance. From this location, the LORD Himself will reign.

4. The Living LORD of The Covenant:

Abraham, through Isaac and Jacob, was the Patriarch of the People who would inherit this Covenant of Promise. The blessings and promises bestowed upon Abraham by the LORD are eternal. [195]They <u>are</u> a Blood Covenant, therefore cannot ever be broken. Israel has tried to break faith with The Abrahamic Covenant, but a covenant is not the same as other agreements. It cannot be broken or annulled while the one who drew up the Covenant is alive. Since The LORD is eternal and alive forever, The

---

[194] Hebrews 8: 13-20, Hebrews 7: 1-28.
[195] Genesis 15: 7-21.

Abrahamic Covenant is eternally valid. Christ's physical death on the cross did not annul this Covenant, as some would have us believe, because in His essence, God cannot die. He is eternal. His incarnated physical frame died, but He did not cease to exist! In fact, while in the state of physical death, He [196]*"led captivity captive,"* and took on Himself the sentence for our sin. But sin was powerless over Him, because although He became sin for us in our place, He Himself was sinless. He was therefore able to be totally victorious over sin and death, and to be physically raised again in total righteousness. No one else could have done it. God had to do it for us Himself!

He is able then, to uphold His eternal Covenant He made with Abraham, Isaac, and Jacob. And as such, He also is rightfully jealous over His Land, over His own City, and over His own Mount Zion. No wonder, when Jesus cleared the Temple in Jerusalem He was absolutely furious, and stated, *"My house shall be called of all nations the house of prayer? But ye have made it a den of thieves."* Mark 11:17. He had every right to be upset! No wonder His wrath will be poured out on those who ignore His Covenant with Abraham, Isaac, and Jacob, and set about to steal the birthright from Jacob! He indeed has a right to be angered! The nations who try to pull off dividing up The Covenant Land of Promise will inherit His wrath. Therefore, the *"Moreover"* of Psalm 105:16 must be taken seriously!

D. Deliverance: Prophetic Types From Israel's Past:

Psalm 105 states in verse 16 that the LORD *"called for a famine upon the land: He brake the whole staff of bread."* This famine led the Children of Israel into Egypt, where Joseph beforehand, through very questionable circumstances orchestrated by his own brothers, was sent ahead by the LORD to prepare for their sustenance and survival. But God also blessed Joseph with great understanding, position, and wisdom. Following a lengthy stint in jail for something he did not do, verse 20. *"The king sent and loosed him; even the ruler of the people, and let him go free.* Verse 21. *He made him lord of his house, and ruler of all his substance:* Verse 22. *to bind his princes at his pleasure; and teach his senators wisdom."*

Joseph was a prophetic type of Christ. His own brothers sold him into slavery. He ministered in a foreign land. He was accused and punished for sins he did not himself commit. He was released from jail, then was elevated to the highest position of power next to Pharaoh. He taught the senators of Egypt wisdom. Christ was despised and sold to the Romans.

---

[196] Ephesians 4: 8-10.

He ministered on earth, having left the portals of Heaven. He ministry was received more by foreigners than by His own people. Many Gentiles accept Him. Most Jews still do not! He was falsely accused, and suffered the unjust punishment of sins He did not commit, willingly bearing the sin of us all. But He was released from the dungeons of Hell by His resurrection, and is the LORD over all the universe, and will declare His victory over Satan. He will return, and His wisdom will become the basis for all government, and He will teach all men, including world leaders, princes, and kings, this world's 'senators,' His ways.

Psalm 105 continues, taking us through the life and rule of Moses, and God's many signs and wonders as He prepared to lead Israel out of Egypt. All the plagues are listed. Verse 28. *"He sent darkness, and made it dark; and they rebelled not against his word. Verse 29. He turned their water into blood, and slew the fish. Verse 30. Their land brought forth frogs in abundance, in the chambers of their kings. Verse 31. He spake, and there came diverse sorts of flies, and lice in all their coasts. Verse 32. He gave them hail for rain, and flaming fire in their land. Verse 33. He smote their vines also, and their fig trees; and brake the trees of their coasts. Verse 34. He spake, and the locusts came, and caterpillars, and that without number. Verse 35. and did eat up all the herbs in their land, and devoured the fruit of their land. Verse 36. He smote all the first-born in their land, the chief of all their strength."*

What were these plagues that came upon Israel's enemies in Egypt all about? Why did God pour them out? Pharaoh, steeped in his pagan worship of the gods each of the plagues highlighted, would not let the people go to worship their God, and he certainly was not going to allow them to return to The Land of Promise, because he would permanently lose his slave-force. Even though God sent these plagues, Pharaoh hardened his heart. The only plague which had any positive result was the death of all the first-born. But even though this plague resulted in a willingness to let the people go, the decision became overshadowed after Israel finally left, and Pharaoh chased them to The Red Sea in order to re-enslave them. Israel's deliverance was not because of the plagues, or even because of the changed mind of Pharaoh, but because of the direct, Divine, miraculous intervention of the LORD Himself, as He made a way where there was no way, and fed and sustained them where there was no natural food or water.

The parallels with what the Israelis will yet be dealing with in gaining full control of The Land of Covenant are striking. During the coming Days of Awe, Israel will lose their absolute jurisdiction over The Land, and will even become a nation with their political and religious leaders in exile, because of the pagan rule of AntiChrist. God will again re-enact almost this entire list of plagues as He pours out His Vials of Wrath. The final deliverance again will not be because of the plagues directly, but because of the intervention of the LORD Himself into the affairs of the nations when He returns. Then The Covenant will be brought to full fruition.

By the way, Christ Himself is referred to as *"the firstborn among many brethren."* Romans 8:29b. He took on Himself the role of succumbing to the plague of the death of the firstborn on behalf of all mankind, to bring about deliverance, not just from Egypt, but from the penalty for all unrighteousness! He did this at the cross, which, as I have already pointed out, took place following His 69th week Triumphal Entry. Although Gabriel explained to Daniel that the death of Messiah, the Prince, will take place at the 62nd week, this is a re-set of the prophetic clock, because He went to the cross chronologically in the 70 Week, tasting the Wrath of God against all sin on behalf of all of us! He did so to provide an avenue whereby mankind could be delivered from the Wrath of God! Daniel's 70th Week deals literally with the wrath of God poured out upon the unrighteous! Jesus Christ took upon Himself the ultimate penalty, and became our Deliverer because of His great love and mercy. Therefore, this plague of the death of the first-born does not have to be re-enacted. The plague of the death of the firstborn, being left out of the duplicated list of the plagues of Egypt when the Vials are poured out, is therefore not an oversight. Rather, it has already been fulfilled, once for all, for all time! All the other plagues are able to be re-enacted, but this one cannot be, because it represents absolute death and separation from God for eternity for the sinner. Christ took this penalty for sin upon Himself. <u>But He was able to be victorious over sin and death</u>, because He, as the perfect Lamb of God offered in our place, was Himself without sin or any blemish. His shed blood is the atonement for our sin! So the way to deliverance is open to all mankind, and will remain so, even during Daniel's 70th Week! All we need do is accept it!

Psalm 105 points out another interesting parallel. Israel was brought out of Egypt, carrying Egypt's wealth, which the Egyptians themselves had willingly given to them, leaving Egypt destitute. Egypt was at first very glad when they left. Fear had come upon all the citizens of Egypt because of The Children of Israel, and because of the plagues. People will again be glad and thankful when Israel is finally settled. The entire world will be tired and fearful of all that has been brought upon them because of Israel! Ultimately, the enemies of Israel and of the LORD will be brought to heel, and will cease to fight. Then the whole Land, and all nations will be at rest. But not before the entire world will have had to suffer great devastation and loss.

E. "God Remembered His Holy Promise, and Abraham His Servant:"

Why did God take Israel through the plagues, through the desert, and through the wilderness? Verse 42. " *He remembered his holy promise, and Abraham his servant."* He led them back to The Covenant Land of Promise. God will take Israel through The Days of Awe to bring them to a place of total dependance on Himself, so that they will have to turn completely to Him in repentance, honesty, and recognition, because He has remembered His Covenant with Israel. He will bring them to the place of Teshuvah so that they will willingly accept the atonement of Jesus, the Christ, and recognize Him and their KING and Messiah. Then He will bring them to the total deliverance of Yom Kippur, fulfilling His Covenant, and He will rule over them in The Land of Covenant as The KING of Righteousness and Peace. Sukkot.

Verses 43 to 45 appear to describe Yom Kippur, Sukkot, and Shemini Atzeret-Simchat Torah. *"And he brought forth his people with joy, and his chosen with gladness:* Verse 44. *And gave them the lands of the heathen: and they inherited the labor of the people:* Verse 45. *That they might observe his statutes, and keep his laws. Praise Ye the LORD."*

Psalm 105 emphasizes The LORD's determination to honor His Covenant, and to ultimately bring it to fruition in The Land He promised to Abraham, Isaac, and Jacob. The terms of this Covenant cannot, and will not be broken, but He will personally bring it to pass. He will again come to His Holy City, and His Holy Temple, and rule over Israel and over all nations. His Word will be sent forth from Jerusalem, and the nations will be made to accept His rule and Law. The KING of Peace will truly reign over all nations. The LORD is certainly to be praised!

It is obvious all this will not take place overnight, but will follow the sequence of God's Convocation Appointments. When this series of Fall Harvests is to begin, is still open to some interpretation, but 2005 will likely see an escalation of the countdown to the fulfillment of The Abrahamic Covenant, addressed in all seriousness. 'The Roadmap,' or a variation of it, will likely become a hot issue, and great strides may in fact be made toward implementing "Peace and Safety' in The Middle East. Then the fall-out will begin!

CHAPTER 26
JESUS CHRIST, VICTORIOUS KING

Now that we have been made aware of the ramifications of the Times and Seasons relative to the Bride and The Covenant with Israel, we are able to fast-forward to where John left off in Revelation chapter 19. The time-frame we are to focus upon takes place at the culmination of The Days of Awe, and John's perspective is no longer on the celebration of The Marriage Supper of The Lamb, which takes place in Heaven during the seven years of the Tribulation portion of Yamim Nora'Im. Rather, he is positioned upon the earth where the Tribulation has reached a crisis. All the nations of the earth have gathered into The Middle East to do battle, each nation with its own provocation and agenda. They are all drawn into The Valley of Megeddo, also referred to as The Valley of Jehosephat, or The Valley of Jezreel, and a war of unprecedented fierceness takes place. It appears Israel is doomed. Not only that, it would also appear all mankind is bent on self-annihilation if left to their own devices and hatreds. But at this juncture, another army no one is counting on shows up. Suddenly all factions forget their petty grievances against one another, because they realize they are facing a truly formidable Foe. They quickly regroup, and focus their weaponry against this surprise Attacker.

Jesus stated in His Olivet Discourse to His disciples: Matthew 24: 27-31. "*For as the lightning cometh out of the east, and shineth even unto the west; so shall also the coming of the Son of man be. Verse 28. For wheresoever the carcase is, there will the eagles be gathered together.* Verse 29. <u>*Immediately after the tribulation of those days*</u> *shall* <u>*the sun be darkened and the moon shall not give her light, and the stars shall fall from heaven, and the powers of the heavens shall be shaken*</u>: Verse 30. *And* <u>**then shall appear the sign of the Son of man in heaven**</u>: <u>**and then shall all the tribes of the earth mourn**</u>, <u>**and they shall see the Son of man coming in the clouds of heaven with power and great glory**</u>. Verse 31. *And he shall send his angels* <u>*with a* **great** *sound of* **a trumpet**</u>, *and they* <u>*shall gather together his elect from the four winds, from one end of heaven to the other*</u>."

Yom Kippur! At the end of The Tribulation, Jesus Christ, The Son of Man, The Messiah, The Deliverer, The Great KING, The LORD of Hosts, will break through the Heavens like lightning. Every person upon the earth will see Him. He will come openly and visibly, in great power, in awesome military parade, riding upon the white horse of the Conquering

KING, accompanied by His forces who will also all be riding upon white horses, wearing white uniforms.

Now, realistically, no army on earth engages in battle wearing white! Some may have white uniforms, but they are not worn on the battlefield, but are worn for ceremonial purposes only. Rather, in combat they wear camouflage so that they can take advantage of stealth, and gain some protection from their enemies. But these forces and their Commander-in-Chief obviously do not need any camouflage. They parade openly! They demand everyone on earth behold in awe and terror! The LORD of Hosts' arrival is announced by the riveting blast of The Great Shofar, Tekiah HaGadol, the final sounding of The Seventh Trumpet, (the other horn of The Ram) <u>revealing The Victorious Lamb to the whole world!</u> All people of all nations are struck with great fear and trepidation. They recognize this really is Jesus, The Messiah, coming in victory.

Israel, and all nations, mourn. Why would they mourn? The nations realize that they have not repented of their evil ways. The enemies of Christ couple their mourning with animosity, haughtiness, and anger. They leave off their grievances against one another, and turn all their military attention to fight this unwelcome Intruder from Heaven, while at the same time, they realize they will never succeed against Him. They mourn out of abject frustration.

But Israel finally recognizes that they have not exercised true repentance during the High Holy Days before the culmination of Yom Kippur. They have not taken advantage of The Ten Days of Tishrei Teshuvah to examine their hearts, so are now found still in their sin, which is exposed for all to see. Israel's Messiah has arrived, and they finally recognize Him in truth, but they are ashamed of their own inadequacy and unbelief. They finally realize they have not given due respect to the One Who ultimately not only deserves it, but requires worship in total repentance, obedience, commitment and righteousness. They recognize their own inability to live up to the demands of One so all powerful, so Almighty.

Notice the whole universe responds to this Triumphal Return of Christ. The sun is darkened, and the moon does not give off any light. The moon is not even giving off a red glow this time! The stars fall from heaven, and the equilibrium of all cosmic bodies, is shaken. These are far more drastic changes than occurred at The Battle of Gog and Magog ten years previous.

At the sounding of The Great Shofar, the angels are sent to gather The Elect (Israel) from the four corners of the earth, and from one end of Heaven to the other (The Tribulation Saints.) This is the Yom Kippur ingathering of the Elect, The Chosen of God from the Days of Awe, who

JESUS CHRIST, VICTORIOUS KING

have their names written in The Book of Life, whether Jew or Gentile. At the sounding of this powerful trumpet, there is a great resurrection of those who became Tribulation Saints during The Days of Awe. These are called to join with those who were resurrected at Rosh HaShanah just prior to The Days of Awe, the Raptured Church, the Bride of Christ. That is why Jesus states the angels gather His Elect from the far reaches of both Heaven and earth. The Jews are The Elect who are gathered to take their place as the chosen nation on the earth, with Christ as their KING. The resurrected Tribulation Saints are The Elect who will rule and reign with Christ, together with the Bride.

I. KING of Kings, LORD of Lords, Victorious Conqueror:

Revelation 19:11-21. *"And I saw heaven opened, and behold a white horse: and he that sat upon him was called Faithful and True, and in righteousness he doth judge and make war. Verse 12. His eyes were as a flame of fire, and on his head were many crowns; and he had a name written, that no man knew, but he himself. Verse 13. And he was clothed with a vesture dipped in blood, and his name is called The Word of God. Verse 14. And the armies which were in heaven followed him upon white horses, clothed in fine linen, white and clean. Verse 15. And out of his mouth goeth a sharp sword, that with it he should smite the nations: and he shall rule them with a rod of iron: and he treadeth the winepress of the fierceness and wrath of Almighty God. Verse 16. And he had on his vesture and on his thigh a name written, KING of KINGS, and LORD of LORDS. Verse 17. And I saw an angel standing in the sun; and he cried with a loud voice, saying to all the fowls that fly in the midst of heaven, Come and gather yourselves together unto the supper of the great God; Verse 18. That ye may eat the flesh of kings, and the flesh of captains, and the flesh of mighty men, and the flesh of horses, and of them that sit on them, and the flesh of all men, both free and bond, small and great. Verse 19. And I saw the beast, and the kings of the earth, and their armies, gathered together to make war against him that sat on the horse, and against his army. Verse 20. And the beast was taken, and with him the false prophet that wrought miracles before him, with which he deceived them that had received the mark of the beast, and them that worshiped his image. These both were cast alive into a lake of fire burning with brimstone. Verse 21. And the remnant were slain with the sword of him that sat upon the horse, which sword proceeded out of his mouth: and all the fowls were filled with their flesh."* KJV.

Jesus Christ is KING of Kings and LORD of Lords. He is claiming His rightful position. He is dressed in Royal, military attire. His Royal Sovereign demeanor, attitude, and authority is evident. He sits on the white horse of sovereign authority as Conqueror, and Victorious KING. When Christ came the first time, He did not ride on a white horse, because

He did not come to take His place as KING at that time. He came as The Lamb of God to take away the sin of the world. Therefore, He came the first time as a Suffering Servant, so He rode into Jerusalem on the day of His Triumphal Entry on a lowly donkey and her colt. But He will ride the white horse of Royalty and of Victorious Conqueror when He returns to the earth in Battle array at Yom Kippur. Then at Sukkot, He will ride through the same Golden Gate of Jerusalem, but this time in Triumphal Procession, to restore The Kingdom to Israel, and ascend The Throne of David.

When Christ returns to the earth, He will come leading His forces into battle against AntiChrist, The False Prophet, and against Satan. This will be a real battle, not just an allegorical show-down as some would have us believe this passage portrays. He will come against all nations who have placed themselves in opposition to His truth, and to His will. All the military might of the earth will be gathered into The Middle East in The Valley of Armageddon, assembled together to do battle against one another. The Battle of Armageddon lasts *"for an hour, and a day, and a month, and a year,"* and fully a third of all mankind is killed. Revelation 9: 15. When Christ returns, the final conflict of this War will take place, <u>The Battle of The Great Day of God Almighty</u> (Revelation 16:14), where all the nations will come face to face with Christ and His armies. Jesus Christ, the Conquering KING, will defeat all Satanic and human forces.

He will not come this time as a meek Lamb to be slaughtered, rather this passage describes Him as having a totally different demeanor. His eyes are as flames of fire, showing His anger, His determination, His judgment, and His ability to carry out righteous justice. He wears many crowns upon His head, showing His complete and absolute Royal Sovereignty over all. His Name is called, "Faithful and True" meaning He is The One who carries out His purposes in righteousness according to, and in faithful fulfillment of the truth of His Own Word. His royal robe is a vesture that has been dipped in blood, showing He holds His position rightfully, because He personally procured salvation for His Creation through His own blood. He is victorious over sin, death, and the grave. Monogrammed in blazing letters on His Royal Vesture, and on the thigh of His white uniform is the title, KING of KINGS, and LORD of LORDS. That title, emblazoned for all to see, will certainly catch the Islamic hoards by surprise and consternation! He also has another Name that no man knows, but He Himself. This is not an earthly man-given name, but His true Heavenly and Holy Name. He bears the title, "The Word of God," indicating He is the power, expression, and essence of eternal God, The Creator of Heaven and Earth.

A sharp Sword goes out from His mouth, speaking of His Word going forth in power to smite the nations, who He will rule over with a rod of iron. He cannot, nor will He be, questioned. His Word will be Law. He will tread out *"the winepress of the fierceness of the wrath of the <u>Almighty."</u> <u>This is the beginning of the Second Sickle Judgment when He</u>* pours the nations into the winepress of His Wrath at Yom Kippur. This Sickle Judgement will be brought to completion at His Court of Justice when He, The Righteous Judge, will hand down His sentence upon the nations as they stand before Him to give account during Sukkot. His poured-out judgment will be totally just.

At the time of this Battle, The LORD takes AntiChrist and the False Prophet, and casts them alive into The Lake of Fire that burns with fire and brimstone. Verse 20 of Revelation 19. *"And the beast was taken, and with him the false prophet that wrought miracles before him, with which he deceived them that had received the mark of the beast, and them that worshiped the image. These both were cast alive into the lake of fire, burning with fire and brimstone. Verse 21. And the remnant were slain with the sword of him that sat upon the horse, which sword proceeded out of his mouth; and all the fowls were filled with their flesh."* KJV.

II. What Becomes of Satan, The Dragon?

Chapter 20: 1-3 of Revelation explains the sentence upon Satan at this juncture. *"And I saw an angel come down from heaven, having the key to the bottomless pit, and a great chain in his hand. Verse 2. And he laid hold on the dragon, that old serpent, which is the Devil, and Satan, and bound him a thousand years, Verse 3. And cast him into the bottomless pit, and shut him up, and set a seal upon him, that he should deceive the nations no more, till the thousand years should be fulfilled: and after that he must be loosed a little season."* Satan is bound and banished from being at liberty upon the earth. He is chained, and cast into The Bottomless Pit for 1000 years, and a seal is placed upon him.

Then he is released. Why would he be set free to roam upon the earth again? He is allowed to try the hearts of men once more. There will be mortal people born during The Millennial Reign of Christ. These will live very long lives, similar to those who lived before The Flood. They will have had no option but to obey under the rule of Messiah. However, the LORD wishes for each person to have a free-will choice whether to serve Him or not. This season of temptation by Satan will clarify the position of the hearts of mortal mankind born during The Millennium. Yes, Satan has already been defeated, but all mankind must be presented with the opportunity to choose between good or evil. All must be presented with the fact that they have need of salvation through Christ, and be allowed of their own free will, to repent. After a short space of time, the length of which we are not told, there will be one final Battle, followed by The Great White Throne Judgment. Then there will be a New Heaven and a New Earth where only righteousness will dwell, and Satan, along with all the Wicked, will be cast into The Lake of Fire where the AntiChrist and False Prophet already are.

So, following The Millennium, Satan will be released from The Bottomless Pit, *"and he shall go out to deceive the nations which are in the four corners of the earth, Gog and Magog, to gather them together to battle: the number of whom is as the sand of the sea,* Verse 9. *And they went up on the breadth of the earth, and compassed the camp of the saints about, and the beloved city: and fire came down from God out of heaven, and devoured them.* Verse 10. *And the devil that deceived them was cast into the lake of fire, and brimstone, where the beast and the false prophet are, and shall be tormented day and night for ever and ever."* Revelation 20: 8-10.

Gog and Magog again wage war against Christ and the Saints after Satan is released following the end of The Millennium. So there are two battles of Gog and Magog, one at the transition to The Days of Awe, and one following the end of The Millennium more than a thousand years later. The nations are deceived again by Satan into thinking they can defeat Christ. Will the Nation of Israel play a part at that time? Absolutely, because the beloved city, Jerusalem, is mentioned, along with the Camp of The Saints being surrounded by the troops of Gog and Magog. But this Battle is short-lived. God reigns fire and brimstone down upon His enemies, and they are all killed. Now we finally see the last of Satan who has managed to again deceive the nations. He is cast into The Lake of Fire where the Beast and the False Prophet already are, and is tormented *"day and night for ever and ever."*

V. The Great White Throne:

[197]The heavens and the earth flee from the presence of Him who sits on The Great White Throne, and the dead (those resurrected for The Second Death) both small and great, stand before God to be judged. This is the resurrection of the unjust. The Books are opened once more, and The Book of Life is also opened. The dead are judged according to what has been written in the Books regarding their works. All the unrighteous dead, whether from the sea, or from death and hell, are judged. This is not a judgment of reward, but of the disobedience of not repenting, and of not accepting the Atonement provided through Christ's shed blood. Death and Hell are cast into The Lake of Fire, and whoever is not found written

---

[197] Revelation 20: 11-15.

in The Book of Life is also cast into The Lake of Fire. Therefore, all the unrighteous from all dispensations are cast into The Lake of Fire. This is The Second Death.

VI. The Resurrection Order:

Where did Paul get his <u>order of the resurrections</u> from? He obviously believed and taught it, even to the Gentile Churches. We must remember, Paul was a Jew, just as Jesus was also a Jew. So were Matthew, Mark, John, Peter, and the rest of the Apostles. The only writer who wrote two books of The New Testament who was not Jewish, was Luke. He was a Greek. But even he had an approach based in analytical thinking, so quickly understood the life and ministry of Christ, and recognized correct doctrine. He rubbed shoulders with Jews daily, living and working among them, and as a Christian, worshiped with them. We tend to forget these snippets of trivia! But they <u>are key</u> in identifying and understanding certain doctrines.

At no time did Paul contradict Jesus, because both, humanly speaking, had the same upbringing in Judaism. And at no time did either of them, or any of the other apostles, contradict true Judaic beliefs. <u>They only attacked error</u>. That being the case, we must realize Judaic belief that is based in the Scriptures, <u>and not tampered with</u>, must be truth. The Jews do have access to truth, only they do not take it to its fulfillment in Jesus Christ, <u>and that is their blindness</u>. Paul received his education under the most revered Pharisee of his day, Gamaliel. Gamaliel must have taught some things correctly! Paul would have understood the order of the resurrections from the doctrines of the Pharisees, who did believe in the resurrection of the dead. In believing this doctrine, they had to interpret their understanding in light of the Scriptures. So Paul already had an education based in Judaic exegesis and doctrinal apologetics.

After Paul was transformed by the saving power of Christ, he did not then throw out all his education, but rather <u>applied it to fulfillment</u>. This understanding was enhanced over the course of the years he spent in The Arabian Desert, where Christ Himself was his Teacher. Paul was privileged to be able to come under Christ's own private Rabbinical Yeshiva instruction. All it took was for Paul to put his education and upbringing into proper perspective, then along with the personal tutoring of Christ, his doctrines became absolutely clear. Since Jesus also was a Jew by Divine Appointment, this private Yeshiva experience would have made perfect sense. After all, they both spoke the same spiritual language, were from the same cultural basis, and examined all doctrine from the same Scriptures.

The Final Schedule Revealed

On top of that, Jesus is LORD, and <u>He gave the Scriptures and the Jewish culture in the first place</u>. His curriculum would have included all The Law and The Prophets. As a result, Paul's doctrinal writings in The New Testament are absolutely flawless, and would have been derived from the logic needed to place Old Testament doctrines into proper interpretation in and through Jesus Christ. It's not rocket science to understand from where Paul derived his observations and interpretations. He wrote down these doctrins, and his writings were anointed and inspired by the Holy Spirit!

What is mystifying is the fact that most of us don't always understand Paul, or Jesus. In reference to a doctrinal dissertation on the end times Paul writes to the Church in Thessalonica, *"But of the times and seasons, brethren, ye have no need that I write unto you."* I Thessalonians 5:1. Our response? "O yeah? I am supposedly already equipped to understand this?" Are we somehow short a few marbles compared to those of the early Church, or is there something missing from our data-base? The truth is, we, in this twenty-first century, have dropped much of the Judaic basis that allows us to arrive at appropriate interpretation and application. Even the early Gentile Church was taught Judaic root reasoning and Scriptural doctrine and culture, because it's in his letters to the Gentile Church that Paul states they already understand the things he is discussing. It's time to revisit the basis of many of our doctrines! In not understanding the order of the Feasts and Festivals, and their ramifications, we do not realize the significance of the order of the Harvests. This lack of background knowledge has left us arguing over how many resurrections there are, who is being resurrected, what the resurrected are to do, when are they resurrected, where they are resurrected, and why. We have placed the Rapture variously as pre-trib, mid-trib, post-trib, pre-millennial, post millennial, and a-millennial with no rapture at all. Our time-lines seem to make some logical sense, but always contain gaps we cannot adequately explain. Then Paul comes along and says, *"You have no need that I write unto you."* Right!

But to be fair, it's not Paul's fault. The early Church very quickly became side-tracked through the pressures of false teachers within, mutual animosities between Jews and Christians, and strong politically motivated persecution of both Jews and Christians from the top down within the Roman Empire. The resultant damage has plagued us down through the centuries since. The Gentilization of the Church, not just in demographic population, but in exegesis, has caused us to lose some of the doctrinal understanding the early first century Church obviously had a handle on.

What is encouraging though, is the fact that the Holy Spirit has cut across our tendency to stray. Obviously, Paul had to bring clarification to the early Church about the timing of the events leading to the fulfillment

JESUS CHRIST, VICTORIOUS KING

of the Rapture, and the restoration of the Kingdom to Israel. We can be encouraged in our day when we understand Gabriel indicated to Daniel that the prophecies would become clarified toward the end of the Age as the prophetic events themselves unfold.

VII. The New Heaven and The New Earth: Revelation 21: 1-15.

Following The Great White Throne Judgment, The New Heaven and The New Earth are formed. The Heavens are rolled up like a scroll, and the earth as we have known it, is destroyed, but the planet is not annihilated. Rather, it is re-formed. It is made new. There is no more sea in The New Earth. The New Jerusalem comes down out of Heaven, prepared as a Bride for her husband, and rests upon the circle of the earth. God dwells again in full fellowship with mankind, and wipes away all tears. There is no more death, sorrow, crying, or any pain, because all these former things that were part of the curse, are now gone.

Revelation chapter 21 gives us a glimpse into this New Heaven and New Earth. John sees The Holy City, The New Jerusalem, descend from God out of Heaven, prepared as a Bride for her Husband. The New Jerusalem is the permanent dwelling place of Christ and His Bride. John hears a great Voice from heaven, saying, Verse 3. *"Behold, the tabernacle of God is with men, and he will dwell with them, and they shall be his people, and God himself shall be with them, and be their God. Verse 4. And God shall wipe away all tears from their eyes; and there shall be no more death, neither sorrow, nor crying, neither shall there be any more pain: for the former things are passed away. Verse 5. And he that sat upon the throne said, Behold I make all things new. And he said unto me, Write: for these words are true and faithful. Verse 6. And he said unto me, It is done. I am the Alpha and Omega, the beginning and the end. I will give unto him that is athirst of the fountain of the water of life freely. Verse 7. He that overcometh shall inherit all things; and I will be his God, and he shall be my son. Verse 8. But the fearful, and unbelieving, and the abominable, and murderers, and whoremongers, and sorcerers, and idolaters, and all liars, shall have their part in the lake which burneth with fire and brimstone: which is the second death."* KJV.

VII. The New Jerusalem: Revelation 21: 9-27.

One of the seven angels who had the Seven Vials of Wrath, comes and talks with John, and says, verse 9. *"Come here. I will show you the bride, the Lamb's wife."* John is taken in spirit to a very high mountain, and is shown The New Jerusalem descending out of Heaven.

This Holy City has some amazing structural and functional characteristics. The Shekinah Glory of God is there. The light is very clear like a precious jasper stone. The City is surrounded by a massive, high wall, containing three gates on each of its four sides, with an angel stationed at each gate. The name of one of the twelve tribes of Israel is inscribed on each gate. The City wall has twelve foundations inscribed with the names of the twelve apostles of The Lamb.

The angel accompanying John on his tour, holds a golden reed. He measures the City, the gates, and the foundations. The City is described as being four-square, which lends itself to perhaps being a cube, each dimension being twelve-thousand furlongs. Some have pictured The New Jerusalem as a pyramid, which is a four-sided geometric shape that also has the mathematical ability to have the same, four-square dimensions. This is not an outlandish concept, because the occult tends to use the pyramid shape as one of its symbols of power and authority. Since the occult is <u>a counterfeit system to righteousness and truth</u>, attempting to undermine the Deity of Christ, and the power of God, it is possible the pyramid shape of the New Jerusalem is not far-out. A counterfeit tries to emulate reality in order to deceive and manipulate the unsuspecting, or to cast doubt. It would be just like Satan to try to cast negative connotations on the eternal dwelling of Christ and the Bride by absconding with, and desecrating the truth through making the pyramid shape into an occult pariah, <u>showing his jealousy</u> of Christ's total authority and power, which is, and will be the eternal reality in The New Jerusalem. Therefore, we will have to wait to verify the exact geometric shape of The New Jerusalem. Personally, I tend to think of it as a cube.

The wall is built of jasper, and the City is made of pure gold, like clear glass. The foundations of the wall are imbedded with twelve types of precious stones, and the twelve gates are twelve pearls. The streets of the City are paved with pure gold. There is no temple building structure in the City, because *"the Lord God Almighty and the Lamb are the temple of it"* Revelation 21: 22. The City does not need the sun or moon to shine upon it, because *"the glory of God did lighten it, and the Lamb is the light thereof."* Verse 23b. The redeemed out of all nations will walk in its light, and the kings of the earth will bring their glory and honor into the City. The City gates will never be shut during the day, which means they will never ever be shut, because there will be no more night. No wise (man's limited wisdom or foolish, devilish, pagan scheming), or anything that defiles, or is an abomination, or tells a lie, will ever enter. Only those who have their names written in The Book of Life will enter the New Jerusalem.

A. The River of Life, and The Tree of Life:

Revelation chapter 22:1-2 describes The River of The Water of Life that issues from The Throne of God and The Lamb. *"And he showed me a pure river of water of life, clear as crystal, proceeding out of the throne of God and of the Lamb. Verse 2. In the midst of the street of it, and on either side of the river, was there the tree of life, which bare twelve manner of fruits, and yielded her fruit every month: and the leaves of the tree were for the healing of the nations."* The Tree of Life that the angel with the flaming sword had guarded in The Garden of Eden after The Fall, has been transplanted, once into The Garden of Paradise for the coming wedding festivities, and it will be transplanted once more to be a prominent feature of the landscape in The New Jerusalem. It will grow in the central median of the main thoroughfare, and its branches will extend over both sides of The River of The Water of Life. It will bear twelve types of fruit, one for each month, and the leaves will be for the healing of the nations.

The Throne of God from which The Lamb will preside, will be located in the New Jerusalem, and His servants will serve Him there, and commune directly face to face with Him. Each will have His Name written in their forehead. Christ and His Bride will reign for ever and ever from The New Jerusalem.

VIII. No More Curse: Revelation 22:3-5.

Revelation 22:3. *"And there shall be no more curse:"* The curse on all Creation will be totally removed in The New Heaven and The New Earth. This is significant, because we generally think of the curse as affecting <u>mankind</u>, as a consequence of breaking our relationship with God, and bringing about <u>man's</u> separation from God, and eternal death and punishment. Although this is certainly true, <u>the curse has affected all Creation</u>. The curse fell upon man, the animal kingdom, and even upon the ground. In fact, the curse fell upon the entire universe and everything in it, both animate, and inanimate.

Originally, there was no sentence of death for any living thing, so there was no negative aging or decay. Neither was there breakdown or erosion of the inanimate. But the entrance of sin brought death, resulting in The First and Second Laws of Thermodynamics. Although, in the natural world, nothing in essence can be either created or destroyed, all does break down to a state of uselessness or chaos. That means all Creation has suffered the consequences of man's sin and disobedience. Scripture indicates *"For we know that <u>the whole creation</u> groaneth and travaileth in pain together until now."* Romans 8:22.

James makes an interesting proclamation, and observation. He reminds us that all good things come from God, and that *"Of his own will beget he us with the word of truth, <u>that we should be a kind of first fruits of his creatures</u>."* James 1:18. The salvation of mankind through the redemptive power of the blood of Jesus Christ, has brought about an ultimate promise <u>of the total reversal of the curse</u>. Since firstfruits are the wave offering of a full harvest, presented unto the LORD in thankfulness, indicating a full harvest is to follow, we who are regenerated through redemption, are the firstfruits of all His creatures, meaning, there will be a full harvest to come of all other creatures as well. <u>The entire Creation will come out from under the curse</u>, and dwell in perfection in The New Heaven and The New Earth. Since it was man's sin that caused the curse to pass upon all Creation, man's redemption as provided through Christ's atonement, breaking the curse of sin, will ultimately also redeem all Creation. So it would appear that everything God created will be part of The New Heaven and The New Earth.

The only thing missing will be the need for the sea. Does that mean there will be no marine creatures? We know all life in the oceans will be destroyed in the pouring out of the Second Vial, but we cannot say that there will be no water creatures in The New Earth. Since all Creation will be released from the curse, and marine creatures are definitely part of Creation, we must assume marine life will then benefit from this reversal of the curse along with all other creatures. Since there will be no more sea, we are able to conclude then, that all marine life may be fresh-water oriented.

A. Exhortation For The Church: Revelation 22:6-20.

The remainder of Revelation chapter 22 is an exhortation to the believers who are alive at the end of The Age of Grace before The Days of Awe begin. This passage is a message to us who are alive on earth just prior to the Rapture. Verses 6 through 20 of Revelation 22 are a targeted message for the born-again believers of today, the twenty-first century Church awaiting the Rapture. <u>WE are the ones who benefit the most from this message</u>, and from the things shown to John, <u>because all these things are shortly to come to pass</u>. This is a message across the centuries targeted directly to us, because we are now living during the days when the prophecies of all the prophets and of Revelation will be shortly fulfilled, and God will keep His final Appointments with mankind. John <u>is told to write us a letter containing information we are going to be in need of just prior to, and at the time of the Rapture</u>. This information will also benefit those who will have to endure the coming Days of Awe. Jesus Christ is soon to be revealed in all His glory and truth, first to His Church (Rosh HaShanah), and then to the whole world (Yom Kippur). This passage is primarily for us who are living in the closing days of The Church Age, so it is for us who are awaiting the coming of the Bridegroom to take us into His presence. Therefore, we would do well to read and heed this message from The LORD!

Since the topic of The Book of Revelation is The Revelation of Jesus Christ, we realize the bulk of the Book addresses the time-frame of the Church Age, and on into The Days of Awe. It gives necessary information the Church needs in order to be prepared for the Rapture, and provides warnings, exhortation, and invitational encouragement for those who will remain on the earth to live through The Days of Awe. Certainly, John is shown projections beyond The Days of Awe into The Millennium, The Great White Throne Judgment, and The New Heaven and The New earth, but these are not the main topic. Rather, these prophecies are intended to focus on the eternal Person, ministry, and position of Jesus Christ. The message of Revelation is particularly directed toward the righteous, starting with Christ's exhortations to The Seven Churches, and culminating with the urgent call to holiness, so we will be ready for when He comes for us.

John's Book of The Revelation of Jesus Christ will also be a comfort and guide for The Tribulation Saints, and for the Jews, revealing the unfolding of the time-table of The LORD's Divine Appointments, and the reason for the manner in which these Appointments will be fulfilled. All must sense the urgency, the grandeur, the terrible wrath, and the fervent love of Christ as portrayed in the pages of this Prophecy. Verse 6 of chapter 22 states: *"These sayings are faithful and true: and the Lord God of the holy prophets sent his angel to show unto his servants the things which must shortly be done."* If these things were shortly to be done in John's day, how much closer and more imminent, and therefore relevant, this message is now!

B. The Predominant Message for The Righteous:

In Revelation chapter 22 verse 7 Jesus states, *"Behold I come quickly: blessed is he that keepeth the sayings of the prophecies of this book. Verse 8. And I John saw these things, and heard them. And when I had heard and seen, I fell down to worship before the feet of the angel which showed me these things. Verse 9. Then saith he unto me, See thou do it not: for I am thy fellow servant, and of thy brethren the prophets, and of them which keep the sayings of this book: worship God. Verse 10. And he saith unto me, Seal not the sayings of the prophecies of* this book: for the time is at hand. Verse 11. He that is unjust, let him be unjust still: and he which is filthy, let him be filthy still: and he that is righteous, let him be righteous still: and he that is holy, let him be holy still." KJV.

Verse 11 is a reference particularly to the separation judgments of Rosh HaShanah and of Yom Kippur. Rosh HaShanah, which judgment takes place at the sounding of Ha Teruah at the beginning of The Days of Awe, is a judgment of separation of the Tzadikim (Righteous) from the Rashim (Wicked), and according to Jewish interpretation, the nominal secular. Those who have remained righteous from the previous Day of Atonement (which Christ fulfilled once and for all) until Rosh HaShanah, will be gathered unto the LORD. Those who are Wicked will remain, and go into The Ten Days of Awe to be tried, and will have one last chance along with the nominal, to repent. <u>But in truthful essence, there is no nominal designation with God. One is either Righteous or Wicked in His eyes</u>. So this verse goes one step further to the final separation judgment of the Righteous from the Wicked at Yom Kippur, when Tekiah HaGadol is sounded. At that time, it will become evident that there is no nominal position with God, but everyone will be <u>permanently sealed</u> as to their eternal destiny. The Wicked will remain wicked. The Unjust will remain unjust. The Filthy will remain filthy. The Righteous will remain righteous. People need to hear this message! The Church needs to hear it, and be awakened out of our complacency! These Divine Scheduled Appointments are soon to take place, ready or not, and the time for repentance will end!

Verse 12 reminds us of the urgency. It repeats "<u>Behold I come quickly: and my reward is with me, to give every man according as his work shall be</u>. Verse 13. *I am Alpha and Omega, the beginning and the end, the first and the last.* Verse 14. *Blessed are they that do his commandments, that they may have right to the tree of life, and may enter in through the gates into the city.* Verse 15. *For without are dogs, and sorcerers, and whormongers, and murderers, and idolaters, and whosoever loveth and maketh a lie.* Verse 16. *I Jesus have sent mine angel to testify unto you these things in the churches. I am the root and the offspring of David, and the bright and morning star."*

Verse 17. *"And the Spirit and the bride say, Come. And let him that heareth say, Come. And let him that is athirst come. And whosoever will let him take the water of life freely.* Verse 18. *For I testify unto every man that heareth the prophecy of this book. If any man shall add unto these things, God shall add unto him the plagues that are written in this book:* Verse 19. *And if any man shall take away from the words of the book of this prophecy, God shall take away his part out of the book of life, and out of the holy city, and from the things which are written in this book.* Verse 20. *He which testifieth these things saith.* <u>**Surely I come**</u>

quickly. Amen. Even so come Lord Jesus. Verse 21. *The grace of our Lord Jesus Christ be with you all. Amen.*"

CHAPTER 27
IRAQ, SYRIA, and ISRAEL'S SHORTCOMINGS

The rapid development in current world events has presented a challenge to keep abreast of while writing this book.

I. Iraq:

When I started, Saddam Hussein was still the President in Iraq, but now has been deposed by the Coalition Forces, and a new regime is being set up. For several months, no one knew for sure whether he was alive. Now he has been found, and is in custody awaiting sentencing for his crimes against humanity. At least his position as the despotic ruler over his land and people has ended. There are some hangers-on trying to pose as his supporters, and although they are not having much success in regaining any position of power, they, along with other Islamic factions opposed to the presence of the United States forces in particular, are managing by using gorilla terrorist tactics, to keep the conflict in Iraq on-going.

Iraq is the seat of the former Babylonian, Medio-Persian Empires, and was a vital part of the Greek Empire. Much of this world's ideologies and economic standards originated from The Babylonian Empire. In fact, the geographical area of Iraq was indeed the cradle of post-Flood civilization, dating back to before Nimrod and the Tower of Babel, and now the international focus is shifting back to this piece of real estate that has had so much world influence down through the centuries. A regime change there, which now is in the throes of taking place, will prepare The Middle East, and indeed the world, for a new era in global political balance and economics.

So are the events taking place in Iraq part of God's timetable? Absolutely. The Daughter of Babylon is poised on the brink of performing her final role in world events before Christ returns. We must keep a sharp eye on Iraq, and even on Iran which was integral to the Babylonian and Medio-Persian Empires as well. Iraq's next regime may be the one that brings a degree of wealth and prosperity to the region. Her ability to control the flow of oil and the distribution of other commodities, coupled with her ideologies, could provide much of the foundation upon which the coming Time of Trouble facing the entire world will be built. We must keep in mind that The Four Horsemen of The Apocalypse appear to be already galloping, and the emergence of a strong economic infrastructure within Iraq could form the basis for the coming stranglehold on commodities, redistributing the wealth of the entire world. The hand that holds the purse-strings has the ability to call the shots, so a manipulated era of economic upheaval may very well be a reality in the days ahead. Economic recovery for one, may in fact produce hardship for many others. The course for these horses and horsemen to gallop world-wide may already be laid out, as the world is now leading up to The Battle of Gog and Magog.

The Whore of Babylon may indeed be poised to mount The Fourth Hybrid Beast. This means The Whore must have some basis upon which to consolidate her influence, so she can act in economic concert with the final Hybrid Beastly Empire that is now beginning to emerge. This Empire will draw upon the highest positions of power and influence of both East and West, particularly as represented through The Arab nations, and The European Union. She is the one who will steer this final Beast, just as she has controlled all the other Empirical Beasts of the past, and she may do so from a renewed position arising out of the recovery of Iraq, and the strengthening of The European Union's economic and political clout.

The ancient City of Babylon which was being rebuilt by Saddam Hussein, may again become a major economic center in the world. This development need not take a lot of time either, because the restored facilities there apparently were not damaged in this latest war. The usefulness of this site may not take long to recognize for those who require a secure base from which to operate. Iraqi domestic political power may still remain seated in Baghdad, but Iraq's economics and culture may shift to emanate from the revived Babylon sometime in the near future.

The United Nations has now officially signed an agreement to send in representatives to assist the United States in the reorganization of the Iraqi government, and to help rebuild the internal domestic infrastructure. Members of The European Union also are now beginning to offer assistance. Therefore, it is important that we watch how Iraq now develops in economic recovery and international affiliation, and not simply observe what transpires on the internal political level.

Will the Iraqi leaders who emerge out of the war and unrest be pliable in the hands of international opinion and policy? Yes, and no. They certainly will not relish any more attacks from the USA or Britain, or from anyone else for a good while. The people of Iraq, although not excited about the presence of Coalition Troops and outside forces manipulating and directing the formation of their next government, are at least grateful to be free from the oppression they suffered under Saddam Hussein, and they certainly will now expect, and work toward, a hopefully much more open and equitable society, tempered of course by the dictates of Islamic shariah doctrine.

However, this metamorphosis will not take place without an under-current of internal animosities between political and rival Muslim groups. But in the final analysis, their fear and hatred of the United States may win the day for the emergence of a new regime that at least has a more progressive outlook. It remains to be seen just what form this progressiveness will take. Also, it will be interesting to track how Iraq develops her new foreign policy, and whether this will result in stronger ties with Russia, and how it will define her place within The Arab World.

Meanwhile, Iraq certainly will not be able to accomplish any of her immediate aspirations on her own. She needs the monetary, military, economic, and medical assistance of the West to settle the nation. This is a very difficult position for many in Iraq to recognize or accept, because they are a proud people, and they have been taught that the United States especially, along with Britain and the other Christian Western nations, are crusading militant impostors and infidels. This Islamic ideological premise is not something that can be shed overnight, even though these 'infidels' have been the very ones to bring about their freedom from overt oppression. But the prophetic spiral is turning, and the new climate in Iraq will definitely bring about further fulfillment.

II. Syria:

The mutual animosities now being voiced by the USA and Britain toward Syria, as the West actively continues the war against terrorism, is furthering the march toward Gog and Magog. Syria is under scrutiny, much to the chagrin of the Russians in particular. Vladimir Putin has voiced serious reprisals may be considered if the USA attacks Syria. President George W. Bush has not stated in so many words that Syria will be attacked,[198] but he has recently signed an agreement in the US House of Representatives to allow sanctions to be imposed if necessary, contending that Syria is a breeding ground for, and a supporter of terrorism. The sanctions are known as The Syria Accountability and Lebanese Sovereignty Restoration Act (HR 1828.) This Bill bans exportation of all 'dual use' technologies to Syria, claws back some of the US diplomatic interaction with Syria, allows the US to freeze Syrian government assets within the United States, and demands Syrian withdrawal of all troops from Lebanon. It even goes so far as to restrict Syrian planes from flying over US air-space. [199]Needless to say, even though

---

[198] Arutz Sheva News Service, www.IsraelNationalNews.com, October 16. 2003, *FOR SYRIAN ACCOUNTABILITY & A FREE LEBANON.*
[199] The Jerusalem Post, OnlineEdition, October 17, 2003, Tovah Lazaroff and Janine Zacharia. www.jpost.com *US votes sanctions, Syria slams Israel.*

these sanctions have not yet been imposed, the Syrian reaction has not been friendly!

But interestingly, Lebanon is not at all happy about the declaration that Syria may be asked to withdraw troops. The current Lebanese government is actually pro-Syria, and views the threatened sanction regarding Syrian troops on her soil as US capitulation to pressure from Israel.

As a precautionary response, Syria has put all military on alert for a possible attack by Israel, and has even threatened reprisal attacks into the Golan. If any of these US sanctions are actually imposed against Syria, there certainly will be repercussions, both for the United States, and inevitably, for Israel and for the world!

According to an Arutz Sheva News Service report, Israel's Defense Minister Sha'ul Mofaz stated on Tuesday, October 28, 2003 that the Israeli army intelligence is aware that Hizbullah is preparing an attack against Israel, "more significant than the usual artillery attacks." Israel has indicated it will take any such attack very seriously, and the IDF Northern Command O.C. Benny Ganz stated "attacking Israel and then hiding amidst civilian populations might cause Israel to have to take very strong action." Hizbullah is not the Syrian military, but Syria obviously does support Hizbullah, and is allowing this terrorist/political radical organization to be a front-line of threats and possible attack against Israel. Needless to say, the US Secretary of State, Colin Powell, is calling on both Israel and Syria to "tone-down." So, everyone is again on edge, waiting anxiously to see what will transpire between Israel and Syria.

Also, the Golan has become a territorial contention between Syria and Israel again. This mountainous area in northern Israel has a history of being used as a threat of Syrian take-over whenever Syria wishes to pressure Israel. With the current animosities raging over the Territories, and the dismantlement of Settlements within Israel, the Golan is again being eyed by the Syrians. Since it appears Ariel Sharon is 'threatening' to take unilateral steps to dismantle settlements and outposts in Gaza and the West Bank in preparation of the formation of a Palestinian State, thus giving Israel the upper hand in saying where the borders of such a State will be, Syria is seeing an opportunity to make certain the Golan is part of this move. Needless to say, Sharon is putting Israel in a most awkward position!

Meanwhile, 'The Quartet,' negotiations regarding 'The Roadmap' means Vladyimir Putin and George Bush still must try to work together toward peace in The Middle East. Tensions obviously are great between these two powerful world leaders, as well as with The European Union leaders following the Iraqi invasion. But the formation of a Palestinian

State carved out of The Land of Covenant is still a number one priority, especially for George Bush, and is being encouraged by Prime Minister Tony Blaire of Britain. Whether the tensions regarding Syria will scuttle the goal of the 'Roadmap' is debatable, because threatened reprisals against Syria may be used as a trump-card to attempt to keep tensions down in The Middle East. Syria definitely wants a Palestinian State to be formed, if for no other reason than to weaken Israel. Concerns regarding Syria may indeed help shift the focus onto Israel and the formation of the Palestinian State as a result. We will have to wait and see what transpires regarding Syria.

But, 'The Roadmap' does appear to be in jeopardy as the Arab Terrorist organizations: Hamas, Fatah, Islamic Jihad, Hizbullah, and other such groups, are becoming more organized and militant. And even though a "hudna" (so-called cease-fire, which really means a time-out to re-arm) was recently called, it quickly fell apart as the acts of terrorism within Israel and in Iraq have increased, with threats of further atrocities planned, particularly against Israeli and USA targets. These groups are on the extreme edge of the Arab policies which are being promoted to annihilate Israel, not simply to form a co-existent State. Therefore, they have in their power the ability to disrupt the 'Road Map' through non-compliance with the terms of the agreement to end all atrocities. Therefore, implementation of 'The Road Map Peace Plan" already has major pot-holes along its path. It will take a very strong hand indeed to bring these terrorists to heel.

[200]Along with the efforts to keep "The Roadmap' viable, Ariel Sharon has devised another controversial plan. He has stated that if negotiations with the Palestinians cannot proceed without violence, he will unilaterally begin withdrawal from Judea, Samaria, and Gaza (together known as Yesha) by a controlled dismantlement and evacuation of Jews from these areas. [201]The response from Israelis has been swift. [202]There is a move now

---

[200] Arutz Sheva News Service, <http://www.IsraelNationalNews.com>, Mar. 21, 2004. *LIKUD MINISTERS HEAR OF DISENGAGEMENT PLAN.* "...Prime Minister Ariel Sharon formally discussed his disengagement plan - under which he wishes to unilaterally withdraw from the Gaza Strip and expel its nearly 8,000 Jewish residents from their homes of 30 years - with the Likud Party ministers... Most Likud Ministers do not support the withdrawal in its current format."

[201] Arutz Sheva News Service, <http://www.IsraelNationalNews.com>, March 15, 2004, *YESHA COUNCIL TO LIKUD MINISTERS: WAKE UP ALREADY!"*... the Council of Jewish Communities in Judea, Samaria and Gaza (Yesha Council) has expressed a sharp protest against the Likud Party ministers still straddling the fence regarding Sharon's unilateral withdrawal plan."

"...Sharon has decided to retreat under fire from Gaza, plans to uproot dozens

The Final Schedule Revealed

afoot to topple Sharon and his coalition Government from power, [203] and call new elections. [204] The Yesha Rabbis Council of Judea, Samaria, and Gaza, (the [205] "Land of Israel Rabbis" have spoken against withdrawal, have promised resistance to Ariel Sharon's initiative, and have vowed to prevent the dismantlement of any Jewish Communities. [206] This resistance, and its vocalization both against Ariel Sharon and against the [207] forced movement of Jews from their homes, has been rising to a crescendo.

Meanwhile, the United States has been carefully watching Sharon's stance, and encouraging him to get on with taking steps toward the formation of a Palestinian State. However, the United States position is caution, and a preference for negotiated agreement with the Palestinian Authority rather than unilateral withdrawal, although George Bush has

---

of communities in Yesha and expel thousands of residents from their homes - all with nothing at all in return." "...The time has come to end the 'silence of the sheep.' Don't let Weisglass continue dragging Sharon into the abyss. For G-d's sake, say something!"

[202] Arutz Sheva News Service, <http://www.IsraelNationalNews.com>, Mar. 16, 2004. *PM BARELY SURVIVES NO-CONFIDENCE VOTE.* "While he emerged with a majority in support of his address to the Knesset yesterday, Prime Minister Ariel Sharon was made to understand that his disengagement plan does not enjoy widespread Knesset support - even among coalition members."

[203] The Boston Globe, www.boston.com/news/world/articles/2004/02/04sharon_could... March 2, 2004, Dan Ephron, *Sharon could face political rebellion, Right-wing parties say they'll leave coalition if settlements dismantled.*

[204] Arutz Sheva News Service, <http://www.IsraelNationalNews.com>, December 18, 2003, *THOUSANDS EXPECTED TO ARRIVE IN MIGRON.* "With leading rabbis of the religious-Zionist public presiding, hundreds of people rallied in Migron last night to declare that they will make sure to stop any plans to uproot a jewish community anywhere in Israel." "The Yesha Rabbis Council of Judea, Samaria, and Gaza declared, "It is halakhically [Jewish-legally] forbidden to uproot a Jewish town in the Land of Israel, and the government has no right to give over parts of the Land of Israel to foreigners."

[205] The Jerusalem Post Online Edition, www.jpost.com/servlet/Satellite?pagename=JPost/JPArticle/Prin..., Dec.18, 2003, *Rabbis call for resistance to Migron dismantlement.*

[206] Arutz Sheva News Service, <http://www.IsraelNationalNews.com>, March 15,2004, *LIKUD BILL TO DEMAND KNESSET MAJORITY FOR YESHA EVACUATIONS*
"The Likud Knesset faction continues to show opposition to Prime Minister Sharon's plans to destroy Jewish communities in Judea, Samaria and Gaza. "...The purpose of the bill," MK Chazan said, "is to curb the government, such that any Cabinet decision to evacuate Jewish communities must also

indicated he will support the idea of unilateral withdrawal from Gaza. The same is being voiced by Kofi Annon from the United Nations. The Palestinians themselves are mixed in their reaction. Some view Sharon's initiative as a victory for Arab terrorism, showing it is really starting to have an effect which will further their cause. Their goals are being reached by Israeli capitulation to terror! Others are not standing around holding their breath, stating they will believe it when they see dismantlement actually begin.

III. The Perspective from The Book of Isaiah:

To put this present day situation into prophetic perspective, come with me to the Book of Isaiah for a few moments. When we read Isaiah, we generally think in terms of what for us is now ancient history. Although there was fulfillment of Isaiah's prophecies in the past, we are dealing with God-breathed prophecy, and the prophetic spiral is definitely in play, so most of Isaiah's prophecies have more than one fulfillment before they are complete. Generally, we look at Isaiah's prophecies and say they were for Judah and Israel. But this conclusion must be qualified to understand the ramifications.

Isaiah was given a vision by the LORD, and he prophesied during the reigns of Uzziah, Jotham, Ahaz, and Hezekiah, who all ruled over Judah, according to verse 1 of chapter 1. So Isaiah's prophecies deal directly with The House of Judah, but are not exclusive. The House of Israel was taken captive by the Assyrians in 722 B.C.E. The House of Judah was taken into captivity by the Babylonians in 586 B.C.E. These dates of when Israel and Judah were taken captive are important, because they put Isaiah's prophecies into perspective.

Isaiah's vision and the Word of the LORD he received, draw upon the past, as well as projects to the future, first of all for The Assyrian Captivity, then for The Babylonian Captivity. But absolute fulfillment does not end

---

receive Knesset approval. We are talking about decisions that touch on the very existence of our Jewish state." Chazan, who heads the Yesha lobby in the Knesset, said that the forum would "fight bitterly against the Prime Minister's disengagement plan, because it stands in the face of Israel's continued secure existence."

[207] Arutz Sheva News Service, <http://www.IsraelNationalNews.com>, December 18, 2003, *RABBI SHAPIRA'S LETTER.* "... We must answer the call and come to the aid of these heroes in every spot in Israel, and take action and prevent the uprooting of communities. Such destruction is forbidden according to our Holy Torah,..."

with the ancient Assyrians and Babylonians. These prophecies also project down to the present, and beyond.

Isaiah's prophecies reveal more about the political climate, and the predominant thinking of the leadership within Judah especially. Judah is the focal-point used for the fulfillment of end-time prophecy regarding present day Israel. Isaiah then, reveals the mind-set of modern Israel!

Apart from obvious idolatry and disobedience, we often do not catch the undercurrent of thinking that was rampant throughout the population and national leadership of either Judah or Israel during Isaiah's ministry.

More importantly, we certainly must be careful that we do not miss the implications and application of Isaiah's prophecies for the present. We have a tendency to somehow put our current Israeli nation on a pedestal, because, after all, Israel is back in The Land, therefore God's hand of blessing must rest upon them, so surely they cannot do anything wrong now. Right? Wrong! Israel still is the nation chosen by God to possess The Land of Covenant, but they have a long way to go before they turn totally back to the LORD in full repentance, recognizing truth, and receiving Jesus Christ as their Messiah and KING. In fact, because of their current half-baked religious, humanistic secular stance, many will again be exiled and/or scattered before the LORD comes and brings them back, and establishes them in The Land.

A. Israel's Iniquity:

Why will the LORD allow what will appear to be a reversal of current blessings? The sin of Israel and Judah <u>was spiritual adultery committed against the LORD</u>, through choosing to buddy-up to, and even participate with, the philosophies and pagan practices of the nations surrounding them. In other words, they tried to compromise in order to make themselves more acceptable on the international scene, because they wanted to fit-in and be recognized. Unfortunately, this mind-set still plagues Israel! They still seek international acceptance and recognition, causing their government leaders to do what really is not best for their own interests. They bow easily to international opinion, especially when threats are being made against them. In other words, they accept opinion and policy that others put forward in order to placate their enemies and win friends. They feel they can tame their enemies through compliance, concessions, and negotiation! Ariel Sharon has even gone so far as to give up on the compliance of Israel's enemies, and has chosen to reward terrorism, through concessions and retreat.

IRAQ, SYRIA, and ISRAEL'S SHORTCOMINGS

What they fail to take absolutely seriously, is the publicly stated position of their sworn enemies. The Arabs have many times stated in no uncertain terms that their ultimate goal is to destroy Israel as a nation. The enemies' ruse is negotiation, along with the use of terrorist tactics. Part of their strategy is to use lies and deception at the negotiating table to hoodwink Israel and the West into believing they are making headway toward a compromised peace in The Middle East that will last. But in the agenda of the Islamic Arabs, The Palestinian State is only a step along the path to several goals: annihilating Israel, destroying the Christians, and bringing in Islamic world domination.

B. Inflammatory Rhetoric:

If we think this is a drastic interpretation of what is taking place in The Middle East, [208] all we need do is refer to the comments recently made by the Malasian Prime Minister, Mahathir Mohammad, during the Organization of the Islamic Conference (OIC.) He called on all Muslims to unite together against Israel, and against Jews world-wide. However, he also stated a somewhat new approach must be taken -- brain-power, not just brawn! (As if they haven't already been bending their brains to their schemes!) He accused the Jews of inventing socialism, communism, human rights, and democracy, "so that persecuting them would appear to be wrong, so that they can have equal rights with others." In his view, this well thought-out strategy has allowed the Jews to survive for the past 2000 years. He stated that Israel, "is the enemy allied with most powerful nations," and "the Jews rule the world by proxy. They get others to fight for them. ... They have gained control of the most powerful countries, and they, this tiny community, have become a world power. We cannot fight them through brawn alone, we must use our brains also." So, the Islamic strategy is to now officially include the jihad of wits. This is the tactic the AntiChrist and his henchmen will use successfully against Israel.

The pincher effect strategy of <u>terrorism</u>, coupled with <u>purposefully thought-out deception and manipulation</u> against Israel and the West, was made known from another source in October, 2003. [209] Muammar Gaddafi of Libya (who by the way, is the current appointed United Nations Secretary of Human Rights) made a speech directed toward the

---

[208] Arutz Sheva News Service, <http://www.IsraelNationalNews.com>, October 16, 2003, *MALASIAN PM: JEWS RULE THE WORLD.*

[209] Arutz Sheva News Service, <http://www.IsraelNationalNews.com> October 14, 2003. *GADDAFI: "ARABS ARE COMPLETELY USELESS"*

The Final Schedule Revealed

Arab world, obviously designed to stir up anger. He accused the Arabs of being "completely useless," and called for Libyan withdrawal from the Arab Organization of Islamic States. He harked-back to the Israeli War of Independence in 1948, pointing out "the Arabs fought as one people and as one nation." What he did not point out was the fact that the Arabs lost that conflict, even though they greatly out-numbered the Israeli forces. He accused the now-generation of Arabs as having "no courage, honor, blood, or pride. ... You cannot speak of Arab unity and pan-Arab nationalism."

He stated, "The U.S. has become Libya's enemy No.1 due to Arab and pan-Arab unity and the Palestinian cause. Libya became the enemy of the Jews and the entire West for the Arabs, and without this there would have been no problems between Libya and the U.S., and between it and the Jews, or between Libya and Europe. If we had not gotten ourselves in trouble in battles because of pan-Arabism and Arab unity, we would have been spared all the tragedies caused us." He basically told all the Arab nations, "Leave us alone! Are you attacking us because we are Arabs? We're fed up. We are Africans. Treat us like Africans; treat us like black Negroes; we'll stay away from you, and you'll stay away from us. Don't talk to us, and we won't talk to you. What is the connection between Libya and Kuwait? One country is situated in Africa, and the other in Asia. We will not meet again until Judgment Day, and then one of us will go to Paradise, and the other will go to Hell..." End of quote.

Has Gaddafi had a change of heart toward the West, the Jews, and Europe? Has he suddenly 'seen the light,' and does not want anything at all to do with the Arabs, as his speech seems to indicate? Is he now preaching <u>true</u> human rights? He states, "The Arabs have become the joke of the world because they do not think of their future... The Arabs are completely useless... The Arabs have written a mark of disgrace in history that they will never be able to eradicate. They watch what is happening in Iraq and in Palestine from the sidelines. They are finished. They have no honor, and they have no blood. There is no longer any Arab blood or pan-Arab blood, Arab unity, Arab manliness, Arab femininity. Today was the most dangerous terror operation in so-called Israel - <u>and it was carried out by a young Palestinian woman</u>, not by a man... The Arabs are completely useless. <u>We must not waste time</u>. The Arabs are through. Tomorrow, Asia will establish great unions, and Africa is already united - and where are you, Arabs?" Underline emphasis mine.

If he wants to distance himself and Libya from Arab causes, why is he so concerned with what is taking place in Iraq and "Palestine?" Why did he zero-in on the recent Maxim Restaurant bombing in Israel as "the most dangerous terror operation," and that it was carried out by a Palestinian

IRAQ, SYRIA, and ISRAEL'S SHORTCOMINGS

woman rather than a man, if he is no longer concerned with what this terror operation was to achieve?

He goes on to apologize to the African nations for having brought many of them into the Arab League, which he states is "a failed nation, a failed regime, and failed people..." He goes on to reiterate that Libya must quit the Arab League, "without wasting time. These people (The Arabs) are useless. Their situation is terrible. We must be rid of them, of their curses and of their problems." Really? Can we believe him?

His speech continues, to reveal where his <u>true aspirations</u> lie. He challenges Islamic women directly, <u>but in contradiction to his previous diatribe against the men not being responsible for the "most important terrorist attack."</u> In other words, he uses double-speak. "The woman must be trained how to fight within the home, how to put together an explosive belt and blow herself up together with the enemy soldiers... We must train the women how to booby-trap the car and blow it up among the enemy, how to blow up the house so it falls on the enemy soldiers. Traps must be prepared." He goes on to indicate women must know how to booby-trap suitcases so that they blow up when inspected, booby-trap clothes, purses, shoes, children's toys, "so that they blow up on enemy soldiers."

First of all, women and children are obviously expendable in his opinion, (along with the lives of the young men who usually do carry out the terrorist suicide missions) so their lives are not important. Secondly, who are the "enemy soldiers?" There are only two sources of "enemy soldiers" at the moment. The Coalition forces in Iraq, and the IDF in Israel. He surely cannot be referring to the UN Peace Keeping Forces which shortly may enter the picture in Iraq, because after all, he is a high ranking respected member of the UN, with an important portfolio himself. Human Rights! We must therefore conclude that innocent Arab women and children fall outside of his human rights portfolio, along with Israelis, US, and British soldiers, since it is obviously his intention that women learn how to blow themselves up <u>along with</u> the "enemy soldiers!" So women are to increase their involvement in doing the dirty work, even if they, and their children, must be killed in doing so.

And what exactly does he mean by saying, "We must not waste time." Waste time doing what? Separating from the Arab goals and organizations, or blowing up the women and children to fulfill these goals? He is purposely ambiguous, leaving those listening to draw their own conclusions!

It is this type of negative psychology, pep-rally speech-making that is designed to anger the Arab community in order to ruffle their feathers, so that they will rise up to prove him wrong. This is rallying the troops

The Final Schedule Revealed

through manipulated mind-control and verbal abuse! All one need do to make someone angry, is to call him useless! Either he will react by punching you out, or he will become intimidated. You will then be able to direct his anger to accomplish your own destructive goals. This is nothing short of bullying the troops, especially in regard to women and children. The entire world should be up in arms about this speech, but most folk do not even know Gaddafi gave it! Has the international media been muzzled too?

Hmm! Gaddafi is the current Human Rights Secretary of the UN! Go figure! What most of us fail to realize is the fact that it is possible Gaddafi, even within his official UN position, may be operating under <u>a valid, but different set of Human Rights principles</u> than the rest of us. Ask any Muslim whether he believes in Human Rights, and he will answer unflinchingly, and honestly, in the affirmative. But what he won't tell you is the fact that his definition and yours are at opposite ends of the Human Rights spectrum. [210]According to Bat Ye'or, a noted author exposing jihad, and 'dhimmitude,' there are two conflicting human rights declarations currently operating in the world. 1. "The Universal Declaration of Human Rights," and "International Bill of Human Rights" which were set up under the UN Charter, and 2. "The Cairo Declaration of Human Rights in Islam" which was approved in 1990 by the Organization of the Islamic Conference (OIC), conforming to Islamic belief as dictated by the Islamic Shariah doctrines of law and conduct, under which many Islamic countries now operate.

At first glance it would appear to be prudent to have someone who understands <u>both declarations</u> to be in charge of Human Rights in the United Nations. But is it? What most of the world fails to grasp is that it certainly is possible Gaddafi is operating in his UN position according to The Cairo Declaration, while purportedly representing The UN Declaration. Most of us do not realize he may have two conflicting declarations within his ability to manipulate as Secretary of Human Rights! He is in a perfect position to use the jihad of deception, even within the UN! Needless to say, the rest of us certainly no longer have a guaranteed Human Rights advocate within the United Nations, because he has an immutable position from which to operate. The fox commissioned to mind the hen house has already raided it! Unfortunately, most of the hens haven't figured it out yet!

---

[210] FRONTPAGE MAGAZINE, www.FrontPageMagazine.com, October 10, 2003. Jamie Glazov, Symposium: *The Muslim Persecution of Christians*.

Therefore, we now have a co-ordinated plan of attack on two fronts. 1. Mind-games, and 2. The escalation of terrorism at the expense of more innocent Arab lives, which are to be used directly as terrorist weapons. So deception and terrorism are not only to be continued, but are scheduled to be stepped up several notches in the days ahead.

So where are we? The world is on the brink of the most dangerous international scenario ever know to man, yet most of the West still does not understand. We are sitting-ducks for manipulation, deception, and rampant terrorism. By the way, just the threat of terror is a form of terror itself. All of us have already been attacked by both pincher-prongs in this war!

C. Israel is Hoodwinked:

Meanwhile, Israel, who is the Islamic target of choice in order to get through to the USA, and ultimately to destroy both, only half-heartedly realizes she is already in a war, so does not recognize the severity of it. She is deceived. How is that possible?[211] Her ability to be hoodwinked lies in her propensity to allow others to run her affairs, and the overwhelming desire to be accepted in the world. She does not give public credence to the God of Israel, but is proud of her own achievements. In other words, she is still willful, proud, and arrogant. This was Israel's idolatry in history, and it still is! Do all Israelis fit this profile? NO! But their overall government attitude is leading Israeli citizens down a very rocky road ahead. And many Israelis are fearful of what is coming down that 'Road!'

---

[211] Women For Israel's Tomorrow (Women in Green), www.womeningreen.org., March 19, 2004. *Plans and Plans* by Gary Cooperberg. "...Threats to our existence are nothing new to the Jewish people. What we must continue to keep, first and foremost, in our minds is the knowledge that Israel and the Jewish People are part of a Divine Plan which no human power can alter. Of course it would be a lot better if we, the Jewish People, could pull ourselves together and act with faith in G-d and true self-confidence in the certainty of our destiny. By failing to do this we are the prime cause of our own needless suffering." "... We Jews have been trying to compromise with our enemies from the moment of our re-emergence as a sovereign entity. Consistently those efforts have brought nothing but war and strife. Never have we gained any advantage as a result of our attempts to appease our enemies. The only times we had any respite from our enemies were in response to inflicting decisive victories against them. Yet, in spite of this observable fact, we have consistently undone those victories by voluntarily surrendering to the losers!"

Notice what Isaiah writes in chapter 1, verse 2: *"Hear, O heavens, and give ear, O earth: for the LORD hath spoken, I have nourished and brought up children, and they have rebelled against me. Verse 3. The ox knoweth his owner, and the ass his master's crib: but Israel doth not know, my people doth not consider. Verse 4. A sinful nation, a people laden with iniquity, a seed of evildoers, children that are corrupters: they have forsaken the LORD, they have provoked the Holy One of Israel unto anger, they are gone away backward. Verse 5. <u>Why should ye be stricken any more</u>? Ye will revolt more and more: the whole head is sick, and the whole heart faint. Verse 6. From the sole of the foot even unto the head there is no soundness in it; but wounds, and bruises, and putrifying sores: they have not been closed, neither bound up, neither mollified with ointment."* KJV Underlining mine.

Both the Heavens and the earth are to take note that the LORD has given His opinion on Israel. He has raised them properly, and provided for them, but they have rebelled. Even animals know who their masters are, and understand where their safety and provision lies, but Israel has sinned, and willingly become participant in corruption. They have forsaken the LORD, and provoked Him to anger. This has resulted in His discipline in the past, but His anger has not been fully carried out -- yet. The LORD will pour out His disciplinary wrath on the entire world, <u>and on Israel</u>, during the coming Ten Days of Awe.

Obviously, Israel still has not repented of their rebellion against the LORD. Why? Because they are absorbed in their wayward, futile thinking, setting out their own misguided agenda, thinking they can solve their own problems without God. But where has this stance gotten them thus far? They perpetuate unhealthy policies, and reap the paralysis of fear. The LORD asks, *"Why should ye be stricken any more?"* The path they are determined to travel has brought them nothing but wounds, bruises, and open sores. Terrorism, suicide bombings, and murders. The LORD is amazed. One would think they would wake-up and realize they are getting it wrong, but apparently they do not have the advantage of clear, sound reason as yet. This blindness was evident in their past, and it still is so today.

D. Jerusalem almost Abandoned:

Isaiah chapter 1 verse 7 describes the devastation of the Land following the original captivities under Assyria, then Babylon. But verse 8 addresses "The Daughter of Zion," current Jerusalem. *"And the daughter of Zion is left as a cottage in a vineyard, as a lodge in a garden of cucumbers, as a besieged city."* It is interesting to note that the Daughter of Zion is described as an abandoned home in a vinyard, or as a lodge in a vegetable garden, and as a besieged city. That means structure is intact, but the inhabitants have vacated. These structures lie within still productive and profitable property, which means the physical infrastructure still exists, but for some reason the resident owners have abandoned it all. Also, since this is Zion, and the *"besieged city"* is mentioned, we know we are dealing with Judah, and specifically with [212]Mount Zion which is The Temple Mount, and Jerusalem. Why would these be intact, yet left empty as if they were under some sort of siege? This scenario did occur in the past under the Babylonians when verse 9 was the result. *"Except the LORD of hosts had left unto us a very small remnant, we should have been as Sodom, and we should have been like unto Gomorrah."* However, it will occur again.

Following The Battle of Gog and Magog, Jerusalem will still be intact, and yes, The Temple will be built. The LORD orchestrates Gog and Magog to save Judah, and to usher in The Days of Awe. During this war it appears nuclear weapons, or at least serious bombing raids, will be exchanged between the fighting international factions, but structural devastation will not fall upon Jerusalem. Jerusalem and Judah will be saved at that time. It is the LORD's will to *"save the tents of Judah first,"* according to Zechariah 12:7. Jerusalem must be preserved to bring about God's will. So how does the reduction in population of the city of Jerusalem take place? This depopulation is the result of several scenarios that unfold over the entire course of The Days of Awe, so it is not simply from one incident. Jerusalem is not directly attacked during the Gog-Magog Battle, but by the same token, there are several logical scenarios which may cause Jews to consider leaving Jerusalem. The war may scare some Jerusalem residents into leaving, so that they return to the safety of Diaspora, or at least to other smaller cities within Israel. Next, many may leave after The Temple is built, because it is very possible that once the initial excitement wears off, the reality of what Temple rituals require may hit home! So some will simply

---

[212] Author's Note: Mount Zion is generally identified as a hill on the north side of Jerusalem near the Temple Mount, according to present maps. And the Temple Mount is currently identified as Mount Moriah. But there is some debate as to where Mount Zion and Mount Moriah really were. Abraham was instructed to sacrifice Isaac on Mount Moriah. Jesus, The Lamb of God, was crucified on Golgotha, and was the literal fulfillment of the Akeidah substitute Lamb, not just on behalf of Isaac, but for the whole world. It is therefore logical, Scripturally, to place Mount Moriah at Golgotha. Scripture also variously identifies Mount Zion as a name for Jerusalem, The City of David, as well as appears to be the location of the future Temple Throne of Messiah. Therefore, it is logical that the Temple Mount may also be referred to as Mount Zion.

turn their back on Temple practices and return to Diaspora just to maintain their Judaism in a passive manner, once they realize the bloodiness of the sacrificial system. But not all leave, a remnant does remain.

Is this interpretation pure speculation? No. The next few verses in the same passage are obviously part of the context, and the topic is clarified, revealing the Jews' attitude toward their Temple practices after The Third Temple is complete. We will look at the ramifications of this in a moment. While some reject Temple practices, many others will embrace the sacrificial rites and customs.

But the numbers vacating Mount Zion and Jerusalem will increase with the rise of AntiChrist unto the scene, and especially after The Temple is desecrated. Half-way through the Tribulation, six and one-half years after Gog and Magog, AntiChrist will take over The Temple and Jerusalem, so that Israel's government, along with many Jerusalem citizens, will be exiled. Because he will take over the Temple, many priests especially will find they must flee -- literally for their lives -- because they will find they suddenly cannot enter the Temple, and AntiChrist will likely hunt them down to eliminate them if possible. Judaism will become illegal, especially in Jerusalem and on the Temple Mount! They will have to leave quickly. Jesus refers to this scenario. He stated in Matthew 24:15-16, *"When ye therefore shall see the abomination of desolation, spoken of by Daniel the prophet, stand in the holy place, (whoso readeth let him understand) Then let them which be in Judea flee into the mountains."*

How do they manage to flee to the mountains? The Eagle of the USA helps many of them, and they end up in Edom as exiles. So the Jewish population of Jerusalem and Mount Zion will be greatly reduced under AntiChrist's regime. Jerusalem will be <u>like a city under pagan siege</u>. The City is not under siege of military battle at this juncture, but abandoned <u>first by those who forsake the LORD</u>, and <u>further emptied as a result of the treachery</u> of AntiChrist's regime. Thus the city seems forsaken, like an intact cottage, or a planted garden that has been abandoned, stripped especially of her priests and government leaders.

However, this is a prophecy with spiral fulfillment ability. Jesus continues, but the scene changes, because He next states there will be a further situation where immediate fleeing will not necessarily be wise! There is a further scenario which will also leave much of Jerusalem intact structurally, but many people dead. Eventually, at the end of The Days of Awe, during the Battle of Armageddon, Jerusalem <u>will</u> actually come under the siege of military battle, and Jerusalem will be directly attacked. Zechariah 14:12 describes the manner in which the LORD Himself fights those attacking Jerusalem. *"And this shall be the plague wherewith the LORD* will smite all the people that have fought against Jerusalem; Their flesh shall consume away while they stand upon their feet, and their eyes shall consume away in their holes, and their tongues shall consume away in their mouth."* This description seems to indicate the use of neutron bombs which attack living flesh, but do not destroy inanimate structures. It also describes massive radiation which may accompany a major meteorite shower if the meteorites themselves are composed of radioactive materials. The factions fighting Armageddon may use neutron bombs, because the city of Jerusalem itself will still remain intact structurally. But at Yom Kippur, the LORD attacks his enemies with fire and brimstone, the cosmic weaponry He used to destroy Sodom and Gomorrah.

According to Zechariah, a similar scenario took place at the time of the destruction of Sodom and Gomorrah. Recall, Lot's wife looked back, and was turned into a pillar of salt. It would appear the fire and brimstone sent to destroy Sodom and Gomorrah gave off massive radiation energy waves. If Lot's wife had simply kept going, the radiation wave would not have caught up with her. But she stopped, or at least slowed down long enough to look back, so that she was engulfed in the radiation energy wave.

Jesus, in His Olivet Discourse, also describes a similar scene which will occur at His Second Coming. Luke 17:30-37. *"Even thus shall it be in the day when the Son of man is revealed.* (Yom Kippur!) Verse 31. *In that day,* (the term "that day" appears to always refer to Yom Kippur) *he which shall be upon the housetop, and his stuff in the house, let him not come down to take it away: and he that is in the field, let him likewise not return back.* Verse 32. **Remember Lot's wife.** Verse 33. *Whosoever shall seek to save his life shall lose it; and whosoever shall lose his life shall preserve it.* (In this prophetic context of the spiral, Jesus is not talking about the eternal ramifications of the Mark of the Beast, but about the folly of trying to escape the bombing and brimstone hail during The Battle of the Great Day of the Almighty.) Verse 34. *I tell you, in that night* (this day will be dark as night because the sun shall be darkened, and the moon will not give off any light, and the stars will not be visible) *there shall be two men in one bed; the one shall be taken, and the other shall be left.* Verse 35. *Two women shall be grinding together; the one shall be taken, and the other left.* Verse 36. *Two men shall be in the field; the one shall te taken, and the other left.* Verse 37. *And they answered and said unto him, Where Lord? And he said unto them, wheresoever the body is, thither will the eagles* (vultures) *be gathered together."*

Traditionally, we have been told this passage is describing the Rapture of the Church, where one is taken and the other left. However, this passage is not about the Rapture. It is not about Rosh HaShanah at all! Rather, in context, it describes the Yom Kippur scene at Christ's

Second Coming when He engages in The Battle of The Great Day of The Almighty against AntiChrist and the nations. The disciples ask where the ones who are "taken," are taken to. Notice Jesus' answer. They are not transported anywhere; rather the eagles (vultures) gather over the dead bodies. Obviously this cannot be the Rapture! Jesus is speaking about the bodies of those killed by the radiation-waves. He even describes the manner in which the energy waves will kill! One will literally be standing or walking right beside another, and the effects of the radiation will jump over one, leaving him or her absolutely untouched, and the other will be zapped. In fact, Jesus seems to indicate the best approach to safety while this phenomenon takes place will be to stay put. Don't move! Or you may end up like Lot's wife!

So, yes, Jerusalem will be almost evacuated because of several prophetic scenarios, like a deserted cottage, or an abandoned vegetable garden; just like a city under siege. At Yom Kippur, this scenario will almost be as it was for Sodom and Gomorrah! But a remnant of living will remain in Jerusalem.

D. The Sin of Ritualism:

Now let's take a moment to examine the attitude of those who embrace Temple practices and Jewish ritualism. According to Isaiah, with the re-institution of Temple Worship after The Temple is built, before AntiChrist takes over, the LORD will have a bone to pick with the Jews. Although they finally gain control over The Temple Mount, and build their Temple after 2000 years, they still will not worship the LORD in true heart-felt repentance. Rather, because those who accept Temple practices will be caught up in the rituals and regulations of the sacrificial Laws, and in the keeping of their Feasts, they will miss the heart of what they are doing. Isaiah 1:11. " *To what purpose is the multitude of your sacrifices unto me? Saith the LORD: I am full of the burnt offerings of rams, and the fat of fed beasts; and I delight not in the blood of bullocks, or of lambs, or of he goats.* Verse 12. *When ye came to appear before me, <u>who hath required this at your hand</u>, to tread my courts?* Verse 13. *Bring no more vain oblations; incense is an abomination unto me; the new moons and sabbaths, the calling of assemblies, I can not away with; it is iniquity, even the solemn meeting.* Verse 14. *Your new moons and your appointed feasts my soul hateth: they are a trouble unto me; I am weary to bear them.* Verse 15. *And when ye spread forth your hands, I will hide mine eyes from you: yea, when ye make many prayers, I will not hear: your hands are full of blood.* Verse 16. *Wash you, make you clean; put away the evil of your doings from before mine eyes; cease to do evil;* Verse 17. *Learn to do well; seek judgment, relieve the* *oppressed, judge the fatherless, plead for the widow.* Verse 18. *Come now, and let us reason together, saith the LORD: though your sins be as scarlet, they shall be as white as snow; though they be red like crimson, they shall be as wool.* Verse 19. *If ye be willing and obedient, ye shall eat of the good of the land:* Verse 20. *But if ye refuse and rebel, ye shall be devoured with the sword: for the mouth of the LORD hath spoken it."* KJV. Underlining mine.

Why does the LORD give them this severe scolding? Just before the Assyrian and Babylonian captivities, Israel and Judah were into ritualistic Judaism, and treated their sacrificial system of worship with disdain, and their Feasts and Festivals with a lack of understanding. Even so, once Temple worship is re-instituted, they will still treat it all as a ritualistic requirement that God insists upon, rather than perform their sacrificial worship and Feasts with the joy of faith and understanding. In fact, the LORD indicates He is sick of all their sacrifices, their Feasts, their incense prayers, and their New Moon Festivals. They are meaningless and obnoxious to Him! Why? The Israelis just don't get it! They think ritualism is how to approach God, rather than understand that He has already fulfilled all the requirements of the sacrifices at the cross, and that He has, and will, fulfill the Feasts and Festivals Himself. Although there is a glimmer of understanding among some of them, the majority will not recognize Jesus Christ as The Lamb of God, LORD, or as coming Bridegroom, KING, and Righteous Judge -- yet!

In fact, as the major point of His scolding, the LORD gives them the salvation message of His grace and love. Therefore, this passage prophetically was not directed only toward those who were under the old Mosaic Law, but describes the fulfillment of the Law through Christ, so is directly applicable for the Israelis now in the Age of Grace, and during The Days of Awe to follow. In context then, this is an end-time prophecy directed specifically to those who will again take up the ritual of Judaic practices and Temple Worship. He tells them to wash, so that they may be made clean. In other words, wash in the true fountain of cleansing. Teshuvah, return to God, and turn from their wicked ways of pride and unbelief.

In verse 18 of Isaiah chapter 1, He appeals to their reason. He invites them to talk this whole issue over with Him. If they will do so, they will discover He has already made provision, so their sins and iniquities are forgiven. There is cleansing already provided in fulfillment of the sacrificial Law, through Christ's atonement sacrifice on the cross. The bloody animal sacrifices are no longer required, or wanted by Him. He invites them to *"Come now, and let us reason together, saith the LORD: though your sins be as scarlet, they shall be as white as snow; though they be red like crimson, they shall be as wool."* This is His provision. This is His grace which can only be received through faith. <u>The Law is fulfilled through Christ</u>! <u>Salvation is of the LORD</u>. They <u>must</u> recognize this truth! Jesus is LORD! He is The Lamb of God. He is The Redeemer.

If they will accept, they will eat of the goodness of The Land. They will be partakers of the fulfilled Covenant. If they refuse and rebel, they will be devoured with the sword! In other words, without true Teshuvah by faith before the LORD Who has fulfilled all the requirements of the Law, there is a conflict of greater proportion to unfold for Israel, and for the entire world. The sword of the nations gathered to Armageddon, culminating with The Sword of His Mouth wielded in fulfillment of Yom Kippur, at the Time Appointed, will devour those of unbelief, and they will not inherit The Land, or benefit from The Covenant.

Notice the areas the LORD will be concerned about regarding iniquity. Doing what is right; using righteous judgment in financial and fiscal matters, relieving the oppressed, exercising judgment in dealing with the fatherless, pleading the cause of the widow, and relieving the plight of the oppressed. Isaiah 1:23. This sounds like the same list Jesus gives in Matthew 25! This is the criteria on which He will not only judge the individual, but the nations when He separates the sheep from the goats. Sukkot! In other words, the LORD is not interested in the ritualistic keeping of the Feasts, but He has, and will, fulfill the essence of these Feasts and Festivals of separation judgment. Israel still keeps their Feasts and Festivals, but they do not recognize Christ's fulfillment of them, and what that will mean for them as a people, or for the other nations of the world. The Fall Feasts and the fulfillment of the New Moon Festivals are still to take place when Christ is fully revealed, first to the Righteous in fulfillment of Rosh HaShanah, and finally to the entire family of nations, including Israel, at His Second Coming in fulfillment of Yom Kippur, and during the fulfillment of Sukkot and Shemini-Atzeret- Simchat-Torah to follow. Because the Jews do not as yet understand, and place only historical or traditional emphases on these celebrations, <u>He would rather they just quit their ritualism</u>, <u>because it is not preparing them for what truly is coming in fulfillment</u>.

Therefore, the LORD will not be impressed with their Temple Worship and rituals, and with their keeping of the Feasts and Festivals, so will not receive their prayers, because they still will not recognize His fulfillment as Redeemer, Messiah, Bridegroom, Priest, Righteous Judge, and KING.

E. Policy Improprieties:

Apart from religious ritual, is Israel even now committing iniquity? Her citizens are continuing to be killed, maimed, orphaned, or widowed, as they are being sacrificed on the altar of humanistic tolerance to the false god of Islamic radicalism and deception. Young, strong IDF soldiers are being sent out like innocent sheep to be slaughtered in Israel's half-hearted war against terrorism. Private citizens are being slaughtered because of tolerating and trying to negotiate with those of pagan beliefs. Israel is not taking decisive steps to end this conflict. Rather she is compromising with other nations, entering into negotiations which will divide The Land, and trying to placate her enemies, believing their half-hearted assertions that they also are against the terrorists and their tactics.

Along with Israel's indecisiveness against her enemies, her government is reducing welfare payments and monthly family assistance cheques, cutting back on social services and medical programs, and even closing some hospitals. In other words, the government is trying to balance the budget on the backs of the poor, the ill, and the fatherless.

Netanyahu's latest budget which just passed in the Knesset, has dealt a severe blow to the underprivileged and weakened in Israel, both for Jewish, as well as for Palestinian Israelis. The LORD is not pleased with these iniquities! If the Israelis do not repent, change their mind-set, and re-set the priorities of their government policies, they will have to endure the sword, because that is exactly where they are headed.

"Woe into the wicked! for it shall be ill with him: for the reward of his hand shall be given him. Verse 12. As for my people, children are their oppressors, and women rule over them. O my people, they which lead thee cause thee to err, and destroy the way of thy paths. Verse 13. The LORD standeth up to plead, and standeth to judge the people. Verse 14. The LORD will enter into judgment with the ancients of his people and the princes thereof: for ye have eaten up the vineyard; the spoil of the poor is in your houses. Verse 15. What mean ye that ye beat my people to pieces, and grind the faces of the poor? saith the Lord GOD of hosts." Isaiah 3: 12-15.

It is not that there is no wealth in Israel to fund social programs, because there is. In fact, Israel has a very strong economy. However, they have been struggling to maintain the gross national product at the rapid growth-rate of expansion it has enjoyed for many years. Even though the slump in the world economy has affected Israel, this does not mean her wealth has diminished overtly. In fact, <u>Israel is the envy of all her neighbors,</u> hence one of the jealous reasons for the unrest in the region. Notice what the LORD says in Isaiah chapter 2:5-9. *"O house of Jacob, come ye, and let us walk in the light of the LORD. Verse 6. Therefore thou hast forsaken thy people, the house of Jacob, because they be replenished from the east, and are soothsayers like the Philistines, and they please themselves in the children of strangers. Verse 7. Their land also is full of silver and gold, neither is there any end of their treasures: their land is also full of horses, neither is there any end of their chariots: Verse 4. Their land also is full of idols; they worship the work of their own hands, that which their own fingers have made: Verse 9. And the mean man boweth down, and the great man humbleth himself: therefore forgive them not."*

These verses show dual fulfillment in the prophetic spiral. The people of the Land were self-satisfied, and self-sufficient before the ancient captivities.

They have again reached this point in Israel today. Their trading partners are from both the East and from the West. They are an exporting as well as an importing nation in all sectors of their economic growth. The Land indeed is full of horses and chariots (horse-powered vehicles, which are a sign of great wealth.) Israel is a world leader in many areas of the technologies, especially in the sciences and medicine. The people enjoy the benefits of education, and many of the world's top scientists have emigrated from other countries as the Jews have been making their way back to their homeland. Their agricultural research and productivity is a marvel. They do have a great deal to be proud of! But their pride is also their downfall. Many do not see the need of relying upon the LORD, since they do so well at 'doing it themselves.' So their land is full of the idols of self-sufficiency and materialism. They worship their achievements, bowing down to the idols of success, *"the works of their own hands, that which their own fingers have made."*

F. Hostages to Those Who are Like The Philistines:

Israel is allowing the idolatry of Islam to remain in The Land, and have not ousted this paganism which still occupies their most holy sight, The Temple Mount. This Islamic idolatrous presence is holding them hostage within their own government, and breeding fear within their own communities. Islam is tying their hands, and slowly but surely undermining their resolve to continue to lay claim to their God-given right to The Land of Covenant. They are falling prey to the underlying false prognostications (*soothsaying*) of those who are like the Philistines.

Who are like the Philistines? The Palestinians! The Palestinians are not Philistines! But many of them operate from covert headquarters of terror from within Israel, and particularly from Gaza, which was the stronghold of the Philistines; and they use similar gorilla tactics against Israel. The

Israelis try to make life more pleasant for themselves by accepting and placating the *"children of strangers,"* but it is not working! Therefore, until they repent of these idolatries and compromising, the LORD will not forgive them.

"How is the faithful city become an harlot! It was full of judgment; righteousness lodged in it; but now murderers." Isaiah 1:21. Who is a murderer? The terrorist organizations. The suicide bombers. The Jihadists. The Islamic Imams and educators who teach and incite to murder. But the Israeli government officials who will not take action to end the terrorism, are in fact becoming accessories to the atrocities, and God will hold all of them accountable.

So, has Israel done everything right since being back in the Land since 1948? Obviously not! Unfortunately, it appears she will continue down her 'Road' to destruction until the LORD Himself will finally intervene.

G. Disobedience to the LORD's Counsel:

Prime Minister Ariel Sharon and his supporters are stepping up their determination to unilaterally withdraw from Gaza and from several communities in the West Bank. Gaza is Sharon's first priority for "withdrawal" of all Jews. The resultant security vacuum which will be created if he goes through with this withdrawal, is of great concern to many within Israel, with many calling for an International Force to monitor Gaza after the withdrawal. Egypt has already been approached to take on this responsibility, but so far has declined. However, Egypt is being pressured.

If Egypt does take on the security role in Gaza, or even sends in personnel as part of an international security force, we would have to regard such a development as equal to sending in the foxes to mind the henhouse. Everyone knows arms and other illegal commodities have been supplied to terrorists by operatives from within Egypt through Gaza. The concern is, if Egypt complies by sending in security forces once Israel vacates Gaza, will this actually open up a door for greater movement of arms to terrorists, because the Israeli IDF will no longer have any direct presence or jurisdiction in Gaza. Withdrawal from Gaza would mean the Palestinians could become better armed, and have a secure base from which to increase attacks against Israel. In essence, security for Israel would be compromised, and her continued existence further threatened.

But, what does the LORD think of this scenario? First of all, He is not in favor of Israel withdrawing from Land He gave to them, or of the invitation to Egypt to provide security. Secondly, He indicates through the prophet Isaiah that such a move would be foolhardy, because it would certainly not benefit Israel in any regard! Thirdly, He would be incensed by Israel giving in to external pressure by other nations, and pagan manipulations by Islamic groups. He therefore would have to follow through on disciplining Israel.

Isaiah chapter 30 almost reads like a news editorial on this exact scenario, written by the LORD through the prophet. Let's read His take, beginning at verse 1. *"Woe to the rebellious children, saith the LORD, that take counsel, but not of me; and that cover with a covering, but not of my spirit, that they may add sin to sin. Verse 2. That walk to go down into Egypt, and have not asked at my mouth; to strengthen themselves in the strength of Pharaoh, and to trust in the shadow of Egypt. Verse 3. Therefore shall the strength of Pharaoh be your shame, and the trust in the shadow of Egypt your confusion."*

Israel's government leaders are not seeking counsel from God! Therefore they are sinning, adding to the treachery against the state of Israel. They are approaching the Egyptian government to take over security in Gaza in the wake of unilateral withdrawal, so that they can then proceed to negotiations for the formation of a Palestinian State. They have approached Egypt without seeking God's counsel on the whole matter. Israel is trusting in the *"shadow"* (enforcement presence to oversee security) of Egypt! But doing so will be Israel's shame, and will result in confusion! Egypt is being invited into Gaza to eliminate friction between the Palestinians and Israel, and to reduce terrorism by thwarting the illegal movement of terrorists and weapons. Israel is seeking to trust in the benevolence of Egypt, who already has indicated they are not really in favor of the whole arrangement. Even though Egypt is in favor of Israel pulling out of Gaza, they are not so sure they want to be the ones to police the consequences.

Verse 5. *"They were all ashamed of a people that could not profit them, nor be an help nor profit, but a shame, and also a reproach. Verse 6. The burden of the beasts of the south: into the land of trouble and anguish, from whence come the young and old lion, the viper and fiery flying serpent, they will carry their riches upon the shoulders of young asses, and their treasures upon the bunches of camels, to a people that shall not profit them."*

Let's observe the situation from Egypt's perspective for a moment. What profit would there be for Egypt to take over security in Gaza, either for Israel or for Egypt? Egypt views Israel as a bone of contention in The Middle East already, so why would they wholeheartedly step into the picture? It really makes no sense for Egypt to do so. They would run the risk of being viewed as compromising with Zionists!

The result will ultimately bring reproach, and will plunge the region into major unrest, resulting eventually in bringing everyone, including the nations of northern Africa, (beasts of the south), the young lions, (USA, Canada, Australia, etc,) and Britain, (the old lion), against AntiChrist and his henchmen (the viper), and the fiery flying serpent, (Satan who indwells AntiChrist) all into the Middle East for an eventual showdown. This will gradually escalate into wars over the course of The Days of Awe, starting relatively slowly with Gog and Magog, but eventually building to Armageddon.

Verse 7. "*For the Egyptians shall help in vain, and to no purpose: therefore have I cried concerning this, Their strength is to sit still.*" Whose strength is best served by sitting still? Israel's! Sit still! Stay in Gaza, Judea, and Samaria! Do not dismantle, withdraw, or retreat!

Verse 8. "*Now go, write it before them in a table, and note it in a book, that it may be for the time to come for ever and ever:*" This admonition from the LORD through the prophet Isaiah was not meant for the ancient past, but for the time we are now living in, and for the situation Israel is now facing. It is directed to Israel today! How do we know that? This prophetic word is to be delivered in a readable, and easily understandable format regarding a "*table*", a written schedule, which will unfold in a prophesied time to come, that will lead to Israel's establishment in The Land forever!

Unfortunately, even in written format, directed specifically to Israel, this prophetic admonition is not being, and will not be heeded. Verse 9. "*That this a rebellious people, lying children, children that will not hear the law of the LORD:* Verse 10. *Which say to the seers, See not; and to the prophets, Prophesy not unto us right things, speak unto us smooth things, prophesy deceits:* Verse 11. *Get out of the way; turn aside out of the path, cause the Holy One of Israel to cease from before us.*" Hello?!! Can anyone be so callous toward the LORD to try to hush His prophets? Who can be so rash as to dismiss the Holy One of Israel? Is there no honor or fear of the LORD? Is this not describing the current stance of Israel's government dignitaries? Is Ariel Sharon choosing to ignore what the LORD is trying to tell him through the residents of Yesha, through Israel's Rabbis, and through the Evangelical Christians regarding the Covenant, The Land, and what is best in policy according to Scripture? Is he listening to anyone? Yes, he hears the protests. But he, and many in authority with him, are choosing to ignore God's messengers telling him what the LORD says! He and his government are choosing to listen to the voices of compromise, leading Israel down a 'road of disobedience!'

Verse 12. "*Wherefore thus saith the Holy One of Israel, Because ye despise this word, and trust in oppression and perverseness, and stay thereon:* (are

The Final Schedule Revealed

determined to be stubborn, acting dictatorially to pursue a dangerous path of oppression and disobedience), Verse 13. *Therefore <u>this iniquity shall be to you as a breach ready to fall</u>, <u>a swelling out in a high wall</u>, <u>whose breaking cometh suddenly at an instant</u>.* Verse 14. *And he shall break it as the breaking of a potters vessel that is broken in pieces; he shall not spare: so that there shall not be found in the bursting of it a sherd to take fire from the hearth, or to take water withal out of the pit."* Because Israel officially, through the government, is thus determined to ignore, and even to despise the prophetic word given by the LORD, it is as a weakness, <u>a swelling in a high wall that will give-way suddenly</u>, causing great devastation. Whoa!!

The Word of the LORD often came prophetically through physical signs. Israel need look no further than toward the Temple Mount to view a prophetic object lesson of dire warning already in progress! The entire southern wall area of the Temple Mount is weakening daily, and there is a swelling (bulge) that began high in the wall, which is threatening to collapse at any time! When it does, Israel will immediately be embroiled in controversy, not to mention the major mess which will have to be cleaned up in order to stabilize the southern aspect of the Temple Mount!

The Islamic presence on The Mount will not be amused! The collapse and crumbling of the wall will not bode well for Israel, because The Mount is one of Islam's holiest sites. The Muslims won't simply walk away from their current holdings on The Temple Mount! In other words, the collapse of the currently swelling south wall will become an instant international incident of mega-proportions!

But why will the wall suddenly crumble? Apart from the already mentioned geological instability of The Temple Mount, Israel is being stubborn and disobedient. Israel is ignoring God! Israel will have to face the LORD! His presence is typified to all Jews by The Temple Mount, the site of The Holy Temple of the LORD twice in the past, and the promise of two more Temples in honor of His Name in the future. (1. The soon to be built Tribulation Temple of The Days of Awe, and 2. Ezekiel's prophesied Millennial Temple to be built by Messiah.) So He will cause the Israelis, and Jews worldwide, to focus their attention toward The Temple Mount. Now, will The Holy One of Israel finally have everyone's attention?

Verse 15. *"For thus saith the Lord GOD, the Holy One of Israel; in returning and rest shall ye be saved; in quietness and confidence shall by your strength: <u>and ye would not</u>."* The Holy One of Israel is calling for Israel to return to Him, so that they can rest in His Word and in His counsel, so they can be delivered. Unfortunately, it does not appear Israel in the immediate, officially will repent of their stance. Instead, Israel <u>will choose</u> a path which will result in two wars, and in fleeing from her enemies. Verse 16. *"<u>But ye</u>*

said, No; for we will flee upon horses; therefore shall ye flee: and, We will ride upon the swift; therefore shall they that pursue you be swift. Verse 17. *One thousand shall flee at the rebuke of one; at the rebuke of five shall ye flee: till ye be left as a beacon upon the top of a mountain, and as an ensign on an hill."* There will arise one (AntiChrist), who will rebuke Israel, and thousands will have to flee. Others will join him in rebuking Israel, and they will have to escape to the mountains of Edom, where they will retain their identity as a nation.

But the LORD will wait patiently while all this unfolds. He will be gracious and show mercy, because He is the God of judgment. When we think of judgment, we usually think of negative harshness and discipline, and legal justice. But one of the sentencing choices of legal justice is the ability of a presiding judge to grant clemency, mercy, as judgment. The LORD, the Righteous Judge, will graciously grant mercy toward Israel. Verse 18. *"And therefore will the LORD wait, that he may be gracious unto you, and therefore will he be exalted, that he may have mercy upon you: for the LORD is a God of judgment: blessed are all they that wait for him.* Verse 19. *For the people shall dwell in Zion at Jerusalem: thou wilt weep no more: he will be very gracious unto thee at the voice of thy cry; when he shall hear it, he will answer thee."* Verse 20. *"And though the LORD give you the bread of adversity, and the water of affliction, yet shall not thy teachers be removed into a corner any more, but thine eyes shall see thy teachers:* Verse 21. *And thine ears shall hear a word behind thee, saying, This is the way, walk ye in it, when ye turn to the right hand, and when ye turn to the left."* Verse 22. *Ye shall defile also the covering of thy graven images of silver, and the ornament of thy molten images of gold: thou shalt cast them away as a menstrous cloth, thou shalt say unto it, Get thee hence."* Israel will finally repent, and turn wholeheartedly to the LORD in truth. They will finally give heed to His voice directing their policies. As a result, all the uncleaness of paganism will be removed from The Land. It will be cast away by decree.

Meanwhile, we must admit Israel is not being obedient to the LORD at the moment. They are looking toward Egypt to bail them out if possible. But Egypt just may choose <u>not</u> to bail them out! Why is it that Israel seems so easily inclined to place themselves under some kind of bondage to Egypt? Just because Egypt was there in history to sustain the sons of Jacob, (and that was orchestrated by God,) does not mean Egypt is still to be a power to assist them now. In fact, Egypt has never been a great buddy of Israel's at any time since the Exodus! Israel is not to trust in Egypt, but in God! Isaiah 31:1 says, *"Woe to them that go down to Egypt for help..."* What part of that statement does Israel not understand?

IV. A Religious Battle of International Proportions:

But is Israel the only one at fault? The rest of the Arab nations, and almost all the other Islamic States are egging-on this conflict, not only targeting Israelis, but Christians and Jews, and other 'infidels' world-wide. This is a battle of religious fervor on the part of the Islamic world. The European Union has already fallen prey to the Islamic trap, and in the name of Human Rights, is harboring more and more Islamic adherents every year. Meanwhile, they also are indirectly funding much of the Intifada in Israel, sending arms and monetary assistance to the Palestinians, and preaching a message of tolerance which is aiding the spread of unrest and terror, allowing the Muslims to then slide in under this Human Rights ruse.

The United States of America, Britain, Australia, Canada, and other so-called bastions of Judeo-Christian ethics and freedom, are also at fault. They are blind to, and therefore do not understand, the forces at work which are undermining democracy, human rights, and religious freedom. Freedom of religion is not an Islamic doctrine. Muslims will 'tolerate' other religions only in so far as it suits their agenda. In most Islamic nations, Jews and Christians are now targets for terrorism and persecution. Saudi Arabia for example, will not allow Jews into their country, and there are no Christian Churches, and no 'preaching' is tolerated, either corporately, or in private conversation. Conversion to either Judaism or Christianity brings an automatic threat of the death sentence if convicted.

Meanwhile, Arafat, Gaddafi, the Princes of Saud, and other Islamic leaders, are getting away with being two-faced. They smile and shake the hands of the Western leaders, speaking platitudes and signing agreements, even holding office in international bodies, all the while delivering inflammatory speeches to their own people -- using deceptive games against us. Their terrorists hurl taunts and accusations in order to weaken the resolve of our leaders to act decisively. They even wield our ideals against us as weapons! If we take action, we are being unkind and intolerant, and are therefore imperialistic bullies. If we refrain from taking decisive action, we are being weak-kneed and lack morals. The separation

---

[213] Christian Week, Canada's National Christian Newspaper, Vol.17, Issue 22, November 2, 2004, Daina Douce, *Ontario introduces institute to uphold Shariah law, Muslims and Christians eye effort with caution* "Have we lost our minds?" cries a Canadian Christian columnist. That's precisely the question echoing in the minds of many concerning the introduction of Muslim Shariah law in Ontario. Where is all this headed?
Rather than whole-heartedly embracing what IslamOnline.net claims to be "the

IRAQ, SYRIA, and ISRAEL'S SHORTCOMINGS

of Church and State, human rights (not based in Islamic Shariah doctrine), freedoms, and pluralism, in their view are proof of the disintegration of our society. Not surprisingly, they have a point, as we in the West particularly have increasingly been pushing God and His Word out of our consciousness. [213]But we do claim to practice tolerance and acceptance of those who adhere to religions other than Christianity and Judaism. [214] What is now considered politically incorrect is to espouse strong Judeo-Christian beliefs! [215] Unfortunately, our stance is a bit too broad-minded, and will lead the West into trouble. <u>The Islamic world knows they are in a war</u>. But apart from having troops in Afghanistan and Iraq, The West does not fully understand that we are <u>already</u> in a world-wide 'knock-em-out' conflict. It would appear Israel is not the only one who must repent!

---

latest effort in a long struggle to have Shariah recognized in Canada," many Muslims are eying the effort with caution.
"It could happen that decisions are based on Islamic law, not Canadian law," Elmasry admits. "They must not do that."
"This is really a backdoor approach by fundamentalists to bring in traditional Islamic law in a country where they otherwise can't," Zuhair Kashmeri of the Muslim Canadian Congress told the Toronto Sun.
[214] World Evangelical Alliance, March 22, 2004, Elizabeth Kendal, *PERSECUTION, CANADA: APPLYING SHARIAH THROUGH ISLAMIC ARBITRATION,* "At a conference in Etobicoke, Ontario, Canada, in October 2003, Muslim delegates elected a 30-member council to establish the Islamic Institute of Civil Justice. The institute is classified in Islamic law as a Darul-Qada, or judicial tribunal. Its bylaws are scheduled to be drafted and approved by 31 December."
"This move can only open the door to social division and conflict. It will polarise Muslim and non-Muslim communities, and it will polarise the Muslim community (as Shariah does). Muslims who choose not to use the Shariah tribunals will doubtless be rejected and persecuted as rebellious or apostate. Muslims in Canada (especially Muslim women and Westernised Muslims) may find that they will lose - or be "persuaded" to abandon - their precious Canadian rights and freedoms."
[215] Author's Note: Ontario, Canada, has accepted, because of the Canadian Charter of Rights and Freedoms, and the revisions of our Canadian Constitution, the right for Muslims in Canada to operate under Shariah Law. Our government obviously has no idea what they have allowed to be unleashed on our Western society! Is Canada being treated as a guinea-pig to see how far Islam can push its agenda before anyone wakes-up? Many Muslims in Canada are very upset, because they came here to escape from the oppression of Shariah.

The Final Schedule Revealed

V. The Phantom State:

Arafat is still the major mover and shaker behind all the Palestinian causes. He appointed Mahmoud Abbas as the Prime Minister of the Palestinian Authority, but Abbas' position only lasted for a few short months. He resigned out of frustration with Arafat, who would not let him make decisions without his approval. He appeared to be a weak leader, not necessarily because of his own bungling, but because of Arafat's pressures. Now there is a new appointed Palestinian Prime Minister, Ahmed Qurei. There is some speculation he also will resign if Arafat does not give him some lateral movement-room. But then, Queri apparently is a respected long-standing henchman of Arafat's, and as such is also not totally innocent in the terrorist planning and support department. But he is somewhat more approachable according to Israeli media analysts, and some Knesset members feel they may be able to work with him.

What I find unusual, and utterly nonsensical, is that there even <u>is</u> a position of Prime Minister within the Palestinian hierarchy. The Palestinian Authority is not a government of State, but merely a Palestinian political body within Israel. How is it possible for there to be a Prime Minister without an already existent country? More importantly, how is it that the Prime Minister of this phantom nation is given international recognition? Also, how can Yassar Arafat be the President of a non-existent State? Holding a position as Chairman of an organization is not the same thing as being the President of a country, yet the international community, the media, and even the Israeli government, are treating him as if he is already President of this phantom Palestinian State, which apparently has a Prime Minister and a ruling government cabinet already in place. They even have a national Constitution! Has such a charade of deception and manipulation ever occurred in the past, anywhere in the world? There have been coup's, planned take-overs, re-defined national borders, but recognized imaginary

---

[216] Women For Israel's Tomorrow, <wfit2@womeningreen.org>, January 2, 2004, The Jerusalem Post Oleg Cartoon, *"Outposts will be Dismantled, Period!" Sharon is NOT the Leader we voted For.*

[217] Arutz Sheva News Service, <http://www.IsraelNationalNews.com>, March 22, 2004 *ARCH-MURDERER IS DEAD IN ISRAELI MISSILE STRIKE* "Reaction in the Cabinet to today's missile strike was overwhelmingly approving, with some saying it was time for the next step: the fulfillment of the cabinet decision to expel or kill Yasser Arafat. The Mukata compound in Ramallah, where Arafat has been holed up for over two years, has gone on high alert. Senior officials have indicated the strike against Yassin is in fact not the last, and that other terrorist leaders are marked as well."

countries? It is as if everyone has unequivocally accepted The Palestinian State as a present reality, before it is a reality!

[216] At the same time, Israel has taken steps of compliance with the demands of 'The Quartet,' by dismantling some of the smaller outposts, with not so veiled promises to destroy and evacuate many larger settlements and communities. [217] And, with the recent increase in terrorist activity resulting in the loss of many lives, Israel has threatened reprisals against Arafat himself, possibly demanding his demise through exile, or worse. Exiling Arafat would not do much good though. In fact, he may be more dangerous outside Israel where no one can keep an eye on him, than he is holed up in Ramallah. Worse yet, if he was to be 'knocked off' he would simply become a martyr to fuel the fire of more terrorism, or even all-out war.

But the real wild-card will ultimately be the jurisdictional control of the city of Jerusalem, the *"cup of trembling."* Ariel Sharon continues to remain solidly in his stance against the division of Jerusalem, while Arafat and Ahmed Qurei stoutly state Jerusalem will be the Capitol of the emerging Palestinian State. God Himself will keep this controversy going over Jerusalem, because He is not in favor of the division of His Covenant Land. Russia, along her allies among the Islamic Arab nations, is positioning herself to wield a great deal of influence, especially against Israel and the United States. Ariel Sharon recently was in Russia for talks with Vladimir Putin. (November 3, 2003.) The whole 'Road Map for Middle East Peace' was brought up on the agenda by Putin, and he is pushing for the Palestinian State to be formed quickly. Russia must work together with the USA, The United Nations, and The European Union to bring about the Palestinian State, but that does not mean she totally agrees in principle with all that the Western members of 'The Quartet' are trying to achieve. Superficially, it appears she is on the same side regarding the Palestinian State, but ultimately, she will use this same scenario for her own ends.

CHAPTER 28
'PALESTINA'

Will a Palestinian State actually come about? I believe it will. Isaiah sheds some light here, as does Joel. But we must place The books of Isaiah and Joel into perspective to understand the real significance of their prophecies.

Lets begin with Isaiah. Isaiah ministered in Judah from 740 B.C.E. to 680 B.C.E., which places his life and ministry definitely pre-Palestine.

Most commentaries and Bible teachers tend to state 'Palestina' is simply another name for 'Philistia,' or 'Palestine.' But is this realistic? An entity called 'Palestine' did not exist until the time of the Romans almost six centuries after Isaiah, and it encompassed roughly the entire area of current Israel, including the West Bank 'territories,' The Galilee, and even included most of what is now Jordan. Therefore, any reference to an existing entity called 'Palestina' by Isaiah was <u>under the anointing of the Holy Spirit, and his knowledge of Torah</u>. Isaiah would have had no contemporary frame of reference to a 'Palestine.' He knew about Philistia, the stronghold of the Philistines, located along the Mediterranean coastal region of what we now call Gaza. But he would not have had any historical, geographical, ethnic, or political ability to know about the existence of 'Palestina,' which will not have anything directly to do with Philistia, other than the fact that it will, along with a much larger geographical territory, likely <u>include</u> the area formerly occupied by the Philistines.

When Israel entered Canaan at the time of the Exodus, 'Palestina' did not exist. Philistia did exist. And, even after Philistia was absorbed under David and Solomon, the Philistines remained as a constant thorn in Israel's side. Much later, the 'Palestine' of the Roman era <u>was a Jewish puppet State, not a Philistine State</u>. By the time of the Romans, the Philistines were no longer a recognized ethnic or national group, or even a geographical-political entity. So, could 'Palestina' have referred to 'Philistia' of the Philistines? No. Therefore, wherever we find 'Palestina' mentioned, <u>fulfillment of the prophecies have not yet been accomplished</u>. Therefore, Isaiah's prophetic 'Palestina' cannot be construed as referring in any way to ancient Philistia, or even to The Land of Palestine of the Roman era. Isaiah's prophecy also had nothing to do with the Ottoman Palestine, which was considered to be ethnically Jewish, and took in much more territory than did ancient Philistia. We must conclude then, that <u>'Palestina' is prophetic</u>

only to the era just preceding when Israel will ultimately be established forever according to the context of the Scriptures where it is mentioned.

A. The Song of Moses:

Some would argue that Isaiah had knowledge of a Torah reference regarding 'Palestina' in The Song of Moses. Yes, he did. But that's just the point! The Exodus chapter 15 reference is a prophecy that relates to the end of this current Age, and to the coming Time of Sorrow, The Days of Awe period, following which Israel will again be ultimately delivered and established forever, fulfilling Moses' prophecy.

Let's examine The Song of Moses for a moment. When we look carefully at The Song of Moses, Exodus 15:1-18, we find that it is broken into two distinct parts. Verses 1 through 13 are historical, and recount the deliverance of Israel from Egypt. But according to the prophetic spiral, verses 14 through 18 have not as yet been totally fulfilled. These verses are futuristically prophetic regarding the process of the establishment of Israel permanently in The Land of Canaan, culminating with the LORD ruling and reigning over them forever.

Let's read, beginning at verse 14. *"The people shall fear, and be afraid: sorrow shall take hold on the inhabitants of Palestina. Verse 15. Then the dukes of Edom shall be amazed; the mighty men of Moab, trembling shall take hold upon them; all the inhabitants of Canaan shall melt away. Verse 16. Fear and dread shall fall upon them; by the greatness of thine arm they shall be as still as a stone; till thy people pass over, O LORD, till the people pass over, which thou hast purchased. Verse 16. Thou shalt bring them in, and plant them in the mountain of thine inheritance, in the place, O LORD, which thou hast made for thee to dwell in; in the sanctuary, O LORD, which thy hands have established. Verse 18. The LORD shall reign for ever and ever."* KJV. Underlining mine.

The inhabitants of 'Palestine' will ultimately experience discipline through dismantlement, and this scenario will take place during a time of sorrow, The Days of Awe. Therefore, an entity called 'Palestine' will have to exist for this prophecy to unfold.

This then explains why The Song of Moses will be sung before The Throne in Heaven by the Tribulation Saints, along with The Song of The Lamb immediately prior to when the LORD returns to fulfill Yom Kippur. The Song of The Lamb celebrates Christ's victorious triumph over Satan and sin through the Atonement, and The Song of Moses celebrates Israel's deliverance in The Land of Covenant, which will be absolutely, and totally fulfilled through and by Messiah. The LORD will reign forever from His sanctuary! The Mystery of the Ages will be complete! The Kingdom of Israel will be established by the LORD *"when sorrow takes hold on the inhabitants of Palestina."*

B. 'The Assyrian' and Babylon:

At the time of The Assyrian Captivity of The Northern Kingdom of Israel, 'Palestina' did not exist. At the time of The Babylonian captivity of The Kingdom of Judah, 'Palestina' did not exist. Philistia did exist. But, as already mentioned, 'Philistia' is not 'Palestina.' They are two separate entities. Also, The Assyrian Captivity did not have anything directly to do with Judah or the Mountain of the LORD, or Jerusalem, but only affected The Ten Northern Tribes, and took place 136 years before The Babylonian Captivity of Judah. But Isaiah refers to both Babylon and 'The Assyrian' in the same context, not regarding separate captivities, but having to do with <u>an identical time-frame of judgment against Babylon and 'The Assyrian.'</u> Therefore Isaiah's prophecy regarding Babylon and 'The Assyrian,' is meant for a time yet to come. Follow me here, because this has much to do with the era in which we now live, why 'Palestina' will be significant, and how The Fall Divine appointment calendar will unfold!

C. The LORD's Response to Israel's Policies:

Isaiah chapter 10 begins with an indictment against those who make unrighteous decrees which will not be beneficial for anyone involved. Verse 1. *"Woe unto them that decree unrighteous decrees, and that write grievousness which they have prescribed:"* What decrees is the LORD referring to here? Verse 2. *" To turn aside the needy from judgment, and to take away the right from the poor of my people, that widows may be their prey, and that they may rob the fatherless!"* Oppressive policies which will affect those least able to cope are exactly what Israel has been passing through the Knesset, pushed through Ariel Sharon's Likud coalition government by Netanyahu and Olmert. In fact, a general strike that was planned in protest to these particular fiscal budget policies was narrowly averted, but has been staged in smaller sectors. If we think the LORD is not paying attention, we must think again!

And then there is the matter of Sharon's policies regarding the Settlements, and the Palestinian State. The LORD asks, verse 3. *"And what will ye do in the day of visitation, and in the desolation which shall come from far? To whom will ye flee for help? And where will ye leave your glory?* Verse 4. *Without me they shall bow down under the prisoners, and they shall fall under* the slain, <u>for all this his anger is not turned away</u>, but <u>his hand is stretched out still</u>." Underlining mine.

Ariel Sharon is decreeing, against his own Likud party policies and membership, the dismantlement of the Settlements and Outposts that are on Covenant Land! They are on land Abraham stood and viewed in the LORD's presence, and was promised, by blood Covenant that his descendants would inherit forever. Genesis 15:7 to 18. *"And he saith unto him, I am the LORD, that brought thee out of Ur of the Chaldees, to give thee this land to inherit it. Verse 8, And he said, LORD God, whereby shall I know that I shall inherit it? Verse 9. And he said unto him, Take me a heifer of three years old, and a she goat of three years old, and a ram of three years old, and a turtledove, and a young pigeon. Verse 10. And he took unto him all these, and divided them in the midst, and laid each piece one against another: but the birds divided he not. Verse 11. And when the fowls came down upon the carcases, Abram drove them away. Verse 12. And when the sun was going down, a deep sleep fell upon Abram; and, lo, a horror of great darkness fell upon him. Verse 13. And he said unto Abram, Know of a surety that thy seed shall be a stranger in a land that is not theirs, and shall serve them; and they shall afflict them four hundred years; Verse 14. And also that nation, whom they shall serve, will I judge: and afterward shall they come out with great substance. Verse 15. And thou shalt go to thy fathers in peace; thou shalt be buried in a good old age. Verse 16. But in the fourth generation they shall come hither again: for the iniquity of the Amorites is not yet full. Verse 17. And it came to pass, that, when the sun went down, and it was dark, behold a smoking furnace, and a burning lamp that passed between the pieces. Verse 18. In the same day the LORD made a covenant with Abram, saying, Unto thy seed have I given this land, from the river of Egypt, unto the great river Euphrates."* KJV.

This Blood Covenant is yet to be fulfilled by Abraham's "Seed" forever. In the meanwhile, Israel is ripe for the LORD's anger, because they are not giving heed to this Covenant. His anger is not turned away, but His hand of judgment is still stretched out. But what form will it take?

VII. The Rod and Staff of the LORD's Wrath:

Isaiah 10: 5. *"O Assyrian, the rod of mine anger, and the staff in their hand is mine indignation."* The LORD will use a coming ruler who He refers to as 'The Assyrian' to be <u>His rod of anger</u>, and <u>His staff of indignation</u>. Who is this 'Assyrian,' and who does he come against? Verse 6. *" I will send him <u>against a hypocritical nation</u>, and <u>against the people of my wrath will I give him a charge</u>, <u>to take the spoil</u>, <u>and to take the prey</u>, and to tread them down like the mire of the streets. Verse 7. Howbeit <u>he meaneth not so</u>, <u>neither doth his heart think so</u>;*

but it is in his heart to destroy and cut off nations not a few." KJV. Underlining Mine.

This 'Assyrian' will be deceptive. He will operate under the deception of apparently not setting-out to destroy Israel, but deep in his heart he will have aspirations to dominate many nations. In other words, he will think he is doing what is ultimately proper and right, but he himself is deceived in what he sets out to do! This certainly has overtones of the Islamic doctrine of not only deceiving Israel and the nations, but in eventually wiping Israel off the map, in order to bring in world Islamic control. Only at first, even he will not recognize the iniquity of this ideological policy. But notice, he will be allowed to take a spoil, and a prey, and walk all over the Israelis for a short time.

Now, if we think this interpretation really has nothing to do with Islamic ideals, just look at the next few verses! Verse 8. *"For he saith, Are not my princes altogether kings?"* Islamic men may be called 'kings, and their rulers also may be referred to as 'princes.' Look at Saudi Arabia. All their leaders are referred to as 'princes.' Verse 9. *"Is not Calno as Carchemish? Is not Hamath as Arpad? Is not Samaria as Damascus?"* Calno, Hamath, Arpad, and the city of Samaria were all in the territory of The Northern Kingdom of Israel. These were taken over by the Assyrians in 722 B.C.E. In our day, these geographical enclaves contain a fairly large Palestinian population, and are also a breeding-ground for radical Islamic terrorist jihadists. This 'Assyrian' will apparently again take over in these enclaves.

Isaiah 10:10. *" As my hand hath found the kingdoms of the idols, and whose graven images did excel them of Jerusalem and of Samaria;* Verse 11. *Shall I not, as I have done unto Samaria and her idols, so do to Jerusalem and her idols?* Verse 12. *Wherefore it shall come to pass, that when the LORD hath performed his whole work upon mount Zion and on Jerusalem, I will punish the fruit of the stout heart of the king of Assyria, and the glory of his high looks."* Underlining mine. The LORD will raise up 'The Assyrian' against Jerusalem and against Mount Zion to punish them for their idolatry, just as He punished Samaria. This was not the case during The Assyrian Empirical conquest, because Jerusalem and Mount Zion are in Judah, which although attacked, were no part of the ancient Assyrian conquest, but will be front and center for conquest by the coming '*Assyrian King*' who will arise to perform God's judgments against Israel's idolatry. Then the LORD will punish this ruler Himself, and come against '*The Assyrian King's*' pride and haughtiness. The LORD will come against AntiChrist's idolatry which will be headquartered in Jerusalem on Mount Zion.

The Final Schedule Revealed

A. 'The Assyrian's' Pride

What will be 'The Assyrian's' pride? Isaiah 10, verse 13. *"For he saith, by the strength of my hand I have done it, and by my wisdom; for I am prudent: and I have removed the bounds of the people, and have robbed their treasures, and I have put down the inhabitants like a valiant man:* Verse 14. *And my hand hath found as a nest the riches of the people: and as one that gathereth eggs that are left, have I gathered all the earth; and there was none that moved the wing, or opened the mouth, or peeped."* This is 'The Assyrian's' arrogance! He will not give any credence to anyone but himself and his own achievements! In fact, he will manage to scatter and weaken the people of Israel, and to plunder the nest of all the eggs. He will take over the wealth, and the pride (Temple) of the people, not just in Jerusalem and on Mount Zion, but also of the whole earth, yet no one will dare to speak out against him while he robs the nest. John states in The Book of Revelation chapter 13 verse 4b, that no one dares challenge him. *"Who is like unto the beast? Who is able to make war with him?"* This scenario has not yet happened, but it will come to pass under AntiChrist.

B. The LORD Deals with 'The Assyrian's' Pride:

How will the LORD deal with him? Isaiah 10, verse 15. *"Shall the axe boast itself against him that heweth therewith? or shall the saw magnify itself against him that shaketh it? as if the rod should shake itself against them that lift it up, or as if the staff should lift up itself, as if it were no wood."* 'The Assyrian' is supposed to be a rod, and a staff in the hand of the LORD to discipline His people, the hypocritical nation, Israel. But this rod and staff raises itself up against Him who wields them! This prideful axe (rod) and saw (staff) exceeds his bounds, and turns his rod and staff against the LORD! Now he is going to feel the wrath of the LORD! Verse 16. *"Therefore shall the Lord, the LORD of hosts, send among his fat ones leanness; and under his glory he shall kindle a burning like the burning of a fire.* Verse 17. *And the light of Israel shall be for a fire, and his Holy One for a flame: and it shall burn and devour his thorns and his briers in one day;* Verse 18. *And shall consume the glory of his forest, and of his fruitful field, both soul and body: and they shall be as when a standard-bearer fainteth.* Verse 19. *And the rest of the trees of his forest shall be few, that a child may write them."* KJV. Underlining mine.

The LORD of Hosts will send a fire upon him, and upon the nations who align themselves with him. He will consume him in one Day, The Day of Yom Kippur. The LORD will appear in glory for every eye to see Him, and He will fight against the nations who align themselves with 'The

Assyrian.' The LORD, the Light of Israel, will be this Consuming Fire! The forest (the nations who have conspired together) will be destroyed, and even a child will be able to write down the names of the few trees (the fighting nations) that will be left intact.

Isaiah 10, Verse 20. *"And it shall come to pass in that day, that the remnant of Israel, and such as are escaped of the house of Jacob, shall no more again stay upon him that smote them; but shall stay upon the LORD, the Holy One of Israel, in truth.* Verse 21. <u>*The remnant shall return, even the remnant of Jacob, unto the mighty God*</u>. Verse 22. *For though thy people Israel be as the sand of the sea, yet a remnant of them shall return: <u>the consumption decreed shall overflow with righteousness</u>.* Verse 23. *For the Lord GOD of Hosts shall make a consumption <u>even determined</u>, in the midst of all the land."* KJV. Underlining mine.

Now, Isaiah's prophecy clinches who 'The Assyrian' is. Verse 24. *"Therefore thus saith the Lord GOD of hosts, <u>O my people that dwellest in Zion, be not afraid of the Assyrian</u>; he shall smite thee with a rod, and shall lift up his staff against thee, <u>after the manner of Egypt</u>.* Verse 25. *For yet a very little while, and <u>the indignation shall cease</u>, and mine anger in their destruction.* Verse 26. *And the LORD of hosts shall stir up a scourge for him according to the slaughter of Midian at the rock of Oreb; and as his rod was upon the sea, so shall he lift it up after the manner of Egypt.* Verse 27. *And it shall come to pass in that day, that <u>his burden shall be taken away from off thy shoulder</u>, and <u>his yoke from off thy neck, and the yoke shall be destroyed because of the anointing</u>."* KJV. Underlining Mine.

Notice, <u>the people who dwell in Zion</u> are not to fear The Assyrian! If this was only about ancient Assyria, this passage would make no sense, because Assyria was unable to conquer Mount Zion or Jerusalem which are in Judah. But obviously, this <u>coming</u> 'Assyrian' will take over Mount Zion and Jerusalem, and he will oppress the Israelis who remain there, just as Egypt oppressed the Hebrews. In fact, as this coming despotic ruler tries to oppress Israel just as Pharaoh did, God Himself will again <u>re-enact most of the plagues of Egypt against him</u> as the Vials of His Wrath are poured out on AntiChrist's empire. But after a very little while, *"the indignation shall cease, and mine anger in their destruction."* Verse 25. The indignation is the desecration of The Temple, The Abomination of Desolation. This will be brought to an end at the same time the LORD's wrath is fulfilled. Yom Kippur!

At that time, The Covenant will be complete, but also, the <u>culmination of the blessings for both Jacob, and for Esau, will be brought to fruition</u>. What is the unfulfilled part of Isaac's blessing that both Jacob and Esau have been fighting over to bring about wrongfully? The yolk of oppression, and the yolk of jealousy. The burden of Esau's brother, Jacob, will finally be lifted from off his shoulder, and Jacob's yolk from off his neck. This yolk will be destroyed *"because of the anointing!"* So both Jacob's and Esau's blessings that they received from Isaac their father will <u>finally</u> be brought to absolute fulfillment, because of the anointing of the LORD! Jacob and Esau will finally be at peace with one another when the LORD rules and reigns upon the earth! When the yolk of oppression will be lifted off the neck and shoulders of Jacob, the yolk of jealousy and anger will be lifted off of Esau's neck and shoulders.

But what does this have to do with Palistine? Stay with me, because we're getting there!

VIII. The Babylon Connection:

Isaiah chapter 13 deals with the rise and fall of The Babylonian Empire, and particularly states that Babylon is a burden. The LORD raised up The Babylonian Empire to chastise The Kingdom of Judah, and to take them into captivity in 586 B.C.E. Subsequently the Babylonians were over-run by the Medes, resulting in The Empire of the Medes and Persians. This is all very neatly described until we get to verses 19 and 20, which state, *"And Babylon, the glory of the kingdoms, the beauty of the Chaldees excellency, shall be as when God overthrew Sodom and Gomorrah.* Verse 20. *It shall never be inhabited, neither shall it be dwelt in from generation to generation..."* Hold it! We were discussing The Babylonian Empire, and suddenly we are observing annihilation <u>in like manner to the destruction of the cities of Sodom and Gomorrah</u>.

When a comparison is put in place, one must be careful to compare apples with apples. One must compare empires with empires, and cities with cities. The comparison is invalid if one tries to equate empires with cities, unless the comparison is directly qualified in the write-up. Now <u>that</u> puts a different slant on the whole prophecy! The destruction of the entire Babylonian Empire by capturing the city of Babylon <u>was not</u> as the destruction of Sodom and Gomorrah when the Medes first attacked and took over. The Medes and Persians ruled the Empire from the city of Babylon! The city of Babylon was still intact. Eventually, Babylon did become a ghost town, but it was never destroyed to the point of being absolutely uninhabitable for any human being. Therefore the destruction of the city of Babylon in like manner to the destruction of Sodom and Gomorrah, <u>by fire and brimstone sent by God from heaven because of abominations,</u> <u>is still to come</u>. It is obvious the prophetic spiral is being played out in this entire passage, meaning there will come a further fulfillment by Babylonian and Mede players, but the circumstances will be more devastating than was the ancient take-over of the Babylonian Empire.

This realization causes us to go back and re-read the entire passage. When we do, we suddenly pick up on the significance of some of the detail, not in relation to the first fulfillment by the ancient empires, but in relation to what is soon to come as judgment from God upon the city of Babylon. We also realize as we continue reading further into Isaiah chapter 14, that we are dealing with Jacob (not just Judah) under circumstances which only will come about in the latter fulfillment.

Just as the ancient Assyrians had no direct captivity dealings with those of the House of Judah, or with Jerusalem, so too the ancient Babylonians had no direct captivity dealings with the House of Israel, because the Ten Northern Tribes were long gone into captivity by the time the Babylonians arose on The Middle Eastern scene. But chapter 14 is obviously a seamless continuance of Isaiah's prophecy, explaining God's reasons for what is to take place. It is the LORD who chooses Jacob, referring to <u>all</u> of Jacob's offspring -- all twelve tribes. So what connection is there between <u>all</u> Israel, Babylon, and the Medes? Before delving into chapter 14, lets look for the answer in chapter 13.

A. The "Medes."

Isaiah 13: 6. *"Howl ye, for <u>the day of the LORD</u> is at hand; it shall come as a destruction from the Almighty.* Verse 7. *Therefore shall all hands be faint, and every man's heart shall melt:* Verse 8. *And they shall be afraid: <u>pangs and sorrows</u> shall take hold of them; <u>they shall be in pain as a woman that travaileth</u>: they shall be amazed at one another; their faces shall be as flames."* This passage, which will yet have a dual fulfillment, speaks of <u>the coming birth-pangs that Jesus spoke about</u>, which are to indicate the nearness of the Rapture, <u>and imminent onset of The Days of Awe</u>, and will continue in increasing intensity until Christ's Yom Kippur Second Coming. Recall, The Whore of Babylon has undergirded the world's political and economic systems, and has bank-rolled all empires, including the current period in which we live. The Roman Empire is being revived, and the line-up representing the Hybrid Empire is now taking shape. When The Battle of Gog and Magog, spear-headed by Russia (the Medes) and the Arabs, but orchestrated by God, takes place, the world's balance of ideological, political, and economic power will also be severely shaken. This will occur during the lead-up to the intense birth-pangs, just before the fulfillment of Rosh HaShanah. That's once.

But there will also be a further fulfillment by the Medes. Verse 9. *"Behold, <u>the day of the LORD</u> cometh, cruel both with wrath and fierce anger, to lay the land desolate: and <u>he shall destroy the sinners thereof out of it</u>.* (This Day of The LORD is Yom Kippur, the second fulfillment.) Verse 10. *For the stars of heaven and the constellations thereof <u>shall not give their light</u>: <u>the sun shall be darkened</u> in his going forth, and <u>the moon shall not cause her light to shine</u>.* Verse 11. *And I will punish the world for their evil, and the wicked for their iniquity; and I will <u>cause the arrogancy of the proud to cease</u>, and <u>will lay low the haughtiness of the terrible</u>.* Verse 12. *I will make a man more precious than fine gold; even a man than the golden wedge of Ophir.* Verse 13. *Therefore <u>I will shake the heavens</u>, and <u>the earth shall remove out of her place</u>, in <u>the wrath of the LORD of hosts</u>, and <u>in the day</u> of his fierce anger."* KJV. Underlining mine.

The second involvement of Russia (the Medes), along with many other nations who will participate in the coalition which sets out to destroy Babylon, The Whore, takes place during Armageddon, and is culminated when the sun is darkened, the moon is not visible, and the stars do not shine. At that time, the wicked will be punished for all their evil and iniquity. Christ Himself will return, and put and end to the pride of the arrogant, and *"will lay low the haughtiness of the terrible."* Who are the those who are haughty and terrible? AntiChrist, The Whore, The False Prophet, and all their henchmen.

Isaiah 13: 17. *"Behold, I will stir up the Medes against them, which shall not regard silver, and as for gold, they shall not delight in it.* Verse 18. <u>*Their bows also shall dash the young men to pieces*</u>; *and they shall have no pity on the fruit of the womb; their eye shall not spare children."* These verses describe true barbarism, a character-trait of the Medes who eventually infiltrated from what is southern Russia into the north. But to be fair, all oppressive regimes of this world have exhibited such barbarism, not just Russia. It is certain AntiChrist, who will not be Russian, will take barbarism to new heights before the Medes (Russia and the southern provinces, along with the nations who now occupy the Mede-Persian Empire former territory) will come against him along with many other nations.

The first Russian 'Mede' alliance invasion at Gog and Magog is tied-in with wealth and prestige, <u>to attempt to take a spoil of The Land</u>. But the second Russian 'Mede' alliance campaign during Armageddon, will have a very different motivation. <u>Wealth will not be the provocation the second time around</u>, but the many nations who will come against AntiChrist and his regime will seek <u>to destroy</u> his oppressive economic system, (The Whore) which if left unchecked would threaten to destroy the world. The Whore of Babylon will have stakes in underwriting AntiChrist's oppressive Image System. Therefore, Babylon, The Whore, and the city of Babylon, will be destroyed in this Armageddon onslaught. Verse 19. *"And Babylon, the glory of kingdoms, the beauty of the Chaldees' excellency, shall be as when God overthrew Sodom and Gomorrah.* Verse 20. *It shall never be inhabited, neither shall it be dwelt in from generation to generation..."* Only wild beasts will live there.

B. Mercy on Jacob:

Why will the Babylonian system that will shore-up the AntiChrist's regime be destroyed? Isaiah 14:1. *"<u>For the LORD will have mercy on Jacob</u>, and <u>will yet choose Israel</u>, and set them in their own land: and the strangers shall be joined with them, and they shall cleave to <u>the house of Jacob</u>. Verse 2. And the people shall take them, and bring them to their place: and the house of Israel shall possess them in the land of the LORD for servants and handmaids: and they shall take them captives, whose captives they were; and they shall rule over their oppressors. Verse 3. And it shall come to pass in the day that the LORD shall give thee rest from thy sorrow, and from thy fear, and from the hard bondage wherein thou wast made to serve, Verse 4. That thou shalt take up this proverb against the king of Babylon, and say, How hath the oppressor ceased! The golden city ceased! Verse 5. The LORD hath broken the staff of the wicked, and the scepter of the rulers. Verse 6. He who smote the people in wrath with a continual stroke, he that ruled the nations in anger, is persecuted, and none hindereth. Verse 7. The whole earth is at rest, and is quiet: they break forth into singing."* KJV. Underlining mine.

This passage certainly was fulfilled when the Medes broke the oppressive rule of the Babylonians, but the context speaks of a time that as yet has not taken place, because the prophecy is regarding Jacob, Israel -- the whole House of Jacob, not just the House of Judah who went into Babylonian Captivity in 586 B.C.E.

C. 'The Assyrian's' Identity:

But who is the ruler that is broken? Isaiah describes this one who is brought down. In Isaiah chapter 10 he is referred to as 'The Assyrian.' Here in Isaiah chapter 14 he is referred to as a personage that is not entirely human. Verse 10. *"All they shall speak unto thee, Art thou also become weak as we? Art thou become like unto us? Verse 11. Thy pomp is brought down to the grave, and the noise of thy viols: the worm is spread under thee, and the worms cover thee."*

According to the context, the next verses take on a relevancy to the coming Days of Awe that perhaps we overlook simply because we usually use these verses to describe Lucifer, to show that he is a fallen archangel -- which is absolutely true. However, we must place our understanding and application into the context of what is being prophesied. The LORD is describing the Satanically possessed 'Assyrian", and his aspirations. Verse 12. *"How art thou fallen from heaven, O Lucifer, son of the morning! How art thou cut down to the ground, <u>which didst weaken the nations</u>! Verse 13. For thou hast said in thine heart, I will ascend into heaven, I will <u>exalt my throne above the stars of God</u>: I will sit also upon <u>the mount of the congregation</u>, in the sides of the north: Verse 14. I will ascend above the heights of the clouds; I will be like the most High."*

Lucifer (Satan), through AntiChrist, will weaken the nations. Satan desires to sit upon a throne that is exalted higher than the Throne of Heaven, and above the Throne of God's people, Israel, The Throne of David. In fact, he has his sights set on ruling <u>from the same location as Christ will rule and reign from</u>, namely from Mount Zion, the *" mount of the congregation, in the sides of the north."* His well thought-out scheme is to usurp Christ, rule the kingdoms of this world, and receive worship <u>above</u> God. Verse 15. *"Yet thou shalt be brought down to hell, to the sides of the pit. Verse 16. They that see thee shall narrowly look upon thee, and consider thee, saying, Is this the man that made the earth to tremble, that did shake kingdoms; Verse 17. That made the world as a wilderness, and destroyed the cities thereof; that opened not the house of his prisoners?"* When AntiChrist is defeated, Satan will be brought down, and corralled. He will be bound, and cast into The Bottomless Pit. So much for his attempt to counterfeit Christ, and to take over Christ's power and position through staging a counterfeit charade! Even the nations will be amazed, and finally realize who has deceived them when he is exposed for his true colors!

Then, 'The Assyrian' is again mentioned, indicating we are definitely dealing with his identity in this entire passage in Isaiah. Isaiah chapter 14, verse 24. *" The LORD of hosts hath sworn, saying, surely as I have thought, so shall it come to pass; and as I have purposed, so shall it stand: Verse 25. That <u>I will break the Assyrian in my land</u>, and <u>upon my mountains tread him under foot</u>: then shall his yoke depart from off them, and his burden depart from off their shoulders. Verse 26. This is the purpose that is purposed upon the whole earth: and <u>this is the hand that is stretched out upon all the nations</u>. Verse 27. <u>For the LORD of hosts hath purposed</u>, and <u>who shall disannul it</u>? And his hand is stretched out, and who shall turn it back? Verse 28. In the year king Ahaz died was this burden. Verse 29. <u>Rejoice not thou whole Palestina</u>, because the rod of him that smote thee is broken: for out of the serpent's root shall come forth a cockatrice, and his fruit shall be a fiery flying serpent. Verse 30. And the first-born of the poor shall feed, and the needy shall lie down in safety: and I will kill thy root with famine, and he shall slay thy remnant. Verse 31. Howl, O gate; cry, O city; <u>thou, whole Palestina, art dissolved</u>: for there shall come from the north a smoke, and none shall be alone <u>in his appointed times</u>. Verse 32. What shall one then answer the messengers of the* nation? *That the LORD hath founded Zion, and the poor of his people shall trust in it.*" KJV. Underlining mine.

It appears 'The Assyrian,' AntiChrist, who is possessed by Lucifer, will be defeated on the mountains of Israel. But notice, there is a process, a purpose -- a pre-determined plan that the LORD has decreed, in His Appointed Times, that will bring him down. Along with this victory, Palestina will be utterly dissolved! No more Palestinian State!

D. The Folly of Compromise:

King Ahaz represents the compromising sin of the leadership of Judah with her enemies. What will be the sin of Israel's governing leaders just before Russia (the Medes) comes down the first time? Allowing the formation of a Palestinian State! This will come about because of the sin of compromising with the nations, and giving-in to Israel's enemies over Judea, Samaria, and Gaza, which are under negotiation to be the Palestinian State lands. There will be something about the process of the formation of the Palestinian State which will upset the balance of power, and Russia will not be pleased about it, and will attempt to take advantage of the whole scene. During the resultant Battle of Gog and Magog, Russia's military power will be broken, but the Palestine State will somehow exist, but with a smaller territory than they desire. Palestine will lose the chance to include Judah and Jerusalem, which will decisively be placed into Israel's hands. Therefore, there will not be much for 'Palestina' to rejoice over!

So, 'Palestina' is cautioned. She is not to rejoice, because something much more sinister is taking place. Verse 29. "*Out of the serpent's root shall come forth a cocatrice.*" This indicates there will arise, out of Satan's (the serpent's) desires and scheming, a deadly Deceiver who will be a world-class politician. The "*fruit*" of this Deceiver will be "*a fiery flying serpent,*" which means this Deceiver will then become Satanically possessed by the fiery serpent. AntiChrist will begin his rise to power out of the fall-out from the formation of the Palestinian State, and The Battle of Gog and Magog, and the need to control the resulting world scene. The Palestinians, then, will be pawns in Satan's game, and he will use them and their State as the excuse to step into the picture in The Middle East. It will take him a little time to get his act together, but he will groom the coming AntiChrist to carry out his diabolical plans. Hence the three year Calm, followed by the relatively benign first three and one-half years of the Tribulation. Then, after possessing AntiChrist, Satan will be in high gear!

E. The Palestinian Spring-Board:

Will AntiChrist be a Palestinian? Since Isaiah refers to him as 'The Assyrian,' it is possible he may come from the geographical area occupied by the former Assyrian Empire, which took in The Northern Tribes of Israel, and extended East to the southern aspect of the Caspian Sea toward the areas of northern Iraq, Turkey, and Kurdistan. Also, one of the anomalies of the Palestinians is that they are an ethnic mixture of Arabic and other peoples who have found themselves in, or have recently emigrated to The Middle East. For example, some who have generational roots within Israel may be descendant from the Samaritans. Others have connections to Egypt, Syria, or Jordan. Many Palestinians live in Jordan, and enclaves of them are found in most other Arab nations. The majority therefore, have no specific identifiable ethnicity of their own, or have abandoned their former identities, so are no longer totally accepted by any other ethnic Arab group. It is as if they are considered to be renegade. That is one reason why they have become a thorn of contention in The Middle East, with no one knowing exactly what to do with them, and why giving them their own State would seem a logical way to address their needs, and quiet The Middle East. So, will AntiChrist be Palestinian? Possibly, but no one will know his identity for certain until he arises on the scene. However, he will likely arise out of the geographical area that was the former Assyrian Empire.

But Middle East peace will not be easy to implement, because there are too many voices trying to decide what is best for the Palestinians, and world leaders are somehow driven by a fixated need to divide The Land of Israel in order to give the Palestinians a State. No nation but Israel is even being considered for the possible partitioning off of land for a Palestinian State, even though all surrounding nations have much more available land. What no one realizes is the fact that Satan also has a plan in motion, and through the unfolding scenario, has designs on arising to a prominent position in counterfeit 'incarnate' form, to take over Judah and Jerusalem, and to rule the world in the stead of Messiah. He will use the Palestinian State as a spring-board, because after The Gog - Magog Battle when Russia comes down against Israel, and loses out on the mountains of The West Bank; Judah will be entrenched as Israeli territory, so he will have to use deception to wrest Judah and Jerusalem from Israel. So AntiChrist, the *"cockatrice,"* will arise, operating deceptively in the apparently noble cause of Middle Eastern 'peace.' But once he is established, Satan will possess AntiChrist, and become the 'ruler,' the *"fiery flying serpent."*

'PALESTINA'

Russia will recover from her defeat during The Gog-Magog Battle, and the next time, along with many other nations who will wake-up to the treachery taking place, will ultimately come down again into Israel against AntiChrist. Notice verse 31 states none shall be alone in *"his appointed times."* These 'appointed times' are plural, meaning, as far as dealing with Palestine and Israel, and all the surrounding nations, there are at least <u>two scheduled appointed times</u> on the LORD's calendar when He will be dealing with the nations regarding The Middle East. Russia and her alliances (The Medes) have a hand in both Gog and Magog, ushering-in The Days of Awe Appointments, and Armageddon during the final days of these ' appointments.' But the ultimate outcome of these 'appointments' is based on one reality that the nations involved must consider carefully, namely, *"The LORD hath founded Zion, and the poor of his people shall trust in it."* Isaiah 14:32b.

IX. Joel Describes Islamic Jihad Motivation, and Palestine's Demise:

So yes, a Palestinian State, referred to in prophetic Scripture as 'Palestina' by Moses and Isaiah, and as 'Palestine' by Joel, will be part of the unfolding of the Fall Divine Appointments. Let's go to Joel chapter 3 to observe further ramifications of the formation of the Palestinian State. Beginning at Verse 2 *"I will also gather all nations, and will bring them down into the valley of Jehoshephat, and will plead with them there for my people and for my heritage Israel, whom they have scattered among the nations, <u>and parted my land</u>.* Verse 3. *And <u>they have cast lots for my people</u>; and have given <u>a boy for a harlot</u>, and <u>sold a girl for wine</u>, that they might drink."* Underlining mine.

This is an obvious reference to those who will hedge their bets against Israel in order to divide up The Land of Covenant, and attempt eventually to destroy Israel as an entity. [218]These will operate from an ideological premise which promises their young men and women that they will gain the rewards of the Islamic Paradise if they sacrifice themselves as terrorist suicide bombers in the cause! Jihad! [219] According to radical Islamic

---

[218] Arutz Sheva Israel National News, www.israelnn.com/news.php3?id=42996, *Teaching Children to Hate and Kill, Firial Hillis, C.E>O. Of the Palestinian children's Aid Assocciation:* "The concept of Shahada for him [the child] means belinging to the homeland, from a religious point of view. Sacrifice for his homeland. Achieving Shahada in order to reach Paradise and to meet his God. This is the best. We also teach our children to protect the homeland, belinging and to reach Shahada,"

[219] Arutz Sheva News Service, <http://www.IsraelNationalNews.com>., , March. 25, 2004, *CHILD BOMBERS IN THE SERVICE OF PALESTINIAN MURDER,* "One of the two new Hamas co-leaders, Khaled Mashal, called two

doctrine, 72 harlots for the guys, and plenty of wine for all, including the young women, await them in Paradise. By the way, this passage in Joel was rather vague in interpretation before 9/11. Since the terrorist attack on The Twin Towers, many Islamic doctrines have become better known. What is amazing is the fact Joel would have prophesied these exact details which describes the Islamic Paradise awaiting terrorists who are attempting to help divide up The Land of Israel! Did Joel have an inside track of understanding? Yes! He may not have totally understood the ramifications, but He had the Holy Spirit's anointing on what he wrote.

Joel chapter 3, verse 4. *"Yea, and what have ye to do with me, O Tyre, and Zidon, and all the coasts of Palestine? Will ye render me a recompense? And if ye recompense me, swiftly and speedily will I return your recompense upon your own head."* Notice the alliance of Israel's destroyers with Tyre and Zidon, referring to Lebanon. It appears Lebanon sides with the Palestinian Islamic cause against The Covenant. We see this stance developing even now, where Lebanon appears to be supporting Hamas and Hizbullah along with Syria, and Iran. They harbor terrorist organizations against Israel. But their recompense against the LORD will be returned upon their own heads! Why? Verse 5. *"Because ye have taken my silver and my gold, and have carried into your temples my goodly pleasant things:"* Israel will be raped of all her wealth by her enemies to accommodate Islamic idolatry.

Verse 6. *"The children of Judah and the children of Jerusalem have ye sold unto the Grecians, that ye might remove them far from their border."* These will sell-out Israel through deception in order to scatter and exile most of the residents of Jerusalem and Judah, giving them over to their enemies, represented here by the Grecians. Greece is a member of The European Union out of which will emerge the vocal, and cerebral political clout of the Fourth Beast confederacy (the heads and horns). The European Union is a member of 'The Quartet' seeking to form the Palestinian State. Perhaps at the time all this unfolds, Greece will hold the rotating presidency of the EU, or have a major Foreign Ministry role, or similar portfolio, and will be

---

years ago for the training of child suicide bombers - and the program seems to be well underway. Yesterday, for the second time in a week, alert IDF soldiers discovered a young Arab boy from the Palestinian Authority wearing an explosives vest designed to kill him and as many Israelis as possible."
"...the Tanzim promised him 100 shekels for his mother and 72 virgins in Paradise. He said that his teacher taught him that waiting for him in Paradise were rivers of honey and wine and 72 virgins, and that "if I do good acts, I will sit there and enjoy." Those "good acts" include, apparently, murdering Israelis.
"

'PALESTINA'

acting in concert with The Ten Horns and AntiChrist. [220]Even now, Greece sides with Arafat in support of the formation of a Palestinian State.

However, there possibly is another Greek connection which may easily be overlooked. The headquarters for the Greek Orthodox Church is in Jerusalem. In August of 2001, the Patriarch of the Greek Orthodox Church, Theodorus, passed away. He had always taken a supportive stance toward Israel. A new Patriarch has not yet been ratified by the Israeli Supreme Court.

[221]However, Irineos, who is under consideration to become Patriarch, has been given a marginal majority vote by the Greek Orthodox Churches to fill the position. Irineous is a rather colorful character. He owns a great deal of key real-estate in Jerusalem, such as the land upon which the Knesset sits, the home of the Israeli Prime Minister, and other major property holdings. Israeli security agencies are in strong opposition to Irineos' appointment because of his apparent connections with Arafat, who is a personal friend. [222] Therefore his recommendation for appointment is now being challenged in the Israeli Supreme Court because of some of his activities and alignments. Apparently there is evidence he wrote at least two anti-Semitic letters to Arafat at the end of January 2004, according to information obtained by Israel National News sources. Irineous has been the subject of previous Supreme Court hearings according to claims made by the General Security Service and the police, with the issue being his qualifications regarding the appointment. Also, another Greek Orthodox leader from the Galilee has filed his own suit against him. So, we have a possible connection to a high ranking Greek Orthodox leader within Israel, who could subversively wield much power and position. Even if the Supreme Court rules against his appointment, he still is in a dangerous position of influence with which to manipulate the Palestinian cause.

But the LORD will have the last word! Joel 3:7. *"Behold, I will raise out of the place whither ye have sold them, and will return your recompense upon your own head. Verse 8. And I will sell your sons and your daughters <u>into the hand of the children of Judah</u>, and <u>they shall sell them to the Sabeans</u>, to a people far off: for*

---

[220] The Jerusalem Post newspaper, Online News From Israel, www.jpost.com/2002/02/14/LatestNews/LatestNews... February 14, 2002, Nina Gilbert, *Greek FM calls for Palestinian Stat*, "Greek Foreign Minister George Papandreou declared his support yesterday for a Palestinian state and Palestinian Authority Chairman Yasser Arafat,..."

[221] Arutz Sheva News Service, www.IsraelNationalNews.com. January 25, 2004. *WHY WAS IRINEOS APPROVED?*

[222] Arutz Sheva News Service, www.IsraelNationalNews.com,. February 3, 2004, *SUPREME COURT BLOCKS IRINEOS APPOINTMENT.*

the LORD hath spoken it." Those who have sold-out the children of Judah to the Grecians, will see their own sons and daughters sold out <u>by the children of Judah, who will sell them into the hands of the Sabeans</u>. [223]"The Sabeans were powerful Arab merchants who occupied the remote southern areas of the Arabian Sinai Peninsula. Does this mean that when Palestine as a State is ultimately dismantled under Messiah, that the Palestinians will end up being exiled to Yemen, Oman, or the United Arab Emirates? Very possibly! But this does not mean the Islamic Sabean-Arabs suddenly seek to recognize Israel, but that they become a tool in God's hand to allow the returned of Judah to remove all those who have fought against The LORD, and have divided The Land, and exiled Judah and Jerusalem. How will this sell-out of the Palestinians to the Sabeans occur? Ultimately, The LORD Himself will bring this about to restore Judah when He sets up His reign from Judah and Jerusalem, then takes all nations to task at Sukkot regarding how they have treated Jacob.

Joel 3 chapter 3 verse 9. *"Proclaim ye this among the Gentiles; Prepare war, wake up the mighty men, let all the men of war draw near; let them come up;* Verse 10. *Beat your plowshares into swords, and your pruninghooks into spears: let the weak say, I am strong.* Verse 10. *Assemble yourselves, and come, all ye heathen, and gather yourselves together round about: thither cause thy mighty ones to come down, O LORD.* Verse 12. *Let the heathen be wakened, and come up to the valley of Jehosephat: for there will I sit to judge all the heathen round about.* Verse 13. *Put ye in the sickle, for the harvest is ripe: come, get you down: for the press is full, the vats overflow; for their wickedness is great.* Verse 14. *Multitudes, multitudes in the valley of decision: for the day of the LORD is near in the valley of decision.* Verse 15. *The sun and the moon shall be darkened, and the stars shall withdraw their shining.* Verse 16. *The LORD also shall roar out of Zion, and utter his voice from Jerusalem; and the heavens and the earth shall shake: but the LORD will be the hope of his people, and the strength of the children of Israel.* Verse 17. *So shall ye know that I am the LORD your God dwelling in Zion, my holy mountain: then shall Jerusalem be holy, and there shall no strangers pass through her any more.* KJV. Yom Kippur! Followed by Sukkot!

The prophet Joel pre-dated Isaiah, ministering from 835 B.C.E. to 796 B.C.E. during King Joash's reign in Judah. What would he have known about the dividing of The Land of Covenant to form a Palestinian State, or about a further scattering of much of Israel during The Days of Awe?

---

[223] Pictoral Encyclopedia of the Bible, Volume 5, Merrill C. Tenney, General Editor, 1976, The Zondervan Corporation, Grand Rapids, Michigan, p 190-191. The Sabeans were descendants of Sheba, living in SW Arabia, in the present area of Yemen and Oman.

Again, he would have been familiar with Philistia, but not Palestine! How would he have gained knowledge of the wanton terrorism to be perpetrated by many Islamic youth, both male and female, in the cause of dividing The Land to gain a Palestinian State, and that they would seek to scatter the Israelis again? [224]And, how would Joel have known they would sacrifice themselves, and their children, [225]through acts of Jihad to the pagan god, Allah, in order to obtain a promised Paradise of harlots and wine? His prophetic knowledge of Palestine, and the role of Islamic doctrine and ideology in brain-washing Islamic youth, could only have come from the anointing of the Holy Spirit telling him what to write regarding the Time and Season we now live in, and The Days of Awe ahead!

---

[224] Arutz Sheva News Service, <http://www.IsraelNationalNews.com>., March. 25, 2004, *CHILD BOMBERS IN THE SERVICE OF PALESTINIAN MURDER* "Nine days ago, Palestinian terrorist elements were willing to sacrifice a 10-year-old boy whom they equipped, without his knowledge, with a bomb inside a bag. They promised him 5 shekels if he would give the bag to someone on the other side of the checkpoint - but planned to detonate the bomb by remote control if he was caught.
The IDF reported that more than 40 other minors who were involved in planning suicide bombings have been arrested by security forces since 2001. Twenty-two shootings and bombings were actually perpetrated by minors during this period.
[225] WorldNetDaily, March 24.2004, Joseph Farah, Between the lines, *Another one bites the dust,* ""The so-called peace path is not peace and it is not a substitute for jihad and resistance," said Yassin. It makes you wonder why his followers are so upset. Yassin got just what he said he wanted _ martyrdom. That's what he had sent countless boys, young men and even girls to carry out in suicide attacks on Jews."

CHAPTER 29
TREACHERY

I. The Geneva Accord:

There is a treachery taking place from within Israel, and very little is being done about it. [226]Any other nation on earth would look upon what is happening with extreme concern, and would even arrest those involved for treason. But neither Israel nor The European Union, or even the USA and Britain, are taking those involved to task. [227]There is a non-official initiative being floated by a renegade group of disgruntled Israelis headed by Labor party members Amram Mitzna and Avraham Burg, in conjunction with former Knesset member Yossi Beilin, who actually put the idea forward. Labor does not form the Government in Israel at the moment, so really has no power to carry out what these people have set in motion. In fact, this is not even a Labor initiative officially put forward from within the Labor Party! Neither is the Likud coalition involved in this! Mitzna, Burg, and Beilin have drawn up what is being referred to as The Geneva Agreement in defiance of the current Israeli elected government, in conjunction with, and backed by the financial support of foreign powers within The European Union membership, namely France, Belgium, and Switzerland. What is this illegal initiative, and why is it so dangerous?

[228]They have unitarily decided that they will sign an agreement, called The Geneva Accord, without the consent of the Israeli Government, that:

---

[226] Arutz Sheva news Service, www.IsraelNationalnews.com., December 2, 2003, *GENEVA: SETTING THE WOLVES LOOSE UPON THE SHEEP*. Quote from Rabbi Druckman in response, "...There is simply no other way of defining their behavior other than as "tratorous." "

[227] Women For Israel's Tomorrow, www.womeningreen.org. October 30, 2003, Ruth Matar, From *AMERICA AND ISRAEL IN THE CROSSHAIRS OF TERRORISM, LETTER FROM RUTH MATAR (WOMEN IN GREEN) JERUSALEM, THE GENEVA AGREEMENT*, "...Labor party leaders Amram Mitzna and Avraham Burg, together with initiator Yossi Beilin, are planning to sign this surrender afreement "on behalf of Israel." In any normal country, negotiations with the enemy on security issues, in defiance of the elected government, would undoubtedly be considered illegal and even treasonous."

[228] Haaretz.com, www.haaretz.com/hasen/pages/ShArt.jhtml?itemNo=3-49832&co... January 5, 2004, Editorial Op. Ed. *The Geneva Accord.* "The Plan, dubbed the Geneva Accord in tribute to the funding and support supplied by the Swiss Foreign Ministry, offers itself as a decisive solution to the Israeli-Palestinian conflict, based on the plan drawn up by former U.S. President

The Final Schedule Revealed

1. The Palestinian Arabs be given control of The Old City of Jerusalem and The Temple Mount, and all Jews be removed permanently from living in East Jerusalem. 2. Ariel, Efrat, and eventually all other Israeli communities in Judea, Samaria, and Gaza be evacuated and dismantled. 3. This is to be done without any concessions from the Palestinians, or the necessity for stopping terrorism. This initiative would not only remove Yesha from Israeli control, but would seal off The Temple Mount permanently from the Jews if the Palestinians so chose. It would also destroy over 100,000 Jewish homes and businesses, and disrupt a fair segment of the local economy. And, it would severely limit Israeli defense, as the Palestinians would occupy the high ground, and Israel would be a sitting-duck in the lowlands. Interestingly, even Arafat is not in support of this initiative, because it undermines his absolute control of what is to transpire, and weakens his own bargaining powers with Israel.

The question is, if this initiative is only a possible alternate plan to 'The Road Map,' why is it being celebrated without official Israeli Government consent, [229]and being signed into recognition with the obvious support of foreign powers as if it is an agreement with the Israeli Government? Is there an insurrection in the making? Meanwhile, would this initiative then mean 'The Road Map' is to become obsolete, and the Palestinian State fast-tracked on a rail-line under the table? Does the Israeli government have any bargaining ability now at all, or are they being made out to be inept? And, why is the Israeli Government not strongly denouncing these renegades and their initiative? Even more amazing, why hasn't the U.S. government and The State Department condemned these Israeli manipulators as traitors, and taken them to task in the International Court in The Hague for committing a security crime against Israel?

Bill Clinton after the breakdown in the July 2000 talks between former Prime Minister Ehud Barak and Yasser Arafat."
"Fifty-eight former presidents, prime ministers, foreign ministers and other global leaders world leaders, among them former presidents Michail Gorbachev of the Soviet Union and F.W. de Klerk of South Africa, issued a statement expressing "strong support" for the plan."
"At the heart of the proposal is a Palestinian consession on the right of return to lands within the State of Israel, in exchange for sovereignty over the Temple Mount. The plan also calls for an Israeli withdrawal from most of the West Bank and the entire Gaza Strip."
[229] Women in Green, ,writ2@womeningreen.org> Letter from Ruth Mater, December 4, 2003. *THE"PEACE CARPENTERS" ARE PUTTING NAILS INTO THE COFFIN OF THE JEWISH STATE.* "The ultimate betrayal is Yossi Beilin's GENEVA SELLOUT."

TREACHERY

And, why has Ariel Sharon apparently adopted these initiatives (except those regarding Jerusalem and The Temple Mount), while stating he is still traveling along the path of 'The Road Map?' In essence, he is a traitor to his own Likud party, the Knesset, and to the citizens of Israel. [230]Prime Minister Ariel Sharon is rewarding the terrorists, and turning against his own citizens who are living in Judea, Samaria, and Gaza. [231]Above all, he is traveling in a direction which will bring about God's judgment upon himself, and plunge Israel into much hardship and war.

[232]His latest unilateral withdrawal initiative is to totally "withdraw" all Jews from Gaza. However, this initiative is being met with varying degrees of opposition. [233]The European Union is not in favor, unless it is negotiated along with the agreement of the Palestinian Authority. [234]The U.S. takes the

---

"Very weird situation. The agreement was signed, not by Israeli and Palestinian officials, but by two individuals WITH ABSOLUTELY NO POWER. On the Palestinain side it was signed by former information Minister Yasser Abed Rabbo. On the Israeli side it was signed by Yossi Beilin..."
"...Hundreds of journalists, rock stars, Hollywood actors and politicians were flown to Switzerland from all around the world, on a plane chartered by the "neutral" Swss government."

[230] Women inGreen, <wfit2@womeningreen.org> December 14, 2003, Nadia Matar, *About Pigs and Transfer of Jews*. "The Prime Minister's mouthpiece, Ehud Olmert, said this: in his opinion, Israel is incapable of controlling the entire area between the Jordan and the Mediterranean, and, therefore, we must withdraw." "What is important to know is that this time, Sharon is serious, and that he wants to be rid of most of Judea, Samaria, and Gaza, to uproot settlements, and to transfer Jews."

[231] Arutz-7 Editor,<autz-7@israelnationalnews.com>. December 16, 2003, De. Hagi Ben-Artzi, Prof. Of Bible Studies. *HINENI! - A Call to Arms for Jewish towns in Israel*. "Rabbi Tzvi Yehuda Kook, of saintly blessed memory, declared, "Over Judea and Samaria will ba a war!" -and the war has started in Migron and Amona."

[232] Arutz Sheva news Service, www.IsraelNationalNews.com., December 16, 2003, *PM SHARON WRITES OFF GAZA*." "It's clear that we won't be able to remain in Gaza forever." So said Ariel Sharon..."

[233] Haaretz Daily News, www.haaretzdaily.com., February 27, 2004. Aluf Benn, *Irish FM: EU opposes transfer of Gaza settlers to West Bank*. "The EU objects to the transfer of settlers from the Gaza Strip to bolster settlements in the West Bank. Disengagement should be carried out with the agreement of the Palestinian Authority, and should be coordinated with it, rather than as a unilateral move. Israel should facilitate the rebuilding of the Gaza Strip after withdrawal."

The Final Schedule Revealed

same stand.[235] In fact, President George W. Bush was somewhat hesitant to meet with Sharon to discuss the initiative.[236] The United Nations supports it.[237] Not all the Likud ministers in the government agree with it, so Sharon is having difficulties gaining full support. Needless to say, the settlers living in Gaza are definitely not in favor of being uprooted from their homes, and they have a great deal of support from many other Israeli citizens for their stance, because none feel it is right to unilaterally give-in to terrorism,[238] or to hand their God-given Land over to those who are not the inheritors of The Covenant according to Torah.[239] Many feel that withdrawing from Gaza, and allowing the Palestinians to take over, would

---

[234] Haaretz Daily News, www.haaretz.com/hasen/objects/pages/PrintArticleEn.JHtml?it... , February 7, 2004, Aluf Benn, Olmert: *U.S. knows Sharon determined to leave Gaza Strip.*

[235] Arutz Sheva News Service, <http://www.IsraelNationalNews.com>, March. 21, 2004, *EXCLUSIVE: SHARON- BUSH MEETING TO BE CANCELLED.* " Until three days ago, Prime Minister Ariel Sharon was still unsuccessful in his bid for a White House reception at which he could propose his Gaza withdrawal plan." ... "President Bush has reportedly noted the growing opposition in Israel to Sharon's Gaza plan – from IDF chiefs, to the Knesset, and even amongst the left-wing. He has therefore taken a step back – deciding not to allow PM Sharon to use an American endorsement of his plan as a way of bypassing Israeli public opinion, as well as that of the prime minister's own Likud party."

[236] The Boston Herald, http://bostonherald.com., February 4, 2004, Associated Press, *Annan backs Israeli plan for Gaza withdrawal, sees momentun for Mideast peace.*

[237] Arutz Sheva News Service, <http://www.IsraelNationalNews.com>, March. 21, 2004, *LIKUD MINISTERS HEAR OF DISENGAGEMENT PLAN*, "For the first time, Prime Minister Ariel Sharon formally discussed his disengagement plan - under which he wishes to unilaterally withdraw from the Gaza Strip and expel its nearly 8,000 Jewish residents from their homes of 30 years - with the Likud Party ministers."... "Most Likud Ministers do not support the withdrawal in its current format. Five are reported to be definitely in favor, and at least seven are opposed. "

[238] Women in Green, wfit2@womeningreen.org., March 23, 2004, *Death Knell to Secular Leadership* "Netanyahu does not take seriously the words of the Prophet Ezekiel that no Jewish Leader is permitted to relinquish the inheritance of the entire Jewish People (Ezekiel 46:18). The inheritance of the Jewish People is not Sharon's or Netanyahu's to give away. Every Inch of this Promised Land, belongs to the descendants of Abraham, Isaac and Jacob, that is the entire Jewish People, whether living in Israel or outside of the Holy Land."

[239] Women in Green, wfit2@womeningreen.org., March 10, 2004, ZOA Report: *Gaza: The Case Against Israeli Withdrawal,* U.S. Joint Chiefs of Staff: *Gaza is crucial to Israel's security* " An Israeli withdrawal means creating a terrorist state in Gaza:

produce another Arab terrorist State, and place Israel in more danger from her sworn destroyers.

[240] Along with all the above, The Palestinians have managed to complain to the UN that Israel is breaking international law by erecting the security fence, so have filed a suit against Israel in the International Court at The Hague. Strangely, most of the other Arab States, even many not close to Israel, have pledged support in taking Israel to the International Court. The United States, Australia, Canada, Great Britain, and India have filed a complaint stating the International Court does not have jurisdiction over the initiatives taken by Israel to protect herself. This is a slight twist, because it does not mean these nations suddenly have changed their tune toward Israel in calling for a halt to the building of, or at least the re-routing of, the security fence.

But notice the unfolding alignment of the nations! The Young Lions are beginning to act together, while the Arab and Islamic-leaning nations are starting to coalesce.

So now we have an internationally recognized imaginary State, and a renegade, self-appointed group of 'diplomats' attempting to sign an agreement into being with other nations on behalf of Israel, when they have no official, or legal business to do so! And, we have Israel's Prime Minister turning against his own citizens, while justice is being turned upside-down by the Palestinians, the UN, and most other nations! Deception and corruption in high places? I wonder what other anomalies of protocol will show up!

Actually, <u>there are more breaches of protocol regarding The Geneva Accord that prophetically should be a 'heads-up!'</u> These subversive traitors, according to a news release by Gideon Alon of Haaretz, January 28, 2004, article: "Palestinian Geneva Accord group invited to Knesset," have been invited to talks <u>at the Knesset</u>, chaired by Labor MK Ophir Pines-Paz and Yossi Beilin. They have invited several Arab leaders to sit down with them to discuss their Geneva Accord initiative. This information session has been thrown open to all Knesset members as well, but the

---

..."The Palestinian Authority regime currently administers parts of Gaza but does has not have sovereignty, because of the presence of the Israeli Army. The PA does not control the borders, does not control sea access to Gaza, and does not have a full-fledged army. If Israel withdraws from the area, the PA will be able to establish a sovereign state."
..."Such a state would certainly be a terrorist state,"

[240] The Jerusalem Post Internet Edition, February, 2, 2004, *Arafat: The Hague must discuss fence.*

The Final Schedule Revealed

right-wing Members of the Knesset are planning to not attend. Aluf Benn, a Haaretz Correspondent, February 4, 2004, states in his article: "Geneva Accord architects look for Arab League blessing," that the Geneva Accord architects, Yossi Beilin and Abed Rabbo (the Palestinian who had input in drawing up this Accord) are going to attempt to have their plan adopted at the up-coming summit of the Arab League in Tunisi. The purpose is to bring about a situation where Israel must face the entire Arab world regarding the issues raised by the Accord, so that Israel is not dealing just with the Palestinians. They have even been meeting with EU leaders to bring pressure on the Arab League, and to have the EU members all adopt the Geneva Accord as the final stage of 'The Road Map.' In other words, the move is now on to completely surround Israel with preemptive agreements made among as many nations as possible to pressure Israel. <u>This has overtones of the confederacy of the *"many"* of Daniel chapters 9 and 11</u>, who assist AntiChrist in placing the abomination, and <u>who he corrupts by flatteries</u>!! The AntiChrist will seek to bring about an agreement <u>among many</u> regarding the terms of the Covenant! Is this the opening round leading to AntiChrist's deceptive negotiations? <u>How close are we to the end of this Age</u>?!

II. Muzzled Media:

There is one other area which should be of major concern for any so-called democratic free society, especially while these strange occurrences are taking place. [241]"The right-wing media is being severely muzzled in Israel. For example, among others whose voices are being censored or ignored, the Arutz-7 Israel National News radio broadcasting ability has been all but shut down, even though the Knesset did vote to give them a license so they could broadcast from within Israeli air space. The Supreme Court rejected the license application, and overturned the Knesset decision. Arutz-7, a nationalist radio voice of the Right, has been broadcasting for 15 years, providing a balance to the Leftist media bias, and offering a venue whereby average citizens can air their views and concerns, as well as listen to cultural and religious programming. Their broadcasts have kept many who are concerned for Israel world-wide informed about the issues in The

---

[241] Women in Green, wfit2@womeningreen.org. April 25, 2003, Jack Englhard, *CNN and the Media Jihad*. " "They teeter in vision," said Isaiah. "They totter in judgment." " " ... This appeasement to the forces of terror is nothing less than a Media Jihad. Media manipulation? You bet. Out in the open. Are we shocked, shocked that we've been misinformed and disinformed?"

TREACHERY

Middle East. [242]Their entire board of directors has been charged, fined, and sentenced for illegally broadcasting without a license. This is strange, since they actually never did broadcast from within Israeli air-space, but from a ship located in international waters, a place from which they should have had continued immunity to broadcast freely until their license officially came through. In that regard, they are not a pirate station. Their board of directors are all respected Israeli rabbis and journalists. It would appear the leftist Shinui Party, (which at the moment does hold the portfolio of Justice, and is in favor of a Palestinian State and the dismantlement of all Settlements, and total withdrawal of Israel from the Territories,) does not want anyone to uncover or question what is taking place, especially at this juncture! Why attempt to shut down the Right-wing voice now, unless there is a greater agenda at stake? Fortunately, Arutz Sheva does still have a television outlet, and the Internet. But it is obvious there are sinister forces at work!

III. An Alternate Ten Nation Scenario:

As this book is now almost ready for print, another development has come to my attention. Ten nations, five from Europe, (Portugal, Spain, France, Italy, and Malta), and five Islamic nations from Western Africa, (Libya, Tunisia, Algeria, Morocco, and Mauritania), have agreed to a new initiative of political, economic, and religious-cultural cooperation. This is the result of what is being called "**The Tunis Declaration**" according to the article "Muslim, EU States Affirm Solidarity" by Andrew Borowiec, that appeared in The Washington Times, December 9, 2003. Apparently Jacques Chirac of France is calling this agreement, "historic," and Italian President Silvio Berlusconi states this will open up "**permanent dialog between Europe and Islam**." Zine El Abidine Ben Ali, the Tunisian host of the summit, stated this is "the beginning of a new process of cooperation and solidarity" **based in what historically was the heart of The Roman Empire**. Interesting!

The goals of "The Tunis Declaration" are: to hold annual business forums, to create a Euro-Mediterranean Bank, to promote open markets, and to allow for easier inter-immigration. They also have agreed to work

---

[242] Women in<wfit2@womeningreen.com>, December 27, 2003, Action Committee for Arutz 7, SENTENCING OF THE DEFENDANTS IN THE ARUTZ 7 CASE! THE PRINCIPLE OF FREE SPEECH DIRECTLY AFFECTS YOU. WHEN THAT STATION IS CLOSED DOWN, SO IS YOUR RIGHT TO HEAR OBJECTIVE RREPORTING.

The Final Schedule Revealed

together to fight terrorism in order to make the entire Mediterranean area a "sea of peace."

This new cooperative ten-nation agreement already carries a recognizable international logo, "**5 Plus 5**."

My question is this. Why is it "historical" for these five European and five African nations to officially agree together for meaningful <u>permanent</u> dialog between Europe (a confederacy of nations) and Islam (a religion), while at the same time Christianity and Judaism are politically incorrect and under attack? There are forces at work here which certainly are not Judeo-Christian friendly, nor are they open to Western ideals!

Another question. Will their "5 Plus 5" logo change to say "6 Plus 6," or "7 Plus 7" if other nations are allowed to participate, or is this a closed exclusive political, ideological, economic, international Mediterranean club?

And why would they be so quick to exhibit a specified logo to identify themselves? Or, has this co-operative alignment really come about so quickly? How long has this alliance been under negotiation behind the scenes before becoming public?

Could this be a major reason why Gaddafi of Libya spoke so vehemently in his diatribe against The Arab League Brotherhood, because he is trying to distance himself and his nation from Islamic in-fighting so that he will appear worthy to be welcomed into this new confederacy?

Could such an alignment result in The Ten Horns which will arise from within the former Roman Empire area, producing <u>the cerebral characteristics</u> of the coming Hybrid Fourth Beast? Or will their cooperative organization simply fizzle-out, like many similar attempts at agreements between nations in the past?

I tend to think this alliance <u>is merely part of the jostling for position</u>, as the nations edge toward the confederacy of the Ten Horns. However, I still feel the Ten Horns are more related to a combination of national groups from the Eastern and Western areas of the former Roman Empire, because eventually Libya, Egypt, and Ethiopia appear to operate separately from the European alignment.

We will certainly have to keep a sharp eye on this new "5 Plus 5" group of 'The Tunis Declaration" nations to see what transpires!

IV. Where is all this Alignment of Nations Leading?

All the political unrest and international terrorism in our present world indicates we are definitely nearing the end of this Age of Grace. The world's leaders are standing on the edge of a global, political and religious precipice, and their precarious positions are going to cause them to make

TREACHERY

decisions which will be devastating for all nations. The Middle East is increasingly becoming the focus, as the emphasis is shifting toward Israel, Jerusalem, Mount Zion, and the formation of a Palestinian State. As the nations follow their agreed upon 'Roadmap' and 'Accord,' Israel will be backed into a corner where she must cry out to God for deliverance.

Scripture indicates all that is taking place right now among the nations is treachery, and will become even more treacherous until Christ returns to set up His rule and reign. Certainly, not all world leaders are bent on evil. Rather, it is as if there is an uncontrollable relentless force picking up momentum, like a steamroller threatening to crush all in its path, driving world leaders to implement decisions that will ultimately result in treachery. How does the LORD plan to deal with Israel and the nations in light of all the treachery?

Let's read Isaiah chapter 24. *"Behold, the LORD maketh the earth empty, and maketh it waste, and turneth it upside down, and scattereth abroad the inhabitants thereof. Verse 2. And it shall be, as with the people, so with the priest, as with the servant, so with his master; as with the buyer, so with the seller; as with the lender, so with the borrower; as with the taker of usury, so with the giver of usury to him. Verse 3. The land shall be utterly emptied, and utterly spoiled: for the LORD hath spoken this word. Verse 4. The earth mourneth and fadeth away, the world languisheth and fadeth away, the haughty people of the earth do languish. Verse 5. The earth also is defiled under the inhabitants thereof; <u>because they have trangressed the laws, changed the ordinance, broken the everlasting covenant</u>. Verse 6. Therefore hath the curse devoured the earth, and they that dwell therein are desolate: therefore the inhabitants of the earth are burned, and few men left. Verse 7. The new wine mourneth, the vine languisheth, all the merryhearted do sigh. Verse 8. The mirth of tabrets ceaseth, the noise of them that rejoice endeth, the joy of the harp ceaseth. Verse 9. They shall not drink wine with a song; strong drink shall be bitter to them that drink it. Verse 10. The city of confusion is broken down: every house is shut up, that no man may come in. Verse 11. There is a crying for wine in the streets; all joy is darkened, the mirth of the land is gone. Verse 12. In the city is left desolation, and the gate is smitten with destruction. Verse 13. When thus shall it be in the midst of the land among the people, there shall be as the shaking of an olive tree, and as the gleaning grapes when the vintage is done. Verse 14. They shall lift up the voice, they shall sing for the majesty of the LORD, they shall cry aloud from the sea. Verse 15. Wherefore glorify ye the LORD in the fires, even the name of the LORD God of Israel in the isles of the sea. Verse 16. From the uttermost part of the earth have we heard songs, even glory to the righteous. But I said, <u>My leanness, my leanness</u>, woe is me! <u>The treacherous dealers have done treacherously</u>; yea, <u>the treacherous dealers have done treacherously</u>!"* KJV. Underlining mine.

Notice the leanness and treachery are emphasized by being repeated. This is not merely literary dramatic emphasis, but indicates the leanness and treachery regarding Israel and the everlasting Covenant will unfold <u>twice</u>. We are even now witnessing the lead up to the <u>first</u> <u>round of treachery</u> which will result in The Battle of Gog and Magog. The second round of leanness and treachery will transpire under AntiChrist leading all nations to The Battle of Armageddon. Both times, the treachery is a direct result of the transgression of God's laws, the changing of His ordinances, and the breaking of the everlasting Covenant. Both times Israel will be devastated, and the nations will be brought to war.

The emphasis in this passage is on the devastation that will ultimately be wreaked on the earth, on the economy, on the people, and especially on Jerusalem as The Days of Awe finally wrap up. How will the LORD deal with the treachery regarding His Covenant? He will entice all nations into the Middle East to engage directly in battle against Him! Then He will bring victory. Notice verses 21 to 23 of this same chapter, indicating how the forces of treachery are ultimately defeated. *"And it shall come to pass in that day, that the LORD shall punish the host of the high ones that are on high, and the kings of the earth upon the earth. Verse 22. And they shall be gathered together as prisoners are gathered in the pit, and shall be shut up in the prison, and after many days shall they be visited. Verse 23. Then the moon shall be confounded, and the sun ashamed, when the LORD of hosts shall reign in mount Zion, and in Jerusalem, and before his ancients gloriously."* KJV.

Who are the hosts of the high ones who will be gathered as prisoners in the pit? This is Satan and his demonic forces! These are the real enemies of Israel, of the nations, and of the LORD! These are the spiritual forces who have spawned all the treachery, and incited the nations and the AntiChrist forces against God, against His people Israel, and against The everlasting Covenant. Satan, who has been behind the whole thing from the start, will be bound, and cast, along with his fallen demonic hoards, into The Bottomless Pit. So, when will this victory over Satan's treachery take place? When Christ returns at the time of the sun being darkened and the moon not giving off any light! Yom Kippur! Jesus Christ will set up His rule and reign from Mount Zion and from Jerusalem, and all the Heavenly host will rejoice as He ushers in the Millennium! The Everlasting Covenant with Israel will be fulfilled!

V. In Conclusion:

The coming Divine Appointments of The Fall Convocations; The Fall Feasts and Festivals, fulfilled by and through Jesus Christ, will wrap up all righteousness, and bring His Peace to the whole earth. The Rosh HaShanah

Seventh Trumpet, revealing The Lamb of God to the Righteous, is soon to sound, and The Bride will be summoned by HaTeurah Shofar to meet her Bridegroom, also fulfilling Rosh HaChodesh -Yom HaKeseh. The Yamim Nora'Im, The Ten Days of Awe, will then unfold, and judgments will be poured out upon the unrighteous and the nations. All enemies: Satan, AntiChrist, The False Prophet, The Whore, will be brought low. Yom Kippur! The Mystery of God will be complete, announced by the blast of The Seventh Trumpet, Tekiah HaGadol, revealing The Lamb of God to the whole world! Revelation 10:7. *"But in the Days of the voice of the seventh angel, when he begins to sound, the mystery of God should be finished, as he hath revealed to his servants, the prophets."* When The Bridegroom, The LORD of Lords, Messiah, The Lamb of God, The Lion of The Tribe of Judah, The KING of Kings comes in fulfillment of Yom Kippur, all enemies will be defeated. All nations will come under the rule of The KING of Israel Who will sit upon The Throne of David in fulfillment of Sukkot, and He will judge the nations of the whole earth from Mount Zion.

Shemini Atzeret - Simchat Torah. The LORD will forgive and restore Israel on The Eighth Day, and He will ascend His Throne administratively to rule over all nations according to His Own Word which will go forth from Jerusalem into all the earth. The Creator of Heaven and Earth, The Word of God, The Light of The World, The Eternal High Priest, The Redeemer, will be victorious!

CHAPTER 30
PERSONAL TESHUVAH

We have examined where we are in relation to the Times and Seasons of God's prophetic time-table, but where are we as individuals in our relationship with the LORD, as this Appointment Schedule is soon to unfold? Have each of us already exercised our own personal Teshuvah? Have we turned to the LORD Jesus Christ, the Messiah Redeemer, in true repentance?

"But how," you ask, "do I repent?"

First of all, recognize that the root cause of why each of us has been separated from God is sin. *"For all have sinned and come short of the glory of God."* Romans 3:23. *"There is none righteous, no not one."* Romans 3:10. This is not a matter of being good enough. Rather, it is our inherited sin-nature that keeps us from God. *"But we are all as an unclean thing, and all our righteousnesses are a filthy rags; and we all do fade as a leaf; and our iniquities, like the wind, have taken us away."* Isaiah 64:6. *"All we like sheep have gone astray; we have turned every one to his own way; but the LORD hath laid on him the iniquity of us all."* Isaiah 53:6.

Upon recognition of our own inability to ever be able to live up to God's righteousness by our own will or strength, we must then admit our inadequacy. Admit it both to ourselves, and to God. Then, we must come to Jesus Christ, The Perfect Lamb of God, and believe He died and shed His own blood as the ultimate legal payment for our sin and iniquity, and recognize that He arose victorious over sin and death, removing forever the curse, fulfilling Passover and The Atonement of Yom Kippur. He is our Redeemer. He has done for us what we cannot do for ourselves.

Isaiah 49:26b states, *"...all flesh shall know that <u>I the LORD am thy Savior and thy Redeemer, the mighty One of Jacob</u>."* This message is for all of us, whether Jew or Gentile. When Paul was referring to those of Israel, he wrote, Romans 10: 1-13. *"Brethren, my heart's desire and prayer to God for Israel is, that they might be saved. Verse 2. For I bear them record that they have a zeal of God, but not according to knowledge. Verse 3. For they being ignorant of God's righteousness, and going about to establish their own righteousness, have not submitted themselves unto the righteousness of God. Verse 4. <u>For Christ is the end of the law for righteousness to every one that believeth.</u> Verse 5. For Moses describeth the righteousness which is of the law, That the man which doeth those things shall live by them. Verse 6. But the righteousness which is of faith speaketh on this wise, Say not in thine heart, Who shall ascend into heaven? that* is, to bring Christ down from above: Verse 7. Or, Who shall descend into the deep? that is, to bring Christ again from the dead. Verse 8. *But what saith it? The word is nigh thee, even in thy mouth, and in thy heart: that is, the word of faith, which we preach;* Verse 9. <u>That if thou shall confess with thy mouth the Lord Jesus, and shalt believe in thine heart that God hath raised him from the dead, thou shalt be saved</u>. Verse 10. <u>For with the heart man believeth unto righteousness; and with the mouth confession is made unto salvation.</u> Verse 11. *For the scripture saith, Whosoever believeth on him shall not be ashamed.* Verse 12. <u>For there is no difference between the Jew and the Greek: for the same Lord over all is rich unto all that call upon him.</u> Verse 13. <u>For whosoever shall call upon the name of the Lord shall be saved</u>." KJV. Underlining mine for emphasis.

Teshuvah. Repent. Return. This is a word few really understand anymore. It means to realize the condition one is in, then consciously turn around, and head in the opposite direction. It means to admit our sin, turn away from it, and ask the LORD to cleanse us through His own blood which He shed in complete atonement for our sin. This is not merely turning over a new leaf, or determining to live differently. By accepting the atonement of Christ, we are not just forgiven and washed clean from sin, but a spiritual new birth occurs. We become born anew as totally righteous, sinless, creatures! " *If any man be in Christ, <u>he is a new creature</u>, <u>old things are passed away</u>; behold, <u>all things are become new</u>. And all things are of God, who hath reconciled us to himself by Jesus Christ, and hath given to us the ministry of reconciliation. To wit, <u>that God was in Christ, reconciling the world unto himself,</u> not imputing their trespasses unto them; and hath committed unto us the world of reconciliation. Now then we are ambassadors for Christ, as God did beseech you by us: we pray you in Christ's stead, <u>be ye reconciled to God. For he hath made him to be sin for us who knew no sin; that we might be made the righteousness of God in him</u>.*" 2 Corinthians 5:17-21. KJV. Underlining mine for emphasis.

The righteousness we receive is a gift. It cannot be earned. It can only be received. *"For the wages of sin is death, but the gift of God is eternal life through Jesus Christ our Lord."* Romans 6:23. Sin has a price-tag attached, an eternal wage that must be paid. The wage of sin is eternal separation form God, Eternal Death. But Jesus Christ has already paid the price for each of us, so all we have to do now is accept it. Christ's gift is eternal life through His blood, His death, and His resurrection. He offers this gift to every person. He does not automatically give this gift to us, but we must reach out and receive it from His hand by faith.

This is true Tzadika! What is Tzadika? The word literally means "a righteous gift." What is a righteous gift? It is a gift purposely purchased in order to meet a real need that the person it is offered to cannot provide for himself. Salvation then, is a true Tzadika! But the word also carries a further fulfilled meaning for the one accepting this righteous gift. The word also means "a righteous one." So, our position as born-again believers means, not only do we have the privilege to receive a very needed gift that we could never provide for ourselves, but once received, we become " righteous ones," Tzadikim. The life we receive, then, qualifies each of us to be 'a righteous gift' that is then listed in The Book of Life. We become new, alive, righteous creatures -- ' righteous gifts' unto the LORD, set apart as His Righteous Bride! No wonder He is coming at Rosh HaShanah to receive all the Tzadikim unto Himself!

Have you accepted Jesus' righteous gift of salvation, and become a Righteous One? You can! Just talk to Jesus Christ, and admit your sinful state. Ask that He cleanse you from your sin through the blood He shed. Turn totally to Him, by turning away from all sin, and allow Him to be the One in charge of your life and destiny. This is Teshuvah! Repentance! He will receive you with much joy, and you will receive the righteous gift of a new life, and have your name entered, right now, into The Book of The Wholly Righteous, The Book of Life.

This is your opportunity to receive the love and forgiveness of Christ NOW. What an invitation!

If you have prayed for salvation today, you are now Tzadika! As a Righteous One, you will want to take care of your new life very carefully. Contact a Bible believing Church near you, and introduce yourself to a Pastor there, telling him/her the decision you have made. They will be able to rejoice with you, and provide you with the help you will need to grow as a Righteous One, a new creature born into the Family of God.

Obtain a Bible, and read it daily. It contains all the inspired words of God, sent to strengthen and sustain you as you live your life while still in this world. And stay in communication with Jesus Christ through prayer. Prayer is not difficult, and does not need to be stilted or 'religious.' All prayer is simply talking to, and with God, just as we would converse with a very close friend. He wants you to voice your thoughts and concerns, and your observations. He also wants to talk to you as you give Him time to answer you through His Word, The Bible, and as you sense His presence, the Holy Spirit, with you in each situation. Sometimes He speaks to us in our prayers and thoughts. Often He speaks through circumstances and other people. Sometimes He speaks directly to us through the preaching of His Word at Church, or when meeting together with others to discuss Scripture. And often He will communicate His will and His presence as we worship and praise Him with music and singing, and as we tell those we meet of what He has done in our lives. God has many ways to speak to us, and we have many avenues to share directly with Him. He wants the closeness of a real relationship.

Accepting Christ and His salvation is the most important decision you will ever make, because your eternal destiny depends on it. In light of the soon unfolding of God's final schedule for this world, the condition of your eternal soul is paramount.

The Divine appointments are no longer far off in the nebulous future, but are already showing signs of quickly coming up on God's prophetic calendar of the Ages. These coming appointed Days of fulfillment (mo'ed) are about to begin within just a few short years, months, weeks, or even days ahead. The Season of The Fall Harvests, The Latter Rain, The final Ten Days of Awe of The Forty Days of Teshuvah, are now almost upon us. The most important question is this: for which of the appointed Harvests are each of us going to take up our role? Now, during the Elul Days of Teshuvah, is the time to make our choice. Now is the time for the Bride to make herself ready to meet her Bridegroom. Therefore, I leave you with the Elul Teshuvah greeting, "May your name be inscribed in The Book of The Wholly Righteous," so you may indeed, at the sounding of Ha Teurah Shofar, participate in the ingathering harvest of Tzadikim at Rosh HaShanah.

BIBLIOGRAPHY

Douglas, J. D. (Ed.) (1962, reprint 1987). *Evangelical Dictionary of Theology.* Grand Rapids, Michigan: Baker Book House Co.

Dowley, Tim. (Ed.) (1982 reprint). *Eerdman's Handbook to the History of Christianity.* Grand Rapids, Michigan: Wm. B. Eerdman's Publishing Co.

Elwell, Walter A. (Ed.) (1984). *Evangelical Dictionary of Theology.* Grand Rapids, Michigan: Wm. B. Eerdmans Publishing Co.

Fox, Rabbi Karen L. and Zimbler Miller, Phyllis. (1992). *Seasons for Celebration.* New York, NY. Perigree Books: The Putnam Publishing Group.

Good, Joseph. (1989) *Rosh HaShanah and the Messianic Kingdom to Come.* Port Arthur, Texas: Hatikva Ministries.

Halley, Henry H. (Ed.) (Twenty-Fourth Edition) (1924, reprint 1976). *Halley's Bible Handbook.* Grand Rapids, Michigan: Zondervan Publishing House.

Henry, Matthew. Reprint Reference Library Edition. Volumes 1 and 4. *Matthew Henry's Commentary on the Whole Bible.* Old Tappan, New Jersey: Fleming H. Revell Company.

Keeley, Robin. Organizing Editor. (1982 Editiion). *Eerdman's Handbook to Christian Belief.* Grand Rapids, Michigan. William B. Eerdmans Publishing Company.

Merriam-Webster, (1995) *Webster's New Complete Dictionary*, Merriam-Webster Inc., SMITHMARK Publishers, New York, NY.

Morey, Robert A. (1996) **Where did Allah Come From?** Research and Education Foundation.

Packer, J.I., Tenney, Merrill C., White, Jr. Wm. (Ed.) (1957 reprint). *The Bible Almanac.* Nashville, Tennessee: Thomas Nelson Publishers.

Paterson JH, Wiseman DJ, Consulting Editors, Bimson JJ, Kane JP, Contributing Editors.(1985). *New Bible Atlas*. Tyndale House Publishers, Wheaton, Illinois.

Strong, James. (1989 Edition) *Strong's Exhaustive Concordance of the Bible, with Greek and Hebrew Dictionary*, Vancouver, B.C. : Praise Bible Publishers, Ltd.

Tenney, Merrill C. (G.Ed.) (1975,1976) Volume 1, Volume 2, Volume 3, Volume 4, Volume 5. *The Zondervan Pictoral Encyclopedia of the Bible.* Grand Rapids, Michigan: The Zondervan Corporation. Regency Zondervan.

Wright, G. Ernest. (1946, 1952,1971). Principal Advisor and Editorial Consultant: Chariman, Old Testament Department, Harvard Divinity School. Pres. American Schools of Oriental Research. *Great People of the Bible and How they Lived.* .New York: The Reader's Digest Association Ltd.

Zimmerman, Martha. (1934) Copyright 1981. *Celebrate the Feasts.* Minneapolis Minnesota: Bethany House Publishers.

PERIODICALS and NEWS ARTICLES:

MIDDLE EAST DIGEST February 1998, www.cdn-friends-icej.ca/medigest/feb98/tragic.html ,Stan Goodenough "Christian ears have not yet become accustomed to Arafat's latest tune 'until the Palestinian flag is hoisted over all the walls, minarets and churches of Jerusalem' This follows another slogan: **'First the Saturday people - then the Sunday people'**.

WorldNetDaily.com , March 20,2000. *Editorial,* ***YOUR PAPERS, PLEASE*** *...Big Brother gets under your skin.* Julie Foster, Ultimate ID badge, transceiver implanted in humans monitored by GPS satellites.

The Voice of the Temple Mount Faithful: Newsletter, Spring 2000. *The Tribe of Menash Discovered in North East India.*

The Voice of the Temple Mount Faithful: Newsletter, Spring 2000. Gershon Salomon, *Water Flowing from the Rock: A Sign of Redemption.*

The Voice of the Temple Mount Faithful: Newsletter, Spring 2000. *The Tragedy of the Destruction on the Temple Mount and the Weakness of the Israeli Government to Stop it Continues.*

The Voice of the Temple Mount Faithful: Newsletter, Spring 2000. *A Demonstration Against the Covenant and the Meeting Between the Pope and Arafat.*

The Voice of the Temple Mount Faithful: Newsletter, Spring 2000. *The Name of G_d is on Jerusalem.*

The Voice of the Temple Mount Faithful: Newletter, Spring 2000. *The Temple Mount as the Key Place in the Fulfillment of Prophecy.*

World Net Daily, November 1, 2000. *Human-Tracking Subdermal Implant Technology makes Debut.*

WorldNetDaily.com November 1, 2000. *Digital Angel unveiledHuman-tracking subdermal implant technology makes debut.*

Crying Voice in the Wilderness: November 5, 2000. *Bible Prophecies About the Mark of the Beast.*

CBC.ca News: CBC News Online Staff, July 19, 2001: *Plague of Grasshoppers descends on Alberta*

The Voice of the Temple Mount Faithful: Newsletter, Summer 2001. *The Beginning of the End-Time Gog and Magog War Against Israel and Against Jerusalem.*

The Voice of the Temple Mount Faithful: Newsletter, Summer 2001. *The Arabs Continue to Destroy the Remains on the Temple Mount.*

The Voice of the Temple Mount Faithful: Newsletter, Summer 2001. *A Cornerstone for the Third Temple Causes an "Earthquake" in the Middle East and all over the World in Tisha B'Av 2001.*

EE Times: Junko Yoshida, Dec. 19, 2001. *Euro Bank Notes to Embed RFID Chips by 2005.*

The Jerusalem Post Newspaper: Online News from Israel: Liason Committee of the President's Office, Sunday September 30, 2001. *Arafat letter incites Israeli Arabs against state.*

One Jerusalem News, <news@onejerusalem.org> January 22, 2002. Related News. "*Yasser Arafar wants a Palestinian state with Jerusalem as its capitol.*

ONE JERUSALEM NEWS: One Jerusalem Breaking News. January 22, 2002. *TERRORIST ATTACK IN JERUSALEM.*

Washington Post: Walter Pincus, February 4, 2002. *'Special Forces' High Special Profile Could Yield a Budget Increase, Pentagon Seeks New Weapons, Equipment for Elite Troops.*

The Jerusalem Post Internet Edition: Arieh O'Sullivan, February 6, 2002. *A portrait of enmity.*

The Jerusalem Post Internet Edition: Tovah Lazaroff, February 13, 2002. *Six-million could be lost again- Meridor.*

The Jerusalem Post Internet Edition: The Jerusalem Post Internet Staff, February 14, 2002. *Report: US formally protests EU position on statehood.*

267 The Israel Report, http://www.cdn-friends-icej.ca/isreport/feb02/horizon.htmlFebruaru 8, 2002, Emanuel A. Winston, Middle East Analyst & Commentator. *The Rolling Horizon Into The Coming War.*

The Jerusalem Post Internet Edition: Nina Gilbert, February 14, 2002. *Report: Greek FM calls for Palestinian state.*

CBN News: George Thomas, Sr. Reporter, February 25, 2002. *Under Suspicion: Faith in France*

ABCNews.com Paul Eng, March 1, 2002. *Implant Chip, Track People I, Chip? Technology to Meld Chips into Humans Draws Closer*

The Jerusalem Post Newspaper: Online News From Israel: Thomas Wagner, The Associated Press. March 1, 2002. *British chief rabbi: Worst anti=Semitism since WWII.*

The Jerusalem Post Internet Edition: Edith M. Lederer, The Associated Press, March 6, 2002. *Saddam rejects Saudi peace initiative.*

Time Archives: Lev Grossman, March 11, 2002. *Meet the Chipsons.*

Jerusalem Post Internat Edition: Al-Ahram Weekly. April 26, 2002. *A Palestinian fighter's version of the Jenine battle.*

Prophecy in the News: Gary Stearman, April 2002. *The Coming Collapse of Israel.*

BBC News: May 11, 2002. *US Family Gets Health Implants.*

Prophecy in the News: J.R. Church, May 11, 2002. Articles List: *The Southern Wall is About to Fall!*

CENTER FOR MONITORING THE IMPACT OF PEACE: www.edume.org/reports.index.htm March 16, 2002. *The Palestinian Authority School Books and Teacher's Guide.*

Prophecy In The News, Gary Stearman, JR Church,, May 2002 *The Southern Wall is About to Fall.*

Jerusalem Post Internet Edition: Michael Freund, June 12, 2002. *Stop Apologizing for 1967*

The Jerusalem Post: June 12, 2002. *The International Criminal Court is to begin on July 1, 2002.*

The Jerusalem Post: Daniel Pipes: June 12, 2002. *Harboard loves Jihad.*

Jerusalem Post Internet Edition, <www.jpost.com/App/cs/ComtentServer?pagename+JPost...> Jun.12, 2002. *Stop Apologizing for 1967.* Michael Freund, Deputy Director of Communications & Policy Planning in the Prime Minister's Office from 1996 to 1999.

Jerusalem Post Internet Edition: Eran Lerman, July 10, 2002. ***Ya'alon's test could come in the North***

Jerusalem Post Internet Edition: Arieh O'Sullivan and Greer Jay Cashman, July 10, 2002. ***PM to Ya'alon: Hard years ahead***

Women for Israel's Tomorrow: Nadia Matar. July 18, 2002. ***Nadia Matar's Speech at the Tisha B'Av Walk***

World Net Daily ExclusiveCommentary, Hal Lindsey, July 10, 2002, ***Participating with Pagans.***

The Jerusalem Post Internet Edition: The Associated Press. July 18, 2002. ***UN Security Council call for Palestinian state within three years.***

CNN.com/WORLD Jill Dougherty, August 17, 2002. ***Envoy: Russia, Iraq close to economic deal***

"Women in Green" Nadia Matar. August 19, 2002, ***NO TO GAZA FIRST!!***

Ruth Matar's Women in Green Hour, Arutz Sheva English Radio, August 22, 2002. ***IS THE SHARON GOVERNMENT IN FACT TRAVELING DOWN THE OSLO PATH?***

"Women in Green" Nadia Matar, August 26, 2002. **FAX Bogie Yaalon and Say Thanks.**

Women in Green, August 26, 2002. Chief of General Staff, Lt-Gen. Moshe Ya'alon, speaking to an assembly of Rabbis in Jerusalem, Aug. 25, 2002. "The current Palestinian leadership does not recognize the State of Israel's right to exist as a Jewish state, and is trying to realize its" doctrine of stages." "...the PLO is still trying to implement its "plan of stages" leading to Israel's destruction..."

israelinsider, Israel's Daily Magazine, August 27, 2002. Ellis Shuman, ***Southern Temple Mount wall reportedly in imminent danger of collapse.***

Ruth Matar's Women in Green Hour, Arutz Sheva English Radio, August 28, 2002. *IS THERE ANY DIFFERENCE BETWEEN ISRAELI ARABS AND ARABS UNDER THE PALESTINIAN AUTHORITY?*

RAIDERS News Update: 2002. **Test Marketing the Mark of the Beast!**

Prophecy in the News: J. R. Church, September 2002. *The Southern Wall is About to Fall.*

Prophecy in the News: J.R. Church and Gary Stearman, September 2002. *Israel's Dilemma.*

aish.com http//www.aish.com/articleToPrint? Rabbi Shaga Simmons. *Symbolism of the Shofar.*

Autz SHEVA: Ruth Matar. September 1, 2002. *Israel's and PA Arabs - Any Difference?*

Arutz SHEVA: Jeff Jacoby. September 3, 2002. OPINION. *With Eternal Friends Like These–*

"Women in Green" Ruth and Nadia Matar, September 3, 2002. Va'ad Rabbanei Yesha and Moetset Yesha *Har Habayit, The Temple Mount - where the Temples stood is the heart of our People, the heart of the World.*

The Jerusalem Post Internet Edition: Gerald M. Steinberg, September 3, 2002. *ANALYSIS: Syria wavering between terrorism and credibility.*

The Jerusalem Post Internet Edition: The Associated Press. September 3, 2002. *Israel preparing by November 1 for possible US attack on Iraq.*

The Jerusalem Post Internet Edition: Barry Rubin. September 4, 2002. THE REGION: *Waiting for Arafat and Bush*

The Jerusalem Post Internet Edition: Haim Shapiro. September 5, 2002. *The Start of a new year.*

The Jerusalem Post Internet Edition: Nina Gilbert, Gil Hoffman, Lamia Lahoud. September 5, 2002. *Sharon sees possible breakthrough with PA.*

The Jerusalem Post Internet Edition: Jonathan Rosenblum. September 5. 2002. *THINK AGAIN: Conservatism's incredible shrinking God.*

The Jerusalem Post Internet Edition, Sep.9,2002, Jonathan Rosenbleum, *THINK AGAIN, Conservatism's incredible shrinking God.*

CNN.com/WORLD: September 10, 2002. *Blair brands Saddam 'outlaw'.*

The Jerusalem Post Internet Edition: Moshe Shamir. September 10, 2002. *Don't sacrifice Israel in this war.*

Women in Green Radio Program, Arutz Sheva, Ruth Matar, September 11, 2002. *MORALITY IN THE ISRAELI DEFENSE FORCES.*

The Jerusalem Post, Sept.11, 2003, Regional Media, Translated by Shira Guttgold, Editorials From The Arab Press: *To Annihilate the Infidels is a divine decree.*

The Jerusalem Post Internet Edition: The Jerusalem Post Internet Staff. September 12, 2002. *UN Secretary General: "We are struggling to reconcile Israel's and the Palestinians concerns"*

The Jerusalem Post, Internet Edition, September 12, 2002. www.jpost.com/servlet/Satellite?pagename=JPost/A/JPArticl... Regional Media, Translated by Shira Guttgold. Editorials From The Arab Press: *To annihilate the infidels is a divine decree.*

HINENI: Rebbetzin Esther Jungreis, September 12, 2002. *Browse: Not Just Tilim - Missils, But Tehillim - Psalms*

HINENI: Rebbetzin Esther Jungreis, September 12, 2002. *Browse: A WAKE-UP CALL -- CHOOSE LIFE*

The Jerusalem Post: September 12, 2002. *A Different Kind of Holiday Ritual.*

One Jerusalem, <news@onejerusalem.org>September 12, 2002, *Save the Temple Mount,* "The walls of Jerusalem's Temple Mount are in danger of collapse..."

Arutz SHEVA, IsraelNationalNews.com *Religious Incitement Throughout the Arab World*

The Jerusalem Post: Regional Media, Translated by Shira Gutgold, September 12, 2002. **EDITORIALS FROM THE ARAB PRESS: To annihilate the infidels is a divine decree**

The Jerusalem Post Internet Edition: Annie Bayefsky, September 12, 2002. *Since Durban: An entrenchment of hatred*

The Jerusalem Post Internet Edition: Special Action Alert, September 12, 2002. **Save the Temple Mount!**

The Jerusalem Post Internet Edition: The Associated Press, September 17, 2002. Sharon: *Israel cannot trust its neighbors to carry out agreements*

The Jerusalem Post: The Jerusalem Post Staff. September 17, 2002. **Bush to US Jews on Yom Kippur: Together we can transform our nation.**

The Jerusalem Post Internet Edition: Michale Freund and News Agencies. September 18, 2002. ***Kuwaiti group aids Palestinian terrorists.***

The Jerusalem Post Internet Edition: Melissa Radler, September 18, 2002. ***Quartet agrees on "roadmap" to peace.***

The Jerusalem Post Internet Edition: Melissa Radler, Janine Zacharia, Lamia Lahoud, September 19, 2002. *Peres urges Palestinians: Let prophets, not terrorists shape our future*

Ruth Matar's Women in Green Hour, Arutz Sheva: Ruth Matar, September 19, 2002. ***TEMPLE MOUNT OUTRAGE***

The Jerusalem Post Internet Edition: Melissa Radler, Janine Zacharia, and Lamia LaHoud. September 19, 2002. **Peres Urges Palestinians: Let prophets, not terrorists shape our future.**

The Jerusalem Post Internet Edition: Kahled Abu Toameh, September 19, 2002. *Final Draft of PA consitiution nearly complete.*

The Jerusalem Post Internet Edition: Melissa Radler, September 19, 2002. *Quartet agrees on 'roadmap' to peace*

The Jerusalem Post Internet Edition: Michale Freund, September 19, 2002. *Because the Bible says so.*

The Jerusalem Post Internet Edition: Matthew Gutman, September 25, 2002. *Fence to trample human rights B'Tselem.*

The Jerusalem Post Internet Edition: A.B. Yehoshua, September 26, 2002. *The War of the Borders.*

"Women in Green": Ruth and Nadia Matar, September 26, 2002. *The Land of Israel Belongs to the People of Israel.*

Women in Green, <wfit2@womeningreen.org> September 26, 2002. *"We are fighting to retain possession of our Biblical Homeland.*

IsraelInsider, Israel's Daily Magazine, September 30, 2002. Ellis Shuman, *Israel Fears Temple Mount may Collapse due to Ramadan Crowds.*

Arutz SHEVA: Lori Milroy, October 2, 2002. *Iraq part of Terrorist Attacks against US.*

The Jerusalem Post Internet Edition: Matthew Gutman, October 2, 2002. *Hamas leader warns US against attacking Iraq.*

The Jerusalem Post Internet Edition: Jamal Halaby. October 2, 2002. **Arabs blast US legislation recognizing Jerusalem as capitol**

CBC Television: October 22, 2002. 9:00 pm.: Public Broadcasting Service, *The Ottomans:* Third in Documentary Series *of Islam: Empire of Faith.* Producer: Gardiner Films, Baltimore, Maryland, in conjunction with PBS and Devillier Donegan Enterprises.

Women In Green Hour, Israel National News, October 23, 2002, www.lisralenetionalnews.com. *What Does the Bible Have to Say About Jewish Settlers?* **Outposts are approved by the government.**

Internet Jerusalem Post: The Associated Press, October 24, 2002. ***What is the latest US peace plan?***

Hineni, A Wake-Up Call – Choose Life. Rebbetzin Esther Jungreis, www.hineni.org/rcolumn_view.asp?id+54&category=1. **"On 9/11, the President called upon the nations to pray, and quoted Psalm 23."**

The Jerusalem Post Internet Edition: Daniel Pipes, October 29, 2002. *The snipers: Crazies or jihadists?*

The Jerusalem Post Internet Edition: Mark Steyn, October 28, 2002. *Muslim ties are no surprise.*

The Jerusalem Post Internet Edition: Etgar Lefkovits, November 4, 2002. *Islamic Movement leader questioned.*

The Jerusalem Post Internet Edition: Adam Sharon Washington, November 5, 2002. *US Jews protest 'Protocols' mini-series outside Egyptian embassy.*

The Jerusalem Post Internet Edition, Nov. 5, 2002, www.jpost.com/servlet/Satellite?pagename+JPost/AJPArticle... Herb Keinon in Ankara,*Islamist party works to calm fears of jittery world after victory,*

"Women in Green": Posted Quote, November 9, 2002. *President John Adams Speaking About the Jew's contribution to mankind.*

The Jerusalem Post Internet Edition: Herb Keinon, November 10, 2002. *Netanyahu pledges to stick by US Mideast road map'*

Women in Green Hour, Arutz Sheva English Radio: Ruth Matar, November 13, 2002. ***THE OVERWHELMING MAJORITY OF THE JEWISH PEOPLE ARE AGAINST A PALESTINIAN STATE***

Jerusalem Post Internet Edition: The Jerusalem Post Internet Staff, November 15, 2002. *EU official supports entry of Israel and Morocco into European Union.*

The Jerusalem Post InternetEdition, November 11, 2002. www,jpost.comservlet/Satellite:pagename=A/JPArticle... Herb Keinon, *Netanyahu pledges to stick by US Mideast 'road map.'*

"Women in Green:" Ruth and Nadia Matar, November 17, 2002. *The Inadequacy of Sharon*

Israel Hasbara Committee: Professor Paul Eidelberg, Scheduled for Publication by the Ariel Center for Policy Research, November 2002. *Democratizing Islam*

"Women in Green:" Media Information Release: Ruth and Nadia Matar, November 25, 2002. *The Government and the Media Refuse to Acknowledge the Will of the Majority!*

Women in Green Hour, November 27, 2002. Ruth Matar. Before elections, Sharon stated in reference to Arafat, Sept, 3, 1993, **"You can't dance with a murderer."**

Prophecy in the News: J. R. Church and Gary Stearman, December 2002. *The Seventh Trumpet.*

Arutz SHEVA, IsraelNationalNews.com Nissan Ratzlav-Katz, December 5, 2002. *OPINION: "In Those Days, At That Time"*

Hineni, Rebbetzin Esther Jungreis, Dec.9,2002, *A Wake-Up Call."*

"Women in Green:" Martin Sherman, December 18, 2002. *The Arabs Themselves Don't want a Palestinian State!*

"Women in Green:" Joseph Farah, December 23, 2002. *THE SETTLEMENT ISSUE.*

Arutz SHEVA: Israel CNN.com *Temple Mount Faithful Turn to the High Court.*

Women in Green Radio Program, Arutz Sheva English Radio: Ruth Matar, January 9, 2003. *ISRAEL'S ELECTORAL SYSTEM*

Arutz Sheva, Israel National News: January 13, 2003. **Message From Yoash, King of Judah**

Women for Israel's Tomorrow: Martin Sherman, January 27, 2003. **Unleashing the Dogs of War**

Women in Green Hour, Arutz Sheva English Radio: Ruth Matar, February 12, 2003. **ISRAEL'S JEWISH ADVERSARIES, LOCALLY AND ABROAD**

Aish HaTorah: Rabbi Pinchas Winston, 1995, **From Y2K to the Intifada to Durban to the WTC attacks, world events are chillingly predicated in the kabbalistic writings.**

The Jerusalem Post: Translations from The Arab Press, By Gutgold, February 13, 2001. **Middle East Notes: Saddam Hussein forms a 'Jerusalem Liberation Army'**

Women for Israel's Tomorrow: Yashiko Sagamori, February 14, 2003. **A Japanese View of the Palestinians**

Women for Israel's Tomorrow: Martin Sherman, February 15, 2003. **Palestinian Lies, Israeli Truths**

Women for Israel's Tomorrow: Ruth and Nadia Matar, February 19, 2003. **KNOWING YOUR ENEMY**

Women in Green Hour, Arutz Sheva English Radio: Ruth Matar, February 20, 2003. **ISRAEL'S JEWISH ADVERSARIES**

Women for Israel's Tomorrow: Harvey Tannenbaum, February 23, 2003. **Our Peace Partners.**

Women for Israel's Tomorrow: Joseph Farah, February 24, 2003. **An Unconventional Arab Viewpoint**

Women in Green Hour, Arutz Sheva English Radio: Ruth Matar, February 27, 2003. Untitled. Topic: **Reaping the bitter harvest of the handiwork of the Israeli Left.**

"Women in Green:" Jack Englehard, February 28, 2003. *A View of the Absurd*

Women in Green. Arutz Sheva Israel National News.com: Ruth Matar, March 5, 2003. *Why Christians should be worried.*

CNN.com Tom Raum, March 6, 2003. *Arab Leaders Back Mideast Peace Road Map.*

The Jerusalem Post Internet Edition: Evelyn Gordon, March 10, 2003. *The real double standard.*

Women in Green,, wfit2@womeningreen.org March 12, 2003, *Who "Invented" Iraq and the Modern Middle East?*

Women in Green Hour, Arutz Sheva English Radio: Ruth Matar, March 13, 2003. *WHO " INVENTED" IRAQ AND THE MODERN MIDDLE EAST?*

News from CNN.com: Catheryn Conroy, March 13, 2003. *War: Bible's End-Time Prophecies True?*

One Jerusalem News: *The One Jerusalem Family,* March 13, 2003. *Textbook study.*

Women for Israel's Tomorrow: Ruth and Nadia Matar, March 22, 2003. *Purim, 5763*

Women in Green Hour, Arutz Sheva English Radio: Ruth Matar, March 27, 2003. *The Laundering of Abu Mazan*

Women for Israel's Tomorrow: Nadia Matar, March 28, 2003. *The Testimony of Livnat Ozeri*

Women for Israel's Tomorrow: Ruth Matar, March 30, 2003. Michael Levi from Jerusalem Post, March 28, 2003. *Ominous Portent of Things to Come*

Women for Israel's Tomorrow: Ruth and Nadia Matar, March 31, 2003. *UNMASK THE CHARADE!*

Women in Green Hour with Ruth Matar: Arutz Sheva English Radio, April 10, 2003. Summarized topic: *Arafat and Abu Mazan are the godfathers of Arab terrorism. Will the US adopt the immoral policy of rewarding its detractors and emenies, and forcing a Palestinian state down Israel's throat?*

Women for Israel's Tomorrow: Joseph Farah, April 12, 2003. *Why Arabs love Israel*

Women for Israel's Tomorrow: Ruth and Nadia Matar, April 25, 2003. Quoted Article: Jack Englehard, *CNN and the Media Jihad.*

Women for Israel's Tomorrow: Naomi Ragen, April 26, 2003. *The Next Wave of Terror.*

Women for Israel's Tomorrow: Ruth Matar, Arutz Sheva English Radio, April 30, 2003. *"THE ROADMAP TO HELL"* Interview with Elyakim Haetzni, former Knesset Member, Prominent Attorney and Columnist, and Jodie Anderson, Head of Deborah's Battallion, A Christian-Zionist Organization.

Women for Israel's Tomorrow: Abraham D. Sofaer, May 7, 2003. *Wrong Turn.*

Arutz Sheva, Israel National News.com : May 8, 2003. *Israel: "Right of Return" is a Non-Starter.*

Arutz Sheva, Israel National News.com: May 8, 2003. *Teaching Children to Hate and Kill.*

Arutz Sheva, Israel National News.com: May 8, 2003. *Message from PM Ariel Sharon.*

Arutz Sheva, Israel National News.com: May 8, 2003. *Message from Pres. Katzav.*

Arutz Sheva, Israel National News.com: May 8, 2003. *Minister Eitam: No Withdrawal In Golan.*

Arutz Sheva, Israel National News.com: May 8, 2003. *Memorial Day Contemplations*

Arutz Sheva, Israel National News.com: May 8, 2003. *P.A. Finds Easy Solution; Abu Mazan's Past.*

Arutz Sheva, Israel National News.com: May 8, 2003. *More Negative Reactions To The Road Map.*

ArutzSheva English Program, Women In Green Hour, www.IsraelNationalNews.com, June, 26, 2003. Ruth Matar, Transcript, *Are Settlements in Judea and Samaria Legal?*

Arutz-Sheva <IsraelNationalNews.com>, Women In Green Hour, May 7, 2003, Some recent quotes by PM Sharon: "**I am ready to make painful concessions.**"

Ruth's Women in Green Hour: Arutz Sheva Israel National Radio: Ruth Matar, May 14, 2003. *The US State Department's Antagonism against Israel.*

The Jerusalem Post Internet Edition: The Jerusalem Post Internat Staff, May 27, 2003. *Sharon: Road map doesn't require settlement freeze.*

Prophecy in the News: J. R. Church and Gary Stearman, June 2003. *Iraq in Prophecy.*

Arutz Sheva English Program, www.IsraelNationalNews.com, Women in Green Hour with Ruth Matar, June 25, 2003. *Are Settlements in Judea and Samaria Legal?*

Jerusalem Post Internet Edition, September 5, 2002, Nina Gilbert, Gil Hoffman, and Lamia LaHoud, *Sharon sees possible breakthrough with PA.*

HonestReporting.com: Communique, September 9, 2003. *Cycle of Arafat.*

FRONTPAGE MAGAZINE.com : Jamie Glazov, October 10, 2003. Symposium: *The Muslim Persecution of Christians.*

Arutz Sheva News Service, <http://www.IsraelNationalNews.com> October 14, 2003. *GADDAFI: "ARABS ARE COMPLETELY USELESS"*

Arutz Sheva News Service: <http://www.IsraelNationalNews.com> October 16, 2003, **GADDAFI: "ARABS ARE COMPLETELY USELESS."**

Arutz Sheva News Service: <http://www.IsraelNationalNews.com> October 16, 2003, ***EVEN ARAFAT IS AGAINST THE LEFT-WING AGREEMENT***

Arutz Sheva News Service: <http://www.IsraelNationalNews.com> October 16, 2003, ***MALASIAN PM: JEWS RULE THE WORLD.***

Arutz Sheva News Service: <http://www.IsraelNationalNews.com> October 16, 2003, ***FOR SYRIAN ACCOUNTABILITY & A FREE LEBANON.***

The Jerusalem Post: Tovah Lazaroff and Janine Zachariah, October 17, 2003. **US votes sanctions, Syria slams Israel.**

Arutz Sheva News Service, <http://www.IsraelNationalNews.com, October 28, 3003. ***MOFAZ: HIZBULLAH IS PLANNING MAJOR ATTACK.***

Women in Green: Ruth Matar, Letter, October 30, 2003. ***AMERICA AND ISRAEL IN THE CROSSHAIRS OF TERRORISM.***

Women in Green: Ruth Matar, Letter, October 30, 2003. ***THE MUZZLING OF ARUTZ 7.***

Arutz Sheva News Service, <http://www.IsraelNationalNews.com> November 2, 2003. ***PM SHARON TO RUSSIA.***

Arutz Sheva News Service, <http://www.IsraelNationalNews.com> November 2, 2003. Europeans: ***ISRAEL IS THE GREATEST THREAT TO PEACE.***

Arutz Sheva News Service, <http://www.IsraelNationalNews.com> November 3, 2003. ***P.A. INCITEMENT AND HATRED DOCUMENTED BEFORE U.S. SENATORS.***

Arutz Sheva News Service, <http://www.IsraelNationalNews.com> November 3, 2003. ***MEGA-STRIKE REPLACED BY PROTEST STRIKE OF 4 HOURS***

Arutz Sheva News Service, <http://www.IsraelNationalNews.com> November 3, 2003. ***WARM MEETING BETWEEN PM SHARON AND PUTIN***

The Jerusalem Post, Janine Zacharia, October 24.3003. ***Poll: Palestinians Back Terror Even With State.***

The Jerusalem Post, Rabbi Stewart Weiss, November 2, 2003, Op. Ed. ***Strangers in a familiar land.***

Arutz Sheva News Service, Arutz-7editor<http://www.IsraelNationalNews.com> November 7, 2003. ***UN EXPERT: REMOVE ISRAEL'S "IMPUNITY"***

Christian Week, Canada's National Christian Newspaper,Vol.17, Issue 22, November 2, 2004, Daina Douce, ***Ontario introduces institute to uphold Shariah law, Muslims and Christians eye effort with caution.***

Women in Green, ,writ2@womeningreen.org> Letter from Ruth Mater, December 4, 2003. ***THE "PEACE CARPENTERS" ARE PUTTING NAILS INTO THE COFFIN OF THE JEWISH STATE. "The ultimate betrayal is Yossi Beilin's GENEVA SELLOUT."***

The Washington Times, Andrew Borowiec, December 9, 2003. ***Muslim, EU States Affirm Solidarity.***

Arutz Sheva news Service, <http://www.IsraelNationalNews.com> December 2, 2003, ***GENEVA: SETTING THE WOLVES LOOSE UPON THE SHEEP.***

Arutz-Sheva News Service, Arutz-7 Editor, December 9, 2003, ***Israeli ambassador responds to UN "hypocritical" decision.***

Women in Green: Ruth Matar, Letter, December 11, 2003, ***YOU CAN'T DANCE WITH A MURDERER.***

Women inGreen, <wfit2@womeningreen.org> December 14, 2003, Nadia Matar, *About Pigs and Transfer of Jews.*

Arutz Sheva news Service, www.IsraelNationalNews.com., December 16, 2003, *PM SHARON WRITES OFF GAZA."*

Arutz-7 Editor,<autz-7@israelnationalnews.com>. December 16, 2003, De. Hagi Ben-Artzi, Prof. Of Bible Studies. *HINENI! - A Call to Arms for Jewish towns in Israel.*

Arutz Sheva News Service, <http://www.IsraelNationalNews.com>, December 18, 2003, *RABBI SHAPIRA'S LETTER.*

Arutz Sheva News Service, <http://www.IsraelNationalNews.com>, December 18, 2003, *THOUSANDS EXPECTED TO ARRIVE IN MIGRON.*

The Jerusalem Post Online Edition, www.jpost.com/servlet/Satellite?pagename=JPost/JPArticle/Prin..., Dec.18, 2003, Rabbis call for resistance to Migron dismantlement.

Women in Green: Ruth Matar, Letter, The Jerusalem Post, JPost Staff, December 18,2003. *Rabbis call for resistance to Migron dismantlemant.*

World Tribune.com Middle East Newsline, December 22, 2003. *Israel bows to U.S. demand for Palestinian state in 2004.*

Women in<wfit2@womeningreen.com>, December 27, 2003, Action Committee for Arutz 7, *SENTENCING OF THE DEFENDANTS IN THE ARUTZ 7 CASE! THE PRINCIPLE OF FREE SPEECH DIRECTLY AFFECTS YOU. WHEN THAT STATION IS CLOSED DOWN, SO IS YOUR RIGHT TO HEAR OBJECTIVE RREPORTING.*

Arutz Sheva News Service, Arutz-7 Editor, Dec. 31, 2003. *STATE OF PALESTINE UNDER ISLAMIC SHARIA LAW.*

Washington Post Staff Writer, Robin Wright, December 31, 2003, Page A15. *Palestinian State Remains Bush's Unfulfilled Goal, Administration's 'Road Map' Stalls.*

Arutz Sheva News Service, Arutz-7 Editor, Dec. 31, 2003. **MORE FENCE PROTESTS**

Arutz Sheva News Service, Arutz-7 Editor, Dec. 31, 2003. **CONDEMNING SENTENCES FOR ARUTZ-7.**

Women in Green, Shalom Freedman, December 31.2003, *Scapegoating the "Settlers."*

The Boston Globe, Dan Ephron, January 1, 2004, Looking Ahead to 2004, Middle East, **Settlements' future could determine Sharon's too.**

Women in Green, Letter from Ruth Matar, January 1, 2004, *AN EMASCULATED GIANT CALLED ARIEL SHARON, Ariel Sharon Then and Now.*

The Jerusalem Post, Women in Green, Oleg Cartoon, January 2, 2004, **"Outposts will be Dismantled, Period!"**

Women For Israel's Tomorrow, <wfit2@womeningreen.org>, January 2, 2004, The Jerusalem Post Oleg Cartoon, *"Outposts will be Dismantled, Period!" Sharon is NOT the Leader we voted For.*

HAARETZ.com, January 4, 2004, Draft December 2002, *Elements of a performance-based road map to a permanent two-state solution to the Israeli-Palestinian conflict.*

washingtonpost.com. The Associated Press, January 4, 2004, *Sharon Orders Two West Bank Settlement Outposts Dismantled.*

Haaretz.com, www.haaretz.com/hasen/pages/ShArt.jhtml?itemNo=3-49832&co... January 5, 2004, Editorial Op. Ed. *The Geneva Accord.*

Fox News Channel, Associated Press, January 5, 2004, **Hard-Line Settlers Defy Israeli Government.**

HAARETZ.com, Aluf Benn, January 5, 2004, *Israel to reject the Hague court's authority on fence.*

HAARETZ.com, January 5, 2004, *The Geneva Accord.*

HAARETZ.com, Aluf Benn, January 5, 2004, *UN vote sends fence discussion to int'l court.*

Arutz Sheva News Service, Arutz-7 Editor, January 8, 2004. *NETANYAHU, STEINITZ, SEE NO REASON TO CEDE THE GOLAN.*

Women in Green, Joseph Farah, January 9, 2004, *Why Palestinian statehood is a mistake.*

Arutz Sheva News Service, Arutz-7 Editor, January 11, 2004. *SYRIA NOT SERIOUS ABOUT PEACE, CONTINUES ARMING HIZBULLAH.*

VOANews.com. Ross Dunn, January 11, 2004, *Sharon: Palestinians Have Themselves To Blame forSecurity Barrier.*

Arutz Sheva News Service, www.IsraelNationalNews.com. January 25, 2004. *WHY WAS IRINEOS APPROVED?*

HAARETZ.com, Gideon Alon, Haaretz Correspondent, January 28, 2004. *Palestinian Geneva Accord group invited to Knesset.*

The Jerusalem Post Internet Edition, February, 2, 2004, *Arafat: The Hague must discuss fence.*

Arutz Sheva News Service, Arutz-7 Editor, February 3, 2004, *SUPREME COURT BLOCKS IRINEOS APPOINTMENT.*

Arutz Sheva News Service, Arutz-7 Editor, February 3, 2004, *NATIONALIST CAMP SAYS IT WILL BRING DOWN SHARON.*

Arutz Sheva News Service, www.IsraelNationalNews.com,. February 3, 2004, *SUPREME COURT BLOCKS IRINEOS APPOINTMENT.*

The Boston Herald, http://bostonherald.com., February 4, 2004, Associated Press, *Annan backs Israeli plan for Gaza withdrawal, sees momentun for Mideast peace.*

HAARETZ.com, Aluf Benn, Haaretz Correspondent, February 4, 2004,. *Geneva Accord architects look for Arab League blessing.*

The Boston Herald, www.Bostonherald.com, Associated Press, February 4, 2004, *Annan backs Israeli plan for Gaza with drawal, sees momentum for Mideast peace.*

Haaretz Daily News, www.haaretz.com/hasen/objects/pages/PrintArticleEn.JHtml?it... , February 7, 2004, Aluf Benn, Olmert: **U.S. knows Sharon determined to leave Gaza Strip.**

The Jerusalem Post, Internet Edition, www.jpost.com/servlet/Satellite?pagename=JPost/JPArticle/Printer&cid=107632529480Feb.9,2004. Gil Hoffman. *Sharon survives close no-confidence vote.*

Washington Post Foreign Service, www.washingtonpost.com , February 10, 2004, John Ward Anderson, *Israel hems In a Sacred City.*

The Washington Post Foreign Service, February 10, 2004, John Ward Anderson, *Israel Hems I n a Sacred City, Encircling of Jerusalem Complicates Prospects for Peace.*

Arutz-7, February 11, 2004, **PROFS: "DISPENSE WITH THE FENCE!"**

Haaretz News Service, www.haaeretz.com, February 11, 2004, *Quake rocks Israel, neighbor countries.*

IsraelInsider, Israel's Daily Newsmagazine, www.israelinsider.com February 16, 2004. Ellis Shuman, *Collapse of embankment near Western Wall shows danger facing Temple Mount.* israelinsider magazine, February 13, 2004. Ellis Shuman *Israel won't participate in Hague court hearings on fence.*

Temple Mount Faithful, Gershon Saloman, Feb.14,2004. **Another Wall Collapses on the Temple Mount Near the Western Wall**, Partially result of the recent earthquake of February 11,2004.

The Temple Mount Faithful, February 16, 2004, Gershon Salomon, *Another Wall Collapse on the Temple Mount Near the Western Wall.*

Jerusalem Post, Internet Edition, February, 23, 2004, Khaled Abu Toameh, *Arafat: Fence prevents PA State; Rage day declared.*

Arutz Sheva News Service, www.israelnationalnews.com. February 25, 2004, *GSS CHIEF: P.A. **TERRORISTS WORKING ON MISSILES TO BYPASS FENCE.***

Arutz Sheva Israel National News, www.israelnn.com/news.php3?id=42996, ***Teaching Children to Hate and Kill****, Firial Hillis, C.E.O. Of the Palestinian children's Aid Assocciation:*

Women in Green, <wfit2@womeningreen.org> February 26, 2004, Letter From Ruth Matar, ***Whose Land Grab?***

Haaretz Daily News, www.haaretzdaily.com., February 27, 2004. Aluf Benn, ***Irish FM: EU opposes transfer of Gaza settlers to West Bank***.

The Boston Globe, www.boston.com/news/world/articles/2004/02/04sharon_could... March 2, 2004, Dan Ephron, ***Sharon could face political rebellion, Right-wing parties say they'll leave coalition if settlements dismantled.***

Arutz-7News Service, <www.IsraelNationalNews.com> March 3. 2004, Daniel Pipes, Director of the Middle East forum. ***The Legality of the Yesha Settlements****, Article for Israel national News.*

Arutz-7. <www.IsraelNationalNews.com>March 3, 2004, Pinchas Wallerstein of Benjamin Regional Council. ***Outposts Again in Danger.***

Arutz-7. <www.IsraelNationalNews.com> March 3, 2004, Quoted in the article, ***The Legality of the Yesha Settlements*** :Eugene Rostow, Distinguished Fellow at the United States Institute of Peace, has written the following (The New Republic, October 21, 1991):

Women in Green, wfit2@womeningreen.org., March 10, 2004, ZOA Report: *Gaza: The Case Against Israeli Withdrawal*, U.S. Joint Chiefs of Staff: *Gaza is crucial to Israel's Security.*

Arutz-7 <http://www.IsraelNationalNews.com> March 11, 2004. ***SAAR IS AGAINST, DEF IS IN FAVOR***

Women in Green, mailto:michael@womeningreen.org , March 11, 2004. Yoram Ettinger , *A PALESTINIAN STATE - A U.S. BLUNDER.*

Women in Green mailtomichael@womeningreen.org, March 11. 2004. Ruth Matar, *LEOPARDS DO NOT CHANGE SPOTS, ONLY TACTICS.*

Arutz Sheva News Service, <http://www.IsraelNationalNews.com>, , March 15, 2004,*YESHA COUNCIL TO LIKUD MINISTERS: WAKE UP ALREADY!"*

Arutz Sheva News Service, <http://www.IsraelNationalNews.com>, March 15,2004, *LIKUD BILL TO DEMAND KNESSET MAJORITY FOR YESHA EVACUATIONS.*

Arutz Sheva News Service, <http://www.IsraelNationalNews.com> , Mar. 16, 2004. *PM BARELY SURVIVES NO-CONFIDENCE VOTE.*

362 www.ABCNews.com, SCI/TECH , March 18, 2004. Paul Eng, *I, Chip? Technology to Meld Chips into Humans Draws Closer.*

WomenForIsrael'sTomorrow (WomeninGreen),www.womeningreen.org., March 19, 2004. Gary Cooperberg, *Plans and Plans* .

Arutz Sheva News Service, <http://www.IsraelNationalNews.com>, March. 21, 2004,*LIKUD MINISTERS HEAR OF DISENGAGEMENT PLAN.*

Arutz Sheva News Service, <http://www.IsraelNationalNews.com>, March. 21, 2004, *EXCLUSIVE: SHARON-BUSH MEETING TO BE CANCELLED.*

Arutz Sheva News Service, <http://www.IsraelNationalNews.com> , March 22, 2004 *ARCH-MURDERER IS DEAD IN ISRAELI MISSILE STRIKE.*

World Evengelical Alliance, March 22, 2004, Elizabeth Kendal, *PERSECUTION, CANADA: APPLYING SHARIAH THROUGH ISLAMIC ARBITRATION.*

Women in Green, wfit2@womeningreen.org., March 23, 2004, ***Death Knell to Secular Leadership.***

WorldNetDaily, March 24.2004, Joseph Farah, Between the lines, ***Another one bites the dust.***

Arutz Sheva News Service, <http://www.IsraelNationalNews.com>., March. 25, 2004, ***CHILD BOMBERS IN THE SERVICE OF PALESTINIAN MURDER.***

Women in Green, www.womeningreen.org. March 30, 2004, Jan Willem van der Hoeven, Director, International Christian Zionist Center, ***Allah is not God.***

Notes and References on Islam by Chuck Missler, www.templemount.org/missler.html (accompanying the briefing package "The Sword of Allah: The Rise of Islam")

A Short Summary of Islamic Beliefs and Eschatology, Collected by Lambert Dolphin, www.templemount.org/islam.html "The pre-Islamic deities of Arabia..."

Notes and References on Islam by Chuck Missler, www.templemount.org/islam.html The Sabeans' Religion (pre-Muhammad) "Astral religion, which involves worshipping heavenly bodies ("the host of heaven") is strongly warned against in the Bible. ..."

Notes and References on Islam by Chuck Missler, www.templemount.org/islam.html "Archaeological and linguistic work done since the latter part of the 19th century has discovered overwhelming evidence that Muhammad constructed his religion and the Quran from pre- existing material in Arabian culture."

Jewish Heritage Online Magazine, **Yom Kippur Basics,** www.jhom.com/calendar/tishrei/yk/basics.html.

Workable Calendar And Fact Sheet On the Feasts of Judaism. www.velocity.net/edju/PForum/Calendar.htm.

Judaism 101, **Shemini Atzeret and SimkhatTorah**, Level Basic, www.jewfaq.org/holiday6.htm.

A quick Overview of the High Holidays, Rabbi Shraga Simmons, www.aish.com/hhElul/hhElulDefault's_quick_overview_of_the_...

Jewish Heritage Online, **The day of the Concealed Moon**, .www.jhom.com/calendar/tishrei/concealment.htm.

Judaism 101, **Rosh Chodesh**, Level Basic, www.jewfaq.org/chodesh.htm

Prophetech, Digital Missions, **The Rapture of the Church. The Rapture of the Bride of Christ**: A Digital Missions Fact Sheet. www.prophetech.com/institute/rapture.htm.

Jewish Heritage Online Magazine, Jeffrey H. Tigay, *How Israelite Rain is different From All Other Rain*, www.jhom.com/topics/rain/different.html

Sacred Texts Bible Index, *Rain*, www.sacred-texts.com/bib/ebd/ebd305.htm

A Quick Overview of the High Holidays, Rabbi Shraga Simmons, www.aosh.com/hhElulDefault/a_quick_overview_of_the...

Judaism 101, **The Month of Elul and Selichot** ,Level: Basic. www.jewfaq.org/elul.htm.

Yeshivat Har Etzion, www.vbm-torah.org/roshandyk/13-eb.htm., Rav Ezra Bick, The Israel Koschitky Virtual Beit Midrash, *The Secret of Selichot: The Thirteen Attributes of Mercy.*

Hadrash Ve-Haiyun - The Torah Page, http://members.aol.com/eylevine/5763pinchas.htm., The Reisha rav HaGoan R' Aaron Levine zt"1, **Torah Insights on the Weekly Parsha**, Pinchas 5763.

Growth and Renewal, Rabbi Ari Khan, *Power of Tzesakah*, www.aish.com/hhGrowth/hhGrowthDefault/Power_of_Tzedaka.

Rosh HaShanah, Rabbi Shraga **Simmons**,*Symbolism of the Shofar* www.Aish.com/holidays/The_High_Holidays/Symbolis...

The Triumphal Entry, **The Prophet Daniel Foretells Jesus' Death**, www.ida.net/users/rdk/ces/Lesson20.

The Temple Mount Faithful Newsletter, *The Beginning of the End-Time Gog and Magog War Against Israel and Jerusalem.* ,www.templemountfaithful.org/Newsletters/2001/5761-2.htm.

Jerusalem Center for Public Affairs, www.jcpa.org/art/knesset4.htm. The Constituent Assembly First Knesset 1949-1951, **Prime Minister's Statement Concerning Jerusalem and the Holy Places**, Sitting 96 – 5 December, 1949, Debate on the Prime minister's Statement.

The Temple Mount Faithful Newsletter, www.templemountfaithful.org/Newsletters/2001/5761-2.htm. *The Beginning of the End-Time Gog and Magog War Against Israel and Against Jerusalem.*

Contact us at:
schedreveald@fa-ct.com

ABOUT THE AUTHOR

Maureen Metcalf is the mother of three grown children, and has two delightful grandchildren. She has been a Pastor's wife for many years, and has taken an active leadership role in music, drama, and in Christian Education. She has experience in leading Bible Studies, and has researched many topics, both from an historical, as well as from a Biblical perspective. Because of her education and experience, she is well qualified to write on the subject matter of this book.

Printed in the United States
22482LVS00003B/79-156